INTRODUCTION

Since the end of World War II, most students and practitioners of Canadian foreign policy have approached their respective tasks with a single vision of the world system that surrounds them and of their own country's place within the globe. They believe that the world order established in the aftermath of the war has been sustained in its central features up to the present day. Led by a United States newly converted to international tasks, the nations of the West joined together to successfully counter the new threat from the Soviet Union and its satellites, rebuild the devastated nations of Europe and Japan, and begin the task of stimulating prosperity for the poor nations of the South. In doing so, they slowly tempered the reliance on force and anarchy that the prewar balance of power bred, and they developed in its place a more collaborative multilateral system, based on a strong network of international organizations in which the small, middle, and great powers alike have had legitimate and influential places.

Within this comfortable configuration, Canada's role has been that of a committed internationalist nation, distinguished by its diligent pursuit of values largely shared by the world community. As a middle power with medium strength, Canada, in this portrait, has rarely exercised its power against others in pursuit of direct national advantage. Rather, acting as a skilled diplomat, it has played an active, responsible, and influential part in a multitude of global issues, developing harmonious, effective, and expansive ties with states of similar strength and common political tradition. And in keeping with the values of contemporary liberalism, Canada has pursued the central purpose of steadily constructing a more durable and just international order for all.

As appealing as this liberal-internationalist vision has been, however, it has long been challenged by critics who have viewed the postwar world and Canada's role from a very different perspective. In their view, it is America alone that has dominated the postwar international system, defending and developing other states with the central purpose and effect of supporting a world capitalist system that it largely controls and from which it derives disproportionate benefit. While garbed in the attractive cloak of internationalist rhetoric, American pre-eminence has been sufficiently overwhelming to ensure a multilateral order created in the American image, casting lesser powers in a dependent position and relatively insignificant role. Thus Canada has been cast into the position of a minor power, operating within limits set by an overwhelming United States and proving increasingly incapable of resisting a pervasive U.S. influence around the globe, on the North American continent, and within Canada itself. As a penetrated, semiperipheral power, Canada has had its internal structure determined largely by sources of public and private power centred in the United States. It has been forced to secure from a globally dominant economic power the resources required to meet basic domestic needs. Its external behaviour has followed, as, in conformance with Marxist predictions, Canada has been induced to collaborate with a preponderant America, provide uncritical support for American actions and purposes, and passively promote those open international regimes and gradual reforms by which the global dominance of imperialist powers is sustained.

During the past two decades, the debate between those who see Canada as an internationalist middle power and those who view it as a dependent satellite has provided the central focus of scholarly exploration and dialogue in the Canadian foreign policy field.[1] Adherents of both positions have been quick to point to the evidence that confirms the validity of their views.

Proponents of the liberal-internationalist perspective emphasize Canada's successful efforts to create and extend international institutions—notably a multiracial Commonwealth, the universal United Nations system, and the multilateral North Atlantic Treaty Organization—in which military power is not always decisive and in which lesser powers have an influential place. Students of peripheral dependence counter that Canada's quest for multilateral institutions operates to enhance the needs and values of an American-dominated security system and capitalist order, by facilitating the Anglo-American harmony and international legitimacy that allowed American pre-eminence to arise and endure. Liberal-internationalists stress Canada's efforts to reduce military tensions through peacekeeping, arms control, and East–West détente, to develop effective international law for the globe's seas and outer space, and to engender stable multilateral regimes for monetary, trade, and investment flows. Their challengers claim, in response, that Canada's military peacekeeping and diplomatic mediation facilitate the extension of American influence into distant regions; they point to Canada's often implicit support for an international law acceptable to the great capitalist powers and its ready retreat from multilateral regimes to continental partnerships in air defence, defence and automotive production, oil exports, and balance-of-payments policies. The liberal internationalists argue that Canada's enlightened internationalism, expressed in its generous aid policies to the Third World, for example, give it the influence and self-confidence to moderate unilateral American action abroad, to secure balanced bargains on the North American continent, and to resist undue

influence from American forces at home. And the advocates of peripheral dependence reply that Canada's penetration by American influences has produced an underdeveloped, fragmented, and vulnerable nation that anticipates and responds favourably to U.S. requests, confines its objections to procedures rather than principles, and retaliates only against the crudest American interventions in the Canadian political process.

Thus, while these perspectives offer diametrically opposed predictions about Canada's foreign policy, each can marshal a considerable amount of evidence. Although any single piece of evidence will support one perspective against its rival, both perspectives, working in combination, are necessary to account for much of the overall record since 1945. Yet both are deficient in one critical respect. Neither seems capable of adequately absorbing the profound changes that have taken place in the international system since the late 1960s and the new trends that have emerged in Canadian foreign policy as a result.

Since the 1960s, the postwar order has changed dramatically, as the pre-eminent America that catalyzed its creation and enforced its effectiveness has experienced a massive decline. The United States defeat in the Tet offensive in Vietnam in February 1968, its desperate assault on the international monetary and trade system in August 1971, and its vulnerability to the oil shocks of October 1973 have highlighted its rapidly declining share of the globe's military and economic capability, led it to retreat from its global commitment, and reawakened its isolationist instincts. With neither the Soviet Union nor any other global power capable of filling the vacuum, a far greater role has been given to a small group of states in the developed world—notably France, West Germany, and Japan—that were formerly confined by America's international pre-eminence to the second tier in the global scale. In this increasingly diffuse international system, they have had the resources and freedom, in concert with a much more modest United States, to shape the global order in keeping with their own interests and values. This role has been performed most obviously at the Western Economic Summits co-ordinating the West's economic and political policies, in the Security Council's Namibia Contact Group fostering a peaceful transition in southern Africa, and in the developed state group in the North–South dialogue.

What have these profound global changes meant for Canadian foreign policy during the past decade and a half? Preoccupied by the debate between "middle power" and "satellite" conceptions of Canada, scholars have provided answers far less convincing than they once were. The peripheral-dependence group, slow to recognize America's decline, implies that the dominant world capitalist system will survive the demise of its leading member and that a declining United States will carry an ever dependent Canada downward in its wake. The liberal-

internationalists see in a more modest American presence enhanced opportunities for Canada's classic multilateral instincts and a renewal in the 1970s of its traditional diplomacy of mediation and constraint. But neither explains how Canada has behaved in an era of diffused international power, when there has been too little, rather than too much, American power in the globe.

A new perspective on Canadian foreign policy, equal in intellectual status to the liberal-internationalist and peripheral-dependence visions, is developed in this book under the label "complex neo-realism".[2] It begins with the premise that America's decline and the consequent diffusion of power in the international system have propelled Canada into the position of a principal power in the globe. Principal powers, like the great powers of old, stand in the top tier of the global hierarchy of power and act autonomously in pursuit of their own interests, rather than as mediators among others or agents for them. Yet this small set of states, unlike former great powers, have the additional task of creating—in concert and on the basis of their own distinctive values—a global order in an age when no single state or set of universal principles can perform the task.

Viewing Canada as a principal power, the perspective of complex neo-realism thus argues that Canadian foreign policy, particularly since the mid-1960s, consists primarily of an expanding effort to advance Canada's distinctive national interests and values through external initiatives and the promotion of a world order directly supportive of Canadian purposes. Believing that Canada's principal-power position in a diffuse system gives the country enhanced opportunities for autonomous and effective activity abroad, complex neo-realism predicts a global Canadian pursuit of defined national interests through the development and management of direct bilateral relationships with carefully selected states. Drawing on realist theory in the field of international politics, it highlights Canada's competitive effort—conducted through unilateral initiatives, temporary alliances, and hard bargaining—to forward its divergent interests and diversify its international affiliations beyond the middle-power coalitions or imperial powers of old. And recognizing the special role of principal powers in creating world order, complex neo-realism underscores Canada's quest to enter and influence those informal, highly restricted concerts within which global order in a diffuse international system is defined.

This vision of Canada as one of the world's leading powers is rather unfamiliar to most Canadians. In fact, their country has rarely exercised the freewheeling autonomy or engaged in the constant struggle for survival and dominance that once characterized the superpowers and great powers. Yet the concept of Canada as a principal power in a diffuse international system is sustained by several strong trends in Canadian

foreign policy during the governments of Prime Minister Pierre Trudeau.

During this time, Canada has grown to rival the United Kingdom in the Commonwealth and even France within francophonie, by offering a strongly sympathetic response to Third World members' requests for development assistance, shaping the agendas and structures of these organizations, and receiving the support of most of their members in this task. Within the United Nations, Canada has slowly shifted from its traditional middle-power associates in the General Assembly and in specialized agencies towards a position of greater equality with the great powers on the Security Council and a broader set of associates in new programs on environment, food, and energy matters. Similarly, in regard to NATO, Canada has departed more frequently from the cautious positions of allied middle powers and adopted the security-oriented concerns of major continental European powers, notably West Germany and France.

Within North America, as the global power of the United States has diminished, Canada has developed a significantly more assertive stance, defining comprehensive strategies grounded in more precise definitions of its national interest, conducting vigorous campaigns of public diplomacy, bargaining on an arm's-length basis, and moving towards a closer linkage of issues across different sectors and spheres. On the global stage, Canada has been more reluctant to pursue open-ended peacekeeping commitments and standard exercises in arms control and international law, and it has moved away from open economic regimes ensconced in multilateral institutions towards covert cartels, state trading arrangements, and bilateral organizations. Through its legitimate, equal place in such exclusive clubs as the Western Economic Summit, the developed states group in the North–South dialogue, and the Namibia Contact Group, Canada has acquired a foremost place in the definition and management of global order in crucial economic and political spheres.

In developing and applying this vision of Canada as a principal power in a diffuse international system, this book seeks to make several contributions to a field of study long dominated by the "middle power" versus "satellite" debate. The first is to broaden this debate beyond the two traditional poles. While the grand dichotomy they form has done much to enrich academic inquiry, it has provided few tools for describing and explaining the significant innovations in Canadian foreign policy since 1968.[3] In particular, it has forced these departures from past practice to be interpreted, unconvincingly, as futile efforts to alter the deep condition of dependence within which individual governments operated, as modern variants of such liberal-internationalist themes as "middlepowermanship" or "functionalism", or as transitory bursts of creativity by an inexperienced prime minister who rapidly discovered and reverted to the internationalist practices of old.[4] There has been too little attention to the precise questions of what has really changed, in what ways, and from what underlying causes.

This study, in contrast, develops, defines, and comparatively tests a "complex neo-realist" perspective that may account more accurately for recent Canadian foreign policy. It begins with the premise that each of the theoretical perspectives of complex neo-realism, liberal internationalism, and peripheral dependence provides a comprehensive, internally consistent, and mutually exclusive set of conceptions about how the Canadian government, in its foreign policy, has actually behaved.[5] By distilling the common logic of authors operating within each of the three scholarly traditions, it identifies the central concepts, specific predictions, and distinctive answers that each theoretical perspective makes about how the record of Canadian foreign policy will unfold.

Identification of these distinctive answers and the common questions they address requires moving beyond the scholarly work on Canadian foreign policy. To be sure, the Canadian government's own agenda has periodically defined the questions that adherents to the middle-power and satellite traditions have long debated. Furthermore, in providing answers, scholars have both drawn from general theories in the broader field of international politics and made selective contributions to them.[6] Yet the controversy has had little resonance or relevance elsewhere. It has largely overlooked the rich and predominant tradition of political realism in the general field of international relations. And it has devoted too little attention to the profound impact of a changing global environment on the international position and behaviour of Canada itself.

The second purpose of this volume, therefore, is to integrate the study of Canadian foreign policy more closely with that of international politics generally. This requires basing the three theoretical perspectives on Canadian foreign policy, at the outset, on those fundamental questions that have long been central to students of general foreign policy analysis and that have proven to be most useful in charting any country's behaviour in the international realm. It demands including among these questions, in a prominent position, the impact of a changing global environment on foreign policy behaviour. And it makes it necessary for the distinctive answers provided by each of the three perspectives to be consistent with appropriate literature in the larger field of international politics. This is particularly true in the case of complex neo-realism, where the body of scholarly material on Canadian foreign policy is far less developed. Together these requirements lead to an emphasis on a stream of realist theory that focuses on the rise and decline of dominant powers in the international system and the structural trends in population, resources, and technology upon which these processes are based.[7]

When constructed on such careful theoretical foundations, it is highly unlikely that any of the three perspectives will account for all the evidence on its own. Each specific piece of evidence can conform to the predictions of only one perspective. And given the rich, multifaceted nature of Canada's international involvement over the past forty years, it hardly can be expected that any one perspective will end up with all the evidence conforming to the theoretical predictions it initially made.

Thus this study is well positioned to meet its third basic objective of moving towards conclusions about which perspective is most accurate—that is, sustained by the bulk of the evidence—most of the time. Did the empirical patterns predicted by the perspective of liberal internationalism in fact prevail in Canadian behaviour in the two decades following the end of World War II? Were there strong traces of the patterns predicted by peripheral dependence during this time? And does the perspective of complex neo-realism provide a more accurate account than its two traditional competitors in the years since 1968?

To answer these questions with confidence, the evidence selected to test the predictions of the three perspectives must be comprehensive and fair. This study passes lightly, therefore, over the usual focus on a state's relative position to focus on its actual behaviour in a wide number of dimensions, including a state's externally oriented behaviour and the processes on which that behaviour is based. Equally important, it avoids the conventional focus on Canada's military or economic relations with the United States, at the United Nations, or in the outer world, since an undue emphasis on any of these standard categories tends to prejudge the answers to the question of which perspective works best. Rather it focuses on the relatively unexplored areas of population, resources, and technology, which, as we explain in Chapter 4, are most likely to provide the fairest and most theoretically secure test.

To fulfill these objectives of broadening the debate, integrating the fields, and moving towards conclusions, we begin with the theoretical task. Chapter 1 identifies the seven central questions that students of foreign policy commonly ask about any state: its international presence, its approach to activity, association, and order in its externally oriented behaviour, and the external, societal, and governmental processes on which this behaviour is based. The distinctive answers to these questions provided by the perspectives of liberal internationalism, peripheral dependence, and complex neo-realism are then outlined.

Chapter 2 begins the task of assessing these competing perspectives against the evidence. A historical survey of Canadian foreign policy since 1945 focuses on two types of evidence: the broad foreign policy declarations a government publicly makes when it first enters office and the major decisions it takes on critical issues in the following years. Such decisions have generally been consistent with initial declarations; together they have produced five basic eras in Canadian foreign policy since 1945. The boundaries of these eras will vary across the issue areas discussed in other chapters, as complex behaviours, interests, and resources intersect.

Chapter 3 turns from discrete declarations and decisions to the routine implementation of policy, and from historical to quantitative forms of evidence. Focusing on Canada's approach to activity, association, and world order since 1945, it uses a range of indicators and evidence to measure each dimension, in order to determine with more precision when major turning points occurred. We find that routine behaviour does tend to reflect major declarations and decisions and that differing blends of the three theoretical perspectives are needed to account for Canada's international behaviour over the years.

In the next three chapters, attention shifts to the processes by which Canada's foreign policy behaviour is produced and sustained. Unlike most conventional treatments of this subject, Chapter 4 begins with changes in the global environment, focusing on underlying structural trends in the global distribution of population, resources, and trade and on the diffusion of power among relevant actors brought about by these trends. Chapter 5 explores how changes in population, resources, technology, and production within Canada have intersected with global developments, created new opportunities and vulnerabilities for Canada, and given rise to a broader and more balanced foreign policy process at home. Chapter 6 examines foreign policy decision making within the executive branch of the federal government to see how the state apparatus has integrated these outside forces into a more comprehensive process and a transcendent conception of the national interest.

In the final section of the book we explore Canada's evolving foreign policy behaviour and processes since 1945 in four critical, politicized policy sectors, each chosen to highlight forces fundamental to the overall process of foreign policy and international change. Chapter 7, highlighting structural trends in population, deals with Canada's refugee policy. Chapter 8, embracing shifts in energy and natural resources, focuses on Canadian policy towards the international flow of oil and gas. Chapter 9, mapping trends in science and technology, deals with Canada's international involvement in the area of satellites and space. Chapter 10 provides a more comprehensive focus by examining Canadian policy towards the Middle East, a geographic region in which the competitive intersection of Canada's population, resources, and technological relationships has been particularly acute, and in which Canadian policy has long been seen as an archetypical expression of either the dominant liberal-internationalist or the competing peripheral-dependence perspective. Together these four cases test the three competing theoretical perspectives in areas fundamental to long-run, sustained shifts in Canada's international orientation.

* * *

What does the evidence suggest about the course of Canadian foreign policy over the past four decades? Which of the three theoretical perspectives offers the most accurate account of this course? As expected, none of the three theoretical perspectives by itself provides a complete or even adequate account of Canadian foreign policy in all sectors, in all dimensions of Canada's foreign policy behaviour and process, and through all periods since World War II. Yet throughout all these explorations of Canada's external behaviour, its foreign policy process, and its approach to critical sectors, a remarkably consistent pattern has emerged.

From 1945 into the 1960s, substantial elements of peripheral dependence have indeed characterized Canadian foreign policy, and traces of such patterns remain to the present day. But during the first two postwar decades, they were always overwhelmed by a liberal-internationalist orientation that rapidly achieved predominance and continues with considerable strength into the Trudeau years. During this latter period, it is the patterns predicted by the perspective of complex neo-realism that have clearly come to dominate.

During the Trudeau years, the relative decline of the United States and the growing diffusion of power in the external environment have endowed Canada with an increasing prominence in the international realm. With this prominence has come an enhanced freedom for Canada's societal and governmental leaders to shape their country's external behaviour in accordance with domestic values and the distinctive conception of world order they engender. Beginning with basic redefinitions of Canada's international relationships in the critical areas of population, resources, and technology, this transition has reshaped Canada's economic and political approaches in such previously remote regions as the Middle East. And while all Canadian leaders have made their contribution to this transition, the governments of Pierre Trudeau have been in the forefront of this profound process of change.

Indeed, when viewed from the vantage point of our three competing perspectives, the revolution in Canadian foreign policy made by Pierre Trudeau and his associates has been real, reliably reflected in their governments' subsequent behaviour, and registered in a wider sphere of behaviour than its progenitors had conceived. Skeptical of the relevance of liberal-internationalist precepts for Canada in the 1970s, the Trudeau government from 1968 to 1972 defined doctrines that conformed to and helped form the conceptual foundation of the complex neo-realist perspective. After the interlude of minority government, the regime continued from 1974 to 1980 to impose these doctrines—by emphasizing diversification abroad and the role of External Affairs as a central agency of government at home—on the patterns and processes of Canadian foreign policy as a whole. Following Prime Minister Joe Clark's short-lived Progressive Conservative government, the new Trudeau government began—through the doctrine of bilateralism, the Western Economic Summit, and the North-South dialogue—to consider Canada's distinctive contribution to shaping a new world order. And most recently, the leading intellectuals of the Trudeau government have started to state explicitly what the record of the past decade and a half clearly demonstrates: that American decline and a diffuse global environment have given Canada an opportunity to attain its true potential as one of the principal powers of the globe.

PART I
AN OVERVIEW OF CANADIAN FOREIGN POLICY: THEORY AND EVIDENCE

CHAPTER 1
THREE THEORETICAL PERSPECTIVES

Despite their differences over themes, interpretations, and values, scholars of Canadian foreign policy share an implicit interest in a single set of fundamental questions about Canada's behaviour in international affairs. These questions have been developed through public debate concerning Canada's role abroad.

The first debate centred on whether Canada should use its new formal freedom from the United Kingdom, attained in the 1931 Statute of Westminster, to sustain the League of Nations, enhance Canada's position as a North American nation, or support Britain in maintaining a broader global balance of power.[1] Although support for this last alternative was reflected in Prime Minister W. L. Mackenzie King's September 1939 decision to enter World War II and in Canada's substantial contribution to the Allied cause, the end of the war saw a new debate between those preferring a retreat to quasi-isolationism and those urging active international participation commensurate with Canada's new material strength.[2] The victory of the latter group gave Canada two decades under Prime Ministers Louis St. Laurent, John Diefenbaker, and Lester Pearson during which the precepts of liberal internationalism evolved. The 1968 election of Prime Minister Pierre Trudeau's Liberal government began a new debate about whether Canada was reverting to the isolationist and continental instincts of the interwar era, modifying its internationalist traditions to reflect new circumstances, or defining a new approach to Canadian behaviour abroad.[3]

Out of this debate has emerged the need for a more explicit, rigorous, and comprehensive analytical framework for the study of Canadian foreign policy. By drawing upon the literature of Canadian foreign policy, general foreign policy analysis, and international relations, it is possible to identify the most fundamental questions about Canada's international behaviour.[4]

Based on the thesis that a country's external activities and international presence are related to its size and capabilities—population, resources, and specialized skills and knowledge—a central question for students of international affairs and foreign policy has been to determine the relationship between these attributes and international behaviour. In the Canadian context, a postwar issue has been whether Canada's attributes are sufficient to propel it from its former status as a minor actor through small- and middle-power ranking to a more prominent place in the community of nation-states. In the shadow first of the United Kingdom and more recently of the United States, Canada has been perceived as a regional power without a region, and recognized as a middle-range partner in the Western coalition. One set of questions relating to this issue concerns Canada's historic position, or *rank*, in the hierarchy of the international system; the next questions provide the explanatory focus for Canada's *activity, association,* and *approach to world order*, examining the relative significance of *external, societal,* and *governmental* determinants.

In this chapter we present the three theoretical perspectives in terms of the seven central questions. We do not make a case for the analytical usefulness and empirical accuracy of one view rather than another. That task is left to the other chapters.

THE CENTRAL QUESTIONS OF FOREIGN POLICY ANALYSIS

International Presence

Rank

Virtually all students of foreign policy begin their explorations with a perception of a state's historical experience. Formulated into models that may try to account for the past, these evolutionary myths are partly the inherited results of exposure to particular historical traditions, partly ideological or philosophic orientations conditioning one's interpretations of evidence, and partly crude summations of easily measurable attributes. Yet in most cases, they are grounded in an underlying conception of whether the state's capacity to pursue its national interests—most basically, self-help in a competitive international system—is being diminished, maintained, or expanded over time.[5]

What is Canada's place in the international system relative to that of other states? The concern with defining Canada's position was heightened by its leading international stature at the end of World War II, when a newly emerging world order was being shaped out of the ruins of global conflict. Canada's ability to influence these efforts was seen as linked directly to its ascribed status. In the study of international relations, this focus on a state's rank has been sustained by mounting evidence of the salience of national capabilities in determining foreign policy behaviour.[6]

The question of rank includes the state's relative capability, as measured by a standard set of objective attributes such as population size and distribution, indigenous fuel supplies, and size of standing armed forces. It is also concerned with the position that it ascribes to itself and that it asserts internationally, and with the acknowledged status ascribed to it by other international actors.[7] It includes the consistency of these elements across varying international systemic configurations, geographic regions, substantive issue areas, and critical power resources.[8] And it is based on the state's maintenance of minimum levels of performance in meeting the basic requisites of statehood—notably security, sovereignty, and legitimacy.[9]

International Behaviour

Activity

The importance of a state's international ranking—both ascribed and achieved — is based upon the hypothesized relationship between rank and externally oriented behaviour.[10] The primary aspect of a state's behaviour is the activity it directs towards other actors in the international realm. Concern here centres on the *degree* of a state's activity, or the simple volume of interaction it has with its "targets" abroad; the *variety* of this activity, or the similarity across time, issues, and targets in the volume and intensity of action; and the *diffusion* of this activity among targets abroad.[11]

Association

Association is the intersection of one state's external activities with those of another, and includes the question of *initiative*—the extent to which the state maintains its membership in an existing group, participates in forming a new or altered group, or acts without direct reference to any group. It embraces a country's *commitment*—the time, resources and effort expended to produce similarity between the country's own position and the group position. And it contains the element of *focus*, or the extent to which the central target of the country's activity lies within or outside existing or emerging groups.[12] Characterized by degrees of conflict and co-operation, association can be measured by the extent to which a country's activity is similar in time, content, and target to that of other states.

Approach to World Order

Also relevant is a state's attempt to foster a global order in which relationships are organized into regimes and institutions that promote a particular distribution of political power and economic resources.[13] The first aspect is the *degree* to which the state considers that order should be registered in a comprehensive, well-developed, interrelated, and autonomous network of international organization and law. A subsequent aspect is that of *scope*—that is, the extent to which a state seeks to ensure that international order, at all levels of institutionalization, has the full, active participation of all members of the state system, and embraces a broad range of subjects. A third aspect is *transformation*, the extent to which a state supports moderate, specific alternatives or more permanent alterations in the structure of existing and emerging regimes and organizations.

Determinants of International Behaviour

External Determinants

To explain a country's particular pattern of activity, association, and quest for order, most scholars focus on the stimuli that a country receives from states and organizations abroad, whether or not these are directed at it. Their initial interest centres on the *relative salience* of this external environment—the extent of variation in a state's foreign policy behaviour caused by these states and organizations as compared with the variations explained by forces at home.[14] A further concern is the *scope* of relevant external determinants—the number and range of states and international organizations with a direct impact on a state's foreign policy behaviour. A third issue deals with a state's *sensitivity* to external stimuli—the immediacy, directness, and specificity with which external events and conditions affect the decisions of leaders and the behaviour they authorize.[15] Finally, interest centres on *actor relevance*—the identity of those particular major powers, groupings of middle and smaller powers, and leading international organizations that have the most salient, wide-ranging, and immediate impact on a state's foreign policy behaviour.

Societal Determinants

A similar set of questions arises in regard to domestic influences on a state's international behaviour.[16] The *relative salience* of domestic organizations is of fundamental concern, as is the issue of the *scope* of societal actors—the extent of differentiated, specialized, and autonomous nongovernmental institutions that have a direct impact on foreign policy behaviour.[17] Further aspects are the *sensitivity* of the government to these organizations and the *relevance* of particular actors, notably Parliament, political parties, interest groups, labour, media, business communities, and provincial governments. Also of importance is the country's profile of population, resources, and technology and the impact of these critical factors on the structure and activity of societal actors.

Governmental Determinants

The final set of questions addresses the influence of the executive branch of a state's central government on foreign policy making and ensuing behaviour.[18] The central questions remain the relative overall *salience* of governmental factors, the *scope* of institutional differentiation and autonomy, the state's *sensitivity* to its foreign policy process, and the *relevance* of specific governmental actors.[19] Attention is directed at the relevance of the prime minister and his closest associates, the

CANADA

AS A PRINCIPAL POWER

A STUDY IN FOREIGN POLICY AND INTERNATIONAL RELATIONS

DAVID B. DEWITT
UNIVERSITY OF ALBERTA

JOHN J. KIRTON
UNIVERSITY OF TORONTO

JOHN WILEY & SONS

TORONTO NEW YORK CHICHESTER BRISBANE SINGAPORE

Canadian Cataloguing in Publication Data

Dewitt, David Brian, 1948-
Canada as a principal power

Includes index.
ISBN 0-471-79885-1 (bound)
0-471-79846-0 (pbk)

1. Canada—Foreign relations—1945- I. Kirton, John J. III. Title.

FC242.D38 327.71 C82-095031-9
F1029.D38

Printed and bound in Canada
10 9 8 7 6 5 4 3 2 1

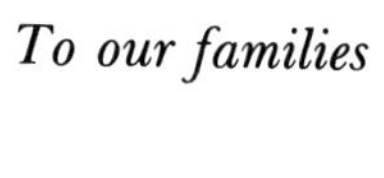

To our families

PREFACE

Over the four years spent researching and writing this book, we have received considerable assistance and support from the community of scholars, in some instances beyond the norms of the profession. The Institute of International Relations at the University of British Columbia and its director, Mark Zacher, provided both the initial catalyst for our collaboration in this work and the intellectual and financial support to sustain it in the critical early stages. Further generous assistance has been provided by the Social Sciences and Humanities Research Council of Canada, through a research grant, and by our home institutions, the Department of Political Science, University of Alberta, and Trinity College and the Department of Political Science, University of Toronto. In many ways, this project has benefitted more than most from the counsel, suggestions, and criticisms of a substantial number of colleagues. Among them, special thanks are due to Howard Adelman, Don Barry, David Cox, Charles Doran, Leslie Green, John Holmes, Brian Job, David Leyton-Brown, Peyton Lyon, Roberta McKown, Tony Miller, Don Munton, Cranford Pratt, Larry Pratt, Denis Stairs, Janice Stein, Garth Stevenson, Don Story, Brian Tomlin, and Harald von Riekhoff for commenting on all or parts of the manuscript. David Leyton-Brown, Garth Stevenson, Cranford Pratt, and Peyton Lyon did much to clarify our thinking on the theoretical perspectives, with David and Garth providing, respectively, the labels of complex neo-realism and peripheral dependence. In addition, informal presentations provided opportunities for discussion with David Bercuson, Peter Busch, David Elkins, Kal Holsti, Jim Keeley, and Kim Nossal. As we have tried to embed our study of Canadian foreign policy in the broader framework of international relations, we are especially indebted to our former teachers Alexander George, Robert Keohane, and Robert North at Stanford University, and George Liska, Charles Burton Marshall, and Roger Swanson at the School of Advanced International Studies of the Johns Hopkins University. As for all who study Canada's foreign policy, our debt to John Holmes is enormous.

In researching this book, we have been equally fortunate in the assistance we have received from officials of the Canadian government and foreign service, within the bounds of our respective professional obligations. We thank all those who generously participated in our program of extensive interviews over the past four years. We also acknowledge the invaluable help provided by our students Martha Konig and Andrew Stark (UBC), Mary Joy Aiken, Ashraful Hasan, and Ian Montgomerie (Alberta), and Blair Dimock, Steven Cobrin, Chris Cooter, Leonard Preyra, and George Takach (Toronto). Elbridge Goode played a very special part as research assistant and critic. His death in the summer of 1982 is a great loss to the scholarly community, for he was clearly headed towards a fine academic career.

The transformation from draft to manuscript to book was made possible by the patience and talent of Darlene Nosko and Darlene Miske (Alberta) and Kathy McCallum and Herma Joel (Toronto). Finally, our work owes much to the people at John Wiley & Sons, who ensured that our ideas would reach the marketplace. Our sincere thanks and appreciation for the perseverance and superb editorial capabilities of Jim Rogerson, Kathryn Dean, and Wiley's editorial personnel.

This book is a collaborative effort. While each of us took the lead for specific research areas and the initial drafts of particular chapters, all material has been worked and reworked together. Although we gratefully acknowledge the excellent comments and criticisms we received from our colleagues, only we are responsible for the presentation in the following pages.

David B. Dewitt
Edmonton, Alberta

John J. Kirton
Toronto, Ontario

February, 1983

CONTENTS

Canada is a large power; to call us a "middle power" is inaccurate. . . . As an immigrant country with a barely developed natural resource base to our economy, and a rapidly adapting capability in technology and processing, we are to some extent only now beginning to reach our true potential.

Allan Gotlieb, Canadian Ambassador to the United States and formerly Undersecretary of State for External Affairs.

government's foreign office, and especially the domestically oriented departments and agencies responsible for critical changes in the state's pattern of growth in population, resources, and technology.[20] The complexity of the modern state requires that attention be given to the central foreign policy co-ordinative structures and processes in attempts to define autonomously and implement overarching conceptions of the national interest.[21]

Table 1.1 provides a schematic overview of the seven basic foreign policy questions and the predictions of each of the three theoretical perspectives.

THE LIBERAL-INTERNATIONALIST PERSPECTIVE

The most common answers to the basic foreign policy questions are contained in the still-dominant liberal-internationalist perspective.[22] This perspective, however, has remained less a systematic theory than a collection of assumptions and descriptions. In part, the flexibility of this perspective reflects the original articulation of these themes by individual practitioners such as Lester Pearson, John Holmes, Hume Wrong, and Escott Reid, each of whom contributed to the evolving body of thought with his own distinctive tone. Moreover, since liberal internationalism was a virtually unchallenged orthodoxy in both policy and academic circles during the decade following 1947, there was little need to defend and distill its elements through scholarly interchange or policy debate.[23] Hence the liberal-internationalist perspective developed less as a single systematic academic theory than as a related collection of central themes produced by the practitioners themselves.

The first central theme developed by the policy makers, indeed the foundation for the entire liberal-internationalist edifice, was "functionalism". Grounded in a theory of representation outlined by Mackenzie King on 9 July 1943, functionalism began with Canada's desire that in the postwar international institutions, effective representation should be neither restricted exclusively to the largest states nor extended equally to all states, but rather that it should be given to those countries "which have the greatest contribution to make to the particular object in question."[24] As this suggested, Canada's first-hand experience with the failure of the League of Nations and the frustrations of great-power dominance of the wartime alliance led it to repudiate the concept of international organizations as vehicles for either small-power egalitarianism or great-power concert. Canadian policy makers asserted that Canada's rapidly enhanced capacity to contribute to the alliance enabled it to be recognized as a middle power and to participate with responsibility and effectiveness in shaping and operating postwar institutions.

TABLE 1.1 Theoretical Perspectives on Canadian Foreign Policy: Predictions Based on Ideal Types

Foreign Policy Questions	*Liberal Internationalism*	*Peripheral Dependence*	*Complex Neo-Realism*
A. International Presence			
1. Rank	middle power	small, penetrated power	principal power
B. International Behaviour			
2. Activity			
Degree	active participation	low interaction	global involvement
Variety	responsible participation	undifferentiated interaction	interest-based involvement
Diffusion	multiple participation	imperial-focused interaction	autonomous bilateral involvement
3. Association			
Initiative	combination	adherence	unilateralism
Commitment	consensus	acquiescence	divergence
Focus	constraint	support	diversification
4. Approach to World Order			
Degree	moderate institutionalization	existing institutionalization	revised institutionalization
Scope	multilateralization	hegemony and marginal universalism	concert
Transformation	reformation	marginal redistribution	modification

C. Determinants of International Behaviour			
5. External Determinants			
Relative Salience	moderate	high	low
Scope	moderate	low	high
Sensitivity	moderate	low	high
Actor Relevance			
United Kingdom	moderate	high	low
United States	moderate	high	low
U.S.S.R.	moderate	low	high
China	moderate	low	high
Large European States and Japan	moderate	low	high
Non-European Middle Powers	high	low	moderate
Small European States	high	low	moderate
Other Small States	high	low	moderate
NATO	moderate	low	high
United Nations	high	low	moderate
6. Societal Determinants			
Relative Salience	moderate	low	high
Scope			
Institutional Differentiation	moderate	low	high
Institutional Autonomy	moderate	low	high
Sensitivity	moderate	low	high
Actor Relevance			
Parliament	high	low	moderate
Parties	high	low	moderate
Associational Interest Groups	moderate	low	high
Labour	moderate	low	high
Media	low	moderate	high
Business Community	low	moderate	high
Provincial Governments	low	high	moderate
Critical Capabilities	resources and technology	resources	population, resources, and technology

TABLE 1.1 Theoretical Perspectives on Canadian Foreign Policy: Predictions Based on Ideal Types
(cont'd)

Foreign Policy Questions	*Liberal Internationalism*	*Peripheral Dependence*	*Complex Neo-Realism*
7. Governmental Determinants			
Relative Salience	moderate	low	high
Scope			
Institutional Differentiation	moderate	low	high
Institutional Autonomy	moderate	low	high
Sensitivity	moderate	low	high
Actor Relevance			
Prime Ministerial Group	moderate	low	high
Department of External Affairs	high	low	moderate
Foreign Service Departments	low	moderate	high
Other Domestic Departments	low	moderate	high
Agencies and Crown Corporations	low	moderate	high
Central Foreign Policy			
Co-ordinative Structures	moderate	low	high

Moreover, by stressing Canada's particular relevance to economic institutions, the functional theme drew on a broader concept of functionalism, originated by David Mitrany. This concept suggested that the international agenda should be divided into issue areas, that military functions should not dominate the others, and that national sovereignty and military force should be eroded by developing a nonpolitical network of discrete international organizations, each dedicated to the performance of a specialized global task.[25]

Reflecting Canada's concern with functional representation was its success in injecting into the United Nations Charter the provision, codified in Article 23, that due regard be given to a state's contribution to peace and security in elections to the six nonpermanent seats on the Security Council. Expressing its broader conception of functional specialization was the leading role Canada played in the formation of a host of agencies, notably the International Monetary Fund, the Food and Agricultural Organization, the United Nations Relief and Rehabilitation Administration, the International Civil Aviation Organization, and the General Agreement on Tariffs and Trade, as well as the Economic and Social Council. The fusion of these two forms of functionalism, their entrenchment in Canadian diplomatic practice, and their extension to new arenas were clearly evident by the end of the decade when Canada succeeded in inserting a clause (Article 2) in the North Atlantic Treaty calling for a variety of nonmilitary functions.

A second central foreign policy theme, developed primarily in the 1950s, was that of "mediatory middlepowermanship", which expanded Canada's commitment to vigorous activity abroad and codified the meaning of the term "middle power" into a more precise, self-defined, but externally encouraged obligation to adopt positions between those of opposing actors and to work actively towards reconciliation.

Developed initially as a consequence of Canada's skill in early United Nations conference diplomacy, the theme acquired a new dimension in the late 1940s and early 1950s as Canada responded to requests for observer and supervisory teams in Asia, the Middle East, and Indochina. It was given generalized prominence by the success of Lester Pearson's peacekeeping efforts in response to the 1956 Suez crisis and reached maturity in the 1964 Cyprus dispute, when Secretary of State for External Affairs Paul Martin emulated Pearson's earlier success.[26] In that same year, the publication of the defence White Paper enshrined peacekeeping as the first priority for Canada's military establishment. After that time its attraction began to fade as a result of the United Nations debates over financing peacekeeping forces in 1964 and 1965, domestic concern over Canadian "complicity" in Vietnam in the mid-1960s, and widespread disenchantment with the concept itself following President Gamal Nasser's successful request for removal of the Canadian contingent in Egypt before the Middle East war of 1967.

A third major theme developed by Ottawa's foreign policy élite, which can be termed "distributive internationalism", evolved as an attempt to address the new demands of the decolonized world of the 1960s.[27] This defined an approach to world order extending well beyond the promotion of peace and security within the *status quo*, which peacekeeping initiatives tended to enshrine. It sought to reduce economic disparities between rich and poor states by the donation, largely under the auspices of multilateral organizations, of large volumes of official development assistance. While this emphasis had its origins in Canada's contribution to postwar assistance to European allies, to new United Nations relief programs, to the Commonwealth's Colombo Plan in the 1950s, and to African and Caribbean Commonwealth states during John Diefenbaker's government, it assumed prominence only during the period of Liberal government and sustained economic growth that began in 1963.

This cumulative thematic portrait of Canada as a middle power with functional capabilities, mediatory roles, and distributive responsibilities emerged out of the combined experience and vision of Canada's postwar foreign policy élite and was predicated upon a powerful, mutually reinforcing, and unifying set of core premises and precepts about Canada's place in the world, its foreign policy approaches, and the processes that formulated them. As interpreted by liberal-internationalist authors, Canada's international experience is based on a constant co-operative endeavour to enhance universal values through the steady development of a more institutionalized and just international order.[28]

Fundamental to this pursuit is Canada's perceived rank in the international system as a middle power.[29] This conception derives less from the term's meaning in international relations, or even the prewar debates over Canada's status, than from preoccupation with Canada's place in the United Nations system, earlier experience with the League of Nations, and the promise of functionalism as a guide to an improved postwar arrangement. The early authors saw a hierarchical, stratified international system in which objective capability, asserted position, and recognized status combined to produce three classes of states.

At the top was a group of seven great powers, composed of the four wartime allies with permanent seats on the Security Council (the United States, the Soviet Union, the United Kingdom, and France) plus three states (West Germany, Italy, and Japan) whose status as major wartime adversaries precluded Security Council membership. China was sometimes listed as the eighth great power.[30] Below came a group of about a dozen middle powers, with considerable capability and political independence. They also had special claims to influence, based on their status as European colonial powers with global concerns (Holland and Belgium), as major Commonwealth contributors to Allied victory

(Canada, Australia, and South Africa), as dominant powers in regions outside Europe (Mexico, Brazil, Argentina, and Egypt), as states at the critical intersection of geopolitical boundaries (Sweden, Yugoslavia, and Poland), or as states with a combination of the above characteristics (pre-eminently India, which embodied the last three). And at the bottom was a collection of small states, which could exert influence only as a group, at best. Within this overall configuration, the existence, boundaries, and even composition of the categories and Canada's location in the middle-power range were remarkably clear.

Over time this conception of Canada was sustained as it evolved from a small state to a stable middle power and was critically reinforced by the dynamic logic of functionalism. The cold war, decolonization, and the revival of defeated powers began to transform the international system. The shifting doctrines of containment, peaceful coexistence, and détente altered both the geographic focus of international concern and the effective instruments of statecraft. Yet throughout this turbulence, Canada continued to be perceived not as "the smallest of the large" or "the largest of the small", but as a vital middle-ranking power.

Canada's high rank in regions such as the Caribbean, Africa, the Commonwealth, and francophonie, in areas such as development assistance, and in assets such as food, energy, and minerals compensated for areas of relative vulnerability (small population) and provided a basis for Canadian entry into geographic regions where it was comparatively weak (the United States and countries in remote regions) and for Canadian participation in select high-technology fields (for example, defence). Secondly, Canada's close relationship with the United States, its sensitivity to developing states' aspirations, its solid reservoir of basic capabilities and infrastructure, and its particular strengths in vital human skills, natural resources, and communications technologies ensured that Canada's variation in rank would not be too severe and that overall equilibrium could be maintained through the *ad hoc* shift of resources from one arena to another with only moderate costs in resources and time.[31] And thirdly, Canada's skilled, developed state apparatus meant that challenges to Canadian boundaries, occasional incursions into its territory, and its potential vulnerability to actors with superior technology could be prevented, pre-empted, or countered.[32]

It is this view of Canada's stable middle-power rank that both allows and stimulates distinctive approaches to the questions of activity, association, and order that define international behaviour. The degree of activity is characterized by a strong emphasis on active participation in international affairs and on the maintenance of substantial, relatively continuous contact with many actors abroad. This active participation stems from a multitude of motives: a vague concern with status; a rejection of prewar quasi-isolationist instincts; a direct concern with differentiating Canada from small powers while tempering the collective dominance of the great; a longer-range wish to acquire an international reputation for reliability and experience; a desire to prevent lapses into anarchy, isolationism, and withdrawal; and a concern with safeguarding core Canadian interests. Although constrained by the realization that influence is limited, actions not decisive, and direct interests often remote, Canadian leaders assume that at least other middle powers can be influenced by their actions. The most visible manifestation is an emphasis on displaying capacity and assuming duties beyond merely monitoring developments or exercising a right to be heard, and extending into taking initiatives, catalyzing action, and exercising leadership within the middle-power range.

The variety of activity is expressed in liberal-internationalist scholarship in terms of responsible participation, meaning that Canadian external behaviour includes a moderate number of independent foreign involvements, ranging beyond narrow national interests to encompass the universal values professed by Canadian leaders. Demanding considerable consistency over time and across issues, "responsibility" is expressed in recurrent injunctions to Canadian representatives to formulate their positions in the light of previous contributions and service, to forward proposals that display objective judgement and a sense of proportion, and to ground advice in well-developed proposals for world security.

The diffusion of activity has focused on multiple participation as a necessary complement to active and responsible participation in international affairs. This means that Canada has directed a substantial amount of its activity towards a considerable number of states and the international organizations in which they cluster. Although admitting Canada's historic focus on the North Atlantic world, the liberal-internationalist perspective points to the need for Canada to become involved in several arenas and coalitions, to maintain membership in many informal or institutionalized blocs or groupings, and to develop ties with both like-minded states and the superpowers. In practical terms, it involves supplementing and balancing North American ties with those in NATO, offsetting these with affiliations in the Commonwealth, maintaining a certain flexibility in behaviour at the United Nations, yet displaying some reluctance to become fully associated with such distant ventures as the Organization of American States, the Central Treaty Organization, and the Southeast Asia Treaty Organization.

Scholars see Canada's initiative, the first characteristic of associative behaviour, in its particular proclivity towards combination. In other words, Canada takes the initiative in forming new coalitions while acting within the existing institutionalized framework. Highlighting its facility at coalition diplomacy, these authors stress Canada's skill in assembling groupings, often of fellow middle powers, to offset the weight of existing blocs and thereby reduce the divisions among them. Furthermore, this process is seen to involve a large number of countries, including both Third World states and great powers, in efforts to forge broader and more enduring associations.

A complementary manifestation of this concern with association is the factor of commitment, wherein Canada is portrayed as expending considerable resources to ensure substantial similarity within coalitions. This contextual concern with consensus aims primarily at securing temporary or medium-range agreements in order to satisfy relevant actors and especially to diffuse disputes that threaten great-power confrontation. The routine expression of this quest for consensus consists of initiating compromises, lobbying sponsors and supporters for resolutions, and, more generally, using existing international organizations for conciliation rather than enforcement. Its most dramatic manifestation is an instinctive thrust towards diplomatic mediation and military peacekeeping in crisis situations.

Inspired by a desire to preserve a precarious global stability, Canada intervenes directly to reduce conflicts between great powers or their clients by the three-stage formula of securing a cease-fire, ensuring a disengagement of forces, and working towards a durable political settlement. This emphasis on mediation and peacekeeping, begun in order to facilitate the retreat of the European great powers from overseas imperial involvements, slowly acquired a broader relevance, including bridge-building between the Soviet Union and the United States and the promotion of accommodation between the developed and underdeveloped worlds.[33]

The focus of such associative behaviour in the liberal-internationalist vision is a particular emphasis on practising the "diplomacy of constraint".[34] This is designed to inhibit the unilateral exercise of preponderant American power in a manner unfavourable to Canadian and global interests. The primary instrument is the creation of a wide multinational regime of common norms and the institutional machinery to make them effective. In overseas relations the exercise of constraint requires Canada to concentrate on those groups in which the United States is involved and to mobilize coalition partners in an effort to lessen American dominance. It further demands a continual effort to channel as much American behaviour as possible through multilateral institutions, where the restraining effects of institutional norms and informal persuasion can be applied most effectively. Tactically, this suggests private persuasion rather than public criticism, operating within defined norms emphasizing co-operation and understanding, making limited concessions on subordinate issues, and, in the end, siding with the U.S., whether right or wrong, in order to maintain influence for the future.

From the perspective of liberal-internationalist writers, the successful pursuit of constraint relies on strategies derived from a conception of the Canada–U.S. relationship as a stable partnership.[35] The use of quiet diplomacy is seen to ensure that the overall level of friction on subordinate North American issues does not impede an effective dialogue on more significant multilateral issues. It calls for the use of joint Canada–U.S. organizations to isolate North American problems from broader issues and to allow them to be dealt with on their merits by experts using technical criteria. Effective constraint also occurs through the maintenance of close contacts with decision makers in the executive branch of the U.S. government. Together these techniques offer Canada the prospect of balanced bargains on bilateral issues and a reservoir of goodwill and influence to deploy in multilateral affairs.

Furthermore, from the Canadian domestic arena the pursuit of constraint is viewed in terms of a government desire to maintain "diplomatic capital" with the United States for use on global issues. Canadian society is seen to be sufficiently secure and its values sufficiently similar to those of the United States to allow effective influence. While Canadian policy encourages national alternatives to U.S.-based organizations and forces, the confluence of Canadian and American interests is perceived to pre-empt the likelihood of countervailing U.S. intervention.[36]

Perhaps the most memorable aspect of the liberal-internationalist vision is its distinctive approach to the question of world order. In terms of degree, the pursuit of a moderately institutionalized order is secured through the persistent preservation, enrichment, and development of the norms of international collaboration and the organizations in which they are enshrined. This quest is partially motivated by a sense of Canada's vulnerability, as a resource-rich but sparsely populated country, to a breakdown of the international legal order. It is, however, more directly inspired by a recognition of the broader, long-term value of enhancing, encoding, and rendering more durable the common values among states, a realization that mediation and peacekeeping are essentially rear-guard actions, and a knowledge that in the absence of further action, an unjust *status quo* will prevail.

Moderate institutionalization requires an incremental strategy of controlled change, limiting objectives to the realm of the feasible, accepting compromises when necessary, and developing a broadly elaborated, internally coherent, institutionally embedded, and widely supported corpus of international law. The hallmark of this effort is outstanding support to international institutions generally, and a particular concern with strengthening the United Nations system and the office of its secretary general. Its major manifestations are the provision of large, well-prepared, high-level delegations, regular, reliable, and vigorous participation in conferences and committees, the constant formulation and sponsorship of resolutions, adherence to the outcome of votes, respect for the autonomy and initiatives of these institutions' secretariats, and the commitment of qualified personnel, financing, and military forces to their purposes.

The liberal-internationalist approach to the second component of world order—scope—is a strong emphasis on multilateralization. Under this imperative Canada consistently seeks to ensure that international law and international organization and their activities embrace and receive the active support of a large number and broad range of states in the international system. It is reflected specifically in active attempts to convert bilateral arrangements and organizations to multilateral ones and to have multilateral bodies include and be effectively influenced by as many states as possible, up to the point where gains in breadth would clearly weaken either the strength of the organization or great-power commitment to it.[37]

Beyond this emphasis on multilateralization, the liberal-internationalist orientation displays little interest in any fundamental, short-term transformation of the international order. Rather, under a liberal-internationalist perspective, Canada is guided by a commitment to a stable framework in which great powers, as full and unquestioned members, are allowed to play their special role, the egalitarian principles of small states remain limited, and power and authority are shared in fair proportion. This view of world-order transformation—reformation—implies gradual, discretionary improvement in existing regimes and organizations while limiting more extensive change to areas where order remains undefined. It extends to modifying the procedures and structures of institutions in anticipation of short-term modifications in the international balance of power, such as those deriving from the existence, strength, and cohesion of the Third World. Also it may inspire support for a redistribution of political and economic power in newer areas of international regulation, such as the sea bed and outer space.[38]

The liberal-internationalist literature also sets forth a particular portrait of the factors that determine international behaviour. First, it assumes the existence of a moderately salient, open, and polycentric international environment displaying the conditions of complex interdependence.[39] External determinants are attributed an overall importance roughly equal to societal and governmental factors, events abroad given a rather immediate, direct, and specific relevance, and a good number of individual actors assigned a substantial weight in determining Canada's external behaviour.[40] In particular, the moderate influence over Canada enjoyed by the United States is portrayed as balanced by a similar amount of influence exercised individually by the United Kingdom, large European states (and later Japan), and, to a lesser degree, the Soviet Union and the People's Republic of China. A high degree of influence is accorded small European states, major non-European middle powers such as India, and groups of other small states. And a particular importance is attached to international organizations as autonomous entities, notably the United Nations and, at a lower level, the North Atlantic Treaty Organization.[41]

Within the domestic societal environment, liberal internationalism accepts the features of a classic constitutional model of parliamentary government as it has traditionally operated in foreign affairs. It attributes only a moderate overall salience to societal determinants in the belief that foreign policy remains largely impervious to internal forces within a large, empty country and that neither American economic penetration nor federal–provincial conflict precludes an active Canadian role abroad. Although moral considerations have some direct and autonomous influence, general public opinion has particularly low salience and legitimacy.[42]

The liberal-internationalist conception of governmental determinants is equally circumscribed, pointing to a moderately salient, reasonably well developed, and autonomous set of executive branch institutions, while remaining skeptical of comprehensive and elaborate decision-making systems. It accords a predominant influence to the Department of External Affairs and its career foreign service officers, and a more moderate but generally reinforcing influence to the prime minister and those within his immediate group. In contrast, those in the other foreign service departments as well as domestic departments and agencies are seen to have a relatively low involvement and influence, partly as a reflection of the somewhat underdeveloped state of large bureaucratic structures within the executive branch. A moderately influential role is assigned to the central foreign policy co-ordinative structure, primarily in recognition of the effectiveness of such informal devices as periodic gatherings of senior officials, the rapid crisis-response capability of politicians and officials, and the easy diffusion of Cabinet attitudes and perspectives within a relatively small executive branch.

THE PERIPHERAL-DEPENDENCE PERSPECTIVE

Over the past two decades the predominant liberal-internationalist interpretation of Canada's international experience has been faced with an increasingly strong challenge.[43] Although partially grounded in basic concepts similar to those of classical Marxism, the work in the tradition of peripheral dependence draws from a diverse set of conceptual approaches, more eclectic than the origins of the liberal-internationalist school.[44] In the field of Canadian foreign policy, peripheral dependence also embraces some who operate from conservative premises as well as those with socialist ones, and who give emphasis to Canada's cultural and political dependence on dominant actors abroad as well as its economic dependence.

Despite these variations, for analytical purposes peripheral dependence can be treated as a coherent theoretical perspective challenging the analysis of liberal internationalism. In its original formulation in the prewar era, peripheral dependence in Canadian foreign policy study suggested that economic and cultural dependence emerge simultaneously from the same forces, reinforce each other, and lead directly, perhaps inexorably, to a diminution in political autonomy.[45] A similar conception pervades the modern phase of this literature, which emerged in the late 1950s and gave critical emphasis to Canada's lack of domestic socio-economic and external political independence from the United States and the world system centred upon it. More recently, dependency theory in the general literature of international relations and comparative politics and the political economy tradition within Canada have begun to provide a comprehensive, self-reinforcing consistency for the peripheral-dependence perspective.[46]

The modern themes of the peripheral-dependence perspective, like those of its liberal-internationalist competitor, were developed as responses to particular challenges and catalysts. The first such theme, dating from the work of the Royal Commission on Canada's Economic Prospects in 1956 and the Gordon budget of 1963, highlighted the constraint on Canada's economic independence arising from its heavy concentration on direct investment from the United States.[47] Although an important focus of government debate during the mid-1960s, this concern with the ramifications of undue concentration had few major implications outside the normal economic issue area until the creation of the Watkins task force in 1967.

A second theme, inaugurated by James Minifie's widely read work in 1960, addressed the autonomy of Canadian foreign policy.[48] Fuelled by such visible issues as Canada's vulnerability during the Cuban missile crisis of 1962 and its acquisition of nuclear weapons in 1963, this theme peaked with Canada's alleged complicity with the United States in the war in Vietnam. Although reflected in rhetoric leading up to the Trudeau government's early foreign policy initiatives, this theme had surprisingly little direct influence on those actions and rapidly receded with the start of the American withdrawal from Vietnam in 1969.

A final theme, expressed most eloquently in George Grant's *Lament for a Nation* in 1965, was concern over irreversible cultural homogenization and consequent deindustrialization experienced by Canada as a result of the global spread of United States liberal and corporate values and industrial techniques.[49] Partly an expansion of the initial concern with concentrated economic penetration and the Massey commission's worry about the artistic and scholarly communities in Canada, this envisaged a threat that was far more pervasive within Canada and linked it far more durably to the United States in the world capitalist system. Its major impact on government policy came in a moderate form in the 1970s, with determined moves to give direct protection to the indigenous print and broadcast media. These major themes provide the context in which authors in the peripheral-dependence school determine their responses to the seven central questions of foreign policy.

Despite the varying emphasis on the economic, political, or cultural forms of domination, students in the peripheral-dependence tradition portray Canada's historical experience, following its attainment of formal autonomy from the United Kingdom, as a steady drift into dependence upon the United States.[50] Adherents differ considerably over the consciousness of this trend in public and private élites in both countries, their intentions in fostering it, and the prospects for arresting or reversing it. Yet they portray the trend as a unilinear decline, taking place with few pauses or reverses, and grounded in the objective forces propelling the United States to a dominant position in the world capitalist economy and international political system. Furthermore, they see comprehensive and extensive regression as U.S. direct investment diminishes Canada's basic productive capability in relation to other equally industrialized countries, truncates and fragments its economic and social institutions, and thus erodes its capacity for an autonomous foreign policy.

From the perspective of peripheral dependence, Canada is ranked as a small, penetrated power within the international hierarchy. While Canada's advanced resource capitalism is acknowledged, its capability is seen as significantly eroded by several forces—its status between the developed North and underdeveloped South and its intermediate level of technology, with an overdeveloped sphere of circulation and an underdeveloped sphere of production. Stemming from the success of the United States, with its early industrialization, in dominating ownership and control of Canadian production and injecting ancillary social and cultural flows into the Canadian environment, this uneven, penetrated development has several consequences. It inhibits Canadians from developing a concept of their country's relevance in the world at large and induces them to focus on a bilateral Canada–U.S. framework  that accentuates their subordinate status and leads to a preoccupation with defensive efforts to limit American power. It also renders it  difficult, so it is argued, for actors to conceive of Canada as autonomous and distinctive in international politics, with more damaging consequences than the earlier reluctance to acknowledge Canada's legal independence from the United Kingdom. In addition, U.S. penetration deprives Canada of the independent productive capabilities essential to engender adaptability and stability in shifting environments and to  ensure prominence in some regional and substantive areas that would make Canada relevant in the world as more than a mere channel of American influence. Furthermore, this distorted development compromises Canadian security, sovereignty, and legitimacy through the presence of an American defence umbrella, the extraterritorial application of U.S. law to American-controlled firms operating in Canada, the adoption of American perspectives and values by Canadian élites, the pervasive intrusion of U.S. media into Canada, and the tendency of Canadians to look southward to centres of decision-making authority and economic reward.

This combination of peripheral status, distorted development, and pervasive penetration leads to a degree of international activity characterized by low interaction with the outside world and the virtual absence of independent, direct contacts in world politics. Such contacts as exist take the form not of a regular flow of activity but of intermittent actions limited to a monitoring and servicing role. This pattern arises partly from the lack of broad, direct Canadian interests, limitations on Canada's physical resources, and a lack of knowledge about affairs abroad.[51] But more importantly, it stems from a lack of interest on the part of recipient countries in sustaining the interaction because they regard Canada as having little power, few interests, and very limited scope for divergence from American policy. Within the United States itself, a similar absence of political concern exists, sustained by the confidence of American decision makers that Canada will operate, without threats, within the framework of American policy; consequently they allocate only limited resources to the maintenance of a policy dialogue with Canadian officials.

From the peripheral-dependence perspective, the variety of Canadian external activity is distinguished by its undifferentiated interaction. Consisting of a single pattern of limited complexity, Canadian behaviour tends to manifest a virtual uniformity in its level of involvement and policy preferences over time and across issue areas. This pattern reflects Canada's fundamental lack of autonomy, the homogenization of its economic and societal institutions, the spread of American multinationals, the U.S. government's promotion of open-door doctrines, trade and capital liberalization, and regional economic integration, and the consequent disincentive for other governments, often similarly conditioned, to inspire creative Canadian actions.

Diffusion, the third dimension of international activity, is portrayed as imperial-focused interaction, the heavy concentration on a predominant power in the global system and on those actors most closely associated with it.[52] For Canada this interaction concentrates on U.S. governmental and private organizations operating within Canada, on the issues of Canadian "nationalism" that they create, and on the formation of special alliances within the U.S. government and the private sector. Additional interactions focus on international organizations reliably controlled by the United States and on geopolitical regions lying clearly within the U.S. sphere of influence.[53] Moreover, given the tendency of dominant centres to draw disproportionate resources from peripheries, reinforced by the existence of "special" bilateral arrangements, the peripheral-dependence vision implies a steady contraction in Canada's relations with the outside world.[54] Together, these forces leave Canada with fewer associations abroad, minimal capacity to develop bilateral or multilateral ties with states outside the U.S. sphere of influence, a plethora of bilateral ties with the United States, and the rigidity in behaviour that such a lack of balance promotes.

From this concentration flows a tendency for Canada, in the realm of association, to adhere to the defined requirements and informal obligations of its membership in existing groups, particularly those that the United States dominates. Lacking distinctive interests and values, an autonomous capacity to calculate consequences, or an indigenous conception of preferred global arrangements, Canada takes few initiatives to form coalitions or modify existing ones. Rather, knowing that action by the United States and the groups it dominates is required for others to act, Canada operates within the framework of existing associations, trying to influence American action to the advantage of élites within Canada and forwarding proposals only when assured of passive support, active co-operation, or subsequent imitation from the United States.

This deference to the legitimacy of American-dominated groupings breeds an acquiescent commitment towards their policy debates. American wisdom and capability are seen to be sufficient to deter challenges from alternative great powers or lesser-power coalitions, and to render unnecessary the active pursuit of consensus and compromise. American positions are adopted as Canada's own. Multilaterally, Canada undertakes mediation and peacekeeping only on U.S. initiative, with a view to protecting American interests in regions and situations where they are challenged. Bilaterally it anticipates and defers in advance to probable U.S. reactions and avoids extended bargaining.

The focus of Canada's associational activity that arises from the acquiescent commitment to U.S.-dominated groups is its active support for American preferences and policies. In defining approaches that will maximize its diplomatic company, Canada focuses first on groups in which the United States is the leading power and within them, on the United States and its closest associates. Multilaterally it provides direct reinforcement for United States foreign policy doctrines and limits its dissent from U.S. positions to marginal aspects.[55] Bilaterally it assigns the highest importance to the themes of harmony and commonality in the "special relationship", relies heavily on "exemptionalism", and encourages a flow of transactions from the United States into Canada.[56]

This deferential preoccupation with the actions of the imperial power both reflects and reinforces a highly limited conception of world order. Realizing that the United States, as the predominant actor, defines the shape of the international order, Canada accepts the internal structure and overall adequacy of existing institutions. Similarly, a preoccupation with the penetrative impact of the United States within Canada gives rise to a preference for marginal universalism, as it leaves little scope, beyond declaratory policy, for promotion of organizations in which large numbers of small powers are fully involved. Canada's dominant concern in practice becomes a preference for marginal redistribution through the reinforcement of an American-inspired "internationalism", which breaks down all possible cultural, institutional, and political barriers to the unlimited expansion of multinational corporations.[57] Canada thus works for the creation of international organizations promoting open-door or free-flow regimes in global trade and investment and the mobility of key professional élites. Within this framework, it supports the expansion of Canadian-based actors, particularly in the financial fields, into regions abroad. And it maintains an attitude towards the internal composition of other governments and societies that heavily favours stability, peaceful change, and reform only by Western democratic norms.

Perhaps the clearest feature of the peripheral-dependence perspective is its highly developed conception of the underlying structures that determine Canada's external behaviour. This view attributes a very high salience to external forces. In this vision, Canada, because of its late development within the world capitalist system, experienced an externally induced industrialization that built into its societal structure a profound economic vulnerability to foreign forces. This process of industrialization coincided with the American rise to global predominance. Domestic vulnerability to the American presence rapidly spread from economic to social and political sectors and was registered in the operational premises of Canadian action. The scope of external determinants in this perspective is low. Although the United Kingdom retained some special influence, the global power of the United States since World War II, its particular weight in bilateral and domestic matters, the role of U.S.-based multinational corporations, and the capacity for U.S.-directed action in crisis situations make it the only state with a direct and noticeable impact on Canadian behaviour. Canadian foreign policy, therefore, is relatively insensitive to the international arena while being particularly sensitive to the United States.

In keeping with the high salience assigned to external forces, the perspective of peripheral dependence places a low weight on the influence wielded by actors within Canadian society, viewing them merely as channels for the direct and indirect transmission of preferences developed in the United States. It portrays a strong set of U.S.-controlled corporations, manufacturing enterprises, and resource interests, guided by American parents and the U.S. government and capable of using superior financial, organizational, and advertising capabilities to influence provincial governments, political parties, interest groups, and public opinion. It considers any countervailing power exercised by Canadian-controlled economic actors to be significantly reduced by several factors: their location in the circulation sectors of finance, transportation, utilities, trade, and foodstuffs; their resulting dependence on servicing U.S.-controlled firms; their overt alliance with this group through interlocking directorships; and the common interest of the Canadian economic, cultural, and educational élites in forwarding the values of corporate capitalism, liberalism, and consumption. In this view, such forces discourage indigenous entrepreneurship and innovation, constrain middle-range Canadian-controlled manufacturing and service industries, and confine them to the relatively strong sectors of pulp and paper, agriculture, mining, and iron and steel. In these areas, Canadian firms, as a consequence of railroad construction and western settlement, experienced early entry, significant government assistance, and a strong technological lead.

In addition, the peripheral-dependence perspective acknowledges the presence in only truncated form of a structure of intermediate interest groups, active media, and public opinion, and of such critical capabilities as markets to mobilize large pools of long-range risk capital, merchant bankers, international trading consortiums, innovation-based manufacturing industries, research and development facilities, private policy planning bodies, and indigenous cultural organizations.[58] It notes that powerful labour unions have been hampered by internal divisions and the state's preference for conservative international bodies over radical independent ones. It assigns somewhat greater influence to the media, which, as vehicles for U.S. penetration, captivate an uninformed, fearful, and reticent mass public opinion and engender rampant homogenization of Canada's cultural life.

A prominent role is assigned to provincial governments, particularly that of Quebec. Generally the peripheral-dependence perspective sees a steady increase in American direct investment during the postwar period eroding the traditional alliance among indigenous large-scale enterprise, the Conservative Party, and the central government. From this perspective the ensuing shift of power towards the provinces is reinforced because all provinces favour rapid exploitation for revenue purposes of the staple resources, critical for industrial capability, that they constitutionally control.[59] Because export markets lie in the United States, a series of specialized north–south economies has developed with few interrelationships, heavily dependent on U.S. markets, management, investment, and general economic conditions, and lacking interest in the overseas-oriented, east–west trade where federal powers and skills are most relevant. An intense competition among provinces for foreign investment lowers the bargaining power of all, but ultimately favours the central region, which enjoys locational and financial advantages, and thereby exacerbates problems of economic disparity and national unity. Special Canada–U.S. trade arrangements in manufacturing sectors further the lead of Ontario and Quebec and prompt demands on their part for separate presences abroad. Quebec in particular, with its secure cultural identity, its need for critical natural and investment resources to undertake a rapid modernization, and its equation of English-Canadian-based and American-based actors, is highly susceptible to inflows of U.S. investment and highly assertive in its demands for greater control in tariff, monetary, immigration, and other economic policy fields.

One of the strongest hallmarks of the peripheral-dependence perspective is the limited, passive, and compliant role it assigns to the state apparatus.[60] In this view the state's low salience, reflected in its inability to calculate autonomously a distinctive national interest, is due to the underlying continental socialization experienced by the governmental élite in Ottawa, through professional training and subsequent interaction, and the absence within Ottawa's decisional apparatus of a capacity for sophisticated, comprehensive, and advanced research and planning. Furthermore the decline of the cold war and the attendant drift of financial and skilled personnel and resources to other institutions have left the federal government with relatively few resources to mobilize on behalf of those national interests it identifies. This low level of institutional autonomy has resulted in the inability of the governmental organizations to act as countervailing powers to corporations based externally. Rather, they have adopted a primary role of assisting and sustaining the needs of the corporate sector, and have aided, as have the provincial governments, Canada's transfer of dependence to the United States.

Within this relatively impotent, unimaginative, and unresponsive state apparatus, only domestically oriented government departments exercise a moderate degree of influence. This arises from the growing need of private corporations for direct state support in the face of the increasing uncertainty fostered by global interdependence, the increasing tendency of governments abroad to assist their home corporations, the state's growing regulatory powers, its subsidies through industrial support programs and grants to business-linked organizations, and its role as entrepreneur, merchant banker, and state trader. Such structural linkages provide the Department of External Affairs with a relatively low impact on policy outcomes and leave little room for the exercise of power by those in the prime ministerial group or by highly placed Cabinet ministers generally.

Moreover, they face no challenge from strong central foreign policy co-ordinative structures that might forward sophisticated versions of overriding national interests. Instead, a small central group of politicians and civil servants, lacking a clear conception of the Canadian national interest, act on the basis of unthinking loyalty, emotion, and ideology and pursue an *ad hoc*, uninformed approach to decision making. More particularly, they lack a prepared policy towards the United States, an appreciation of Canadian vulnerabilities, advance surveys of possible U.S. countermoves, a sophisticated view of U.S. public opinion and public diplomacy, and the research and policy planning capability to examine costs and explore alternative policies. With the relative lack of institutional differentiation and associated specialized capacity, both the central decision makers and the state apparatus are reduced to responding, in quasi-automatic fashion, to large corporations and the external forces they represent.

THE COMPLEX NEO-REALIST PERSPECTIVE

Preoccupied with the powerful challenge that peripheral dependence presents to liberal internationalism, students of Canadian foreign policy have devoted relatively little attention to the possible relevance of a third interpretive perspective, one derived from the realist theory that has dominated the study of international relations as a whole. As expressed in the major work of its most popular proponent, Hans Morgenthau, classic realism highlights the ceaseless interplay among great powers preoccupied with maximizing their military security by manipulating the balance of power to secure a fragile stability within an international system characterized by anarchy.[61] It portrays this central theme of the history of international relations as a cyclical pattern in which the short-term stability produced by a balance of power is followed by a breakdown of this equilibrium, leading to war and the creation of a new transitory balance. It focuses almost exclusively on the small set of great powers involved in arranging the balance, the military security interests that motivate their activity, the conflictual quest for advantage relieved only by temporary military alliances, and the structure of the resulting balance of power as the only form of order that a context of anarchy allows.

Given the fundamental fact of anarchy, states are portrayed as giving predominant weight to external determinants, as each is preoccupied with monitoring and adjusting to shifts in the balance abroad. Neither societal nor governmental processes are given significance as determinants, since they are forced by the requirements of the security dilemma to be aggregated in advance, within the impermeable shell of the sovereign state, as "factors of national power" and "quality of leadership", respectively.

This standard realist portrait has had little appeal to students of Canadian foreign policy, for several reasons. Generally, it seemed intuitively irrelevant to the dilemmas of a newer country, beset internally by regional and ethnic cleavages and foreign penetration, preoccupied by a full array of nation-building imperatives, and confronted externally with the necessities of managing interdependencies in collaboration with like-minded but vastly more powerful neighbours. More precisely, preoccupation with security dilemmas, military interests, and the instruments of force appeared secondary to practitioner and scholar alike. For both, armed conflict had been an intermittent, somewhat discretionary concern, always conducted in association with larger external powers, and aimed centrally at sustaining the systems of deterrence within which the primary tasks of foreign policy were pursued.

Realist precepts seemed to be contradicted also by the fundamental features of Canada's historic emergence as a nation. Until well after World War I, Canada's external vision had been affected by a profound and practical attachment to a stable and benign British imperial system.[62] During the interwar period, in a deliberate effort to distinguish themselves from the United Kingdom and the central European system, Canadian leaders eagerly embraced a North American identity defined by the very absence of power politics and by the invention of a uniquely co-operative and peaceful form of international relations.[63] And after World War II, the very tenacity with which American leaders adopted realism as a justification for their policy of global containment engendered skepticism on the part of Canadian leaders, armed with the legacy of distinctive visions and experienced in detaching themselves from the doctrines and accompanying demands of their imperial leaders abroad.

To the attitudes of heritage was added an accident of history. It was the fate of the modern phase in the study of Canadian foreign policy to emerge at a time when the dominant actor in the international system, the United States, was itself moving beyond the immediate demands of the security dilemma, and when the precepts of realism were beginning to lose their intellectual appeal.[64] At the outset of the 1960s, the emergence of an apparent bipolar stability, confirmed by the outcome of the Berlin and Cuban crises, provided American scholars and their Canadian counterparts with the vision of a system in which security was assured in the short term, rendered permanent by the new nuclear balance, and superseded by the tasks of enhancing abroad a range of values formerly perceived as subordinate.[65] In such a mood, there was little incentive to continue debates about Canada's precise role in North American defence and nuclear deterrence or general concerns about its place in a North Atlantic alliance.[66] Realism seemed to have little to offer the student of Canadian foreign policy.

As America's global dominance faced new challenges in the late 1960s, so too did the precepts of standard realism. The emerging dynamics of global politics provided an empirical foundation for a renewed interest in a realist theory considerably more complex, as were the dilemmas it addressed.[67]

The "complex neo-realist" perspective begins by accepting the fundamental premise of standard realism: the primacy of politics. It sees separate states pursuing distinctive interests in an international milieu in which no natural harmony of interests exists. Its new contribution is the emphasis it places on the prevalence of international order—tentatively defined by the convergence of the interests of principal actors leading to an emerging stable global system, but still grounded in the values of an internationally predominant power.[68] Most importantly, it highlights the complex constellation of interests and values that states and nonstate actors in such an ascendant, system-defining position are able to pursue.[69]

Complex neo-realism thus focuses on the role of hegemonic powers in ensuring, defining, and extending international order in a system in which universal values remain secondary, in which a common security calculus and interest in balance provide no substitute, and in which leadership is required to transform convergent interests into stable order.[70] It sees the history of international relations characterized by the rise to positions of international primacy of a succession of hegemonic powers, with periods of balance among roughly equal powers as relatively rare, temporary, and particular to periods in which one state has lost its hegemony before another has emerged.[71] And in the critical transition from balance to hegemony, it highlights the way in which order may be defined by a concert of principal powers.

Collectively substituting for states exercising individual hegemony, such "principal powers" are not merely the familiar great powers of realist theory.[72] Rather they are principal states in three senses. First, they are the states in the international hierarchy that stand at the top of the international status ranking, collectively possessing decisive capability and differentiated from lower-ranking powers by both objective and subjective criteria. Secondly, they act as principals in their international activities and associations, rather than as agents for other states or groupings or as mediators between principals. And thirdly, they have a principal role in establishing, specifying, and enforcing international order.

At the heart of a state's position as a principal power is its possession of surplus capability: a margin of strength in a broad array of sectors well beyond that required to meet the basic requisites of statehood and the minimal performance expected of modern states.[73] Surplus capability relieves principal powers from the tyranny of responding to short-term security dilemmas and provides them with the luxury of basing their international behaviour on the outcomes of political debates within their societies and on the definitions provided by their state apparatus. Surplus capability thus provides such states the discretion to act autonomously, on the basis of internal choices, on a global stage. Such choices derive not from an exclusive or predominant concern with security but from a multiplicity of values in which priority is given to those political interests that integrate, assign weights to, and provide coherence to specific concerns of military, economic, social, and cultural spheres.[74] This configuration of internal values is embedded in a historically evolved and distinctive array of specialized capabilities, which channels the external activity of a principal power and renders it competitive with those of its counterparts.[75] Surplus and specialized capability together enable principal powers to define the characteristics of international order in a way that disproportionately reflects their distinctive values and to extend that order, and hence their values, into member states throughout the international system.[76]

Traditionally, scholars of Canadian foreign policy have not conceived of their country as having the capabilities or performing the functions of a principal power. Yet, led by key individuals within the state apparatus, they have begun in the past two decades to develop major themes that move in that direction.[77] The first such theme, developed from 1960 to 1968, was a thrust towards globalism, especially significant because of the intent to employ aid as an instrument to advance specifically Canadian interests worldwide, on a bilateral basis. Canada extended its formal diplomatic presence to all regions and major capitals in the world, dealt with quite distinctive cultural groupings, and supplemented conventional diplomacy by the deliberate use of such new techniques as cultural relations and development assistance.[78]

The most dramatic manifestation was the programmatic and geographic expansion of Canada's development assistance. Constituting the major division between the distributive thrust of liberal internationalism and the globalist thrust of complex neo-realism, this transition was initiated in the 1960s when significant Canadian aid began to be deployed in specific francophone countries for the domestic political purpose of meeting the challenges to Canadian foreign policy from Quebec and France.

A second major theme, which emerged from 1968 to 1971, advocated an interest-based initiation of external behaviour. Rejecting the reactiveness that they thought characterized Canadian foreign policy in the Pearsonian approach, dissatisfied domestic critics and officials of the new Trudeau government sought to ensure that the Canadian government would be capable of discerning future trends at home and abroad, identifying their impact on Canadian interests, and formulating policies in advance, enabling Canada to withstand the impact of forces from abroad and thereby maximize its self-determined interests. This emphasis presumed both a direct focus on national interests as the basis for policy calculation and the initiation of policies and programs having little direct dependence on the international situation at the time.[79] In its initial form, this theme of internationally projected values offered the image of a "new" Canada whose policies—concerned with such values as bilingualism, ethnic relations, federalism, techniques of parliamentary government, income redistribution, and environmental protection—provided an example for other states to emulate and a foundation for Canadian behaviour abroad. And after 1973 it was enriched by an emphasis on a third major theme: the way in which unique Canadian assets—deriving from its small, diverse, skilled population, extensive resource base, and developed technology—gave Canada a more active role in defining a new international order based on these values.[80]

The emergence of these major themes of principal-power capability and behaviour are logically based on a series of premises and precepts that address the seven central questions of foreign policy analysis from the perspective of complex neo-realism. In application to Canada's post-World War II foreign policy experience, this begins with a view, similar to the other perspectives, of an international system characterized by the disappearance, over the years 1945 to 1957, of the United Kingdom's hegemonic legacy and its replacement by an American hegemony. However, in contrast to liberal internationalism and peripheral dependence, complex neo-realism sees the key factor as the erosion of the hegemonic position of the U.S. from 1968 onward.[81] Canada's international experience is seen as one of secular, sustained development, reflected most profoundly in its steadily increasing ability to define, advance, secure, and legitimize distinctive national interests and values in a competitive process with adversaries and associates.[82]

In response to the question of international rank, the complex neo-realist perspective portrays Canada, particularly since 1968, as an ascending principal power in an increasingly diffuse, nonhegemonic international system.[83] Placed in the context of the most prevalent global configuration—a top tier of eight powers, with an average of seven involved in the central, European-based system, and nine on a global basis if the central and peripheral systems are combined—Canada is argued to be part of the classically defined "top tier" group.[84]

In addition to a location in this configuration, principal powers have three specific characteristics. The first is a rank roughly comparable to other states in the top range, unexcelled by states outside it, and closer to those within than to outside states immediately below.[85] The second is a set of organizations and instruments sufficient to help deter significant direct assaults on its homeland and to provide a strategic presence abroad. The third consists of special rights in determining and preserving international order in political, military, and economic spheres, together with distinctive values and sufficiently strong influence to attract the attention of other principals and to help define the orientation of some lesser states.

With these criteria, the complex neo-realist argument asserts that Canada's objective capability—grounded in the relative size, breadth, and diversity of its natural resources, advanced technology, and skilled population and in other standard calculations of national power—places it predominantly within the top tier of the system.[86] Canada's designated rank is reinforced by its involvement in groupings composed of members drawn exclusively or predominantly from this top tier.[87] While acknowledging Canada's lack of independent nuclear and conventional military deterrence, complex neo-realism recognizes that Canada's military capability at home and abroad directly contributes to strategic stability in several critical regions. Moreover, it assigns Canada a prominent position within the top tier in defining and managing global regimes in major issue areas, and leadership within a distinctive grouping or network of lesser states on such questions.[88]

The degree, variety, and diffusion of Canada's external activities provide the initial indication of aspects of its international behaviour that characterize it as an emerging principal power. The degree of Canadian activity is expressed by the maintenance of a permanent political involvement in virtually all regions, sectors, and forums of world politics. Such global involvement is registered in the consistently high volume of interactions that Canada exchanges with a large number of actors abroad. Grounded in a need to manage continuously a state's immediate, direct, durable interests, global involvement arises when several relatively stringent conditions are met: the existence of societal actors sufficiently powerful to influence behaviour and critical security interests or commitments; the presence of a full range of concerns and values that give the international behaviour additional significance; the recognition that behaviour be based at least partly on state-specific interests, vulnerabilities, and values, rather than universal doctrines; and the desire of partner countries to maintain the involvement.

From these conditions, the variety of activity is defined as one of interest-based involvement predicated on the distinctively national interests and values previously identified as the touchstone of Canadian participation. Canadian policy and behaviour are likely to exhibit some inconsistency over time and across issues as officials also seek to make their contributions in the context of past efforts while maintaining congruence with the accumulated expectations and interests of others. Such activity may appear as a large number of highly complex patterns quite distinct from one another, irregular and seemingly unpredictable as a variety of interests and decision strategies compete.

As a further consequence of Canada's global behaviour, the diffusion of activity is seen as a tendency towards autonomous bilateral involvement. Reflecting the need to develop and maintain direct ties worldwide, distinctive effort is made on specific state-to-state relations while relatively less involvement occurs with international organizations having universal membership. In this mode, new and multiple membership, concern with balance across affiliations, and stress on fluidity assume lesser prominence. Priority is given to employing the state's resources in servicing the particular interest of each specific bilateral relationship. In practice, this suggests a more full and equal association with a larger number of nonuniversal organizations and, more importantly, the development of direct bilateral relations with groups and actors beyond the Anglo–American sphere. More specifically, in this thrust bilateral diplomatic representation on a resident basis is given and received with most actors, posts acquire a "multiprogram" character, regular visits by heads of government increase, and joint organizations are formed with regional bodies and individual countries.

From the complex neo-realist perspective, this tendency towards global, interest-based, bilateral activity is supplemented by associative behaviour characterized by a set of competitive orientations: a predisposition towards unilateral initiatives, a divergence in policy commitment, and a diversification of focus away from any associated imperial state. Emphasizing unilateral initiatives, Canada's diplomatic behaviour does not necessarily concentrate on inducing other states to act, does not require their active co-operation, passive support, or subsequent imitation for success, and is therefore not heavily dependent on calculations of their likely behaviour for its initiation. In short, this diplomatic behaviour is not a heavily context-dependent attempt to preserve or engender co-operative arrangements, but a self-motivated effort to operate within the confines of the existing system to national advantage. A desire to act primarily with equivalent states, on the one hand, and to maintain relatively exclusive spheres of influence, on the other, reinforces this emphasis on selective involvement of other actors as dictated by each issue.

The second competitive tendency, divergence, is reflected in actions in which relatively little effort is made to ensure consistency with the actions of other states and in which dissimilar actions often result. Positions may be taken at variance with those of members in existing groups, and sometimes this exercise of leadership will initiate a new grouping. Little emphasis is given to offsetting the weight of a given bloc or eroding bloc cleavages. As a result, Canada often adopts positions on major issues discrepant with those of traditionally associated states.

The third and most significant competitive tendency is that of diversification, manifested in active efforts to concentrate behaviour on actors other than an associated imperial power or its groups, with the aim of obtaining alternative sources of resources such as information, markets, investment, and general political support. In particular, it involves a deliberate attempt to forge relations and assume compatible positions with other states that are roughly equivalent in status or even more powerful and thus capable of serving as a substitute for, or rival to, the traditional imperial power. Diversification rests on the belief that in the absence of such action, existing behavioural domination by the prevailing imperial power would continue, that this is not in Canada's interest, that Canada has the power to force a more acceptable balance by itself, and that this effort can be sustained even in the face of active opposition from the imperial power.

In overseas relations, the rivalry induced by diversification is constrained somewhat by the fundamental responsibility of all major powers to preserve a general balance of power and reduce the likelihood of war. However, these tasks are performed by individual as well as collective actions, rest on negotiated settlements among equals more than on compromises forwarded or facilitated by other parties, and provide only an overarching framework in which major power interests are pursued in a competitive fashion. Within this framework, diversification engenders the establishment of co-operative relationships with other major or emerging powers as an alternative to its affiliation with an associated imperial power. At that point the process may extend into an intensive and increasingly competitive relationship in which Canada becomes involved in the internal political processes of its new partner, incompatible interests become apparent, and diplomatic conflict results. Alternatively, the continuation and reinforcement of a close, co-operative relationship may result in an effort at counterweight, in which the new partner is deliberately invoked as an ally directly against the preferences of the previous imperial power.

Canada's pursuit of diversification within North America breeds an emphasis on arm's-length diplomacy. Bilateral relations with the United States resemble those between any two sovereign states, with unified governments, formally equal while differing in objective, formulating national positions in advance, guarding information, and seeking to outmanoeuvre adversaries, link issues, and dominate policy implementation. Within Canada itself, the corresponding value of an autonomous society prompts a reliance on strategies that prohibit outright further American penetration and actively reduce the existing American presence.

In an emerging principal power, in the complex neo-realist view, the defence of national interests and the promotion of distinctive values engender a strong incentive to follow and promote a detailed conception of world order compatible with its purposes. The first manifestation of this incentive is an active effort to revise the existing patterns of international institutionalization. Believing that such frameworks preserve old values and inhibit emergent powers from securing equality with their established counterparts, these states reduce their verbal and material support for the standard set of international institutions, seek to forge alternative organizations or informal groupings, and forge alliances with new states that have attained success within the existing order. Moreover, efforts to promote a well-developed, highly autonomous, and fully consistent structure of international law are reduced, on the grounds that such constructions introduce rigidities that impede the process of revision.

A second component of a complex neo-realist approach to world order is the promotion of principal-power concerts through the creation of groupings in which effective participation is restricted to states within the top tier, and more particularly to states with a rank equal to or greater than one's own. Premised on the recognition of Canada's principal-power rank and claims, this tendency is directed at strengthening the distinction between groups made up exclusively of principal powers and mixed groups of principal and lesser powers, and increasingly transferring important questions from the latter into the former, in the interests of a more rapid and realistic revision and more effective management of the international order.

Modification of the existing international order in keeping with its distinctive interests and values is the third criterion of a principal power's approach to world order. Accepting the basic legitimacy of those structures that allowed it to ascend to principal-power status, Canada devotes few resources to conducting direct, comprehensive assaults on the formal framework of existing institutions. Yet, in an attempt to reinforce its new position, it seeks to forge alliances with those who have manipulated the existing system successfully, and who are likely candidates for major-power status in the near future. And in an effort to register the particular contribution it can make to the management of the global system and to secure the support of emerging powers who sustain its position, it forwards distinctive conceptions of what a new international order should be.

Implicit in complex neo-realist writing is the assumption that these action tendencies and doctrines are sustained by an external environment rather more open and less concentrated than in the classical formulation. This configuration, when combined with Canada's principal-power status, reduces to a low level the overall salience of the external environment, disperses its influence across a wide number of states, and endows a multitude of states with a noticeable if minor impact on Canadian behaviour. Thus complex neo-realism assigns the "imperial" actors—the United Kingdom and the United States—a significantly reduced role in providing a stimulus, framework, and referent for Canadian behaviour. At the same time it allows the major European powers and Japan, the Soviet Union, and China a relatively high impact, not only by providing a broader affiliation to balance Canada's relations with the United States but also in serving as comparable, autonomous actors in their own right.

The significant weight attached to the positions and initiatives of these major states reduce to a moderate level the significance of the smaller European and overseas middle powers as associates of Canada in international diplomacy and as a factor when Canada undertakes autonomous action. Within this sphere, attention shifts from states with a historical relationship with Canada to those with similar sociocultural attributes or convergent population, resource, and technology characteristics and to those emerging into the major-power realm. Finally the United Nations, as the institutional codification of an increasingly obsolete pattern of international relations, declines to a moderate position as an influence on Canadian behaviour, while NATO, as a more restricted body with a direct role in security and in defining systems, experiences an offsetting increase.[89] Moreover, a much greater influence is enjoyed by such new, restricted-membership, task-specific bodies as francophonie, the Namibia Contact Group within the Security Council, the Organization for Economic Co-operation and Development, the International Energy Agency, the London Suppliers Group on nuclear materials, and the Western Economic Summits held since 1975.

A complex neo-realist orientation perceives the domestic environment as being marked by the emergence of highly salient, ongoing disputes over foreign policy issues, grounded in the interest of autonomous major organizations throughout the national society. The high importance of domestic organizations rests in the first instance on the likelihood that the country's possession of a surplus margin of capability allows for and prompts an effective debate within society about the purposes for which that power should be employed. Furthermore, the existence of routine global involvements by societal organizations increases the number of actors whose primary interests are affected by foreign affairs, who possess direct, specialized international expertise, and who thus have legitimate, divergent perspectives about the best course to pursue. Moreover, the stress on national interest and initiative emphasizes the desirability of considering domestic sources and taking the time for domestic actors to mobilize, organize, and debate. Together these factors produce a domestic process that, in conformity with a pluralist conception of politics, contains a highly developed set of differentiated institutions, each autonomously defining and pursuing specific interests among societal competitors and organizations in the external and governmental realm. Thus, Canada's international behaviour becomes highly sensitive to such societal factors.

The depth and durability of these societal interests give the overtly political and directly accessible institutions—Parliament and the party system—only a moderate role in influencing government behaviour. In contrast, associational interest groups, labour, the media, and the business community all enjoy a high degree of influence, in keeping with the precepts of interest-group theory. Finally, provincial governments possess a moderate degree of influence. The result is a highly dispersed and evenly balanced process, in which all types of institutions and those organizations whose strength is based on population, resource, or technological capabilities have substantial impact.

Within the executive branch of the federal government, complex neo-realism predicts the existence of a decision-making process resembling bureaucratic politics, but one in which strong central co-ordinative mechanisms operate to produce overall order. The decision-making process of government is viewed as highly salient in foreign policy behaviour, resulting from the vigorous debate taking place among a well-developed constellation of organizational subunits capable of registering their missions with considerable specificity. Within this constellation, a relatively moderate influence is assigned to the Department of External Affairs and its career foreign service officer corps, and a high degree of influence, in contrast, is assigned to other foreign service departments and domestic departments. Exercising dominant influence are those within the prime ministerial group and in the central foreign policy co-ordinative structures closest to it, given their role in defining overarching values and the overall national interest. Indeed, great emphasis is placed on the emergence of a large, highly specialized, and tightly controlled set of such co-ordinative structures as a means for integrating and transcending the multitude of powerful competing missions within the government and competing interests within domestic society. Therefore, Canadian foreign policy behaviour is argued to be, in the context of complex neo-realism, highly sensitive to key governmental actors but durable, interrelated, and comprehensive nonetheless.

* * *

These three theoretical perspectives on Canadian foreign policy provide our entry into the study of Canada's postwar international behaviour. Determinations about the usefulness, accuracy, and validity of each one must be made in the context of the empirical record, not on an *a priori* basis. Each of the following chapters is organized around the seven central foreign policy questions that provide the common structure for the comparative testing of each perspective.

CHAPTER 2
MAJOR DOCTRINES AND DECISIONS

Foreign policy doctrines—the public statements of government intent—provide a bench-mark against which decisions and ensuing external behaviour can be assessed.[1] In the study of Canadian foreign policy, such doctrines have not always been considered for analysis, a legacy of the interwar period when foreign policy declarations were largely confined to brief prime ministerial statements in the House of Commons. The pre-eminent doctrine of those years—"Parliament will decide"—was in part a declaration of Canadian autonomy in foreign affairs, establishing the limits to Canadian participation in secondary, non-European conflicts without questioning support for Great Britain on central issues. But primarily it was an assertion that Prime Minister Mackenzie King would initiate foreign policy only when circumstances required. It was not until after World War II, when Canada began to define its role in the postwar order, that any more precise unifying philosophy could be seen behind declarations from Ottawa. At that time, the need to build a new international system, Canada's increased strength, and the presence of an experienced diplomatic team in Ottawa inaugurated a tradition of producing regular full-scale assessments of Canada's place in the emerging global order.[2]

As this doctrinal tradition has developed, however, so too has skepticism about what such doctrines mean. Critics have quite properly pointed out that general, internally contradictory statements of intention, often designed for the purpose of converting particular audiences, can lack the precision, scale of priority, and commitment required for reliable implementation.[3] Yet there remains the need for leaders to state to constituencies at home and abroad their vision of their country and its place in the community of nations.[4] And especially in crisis situations, when time is short and threat and surprise high, previously internalized guidelines have a profound effect.[5] Furthermore, past successes establish precedents for action that may in turn set the pattern for future responses.[6]

By examining seminal decisions along with major doctrines, it is possible to determine, first, whether governments in fact do what they declare and, secondly, which of the three perspectives best accounts not only for articulated policy but also for the government's actual behaviour. This chapter presents the major foreign policy doctrines and key foreign policy decisions that highlight the official record of Canada's postwar international activity. The doctrines and decisions of each of the five main postwar periods are then assessed in terms of the three theoretical perspectives.

THE ERA OF INTERNATIONALISM, 1947–1957

Doctrine

Canada's first major and comprehensive foreign policy declaration came in a lecture delivered by Secretary of State for External Affairs Louis St. Laurent at the University of Toronto in 1947.[7] In the Gray Lecture, which was to serve as the touchstone of Canada's external behaviour in the decade to follow, Mackenzie King's leading French-Canadian minister and Canada's first full-time foreign minister mobilized the experience of the wartime generation to replace past quasi-isolationist practices with an internationalist orientation broadly acceptable to English-Canadians and French-Canadians alike.

The Gray Lecture has most often been cited as evidence of Canada's presence or international rank as a middle power. The main thrust of the speech was to establish for Canada greater international responsibility, comparable to that assumed in the war. In essence, this declaration and the perceptions that supported it are best explained by the liberal-internationalist model, and represent active, responsible, and multiple participation.

Canada's acknowledgement of its new role in international affairs in the postwar order was highlighted by St. Laurent's emphasis on the necessity of continuing aid and assistance. This acceptance of the responsible participation appropriate to middle powers was supported by St. Laurent's strident rejection of the quasi-isolationism of the prewar years, most clearly articulated in his call for participation with multiple actors beyond the United Kingdom and the United States, including Commonwealth middle powers such as India and broadly based international organizations. It received further emphasis in his recognition of the unique role Canada, with its European heritage, could play both in rebuilding Europe physically and in supporting countries such as France that were struggling to rebuild Europe's democratic foundations.

In pursuit of this revolutionary change in Canada's external behaviour, St. Laurent called for association with equivalent states who shared the values of political liberty, supported democratic institutions, and recognized the humanitarian standards of Judeo-Christian civilization. Out of such combinations of states would come a common commitment and an evolving consensus necessary for the tasks facing the postwar world. Responding to the fears and anxieties of a war-weary world, St. Laurent called for a foreign policy focused on the politics of constraint, using Canada's close association with the United Kingdom, the United States, the Commonwealth, and specific European powers to temper the excesses of state interests. Therefore it would be necessary, in his view, to win the confidence and respect of key powers and other members of international organizations, especially in the newly formed United Nations. The intent of this declaration was to reinforce St. Laurent's strongly held belief that the pursuit of global economic and political stability and the avoidance of further major international war required the establishment of an international network of powerful states acknowledging the primacy of international law. Dealings with Canada's major partner, the United States, could not be based merely on policy but would have to evolve through compromise, daily problem solving, and common efforts to enhance continental welfare.[8]

These declarations concerning activity and association implicitly addressed the issue of world order. In his Gray Lecture, St. Laurent vigorously defended the need to develop new international institutions in a reformed international system, with the gradual widespread acceptance of norms of state conduct based on accepted legal practice.

In presenting his liberal-internationalist vision of Canada's place in the postwar international environment, St. Laurent referred to aspects of the external, governmental, and societal factors affecting foreign policy. He acknowledged Canada's pronounced dependence on external markets and recognized the rise of a new politico-military threat to the West in his arguments against isolationism. Furthermore, Canada's particular sensitivity to the West European states, the United Kingdom, and the United States was central to his commitment for an ongoing effort to establish a powerful United Nations. The policies of state would be enhanced by the growth of a modern state apparatus, particularly a highly skilled and professional Department of External Affairs that would build the requisite diplomatic apparatus abroad. However, the combination of financial constraints and Canadian societal factors would impose limitations on the role of government in introducing new foreign policy orientations. Foremost in St. Laurent's mind was the need for Canada to act as a unified nation, with a foreign policy acceptable to both English- and French-speaking communities. And as a democracy, the government must secure the support of large groups of people dispersed throughout the country, rather than particular regions or representatives of special classes. As a result, foreign policy must be discussed inside and outside Parliament without becoming a matter of partisan controversy among political parties.

Despite the predominantly liberal-internationalist character of the Gray Lecture, examination from the perspective of peripheral dependence reveals the deeply embedded residue of Canada's wartime and prewar experience. St. Laurent's initial goal of national unity and his concern with French–English conflict as a threat to the Canadian fabric showed the deep scars of the 1917 and 1944 conscription crises and

Canada's vulnerability to forces from abroad. Similarly, his acknowledgement of Canada's dependence on external markets and the prominence he gave to Canada's relationships with the United Kingdom and the United States indicated Canada's small, penetrated status and its focus on its associated imperial powers.

St. Laurent also projected aspects of a vision of Canadian foreign policy that conform to a complex neo-realist perspective. The clearest sign of this was St. Laurent's introduction of France as a partner equal to Britain and the United States in Canada's list of close relationships, an associate for political rather than simply cultural or historic reasons and a key actor to whom Canada would be sensitive. St. Laurent thus implied that Canada had the international presence and domestic capability to combine with major actors in the international arena.

The Gray Lecture had a profound impact on the Canadian foreign policy community, for it set the tone for the next decade, indeed previewing a number of the more central guiding themes in Canada's external behaviour in the postwar era. Although projecting elements of interest, components of determination, and aspects of behaviour consonant with either peripheral dependence or complex neo-realism, St. Laurent's vision most completely and logically conforms to the expectations of the liberal-internationalist perspective of a middle-power state.

Decisions

Presented at the dawn of the cold war, St. Laurent's declaration reflected less the recent achievements of Canada in shaping the United Nations framework than its concern with adapting and supplementing the structure of the international organization to meet the emerging Soviet-inspired threat. Within the United Nations, Canada's pursuit of functionalism had, by 1947, given it a fairly secure place as a middle power in the economic and political spheres, although the victories had been hard-won and remained incomplete. During the critical four years from 1943 to 1947, when the UN system was structured, Canada's basic approach was to favour strongly "a policy of international collaboration and co-operation. . .best calculated to serve not only the immediate national interests of Canada but also our *overriding* interest in the establishment of an international order which will prevent the outbreak of another world war."[9] In practice, this meant establishing international organizations as quickly as possible, in spite of the isolationists in both the American Congress and the Canadian Cabinet, and, where possible, setting up these organizations in an orderly fashion, on the basis of principles that were general rather than *ad hoc*, produced at the UN rather than by Anglo–American or four-power initiatives, and consistent with the functionalist logic.

To what degree were these intentions carried out? How successful were the leaders of this era in establishing and maintaining St. Laurent's vision of Canada as a preserver of international order? An examination of the key decisions in the era of internationalism will reveal the extent to which those decisions conformed to the doctrines set forth in the Gray Lecture and the relative appropriateness of the three foreign policy perspectives.

The United Nations

In the formative 1943–1947 period, Canada's participation in the United Nations was already informed by functionalism. In 1943, at the establishment of the United Nations Relief and Rehabilitation Agency (UNRRA), Canada attempted to prevent the domination of the central executive committee by the four great powers, the U.S., the U.K., the U.S.S.R., and China. Although the effort was unsuccessful at first, Canada secured admission to the body in 1945, along with France.

Canada's characteristic middle-power stance was also reflected in its approach to the International Monetary Fund (IMF), the International Bank for Reconstruction and Development (IBRD), and the International Civil Aviation Organization (ICAO). In all these areas, Canada attempted to replace bilateral negotiations with multilateral negotiations in order to reduce the power monopoly of the great powers and to encourage harmonious relations among participating countries. Proponents of peripheral dependence have nevertheless taken Canada's "harmonizing" role as evidence of this country's sensitivity to the needs of the Anglo-American world.

Canada's approach to the task of constructing the United Nations bodies was marked again by functionalism and mediatory activity. In practice, this meant ensuring that all the great powers participated and maintained a unity of purpose, preventing military and security functions from dominating economic and other areas, and, finally, securing a significant position within the UN for middle powers. As an important participant at San Francisco in 1945 and afterward, Canada attempted to increase the autonomy and power of the General Assembly and to reduce the power of veto of the great-power-dominated Security Council. This, along with Canada's efforts to reduce great-power domination of other UN bodies—notably the United Nations Educational, Scientific and Cultural Organization (UNESCO), the International Telecommunications Union (ITU), and the International Labour Organization (ILO)—made Canada's world-view and individual requests more influential within and outside the UN.

Although Canada had a relatively minor role in the peace settlements with Germany, Japan, and other defeated belligerents, it continued the active and responsible international participation it had assumed during the war with its $1.25-billion postwar loan to the U.K. and, after 1947, a generous acceptance of European displaced persons. This activity was still in the nature of reactive peacekeeping, but evidence of the anticipatory peacekeeping of distributive internationalism can be seen in Canada's role in the United Nations Atomic Energy Commission (UNAEC). Canada's uranium resources, advanced technology, and industrial capacity, along with its provision of wartime sanctuary to British and French scientists, made it a logical choice as a key participant in the commission although it was not a permanent member of the Security Council. Canada worked as an equal partner with the U.S. and the U.K. until the commission collapsed under the strains of the emerging cold war.

Strong indicators of liberal-internationalist activity, association, and approach to world order are revealed in Canada's early UN involvement. These were the perseverance with which Canada pursued multilateralism and institutional reformation, the primacy it assigned to broad representation and functional specialization in UN organizations, and the responsible and active role Canada took in the establishment of these organizations and the introduction of constraints to great-power domination. At the same time, the Canadian government's decisions on these matters reflect certain aspects found in both peripheral dependence and complex neo-realism. Canada's inability to limit still further the veto power and overall influence of the permanent members of the Security Council, as well as the decision to place UN headquarters in the U.S. rather than in Europe, can be viewed as concessions to the interests of the United States. But Canada's position as near-equal of the U.S. and the U.K. in the IMF/IBRD, the ICAO, and the UNAEC suggest an implicit recognition of Canada's upper-tier stature and range of influence during this period.

The Creation of NATO

Canada felt the impact of the cold war first as a member of the UN, secondly because of the discovery of a Soviet spy network in Ottawa in 1945, and thirdly because of the threat that the 1948 coup in Czechoslovakia posed to a free Western Europe. A final but less important factor contributing to Canada's involvement in the cold war consisted of the anti-Soviet preachings from south of the border.[10] Hence, Canada's role in establishing the North Atlantic Treaty Organization to ward off the Soviet threat to Europe appeared to be that of a middle power, acting in the international interest, not that of a minor power acting in the wake of U.S. initiative.

In fact, the creation of NATO was largely an Anglo-Canadian initiative, in alliance with the U.S. State Department, to design a multilateral organization that would give France in particular and Europe in general the political stability needed to ward off Soviet encroachments. Canada's main objective was to use the combined associations of the UN to create a fully multilateral framework for NATO, rather than a merely European–North American base, and to set up reciprocal guarantees among all NATO members that would make the NATO arrangements directly relevant and complementary to Canada's growing bilateral defence co-operation with the United States. Canada also cited Article 51 of the UN Charter and pressed for U.S. commitment to an organization that would embrace economic, social, and political as well as military functions.

In a September 1947 speech to the UN General Assembly, St. Laurent was one of the first leaders to propose the concept of a new organization. Canada continued to play a key role as it participated in secret tripartite talks with the U.S. and the U.K. to develop an Atlantic community and as it urged, albeit unsuccessfully, that France be included in these early talks as a key continental power. In establishing the organization, Canada proved successful in achieving a multilateral, reciprocal treaty linked to Article 51; it was less successful in de-emphasizing NATO's military functions, despite the language of Article 2, and quite unsuccessful in limiting its membership and territorial application to North Atlantic democracies. Yet Canada, acknowledging its overall responsibility and commitment to the alliance, provided substantial contributions to NATO's military functions over the next decade through training programs, armaments for a division, and, in October 1951, an army brigade and aircraft squadrons sent to Europe to meet the cold war emergency.

These NATO-related decisions indicate the characteristics of all three perspectives. Canada's initiative, its initial position as one of the big three, its concern with France, and its quest for Article 2 are strong signs of complex neo-realism. The successful quest for a multilateral alliance demonstrates the dominance of liberal internationalism. And the ability of the U.S. and the U.K. to hold sway over membership and primary functions and Canada's final acquiescence and adherence to this definition are indicative of a small-power position in matters vital to security in Canada's sphere of influence.

The Commonwealth

During the 1947–1957 period, Canada's main achievement within the Commonwealth was to ensure, in 1947, that India became part of the association and that it retained its Commonwealth membership once it became a republic in 1949. This was achieved in spite of the bipolar rigidity and Atlanticist preoccupations bred by the cold war.[11] The presence of India and Pakistan within the Commonwealth motivated a bold extension of Commonwealth co-operation into the realm of economic and social development in the Asian region.

Canada was initially reluctant to attend the Commonwealth foreign ministers' meeting in Colombo, Ceylon, in 1950 and to participate in an

Australian–Ceylonese plan for capital assistance (later revised to technical assistance). However, Canada finally agreed to participate as a full member at the ministerial level and provide a financial contribution should the British do so. When the British agreed to a considerable sum, the Canadians followed with a contribution of $25 million. This direct attempt to reduce economic disparity between rich and poor nations points to the distributive internationalism typical of a liberal-internationalist middle power.

The Korean War

The war in Korea, which began in June 1950, cemented the Canadian special relationship with India, developed within the Commonwealth and later confirmed in a program of nuclear co-operation.[12]

While Canada's acceptance of a place on the United Nations Temporary Commission on Korea in 1947 had confirmed its decisive transition from quasi-isolationism to postwar internationalism, the outbreak of hostilities in 1950 found its military weak, focused on its Atlantic responsibilities, and preoccupied with a Soviet threat to Europe. Yet when it was clear that the United States would respond with military force to the North Korean invasion, Canada, through diligent diplomacy and later a military contribution, sought as a priority to channel American action through the multilateral framework of the United Nations. Its twin objectives of constraining the American threat to conduct an unlimited anti-Communist crusade and enhancing the strength of the United Nations in its critical collective security function were largely shared by India, which provided a reinforcing skepticism of American instincts, a crucial regional perspective, and a critical channel of communication with the People's Republic of China, not yet diplomatically recognized. Working with India and the United Nations secretary general, Canada tried to prevent UN forces in Korea from moving too close to the Chinese border and attempted to secure an armistice before the danger of provoking Chinese intervention loomed. After the Chinese had entered the conflict, Canada tried to secure a cease-fire that the Chinese would accept, so that China would not be branded an aggressor. And finally, at the Geneva Conference of 1954, Canada argued strongly for an invitation for India, fostered American communication with the U.K. and India, and conducted a dialogue with the Chinese.

These activities not only established a special relationship between the governments of Canada and India, they also epitomized Canada's self-perceived and self-appointed role as a middle-power state committing its resources to managing conflict, constraining the unilateral activities of the great powers, and seeking consensus and support within the international community for any interventionist activity. Yet it is also true that in spite of these efforts and those of other middle powers, especially India, the prosecution of the Korean war proceeded. That the United States was able to gain UN sponsorship for the pursuit of its interests in Korea while supporting Canada's preference for broadly based multilateralism can be viewed as indicative of the inordinate influence of the United States and the use it made of small allies such as Canada and India in the legitimation of its actions.

Indochina and the Geneva Conference

Canada's special position in the Commonwealth reinforced its preferred role in the UN and *vis-à-vis* the U.S. over Korea; it also provided an entirely separate sphere for creative action on the other major issue at Geneva in 1954, the question of Indochina.[13]

The British and Soviets, as conference co-chairmen, invited Canada to serve with India and Poland on three international commissions in Vietnam, Laos, and Cambodia to supervise the implementation of the Geneva accords. Canada was most reluctant to accept, as this was an operation without UN sponsorship or U.S. association, it imposed a heavy burden on an undermanned diplomatic and military establishment preoccupied with Atlantic affairs, and it threatened to go beyond the framework of aid to European deimperialization within which Canada's previous supervisory and peacekeeping experience had been confined. If Canada had declined the British–Soviet invitation, it would have shown the acquiescence and support typical of the association of a minor power.

However, Canada engaged in the responsible participation of a middle power. It acknowledged responsibility in this affair partly because it alone had the requisite number of skilled, objective, French-speaking officers. Canada's close relationship with India was also a partial incentive for involvement since, as in Korea, India provided regional input and representation from a nonwhite, non-European country, was a leading member of the Commonwealth, and contributed to offsetting the real or perceived biases of current or former colonial powers. In addition, the belief that even precarious multilateral accommodations were preferable to continued fighting or unilateral interventions from any quarter led Canada to accept, in a distant region, a thankless task that was to cost it much in its diplomatic resources, domestic support, and reputation for objectivity abroad.

The St. Lawrence Seaway

These constrained departures from American purposes on overseas politico-military matters were matched by attempts to show independence on functional projects in the North American sphere.[14] The greatest project, both in size and in the longevity of the diplomacy underlying it, was the St. Lawrence Seaway.

Two decades of discussion over the possibility of a joint or co-operative Canada–U.S. project to develop the navigational and hydroelectric potential of the waterway had ended in stalemate by July 1951, when the U.S. House of Representatives had refused to pass enabling legislation. Despite a Canadian preference and presidential support for a co-operative venture, pressures began to mount within Canada for Ottawa to move alone. In the end, the Canadian–American Permanent Joint Board on Defence (PJBD) called for quick collaborative action in the interest of national security. The U.S. passed legislation in 1954 that provided for co-ordinated projects by the respective countries, without an overall formal treaty or single administrative authority. Each government retained responsibility over its own territory, and Canada's right to build an entirely national system in the future was preserved.

The ability of the Canadian government to withstand considerable congressional pressure, secure its preferred outcome, and thereby enhance current and future security over territory and resources was balanced by equivalent American benefits and the joint recognition that bargaining and negotiation between partners would lead to the common goals of economic development and defence co-operation. Although Canada was therefore essentially in the position of a minor power gaining derivative military and economic benefits from its great-power neighbour, its ability to tip the balance of negotiation in its own favour was indicative of a middle- or principal-power position.

The Suez Crisis

The classic expression of convergent Canada–U.S. interests being sublimated into an overriding structure of co-operation in overseas diplomacy came in the Suez crisis of 1956.[15]

Although Canada had few historic interests or involvements in the Middle East region itself, the Egyptian nationalization of the Suez Canal and ensuing invasion by the French, the British, and the Israelis provided a severe threat to British–American harmony and to the stability of the multiracial Commonwealth. It also offered an opportunity to extend the effectiveness of the United Nations in the realms of diplomatic mediation and military peacekeeping. Canada felt the need to provide some support to Britain in its desperate gamble, and Pearson, with Louis St. Laurent's firm support, took Canada's response to the United Nations. Using skillful tactics, the reputation of a decade, his longstanding alliance with the secretary general and India, and his special relationship with the British and the Americans, Pearson succeeded in avoiding a UN condemnation of the British and the French, preventing the escalation of a public divergence between Washington and London, establishing a cease-fire and disengagement in the region, and interposing a newly created United Nations peacekeeping force. Pearson's actions and the Nobel Peace Prize they earned provided both the culminating symbol of the internationalist traditions developed over a decade and an instinctive inspiration for Canadian diplomacy in the next ten years.

Conclusions

The two dominant characteristics of this period were the establishment of universal and specialized international institutions and the development of cold war politics. In this context of fairly high levels of tension, the focus on military security and the recognition that economic progress was a prerequisite to political stability compounded the already difficult task of bringing order to a world torn by war and growing disparities of wealth. Canada's position and role during these turbulent times show evidence of a middle-power state partially constrained by its links to the United States, and somewhat less by the United Kingdom, yet also emerging in some areas as a major international actor.

Canada's main foreign policy decisions of this period, while guided by the doctrine enunciated in the Gray Lecture, necessarily responded to the various exigencies of the day. Canada's decisions and actions concerning the early days of the UN, the founding of NATO, the consolidation of the Commonwealth, and the Korean and Suez crises were focused upon multilateralization, efforts to constrain great-power activity through the creation of compromise or alternative responses, and the need to establish effective coalitions through consensus, common interests, functional necessity, and international ranking. Therefore Canadian foreign policy, in both doctrine and decision, conformed most closely to the expectations of the liberal-internationalist perspective. Although some aspects of peripheral dependence are evident, especially in the weight of U.S. positions on military and security matters, it does not seem to provide a sufficiently comprehensive account of the period. Similarly, Canada's carefully constructed linkage with France as a partner equal to the U.S. and the U.K., reflected in NATO and the Geneva Conference, and the government's near-equal position with the U.K. and the U.S. in UN agencies offer strong elements of principal-power action in the context of a complex neo-realist perspective, but they do not constitute a strong overall pattern of principal-power behaviour.

THE ERA OF INDEPENDENCE, 1957–1963

However successful, Pearson's decisions in the Suez crisis gave rise to growing domestic dissatisfaction with the course of Canadian diplomacy, based on a desire to back Britain more strongly, to detach Canada from American purposes and influences, and to forward United Nations-based internationalist traditions. This dissatisfaction proved strong enough to help elect a Progressive Conservative government under John

Diefenbaker in June 1957, but the new government's revised international approach did not have the coherence of that of the Pearson government.[16] There was no single declaration of Canada's new purposes in the international realm, but the new balance was seen in a series of statements made by Diefenbaker from 1957 to 1960, before division within his government and the changing external environment imposed unmanageable strains.[17]

Doctrine

Upon entering office, John Diefenbaker was quick to reassure his counterparts abroad that his victory involved no change in such fundamental principles as Canada's support for the United Nations, the high priority it placed on its NATO contribution, and its significant involvement in Commonwealth affairs. Showing the constraint of a middle power working within existing associations, Diefenbaker proposed increasing the scope of the UN, the Commonwealth, and NATO through institutionalization. He affirmed Canada's willingness to go to the "utmost limits" of safety to ensure disarmament and proposed the creation of a permanent United Nations peacekeeping force, a Commonwealth financial institution and scholarship program, and a world food bank. Multilateralization of scope was further reflected in Diefenbaker's plan to extend the horizons of the Commonwealth to the new nations of Asia and Africa, the non-Commonwealth states of Southeast Asia, and the less developed countries of the world as a whole.

Diefenbaker proposed extending NATO's limits to cover these same areas, and, showing the middle-power concerns of functionalism and distributive internationalism, he recommended that NATO's functions should go beyond the military to encompass disarmament, economic and political questions outside the Atlantic sphere, and the aid and investment concerns of less developed countries. He showed the liberal-internationalist concerns of combination and consensus, with his heavy emphasis on the value of advance consultation within NATO, tighter integration of member countries, and more equal participation. Diefenbaker continued to assert the primary claims of this body over less multilateral forums by deploring the fact that separate arrangements for political consultation among NATO members had sprung up outside the alliance framework.

Diefenbaker's liberal-internationalist attitude was tempered by a view of Canada as one of the globe's largest industrial and trading countries, with economic growth more rapid than that of the United States and the United Kingdom and with the prospect of surpassing the U.K. in economic power within the next twenty-five years. But Diefenbaker was also acutely concerned by Canada's enhanced vulnerability in the era of the intercontinental missile. Canada's trade was increasingly concentrated on the United States, and the country continued to depend on inflows of American capital. This was further exacerbated, in Diefenbaker's eyes, by the apparent decline of the U.K. as a global power in the wake of its Suez débâcle, the creation of the European Economic Community, and Canada's heavy defence responsibilities in the North American sector, which set limits to its NATO contributions.

While Prime Minister Diefenbaker's personal commitment to internationalism and desire for procedural continuity led to a strong reaffirmation of Canada's traditional multilateral associations and relationship with the U.S., his consciousness of Canada's enhanced capability and vulnerability fostered a more active, adventurous, and autonomous approach within these spheres.

Within North America, Diefenbaker accepted Lester Pearson's earlier judgement that the days of "easy and automatic" relations with the U.S. were over. This, in addition to the disquiet caused by a record trade concentration and imbalance, led the prime minister to declare that he would approach the relationship by placing Canadian interests first. The moderate institutionalization typical of a liberal-internationalist approach still influenced proposals to establish new joint organizations that would enhance trust and confidence between the two nations. However, Diefenbaker indicated his intention to speak with greater forthrightness on bilateral concerns. More importantly, he pledged to diversify Canadian trade away from the U.S. and to ensure that American action in regard to Canada took full account of Canadian interests. Both these declarations reflect the interest-based and autonomous bilateral involvement more typical of a principal power.

Although the liberal-internationalist doctrines reflected in Diefenbaker's declarations were carried out to some extent in key decisions of the period, the paradoxical combination of Canada's increased military vulnerability and economic and technical capability, along with the prime minister's sometimes courageous, sometimes naive approach, led to a number of decisions that did not conform to the pattern.

Decisions

Economic Relations with the United States

To counter a growing concentration of Canadian trade on the U.S., the Diefenbaker government began, on the overseas front, with an ill-considered scheme to divert 15 per cent of Canadian trade from the United States to the United Kingdom and to oppose British entry into the European Economic Community.[18] On the bilateral front, Canada sought to channel American influence through joint institutional structures by creating the North American Air Defence Command (NORAD), the Joint Ministerial Committee on Defence, and the Canada-U.S. InterParliamentary Group and by pursuing a co-operative development of the Columbia River Basin.[19] Within Canada, the government moved to conduct comprehensive surveys of continental trends in the fields of energy and culture by establishing royal commissions on energy, banking, and Canadian periodicals.[20] While these efforts show strong, if largely unsustained, signs of complex neo-realism, the stress on constraint through joint organizations in North America shows the ultimate dominance of the liberal-internationalist approach.

The limits of the government's freedom, however, seemed to be dramatically exposed in its February 1959 cancellation of the Avro Arrow, an advanced interceptor aircraft developed by Canada that fell prey to mounting costs, a lack of U.S. and other foreign markets, and a shift in the Soviet threat from manned bombers to intercontinental missiles.[21] Proponents of liberal internationalism claim that in shifting scarce domestic resources in aerospace electronics and ballistics into the new field of satellites, the government showed political courage; it also displayed defence production sharing arrangements (DPSA) with the U.S. that allowed conventional defence hardware to be produced on a co-operative basis. Patterns of peripheral dependence are strong, however, in this issue. It showed Canada's dependence on American weaponry, export markets, and military assessments. The absence of American or allied markets, the Soviet threat, and the concerns of Canadian economic departments combined to render continuation of the Arrow project unfeasible even while leaving open the nature of the alternative. The ensuing loss of a Canadian-based team of aerospace and high-technology leaders to the United States exacerbated still further Canada's dependence on American military capacity.

The Commonwealth

Diefenbaker's proclaimed commitment to the liberal and universal values underlying the Commonwealth was demonstrated, to much public acclaim, in 1961 over the issue of South African membership in the Commonwealth.[22] South Africa's move towards republican status and its attendant reinforcement of its apartheid policies led John Diefenbaker to urge South Africa to modify its racial policies, as they were inconsistent with the norms of a multiracial Commonwealth, especially repugnant to India and such new members as Ghana and Malaya, and distasteful to his own belief in individual human rights. Believing that Commonwealth pressures might improve South African policies, Diefenbaker first sought a compromise that would preserve Commonwealth values and keep South Africa in the club. But when South African intransigence rendered compromise impossible, he firmly supported the Commonwealth prime ministers' March 1961 declaration on racial equality, which led to South Africa's withdrawal. In these actions, the prime minister confirmed his belief in the need to seek consensus through active, responsible, and multiple participation with institutional members, but also, when that failed, to support the agreed-upon decision of the membership. His lead in this Commonwealth crisis, while confirming middle-power status through diplomatic style, brought with it the influence of a principal international actor.

The Cuban Missile Crisis

After 1961, the creative adaptations in John Diefenbaker's internationalism increasingly fell prey to its internal contradictions and the growing strains of the external environment. These tensions were dramatically revealed in the Cuban missile crisis of 1962, when the U.S. asked Canada to support its naval blockade of Cuba and the Soviet missiles it harboured.[23] Inspired by the classic internationalist calculus of mediation and peacekeeping and by the consultative obligations of the NORAD agreement, Diefenbaker responded by urging caution, refusing to endorse President John F. Kennedy's action, declaring that "the United Nations should be charged at the earliest possible moment with this serious problem,"[24] and suggesting an independent inspection of Cuba by the nonaligned members of the United Nations Disarmament Committee. Only when the crisis peaked did he provide full, unequivocal support, thereby moving towards the position of his defence minister, who had covertly provided practical support at an earlier stage.

Diefenbaker's reaction to this crisis perhaps typifies his government's equivocation between the stances of a middle power and a small power. Canada's desire to inhibit potential American overreaction, involve the UN, use its nonaligned members, and create a new inspection and peacekeeping force dramatically displayed its profound, instinctive attachment to the precepts of constraint, moderate institutionalization, multilateralization, and reformation respectively. At the same time, the failure of the consultative obligations of the NORAD agreement and the close ties of the Canadian defence establishment with American counterparts produced, *de facto,* an acquiescent Canadian support for U.S. military moves.

The Nuclear Weapons Controversy

The final important foreign policy issue of the Diefenbaker government arose out of early contradictory policies that reflected Canada's international obligations in NORAD and NATO, on the one hand, and belief in the disarmament process at the UN, on the other.

Since 1957, John Diefenbaker's strong support of Canada's NATO and NORAD alliances had led him to acquire four weapons systems that depended upon nuclear armaments for maximum effectiveness. Yet his active efforts to forward the cause of disarmament at the United Nations increasingly induced him to delay the full implementation of his pledges. When the issue came to a head in 1963, he remained adamant in his refusal to add the nuclear components to the weapons, despite the combined opposition of the United States, Canada's NATO allies, the opposition Liberal party, and a Cabinet coalition led by his minister of defence.[25] His defiance cost him the solidarity of his Cabinet and his prime ministership in the 1963 election, leaving the successor Liberal government of Lester Pearson to accept the weapons, in fulfillment of Canada's alliance obligations, until they could be negotiated away.

Such behaviour was uncharacteristic of Canada, whether as a middle power with an overriding commitment to the security alliances or as a small power standing defiantly against substantial American and British pressure. While the unilateral nature of Diefenbaker's decision conforms to the expectation of a principal-power perspective, the resulting domestic dissension, loss of Cabinet solidarity, and eventual defeat at the polls compromise this interpretation. The conflict between the commitments of alliance and disarmament was a principal-power problem, but solved in a middle-power mode.

Conclusions

Prime Minister Diefenbaker's profound belief in individual human freedoms and the representative democratic process of government, combined with his strident Canadian nationalism, was expressed in a foreign policy that tried to cope simultaneously with a liberal-internationalist world-view and commitment to association, a complex neo-realist policy defined in terms of Canada's "national interests", and a peripheral-dependent recognition of Canada's minimal military capability. The military situation was not, in Diefenbaker's view, to be confused with the continuation of American economic penetration, which he hoped would change through efforts at trade and market diversification.

Although the cases reviewed provide substantial support, in both doctrine and decision, for the liberal-internationalist perspective, along with some evidence of peripheral dependence on economic and security matters, some of the behaviour conforms more readily to the complex neo-realist perspective. The rhetorical stress on Canada's rapid growth rates, ties with Commonwealth Africa and Asia, Southeast Asia, and less developed countries, and on placing Canadian interests first in the bilateral relationship, indicated a move towards a principal-power position and global, interest-based involvement even if the referents and frameworks remained those of peripheral dependence and liberal internationalism. Similarly, the themes of independence from the U.S., speaking out publicly on bilateral issues, trade diversion, and reconsidering Canada's military contribution to NATO in Europe indicated the attraction of unilateralism, divergence, diversification, and revised institutionalization respectively.

Yet actions showed the clear limits that existed to any decisive breaks from old patterns. In the freest sphere—the Commonwealth—Canada's approach to South Africa indicated the impact that the domestic value of human rights might have in helping to transform an international institution, even at the overt cost of reducing its membership. However, the pause for reconsideration produced by the royal commissions and the short life of the trade diversion effort highlighted the constraints within the North American sphere. And while the unilateral divergence, party divisions, and Cabinet conflict of the nuclear weapons crisis showed the strong thrust towards complex neo-realism, the fall of the Diefenbaker government confirmed the overriding claim of U.S., NORAD, and NATO obligations and the liberal-internationalist patterns on which they rested.

THE ERA OF FEDERALISM, 1963–1968

Given the international pre-eminence Prime Minister Lester Pearson had achieved in foreign policy as St. Laurent's secretary of state for external affairs, and the experience Pearson's foreign minister, Paul Martin, had acquired since his first international exposure in 1945, it was natural that the rhetoric of the new Liberal government should mark a return to the themes of the St. Laurent era.

As in the Diefenbaker government, Canadian foreign policy under Pearson reflected both the dominance of liberal-internationalist patterns and the incoherence introduced by new peripheral-dependence and complex neo-realist trends. But in the Pearson era, complex neo-realist tendencies had somewhat greater scope for success. A new element was the deep interest of both Pearson and Martin in fostering consensus between Canada's English- and French-speaking communities and the allied challenge of Quebec and France to anglophone dominance and orientations at home and abroad. Particularly after 1965, the challenge slowly forced a more direct fusion of international and domestic objectives and a search for a new conceptual foundation for foreign policy.

Doctrine

The most representative initial statement of the government's foreign policy was delivered by Paul Martin before the House of Commons Special Committee on Defence in July 1963.[26] While both the context and the content of the speech reflected the recent debates over foreign and defence policy, it defined well the new Liberal government's approach. The speech placed heavy emphasis on the continuity of Canada's position and policy, as an established middle power, in preserving international peace and promoting trade, national interests, and Canada's image abroad. It defined Canada's five aims as: (1) ensuring Western deterrence and hence collective security through

NORAD and NATO; (2) fostering arms control at the UN; (3) developing peaceful responses to limited wars through UN peacekeeping and mediation; (4) reducing economic disparities abroad, with their resulting instability, by giving aid through multilateral channels; and (5) developing the international peacekeeping envisaged in the United Nations Charter.

The traditional liberal-internationalist precepts of mediatory middlepowermanship (for example, peacekeeping) and of de-emphasizing military functions can be seen in the continued commitment to the UN, the Commonwealth, NATO, and NORAD. Active responsible participation and adherence to distributive internationalism were inherent in the goal of reducing global economic disparities.

Such roles were, in Martin's view, partly prescribed by the search of other nations for a country of fair-mindedness and no international ambition to perform peacekeeping functions as bipolarity, in an age of nuclear deterrence and decolonization, pushed superpower rivalry into the Third World. Yet Martin emphasized Canada's domestic situation as the factor that made Canada the primary choice. The only hints that domestic demands might not be absorbed by the easy translation from biculturalism to mediation came in Martin's stress on the close interrelation of defence, foreign economic policy, and overall national policy and on the need for much tighter integration, planning, and co-ordination of the government's total foreign policy process. In this sense, while Martin's vision of world order conformed to his personal roots in the liberal-internationalist ethos, his stress on the opportunities offered by Canada's domestic profile—as a sophisticated institutional apparatus founded upon a rich, diverse human and natural resource base—implied opportunities for external behaviour beyond the standard capabilities of a middle power.

Decisions

Defence Policy

A concern with coherence and with restoring Canada's reputation as a reliable ally and effective internationalist animated Canadian foreign policy during the first two years of the Pearson government. After immediately fulfilling Canada's earlier NATO commitment to accept nuclear weapons, the government began, in a defence White Paper, to integrate Canada's armed forces and define a new defence policy in which peacekeeping under UN auspices occupied the primary place. This commitment was demonstrated in 1964 in Paul Martin's successful initiative to form a United Nations force, with a substantial Canadian contribution, for peacekeeping operations in Cyprus.

The reorganization of the Department of National Defence and Canada's presence in Cyprus have been cited by proponents of liberal internationalism as evidence that Canada was not only returning to the sphere of activity of a mediatory middle power, but was single-mindedly pursuing a consensus through mediation and peacekeeping, which led to the later mediatory missions in Indochina.

Economic Relations with the United States

If Canada appeared to be re-establishing its reputation as a mediatory middle power in the Cyprus case, it began to break away from liberal-internationalist patterns in its relations with the U.S. In 1963, Minister of Finance Walter Gordon introduced a budget that contained major provisions to stem the American take-over of Canadian industry.[27] This might have been interpreted as the interest-based activity of a principal power, if not for the resulting outcry from the domestic financial community and some Cabinet colleagues. Gordon was forced to withdraw the most significant provisions, a move that seemed virtually to acknowledge American penetration of Canada's industrial sector and the impossibility of anything but low, undifferentiated, imperial-focused interaction in this sphere.

When the U.S. curtailed the outflow of its capital in 1963, 1965, and 1968, Canada was forced to seek exemptions and, in return, to accept restrictions on the use of Canadian foreign exchange reserves. Walter Gordon's rapid retreat and the foreign exchange restrictions can be seen as specific examples of the penetrative impact and exclusive influence of the United States on Canada.

Yet Gordon secured a change in the previous relatively open treatment of direct foreign investment. He moved to protect Canada's banking sector from American competition and proposed a Cabinet-mandated study of direct foreign investment that prepared the intellectual framework for initiatives to come. The end result, then, was that Gordon set the stage for the interest-based involvement of a principal power although his own attempts were thwarted. Canada's success in securing a sectoral trade liberalization agreement with the United States in the automotive field in 1965 was one major example of such involvement, leading to a liberal-internationalist end.

The Temple University Speech

Surprisingly enough, Prime Minister Pearson himself was the second minister to depart from the classic internationalist pattern.[28] The issue was the war in Vietnam; the occasion, a speech in April 1965 at Temple University in Philadelphia. Seeing the critical move towards a massive buildup of U.S. ground forces in Vietnam, and perhaps recalling his earlier successes with public diplomacy in the United States, Pearson cast aside the norms of quiet diplomacy to call for a pause, at an appropriate time, in the American bombing of North Vietnam. The speech earned him a rebuke from President Lyndon Johnson and damaged their once close relationship, but it served to move Canadian involvement beyond military supervision and "mediatory" missions to Peking and Hanoi.

This surprising departure was one of the most telling signs of a new association with the U.S., characterized by unilateralism and divergence. While Pearson's speech may have reflected the growing concern of Canada's major NATO allies over American involvement in Vietnam, it marked a move into public diplomacy, destroyed the assumption of commonality, strained the practice of a close summit-level relationship between the U.S. and Canada, and aligned Canadian policy with that of Britain and France. Such behaviour, especially given the range of likely consequences, conforms most closely to the activities of a principal power, as outlined in the complex neo-realist perspective.

The 1967 Mideast Crisis

Pearson followed his Temple initiatives with moves to prompt a rethinking of Canada's traditional approach to NATO and of the broader edifice of foreign policy erected on this foundation.[29] However, this revised institutionalization, indicative more of a principal power than of a middle power, did not extend to the sphere of Middle East peacekeeping, where Pearson's reputation as a peace and security mediator had been anointed and crowned.[30] When Egyptian President Gamal Abdel Nasser asked in May 1967 for the removal of the UN peacekeeping force at Suez, which included a Canadian contingent, Canada, along with the United Kingdom and the United States, was reluctant to comply. Yet Egyptian determination, reinforced by Indian and Yugoslavian sympathy, rendered Canada's resistance futile. And with the outbreak of hostilities in June, Canada's call for compromise and a meeting of the big four and its presentation of a six-point peace plan similarly proved to be of no avail.

Although at the war's end, Canadian forces returned to the area as part of a UN operation, the ease of their initial removal and the inefficacy of Canadian diplomacy seemed to reveal vividly the obsolescence of the traditional peacekeeping and mediatory roles. According to the perspective of peripheral dependence, Canada's failure to stop the conflict was also the result of supporting and associating too closely with the Americans and the British alone. Hence, Canada's failure to act as a principal power in the 1967 Mideast crisis cast it from its previous role as middle power into the ignominious position of a failed mediator and perhaps a minor power.

The French Challenge

By 1967, the instinct towards compromise also seemed chillingly irrelevant to the much more immediate and fundamental threat posed by Quebec and France.[31] Since 1963, the Pearson government had acquiesced as Quebec increasingly asserted its claims to direct involvement in foreign affairs; Ottawa hastily concluded umbrella agreements that endowed provincial initiatives with a retroactive legal legitimacy. And, more out of intellectual incomprehension than because of calculated policy, Ottawa had spurned France's effort to erode Anglo–American dominance of the Western alliance by departing from the military framework of NATO and seeking the uranium and aircraft sales by which the French claim to great-power status would be achieved. Yet when on 24 July 1967, Charles de Gaulle cried "Vive le Québec libre!" from the balcony of the Hôtel de Ville in Montreal, Ottawa was forced into a much stiffer stance. Pearson declared the statement unacceptable. And, in March 1968, when Gabon invited Quebec to participate as a separate government in an international conference of francophone education ministers, Canada suspended diplomatic relations with the hapless agent of France.

In this context, liberal-internationalist patterns of activity and association no longer account for Canada's changing relationship with France. The middle-power precepts of conciliatory negotiation and compromise became things of the past. Compared with the immediate postwar decade, when Canada's emergent interests coincided with those of France and the Canadian government used its "French connection" as a means to ensure its place in the upper tiers of Western security, economic, and political affairs, the Pearson–de Gaulle years saw two emerging principal powers competing for influence and international presence and, consciously or not, employing both bilateral and multilateral linkages in pursuit of national definition and international stature.

Conclusions

This was a period of direct challenges to the Canadian government, at home and abroad. Two of the principal architects of Canada's postwar internationalism, Lester Pearson and Paul Martin, presided over events and decisions unlike those of earlier periods. The mid-1960s brought attempts at political, economic, and military penetration by France and the United States, challenges to the Western alliance over Vietnam and to Canadian defence policy in the nuclear era, and a crisis of legitimacy at the United Nations over peacekeeping and financing. The novel responses of the Pearson government to these and other foreign policy issues cannot be accounted for sufficiently by the middle-power, liberal-internationalist thesis alone. The deviations from past patterns of international behaviour were movements towards the expectations of the complex neo-realist perspective. Canada's responses to aggressive associates in terms of both domestic penetration and overseas involvements were more typical of a principal than a middle power.

THE ERA OF NATIONAL INTEREST, 1968–1980

Doctrine

With the election of Prime Minister Pierre Trudeau's majority Liberal government in the spring of 1968, the foreign policy objectives of the Pearson government and the internationalist instincts underlying them were subjected to a direct challenge and full-scale replacement by a foreign policy framework differing significantly in emphasis, content, and conceptual form. The new Trudeauvian edifice was articulated in greatest detail in a series of six booklets, collectively titled *Foreign Policy for Canadians,* published in the spring of 1970 and elaborated in a paper entitled "Canada-U.S. Relations: Options for the Future," issued by the secretary of state for external affairs in autumn 1972.[32]

The number, detail, comprehensive coverage, and conceptual consistency of the government's foreign policy declarations and the core concepts of the policies themselves showed a decisive thrust towards global, interest-based involvement implemented through unilateral initiatives. *Foreign Policy for Canadians* propounded the basic doctrine that foreign policy was "the extension abroad of national policies," noted the two inescapable realities of national unity and living with the United States, and identified the six themes of economic growth, sovereignty and independence, peace and security, social justice, quality of life, and harmonious natural environment.[33] In "Options for the Future," Trudeau's government rejected the alternative of maintaining the present relationship with the United States and deliberately pursuing closer integration with it in favour of a "comprehensive long-term strategy to develop and strengthen the Canadian economy and other aspects of its national life and in the process to reduce the present Canadian vulnerability."[34]

As significant as these documents were, the declaration closest to the approach of the prime minister and his government was a statement issued in May 1968, entitled "Canada and the World."[35] This statement announced the government's intention to conduct a "thorough and comprehensive review of Canadian foreign policy," identified seven areas requiring particular attention, defined the central concepts that were to guide the review process, and announced a series of specific policy changes in accordance with these precepts.[36] The changes in policy were based on general dissatisfaction with the premises and public posture of foreign policy under Paul Martin and propelled by a specific interest in countering Quebec's claim to international status. According to the new doctrine, the requirement of national unity was to be directly reflected in the full range and overall structure of Canadian behaviour abroad.

"Canada and the World" provided the clearest signal of the new, decisive shift towards complex neo-realism. Unlike previous declarations, it emphasized a break away from the traditional focus on the United Nations, NATO, and the Commonwealth. Global, interest-based, autonomous bilateral involvement was reflected in the strong emphasis on developing ties with Europe, Latin America, the Pacific, Africa, and the francophone world, in the declaration that Canada's bilingual character and self-interests were directly relevant to this task, and in the concentration on bilateral actors and regional organizations in forging such ties. The statements on the recognition of China and review of military roles in NATO and NORAD constituted unilateral moves divergent from American policies, while the government's desire to strengthen ties with overseas partners indicated an instinctive leaning towards diversification, if not its precise targets and mechanisms. And the announcement in "Canada and the World" of aid to francophonie and creation of the International Development Research Centre suggested a move towards revised institutionalization.

Equally important was the vision of a new foreign policy process. The rise of China, Europe, Latin America, and the Third World and the declining relevance of existing international institutions indicated the broader scope and diminished salience of external determinants. In contrast, domestic processes were given a high salience, direct relevance, and precise specification, notably in the attention given to including provincial governments and university experts in policy formulation procedures. And while the stronger stress on comprehensive, co-ordinated, planned foreign policy indicated a high salience, broad scope, and direct sensitivity for the governmental process, the stress on having foreign policy directly serve overall government priorities suggested that in this process, central foreign policy co-ordinative structures and the prime minister himself would prevail.

Despite Trudeau's assault on the rhetoric of Martin and Pearson, this move to a new doctrine that promoted domestic interests abroad was not as great a blow to liberal internationalism as it might appear. The continuing existence, though not dominance, of liberal-internationalist patterns was reflected in the functional emphasis on Canada's special characteristics as a basis for its international participation, its repudiation of crusades or proclamations of independence in its approach to association, and in the inclusion of the traditional world-order objective of "peace and security" as one of the six objectives of *Foreign Policy for Canadians.*

The Trudeau doctrines also reveal certain patterns of peripheral dependence. The stress on Canada's small-power position, the warning against exaggerating its influence, the concern with Canada's "survival" and with the "basic" realities of national unity and living with the United States all point to Canada's rank below and vulnerability above the limits of the liberal-internationalist perspective.

Decisions

China and the United Nations

These conceptual innovations were soon registered in three far-reaching decisions that fundamentally altered Canada's traditional approaches to the critical spheres of relations with the United Nations, NATO, and the United States. The first, announced in the May 1968 statement itself, was to seek diplomatic relations with the People's Republic of China and support its admission to the China seat in the United Nations.[37]

After overcoming Chinese suspicions that Canada might be proposing a variant of the dreaded "two China" formula as a surrogate for the United States, Canada and China reached an agreement. Under its terms Canada merely "took note" of the Chinese claim to Taiwan and proceeded to recognize the People's Republic. The Canadian government's action, taken primarily in recognition of global and bilateral realities, marked a shift towards complex neo-realist patterns. It was a unilateral action, extending Canada's global involvement, diverging from American policy, and showing compatibility with French foreign policy. The action preceded a U.S. move in the same direction, seemed to catalyze recognition of China by several other states, and provided the diplomatic formula that some of them, notably Italy and Belgium, later employed.

NATO Force Reductions

A second initiative, also announced in the May 1968 statement, was a review of Canada's force posture in NATO.[38] After much internal agony and extensive consultations with major European allies and the United States, the government announced its decision on 3 April 1969. Dismissing American objections that a Canadian reduction would fuel demands for similar U.S. action and British complaints that it would merely shift the defence burden onto the U.K., Canada reduced forces stationed in NATO's central European theatre by half, began to phase out its nuclear role, and moved its remaining 5000-man contingent and three aircraft squadrons to reserve status. The government argued that its force redeployments enhanced NATO security in the North American sector and that Canada remained fully committed to reinforcing NATO's European theatre from its base in Canada. Like the move to recognize China, the NATO decision displayed unilateralism, divergence, compatibility with France, and a thrust towards revised institutionalization. However, some evidence of liberal-internationalist patterns of combination, consensus, and constraint were seen in Canada's extensive consultation of its allies before the decision and in its willingness to absorb their views in determining the size of the reduction and redeployment.

The Arctic Waters Act

The most unilateral decision in the early Trudeau years, and the one most directly antithetical to American interests, was the passage in April 1970 of the Arctic Waters Pollution Prevention Act.[39] Introduced to enhance Canada's "sovereignty and independence" over the Arctic and cloaked in the garb of ensuring a "harmonious natural environment," this act established a 100-mile pollution control zone in the Arctic. Thus, together with an extension of the territorial sea to 12 nautical miles, it effectively closed the Northwest Passage to unrestricted American shipping. By hampering American ability to disperse its naval nuclear deterrent freely, this action reflected Canada's shift in emphasis from the collective security of North America *vis-à-vis* the Soviet Union to the direct political, environmental, and economic threat posed by the United States itself.

This action constituted more evidence that complex neo-realist patterns were being established at the expense of the small-power, peripheral-dependence posture of past Canada–U.S. relations. By reserving this action from the jurisdiction of the International Court of Justice, Canada displayed its suspicion of established conservative international bodies whose approach to international law might reflect unduly the precepts and patterns of dominance of an earlier age. The Arctic Waters decision not only reinforced unilateralism, divergence, and revised institutionalization, it also represented a direct effort to reduce American penetration and constituted a move towards modification of the global order through leadership in defining and legitimizing a new approach to international law.

The August Surcharge

By 1970 the early burst of Prime Minister Trudeau's reforming initiative had been largely spent and the pace of foreign policy innovation slowed. This pause reflected more the need to turn attention to the demands of the upcoming 1972 election and to allow a largely converted bureaucracy to absorb the new changes than any conversion to internationalist precepts on the prime minister's part or a decreasing conviction of the need for reform. For when new external threats arose and when the return of a majority Liberal government in 1974 gave an experienced prime minister greater scope for innovation, deeper modifications of Canada's traditional approach to the U.S., the European NATO system, and the global UN framework quickly ensued.

The first modification came in response to the American imposition of a 10 per cent surcharge on dutiable Canadian imports into the United States, in August 1971.[40] Canada's first reaction to the surcharge conformed to the conciliatory patterns of peripheral-dependence and liberal-internationalist behaviour. Assuming that the surcharge was primarily directed to America's similarly affected European trading partners and Japan, Canada fell back on its classic argument about the interdependence of the two North American economic entities and the consequent need for a special Canadian exemption. Traces of the acquiescent and imperial-focused interaction of a peripheral-dependent nation can be discerned in Canada's request and especially in the surprise U.S. refusal.

However, the August surcharge prompted immediate and longer-range moves to protect Canada's apparently vulnerable economy unilaterally and to restructure the country's broader relationship with America so that such manipulations of Canadian vulnerability would not happen again. The first objective was met by a government assistance program to affected Canadian industries, the second by a rethinking of the entire Canadian–American relationship that culminated in the "third option" policy of "Options for the Future" in 1972. Thus, Canada's association with the U.S. was directed into the patterns of unilateralism and divergence typical of a principal power.

Contractual Links with Europe and Japan

While the quest to reduce vulnerability was further manifested by Canadian initiatives in the bilateral fields of energy and direct foreign investment, an equally important response to the August 1971 surcharge took place on the overseas front. The surcharge had highlighted the need for Canada, along with other similarly shaken allies, to diversify trading partnerships.[41] With *Foreign Policy for Canadians* proclaiming the new importance of Europe and Japan for Canada, and the 1969 decision to reduce Canada's NATO forces in Europe de-emphasizing the traditional transatlantic relationship, a reliance on new bilateral ties was free to emerge. With persistent prime ministerial diplomacy in Europe, French misgivings were overcome and the "contractual link" with the European Community concluded in 1975 and 1976. While subsequent fluctuations in short-term exchange rates among Western countries prevented dramatic progress in supplementing Canada–U.S. trade with European trade, the long-term goals of altering political perceptions and the structure of resource and technological relationships were slowly achieved. And in 1976, the process was geographically extended when Canada concluded a separate contractual link with Japan.

The Indian Nuclear Explosion

As Canada developed these new forms of associations with emerging major powers, it revised its relationship with the traditional middle-power associates that had formerly sustained its mediatory diplomacy in the United Nations. The most dramatic revision came in May 1974 in the relationship with India, when that country exploded a nuclear device with the aid of Canadian materials.[42] Canada abruptly suspended nuclear co-operation with India and announced a stronger nuclear safeguard policy in December 1974. While the suspension ended the special Canada–India relationship begun in the Commonwealth in 1947 and enriched in the UN in the following decade, the new safeguard policy catalyzed a flurry of hard bilateral bargaining with other recipients of Canadian uranium, an active role in reinforcing nonproliferation regimes in the London Suppliers' Club, and after 1976, a quest for similar objectives with a newly converted United States government.

Co-operation with the United States

After the election of U.S. President Jimmy Carter in November 1976, Canada–U.S. co-operation flourished, not only in nuclear diplomacy and in overseas arenas but on North American issues as well.[43] A number of agreements seemed to indicate a return to liberal-internationalist patterns of behaviour. In September 1977, President Carter and Prime Minister Trudeau initialled a joint agreement authorizing construction of a new Alaska Gas Pipeline, designed primarily to carry Alaskan natural gas to the lower forty-eight states. In spring 1978, the executive branches of the two governments concluded an interim agreement on east coast fisheries management; they also negotiated a treaty to solve their east coast fishery and maritime boundary dispute permanently. Throughout the 1976–1980 period, the bilateral oil and gas relationship, which had atrophied in the wake of the 1973 Arab oil embargo, slowly moved towards a more co-operative tone.

One catalyst for these co-operative attitudes was the election in November 1976 of a Parti Québécois government, dedicated to Quebec's political separation from Canada.[44] The Trudeau government, feeling that Canada was vulnerable, turned anxiously to see the U.S. reaction, and the U.S., in its own national interest, responded with a pro-federalist co-operative program symbolized in an American invitation for Pierre Trudeau to address the United States Congress in February 1977. To proponents of the theory of peripheral dependence, Canada's implicit request for positive neutrality from the United States revealed imperial-focused interactions and adherence.

Defence Spending Increases

If Quebec was the catalyst, the deeper cause of Canada–U.S. co-operation was the profound need of the United States, with its diminished power and increased global isolation, for allies to help it in its quest for Western security and global order abroad. For Canada, this implied a revision of its earlier approach to the politico-military demands of NATO in its Atlantic and central European theatres.[45] From 1975 onward, Canada purchased new tanks, long-range patrol aircraft, and interceptor aircraft to replace the aging weaponry that implemented its NATO military roles. Politically it resumed its quest to harmonize differing European and American perspectives over the introduction of theatre nuclear forces and enhanced radiation weapons into Europe, and over the allied response to disruptions in the Middle East and the Soviet invasion of Afghanistan. In 1978 Pierre Trudeau pledged, along with his NATO partners, to increase his nation's real defence expenditures by 3 per cent annually; he moved with surprising determination in subsequent years to fulfill this pledge. Canada's acceptance of the defence spending increases and its participation in efforts to co-ordinate American and European policies and thereby solidify NATO indicate a mix of middle-power and principal-power policy, with the emphasis on responsible participation in Western security.

The Namibia Contact Group

Support for NATO and the search for compromise in that body extended into equal leadership with major Western powers on critical global issues. In many ways the hardest test came over the question of Namibian independence, where the historic task of facilitating decolonization intersected with renewed fears of Soviet incursions into the Third World.[46]

Working under the auspices of the United Nations, Canada joined with the United States, Britain, France, and West Germany in a contact group to secure a plan for Namibian independence through free, fair, UN-supervised elections. Reinforced by its temporary membership on the United Nations Security Council, Canada helped to initiate and draft a settlement plan in 1978 and subsequently coped with South African, United Nations, and American reservations to keep alive the prospects of a peaceful transition to majority rule. Unlike the UN peacekeeping operations, which strive to include a diversity of nations, the Namibia Contact Group was composed of states considered comparable to one another. In this context, Canada's participation places it in the upper hierarchy of the Western state system, among the principal powers, because of its experience in other conflict-prone arenas in the Third World and its stature in relation to its co-participants.

The Boat People and the Tokyo Summit

During the Conservative government of Joe Clark, from May 1979 to February 1980, the durability of shifts towards complex neo-realist patterns was severely tested and substantially confirmed. With no parliamentary majority, no experience in government, and less interest in foreign policy than in domestic problems, Prime Minister Clark had neither the time nor the inclination to articulate a distinctive Conservative approach to foreign affairs.[47] Yet while he sought refuge in traditional policies within the comfortable embrace of alliance relationships, the underlying Canadian strengths and shifting external relationships forced action on his part. The most successful venture came in refugee policy, where Canada's generous acceptance of large numbers of "boat people" fleeing from Communist persecution in Indochina brought Canada's efforts into a new geographic region, beyond the European and Commonwealth countries for the first time. In response to the 1979 rise in global oil prices, Prime Minister Clark joined with his associates at the Western Economic Summit in Tokyo to devise a strict regime of conservation and moved at home to implement its obligations, in part through the Crosbie budget that caused his government's defeat.

The Argentine Reactor and the Jerusalem Embassy

The need to sustain Canada's sophisticated high-technology industries conflicted with the government's emphasis on promoting human rights abroad in the case of a prospective sale of a nuclear reactor to Argentina. The Cabinet, after much internal conflict, finally authorized an ultimately unsuccessful bid. To be sure, the government's one foray into the "high" sphere of foreign policy—its promise to move the Canadian embassy in Israel to Jerusalem and its subsequent cancellation of this move—seemed to reveal its lack of skill in foreign policy matters, its susceptibility to organized domestic pressure, and its ultimate deference to opposing forces abroad. But it also suggested the ability of even inexperienced Canadian leaders to take initiatives that critically affect delicate situations in distinct regions, the new strength of ethnic and corporate groups within Canada, and the efficacy of personal moral conviction in animating Canadian behaviour abroad.

Conclusions

The Trudeau government's decisions, as much as its declarations, demonstrated that the decisive shift from a predominantly liberal-internationalist, middle-power perspective to intent and behaviour indicative of a principal power conforming to complex neo-realist patterns was real. This shift received only minor interruption during the Clark government. Doctrine and decision were reasonably reinforcing. In the various dimensions of international behaviour in the categories of activity, association, and approach to world order, the cases examined provide a portrait of Canada beginning to articulate its foreign policy clearly and forcefully in terms of its national political and economic interests, while still joined in a special relationship with the United States and still committed to multilateral responsibilities. Although, as in the previous eras, the three perspectives coexist, foreign policy in this era was increasingly weighted towards interest-based involvement through bilateral relationships the world over.

THE ERA OF BILATERALISM, 1980–

With the return of a majority Liberal government under Pierre Trudeau in the spring of 1980, the stage was set for even more fundamental change. The first three Trudeau governments had done much to institute complex neo-realist patterns in Canada's activity, association, and approach to world order. It was left to his fourth government to consolidate and complete these developments.

Doctrine

The major codified expression of the government's thinking about foreign policy came in a little-noted speech given by Secretary of State for External Affairs Mark MacGuigan before the Empire Club in Toronto in January 1981.[48] This speech, outlining the new official policy of "bilateralism", marked the culmination of an extensive rethinking of Canadian foreign policy within Ottawa during the preceding year.

The Empire Club address argued that Canada's past emphasis on multilateralism and even the revisions of *Foreign Policy for Canadians* provided an inadequate foundation for Canadian policy in the 1980s. While Canada's past multilateralist successes meant that this tradition would continue, and indeed be enriched by the new stress on bilateralism, the new theme was to be developed as a parallel emphasis. The new policy drew on the earlier concern with national interests, specific goals, the quest for counterweights, and the need for a co-ordinated approach to the United States, but a much more ambitious approach was suggested by the disappointment in some quarters with the results of the contractual links with Europe and Japan, the need to seek even more counterweights, and the desirability of establishing priorities among these relationships.

In the eyes of its authors, bilateralism was based on several profound changes taking place abroad, in Canada, and within the government itself. In the international sphere, since 1973, energy-related events and the effect of technology on traditional societies had produced profound shifts in power among various actors and eroded the traditional distinction between political and economic power. In short, the world situation was beginning to conform to the patterns of classic realism—that is, to patterns of interplay among self-contained, cohesive great powers in an international system characterized by anarchy. But also emerging was a more unpredictable, unstable, dangerous world in which the cold war of East–West competition posed less threat than the multitude of states that had acquired enough independence either to play superpowers off against each other or to be used by other powers as pawns and proxies in pursuit of greater interests. In either situation, national self-interest defined international behaviour.

Other phenomena, less directly linked to classic realist theory, led

Canada to consolidate its approach to world order. A regionalized, competitive economic system had established itself, causing Canada's industrialized partners to restrict their open-market economies. Within the new system, regional blocs such as the European Community countries were achieving prominence and, in combination with industrial states and low labour costs in the Third World, had begun to pose significant competition for Canadian manufacturing industries. Moreover, the transfer of wealth to oil producers and industrial development elsewhere had dispersed economic power well beyond Canada's traditional European, Japanese, and other industrialized partners to states such as Saudi Arabia, Brazil, Venezuela, and Mexico. These states had developed a strong tendency to conduct economic transactions on a government-to-government basis, under umbrella agreements in which overall political and economic relationships were integrally linked.

Canada's societal climate was also beginning to develop into the complex neo-realist configuration of high salience, broad scope, and high institutional differentiation. Basically, this was reflected within the country in the entrenched, divergent views among various regions, linguistic groups, and sectors about which countries and objectives were of central importance to national policy as a whole. This fragmentation was compounded by the success of single-interest groups in capturing intellectual support and media attention, hence effectively defining the national interest, at the expense of business groups. This imbalance seemed particularly costly to Canadian multinationals incapable of effective individual action abroad in the face of increased threats to Canada's traditional manufacturing industries, the need to develop specialty technologies tied to the resource base, the proliferating financial and technological complexity of major projects, and the vast requirements of energy and industrial development in Canada. The Canadian corporate community recognized the need to secure consensus, in Canada's mixed market economy, among themselves and with the government on efforts to combat these difficulties.

Another concern within the country was related to the government's foreign policy decision-making process. The climate of austerity prevailing since the summer of 1978 and the prospect of continuing limitations on Canada's human and financial resources forced a recognition in the foreign policy sphere that Canada was no longer capable of being equally active in all sectors and regions abroad. In addition, since 1977 the Department of External Affairs had been acting as a central policy agency. This furthered its desire to provide leadership in erecting explicit policy frameworks and related operational priorities to guide credible, coherent, and planned Canadian action abroad, reflecting the overall government priorities defined at Cabinet sessions in the summers of 1979 and 1980. Analytically, the new policy consisted of three elements conforming to complex neo-realist definitions of international activity: (1) in variety, a direct pursuit of national self-interests; (2) in degree, the systematic selection and assignment of priority to those countries best able to contribute to the defined national objectives; and (3) in diffusion, the planned development of stable, long-term relationships with these countries of concentration.

The new policy of grounding Canada's international behaviour, in a ruthlessly realistic fashion, in the pursuit of Canadian interests required an acceptance, comparable to that in the United States and other countries, of a distinctive, entirely indigenously defined set of objectives that placed Canadian needs first. The objectives embraced the concerns of the entire country and had a long-term relevance to Canada's national development. In practice, they had to be expressed in clearly defined, partially quantified criteria and balanced among economic and political considerations, but with the latter taking precedence.

Within the economic sphere, the list of relevant objectives extended beyond the traditional concern with markets to finding outlets for Canadian investment and entrepreneurship and securing investment, labour, technology, and strategic natural resources for Canada's internal development. Within the political sphere, they embraced such factors as the compatibility of Canadian values with those in other countries, cultural linkages, serious interest in developing such institutions as the International Monetary Fund and the World Bank, and a common approach to North–South questions. This emphasis on pursuing narrowly defined, domestically based global interests through the establishment of numerous bilateral relationships as well as the concern given to nonuniversal international organizations in seeking a pragmatic approach to world order matched a principal-power analysis of foreign policy.

Similarly, a complex neo-realist pattern was evident in the second element of bilateralism, giving priority to countries that could further Canada's interests. This required the establishment of a global, differentiated foreign policy extending far beyond traditional partners such as the European countries, Japan, and other states in the industrialized world to include new affiliations in all regions, from among the newly industrializing countries, and within the Third World. Within this potential set, the government sought to secure geographical, economic, and political balances among targetted states and to penetrate the tariff walls of regional blocs such as the European Community by developing relationships with their individual members. Most importantly, within this framework it sought to concentrate its limited financial and personnel resources and attention on twenty to forty carefully selected countries where Canadian interests could best be achieved. Among these were emerging nations such as Mexico, Venezuela, Brazil, Indonesia, Singapore, South Korea, Nigeria, Algeria, Saudi Arabia, and major Commonwealth Caribbean states.

The third and most important component of bilateralism was the planned development of stable, long-term relationships with these countries of concentration. This required, among other things, increasing DEA's capacity in order to enable the government to manage relations with these priority states as effectively as it had operated with the United States, Europe, and Japan.

From this internal foundation, the government sought to develop enduring relationships with priority states, relationships that would withstand their adopting individual actions of which Canada disapproved and that would ensure, at times of Canadian weakness and global instability, strong support rather than merely perfunctory friendliness. To secure such longstanding relationships, the policy of bilateralism demanded the coherent political pursuit of relationships that would include economic interactions. At a minimum, this required the injection of a political dimension into relationships that were essentially economic, and the use of political processes to create the conditions for economic exchange. More importantly, it involved the active use of linkage, whereby private economic affiliations expanded into political solidarity, and leverage, whereby good political relationships were employed to secure economic advantages, particularly with governments where democratic values did not prevail. In the case of the United States, linkage included a willingness to overlook specific economic divergences in the interests of pursuing closer associations in fields where common values prevailed. In all cases, the aim was to develop a multi-interest thrust that would provide resilience when international instabilities emerged.

On a more practical level, Canada began establishing a more visible and active presence in priority countries. Following the Japanese model, political, cultural, and social relationships were to be facilitated by the Canadian government in order to create an image and climate conducive to private sector economic interchange, and government-to-government relationships were developed to nurture a wide variety of economic ventures. More ambitiously, it dictated the coherent, unidirectional, selective deployment of all relevant political instruments of state to ensure the sustenance of these priority relationships. These included trade policy, access to Canadian resources, bilateral defence understandings, cultural and information programs, and, in some instances, development assistance in states having considerable overall wealth. Instruments of state included a concentration of summit and ministerial visits to selected countries, formation of governmental contractual links, establishment of ministerial committees, active pursuit of bilateral and umbrella agreements, strengthening Canadian posts, and often, conducting multilateral diplomacy with bilateral considerations in mind.

Perhaps most importantly, bilateralism was meant to have a greater direct impact on the treatment that Canada received in turn from priority countries. This required increased recognition, by public and private sector actors alike, of foreign policy as a vehicle for pursuing national objectives and a willingness to deploy it in that pursuit. Consistent with this orientation was a readiness to establish issue-specific linkages within a bilateral relationship on occasion so that consideration of one question could be used to further the achievement of other goals.

Decisions

Since the return of the Liberal government in 1980, Canadian foreign policy has been directed quite strongly at implementing the logic of bilateralism, most notably in the meetings of the prime minister and secretary of state for external affairs with counterparts from such central, preferred partners as Mexico, Australia, and Brazil. Yet despite this emphasis, bilateralism remains only one of four central poles of Canadian foreign policy in the 1980s. The second pole is the attempt to revive and extend the Third Option policy in Canada's dominant bilateral relationship with the United States, as seen in the announced desire to extend FIRA and in the introduction of the National Energy Program in 1980.[49] Of greater significance are the third and fourth poles, two policy orientations designed to cope with the dual dilemmas of America's decline as an imperial power and its increasing temptation to retreat into a defensive, quasi-isolationist unilateralism. The focus of both orientations has been to manage the most critical arenas of global politics by establishing overlapping groupings among the West's major powers in which the United States, European powers, and ascending states such as Japan, Canada, and Mexico have an integral and often equal role.

The Western Economic Summit

The first and in many ways the most significant of the new concert processes has been the annual meetings of the heads of government of the Western world's seven principal powers, which collectively account for about half of the world's production and trade.[50] Established in 1975 as a French and German initiative, the summit has grown to provide a periodic and apparently permanent forum in which the West's leaders can reliably harmonize perspectives and policies on a full range of economic and political problems, replacing American leadership with a collective management of the challenges of an increasingly interdependent and unstable world. Within this framework, Canada has progressed from the status of a late and initially insecure entrant to a position of full unquestioned membership that has enabled it to participate equally in discussions and to exercise selective leadership in defining the common agenda and guiding the collective consensus.

Although not invited to the initial gathering, Canada joined the group at its second meeting, held in Puerto Rico in 1976. Both President Gerald Ford of the United States and the Japanese leadership found it desirable to have an additional non-European perspective represented at the gatherings, and the Europeans themselves offered little resistance, recognizing that Canada's economic weight approximated that of the United Kingdom and Italy and was substantially greater than that of other Western states besides themselves. At Puerto Rico and during subsequent meetings at London in 1977 and Bonn in 1978, Prime Minister Trudeau, at times with the aid of President Carter, succeeded in injecting such distinctive Canadian concerns as the world wheat trade into the collective discussions. But from that point onward, the North American character of Canada's membership and contribution quickly dissipated. At Bonn, Canada and Japan raised the difficult, political issue of aircraft hijacking, and Prime Minister Trudeau, encouraged by the West German leader, Helmut Schmidt, returned to Canada to introduce a program of austerity in government expenditures in fulfillment of the summit consensus. At Tokyo in 1979, Prime Minister Clark, despite his inexperience, performed fully and credibly as the summit leaders produced specific commitments to deal with the broader political issue of global energy prices and supply. At Venice, Canada was at the centre of discussions between the United States and Europeans, as the leaders grappled with such fused economic and political issues as the response to the Soviet Union's invasion of Afghanistan, the North–South dialogue, and refugees.

The culmination of Canadian participation came in the final session of the first round of summits, held in Ottawa in the summer of 1981. Employing Prime Minister Trudeau's virtually unique experience in the summit forum and his discretion as host of the gathering that year, Canada was able to shift the process from negotiating the specifics of communiqués to exchanging frank, fully political, and notably divergent views among the leaders themselves. Equally important, Canada succeeded with its European and Japanese partners in sensitizing the United States to the problems of its interest rate policy and securing from President Ronald Reagan commitments to participate in the North–South dialogue at Cancùn, Mexico, and to join, however tentatively, in a process leading to "global negotiations" on matters of economic redistribution.

The North–South Dialogue

Although Canada's economic and political capability has propelled it into summit membership, the strength and distinctiveness of its contribution has stemmed partly from the central role it has played in inducing the West's largest powers to accommodate the far-reaching demands for economic justice of an increasingly well organized South.[51] In addition to the initiatives Canada took unilaterally, at the United

Nations, and in other multilateral bodies, it was among the twenty-seven states represented at the Conference on International Economic Co-operation held in Paris in 1976 and 1977, served with Venezuela as a co-chairman of the conference, and exercised an exemplary leadership in writing off the debt of some of the world's least developed countries.

This Canadian role became more apparent at the meeting of twenty-two leaders of Northern and Southern states held at Cancùn in October 1981. As one of the eight Northern states invited, a key participant in recent UN and Commonwealth discussions on the same issue, and a close associate of states such as France, Sweden, Austria, and Commonwealth countries that shared similar positions, Canada was well situated to overcome the strange alliance of Third World radicals seeking self-sufficient development and an American administration reducing aid through multilateral institutions in favour of private sector investment. Moreover, Prime Minister Trudeau, acting as the Northern co-chairman of the conference (replacing the Austrian leader, who was ill), creatively steered towards this goal by ensuring a free exchange of views among leaders on the central general issue of global negotiations. While Canada failed, at the eleventh hour, to secure acceptance of its compromise proposal to have such negotiations begin by year's end in a forum acceptable to Northern and Southern states alike, it did obtain real, if restrained, progress in the form of a concluding consensus on the desirability of initiating such negotiations under "mutually agreed procedures".

The advent of summitry and the concert process during this period bears witness to the rapid changes occurring in the global environment. Canada's central role in these meetings gives clear evidence of its presence in the highest ranks of the international hierarchy of states. The Canadian government's role there has been one of moderation and consensus-building when deemed appropriate, but unilateral expression of interests and divergence from traditional partners when this seemed necessary. In all cases involving non-OECD states, the Canadian government, especially when led by Prime Minister Trudeau, has not hesitated to move well beyond either its former middle-power behaviour or the preferred policies of other OECD members, nor has it failed to cross Commonwealth or francophone counterparts when it appeared to be in Canada's best interests. In terms of international behaviour as exemplified through its participation in these summits, the expectations of complex neo-realism are clearly observed.

Conclusions

Bilateral relationships have always been part of Canada's international behaviour. However, until the past few years, multilateral diplomacy and the appropriate associative and world order behaviour have dominated Canada's foreign policy doctrine and decision making, except with regard to the U.S. and the U.K. The recent years belie this middle-power tradition. The evidence, in both statement of intent and application of policy, shows shifts in the government's priorities and criteria for the commitment of its institutional resources from combination, consensus, and constraint to unilateralism, divergence, and diversification; from selective active participation to global involvement; from multilateralism to bilateralism; and from mediatory diplomacy to interest-based involvement. Although residues of both liberal internationalism (for example, continued commitment to the UN) and peripheral dependence (for example, military security) remain, the evidence shows dramatically that Canada is emerging as a principal power and, hence, that the complex neo-realist perspective is most applicable.

DOCTRINES AND DECISIONS: CONCLUSIONS

The first few years of the 1980s have shown the declared intent and clear ability of the Trudeau government to extend Canadian foreign policy beyond nominal bilateralism and modified multilateralism. With the government's reaffirmation of the integral tie between perceptions and definitions of national interest and supportive external behaviour, and with the recognition of the increasingly diffuse character of the international system, Canadian foreign policy has emerged into a distinctively complex neo-realist pattern of behaviour.

Moving beyond the important precedents of the 1970s, Canada's external activity has concentrated on selective interest-based bilateralism worldwide and, either by initiative or invitation, participation in a supportive and equally diversified set of relatively fluid nonuniversal associations. This has pushed Canada beyond the initial narrow objective of domestic economic development into direct involvement with a distinct group of OECD states and newly industrialized countries; the pursuit of a revised world order reflecting long-term mutual political and economic interests among this group has taken place at the annual Western economic summits and in the North–South debate. This pursuit of a modified world order, in which the parameters are defined no longer by East–West tensions but by the concert process, has provided Canada with an increasingly influential role within a select group of states and the ability to represent and protect Canadian interests, internationally or by domestic actions, with relative autonomy.

The capacity to behave in this manner has been predicated upon domestic capabilities and an understanding of the relationship between Canada's national interests and foreign policy. The preferred balance between economic development and political cohesion has provided an environment conducive to increasingly active participation by a broad range of domestic interests and has necessitated the development of overarching governmental structures to co-ordinate the new demands posed by the developing domestic constituencies, the widening set of political, economic, and bureaucratic concerns, and the expanding number and type of bilateral relationships. The revised Department of External Affairs, by reorganizing and co-opting areas of responsibility, has regained its pre-eminence in the foreign policy arena, but it must contend with direct, independent, and increasingly competitive external interests of other governmental departments, their ministers, and the domestic interests they represent.

If the doctrines of Canadian foreign policy as envisioned in the opening declarations of the 1980 Trudeau government remain the guidelines for Canada's external behaviour in the coming years, then autonomous interest-based bilateralism in an increasingly diffuse international system will heighten the vital importance of the concert process in efforts to mediate competition, negotiate co-operation, and constrain the more pernicious effects of unilateral behaviour undertaken in the cause of Canada's national interest. The main foreign policy concerns since the return of the Trudeau government—FIRA, NEP, GATT, Western economic summitry, North–South dialogue, disarmament, Canadian–American relations, and the development of a distinct Canadian periphery in the Caribbean Basin, the Pacific Rim, and in Latin America—indicate the need, as yet unfulfilled, for the foreign policy decision makers and political élite in Ottawa to comprehend more fully the implications of co-ordinating a multifaceted program of globally diffuse bilateral relations, especially with regard to linkages between actors and across issues, and within the context of contending interests of the segmented, sectorally divergent domestic environment.

CHAPTER 3
ACTIVITY, ASSOCIATION, AND APPROACHES TO WORLD ORDER

The study of international politics and foreign policy requires one to distinguish among declaratory policy, seminal decisions, and the implementation of objectives and decisions in routine diplomatic and bureaucratic life. Just as broad declarations may not be faithfully reflected in major decisions, so too the dramatic, seminal shifts of course at the top of the government hierarchy may not penetrate the ingrained habits and procedures of the large bureaucratic institutions below. Yet as the government moves from professed goals to the commitment of its scarce resources—money, personnel, functional expertise, international presence and prestige, and political capital—it provides a more precise, stable, and durable record of its international behaviour, which we can use to test the perspectives of liberal internationalism, peripheral dependence, and complex neo-realism.[1]

Activity: Degree, Variety, and Diffusion

The first test of the three perspectives lies in their ability to account for Canada's basic involvement in world affairs since the end of World War II. The issue here is not simply how the agenda of Canadian activity expands in response to the changing global environment, but whether the Canadian government commits more or less of its scarce resources to the pursuit of its foreign policy interests. The most fundamental aspect of Canadian activity, the degree of involvement that Canada has maintained, can be assessed by examining Canada's network of posts and personnel abroad, the organization of the Department of External Affairs at home, and the involvement of the prime minister in summit diplomacy against the theoretical predictions of liberal internationalism's active participation, peripheral dependence's low interaction, and complex neo-realism's global involvement.

Since 1945 the number of Canada's operational posts overseas has grown steadily. Table 3.1 charts this growth; it also shows brief reductions in 1959, 1969, 1978, and 1979. To be sure, with decolonization the world has provided ever more countries to which Canadian diplomats can be sent. But Canada still has the choice of whether to pursue these opportunities and, in choosing, has done more than simply keep up. Apart from sustained reversals during the late 1950s, Canada's diplomatic network has embraced a growing percentage of states in the international system. Moreover, Canada has had substantial representa-

TABLE 3.1 Canadian Posts Abroad, by Area, 1945–1979

Year	*United States*	*Europe*	*Latin America*	*Africa & Middle East*	*Asia & Pacific*	*International Organizations*	*Total*	*UN Members*	*Ratio of Coverage*
1945	2	12	6	1	3	—	24	51	47%
1946	2	14	6	1	3	—	26		
1947	4	18	7	1	4	—	34		
1948	7	18	7	1	4	2	39		
1949	7	20	7	1	5	2	42		
1950	7	21	7	1	6	3	45	60	75%
1951							N/A		
1952	8	23	9	1	6	4	51		
1953	10	24	10	1	8	4	57		
1954	10	24	12	4	8	4	62	76	83%
1955							N/A		
1956	10	25	12	4	8	4	63		
1957	10	25	12	5	8	4	64		
1958	10	25	13	6	10	4	68		
1959	10	23	12	6	9	4	64		
1960	10	23	14	7	8	5	67	101	66%
1961	11	24	15	8	8	8	74		
1962	11	24	17	10	8	8	78		
1963	10	25	17	10	9	8	79		
1964	11	26	17	10	9	8	81		
1965	11	27	17	11	9	10	85	115	74%
1966	11	28	18	14	9	10	90		
1967	12	29	18	16	10	7	92		
1968	13	30	18	16	11	7	95		
1969	13	30	15	15	11	9	93		

1970	15	30	15	16	12	8	96	124	78%
1971	15	31	14	18	12	8	98		
1972	15	31	15	17	12	8	98		
1973	16	32	16	17	17	8	106		
1974	16	36	17	20	17	10	116	135	85%
1975							N/A		
1976							N/A		
1977	18	38	17	25	17	9	124		
1978	15	35	17	25	17	9	118		
1979	15	35	17	25	17	8	117		

SOURCE: Statistics Canada, *Representation of Government of Canada Abroad, 1867–1960*, Series W214-217. For period from 1959, Department of External Affairs, *Annual Report*, *Annual Review*.

TABLE 3.2 Department of External Affairs Foreign Service Officer Staff at Home and Abroad, 1948–1976

Year	*Home*	*Abroad*	*Portion Abroad* %	*Total*
1948	100	116	53.7	216
1949	116	123	51.5	239
1950	131	128	49.4	259
1951	120	134	52.8	254
1952	124	134	51.9	258
1953	120	147	55.1	267
1954	112	165	59.6	277
1955	136	162	54.4	298
1956	150	214	58.8	364
1957	174	209	54.9	381
1958	176	219	55.4	395
1959	177	225	60.0	402
1960	192	222	53.6	414
1961	187	246	56.8	433
1962	199	245	55.2	444
1963	196	269	57.8	465
1964	224	273	54.9	497
1965	249	306	55.1	555
1966	289	327	53.1	616
1967	350	355	50.4	705
1968	427	388	47.6	815
1969	448	369	45.2	817
1970	397	328	45.2	725
1971	456	358	44.0	814
1972				N/A
1973				N/A
1974	350	440	55.7	790
1975	327	450	57.9	777
1976	333	453	57.6	786

SOURCE: Based on Department of External Affairs, *Annual Report*, 1948–1971; *Annual Review*, 1972–1976. All figures are of December 31.

tion since 1954 and a major presence since 1966 in all regions of the globe.

This relatively consistent expansion towards complex neo-realism's global involvement has been reflected in the willingness of the Department of External Affairs to deploy its scarce professionals for overseas operations and to undertake the institutional rearrangements necessary to ensure that the concerns of all global regions are reflected in a permanent, focused fashion within the internal structure. As Table 3.2 demonstrates, the number of Canadian diplomats stationed abroad has grown steadily since 1945, despite temporary declines in 1955, 1957,

TABLE 3.3 Summit Visits, 1947–1979

Year	*Heads of Govern-ment Received in Canada*	*Canadian PM Visits Other Heads of Government*	*Balance for Canada*
1947	1	2	−1
1948	3	2	+1
1949	2	0	+2
1950	4	0	+4
1951	4	2	+2
1952	3	2	+1
1953	1	2	−1
1954	8	9	−1
1955	6	0	+6
1956	9	4	+5
1957	2	3	−1
1958	5	13	−8
1959	6	0	+6
1960	0	1	−1
1961	1	1	—
1962	1	1	—
1963	3	0	+3
1964	11	2	+9
1965	7	6	+1
1966	10	2	+8
1967	66	1	+65
1968	11	0	+11
1969	10	3	+7
1970	7	6	+1
1971	11	10	+1
1972	2	1	+1
1973	13	1	+12
1974	7	8	−1
1975	6	13	−7
1976	8	9	−1
1977	15	6	+9
1978	10	10	—
1979	16	8	+8

Note: From 1960 through 1963, the *Annual Report* gave much less detail about Canadian activity with the United States, Western Europe, and Asia.

SOURCE: Based on Department of External Affairs, *Annual Report, Annual Review*.

1960, and 1962 and, more seriously, in 1969 and 1970. And internally, within its headquarters in Ottawa, the department supplemented its initial concern with American, Commonwealth, European, and United Nations affairs by adding divisions for Far Eastern, Middle Eastern, and Latin American affairs during the 1952–1960 period and by achieving essentially global coverage in 1967 with the formation of a unit to co-ordinate relations with francophone states.

This expansionary process has been evident in the increasing readiness of the Canadian government to devote its scarcest resource, prime ministerial time, to a high involvement in international affairs. As Table 3.3 shows, the number of head-of-government visits received by Canada grew rapidly from 1947 to 1956, dropped from 1957 to 1963, and reached a sustained normal level of about ten visits a year from 1964 to the present. Moreover, participation in external summits during the 1970s increased to a new level. Furthermore, after 1968, Prime Minister Trudeau displayed a consistent willingness to conduct numerous visits abroad rather than undertake a single world tour. This interest took the prime minister to all major regions of the globe, as summarized in Table 3.4.

The final indicator of degree of international involvement is the extent of Canadian bilateral activity, as measured by the number of discrete events Canada has initiated with other countries each year. Although the data in Table 3.5 are not representative of all bilateral behaviour, only of that recorded on select non-Canadian media sources (thus tending to underrepresent the frequency of Canadian events), they do present a reasonable picture of Canadian participation. The most obvious trend is the gradual but consistent expansion of worldwide bilateral activity for Canada. The dominance of OECD members as targets over the entire thirty years, especially after 1965 (not counting the United Kingdom and the United States), is a striking confirmation of the stated government policy of increasing Canada's international presence. This is enhanced by a similar expansion of activity outside industrialized areas. Moreover, Canada, especially since the mid-1960s, has at least kept pace with the general increase in state-to-state activity.

When taken together, these measures suggest that the peripheral-dependence perspective provides a far less accurate account than either liberal internationalism or complex neo-realism of the degree of Canada's international activity since 1945. Support for peripheral dependence comes only from the low involvement of the prime minister in foreign summit travel before 1969. In contrast, with the partial exception of the Diefenbaker years, the active participation predicted by liberal internationalism predominates from 1945 to 1968 on virtually all indicators. Most importantly, the global involvement of complex neo-realism emerges as the central feature of Canadian activity abroad from the 1964–1968 period onward. Beginning in 1964 with a substantial increase in the number of visits received from foreign heads of government, and reinforced in 1966 by the expansion of Canada's diplomatic network and headquarters apparatus into areas of francophone Africa, the trend towards global involvement became paramount with the large increase in foreign service officers serving

TABLE 3.4 Prime Ministerial Visits Abroad, by Region, 1968–1980

Region	*1968*	*1969*	*1970*	*1971*	*1972*	*1973*	*1974*	*1975*	*1976*	*1977*	*1978*	*1979*	*1980**
United States	—	3	—	1	—	—	2	1	1	1	—	—	—
Western Europe	—	2	1	1	1	—	5	8	—	2	4	—	6
Asia & Pacific	—	—	5	5	—	1	—	—	1	—	—	—	—
Middle East	—	—	—	—	—	—	—	—	—	—	—	—	3
Africa	—	—	—	—	—	—	—	—	—	—	—	3	—
Latin America	—	—	—	—	—	—	—	—	2	—	—	—	—
Multilateral	—	1	—	1	—	1	2	3	1	3	2	2	1
TOTAL	—	6	6	8	1	2	9	12	5	6	6	5	10

* Through November, 1980.

Note: Visits include both meetings with foreign officials and speeches in foreign countries. Each country or organization visited counted as a separate entry.

SOURCE: Based on Canadian Institute of International Affairs, *Monthly Report on Canada's External Relations*, until 1970 when replaced by Canadian Institute of International Affairs and Parliamentary Centre for Foreign Affairs and Foreign Trade, *International Canada*, monthly.

TABLE 3.5 Canadian-Initiated Activity with Select States and Regions, 1948–1978

In each pair, the first number represents co-operative activities and the second represents activities of conflict.

Year	*United States*	*United Kingdom*	*OECD*	*Socialist Bloc*[1]	*OPEC*	*Middle East*[2]	*Newly Industrializing Countries*[3]	*Less Developed Countries*[4]	*World Total*[5]
1948	7/1	5/0	17/1	1/2	—	4/1	5/1	—	27/4
1949	4/0	6/0	23/0	0/0	—	—	—	—	23/0
1950	3/0	2/0	5/0	1/1	1/0	1/0	1/0	—	8/1
1951	7/0	5/1	16/1	0/2	1/0	2/0	—	2/0	19/3
1952	5/1	8/0	31/1	0/1	—	1/0	1/0	1/0	33/2
1953	12/7	3/0	22/7	1/1	—	—	—	4/1	27/9
1954	2/0	—	8/0	2/2	—	2/0	—	1/1	12/3
1955	7/1	7/0	28/1	7/3	—	1/1	5/1	9/0	50/10
1956	4/1	5/0	17/1	8/3	—	6/3	2/1	8/0	43/8
1957	8/3	7/0	26/3	2/3	1/0	5/5	—	5/0	38/11
1958	10/4	5/0	23/6	15/7	1/0	4/0	0/1	4/0	45/14
1959	11/4	4/0	32/5	8/4	—	1/0	1/0	3/0	45/9
1960	3/2	3/0	24/2	4/1	—	1/0	2/0	9/0	39/3
1961	13/3	3/1	39/4	7/6	1/1	2/1	2/0	11/2	61/13
1962	5/6	2/0	18/6	6/2	—	3/1	0/1	6/1	32/11
1963	8/3	2/0	19/4	11/0	—	2/0	—	7/0	39/4
1964	4/1	1/0	11/2	3/2	1/0	2/0	2/0	14/1	33/5
1965	1/0	—	2/0	4/3	—	3/0	3/0	10/1	22/4
1966	11/4	2/0	26/5	20/3	3/0	5/0	2/0	10/4	64/13
1967	11/5	5/0	24/8	4/3	—	10/2	1/0	8/1	46/14
1968	5/0	1/0	18/2	6/3	3/0	8/0	6/0	10/1	48/6
1969	8/3	4/1	41/8	8/3	4/0	4/0	8/2	37/2	103/16

1970	2/1	4/2	28/3	14/3	1/0	5/0	4/2	21/1	72/9
1971	6/7	3/0	24/7	12/4	2/0	7/0	2/1	11/1	57/12
1972	3/0	1/0	4/1	5/3	2/0	4/1	2/1	14/1	29/7
1973	5/8	2/0	17/12	9/2	2/0	2/0	2/0	18/0	48/14
1974	5/3	3/0	25/4	4/1	2/0	8/1	7/0	15/6	59/12
1975	7/2	7/0	60/2	16/3	2/0	3/0	6/0	31/1	117/6
1976	5/2	3/1	35/3	8/2	—	13/1	7/1	21/3	88/10
1977	14/2	4/0	35/9	6/6	—	8/0	6/0	25/2	83/20
1978	11/2	8/0	91/2	2/4	—	7/0	1/0	5/1	105/8
TOTAL	207/73	119/6	789/110	194/86	38/2	124/17	78/11	320/31	1 515/261

[1] Socialist Bloc includes East Germany, Poland, Hungary, Czechoslovakia, Albania, Yugoslavia, Bulgaria, Rumania, U.S.S.R., People's Republic of China, Mongolia, North Korea, Vietnam.

[2] Middle East includes Maghreb, Mashrek, Afghanistan, Gulf States, Israel, Iran, Turkey, and P.L.O.

[3] Newly Industrializing Countries include Mexico, Brazil, Argentina, Kenya, Israel, Taiwan, South Korea, Malaysia, Singapore, Philippines, Indonesia, Venezuela.

[4] Less Developed Countries are those *not* included in previous categories.

[5] Not the total of columns shown because categories overlap.

SOURCE: Based on Edward E. Azar, Conflict and Peace Data Bank, University of North Carolina, Chapel Hill, North Carolina, 1 January 1980.

overseas in 1968, the sustained increase in prime ministerial visits abroad commencing in 1969, the spread of these visits to all major global regions, and the significant increase in bilateral activity.

This broad shift to complex neo-realist predominance further suggests the existence of five distinct policy eras whose boundaries conform largely to the dates in which individual governments have served in office and whose patterns conform to the major declarations and decisions those governments have made. The first period, from 1947 to 1957, was characterized by a consistent move to develop posts and personnel abroad, departmental structure at home, and contact with visiting leaders. From 1957 to 1963, this process was halted, and in some cases reversed, by a prolonged but somewhat erratic effort to curtail the number of professional foreign service officers serving abroad, the comprehensiveness of the mission network, and the number of resident posts. The return of the Liberals in 1963 brought a sharp, decisive reversion to the internationalist thrust of the St. Laurent era, supplemented by attempts, particularly in francophonie, to add an entirely new dimension. The Trudeau government's 1968 pledge to implement new foreign policy priorities, supplemented by its suspension of other changes pending completion of the foreign policy review and by the 1969 austerity program, was initially registered in a brief but significant reduction in the number of posts and personnel. By 1974, however, there was a general and sustained shift back to previous patterns of conducting summit diplomacy abroad, increasing DEA strength, and encouraging a growth of activity throughout the globe.

The boundaries of these five periods and the shift towards complex neo-realist patterns are evident also in the indicators of the second component dimension of Canadian foreign policy activity, the variety of Canada's actions over time and across issues and targets abroad. Ranging from peripheral dependence's undifferentiated interaction through liberal internationalism's responsible participation to complex neo-realism's interest-based involvement, this variety can be assessed by focusing on the internal consistency or complexity of patterns of diplomatic representation, summit diplomacy, and foreign service officer concentration. Complexity itself can be measured with reasonable confidence by the magnitude, duration, and direction of changes over time and by the simultaneous existence of policy processes proceeding at different rates and in different directions. Such variety might well reflect the attempt to respond to the special character of each bilateral relationship and the effort to establish meaningful priorities as a guide to overall behaviour.

The growth in Canada's diplomatic representation, seen in Table 3.1, was relatively undifferentiated from 1947 to 1959, as all regions received a greater number of posts, albeit at varying rates. In 1959 and again in 1963, an effort was made to establish priorities by reducing representation in some regions while holding or increasing the level in others. However, from 1967 through 1973, major internal modifications of this sort appeared as a matter of course, and from 1973 onward significant changes in the magnitude and the direction of change took place. Similarly, as Tables 3.3 and 3.4 indicate, the number of prime ministerial visits annually and the regions in which they have been concentrated varied considerably from year to year in the post-1969 period, as the prime minister's priorities and the domestic process dictated. As Table 3.2 indicates, the steady concentration of foreign service officers at home rather than abroad between 1966 and 1971, as a means of serving the domestic needs of financial austerity and functional units rather than foreign constituencies, further underscores the trend towards interest-based involvement. Finally, the increase in bilateral activity over the last decade, as shown in Tables 3.4 and 3.5, especially with the newly industrialized countries and specific less developed countries, is an example of Canadian government policy in pursuit of new external relations perceived to be both extending Canada's domestic interests and supporting the evolving Third World–dominant international structure.

The third component dimension of Canadian foreign policy activity, the degree of diffusion among targeted actors, supports even more strongly the trend towards complex neo-realist dominance over these five eras. As Table 3.1 shows, the period from 1945 to 1956 indicates a pattern of imperial-focused interaction in accordance with the peripheral-dependence perspective. The number of Canadian posts in the U.S. grew fivefold; together with those in Europe, they accounted for more than half of all Canadian posts abroad. From 1957 to 1963, the trend turned sharply towards multiple participation and autonomous bilateral involvement, as missions to international organizations, Africa and the Middle East doubled, smaller increases took place in Latin America and Asia and the Pacific, and no net change occurred in Europe or the United States. The period from 1963 to 1968 saw a minor repudiation of the liberal-internationalist commitment to multilateralism, as missions to international organizations declined after reaching an all-time high in 1965 and 1966, while missions in the United States increased by 30 per cent. At the same time a solid shift towards the complex neo-realist pattern of autonomous bilateral involvement occurred as missions to Africa and the Middle East increased substantially and those to Asia and the Pacific, Europe, and Latin America grew at a lower rate. The period from 1969 to 1979 saw the rise of autonomous bilateral involvement as the greatest increases were registered in Africa and the Middle East, Asia and the Pacific, and to a decreasing extent in Europe, the U.S., Latin America, and international organizations. Similarly, as Table 3.4 indicates, from 1969 to November 1980 the United States was replaced by Asia and the Pacific, then Europe, and most recently the LDCs as the dominant targets of prime

TABLE 3.6 Canada's Bilateral Organizations with States other than the United States, 1948–1978

1948	• Canada–United Kingdom Continuing Committee on Trade and Economic Affairs
1950	• Canada–France Economic Committee
1961	• Canada–Japan Ministerial Committee
1965	• France–Canada Joint Commission on Cultural and Scientific Relations
	• France–Canada Interparliamentary Association
1966	• Canada–United Kingdom Ministerial Committee on Trade and Economic Affairs
1967	• Belgium–Canada Joint Cultural Commission
1968	• Canada–Mexico Joint Ministerial Committee
	• Canada–Tunisia Joint Commission
1970	• Canada–New Zealand Consultative Committee
1971	• Canadian–German Scientific and Technological Co-operation Committee
	• Joint Canada–U.S.S.R. Committee (for Arctic scientific co-operation)
	• Canada–U.S.S.R. Mixed Commission for Co-operation in the Industrial Applications of Science and Technology
	• Canada–Belgium Mixed Commission for Scientific, Industrial, and Technological Co-operation
	• Canada–U.S.S.R. Annual Foreign Minister Consultations
1972	• Canada–U.S.S.R. Joint Consultative Committee on Trade
1973	• Canada–China Joint Trade Committee
	• Canada–France Joint Commission on Scientific Co-operation
1974	• Canada–Iran Joint Economic Commission
	• Annual Japan–Canada Consultations on United Nations Questions
	• Canada–Australia annual senior official consultations on foreign policy
1975	• Cuba–Canada Joint Committee on Economic and Trade Relations
	• Canada–Federal Republic of Germany Committee on Cultural Relations
	• Canada–U.S.S.R. Fisheries Commission
1976	• Canada–Japan Joint Economic Committee
	• Canada–Mexico Joint Commission
	• Canada–Brazil Joint Committee on Trade and Economic Matters
	• Canada–Venezuela Economic Commission
	• Joint Canada–Saudi Arabia Economic Committee
	• Canada–Israel Joint Economic Committee
	• Canada–EEC Joint Co-operation Committee
	• Canada–U.S.S.R. Mixed Economic Commission
1978	• Canada–West Germany annual high-level consultations on political, economic, and financial issues

SOURCE: Based on Department of External Affairs, *Annual Report* or *Annual Review*, and Canadian Institute of International Affairs and Parliamentary Centre for Foreign Affairs and Foreign Trade, *International Canada*, monthly.

ministerial visits. Furthermore, as seen in Table 3.5, until the late 1950s Canadian bilateral activity was primarily focused on the U.S. and Britain, shifting to a more diffuse set of relationships in the 1960s although still OECD-dominant, and in the following decade exhibiting a more broadly based pattern, with non-OECD states accounting for more than half of all such activity. Table 3.6 reinforces the emergence of complex neo-realism in the 1970s with the rapid expansion of autonomous bilateral involvement outside the special Canada–U.S. relationship.

Association: Initiative, Commitment, and Focus

As useful as these measures of overall activity are in assessing the validity of the three perspectives, Canada's process of association with other actors provides a more difficult and discriminating test. The initial subdimension of association, Canada's initiative in joining existing or new groups or acting on the basis of membership in them, includes Canada's basic tendency to structure its ongoing exchanges with the outside world by becoming a part of international organizations and coalitions, to achieve a balance between action and reaction in these and other exchanges, and to reduce or expand its association with its major partner, the United States.

The first component can be measured by Canada's relative eagerness to accept membership in international organizations, to increase the number and range of bodies to which it belongs, and to maintain particularly intense ties with a selected group of closely associated states.[2] As predicted by the liberal-internationalist perspective, Canada was eager to combine with others in international organizations during the 1960–1977 period. By doubling its memberships during this time, Canada joined new bodies at a relatively higher rate than West Germany, France, the United Kingdom, the United States, and Norway and only slightly less assiduously than Australia and Japan. However, since 1966 the rate at which it joined these organizations slackened considerably, from a 41 per cent increase over the six years ending in 1966 to only a 36 per cent increase over the longer, eleven-year period ending in 1977. Diminished enthusiasm for multilateralism and a saturation in the number of useful organizations available probably account for this trend.

The growth in memberships in international organizations is reflected further in a general increase in the number and range of intergovernmental organizations to which Canada belonged in the 1950s and 1960s. As Table 3.7 indicates, Canada's overall membership experienced a steady and often rapid growth, with the exception of a prolonged pause from 1957 to 1964, and a brief reduction in 1969. During this time, francophone nations emerged as a fifth major grouping in

TABLE 3.7 Canadian Membership in Intergovernmental Organizations, 1951–1971

	1951	1952–1955	1956	1957	1958	1959	1960	1961	1962	1963	1964	1965	1966	1967	1968	1969	1970	1971
Multilateral Organizations																		
United Nations	11		26	33	32	32	32	31	34	34	34	30	30	34	32	34	34	51
Commonwealth	8		12	12	12	12	13	16	14	15	15	13	15	14	14	14	12	14
Pan-American Group	4		4	4	4	4	4	4	4	4	4	4	4	4	4			
NATO & OECD	2		2	2	2	2	2	2	2	2	3	4	2	2	2	2	2	2
Francophonie															1	2	4	4
Bilateral Organizations																		
United States	7		8	4	5	5	5	8	8	8	9	10	12	13	13	17	16	16
United Kingdom	1		1	1	1	1	1	1	1	1	1	1	2	2	2	2	2	2
Japan								1	1	1	1	1	1	1	1	1	1	1
Other Organizations	23		21	26	25	26	26	14	18	18	16	24	15	29	35	23	43	58
TOTAL	56	N/A	74	82	82	82	83	77	82	83	83	87	81	99	104	95	114	148

SOURCE: Based on Department of External Affairs, *Annual Report*, 1951–1971, *Annual Review*, 1972. After 1971, the *Annual Review* ceased providing the data upon which this table is based.

Canada's multilateral diplomacy. Table 3.8 shows that Canada's bilateral dispersion became more pronounced during the 1970s, as the number of diplomatic missions Canada had exchanged with its most closely associated partners experienced an absolute reduction. During this same period, bilateral activity with non-OECD countries recorded a substantial increase (Table 3.6).

Accompanying this trend towards broader affiliations was the growth of a more balanced exchange of behaviour between Canada and the outside world. As Table 3.3 indicates, in visits between heads of government, Canada recorded a significant negative balance—that is, more visits were given than were received—only twice, in 1958 and 1975.[3] Discounting 1967, the year of Canada's centennial celebrations, two patterns emerge. First, summitry seems to have been, on the average, a balanced phenomenon; when aberrations did occur, they were generally in Canada's favour, a minor though not trivial indication of Canada's international importance. Second, there was a consistent increase in the number of summit visits by foreign heads of government, beginning with Pearson's tenure as prime minister and continuing through the Trudeau years. This period was balanced by an equally active record of Canadian participation in foreign summits. The source of this increasing Canadian presence can be traced to the St. Laurent period, when Pearson was secretary of state for external affairs and

TABLE 3.8 Canadian Diplomatic Missions and Personnel Exchanged with Seven Major Actors, 1969–1980

Year	*Missions Given*	*Personnel Given*	*Personnel Received*	*Balance*
1969	42	288	295	+7
1970	40	279	305	+26
1971	52	271	297	+26
1972	46	268	312	+44
1973	46	287	312	+25
1974	45	327	334	+7
1975	47	341	343	+2
1976	43	341	344	+3
1977	44	348	339	−9
1978	49	357	323	−34
1979	39	331	342	+11
1980	39	347	348	+1

Note: The seven states are the United States, the United Kingdom, France, Germany, Norway, Australia, and Japan.

SOURCE: Based on Department of External Affairs, *Canadian Representatives Abroad* and *Diplomatic Corps and Consular and Other Representatives in Canada*, 1969-1980.

there was a clear move by Canada to initiate and participate in international summitry.[4] This trend towards Canadian initiative and reciprocity was complemented, after 1974, by an attempt to redress the previous imbalance of the exchange of diplomatic personnel between Canada and major associated states (Table 3.8).

A further focus on Canada's behaviour from 1957 to 1970 with two major actors, the United States and the Soviet Union, also shows Canada's capacity for initiative—in this case, the initiation of conflict. As Figures 3.1 and 3.2 indicate, only for a very brief time in 1961 and for a sustained period from 1967 to 1970 did Canada adopt a more conflictual approach to the United States than Canada was receiving in return. And only in the periods 1958–1961, 1965–1966, and 1968–1970 did it undertake a similar shift *vis-à-vis* the Soviet Union.[5]

Canada's increasing willingness to pursue unilaterally its distinctive interests in relations with the United States is evident in Joseph Nye's study of Canadian–American bargaining from 1950 to 1969 over issues

FIGURE 3.1 Mean Conflict Levels of U.S. Stimuli and Canadian Responses, by Six-month Periods, 1957–1970

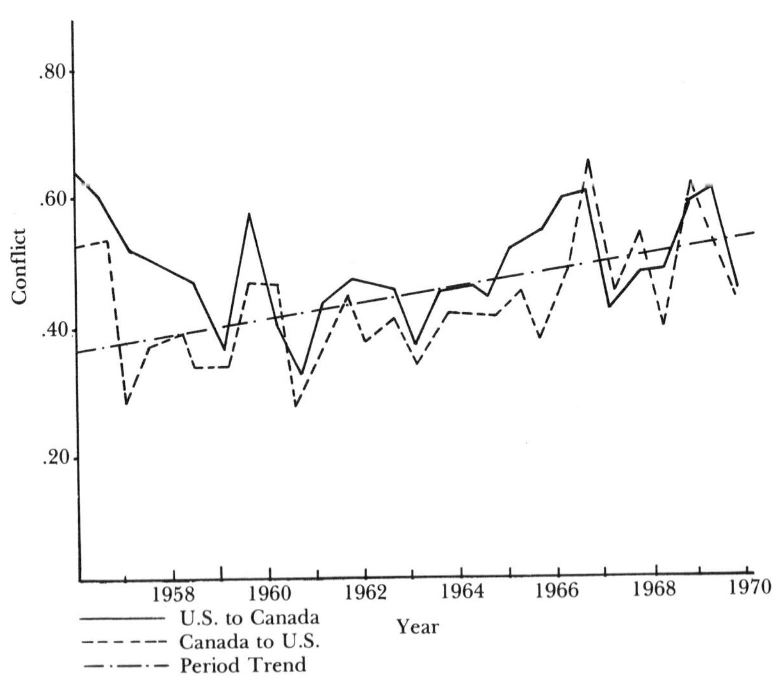

SOURCE: Don Munton, "Stimulus-Response and Continuity in Canadian Foreign Policy Behaviour During Cold War and Détente," in Brian Tomlin, ed., *Canada's Foreign Policy: Analysis and Trends* (Toronto: Methuen, 1978), pp. 16–17. Copyright © 1978. Reprinted by permission of Methuen Publications.

FIGURE 3.2 Mean Conflict Levels of U.S.S.R. Stimuli and Canadian Responses, by Six-month Periods, 1957–1970

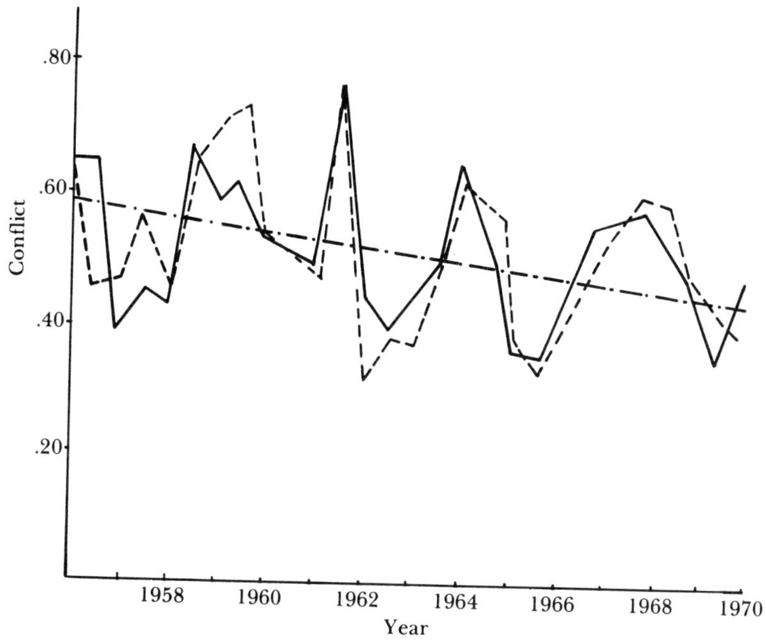

SOURCE: Don Munton, "Stimulus-Response and Continuity in Canadian Foreign Policy Behaviour During Cold War and Détente," in Brian Tomlin, ed., *Canada's Foreign Policy: Analysis and Trends*, (Toronto: Methuen, 1978), pp. 16–17. Copyright © 1978. Reprinted by permission of Methuen Publications.

that involved a basic incompatibility of objectives between the two governments and that were of sufficient importance to attract the attention of the United States president.[6] Nye's results, displayed in Table 3.9, indicate that from 1950 through 1969, the bilateral relationship usually followed the peripheral-dependence pattern of Canada issuing the first interstate request, often in the form of requests for exemptions or special consideration, in response to actions initiated by the United States government alone. In contrast, the data from 1964 to 1969 indicate an increased tendency towards Canadian unilateral action impinging on U.S. interests, and a slightly reduced concern with responding as a government to U.S. moves. Moreover, in the separate category of conflicts involving relations with third countries, the shift towards the United States as the initiator of the first interstate request took place as early as 1961 and was sustained, with one exception, through the decade.[7]

The second subdimension of association, commitment, also reveals a

TABLE 3.9 Conflicts in Canada–U.S. Relations, 1950–1969

Conflict	*First Govern-ment Action*	*First Interstate Request*	*Outcome Closer to Objectives of*
St. Lawrence Seaway, 1945–58	Canada	Canada	Equal
U.S. agricultural import quotas, 1953–	U.S.	Canada	U.S.
Gouzenko interview, 1953	U.S.	U.S.	U.S.
Chicago water diversion, 1954–59	U.S.	Canada	U.S.
U.S. lead and zinc quotas, 1954–	U.S.	Canada	U.S.
Columbia River development, 1944–64	U.S.	U.S.	Equal
Carling Brewery, 1956	U.S.	Canada	Canada
Magazine tax, 1956–65	Canada	U.S.	U.S.
Security information, 1957	U.S.	Canada	Canada
Oil import quota exemption, 1955–70	U.S.	Canada	Canada
Extraterritorial control of corporations, 1956–	U.S.	Canada	U.S.
BOMARC procurement, 1959–60	U.S.	Canada	Canada
Nuclear arming of Canadian weapons, 1961–63	Canada	U.S.	U.S.
U.S. restriction of lumber imports, 1961–64	U.S.	Canada	Canada
Seafarers' International Union, 1962–64	Canada	Canada	U.S.
Renegotiation of civil air routes, 1962–1965	Canada	Canada	Equal
Extended fishing zones, 1963–	Canada	U.S.	Canada
Interest equalization tax, 1963	U.S.	Canada	Equal
U.S. balance-of-payments guidelines, 1965–68	U.S.	Canada	Equal
Auto pact, 1962–73	Canada	U.S.	Canada
Arctic pollution zone, 1969	Canada	U.S.	Canada

SOURCE: Joseph S. Nye, Jr., "Transnational Relations and Interstate Conflicts: An Empirical Analysis," *International Organization* 28 (autumn 1974): 961-96, Tables 2 and 3.

general shift towards liberal-internationalist and, more recently, complex neo-realist patterns. Throughout the 1968–1978 Trudeau period, the number of international agreements to which Canada assented generally increased. In its voting and verbal behaviour, Canada departed increasingly from close concurrence with the positions of the United States and other traditional allies.[8] As Table 3.10 indicates, on the central, enduring North–South issue of colonial and racial questions at the United Nations, Canada has moved steadily since 1965 from a high degree of agreement with the United States to unprecedented levels of consensus with the Scandinavian states. This shift was preceded by Canada's increasing tendency from 1950 to 1965 to move from the hostile fringe of NATO towards its consensus on the central East–West issue of maintaining NATO solidarity towards the Soviet bloc.[9]

More recently, these liberal-internationalist trends have been supplemented by an increase in divergence between Canada and its allies, another indicator of a shift towards complex neo-realism. For example, as Figures 3.1 and 3.2 show, there was a tendency for the average level of conflict in Canadian–American relations to rise and that in Canadian–Soviet relations to fall during the 1957–1968 period. Moreover, as seen in Figure 3.3 and to a lesser extent in Figure 3.1, Canada's increasing friendliness towards the United States during the Diefenbaker–Eisenhower years was followed by a sharp turn towards a conflictual approach during the latter part of the Diefenbaker government, a return to a more co-operative approach until 1969, and a rapid and generally sustained increase in conflict from 1969 to 1973.

The final subdimension of association is the focus, including underlying purpose and impact, of Canada's behaviour within its coalition and bilateral diplomacy. In order to determine whether Canada has concentrated on providing unqualified support to the United States, as peripheral dependence predicts, building coalitions to constrain American behaviour, as liberal internationalism suggests, or diversifying Canada's relations from the U.S. to other countries, as complex neo-realism indicates, it is useful to examine shifts in the character of the organizations with whom Canada has chosen to associate.

Table 3.7 indicates that the ones in which Canada is likely to face the most severe pressure to support American perspectives and positions—the pan-American group, NATO, and OECD—have been a constant yet minor target of Canadian commitment, with the exception of a brief turn towards NATO in 1964–1965, and towards the pan-American group from 1968 to 1971.[10] The various organizations and agencies under the United Nations umbrella most suitable for practising the diplomacy of constraint increasingly occupied Canadian attention from 1951 to 1957 and have generally remained constant since that time. Canada's ties with the Commonwealth and francophonie, where cultural, intellectual, and political diversification is most likely to occur, increased slowly from 1951 to 1956, substantially from 1959 to 1961, and even more from 1968 to 1971.

Within the bilateral sphere, where the most stringent tests of

TABLE 3.10 Indices for Agreement for Resolutions on Colonial and Racial Questions

Period	*N* (=*number of questions*)	*U.S.*	*U.K.*	*Australia*	*India*	*Scandinavia*	*Belgium*	*Netherlands*
1946–50	12	62.5	79.1	79.1	54.1	70.8	75.0	75.0
1951–55	13	80.7	80.7	84.6	50.0	80.7	84.6	92.3
1956–60	14	89.2	57.1	71.4	75.0	85.7	75.0	85.7
1961–65	32	89.0	75.9	89.0	67.1	85.9	85.9	96.8
1966–70	41	74.3	72.3	82.9	56.0	91.4	89.0	87.8
1971–75	73	67.3	78.0	78.0	69.1	90.4	87.6	89.0
MEAN AGREEMENT	185	77.2	72.2	80.8	61.9	84.1	82.8	87.8

SOURCE: Reproduced from Thomas F. Keating and T.A. Keenleyside, "Voting Patterns as a Measure of Foreign Policy Independence," *International Perspectives* (May/June 1980): 24.

FIGURE 3.3 Canadian Behaviour Towards the United States, 1960–1973 (Conflict-Behaviour Index*)

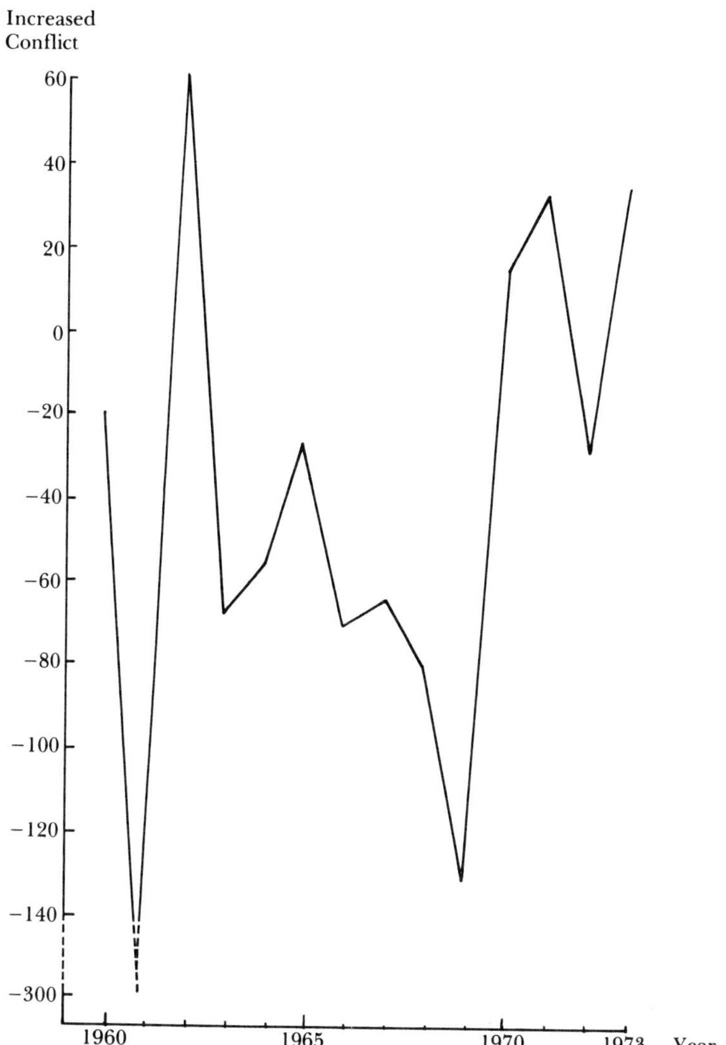

* The conflict-behaviour index, developed by E. Azar and T. Sloan, is defined in Lyon and Tomlin, *Canada as an International Actor*, as having been "calculated by subtracting the co-operative Canadian behaviour towards the United States from the conflictual for years 1960-1973."

SOURCE: Peyton V. Lyon and Brian W. Tomlin, *Canada as an International Actor* (Toronto: Macmillan, 1979), Figure 7.4. Calculated from E. Azar and T. Sloan, *Dimensions of Interaction*, Occasional Paper No. 8, International Studies Association, Pittsburgh, 1975. Reprinted by permission of Macmillan of Canada, a Division of Gage Publishing Limited.

diversification arise, the number of Canada's organizational affiliations with the initial imperial power, the United Kingdom, have remained virtually constant since 1951; those with the United States have risen slowly, despite a drop from 1957 to 1960 and a sharp jump in 1969; and those with associated states such as Australia have been virtually nonexistent. In contrast, ties with the great powers required for meaningful economic and politico-military diversification began in 1961 and increased significantly in 1965 and 1966. Table 3.7, while not conclusive, suggests a strong overall shift towards a multilateral focus from 1955 to 1957 and a slow shift to bilateralism from 1961 through 1970.[11]

A more detailed confirmation of this last trend is provided by Table 3.6, which lists, in order of their creation, Canada's thirty-three bilateral organizations with states other than the United States. Following early ventures with the United Kingdom, France, and Japan, Canada created bilateral bodies from 1965 onward in every year except 1969 and 1977; it was particularly active in 1971 and 1976. From 1967 to 1978, the number of countries with whom Canada had such formal arrangements rose from four to eighteen, and the range of regions represented expanded from Europe and Asia to embrace Latin America, Africa, and the Middle East. Although their importance is often merely symbolic and their procedures often sterile, the significance of these bodies as instruments of genuine diversification is indicated by Canada's concentration on the Soviet Union, France, West Germany, Japan, the United Kingdom, Belgium, and Mexico as its major partners. Also significant were the shifts in attention from francophone states (France, Belgium, and Tunisia) from 1965 to 1968, to global scientific, economic, and political powers (Soviet Union, China, West Germany, France, Japan) from 1969 to 1974, as well as to emerging regional industrial and energy powers (Iran, Mexico, Brazil, Venezuela, Saudi Arabia) from 1974 to the present. Finally, the impact of these new bilateral affiliations in fostering sustained co-operation is reflected, as Table 3.11 demonstrates, in the shift since 1968 from concluding agreements with the United States and multilateral organizations towards forming bilateral arrangements with other states as well.

The impact of these shifts on bargaining over major issues within the Canadian-American relationship is evident from a detailed look at the dynamics and outcomes of significant bilateral disputes from 1945 to 1969. To be sure, the numbers are small and the judgements difficult. But Table 3.9 indicates that from 1945 to 1956, the United States secured relatively favourable outcomes in three such disputes, Canada in two, with two equal outcomes. From 1956 to 1963, the United States was favoured in four and Canada in four, with one equal. And from 1963 to 1969, the United States obtained advantageous outcomes in none while Canada gained three, with two equal. A similar shift from the

TABLE 3.11 Canada's International Agreements with Various Actors, 1968–1978

Year	*With U.S.*	*With Other Bilateral Actors*	*Multilateral*
1968	3	10	12
1969	2	20	13
1970	6	14	17
1971	4	32	16
1973	2	27	18
1974	3	27	24
1975	7	37	24
1977	5	36	11
1978	4	22	14

Note: Numbers are totals of agreements signed, renewed, and amended, minus those terminated. Bilateral agreements signed under the rubric of a multilateral organization are categorized as multilateral.

SOURCE: Based on Department of External Affairs, *Annual Report; Annual Review*.

liberal-internationalist pattern of partnership to the complex neo-realist prediction of Canadian predominance in an era of U.S. decline is evident in Canadian disputes with third parties, where the pattern of two American and two Canadian victories prior to 1957 was replaced in the following years by two U.S. victories, three Canadian victories, and one equal. Moreover, this pattern recurs in the more limited but still salient issue area of bilateral disputes involving American-owned multinational enterprises operating in Canada; the Canadian government secured four favourable outcomes and five unfavourable ones from 1945 to 1959, compared with eight favourable, eight unfavourable, and two neutral outcomes in subsequent years, in disputes generally involving a significantly higher level of conflict.[12]

Approaches to World Order: Degree, Scope, and Transformation

The third major dimension of Canadian foreign policy behaviour is the country's activity in constructing, managing, and transforming the global order. The first subdimension, the degree to which this order is expressed in a well-developed, comprehensive, internally consistent, and autonomous set of international organizations and body of international law, can be considered by focusing on Canada's efforts to create and sustain the United Nations system as the central edifice of international politics. A 1973 study by Robert Angell, examining seven indicators of such support, suggests that Canada was in the global vanguard of such efforts from 1963 to 1967.[13] According to Angell's calculations, Canada ranked seventh during this period in its overall support for world order.

Moreover, Canada led the global community in the basic institutional indicator of the size of a state's UN mission in relation to other posts in its diplomatic network.

A further measure of Canada's approach to institutionalizing global order, the frequency of legislative initiatives in the General Assembly, suggests the pattern of Canadian support. As Figure 3.4 reveals, the number of such initiatives taken by Canada fell from 1952 to a low in 1963, rose sharply with the return of the Liberals until 1966, remained constant during the next four years of foreign policy debate, and climbed rapidly to unprecedentedly high levels well above the position

FIGURE 3.4 Frequency of Legislative Initiatives in the General Assembly

Sponsorship and Co-sponsorship of Draft Resolutions and Amendments

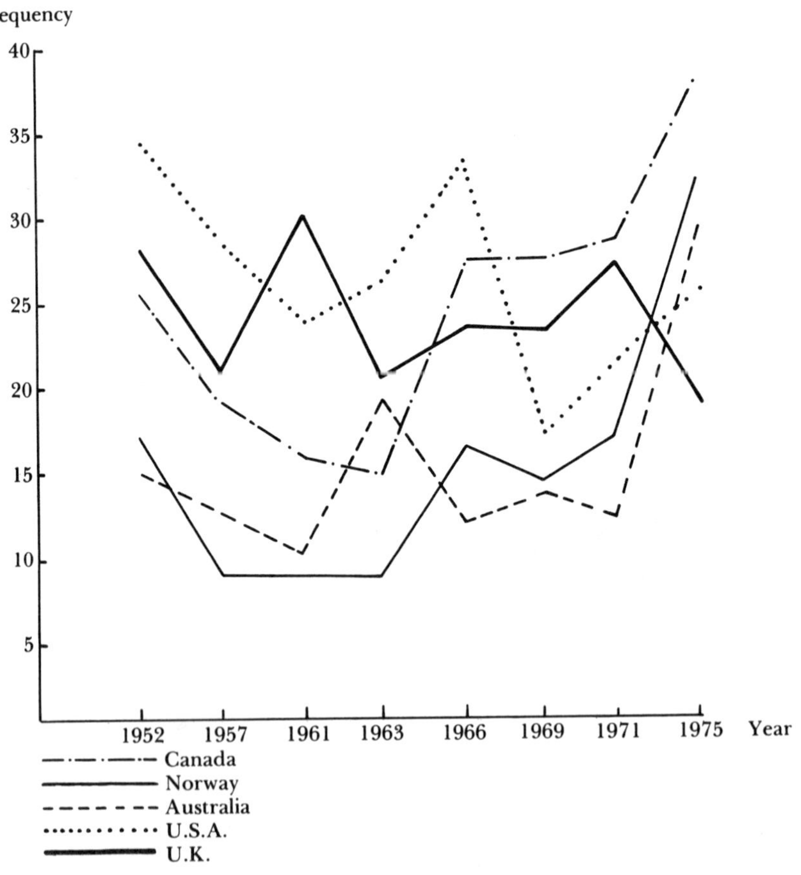

SOURCE: Peyton V. Lyon and Brian W. Tomlin, *Canada as an International Actor* (Toronto: Macmillan, 1979), Figure 9.2. Based on United Nations General Assembly, *Annexes*, various years.

of Norway, Australia, the United States, and the United Kingdom from 1971 to 1975.

A rather more sequential pattern emerges in the second component of Canada's approach to world order, the scope of its efforts to have such order embrace and attract the active involvement of all members of the interstate system. An initial indication of Canada's effort to extend the confines of the United Nations system comes from Brian Tomlin's study of Canada's tendency, in the face of strong divisions among opposing power blocs, to depart from the positions of its bloc leader in key issue areas in order to pursue a more moderate position.[14] In the period from 1946 to 1959, this study found a dichotomy in Canada's approach, as increases in polarization within the General Assembly tended to propel Canada into the peripheral-dependence role of a tightly aligned follower on issues dealing with supranationalism and the cold war, and the liberal-internationalist role of less aligned mediator on matters of self-determination and anti-intervention. After 1959, however, there was a general strengthening of the liberal-internationalist orientation, reflected in a tendency to respond to polarization with a major increase in nonalignment on supranationalism issues, a slight increase on self-determination and cold war questions, and a major reversal to tight alignment only on questions of anti-intervention.

This general post-1960 shift towards mediation and nonalignment, while not convincing in itself, receives considerable support from two further studies. Chadwick Alger's examination of interaction patterns in the General Assembly sessions in 1962 and 1963 indicates that Canada approached such tasks in a strongly liberal-internationalist fashion; its delegates had the highest or second-highest number of interactions during the proceedings and hence a wide relevance and great centrality in the consultative process.[15] In contrast, Thomas Volgy and Jon Quistgaard's examination of participation and voting behaviour at the United Nations from 1963 to 1969 identifies Canada, in accordance with the complex neo-realist expectation, as a dissident along with France, the Soviet Union, and the United States, rather than as the facilitator, along with Scandinavian states, that the liberal-internationalist framework would predict.[16]

This tendency for Canada to move from its traditional emphasis on multilateralization, and towards a great-power concert rather than an isolated support for American hegemony, is further reflected in Canada's record of co-sponsorship and voting at the United Nations. Since 1963, and particularly since 1966, Canada increasingly joined with the United States rather than with associated states such as Norway and Australia in co-sponsorship of General Assembly resolutions, but from 1969 rapidly increased its co-sponsorship with these two states as well as with the United Kingdom. By 1975 Canada and the United Kingdom shared top place as co-sponsors of UN resolutions, with Norway and

Australia well behind. And Canada reduced its voting disagreements with the United States and the United Kingdom while generally increasing those with Australia and Norway.[17] Although the tendency of many of the OECD states to band together in the face of increasing challenges from the South may partially account for this growth in Canadian cohesiveness with the U.K. and the U.S., the divergence from the equally compatible countries of Australia and Norway suggests that Canada was focusing more narrowly on acting with the small group of great powers that count. The presence of the United Kingdom within this group indicates that it was a multimember concert, rather than an attachment to the United States alone, that Canada sought.

From 1968 to the mid-1970s, Canada's traditional multilateral, liberal-internationalist emphasis in constructing world order acquired growing force in one area. From 1961 to 1976, the portion of Canada's official development assistance (ODA) disbursed through multilateral channels increased from 27 per cent to 40 per cent of Canada's program, with most of this growth coming in the mid-1960s.[18] As Table 3.12 demonstrates, since 1971/72 the portion of the Canadian efforts devoted to regular multilateral aid, multilateral food aid, nongovernmental organizations, and the International Development Research Centre increased substantially and on a fairly consistent basis. However, since 1975 Canadian bilateral aid programs have grown in value while expanding from serving thirty-three countries in 1961 to embrace eighty-four in 1976. Furthermore, as Figure 3.5 indicates, Canadian aid policy has achieved a greater balance among regions of the globe. While the rapid rise of francophone Africa as a recipient served direct national needs, recent aid policy indicates a concern on the part of the Canadian government to seek a balance between bilateral and multilateral commitments and their respective national requirements.[19]

The final subdimension of Canada's approach to global order, its impact on transforming the global system through a redistribution of wealth and power, raises further reservations about the continuing applicability of the liberal-internationalist prediction. As Table 3.13 demonstrates, on the fundamental political question of rearranging the global order by eliminating colonialism and racism, Canada, in its UN voting behaviour, has moved from a deep, NATO-inspired reluctance to support such resolutions, from 1946 to 1955, to moderate support during the 1960s, to reasonably high support, in the range of the Belgians and Dutch, from 1971 to 1975. However, even in this latest period, Canadian support has remained significantly below its past peak of 1956–1960 and below that of associated governments outside continental Europe and NATO, such as Sweden, Australia, and India.

On the basic question of willingness to redistribute income to the less developed countries, Canada has remained since 1960 in the top ten countries in its provision of official development assistance as a

TABLE 3.12 Canadian Official Development Assistance by Program, 1971–1980

Amounts are in millions of dollars; percentages refer to portion of total ODA.

Program	*1971/72*	*1972/73*	*1973/74*	*1974/75*	*1975/76*	*1976/77*	*1977/78*	*1978/79*	*1979/80*[3]
Bilateral[1]	270.75	319.61	367.34	502.20	523.71	465.80	541.43	559.32	598.79
(Includes Food Aid)	(68.3%)	(63.0%)	(62.5%)	(67.5%)	(58.0%)	(47.9%)	(51.5%)	(48.0%)	(48.3%)
Multilateral[1]	97.38	153.13	184.46	195.73	318.08	432.60	425.52	490.44	500.50
(Includes Food Aid)	(24.6%)	(30.2%)	(31.4%)	(26.3%)	(35.2%)	(44.5%)	(40.5%)	(42.1%)	(40.3%)
Other Programs[2]	28.24	34.62	35.61	45.87	61.24	74.10	83.55	116.22	141.77
	(7.1%)	(6.8%)	(6.1%)	(6.2%)	(6.8%)	(7.6%)	(8.0%)	(10.0%)	(11.4%)
TOTAL ODA	396.37	507.36	587.41	743.80	903.03	972.50	1 050.50	1 165.98	1 241.06

[1]Over these years bilateral food aid remains in the 13%–20% range of total ODA; multilateral food aid fluctuates from 2.2% to 14% of total ODA.

[2]Other programs include nongovernmental organizations, International Development Research Centre, International Emergency Relief, scholarship programs, miscellaneous programs. Over recent years, NGO have accounted for about 50% of this category and IDRC for slightly over 25%.

[3]Preliminary figures.

SOURCE: Leonard Dudley and Claude Montmarguette, *The Supply of Canadian Foreign Aid: Explanation and Evaluation* (Ottawa: Minister of Supply and Services, 1978), Chart 2.4, p. 16. Prepared for the Economic Council of Canada. Based on OECD and CIDA statistics.

FIGURE 3.5 Per cent Distribution of Canadian Bilateral Development Assistance by Area, 1965–1974

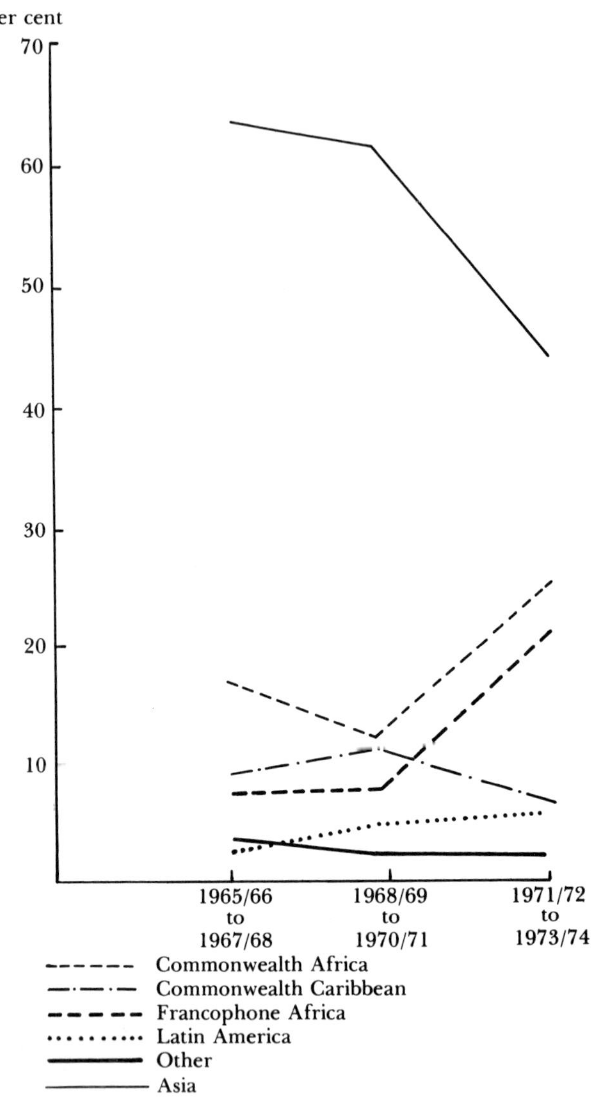

SOURCE: Peyton V. Lyon and Brian W. Tomlin, *Canada as an International Actor* (Toronto: Macmillan, 1979), Figure 8.2. Based on Canadian International Development Agency statistics.

percentage of donor GNP.[20] From 1963 to 1973, Canada steadily increased its voluntary financial contributions to the United Nations Development Programme as a portion of its regular budget assessment. However, since 1973 it moved from its past behaviour and the trends set by its Scandinavian counterparts to join the United States, the United

TABLE 3.13 Indices of Support for Resolutions on Colonial and Racial Questions, 1946–1975

Period	*N (=number of resolutions)*	*Canada*	*U.S.*	*U.K.*	*Australia*	*India*	*Scandinavia*	*Belgium*	*Netherlands*
1946–50	12	20.8	50	−2	0	100	41.6	−4.5	−0.5
1951–55	13	19.2	53.8	0	3.8	100	46.1	3.8	11.5
1956–60	14	82.1	82.1	17.8	39.2	92.8	96.4	42.8	75.0
1961–65	32	48.4	31.2	18.5	37.5	100	79.6	29.6	48.4
1966–70	41	43.9	0	−4.5	12.1	95.1	54.8	33.7	32.9
1971–75	73	68.4	9.0	23.6	82.1	100	76.7	60.2	65.7
Mean Support	185	47.1	37.6	9.9	32.4	97.9	65.8	26.3	38.9

SOURCE: Reproduced from Thomas F. Keating and T.A. Keenleyside, "Voting Patterns as a Measure of Foreign Policy Independence," *International Perspectives* (May/June 1980): 23.

Kingdom, and France in a sharp reduction of its assistance in this category. This movement away from multilateralism complemented the new Canadian emphasis on bilateral aid programs, but it was also reflective of the government's willingness to engage in tied aid in response to domestic economic interests. Furthermore, the average Canadian contribution to ODA as a percentage of its GNP remained well below the official United Nations target of 0.7 per cent of GNP, with decreases throughout the 1970s, indicating perhaps a concern for global modification rather than any radical transformation.[21]

Conclusions

The commitment by the government of Canada to an active presence in international affairs is indisputable. A large and complex bureaucracy housing the expertise necessary to function effectively in an increasingly demanding global environment grew out of Canada's significant role in World War II and its participation in the Western alliance system and the United Nations. The resulting foreign policies reflected those concerns and the perceived priorities of Canada's leading statesmen, politicians, and career diplomats.

The record shows a generally consistent movement of Canadian foreign policy behaviour from that of a government working on the premises of liberal internationalism towards behaviour predicted by our complex neo-realist model. On the major dimensions of activity, association, and order, the liberal-internationalist perspective is most clearly evident throughout the St. Laurent, Diefenbaker, and Pearson governments, with minor expressions of peripheral dependence as well. From the last years of the Liberal government under Pearson through most of the Trudeau period and including the Clark interlude, Canadian foreign policy behaviour becomes increasingly indicative of the complex neo-realist perspective.

Canadian activity moved from being primarily an active, responsible participant in multilateral forums to complementing this commitment with a focus on interest-based, bilateral involvement. Canadian association had started with a primary interest in combining with states of similar character and allegiances to achieve consensus on significant international issues through multilateral involvement. It thereby sought to constrain unilateral activity of other states, especially great powers, in a manner divergent from other similar states. It then moved to pursue its increasingly diversified set of foreign policy interests. Canadian concern with world order, though its political rhetoric contained the liberal-internationalist elements of pursuing fundamental reformation through multilateral forums of equal participation, exhibited in practice the distinctly complex neo-realist implementation of the recognition that, while modification is necessary, it cannot be pursued in such a way as to jeopardize the interests of the leading members of the international community, especially the OECD states.

This brief overview of patterns of Canadian foreign policy behaviour strongly suggests that Canada has evolved from a middle power, as it was designated in the St. Laurent–Pearson days, to a principal power acting in ways that combine its commitment to a functioning, stable international system with the pursuit of policies reflecting unique Canada-based interests. This profile of external behaviour conforms closely to the complex neo-realist perspective of Canada as a significant actor in an increasingly diffuse international system.

CHAPTER 4

POPULATION, ENERGY, AND TRADE

In the broad declarations, major decisions, and routine implementation of its foreign policy, Canada since 1945 and particularly since 1968 has moved steadily towards a structure dominated by the patterns predicted by the theoretical perspective of complex neo-realism. What forces have permitted and propelled a transition of such magnitude, durability, and revolutionary dimensions in such a relatively short space of time? In searching for an answer, most Canadians have focused on the new ideas and related policies introduced by Prime Minister Pierre Trudeau and his associates since taking office in 1968 and on the domestic changes within the "new Canada" that have allowed their innovations to take effect during this time.[1]

Yet an adequate explanation requires, from the outset, a much broader vision. For while forces within Canada have permitted the country to move towards new foreign policy behaviours, it has been profound shifts of power within the international system that have propelled the transition and in some respects forced Canada's new foreign policy patterns to emerge. In short, Canada is not, in and of itself, a principal power. It is a principal power within an increasingly diffuse international system, whose structure and order are no longer defined by the dominant powers of old. To fully comprehend Canada's new international position and the foreign policy patterns that sustain it, it is thus necessary to examine these fundamental shifts in position and power within the globe as a whole.

Traditionally, the assessment of global power and position has begun with a calculation of a single state's capability and the rank this has given it, relative to other states, in the hierarchy of international power.[2] Such calculations remain fundamental, but they are by no means enough. High capability is less useful as an indicator of influence when the international system is dominated and international order defined by a small number of great powers, whose collective capability is overwhelming and whose ranks remain closed to those below.[3] Conversely, the influence of a state with even moderate capability can be enhanced when the top tier of the system is occupied by many states, when its ranks remain relatively open, and when its incumbents enjoy relative equality among themselves.

Throughout history, probably the most prevalent form of international system has been that dominated by the overwhelming capability and unilateral influence of a single imperial state.[4] In such a system, the boundaries of the top tier close immediately below this hegemonic power, all other states become secondary, and their influence is less relevant for most systemic tasks. However, as the dominant capability of an imperial power declines, the boundaries of the top tier widen to embrace other great powers, and they assume greater influence, along with a broader coalition of middle powers below. And in a system in which no imperial power enjoys dominance, the boundaries of the top tier broaden, further power diffuses over a larger and more graduated set of states, and more powers become eligible for inclusion in the upper ranks. Such a system can easily fall prey to an intensively competitive instability and anarchy, in which emerging powers strive for dominance, usually through the destructive cataclysm of a hegemonic war.[5] Yet in an era where revolutionary military technologies and intense economic interdependence impose inhibitions on the unrestrained use of force, they can equally call forth a new set of principal powers to provide, through informal co-operation or more institutionalized concerts, a restructuring of the system and a redefinition of the international order that a former hegemonic power can no longer ensure or enforce. These three basic international configurations of imperial dominance, great power competition, and open diffusion conform in broad strokes to the predictions about the international environment of peripheral dependence, liberal internationalism, and complex neo-realism respectively.

In the calculus of power and the structure of the global system, the possession of military capabilities by individual states is far less central than has traditionally been assumed.[6] For while military power is fundamentally relevant—perhaps exclusively so—to the dramatic and often decisive phenomenon of hegemonic conflict, such events are rare and not necessary paths to systemic restructuring; nor is military power as directly relevant. In examining such configurations, economic capability may provide a more adequate foundation, for economic power projected throughout an open system is the most visible sign of an imperial power's global presence. Rates of economic growth provide critical clues to whether imperial powers are ascending or declining, which powers might replace them, or which must act as principal powers in creating order in their absence. Yet imperial powers can maintain their economic centrality in the system—and inhibit their rivals from emerging—long after they have the internal power to warrant the position. Their previous role in creating an international order centred around themselves provides a period of historical grace.

Less limited than military and economic capability as a focus for examining global power are its structural foundations: population, resources, and technology. These elements allow a relatively neutral and unbiased position in the new great debate between those who argue that military capability has retained its primacy and those who counter that in an era of interdependence, economic assets and instruments have come to dominate.[7] Secondly, the population–resources–technology triad provides the constituent elements of both military and economic capability, either as the skilled manpower, secure commodities, and sophisticated weaponry on which military success depends or as the labour, land, and capital that are the factors of production generating economic growth. Thirdly, most students of international politics agree—even if they often do not emphasize—that a nation's overall power and foreign policy capability are significantly dependent upon population size and structure, the resources available to that population, and the ability of that population to harness the potential wealth available to it by applying technology to exploit the resources at hand.[8]

Three additional reasons are equally compelling in determining our choice. First, we are interested not only in short-term fluctuations in Canada's international activity and association, but also in long-term shifts since 1945 in the pattern of its approach to world order, the most comprehensive and durable realm of international behaviour. Thus we need master variables that change slowly but, once changed, are not easily reversible; they remain central to the pattern of behaviour at a later time. Secondly, Canada's emergence as a principal power in a diffuse international system is probably a relatively recent phenomenon, and the consequent transition to dominant complex neo-realist patterns probably even now remains incomplete, particularly in the difficult realm of the approach to world order. So while our purpose is not prediction, we need master variables that can serve as early warning indicators in order to comprehend the full nature and logic of this transition. Military and economic capability adequately reflect the recent and current distribution of power; population, resources, and technology show the promise and potential for further military and economic capability, thereby suggesting the future pattern of overall power as well.

Finally, whether Canada will emerge as a principal power in a more diffuse international system is a matter not only of long-term systemic possibility but also of internal Canadian forces and individual policy choice. Here there is increasing evidence that the growth and intersection of a country's capabilities and its needs for population, resources, and technology determine its propensity for a pattern of national expansion and the array of specialized capabilities with which it pursues this task.[9] By exploring Canada's endowments within their international context, we can determine whether Canada is likely to have the internal capacity and incentive for choice to sustain complex neo-realist patterns and engage in the longer range order-building tasks abroad.

The first section of this chapter examines the primary factors of demography, focusing not simply on the aggregates of population but on its composition and skill levels, in an effort to incorporate the "soft" forms of technological development as well. The second section chooses energy as a composite indicator of two categories, since fuels are the primary resources for mankind and fuel production and usage is an effective measure of a society's level of technological development. The third sector explores international trade, another composite indicator of resources and technology and also an indirect indicator of comparative differences in demographic, productive, and consumptive capabilities.

Throughout this chapter, and within each of its three major sections, attention is devoted to three dimensions. The first, and most important, is the shifts in the distribution of capability and transactions in the global environment, away from a single dominant, invulnerable imperial power at the centre of global exchange networks towards a much broader and more balanced set of states. The second is Canada's relative rank within this more diffuse global environment, and in particular how changes in the individual positions and class boundaries within the international hierarchy have brought Canada into the top tier. And the third is the way in which the global diffusion of power and Canada's increasing prominence have induced Canada to act with greater strength on a fully global basis.

Population

Of all the master variables determining the distribution of wealth and power in the international system, population has traditionally been regarded as the most fundamental.[10] The size and skill of a nation's population provide a basic measure of its capacity to generate wealth, its productivity in this task, and its ability to mobilize large volumes of effective manpower to ensure territorial defence at home and the projection of force abroad. Conversely, because the size of a nation's population significantly affects its level of consumption and the magnitude of the task of defending its citizenry, population is also a critical component of a state's vulnerability. The dynamics of changes in population affect access to and control over the goods and services in a society. The three central processes of demographics—fertility, mortality, and migration—have long been a central concern of a nation's political life, particularly in a state's international experience. States with large populations, when reinforced by abundant natural resources and advanced technologies, exert influence on contiguous regions and emerge as dominant states or empires beyond.

Canada's basic demographic position in the globe would appear, at first glance, to make it a poor candidate for this category. Canada provides only a minuscule 0.6 per cent of the world's total population, and its share has slowly shrunk over the years since World War II. Moreover, its apparent weakness has been exacerbated by three trends in the global system. First, global population growth, at an alarming rate of almost 2 per cent per year, has combined with burgeoning technology

TABLE 4.1 Global Population by Regions, 1950–1977 (population in millions and percentage of global population)

Region	*1950*	*1955*	*1960*	*1965*	*1970*	*1976*	*1977*	*Annual Increase (1965–1977*
Most Developed Countries	565.9 (22.6%)	600.9 (22.1%)	637.1 (21.3%)	675.2 (20.5%)	705.6 (19.5%)	736.6 (18.2%)	745.5 (18.1%)	0.73%
Least Developed Countries	1 110.0 (44.4%)	1 238.0 (45.5%)	1 384.0 (46.3%)	1 571.0 (47.8%)	1 786.0 (49.5%)	2 082.0 (51.5%)	2 136.0 (51.8%)	2.03%
Centrally Planned Economies	827.0 (33.1%)	894.0 (32.8%)	965.0 (32.3%)	1 041.0 (31.7%)	1 118.0 (31.0%)	1 217.0 (30.1%)	1 234.0 (29.9%)	1.2%

SOURCE: United Nations, Statistical Office, *Demographic Yearbook*, 1977.

and consumption to impose ever-multiplying demands on the natural environment and human organizations.[11] Secondly, as Table 4.1 shows, the advanced industrial world, the one-fifth of the global population in which Canada resides, is growing at less than replacement rate, while the less developed world, with more than half the earth's population, is growing at more than 2 per cent annually. And thirdly, the North is challenged by the Communist East, as the centrally planned states, which contain one-third of the world's population, grow at a 1.2 per cent annual rate.

The critical question, however, is whether the composition of Canada and the world's population provides Canada with a source of internal weakness or of exportable strength. The answer to this question lies in examining a country's total population in relationship to its socio-economic structure, using the two critical dimensions of total dependency ratio (TDR) and effective population.[12]

The first dimension, TDR, is a "statistical index relating the proportion of the population in the non-active age-groups to that in the active age groups" and provides an adequate measure of a country's suitability for economic and military pursuits.[13] In general, a low TDR indicates a good labour potential, a potentially more efficient use of manpower and associated resources, and hence a relatively greater contribution to the country's national strength. As Table 4.2 indicates,

TABLE 4.2 Dependency Ratios in Selected Countries, 1960–1977

	Dependency Ratio			*Population Growth Rate (%)*		
	1960	*1970*	*1977*	*1960*	*1970*	*1977*
Developing Countries	*83.0*	*85.4*	*83.2*	*2.2*	*2.4*	*2.4*
Argentina	57.0	57.0	58.7	1.8	1.4	1.3
Brazil	85.9	84.2	81.5	3.0	2.9	2.9
Egypt	81.8	82.8	78.7	2.4	2.3	2.1
India	79.5	83.2	81.8	1.9	2.3	2.1
Indonesia	78.3	86.9	78.6	2.1	2.2	1.8
Iran	96.1	100.1	96.1	2.4	2.8	3.0
Iraq	94.6	96.1	96.1	2.8	3.2	3.4
Israel	69.2	66.1	68.5	5.2	3.5	2.8
Mexico	96.1	100.0	97.6	3.1	3.3	3.3
Nigeria	84.8	88.7	92.3	2.4	2.5	2.6
Pakistan	93.1	98.0	100.0	2.3	2.8	3.1
South Africa	77.9	81.2	81.8	2.2	2.6	2.7
South Korea	85.9	79.5	66.7	1.9	2.4	2.0
Spain	53.9	60.0	58.7	0.8	1.1	1.0
Turkey	81.2	85.2	85.2	2.8	2.5	2.5
Venezuela	94.9	98.8	88.7	4.0	3.4	3.4

TABLE 4.2 (cont'd) Dependency Ratios in Selected Countries, 1960–1977

	Dependency Ratio			*Population Growth Rate (%)*		
	1960	*1970*	*1977*	*1960*	*1970*	*1977*
Capital-Surplus Oil-Exporting Countries	*85.0*	*88.3*	*91.9*	*2.2*	*3.3*	*3.8*
Kuwait	58.7	81.8	100.0	6.0	10.3	6.0
Libya	89.4	89.0	92.3	2.7	4.0	4.1
Saudi Arabia	85.2	88.7	91.2	2.0	2.6	3.0
Industrialized Countries	*58.6*	*57.3*	*53.9*	*0.8*	*0.9*	*0.5*
Australia	62.9	59.1	56.3	2.3	1.9	1.7
Belgium	55.0	58.7	56.0	0.6	0.5	0.2
Canada	69.5	61.6	51.5	2.7	1.8	1.2
France	61.3	60.5	58.7	0.9	1.1	0.7
Italy	52.0	53.8	53.8	0.7	0.7	0.7
Japan	56.0	45.1	47.1	1.0	1.2	1.0
Norway	58.7	59.7	58.7	0.9	0.8	0.7
Sweden	51.5	52.7	56.3	0.6	0.7	0.4
United Kingdom	53.6	59.2	58.7	0.4	0.5	0.1
United States	67.5	61.6	56.5	1.7	1.3	0.8
West Germany	47.3	57.0	53.8	1.0	0.9	0.2
Centrally Planned Economies	*59.3*	*56.1*	*54.4*	*1.6*	*1.2*	*1.0*
China	—	—	63.9	2.0	2.1	1.6
Cuba	65.0	76.5	75.4	1.8	2.0	1.6
Poland	64.6	54.3	49.3	1.7	0.9	1.0
U.S.S.R.	59.9	57.2	51.5	1.7	1.3	0.9

Note: Dependency ratio $= \frac{\text{number of people under 15 and over 65}}{\text{number of people 15-64}} \times 100$

SOURCE: Based on the World Bank, *World Tables*, 2d ed. (Baltimore: Johns Hopkins University Press, 1980), Series IV, pp. 436–41.

there is a sharp division in the globe among the advanced industrial countries and the U.S.S.R., with low TDRs, the less developed countries, with high TDRs, and an intermediate group of newly industrializing countries such as South Korea, Argentina, Israel, Spain, and China, with TDRs approaching those of the industrialized countries. Canada, despite the demands on employment, economic infrastructure, and social services generated by the postwar baby boom, has had a relatively low TDR, steadily decreasing since 1960 and as of 1977, the lowest in the industrialized North except for Japan's.

Canada's internal age composition represents a source of considerable strength in terms of effective population; this is the concept that "a nation is no larger than the portion of its population that makes a contribution to the furthering of national goals."[14] Table 4.3, which measures effective population by the number of nonagricultural workers in the labour force, shows again the gulf between the industrialized North, the centrally planned East, and the developing South; but, more dramatically, it highlights the favourable position and prospects of the capital-surplus oil-exporting countries. The measure of effective population confirms that Canada is a legitimate member of the "summit seven" Western economic powers. Within the seven, its effective population as a percentage of total population places its internal demographic strength below that of the United Kingdom, Japan, United States, and West Germany but above that of France and Italy.

Table 4.4 reinforces this view of Canada's demographic strength among the world's ten largest economic powers. Although Canada's total population gives it a global rank of twenty-sixth, in the small-power range, its effective population rank of fifteenth places it within the middle-power range. The productivity of the population, as measured by overall GNP, ranks ninth, and Canada's proportion of effective to total population brings it within the range of the principal powers as eighth.

Another measure of demographic strength is Canada's central role, as a recipient country, in the massive postwar migrations.[15] To be sure, large population inflows can strain national capabilities and produce ethnic heterogeneity, leading to internal political disharmony, instability, and weakness. Yet such inflows represent a global recognition of the attractiveness, strength, and absorptive capacity of the recipient country, a way of increasing its population without enduring the costs of high dependency ratios, and incentives towards permanent global involvement and pluralistic foreign policy debate.

Transboundary migration is sometimes forced, in response to political and military pressures, and sometimes voluntary, generated by economic incentives. Between 1920 and 1970, over 100 million persons were involved in forced migration. From Italy alone, more than 25 million people, or close to one-half the current population, have emigrated.[16] Since 1945 international migration patterns have been characterized by unanticipated and unprecedentedly massive flows of both forced migration and voluntary migration, the latter from the underdeveloped South to the developed North.[17]

These developments have brought into being a global demographic environment considerably more diffuse than that of previous eras. First, migration from South to North has helped compensate in a minor way for the diminishing share of the developed West in internal population

TABLE 4.3 Effective Population in Selected Countries, 1977

	Percentage of Labour Force Not in Agriculture	*Total Labour Force (millions)*	*Total Effective Population (millions)*	*Total Population (millions)*	*Percentage of Total Population in Effective Population*
Developing Countries	*50.6*	*806.8*	*408.2*	*2 082.7*	*19.6*
Argentina	86.0	10.0	8.6	26.0	33.0
Brazil	58.0	34.1	19.7	116.1	17.0
Egypt	49.0	9.6	4.7	37.8	12.4
India	27.0	261.0	70.5	631.7	11.2 (9)
Indonesia	39.9	51.0	20.3	133.5	15.2 (9)
Iran	59.0	9.4	5.5	34.8	15.8
Iraq	57.0	2.8	1.6	11.8	13.6
Israel	92.0	1.2	1.1	3.6	30.6
Mexico	66.0	16.6	11.0	63.3	17.4
Nigeria	44.0	27.7	12.2	80.0	15.4
Pakistan	42.0	20.4	8.6	74.9	11.5
South Africa	70.0	9.2	6.4	27.0	23.8
South Korea	55.4	13.1	7.3	40.0	20.3
Spain	81.0	13.3	10.8	36.3	29.8
Turkey	38.0	17.1	6.5	42.0	15.5
Venezuela	79.0	3.7	2.9	13.5	21.5
Capital-Surplus Oil-Exporting Countries	*63.4*	*3.8*	*2.4*	*12.2*	*19.7*
Kuwait	98.0	0.3	0.3	1.1	26.4
Libya	78.0	0.7	0.5	2.6	19.0
Saudi Arabia	37.0	2.4	0.9	7.6	11.8

TABLE 4.3 (cont'd) Effective Population in Selected Countries, 1977

Industrialized Countries	*90.8*	*299.3*	*271.8*	*660.8*	*41.1*	
Australia	93.9	5.9	5.5	14.1	39.1	
Belgium	97.0	3.8	3.7	9.9	37.6	
Canada	94.0	9.9	9.3	23.3	39.0	
France	90.0	22.5	20.3	53.1	38.3	(32)
Italy	87.0	20.9	18.2	56.5	32.2	(28)
Japan	86.0	58.7	50.5	113.2	44.6	
Norway	92.0	1.5	1.4	4.0	34.7	(33)
Sweden	95.0	3.6	3.4	8.3	41.2	
United Kingdom	98.0	26.1	25.5	55.9	45.6	(42)
United States	97.0	98.9	95.9	216.7	44.3	(33)
West Germany	95.0	28.3	26.9	61.4	43.8	(42)
Centrally Planned Economies	*77.3*	*620.5*	*479.6*	*1 297.2*	*37.0*	
China	37.0	422.5	156.3	934.6	16.7	(10)
Cuba	74.0	3.0	2.2	—	—	
Poland	49.0	11.8	5.8	34.7	16.7	
U.S.S.R.	81.0	129.4	104.8	254.4	41.2	(27)

Notes: The category of Centrally Planned Economies places the U.S.S.R. and China together, distorting international political realities. Figures in parentheses to the right provide an indication of changes in effective population. These figures are reported in A.F.K. Organski, Bruce Bueno de Mesquita, and Alan Lamborn. "The Effective Population of International Politics," in Richard L. Clinton, William S. Flash, and R. Kenneth Godwin, eds., *Political Science in Population Studies* (Lexington, Mass.: D.C. Heath, 1972), p. 86; based on 1959-1961 population data.

SOURCE: Based on The World Bank, *World Tables*, 2d ed. (Baltimore: Johns Hopkins University Press, 1980), Table 5, pp. 460–65, and select tables Series I, pp. 30–269; and The World Bank, *The World Bank Atlas* (Washington: International Bank for Reconstruction and Development, 1979). Figures for China and U.S.S.R. showing *total population* and *percentage of total population in effective population* come from the Medium Series 1975 population figures published by the U.S. Bureau of the Census and report in *The Global 2000 Report*, Table 2.10, p. 21.

TABLE 4.4 Power as Indicated by GNP, Total Population, and Effective Population, 1977

Country	GNP (billions $U.S.)		Rank in Total Population		Rank in Effective Population		Rank by Percentage of Total Population in Effective Population
United States	1 896.6	(1)[1]	4	(4)	3	(2)	3
U.S.S.R.	861.2	(2)	3	(3)	2	(3)	6
Japan	737.2	(3)	7	(7)	5	(5)	2
West Germany	529.4	(4)	12	(10)	6	(6)	4
France	397.7	(5)	15	(13)	8	(8)	9
China	372.8	(7)	1	(1)	1	(1)	very low
United Kingdom	254.1	(6)	14	(11)	7	(7)	1
Italy	199.3	(8)	13	(12)	11	(9)	13
Canada	194.7	(9)	26	(26)	15	(13)	8
Brazil	163.8	—	6	—	10	—	very low
Spain	118.2	—	19	—	14	—	15
Poland	114.3	—	21	—	21	—	very low
India	100.2	10	2	(2)	4	(4)	very low

[1]Figures in parentheses show 1968–1970 rankings, based on Organski's work; see Table 4.3.

SOURCE: Based on The World Bank, *World Tables*, 2d ed. (Baltimore: Johns Hopkins University Press, 1980), Table 5, pp. 460–65 and select tables Series I, pp. 30–269; and The World Bank, *The World Bank Atlas* (Washington: International Bank for Reconstruction and Development, 1979). The table follows the format of A.F.K. Organski's presentations but is based on updated research and original calculations.

growth, although it exacerbates the inequalities in effective population between the developed and the underdeveloped. Secondly, it has given the United States a slowly diminishing share of the global intake, as the intake rate of other New World states has grown relatively, as Europe has emerged as an attractive target, and as the U.S. itself has offered a less attractive economic and social environment and more restrictive isolationist policies. And thirdly, migration has highlighted the new importance and attractiveness of Europe, for while Europe lost more than 1.4 million of its own people from 1970 to 1974, it gained in 1974 alone more than 6.5 million new immigrants.[18]

These trends assume greater significance when it is recalled that migration patterns often closely map the flow of imperial power. In the post–World War II period, the dominant exchange networks have been among OECD states and between their individual members and certain LDCs that are either geographically proximate—between Europe and North Africa and Turkey, for instance, or between the U.S. and Mexico and Latin America—or historically part of imperial peripheries—between European countries and former colonies or between Commonwealth states. Yet during this period, there has been a basic shift of demographic power in the globe away from the U.S. to Europe and other developed nations, because that is where internationally mobile people prefer to be.

Among the Northern countries who have received these migrants, two groups of states have historically stood out. The New World states of the United States, Canada, Australia, and New Zealand, who have long depended on immigration for overall population growth, have on the whole taken relatively skilled migrants on a permanent basis from the European continent in which their mother countries and imperial powers reside. The states of continental Europe, on the other hand, have generally taken much more ethnically and culturally heterogeneous unskilled persons, on a temporary basis, from the less developed world in general and their geographically proximate or imperially peripheral states in particular.

Canada's position is a particularly advantageous combination of the patterns of these two groups. As Table 4.5 indicates, Canada, like other New World countries, has long had a high intake of migrants. From 1950 to 1974, Canada attracted almost half as many immigrants as the much larger United States, although the proportion has declined since the early 1950s. As this performance suggests and Table 4.6 confirms, Canada has relied on net migration for a high share—more than one-fifth on average—of its total population growth.[19] After the high baby boom years of the early 1960s, this reliance increased dramatically to the one-third share of 1971–1976. Figures on net migration show that, apart from the war-induced movements of the early 1950s and the dampening effect of recession in the early 1960s, Canada's attractiveness has remained constant at a relatively high level. Even as many Western governments move to reduce immigration in the 1980s, Canada's posture has remained relatively open, if increasingly selective.

Given the importance of immigration to Canada's overall population, the quality of the immigrants assumes particular significance. Canada, like its New World partners, has been fortunate to receive a selective, migratory population, generally reflecting the overall demographic characteristics already present in the country. It has been able to use immigration as a means of supporting domestic demands, for professional and skilled labour requirements or for family reunification. And unlike Western Europe, which has come to depend upon the temporary influx of unskilled transient people to maintain stable economic growth, or less developed countries, which often encourage emigration to alleviate domestic pressures and bring in hard currency, Canada has been free to take a long-range economic perspective and accept immigrants without enduring disruptive political and economic costs. In short, Canada attracts and admits highly qualified people who attain

TABLE 4.5 Immigrants to Selected New World Countries by Region of Last Residence, 1950–1974

	Region of Last Residence (thousands of immigrants)					
	Europe	*Asia*	*Africa*	*Latin America*	*Other*	*Total*[5]
Canada						
1950–1954	671.0	19.3	2.9	10.1	52.6	755.9
1955–1959	680.0	20.7	6.8	16.6	78.0	802.0
1960–1964	340.0	19.3	9.3	15.9	71.5	456.1
1965–1969	623.4	91.5	20.5	53.7	120.8	909.9
1970–1974	338.4	161.5	33.4	118.1	142.8	794.3
Total 1950–1974	2 652.8	312.3	72.9	214.4	465.7	3 718.2
United States[1]						
1950–1954	716.3	35.7	4.9	173.8	168.4	1 099.0
1955–1959	688.6	96.2	8.2	394.6	212.6	1 400.2
1960–1964	547.2	108.7	9.6	503.6	250.0	1 419.0
1965–1969	586.1	250.1	14.2	737.5	206.9	1 794.7
1970–1974	459.2	552.1	29.2	769.8	113.2	1 923.4
Total 1950–1974	2 997.4	1 042.8	66.1	2 579.3[2]	951.1	7 636.3
Australia						
1950–1954	538.8	32.7	10.9	0.7	30.8	613.8
1955–1959	509.4	38.8	10.8	1.0	47.1	607.2
1960–1964	522.0	51.0	19.7	2.5	84.1	709.3
1965–1969	746.0	86.8	27.0	6.8	173.3	1 039.9
1970–1974	524.0	114.3	28.9	19.9	196.0	833.1
Total 1950–1974	2 840.2	323.6	97.3	30.9	531.3	3 803.3
New Zealand[3]						
1950–1954	80.5	4.7	1.2	—	30.1	116.5
1955–1959	73.1	4.5	1.6	—	36.1	115.3
1960–1964	79.9	6.4	3.4	—	66.8	156.5
1965–1969	74.5	8.0	1.2	—	71.4	155.0
1970–1974	76.2	7.0	1.0	—	73.2[4]	157.4
Total 1950–1974	384.2	30.6	8.4	—	277.6	700.7

[1]Years running from July to June.
[2]Excluding inflow from Puerto Rico.
[3]For years running from April to March.
[4]Including Latin America.
[5]Totals may be inexact because of rounding off.

SOURCE: Based on United Nations Statistical Office data.

TABLE 4.6 Growth Components of Canada's Population, 1941–1976

	Natural increase (thousands)	*Natural increase as percentage of total growth*	*Net migration (thousands)*	*Net migration as percentage of total growth*	*Total population growth (thousands)*	*Total population (thousands)*
1941–1951	1 992	92.3	166	7.7	2 503	14 009
1951–1956	1 473	71.1	598	28.9	2 071	16 081
1956–1961	1 675	77.7	482	22.3	2 157	18 238
1961–1966	1 518	85.4	259	14.6	1 777	20 015
1966–1971	1 090	70.2	463	29.8	1 553	21 568
1971–1976	934	65.6	490	34.4	1 424	22 993

SOURCE: *Canada Year Book 1978/79* (Ottawa: Minister of Supply and Services, 1978), Table 4.2, p. 154.

TABLE 4.7 Immigration to Canada by Region of Last Permanent Residence, 1973–1979

(Figures in brackets show percentage of global total immigration.)

	1973	*1974*	*1975*	*1976*	*1977*	*1978*	*1979*	*Total*
Europe	71 883 (39.0%)	88 964 (40.7%)	72 898 (38.8%)	49 908 (33.4%)	40 748 (35.5%)	30 075 (34.8%)	32 858 (29.3%)	387 334 (36.8%)
Africa	8 307 (4.5%)	10 450 (4.8%)	9 867 (5.3%)	7 752 (5.2%)	6 372 (5.5%)	4 261 (4.9%)	3 958 (3.5%)	50 967 (4.8%)
Asia	43 193 (23.5%)	50 566 (23.2%)	47 382 (25.2%)	44 328 (29.7%)	31 368 (27.3%)	24 007 (27.8%)	50 540[2] (45.1%)	291 384 (27.7%)
Australia	2 671 (1.5%)	2 594 (1.2%)	2 174 (1.2%)	1 886 (1.3%)	1 545 (1.3%)	1 233 (1.4%)	1 395 (1.2%)	13 498 (1.3%)
North and Central America	45 946[1] (24.9%)	27 932 (12.8%)	21 665 (11.5%)	18 671 (12.5%)	14 218 (12.4%)	10 895 (12.6%)	10 349 (9.2%)	149 676 (14.2%)
South America	11 057 (6.0%)	12 582 (5.8%)	13 270 (7.1%)	10 628 (7.1%)	7 840 (6.8%)	6 782 (7.9%)	5 898 (5.3%)	68 057 (6.5%)
Caribbean	—[1] —	23 885 (10.9%)	17 973 (9.6%)	14 842 (9.9%)	11 911 (10.4%)	8 328 (9.7%)	6 366 (5.8%)	83 305 (7.9%)

TABLE 4.7 (cont'd) Immigration to Canada by Region of Last Permanent Residence, 1973–1979

(Figures in brackets show percentage of global total immigration.)

	1973	*1974*	*1975*	*1976*	*1977*	*1978*	*1979*	*Total*
Oceania	1 143 (0.6%)	1 816 (0.8%)	2 652 (1.4%)	1 414 (0.9%)	919 (0.8%)	777 (0.9%)	772 (0.7%)	9 493 (0.9%)
GLOBAL TOTAL	184 200	218 465	187 881	149 429	114 914	86 313	112 096	1 053 298

Note: Percentages may not add up to 100 because of rounding off.
[1]Caribbean is included under Central America.
[2]Much of this increase is due to the influx of Indochinese "boat people" refugees.

SOURCE: Based on Department of Manpower and Immigration data.

permanent status and who therefore become, rapidly and continuously, a part of the nation's effective population.

At the same time, however, Canada's migration patterns resemble those of Europe in one crucial respect. As Table 4.7 indicates, the source of Canada's immigrants has steadily become more diffuse. Until the 1960s Canada attracted immigrants from Europe but lost its own population to the wealthier and more attractive United States. However, from 1965 to 1969, the process of globalization in immigration to Canada began in a major way, as Asia, Africa, and Latin America dramatically increased their shares.[20] In the next five years, this process intensified and was reinforced by two major trends. The first was a substantial drop in the number and share of immigrants from Europe, due in large part to renewed prosperity and political stability there. The second was a dramatic reversal of the longstanding Canadian "brain drain" to the U.S.; Canadian flows southward dropped by more than half from the 1965–1969 period, migrations northward rose sixty per cent, and for the first time, the northward flow on the continent exceeded the flow to the south. Table 4.7 strongly suggests the durability in the 1970s of these trends; most dramatically, the fully global sources of Canada's immigration. For by 1979, Asia had surpassed Europe for the first time as the primary source of immigrants to Canada; the combined European–North American share, even with the new strength of northward migrations from the United States, had fallen to only one-third of the total Canadian intake.

These trends are shown more precisely in Table 4.8. During the 1960s, Canada became much more attractive to its imperial associates,

TABLE 4.8 Immigration to Canada from Selected Countries of Last Permanent Residence, 1956–1979

(Figures in brackets show percentage of global total immigration.)

	1956–1960	*1961–1965*	*1966–1970*	*1971–1975*	*1976–1979*	*Total*
Britain (U.K.)[1]	171 573 (21.9%)	121 212 (24.3%)	222 074 (24.3%)	134 055 (16.1%)	64 199 (13.9%)	713 113 (18.0%)
France	17 052 (2.2%)	18 340 (3.7%)	36 137 (4.0%)	17 417 (2.1%)	9 662 (2.1%)	98 608 (2.5%)
West Germany	89 576 (11.4%)	33 442 (6.7%)	40 081 (4.4%)	13 952 (1.7%)	7 720 (1.7%)	184 771 (4.7%)
Italy	129 058 (16.5%)	87 924 (17.6%)	100 370 (11.0%)	26 170 (3.1%)	12 886 (2.8%)	356 408 (9.0%)
Netherlands	37 818 (4.8%)	9 718 (2.0%)	15 824 (1.7%)	8 221 (1.0%)	5 322 (1.2%)	76 903 (1.9%)

TABLE 4.8 (cont'd) Immigration to Canada from Selected Countries of Last Permanent Residence, 1956–1979

(Figures in brackets show percentage of global total immigration.)

	1956–1960	*1961–1965*	*1966–1970*	*1971–1975*	*1976–1979*	*Total*
U.S.S.R.	157 (0.02%)	430 (0.09%)	988 (0.1%)	1 777 (0.2%)	2 378 (0.5%)	5 730 (0.15%)
South Africa	1 963 (0.3%)	2 129 (0.09%)	4 427 (0.5%)	4 656 (0.6%)	7 061 (1.5%)	20 236 (0.5%)
China	— —	— —	— —	1 414 (0.2%)	4 333 (0.9%)	5 747 (0.15%)
Hong Kong	6 397 (0.8%)	8 789 (1.8%)	—[2] —	49 894 (6.0%)	27 832 (6.0%)	92 822 (2.4%)
India	1 855 (0.2%)	5 229 (1.05%)	20 493 (2.2%)	42 577 (5.1%)	21 915 (4.7%)	92 069 (2.3%)
Japan	940 (0.1%)	776 (0.16%)	3 695 (0.4%)	4 200 (0.5%)	1 935 (0.4%)	11 546 (0.3%)
Taiwan	4 268 (0.6%)	922 (0.19%)	32 534[2] (3.6%)	5 505 (0.7%)	3 421 (0.7%)	46 650 (1.2%)
Australia	8 630 (1.1%)	7 586 (1.5%)	18 993 (2.1%)	9 766 (1.2%)	4 002 (0.9%)	48 977 (1.2%)
Mexico	512 (0.07%)	643 (0.13%)	1 502 (0.16%)	3 189 (0.4%)	2 461 (0.5%)	8 307 (0.2%)
United States	54 216 (6.9%)	62 603 (12.6%)	104 183 (11.4%)	118 922 (14.3%)	49 765 (10.8%)	389 689 (9.9%)
Subtotal	524 015	359 743	601 301	441 625	224 892	2 151 576
Subtotal as Percentage of Total Immigration	66.9%	72.1%	65.8%	52.9%	46.3%	54.4%
Total Immigration	782 911	498 790	913 837	834 452	462 752	3 955 194

[1] Select Countries.

[2] For the 1966–1970 period Statistics Canada—Immigration records do not list Hong Kong separately and evidently have combined Hong Kong data with Taiwan/China prior to a separate PRC designation. Hence, the proportion of immigrants from Hong Kong to total immigration is understated, while the ratio for immigrants from Taiwan is relatively overstated.

SOURCE: Based on Department of Manpower and Immigration data.

the United Kingdom and the United States, as their combined share as a source of immigrants to Canada rose from 28.8 per cent in the late 1950s to 35.7 per cent in 1965–1970. This reflected the diminished attractiveness economically of Britain and socio-politically of the United States in contrast to the prosperity and stability of Canada and provided Canada with valuable sources of economic strength. Yet at the same time, it represented a new threat of penetration: an acute anglicization of the country, just when the indigenous growth of the baby boom was receding and Quebec's traditional high birth rates were declining under the influence of the Quiet Revolution. Francophone Quebec's fears for its survival, expressed in the 1960s through new demands for greater power within Confederation and a more direct presence abroad, had considerable basis in demographic fact.

But in the 1970s, the threat of anglicization through highly concentrated immigration diminished as the imperial share of sources fell to 30.4 per cent in 1971–1975 and to 24.7 per cent in 1976–1979. The stable share from other OECD states provided a more demographically neutral inflow, a strong incentive towards multiculturalism, and new ties with major European countries and OECD states beyond. The strong increase in the share of Third World immigration provided new "francophonizable" citizens at home and fully global ties abroad. And as the sharply increased share of immigrants from Commonwealth members India and Hong Kong suggests, a distinctive demographic periphery for Canada in the world at large began to emerge.

This pattern of population growth and transfer in the post–World War II world provides a strong challenge to those Canadians, preoccupied with their small, linguistically divided population, who think naturally of their country as a minor power in the globe. For it reveals quite dramatically the diffusion of global population power, the comparative prominence of Canada's effective population, and the steady globalization of Canada's demographic affiliations. To be sure, traces of the patterns predicted by the theoretical perspective of peripheral dependence remain. Our overall rank as the twenty-sixth largest state in population places Canada just within the range of the small states in the international system, and the intensified influx of American and British immigrants in the 1960s gave rise to profound internal strains over the central issue of the relationship between Canada's anglophone and francophone communities. More visible, however, are the patterns predicted by the liberal-internationalist perspective. For the most useful indicator, effective population, places Canada's rank at fifteenth, clearly within the middle-power range. Our substantial reliance on immigrants from Europe, OECD countries, and states such as India reinforces our multilateral ties within the Atlantic world and with our traditional middle-power partners beyond.

Yet by looking at Canada's demographic rank and exchanges within a fully global context, the recent shift to dominant complex neo-realist patterns is strikingly revealed. The postwar era has seen a dramatic diffusion of demographic power, as growth in the industrialized West has been outstripped by that in the Communist East and less developed South, and as Europe has replaced the United States as the most appealing destination for migrants within the West. Partly because of these migratory changes, Canada's rank in the portion of its effective population to total population was a high eighth in 1977, placing it within the ranks of the principal powers on the globe. It has had the luxury of choosing immigrants who directly enhance its national interests.

The demographic patterns of global interest-based involvement predicted by complex neo-realism are now clear in Canada. It has a high, sustained volume of immigration. It has reversed the historic continental balance in North America by attracting more migrants from the United States than have been lured southward. And by shifting in the 1970s from its former reliance on British, American, and European sources towards the Third World and Canada's distinctive peripheries throughout the globe, it has benefitted from anglophone immigration without unduly exacerbating the internal linguistic balance on which Canada's stability ultimately depends.

Energy Resources

Whether one considers natural resources "the raw material input into production and consumption" or, more broadly, "all the original elements that comprise the earth's natural endowments," it is clear that they are humanity's "life support system."[21] To be sure, resources can be extracted, consumed, transformed, and hence expanded by the living population, as its repertoire of skills and hard technology allows.[22] Indeed technological advancement can mean that less potential energy is lost in a fuel or raw material conversion process, thus providing more output from a given resource base or the same output from fewer supplies. Yet technology, to be effective, requires some resources upon which to work. In the world of science and engineering, "the rate of flow of useful energy" provides the very definition of power itself.[23]

Thus the primary natural resource grouping is that which, when consumed, is transformed into energy output: "the capacity to take action" or do work, whether human or mechanical.[24] Such primary resources as coal, petroleum, natural gas, water, and uranium, like wood, wind, and sunlight before them, have become as essential to us as food itself. Now the need to satisfy the demands of new technologies and expanding consumption has given energy a proliferating significance far beyond the requirements of subsistence.[25] Whether for the development of domestic economic strategies, the logistics of military planning, or the "high politics" of international diplomacy, control over, or at least reasonable access to, sufficient fuel sources is now an essential aspect of the socio-economic well-being and political survival of every nation-state and a central factor in global power.[26]

For most Canadians, the vital significance of energy to national power and international politics was poignantly, indeed brutally, brought home in the oil embargo and four fold rise in the price of world oil in 1973 and the further doubling of world oil prices in 1979. On the implications of these events for their nation's position in the international system, however, Canadians were profoundly divided. On the one hand, the embargo and price rises revealed the dependence of eastern Canadians, who import their oil, on decisions in distant regions beyond Canadian influence. Other states upon whom Canada relied were revealed to have the same vulnerability, and the penetrative influence of American-controlled companies, which controlled close to 90 per cent of Canadian-located oil production, was highlighted. On the other hand, the prospect of permanent global oil scarcity fuelled visions of a new international prominence for Canada as a net oil exporter, with abundant reserves of undeveloped petroleum and natural gas, unconventional hydrocarbons, coal, hydroelectricity, and high-quality uranium as well.[27]

On the whole, it has been the second vision that has proven to be correct. The most important effect of the embargo and price rises was to propel a global diffusion of power, away from the United States and major OECD economic powers towards a broader range of compatible states in both the North and the South. Global scarcity and diffusion gave enhanced international recognition to Canada's resource power and engendered profound changes in its international activity as a result.

Canada's supply reduction and the price rise in its oil and gas exports to the United States reduced the imperial-focused interaction of its traditional export pattern, while its search for new sources of imported oil propelled it into interest-based, autonomous bilateral involvement in several new arenas. And while its reliance on the atlanticist International Energy Agency in the quest for a new global stability showed the durability of liberal-internationalist instincts in Canada, there were strong signs that its approach to the questions of association and order would shift to complex neo-realist patterns as well.

The conclusion drawn immediately by many observers from the 1973 and 1979 oil embargo and price rises was that the world had become afflicted by permanent scarcity. The scarcity was physical in the sense that global demand could outstrip supply before alternatives became available; economic in the sense that producers could restrict supply development to maximize long-term profit. But despite the dire predictions of groups such as the Club of Rome, a third concept of scarcity—political scarcity—has proven clearly to be the most critical.[28]

Producers are organizing to restrict current supply while consumers lack the political will to organize to promote conservation or the development of alternatives.[29]

In fact, world production of oil, gas, and solid fuels stayed comfortably ahead of global consumption throughout the 1970s.[30] At times, notably in the aftermath of 1973 and 1979, when industrialized countries were thrust into demand-inhibiting recession, there was even a considerable surplus of available oil.

Yet seldom has the world's cushion between production and consumption been sufficiently large to free states on either side of the oil exchange from the temptations and burdens of political management. Indeed, the narrow margin of surplus during the 1970s had taken the world from the "first oil regime", characterized by low oil prices and control of markets through the integrated workings of the multinational oil corporations, to the "second oil regime", defined by political scarcity: a greater fragmentation of organization, higher prices, and control of sources and hence supplies by the host countries.[31]

What political scarcity at the global level has done is to highlight the vastly different physical resource endowments among regions and thereby alter the global distribution of power. It has shifted power away from a dominant industrialized West and the newly industrializing countries, transferring it marginally to some centrally planned economies and substantially to a new bloc of oil-exporting developing states. While these trends are well known, closer examination indicates that they were less dramatic that they might appear.

As Table 4.9 indicates, the growth in energy consumption in industrialized countries continues to outstrip the growth in their production, but the margin of vulnerability is significantly smaller than in the period before 1974.[32] The centrally planned economies have made even greater progress, moving from equality before 1974 to a 1.1 per cent margin in favour of production.[33] While middle-income LDCs have suffered acutely since 1974, the lower-income LDCs have increased their growth rates for production and consumption as well as their margins in favour of production during this time.[34] And the capital-surplus oil exporters have experienced a decrease in growth rates of production, an increase in consumption, and an increasing margin, now in favour of consumption.

In interpreting these figures, one must bear in mind the recessions dampening Western consumption, the lower base from which centrally planned and low-income developing countries started, and the vast surpluses with which capital-surplus oil exporters have to meet their increased consumption demands. But political factors, such as conservation, forced production, and demands for development, can alleviate unchecked economic and physical trends.[35] And it is possible that these offsetting forces have some basis in economic and physical factors; since

TABLE 4.9 Energy Production and Consumption Growth Rates, 1960–1978

	Average Annual Growth Rate (%)			
	Production		*Consumption*	
	1960–74	*1974–78*	*1960–74*	*1974–78*
Low-income LDCs	6.8	8.2	5.7	6.8
Mid-income LDCs	6.0	1.7	7.9	6.2
Capital-Surplus Oil Exporters	11.5	1.4	9.2	11.7
Centrally Planned Economies	4.8	6.5	4.8	5.4
Industrialized Countries	3.2	0.8	4.9	1.5
United States	3.5	−0.5	4.1	1.6
Canada	8.9	−1.3	6.0	1.7
Norway	6.8	37.5	5.9	4.0
West Germany	−0.7	−0.7	4.5	1.5
France	−1.3	0.6	5.8	1.6
Great Britain	−1.2	13.5	1.7	0.3
Japan	−1.7	−0.8	10.7	1.8
Australia	11.1	5.3	5.6	3.6
Netherlands	16.2	−1.6	8.7	−1.5

SOURCE: The World Bank, *World Development Report* (1980), Table 7, pp. 122–23.

1974 estimated proven oil reserves have in fact been declining in the world as a whole, but increasing in the Western hemisphere.

In many respects the most significant effects of the new political scarcity have been not the transfers of power among existing blocs but the shifts it has induced *within* each bloc and the new transbloc affiliations that have begun to emerge as a result.

The most significant intrabloc shifts have taken place within the industrialized OECD world. Here, as Tables 4.9, 4.10, and 4.11 indicate, the most dramatic development has been the declining dominance and new vulnerability of the United States.[36] Since 1974 American growth rates of energy production have fallen substantially and turned negative, while the gap between growth rates of production and consumption accentuated the burden on the consumption side. American aggregate total energy requirements have continued to expand, except in the recession years of 1974 and 1975. Yet U.S. energy production remained virtually constant during the 1970s, with the 1978 figure of 1451 million tons of oil equivalent (MTOE) slightly lower than the 1970 figure of 1466 million tons. Thus during this eight-year period American net import requirements increased fourfold, to 405.5 MTOE in 1978.

TABLE 4.10 Total Energy Requirements, Production, and Consumption of Select OECD States, 1960–1978 (million tons oil equivalent)

		1960	*1965*	*1970*	*1971*	*1972*	*1973*	*1974*	*1975*	*1976*	*1977*	*1978*
Australia	TER	26.7	37.1	47.7	49.8	52.1	55.5	61.2	61.6	11.0	66.5	69.0
	IP	18.3	26.5	45.9	53.4	61.8	66.3	70.5	75.0	82.0	87.8	85.9
	TFC	16.8	22.9	30.5	32.0	33.2	36.1	40.5	40.1	42.5	44.4	44.8
Canada	TER	96.1	118.4	159.6	162.1	180.5	194.0	196.6	200.4	204.1	210.2	219.2
	IP	77.2	113.9	170.6	183.4	212.8	235.7	234.7	223.0	214.6	222.6	226.4
	TFC	62.7	81.5	108.5	113.1	126.1	132.3	130.8	126.2	133.1	136.5	141.6
France	TER	90.4	116.2	150.2	157.0	163.9	182.3	177.5	166.9	177.0	178.5	190.2
	IP	58.1	58.0	50.9	47.0	44.9	42.5	41.1	41.9	38.4	46.4	46.3
	TFC	63.5	85.3	116.0	119.8	126.7	140.4	139.3	131.3	137.0	137.2	145.3
Netherlands	TER	21.9	31.8	49.2	50.8	58.6	61.8	61.1	59.1	65.0	63.2	64.4
	IP	11.2	12.0	29.6	38.2	48.8	57.8	67.9	72.3	77.4	77.1	70.7
	TFC	15.2	23.4	37.8	39.2	46.2	49.7	48.8	48.3	53.7	52.4	54.0
Norway	TER	9.0	12.9	17.5	17.8	18.4	19.5	19.6	19.8	20.7	20.2	22.2
	IP	5.0	7.7	9.0	10.1	12.1	12.8	13.6	21.4	26.9	27.7	41.7
	TFC	6.5	9.0	13.0	12.9	13.1	13.8	13.6	13.7	14.2	13.8	15.0
Japan	TER	94.7	151.4	284.0	290.6	311.8	336.4	340.5	333.1	344.4	348.6	357.2
	IP	58.2	62.2	54.0	51.3	47.7	39.1	44.5	44.0	47.2	44.1	50.0
	TFC	61.3	107.4	218.3	224.4	242.3	267.6	240.0	231.4	254.2	256.1	264.5
West Germany	TER	145.8	184.6	236.2	238.4	250.1	266.7	260.2	243.1	263.7	262.6	272.7
	IP	129.1	130.1	123.1	123.0	120.5	120.1	120.8	119.0	118.5	117.9	117.1
	TFC	102.1	134.8	177.3	178.2	188.0	202.8	196.1	183.9	190.6	189.6	200.5

United Kingdom	TER	169.7	193.2	212.5	210.4	215.1	223.8	214.5	203.1	206.5	211.5	211.6
	IP	125.5	123.7	106.5	134.0	104.9	112.3	105.5	116.7	127.7	155.8	170.5
	TFC	122.7	132.4	146.3	143.8	146.4	154.4	147.3	139.8	143.5	146.7	147.6
United States	TER	1 014.2	1 225.5	1 570.3	1 613.6	1 691.1	1 756.4	1 716.3	1 666.9	1 766.7	1 817.3	1 857.3
	IP	965.0	1 150.8	1 466.5	1 457.0	1 484.6	1 483.1	1 448.8	1 420.3	1 428.4	1 440.2	1 451.8
	TFC	772.6	959.7	1 159.1	1 182.6	1 316.8	1 346.5	1 257.6	1 211.5	1 289.7	1 324.7	1 353.4
EEC	TER	519.4	654.2	838.1	844.6	889.2	945.8	922.8	870.2	923.8	930.5	953.7
	IP	366.1	362.8	348.6	357.2	354.7	367.2	368.4	384.3	397.1	435.0	440.5
	TFC	370.4	473.8	625.4	632.3	666.7	7.516	696.5	660.7	691.6	689.6	715.0

Notes: Total Energy Requirements (TER): indigenous production plus imports, minus exports and marine bunkers.
Indigenous production (IP): includes solid fuels, crude oil and natural gas liquids, natural gas, and nuclear, hydro, and geothermal power.
Total Final Consumption (TFC): TER minus the energy used for transformation from fuels to electricity, other energy forms, and refinement within the energy sector.

SOURCE: Based on International Energy Agency, *Energy Balances of OECD Countries 1960/1974* (Paris: Organization for Economic Co-operation and Development, 1976); and International Energy Agency, *Energy Balances of OECD Countries 1974/78* (Paris: OECD, 1980).

TABLE 4.11 Actual Energy Demand of OECD Countries, 1964–1977

Year	*OECD*	*United States*	*Canada*	*Japan*	*Western Europe*
	(millions of barrels per day of oil equivalent)				
1964	44.9	24.3	2.3	2.6	15.8
1965	47.4	25.4	2.5	3.0	16.5
1966	49.9	27.0	2.6	3.2	17.2
1967	52.3	28.3	2.8	3.6	17.6
1968	55.3	29.5	3.0	4.2	18.6
1969	58.7	31.1	3.2	4.8	19.7
1970	63.1	32.7	3.4	5.5	21.5
1971	64.9	33.2	3.5	5.8	22.3
1972	67.8	34.7	3.9	6.2	23.1
1973	72.0	36.2	4.1	7.2	24.5
1974	71.0	35.4	4.1	7.2	24.3
1975	68.9	34.9	4.1	6.7	23.2
1976	72.2	36.2	4.2	7.1	24.7
1977	74.3	38.0	4.3	7.2	24.8

SOURCE: U.S. Central Intelligence Agency, Office of Economic Research, *The World Oil Market in the Years Ahead* (Washington: 1979), Tables F-9 to F-13, pp. 61–62.

A similar increase in vulnerability, although less dramatic, has afflicted the dynamic major economic powers of Japan, West Germany, and France. While all three moved strongly to bring growth rates of production and consumption closer together after 1974, their total energy requirements increased during the 1970s except for variable, recession-induced reductions from 1974 to 1977. More important, from 1970 to 1978 the net import requirements had increased from 230 to 307.2 MTOE for Japan, from 113.1 to 155.6 for Germany, and from 99.3 to 143.9 for France. Even so, the 1970–1978 increase in the net energy import requirements for these three engines of growth in the Western world was, at a combined figure of 164.3 MTOE, only just over half of the equivalent 301.7 figure for the United States. Thus, while these three states made a substantial contribution to the Western world's new energy vulnerability, their role and responsibility was far less than that of the United States.

Within the ranks of the Western Economic Summit seven, only two states moved to offset the collective vulnerability caused by the decline of the big four. The United Kingdom after 1974 dramatically transformed declining production growth rates into major increases, lowered consumption growth rates, kept its 1978 total energy requirement at the 1970 figure, and reduced its net imports from 106 to 41.1 MTOE. And

Canada, while it suffered a dramatic decline into the negative range of growth rates after 1974 and increased its overall requirements from 1970 to 1978, reduced consumption growth rates considerably after 1975 and shifted from a net import requirement of 18.9 MTOE in 1960 and 4.5 MTOE in 1965 to a surplus of indigenous production from 1970 to 1978. During this period, it was the only member of the Western Economic Summit seven with such a surplus.

As these figures indicate, the Western industrialized bloc has experienced three profound shifts in its internal distribution of power since 1960 and particularly during the 1970s. The first has been the massive decline in the position of the United States, taking it from its hegemonic position of reserve supplier to the West, to the vulnerable position of a major net importer, and finally to its current position as the greatest source of weakness and instability in the alliance as a whole. The second shift has been an equalization of economic power among the summit seven, including Canada's critical transition to net exporter status. This has led to the third development, Canada's unique position as a state critically capable of taking a leading role in moving the West towards greater self-sufficiency.

This potential role could be significant at a time when the increased vulnerability of the West has bred dissension within the bloc. Transbloc bilateral affiliations are developing as Japan and the Europeans, with an eye to the drain imposed by a declining America, have forged special arrangements with states in OPEC and the Communist East.[37] To be sure, Canada's surplus capacity remains small in the context of Western demands, and its surplus has been declining since its peak in 1973. Yet this surplus provides the critical physical and economic foundation for a position of pre-eminence that can become a leadership role in the political realm.

A more detailed examination of Canada's position and behaviour reveals that this potential has begun to be realized.[38] Within the summit seven (excluding Italy, for whom figures are not readily available), Canada's rank based on the net energy surplus/importer criteria rose from second (after West Germany) in 1960 to first from 1970 to 1978, while the gap between its position and that of the United States rose from 30.1 MTOE in 1960 to 115 MTOE in 1970 and 413.2 MTOE in 1978. On the more specific criterion of indigenous production, Canada's position rose from fourth in 1960 (after the U.S., Germany, and the U.K.) to second in the 1970–1978 period (after the U.S.).

These figures suggest that Canada's pre-eminent rank in the summit group's external transactions balances from 1970 to 1978 is reinforced by an internal productive potential, enabling it to help assume America's former imperial position as supplier of last resort to the summit seven and the industrialized world as a whole. Certainly the United States, while still the productive leader and generating almost seven times as much energy in 1978 as Canada, can no longer perform this role, given its massive net import requirements. Canada's ability to move into this position will depend on two criteria: its potential for domestic conservation and the availability of reserves that can be brought on stream economically.[39] The data suggest a favourable position for Canada on both counts.

Certainly Canada, as a large, cold, sparsely populated country, has the highest per capita use of energy consumption in the world; and, as Table 4.11 indicates, from 1970 to 1977 our energy demand increased at a faster rate than that of our American and Western European associates and just behind that of Japan. Yet as Japan's experience demonstrates, high consumption carries with it the greatest potential for gains in conservation, and from 1973 to 1975 Canada demonstrated that it could, despite its uniquely favourable position on production, join its associates in stabilizing or reducing energy demand.

On the side of reserve productive potential, the prospects are equally favourable. Canada's overall production of the five major sources of energy is generally within the range established by the U.S. at the top, Europe combined in the middle, and Japan at the bottom, and it is likely to remain there in the future. Therefore, even assuming a united Europe, Canada is a legitimate member of the big four. As Table 4.12 indicates, the prospects for Canada developing surpluses of energy sources other than oil are particularly bright, with gas, coal, hydro, and nuclear power providing the surplus margin. These prospects reflect a long historical transition and a process that is already well under way; strong exported surpluses in natural gas, coal, and hydro have been generated since the early 1970s.

Canadian potential in domestic conservation and production has been reinforced by its demonstrated success in reducing its vulnerability to the outside world. Canada has steadily reduced its concentration on a few states from which it imports fuel, while expanding the number of states to whom it exports both fuel and energy. In both cases, the United States has experienced the most dramatic decline in share.

These opportunities for Canada in the energy field depend, for their full impact, upon the imposition of political will. Governmental leadership, which has been building in Canada over the past decade, received its most advanced expression in the National Energy Program, introduced by the Canadian government in the autumn of 1980.[40] In its first two years, the objectives of the program have given Canada's moves to convert potential into performance a strong boost.

In 1981 Canada reduced its crude oil demands by 7 per cent and its total energy needs by more than 2 per cent; at the same time, its domestic prices moved towards world levels, even though real world oil prices were falling and Canada's economic growth was stronger than in the year before. With the Hibernia discovery, Canada's established oil

TABLE 4.12 Energy Production, Consumption, and Imports in Canada, 1974, 1980, and 1985

	1974	*1980*	*1985 (Projected)*
Oil (million barrels per day)			
Production	1.9	1.5	1.4
Consumption[1]	1.6	2.2	2.4
Net Imports	−0.2	0.8	1.1
Natural Gas (trillion cubic feet per year)			
Production	2.5	3.0	3.6
Consumption	1.5	2.1	2.3
Net Imports	−1.0	−0.9	−1.3
Coal (million short tons per year)			
Production	23.3	41.6	57.9
Consumption	27.4	39.8	49.5
Net Imports	2.4	−1.8	−8.4
Nuclear Power (terawatt-hours per year)	14.3	35.4	52.4
Hydro Power (terawatt-hours)	212.5	242.4	299.0
TOTAL ELECTRICITY (terawatt-hours per year)	284.8	365.0	455.1
TOTAL ENERGY REQUIREMENTS (MTOE per year)	190.2	243.8	279.1

[1]Marine bunkers are included in imports, but are excluded from consumption.

SOURCE: *World Energy Outlook* (Paris: Organization for Economic Co-operation and Development, 1977), p. 33.

reserves began to move upward, reversing the steady downward trend of the previous decade. Even more impressive have been the moves towards reducing vulnerability to OPEC producers and the American firms that dominate Canada's oil and gas industry at home. From 1980 to 1982, OPEC's share of world oil production fell from 45 per cent to 35 per cent, that of the centrally planned economies remained relatively constant at about 25 per cent, while that of the rest of the world (the developing South and developed North) rose from 31 per cent to 38 per cent. During this time, Canada's net energy exports rose slowly, while exports of energy commodities other than oil moved sharply up. And

Canadian control of the domestic oil and gas industry rose from 22.3 per cent to 33.1 per cent, while Canadian ownership advanced from 28 per cent to 34.7 per cent.

Trade

The international exchange of goods and services—trade—is one of the major ways nation-states and their citizens seek to redress distorted distributions of resources and population among themselves, thereby enhancing their own economic capabilities and potential political power.[41] As exports require both economically competitive, domestically produced goods and services and the specialized capabilities to transfer them to market, the great trading nations throughout history have been those countries combining access to and control over demanded products with efficient and reliable delivery systems. Similarly, importing countries need to be able to pay for and distribute the desired goods and services. Taken together, these features make trade an excellent composite indicator of the balance among population, resources, and technological capability in a country, the capacity of its organization system, and the patterns of exchange and influence within the overall system of states.

A familiar topic to economists, trade also lies clearly within the political realm. From Thucydides to Machiavelli, political theorists have recognized the vital link between the viability of a sovereign political entity, the vitality of its economic base, and the security of its trading relationships. The protocols of European diplomacy and the rules governing the affairs of state evolved out of this link and the need to regulate transboundary commerce. Between the fifteenth and eighteenth centuries, the doctrine of mercantilism made the economic realm "the main arena for political conflict," regulated "all international economic transactions. . .for the purpose of state power," and spawned the global trading corporations within the European imperial powers that foreshadowed the multinational corporation.[42] These imperial powers competed, through state and private entities, for economic and political advantage on the peripheries. In the nineteenth and early twentieth centuries, an imperial power—Britain—produced an international regime of free trade, as Germany and the United States resorted to protectionist practices. America again mobilized trade for political purposes in the 1930s, in Cordell Hull's vision of multilateral free trade as the key to reducing international conflict; later the Marshall Plan aimed to revive Western Europe and replace continual conflict with permanent co-operation in Europe and the Atlantic world.

The American vision proved remarkably successful, for in the two decades after 1948, world trade expanded steadily at a vibrant rate.[43] With a surplus demand in the global system, the Bretton Woods monetary regime introduced in 1944 and the General Agreements on

Tariffs and Trade (GATT) begun in 1947 enabled the market economies of the advanced industrialized countries to aggressively pursue economic growth at home and the expansion of trade and investment abroad. Population movements from south to north and east to west also stimulated and responded to economic recovery, low unemployment, and improving productivity; the era of low energy costs, which arrived in 1953, provided a further boost.[44] And underlying this structure were the political actions of an ascending imperial America that provided, through the policy of containment, a secure framework for growth and the critical aid to Europe, Japan, and later the developing South that catalyzed the process.

By 1978, the era of surplus in global demand had given way to a period of scarcity, and the stability of the postwar trading system began to erode.[45] America's withdrawal from Vietnam after the Tet offensive of 1968 indicated that it was no longer willing to bear the global security burden and provide the economic stimulus abroad that flowed from this role. In 1971, the imposition of a 10 per cent tariff surcharge on dutiable imports into the United States and the suspension of the convertibility of dollars into gold signalled the replacement of multilateralism with unilateralism, a rise in protectionism, and the removal of one pillar of the international monetary system. The quadrupling of world oil prices after the 1973 Arab embargo drastically dampened world demand and increased energy costs. Despite new initiatives at GATT and the IMF and in new forums such as the Western Economic Summits, the expansion of world trade—stripped of the mirage caused by inflationary excesses—began to slacken. And under the impact of demand scarcity, tensions among and within the world's major trading blocs began to mount.

The world trading network had been divided into its three current major systems by the 1970s.[46] The first is the East–West system of independence, with the advanced centrally planned economies of COMECON on one side and the advanced market economies of the OECD on the other; interaction is low but growing between the two self-contained groups, and the balance of vulnerability is in favour of the West. The second is the North–South system of dependence, with the OECD and, to a lesser extent, COMECON on the one hand and the less developed countries of Africa, Asia, and Latin America on the other; interaction is moderate and the balance of vulnerability favours the North. And the third is the intra-West system of interdependence among the advanced industrial "free"-market economies of North America, Western Europe, Japan and Oceania, characterized by intense interaction and a balance of vulnerability spread among all.

The East–West system of independence, while the least significant in purely economic terms, has long had the most obvious and direct relationship to the overall politico-military relationships in the international system.[47] What is most striking about this relationship is the vast disparity between its two poles. Economic data reveal the staggering inequalities between the Western alliance and its Communist adversaries in sheer productive capacity, the global reach of trading relationships, the diversity of trading partners, and the need of each partner for the other.

As Table 4.13 indicates, in 1977 the centrally planned economies (CPEs) accounted for the smallest share of overall international trade: only 10 per cent, compared with 65 per cent for the highly developed market economies (HDMEs) and 25 per cent for the less developed market economies (LDMEs). Moreover, from 1960 to 1977, their growth in exports was the lowest of the three groups, and almost two-thirds of their trade was internal to COMECON.[48] Indeed the CPEs remain a very minor player in the whole panoply of North–South economic interac-

TABLE 4.13 Global Exports, 1977, and Export Growth, 1960–1977

	Value (billions $ U.S.)	*Distribution (per cent)*	*Average Annual Growth (per cent)*		
			1960–69	*1969–77*	*1960–77*
Highly Developed Market Economies	729	65	9.6	18.0	13.4
Less Developed Market Economies	283	25	6.6	24.6	14.7
OPEC	147	13	7.4	32.8	18.7
Centrally Planned Economies	108	10	7.2	17.3	11.8
Canada	42	4	10.3	14.8	12.4
United States	119	11	10.6	15.6	12.9
Japan	81	7	15.1	22.4	18.5
EEC of 9	376	34	8.9	18.5	13.4
Other Developed Market Economies	112	10	7.8	17.5	12.3
Developing Africa	44	4	8.8	18.5	13.2
Developing America	63	6	4.6	19.6	11.4
Developing Asia	175	16	7.2	29.5	17.2
TOTAL	1 121	100	8.8	19.3	13.6

Note: Data exclude trade between centrally planned economies of Asia and, for 1977, between West and East Germany.

SOURCE: Department of Industry, Trade and Commerce, *Canada's Trade Performance, 1960–1977*, vol. 1, *General Developments* (Ottawa: Supply and Services, 1978), p. 3. Based on United Nations data. Reproduced by permission of the Minister of Supply and Services Canada.

tions. Total trade between the Soviet Union and Africa in 1974, for example, was less than $2 billion, accounting for about 3 per cent of Africa's trade and 4 per cent of the Soviet Union's. And while the CPEs sent 24 per cent of their worldwide exports to the HDMEs in 1973, in that year the HDMEs sent only 4 per cent of their total global exports to the CPEs in return.

In one critical area, however, this balance has been reversed and the designation of "independence" becomes much less appropriate. Soviet and East European trade with Western Europe has grown steadily since the mid-1960s to the point where, in 1978, it represented almost 80 per cent of total East bloc trade. Western Europe's position in Communist bloc trade was eight times as large as any competitor's, including the United States. In addition, the balance of vulnerability strongly favoured Western Europe, which imported mostly food and raw materials in exchange for manufactures, particularly industrial and technological products vital to Soviet development. Moreover, given the Communist states' shortage of hard currency, much of this trade has been financed by credits extended by Western Europe. These credits can also serve as hostages for future collaboration, although Western European trade with the Soviet Union and Eastern Europe accounts for less than 10 per cent of total Western European trade and less than 1 per cent of the European Community's gross domestic product. In short, East–West trade is a Western European rather than American relationship, and in this relationship the Western European position is highly secure.

The second major international trading system—the North–South system of dependence—stands in notable contrast to the East–West relationship in volume of trade and balance of vulnerability, yet highlights once again the emerging importance of Western Europe and Japan in the globe.[49] North–South trade developed rapidly from a very low base and now represents a substantial portion of the global total. As Table 4.13 indicates, in 1977 the LDMEs accounted for 25 per cent of global exports, with OPEC providing over half of this share (13 per cent of global exports), developing Africa, 4 per cent, developing America, 6 per cent, and developing Asia, a significant 16 per cent. The vulnerability of this trade is heavily in favour of the North, despite the increasing volume, the improved positions of OPEC states and other net oil exporters since 1973, and the striking success in manufacturing exports of the newly industrializing countries of Hong Kong, India, Israel, Mexico, Iran, the Philippines, Taiwan, Pakistan, Argentina, and Brazil.

Three distinct subsystems have emerged in North–South trade. The first embraces Latin America and its northern metropolitan power, the United States, which has traditionally taken about 40 per cent of Latin America's total trade. Yet Latin America accounts for only 6 per cent of world trade, and its average annual growth rate over the 1969–1977 period was a moderate 19.6 per cent.

Latin American vulnerability to the United States is offset by several factors. The U.S. share of Latin American trade has been generally declining, except in 1978, while Western Europe and the other states of Latin America have come to occupy first place at times in recent years. Nine trading blocs account for three-quarters of Latin American import sources, and the relatively strong industrial bases of Latin American states offer many opportunities for import substitution.

The second North–South subsystem, Asia and Japan, has both a larger global presence and a balance of vulnerability more favourable to the southern metropole. With 16 per cent of world trade, Asia is a larger trading region than Latin America, and it grew faster—at an average rate of 29 per cent—from 1969 to 1977. Trade with Japan has steadily risen, except for 1978, to a 20 per cent to 25 per cent share, replacing trade with the United States in top spot. Yet with the United States, Western Europe, and other Asian states coming close behind in their trade shares, and with the newly industrializing countries of the region experiencing rapid internal growth, the vulnerability of Asia to Japan is considerably reduced.

The third subsystem, Western Europe and Africa, is the extreme case in terms of both global size and Southern vulnerability to the North. Contributing only 4 per cent of global trade in 1977, and growing at an annual average rate of 18 per cent from 1969 to 1977, developing Africa is a small player in world trade. During the postwar period, Western Europe alone has taken well over 60 per cent of African trade. And while this share has been diminishing, the United States share has been rising. The resulting vulnerability of Africa to Western Europe is seen in the fact that in 1974, the $41 billion of goods and services exchanged between the two constituted 64 per cent of developing Africa's total exports, 54 per cent of its total imports, but only 6 per cent of Western Europe's total trade. While these figures reflect the legacy of the colonial era, they also show the results of the preferential trading arrangements made by the European Community and other developing states in the Yaoundé Convention of 1963 and in the Lomé Convention of 1976.

The powerful position of Western Europe is seen, finally, in an examination of the third international trading system, Western interdependence.[50] This system, embracing Western Europe, North America, and Oceania, remains predominant in the global trading system because it accounts for more than two-thirds of all world trade and is composed of members who conduct most of their trade with one another.[51] Yet within the comfortable confines of this club, the postwar shift of influence has been profound.

By far the most consequential change—and in many respects, the central fact of international life in the postwar era—has been the massive, sustained decline in the pre-eminence of the United States.[52]

The U.S. share of the combined global GNP has declined "by 10 percent with every decade: from 52 percent in 1950 to 40 percent in 1960, to some 30 percent in 1970"; in 1982 it is 22 per cent.[53]

As Table 4.14 indicates, at the outset of the seven-power Western Economic Summits in 1976, U.S. gross domestic product of $1702 billion was equalled by the four major European powers plus Japan, with Canada's GDP of $194.6 billion providing the critical margin of surplus to either grouping. In that year, U.S. exports of goods and services were exceeded by those of West Germany and Japan together, and America's six summit partners' exports exceeded its own by a factor of three. To be sure, the American export share of GDP is markedly lower than that of its summit partners, and U.S. trade is well dispersed in relatively balanced fashion among five major countries and blocs.[54] Yet during the 1970s, the share of trade in the U.S. economy doubled, and Western Europe, Japan, and Canada accounted for over half of American trade. What the oil shock of 1973 signalled, the influx of Japanese automobile imports into the United States in 1981 and 1982 confirmed: that foreign products had become an integral, pervasive component of everyday American life.

These figures demonstrate America's diminishing share of the West's economic activity, but they understate the degree and significance of the American decline.[55] For it was the surplus capacity and the leadership of imperial America that provided the foundation for postwar economic

TABLE 4.14 Gross Domestic Product and Trade of Twelve Leading Developed Countries, 1976

	GDP (billions $ U.S.)	*Exports of Goods & Services (billions $ U.S.)*	*(% of GDP)*	*Exports of Goods (billions $ U.S.)*	*(% of GDP)*
United States	1 702.0	141.3	8.3	115.0	6.8
Japan	555.1	76.6	13.8	67.2	12.2
West Germany	445.9	115.9	26.0	102.0	22.5
France	346.8	70.4	20.3	55.8	16.1
United Kingdom	219.2	63.8	29.1	46.3	21.3
Canada	194.6	44.4	22.8	38.6	20.4
Italy	170.8	45.6	26.7	36.9	22.6
Spain	104.6	14.5	13.9	8.7	8.5
Australia	94.1	15.0	15.9	13.1	14.1
Netherlands	89.5	48.6	54.3	38.7	43.9
Belgium/Luxembourg	68.2	33.5	49.2	32.8	48.2

SOURCE: Department of Industry, Trade and Commerce, *Canada's Trade Performance, 1960–1977* vol. 1, *General Developments* (Ottawa: Supply and Services, 1978), p. 8. Based on United Nations data. Reproduced by permission of the Minister of Supply and Services Canada.

independence around the world. America's dollars, banks, and multinational corporations provided the lifeblood of economic circulation, while American initiative in creating the IMF, GATT, and even the European Community provided the stable institutional channels through which it flowed. But August 1971 saw the end of the U.S. dollar's position at the centre of the international monetary system, and of the very stability of that system. In the new reality of international trade, only Western Europe and Japan could claim to be global traders, while the U.S. remained confined to nearby, ideologically compatible partners, lacking the global reach to cross the East–West divide, for example, in significant measure. To be sure, the United States, as an ordinary country within the system, remains in a stable position; what has diminished to the point of disappearance is America's special role in defining and ensuring the successful operation of the system itself.

To some degree, America's reduced role can be accounted for by the rise of Japan.[56] By 1976 Japan had become the second-largest economy and third-largest exporter in the West, while maintaining a closed and hence invulnerable economy rivalling that of the United States itself. Since the mid-1960s, Tokyo has diversified its raw material suppliers, specialized in heavy industry and chemical products, and pursued broader export markets. It has long had a very balanced trade profile, with a distinctive periphery of other Asian states; more recently, Western Europe has rivalled the United States as Japan's leading trade partner. And under the domestic pressures of rising wages, labour shortages, and trade surpluses, Japan has become a major exporter of investment capital and technology.

As significant as Japan's rise has been, however, the growth of Western Europe is more important in accounting for America's declining share of world trade.[57] Led by West Germany, which in 1976 was the West's third-largest economy and second-largest trader, Western Europe has become the pre-eminent force in international trade. In 1977 the nine-member European Community accounted for 34 per cent of global exports, three times more than the 11 per cent share of the United States. Western Europe's extensive global reach is reflected in its first-rank position as a trading partner for its contiguous regions, the Soviet Union and Eastern Europe, the Middle East, Africa, and the United States, in its very close second to the United States in Latin America, and in its third place in Asia and Japan. And despite a high exports-to-GDP ratio for most European countries, their vulnerability is much lower than the figures would suggest.

A steadily growing majority of Western Europe's trade, almost 70 per cent in 1978, takes place within the Western European region itself, and the vast majority of this occurs among states bound by the increasingly institutionalized regimes of the European Community. Outside the region, the United States is a significant, if declining, partner, ensconced with the Western Europeans in the regimes of GATT, OECD, and the Western Economic Summit. The only other outsider—and a very important one—is the Middle East, which has grown to a significant position since 1973. Indeed, in 1974 Western Europe's trade with the Middle East became more important than its trade with the United States.

The massive shifts of power in the global economic and trade system have exerted a strong corrosive pull on Canada, a state highly interdependent with its much larger neighbour in North America. Yet the dominant trend over the past decade and a half has been Canada's success in sustaining or strengthening its position; the more diffuse global environment has highlighted Canada's relevance and offered it a host of new partners with which to deal.[58]

As Table 4.14 indicates, Canada had the sixth-largest economy in the Western world in 1976, with a GDP ahead of that of the last-ranked Western Economic Summit partner, Italy, and just behind the United Kingdom's. Canada ranked eighth in exports of goods and services, behind its summit partners and the Netherlands, but its position was virtually identical to that of Italy in seventh spot. As Table 4.13 indicates, Canada, with less than one-tenth the population of the European Community, exported 4 per cent of total world exports in 1977, compared with 11 per cent for the United States and 34 per cent for the nine-member EC. And since 1960, growth in Canadian trade by volume of commodities and manufactured goods has generally kept pace with world trade or surpassed it, with the exception of several years from 1970 to 1975.

In comparison with the U.S., Canada has a highly open economy, heavily dependent upon exports and imports for economic growth. But in a less myopic comparison, Canada's degree of openness and its accompanying potential for vulnerability are much less pronounced. For as Table 4.14 indicates, Canada's exports of goods and services as a percentage of GDP, at 22.8 per cent in 1976, was less than half that of European middle powers such as the Netherlands and Belgium/Luxembourg, and below that of Canada's major summit partners, the United Kingdom, Italy, and West Germany. Indeed, Canada's export dependence places it in the middle of the top tier of the international system represented by the summit seven.

Another longstanding, well-known, and potentially troublesome feature of Canada's trade posture is the very high concentration of its exports and imports on a single partner, the United States. As shown in Figures 4.1, 4.2, 4.3 and Table 4.15, Canadian exports to the United States have accounted for between 50 per cent and 72 per cent of total Canadian exports, while imports from the United States have represented 67 per cent to 73 per cent of total imports during the three decades from 1948 to 1978.

FIGURE 4.1 Canadian Trade with Selected Regions in Proportion to Total Trade, 1948-1978

(U.S. only on left axis scale)

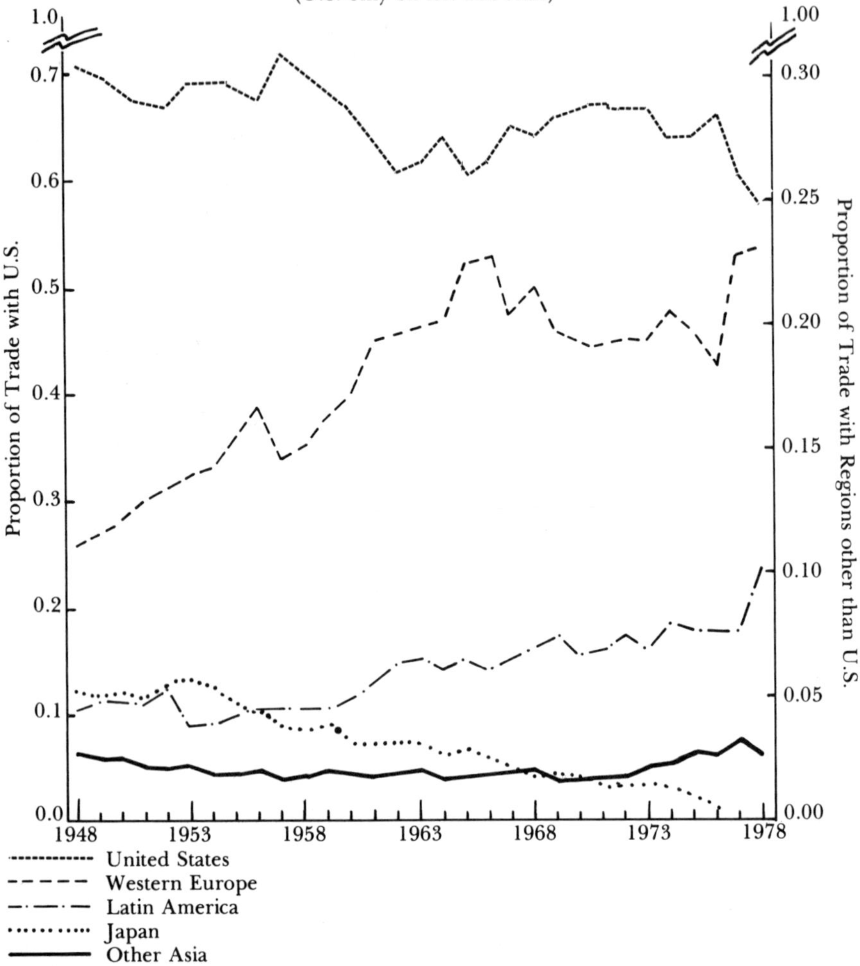

Proportion of Trade with U.S.
1.0
0.7
0.6
0.5
0.4
0.3
0.2
0.1
0.0

Proportion of Trade with Regions other than U.S.
1.00
0.30
0.25
0.20
0.15
0.10
0.05
0.00

1948 1953 1958 1963 1968 1973 1978

United States
Western Europe
Latin America
Japan
Other Asia

SOURCE: Based on International Monetary Fund statistics.

On the face of it, this heavy concentration conforms directly to the peripheral-dependence prediction of imperial-focused interaction. Recognizing this as a danger, the Canadian government in 1972 produced its much misunderstood Third Option policy, aimed at a diversification of overseas relationships, arm's-length diplomacy on the North American continent, and, above all, reduced vulnerability of the domestic Canadian economy to disruptions from outside.[59] However, a closer examination of the evidence reveals that, on the whole, the portrait of peripheral dependence was substantially incorrect.

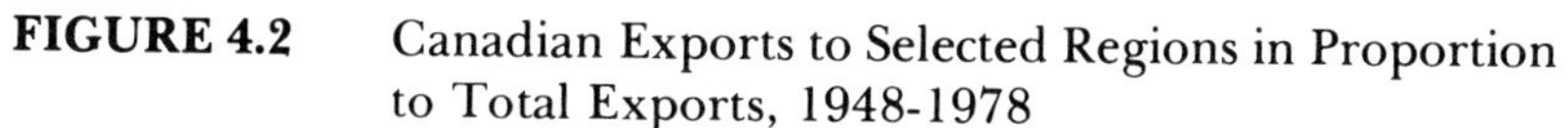

FIGURE 4.2 Canadian Exports to Selected Regions in Proportion to Total Exports, 1948-1978

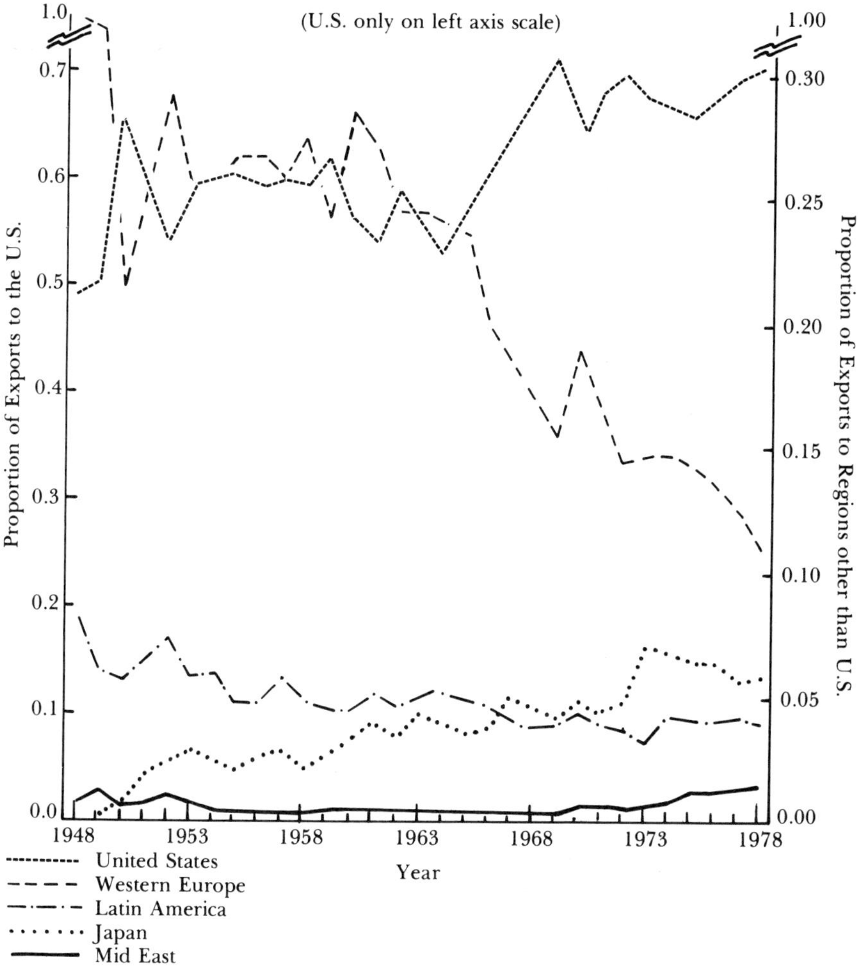

SOURCE: Based on International Monetary Fund statistics.

In the first instance, it is clear that Canada's trade concentration on the United States has generally, if slowly, *declined* over the postwar period. The major offsetting factor came in a rapid rise in Canadian exports to the United States beginning in 1965 and peaking in 1969. This export burst came from a sharp increase in manufactured end products and inedible crude materials, related to several factors:

> The most important was the Canada/United States Automotive Products Agreement of 1965. Others include: the Canada/United States Defence Production Sharing Arrangements; the rationalization of machinery production by large multinational companies between their plants in the United States and those of their

FIGURE 4.3 Canadian Imports from Selected Regions in Proportion to Total Imports (1948-1978)

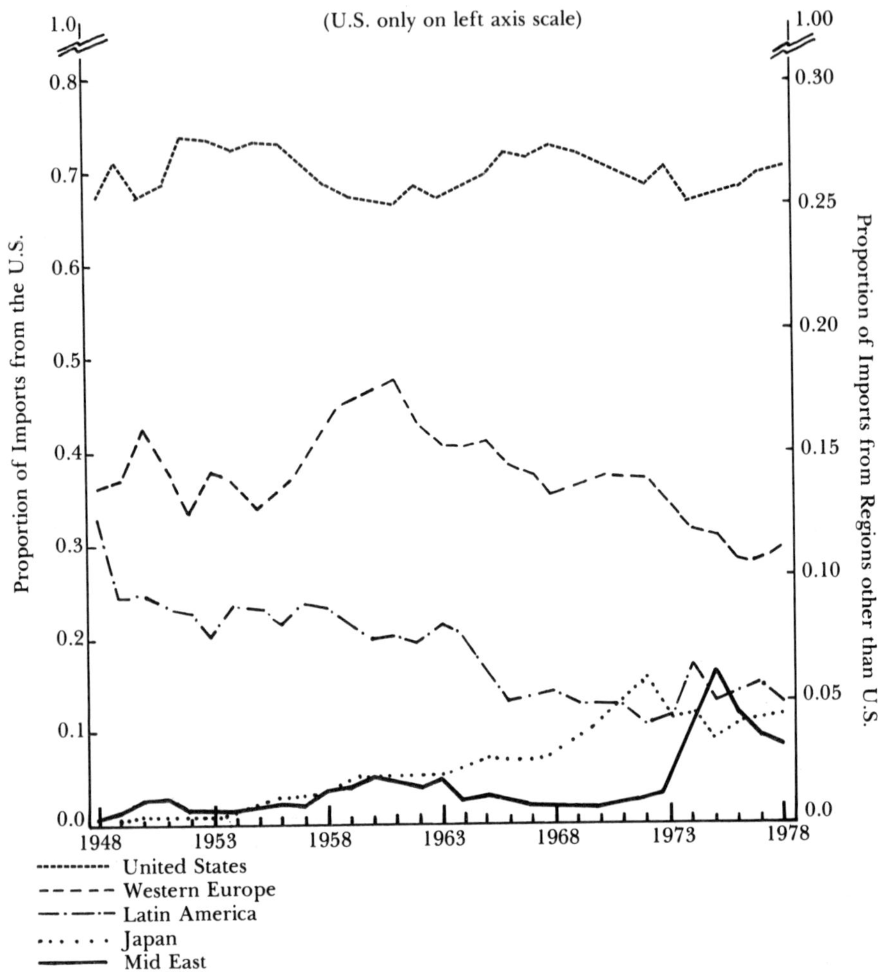

SOURCE: Based on International Monetary Fund statistics.

> subsidiaries in Canada; and the negotiation of special production and sales agreements by Canadian authorities when they awarded large contracts to multinational companies for such items as commercial or military aircraft.[60]

The cause of the increase was thus the vital need of the United States for additional productive capacity in military and military-related sectors, as it sought to conduct full-scale warfare in Vietnam and maintain consumption and prosperity at home as well. Starting from a convergent geopolitical outlook and common values, Canada took the initiative to secure deliberately the integrative regimes to meet this demand. This was a substantial move from an export profile and industrial structure

TABLE 4.15 Canadian Trade with the United States, 1960–1977

	Exports to U.S. (millions $)	*Percentage of Total*	*Total Exports*	*Imports from U.S. (millions $)*	*Percentage of Total*	*Total Imports*
1960	3 036	56.4	5 387	3 687	67.2	5 483
1961	3 215	54.5	5 895	3 864	67.0	5 769
1962	3 745	59.0	6 348	4 300	68.7	6 258
1963	3 913	56.1	6 980	4 445	67.8	6 558
1964	4 437	53.4	8 303	5 164	69.0	7 488
1965	5 033	57.4	8 767	6 045	70.0	8 633
1966	6 234	60.4	10 325	7 136	72.3	9 866
1967	7 332	64.2	11 420	8 017	72.4	11 075
1968	9 285	67.9	13 679	9 051	73.2	12 360
1969	10 551	71.0	14 871	10 243	72.5	14 130
1970	10 900	64.8	16 820	9 917	71.1	13 952
1971	12 025	67.5	17 820	10 951	70.1	15 618
1972	13 973	69.3	20 150	12 878	69.0	18 669
1973	17 129	67.4	25 421	16 502	70.8	23 323
1974	21 399	66.0	32 442	21 387	67.4	31 722
1975	21 697	65.1	33 328	23 641	68.1	34 716
1976	25 894	67.4	38 397	25 752	68.8	37 444
1977	31 027	69.9	44 375	29 630	70.3	42 156

SOURCE: Economic Intelligence Directorate, Office of Policy Analysis, Department of Industry, Trade and Commerce, *Canada's Trade Performance, 1960–1977*, vol. I, *General Developments* (Ottawa: Supply and Services, 1978), pp. 82–86. Based on Statistics Canada data.

based on raw materials to one centred on a manufacturing sector that was large, competitive, and technologically sophisticated, although formed on a specialized basis.[61] Therefore, Canada's apparent move towards peripheral dependence represents instead, in major respects, successful Canadian initiatives to secure a vibrant manufacturing sector when the opportunity presented itself.

What the policy choices of one era produced, those of another can readily change. In the post-Vietnam era, Canada moved, in a different direction, further towards a complex neo-realist posture. As American withdrawal from Vietnam led directly to the new U.S. economic policy of August 1971 and then to Canada's Third Option policy of autumn 1972, Canada moved strongly towards trade diversification abroad and the reduction of economic vulnerability at home. Canada's concentration on American imports was halted and slowly reversed, as the American share dropped from a peak of 73.2 per cent in 1968 to 70.3 per cent by 1977. Similar trends occurred in exports, as the American share fell from its peak of 71 per cent in 1969 to 69 per cent in 1977. In both cases, only exchange-rate fluctuations prevented more dramatic progress from being made.

It is true that Canada's traditional partner and initial diversification target, Western Europe, has failed as yet to play its designated role in the field of trade; its shares of Canadian exports and imports have continued their steady drop. But a broader range of countries has contributed to diversification, such as Japan, in both exports and imports, and the Middle East, in exports alone. Yet as Tables 4.16, 4.17, and 4.18 indicate, the contribution was much more broadly based. In addition to traditional partners, Venezuela and Saudi Arabia, fuelled by the oil trade, ranked fifth and sixth, and the Soviet Union, China, and newly industrialized countries occupied the twelfth to seventeenth slots. While Canadian trade with the U.S. continued to dominate in sheer volume, the rates of increase in exports strongly favoured Canada's

TABLE 4.16 Canada's Most Important Trading Partners, 1979

Rank	*Exports to*	*Imports from*	*Total Trade with*
1	United States	United States	United States
2	Japan	Japan	Japan
3	United Kingdom	United Kingdom	United Kingdom
4	West Germany	West Germany	West Germany
5	Netherlands	Venezuela	Venezuela
6	U.S.S.R.	Saudi Arabia	Saudi Arabia
7	Italy	France	France
8	Venezuela	Italy	Italy
9	Belgium/Luxembourg	Taiwan	Netherlands
10	France	Australia	Australia
11	China	South Korea	Belgium/Luxembourg
12	Australia	Hong Kong	South Korea
13	Brazil	Sweden	U.S.S.R.
14	South Korea	Iran	China
15	Argentina	Switzerland	Brazil
16	Norway	Brazil	Taiwan
17	Poland	Netherlands	Hong Kong
18	Cuba	Belgium/Luxembourg	Sweden
19	Saudi Arabia	South Africa	Switzerland
20	Mexico	Mexico	Mexico
21	India	Spain	Spain
22	Spain	China	Iran
23	Algeria	Singapore	Norway
24	Switzerland	New Zealand	Cuba
25	Sweden	Denmark	Argentina

SOURCE: Department of External Affairs, Policy Planning Secretariat, *Canada's Bilateral Relations: Some Key Statistics* (December 1980), Table IV. Based on Statistics Canada data.

TABLE 4.17 Canadian Exports to Most Important Markets, 1979

Rank	*Country*	*Value of 1979 Exports (thousands C$)*	*Percentage Change since 1978*	*Percentage of 1979 Total Exports*
1	United States	43 438 502	+18.52	67.67
2	Japan	4 076 925	+33.56	6.35
3	United Kingdom	2 588 518	+30.37	4.03
4	West Germany	1 368 290	+75.11	2.13
5	Netherlands	1 081 932	+78.80	1.69
6	USSR	762 953	+34.56	1.19
7	Italy	729 336	+46.48	1.14
8	Venezuela	671 116	−2.22	1.05
9	Belgium/ Luxembourg	667 642	+40.53	1.04
10	France	619 611	+34.63	0.97
11	China	596 108	+18.41	0.93
12	Australia	556 598	+34.96	0.87
13	Brazil	421 563	+1.00	0.66
14	South Korea	364 300	+68.39	0.57
15	Argentina	284 249	+195.67	0.44
16	Norway	279 321	+87.12	0.44
17	Poland	261 623	+16.97	0.41
18	Cuba	257 371	+18.16	0.40
19	Saudi Arabia	251 638	+7.27	0.39
20	Mexico	236 459	+3.13	0.37
21	India	225 784	−12.47	0.35
22	Spain	218 000	+63.63	0.34
23	Algeria	214 751	+33.59	0.33
24	Switzerland	184 342	+71.18	0.29
25	Sweden	172 808	+41.94	0.27
	TOTAL/AVERAGE	60 529 740	+41.57	94.32

SOURCE: Department of External Affairs, Policy Planning Secretariat, *Canada's Bilateral Relations: Some Key Statistics* (December 1980), Table VI. Based on Statistics Canada data.

other summit partners and the Soviet Union, and import growth promised a more geographically diverse set of partners beyond the world of the North.

Success in trade diversification abroad has been accompanied by gains in reducing the vulnerability of the domestic economy, particularly in the area of deepest structural penetration: direct foreign investment.[62] To be sure, Canada remains one of the highest repositories of direct

TABLE 4.18 Canadian Imports from Most Important Sources, 1979

Rank	Country	*Value 1979 Imports (thousands C$)*	*Percentage Change since 1978*	*Percentage of 1979 Total Imports*
1	United States	45 419 508	+28.17	72.41
2	Japan	2 157 120	−5.22	3.44
3	United Kingdom	1 928 516	+19.82	3.07
4	West Germany	1 556 239	+25.00	2.48
5	Venezuela	1 504 969	+20.49	2.40
6	Saudi Arabia	1 241 973	+69.00	1.98
7	France	777 670	+14.46	1.24
8	Italy	636 003	+22.19	1.01
9	Taiwan	522 003	+31.43	0.83
10	Australia	466 099	+32.00	0.74
11	South Korea	462 864	+27.51	0.74
12	Hong Kong	427 084	+28.70	0.68
13	Sweden	383 457	+18.04	0.61
14	Iran	351 125	−40.87	0.56
15	Switzerland	323 472	+13.36	0.52
16	Brazil	313 188	+26.09	0.50
17	Netherlands	251 763	+10.82	0.40
18	Belgium/ Luxembourg	241 443	+16.01	0.38
19	South Africa	240 364	+60.97	0.38
20	Mexico	208 320	+12.89	0.33
21	Spain	177 395	+31.08	0.28
22	China	167 451	+77.01	0.27
23	Singapore	164 029	+63.14	0.26
24	New Zealand	135 088	+34.33	0.22
25	Denmark	117 782	+21.45	0.19
	TOTAL/AVERAGE	62 724 005	+25.19	95.92

SOURCE: Department of External Affairs, Policy Planning Secretariat, *Canada's Bilateral Relations: Some Key Statistics* (December 1980), Table X. Based on Statistics Canada data.

foreign investment in the world. As Tables 4.19 and 4.20 indicate, the U.S. provides an overwhelming 80 per cent of the total. Because it has long provided not only capital that could not be mobilized at home, but also critical inputs of entrepreneurship, management, technology, and markets, it has done much to fuel Canada's strong economic development in the postwar era.

Yet once America's centrality as the global generator of the elements of growth began to decline, the postwar trends began to shift. From 1975

TABLE 4.19 Foreign Direct Investment in Canada by Area of Ownership (millions C$)

	1974	*1975*	*1976*	*1977*
North America and Caribbean	29 198	32 466	34 920	37 835
United States	29 045	32 251	34 707	37 602
Bahamas	77	90	97	104
Bermuda	51	77	75	95
Mexico	10	14	1	1
Netherlands Antilles	5	15	19	17
Other	10	19	21	16
South and Central America	61	78	69	118
Panama	51	71	64	113
Venezuela	1	4	3	3
Other	9	3	2	2
Europe	6 603	7 156	7 875	8 408
EEC	5 757	6 242	6 866	7 357
United Kingdom	3 533	3 680	3 948	4 153
Belgium/Luxembourg	360	443	508	544
France	587	667	742	816
Italy	79	80	93	106
Netherlands	613	684	746	795
West Germany	561	666	806	918
Denmark	21	17	18	20
Ireland	3	5	5	5
Norway	14	12	10	13
Sweden	214	222	234	232
Switzerland	424	494	586	647
Austria	4	4	4	5
Other	190	182	175	154
Africa	185	93	88	133
Asia	288	299	327	395
Japan	258	258	293	335
Hong Kong	18	25	26	48
Other	12	16	8	12
Australasia	50	45	56	62
Australia	40	37	45	57
Other	10	8	11	5
Developed Countries	36 087	39 737	42 944	46 477
Developing Countries	284	380	359	433
Centrally Planned Economies	14	20	32	41
TOTAL	36 385	40 137	43 335	46 951

Note: Direct investment covers investment in branches, subsidiaries, and controlled companies. It is defined as long-term capital provided by or accruing to residents of the foreign country of control for use in Canada by direct investment enterprises. It covers long-term debt (bonds, debentures, loans, advances, etc.) and equity (common and preferred shares and retained earnings).

SOURCE: Department of External Affairs, Policy Planning Secretariat, *Canada's Bilateral Relations: Some Key Statistics* (December 1980), Table XV. Based on Statistics Canada data.

TABLE 4.20 Canadian Direct Investment Abroad by Location of Investment (millions C$)

	1975	*1976*	*1977*
North America and Caribbean	6 493	6 988	7 943
United States	5 559	6 092	7 027
Mexico	75	68	65
Bahamas	147	135	148
Bermuda	462	439	408
Jamaica	118	102	112
Trinidad/Tobago	24	24	29
Other	108	128	154
South and Central America	1 199	1 371	1 603
Venezuela	19	25	22
Argentina	39	46	57
Brazil	1 039	1 157	1 403
Other	102	143	121
Europe	1 865	2 034	2 660
EEC	1 652	1 749	2 239
United Kingdom	1 019	1 037	1 410
Belgium/Luxembourg	36	52	48
France	215	221	187
Italy	36	49	74
Netherlands	72	98	176
West Germany	156	151	190
Denmark	54	70	70
Ireland	64	71	84
Switzerland	72	107	184
Norway	56	54	69
Spain	35	54	84
Other	50	70	84
Africa	167	178	198
South Africa	126	126	123
Other	41	52	75
Asia	317	418	559
Japan	74	68	61
Indonesia	98	186	276
Other	145	164	222
Australasia	485	512	480
Australia	453	478	442
Other	32	34	38
Developed Countries	8 070	8 756	10 243
Developing Countries	2 456	2 745	3 200
TOTAL	10 526	11 501	13 443

SOURCE: Department of External Affairs, Policy Planning Secretariat, *Canada's Bilateral Relations: Some Key Statistics* (December 1980), Table XVI. Based on Statistics Canada data.

to 1977, the growth in direct foreign investment into Canada, at 17 per cent, was far exceeded by the growth in Canadian direct investment abroad, at 27 per cent; the ratio of direct foreign investment in Canada to investment abroad by Canadians dropped from 3.8 to 3.5. During this time the U.S. share of Canada's accumulated intake dropped marginally, as did the U.S. share of Canada's outward investments. Europe and especially Asia provided the most dynamic targets for Canadian investment abroad. While some of this shift undoubtedly reflects speculative flights of capital, in response to such transitory factors as the election of the Parti Québécois government in 1976, it is part of a longer trend showing Canada's increasing strength as a capital exporter on a global scale.

This position is underscored by an examination of Canada's balance of payments from 1969 to 1978. A country's balance of payments serves as a sensitive indicator of short-term trends, but it is also a comprehensive

TABLE 4.21 Selected Components of Canada's International Balance of Payments, 1956–1978 (millions C$)

	Merchandise Trade	*Services*	*Transfers*	*Current Account*
1956	−728	−599	−45	−1 372
1957	−594	−806	−51	−1 451
1958	−176	−836	−125	−1 137
1959	−421	−953	−113	−1 487
1960	−148	−959	−126	−1 233
1961	173	−1 029	−72	−928
1962	184	−995	−19	−830
1963	503	−996	−28	−521
1964	701	−1 111	−14	−424
1965	118	−1 277	29	−1 130
1966	224	−1 438	52	−1 162
1967	566	−1 137	72	−499
1968	1 471	−1 752	184	−97
1969	964	−2 024	143	−917
1970	3 052	−2 099	153	−1 106
1971	2 563	−2 398	266	431
1972	1 857	−2 527	284	−386
1973	2 735	−2 971	344	108
1974	1 689	−3 706	557	−1 460
1975	−451	−4 686	380	−4 757
1976	1 388	−5 760	530	−3 842
1977	2 737	−7 453	417	−4 299
1978	3 382	−8 727	43	−5 302

SOURCE: Daryll G. Waddingham, *The Canadian Balance of Payments to the Year 2000* (Royal Bank of Canada, n.d.), Tables 1.1 and 1.2. Based on Bank of Canada data.

measure, encompassing both trade and investment, that reflects a country's longer-term structural strength in the international system. As Table 4.21 demonstrates, Canada's balance of payments has changed markedly since 1956. In 1961 Canada's merchandise trade balance went from continual, if declining, deficit to a growing surplus, and since 1968 it has shown a strong, sustained surplus except in 1975. Moreover, from 1973 to 1978, total manufactures in Canadian export trade almost doubled (to $23.8 billion) while primary product exports rose only 54 per cent (to $20.16 billion). The service sector has lagged badly, as Canadians' preference for foreign travel and repayment of rents on past investments from abroad have produced a large, steadily growing deficit on service account since 1968.[63] As a result, Canada's dramatic move to a

TABLE 4.22 Components of Current Account as a Percentage of Gross National Expenditure, 1956–1978

	Merchandise Trade	*Services*	*Transfers*	*Current Account*
1956	−2.27	−1.87	−0.14	−4.28
1957	−1.77	−2.40	−0.15	−4.33
1958	−0.51	−2.40	−0.36	−3.27
1959	−1.14	−2.59	−0.31	−4.04
1960	−0.39	−2.50	−0.33	−3.21
1961	0.44	−2.59	−0.18	−2.34
1962	0.43	−2.32	−0.04	−1.93
1963	1.09	−2.17	−0.06	−1.13
1964	1.39	−2.21	−0.03	−0.84
1965	0.21	−2.31	0.05	−2.04
1966	0.36	−2.33	0.08	−1.88
1967	0.85	−1.71	0.11	−0.75
1968	2.03	−2.41	0.25	−0.13
1969	1.21	−2.54	0.18	−1.15
1970	3.56	−2.45	0.18	1.29
1971	2.71	−2.54	0.28	0.46
1972	1.76	−2.40	0.27	−0.37
1973	2.21	−2.40	0.28	0.09
1974	1.14	−2.51	0.38	−0.99
1975	−0.27	−2.83	0.23	−2.88
1976	0.73	−3.01	0.28	−2.01
1977	1.31	−3.56	0.20	−2.05
1978	1.47	−3.79	0.02	−2.30

SOURCE: Daryll G. Waddingham, *The Canadian Balance of Payments to the Year 2000* (Royal Bank of Canada, n.d.), Tables 1.1 and 1.2. Based on Bank of Canada data.

surplus position on overall current account in 1970, 1971, and 1973 has been followed by escalating deficits since that time (see Table 4.22).

While these deficits reflect the necessary costs of the rapid growth of past foreign investment and the luxury items that high discretionary personal incomes allow, the critical structural shift lies in the way in which they have been financed.[64] In themselves, the deficits are not a major problem, for a rising Canadian gross national expenditure has made them a stable and manageable portion of national wealth since 1975, markedly below pre-1961 levels. More importantly, they have not been financed by new direct foreign investment, nor by reductions in Canada's growing trend towards direct foreign investment abroad. Indeed, 1975 marked the first year in which Canada became a net direct investor abroad, and that trend has been sustained since. Rather the deficits caused by current account and reinforced by foreign investment abroad have been financed by rapid inflows of portfolio investment, in which Canadians maintain control and ownership but assume the financial risk. In a marked departure from the dominant trend of the postwar period, this dramatic shift from direct to portfolio investment indicates that Canadians are now able and willing to gamble, in large measure, on the economic future of Canada itself.

CHAPTER 5
THE SOCIETAL PROCESS

Today it is harder than ever for practitioners and observers of international relations to impose the classic distinction between international and domestic politics. Activities that may originate in one sphere have consequences, intended or not, in the other. The movement of capital, for instance, can often have repercussions abroad even when capital flows do not cross boundaries. As the division between the international and domestic spheres erodes, societal organizations acquire a much greater role in international politics.

The interests of nonstate actors and nongovernmental organizations now compete or even conflict with the interests of nation-states. Such is their importance that they have added to the global agenda such issues of "low politics" as environmental pollution, deep-sea mining, and telecommunications, inducing nation-states to assert their sovereignty and control in response. At the same time, the increasing complexity of international relations has made the societal process more important in the making and conduct of foreign policy.[1] In this chapter we assess the changing significance and roles of societal actors in Canada's foreign policy behaviour since World War II.

The Three Theoretical Perspectives and the Societal Process

Why does a country pursue certain policies and activities beyond its own geographic borders? Some reasons relate to the structure of the international system; others to the country's social, economic, and political systems and to its leaders. Both groups of reasons must be examined to explain foreign policy behaviour.[2] Indeed, it is often very difficult to separate the internal from the external factors.[3] We can use our three theoretical perspectives on Canadian foreign policy to guide our explanation of how societal actors within Canada have played their foreign policy role.

In the liberal-internationalist conception, society's role is limited to defining the moral parameters of state action, ensuring that societal actors have access to government and an opportunity to influence it, and establishing the procedures by which attempts at influence are made. Canada's relative international power position provides it with some autonomy to respond to these internal dictates, while not relieving it from the necessity of sensitively monitoring and responding to the world beyond. The salience of the societal process is thus moderate, equally balanced by forces in the government and in the external world. The scope of the societal process—the number and range of relevant actors involved in foreign policy—is also moderate, with the limits set by the procedural norms of constitutional government. And similarly, the government's sensitivity to its domestic environment is moderate, as constitutional procedures within a middle power guarantee access for societal groups while structuring their impact on the decision makers themselves.

The importance attached to constitutional democratic values in the liberal-internationalist perspective suggests a considerable role for the citizenry at large or broad groupings within it, as distinct from concentrated élites. Yet the stress on constitutional procedures indicates that the populace will exert an influence primarily through established political forums. Therefore Parliament and the supporting political parties, acting both in their own right and as representatives of other groups, are significant contributors to the foreign policy process. Conversely, the autonomous influence of the media and that of the private corporate sector are relatively slight, since salient domestic concerns are encompassed by the élite party, the parliamentary process, or associational interest groups. These interest groups, along with organized labour and provincial governments, are seen as relatively important autonomous actors, as they have legitimate constituencies, internal cohesion, ample resources, and ready access to government.

The perspective of peripheral dependence paints a very different portrait of societal actors in Canadian foreign policy. Its concept of Canada as a small country penetrated by and dependent on a dominant United States offers little room for an effective, autonomous societal process. Its frequent use of neo-Marxist concepts leads it to suggest concentrated élite influence, exercised on behalf of external actors and located in the standard industrial or manufacturing sphere. And its focus on natural resources as Canada's only critical capability leads it to suggest that the resource and manufacturing sectors are by far the greatest sources of societal influence.

The domestic process, therefore, has a low relative salience overall, based on a concentrated set of relevant actors without much autonomy, to whom policy makers have a low sensitivity. Within this context, the media, the private corporate sector, and provincial governments are the only actors with a high relevance. The importance of the media and the corporate sector emerges from their special relationships with their American partners, through shared élite interests and direct financial and managerial ties. Provincial governments, externally dependent but internally assertive, weaken the countervailing power of the central state.

In marked contrast, the perspective of complex neo-realism predicts a much larger and richer role for a broader array of domestic actors. It suggests that Canada, as a principal power, has the surplus capability in the international system that enables its government to respond to the demands of its own society rather than to the requirements of forces abroad. Reinforced by the concepts of democratic pluralism, it predicts that a domestic process of high salience will call forth a broad range of domestic actors to compete with and balance one another in a vigorous domestic debate. And because it sees Canada developing technology, along with population and resources, as a critical capability, it suggests that this debate will encompass issues and actors of a very great scope.[4]

Because societal actors can help move the world outside their country's boundaries, they have a direct interest in a foreign policy that supports their concerns and assists their participation in an internationally competitive world. Foreign policy in this sense is viewed as an extension abroad of domestic interests. Organized labour, associational interest groups, the provincial governments, and the media thereby come to play significant roles in the foreign policy process. Parliament and parties, while still influential, are diminished. The private corporate sector, reflecting the development of independent Canadian economic concerns, has an enhanced influence in the decision-making process. The corporate sector and other organized societal actors are also able to pursue their interests through direct action abroad and by forming transnational coalitions with similar actors from other states.

The Influence of Societal Actors

Within a relatively open, democratic, and representative polity such as Canada, societal institutions and organizations are the means to mobilize and transform resources and skills into capabilities and into the political activities of policy articulation, input, and implementation. How do these activities influence foreign policy?

In 1968 one noted Canadian scholar, Franklyn Griffiths, suggested that "enlarged participation is necessary both for a fuller realization of the parliamentary democracy to which we are committed and for a better integration of the Canadian political community."[5] Yet a few years later, Denis Stairs, another noted foreign policy analyst, argued that "the principal consequence of the growing complexity of the domestic foreign policy environment in Canada will be an increase in the amount of attention given by decision-makers to the problem of defending themselves and their organization against the impact of domestic pressure."[6]

What had changed between these two observations was the swearing in of Pierre Elliott Trudeau as prime minister on 20 April 1968. In contrast to his predecessors, Pierre Trudeau entered office with a highly developed and deep personal philosophy of individual liberty and the centrality of the political process. A logical extension of this philosophy was a call for a foreign policy more reflective of Canadian interests and aspirations. Indeed, it was Trudeau himself who demanded that "policies in the future accord with our national needs and resources," and it was *Foreign Policy for Canadians,* in 1970, that defined Canadian foreign policy as "the extension abroad of national policies."[7]

It is the Trudeau imprint that divides societal participation in Canadian foreign policy since 1945 into two eras, the first conforming largely to the predictions of the liberal-internationalist perspective and the second far closer to complex neo-realism. Beginning with Mackenzie King in the closing days of World War II, the Liberal government pursued a bipartisan foreign policy, in which the secretary of state for external affairs and his prime minister took the lead in shaping parliamentary and public opinion. John Diefenbaker, with his strong attachment to human rights and his western Canadian political base, proved more directly responsive to public opinion and associational interest groups, especially on the East–West issues of the cold war. Yet it was only in the nuclear weapons controversy of 1963 that the domestic forces of Parliament, the parties, and public opinion had a major impact beyond the control of the government.

During the Pearson government, Walter Gordon's 1963 budget and public disenchantment over the Vietnam war reflected a growing public concern about Canada's ties to the United States, injecting new interests and organizations into the foreign policy process. Evidence of the influence of these new forces was first seen at Canada's first constitutional conference in February 1968. Here, under Minister of Justice Trudeau, the attempt to resolve federal–provincial jurisdictional disputes led to, among other things, a government study entitled *Federalism and International Relations;* the conference also implied recognition of the need to accommodate bilingualism and growing provincial interests in Canada's international activities.[8]

Cabinet responsibility makes it exceedingly difficult to assess the influence of the new forces with accuracy. The traditions of secrecy and public solidarity among Cabinet members and the professionalism of Canadian public servants make background discussions on key foreign policy decisions virtually inaccessible. Without the ability to identify cause and effect in the government's reactions to proposals it receives, scholars are largely limited to general assessments based on circumstantial evidence.

There is another theoretical guideline that can help, however, in assessing the evidence about societal influence. Denis Stairs has suggested that societal actors can influence a government's foreign policy in four ways:

1. agenda setting—influencing the legitimacy and importance of particular issues;
2. parameter setting—establishing limitations on the range of acceptable options and ensuing activity;
3. policy setting—narrowing the parameters of choice and thereby

effectively determining the acceptable single option; and

4. administration setting—introducing constraints on the actual implementation of policy.[9]

These four types of influence provide a crude scale of the degree of societal influence, with agenda setting and parameter setting reflecting the most nominal aspect of a liberal-democratic polity, and policy setting and administration setting suggesting the strongest impact of non-governmental actors on the decision-making process. The scale implies an increasing specificity of influence, an increasing differentiation and scope in demands and in competition to register those interests, and an increase in the salience of societal inputs in the decision-making process. In addition, an increase in the diversity of salient actors competing for the scarce resources of government may actually increase the government's ability to co-ordinate, direct, and control the policy process, especially in areas deemed vital to the national interest.

This scale of influence complements our three perspectives on Canadian foreign policy. The peripheral-dependence model predicts that agenda setting will be the dominant activity of the societal process. Liberal internationalism implies that parameter setting and, on specific issues, policy setting will dominate. And complex neo-realism predicts that the impact of the societal process will extend to administration setting as well as policy setting.

Parliament and Political Parties

Within the liberal-democratic state, political parties function as the key link between citizens and their government. Influence within Parliament requires coalition building and the ability to be guaranteed, or at least be able systematically to draw upon, organized systemic support. The party provides the organizational cohesion, the legislative alliance, and the foundation for the hierarchy of influence. While Parliament provides the locus for debate, political parties act outside of Parliament to mobilize opinion, co-ordinate political activity, and offer an intermediate instrument of political activity for those not elected to legislative office. Given these complementary roles, of what significance are parties and Parliament in the determination of Canadian foreign policy?[10]

At the end of World War II, Mackenzie King wanted to see Canada retreat from its international activities; but the exigencies imposed by an increasingly complex, conflictual, and interdependent world contributed to a formal change in the conduct of Canadian foreign policy. Louis St. Laurent's appointment as secretary of state for external affairs ushered in what historian Robert Spencer has called "a more extensive and more mature consideration of foreign policy by Parliament, and . . . a tendency to abandon, at least in part, the secrecy with which Mackenzie King had previously cloaked external affairs."[11] When Lester B. Pearson succeeded St. Laurent at External Affairs and St. Laurent became prime minister, the foreign policy debate was pushed still further out of the isolated corridors of power into the public arena.

From 1948 on, one of Pearson's goals was to increase public awareness of Canada's newly emerging roles and interests in international affairs and to encourage articulate and informed foreign policy debate within Parliament.[12]

But the influence of Parliament and the parties in opposition remained constrained by the traditional government control over information. At the most basic level, as John Holmes has pointed out, diplomacy of necessity must be "quiet" and done in confidence.[13] Although the cold war generated interest and discussion throughout the nation, only the government had the sophisticated research apparatus, international channels of communication, and access to information necessary to this area of policy making. Not even the parties in opposition had the wherewithal to counter the government's positions effectively.[14]

Nevertheless, neither Parliament nor the national political parties were impotent or acquiescent in the decisions of Prime Ministers St. Laurent, Diefenbaker, and Pearson and their foreign policy advisers. Within Parliament, the House of Commons served its traditional role of articulating a consensus on issues of importance (agenda setting) and on the range of options available (parameter setting). Canada's participation in international organizations and alliances was acknowledged by all parties, although differences arose on specific aspects of each. This explicit recognition of an internationalist posture was enshrined in the early nonpartisan debates concerning support for Canadian participation in the United Nations, NATO, and NORAD, and in the decision to convene all-party committees on external affairs and defence, thereby enhancing both the importance of foreign policy for Canada and the role of MPs in determining that policy.

Although the centrality of the executive branch in determining foreign policy was never seriously challenged, bald pronouncements of policy to the Commons were replaced over the years by heated and often penetrating debate, augmented by the cross-examination within committees of both government and nongovernment expert witnesses.[15] Two outstanding examples in length of debate, division in the House and within parties, and media and public attention are the Suez crisis of October 1956 and the nuclear warheads issue debated in the Diefenbaker years.[16]

The Suez crisis—in which the Liberal government and the CCF supported the American-sponsored efforts to force the British, the French, and the Israelis to withdraw from captured Egyptian territory—stimulated heated debate throughout the country and divisions among the federal parties. The major split was between the Liberal policy and the pro-British stand taken by the Progressive

Conservatives and Social Credit. The fall of the St. Laurent Liberals in the 1957 federal election has been attributed at least in part to the ability of Diefenbaker, then the opposition leader, to call into question the loyalty of the Liberal government to Mother England, tying this in to the latent fear of growing American domination.[17] Parliament and the federal parties were crucial in transforming the St. Laurent policy into a *cause célèbre,* the first time since the conscription crises when a foreign policy became an integral part of the campaign. However, the government's position was not altered in any significant way by the criticism it received. While related issues, such as the earlier decisions concerning the sale of military equipment to Israel and Egypt, were affected by parliamentary debate and party politics, this high-level foreign policy in the throes of an international crisis was not. The decisions emanated directly from Cabinet under the direction of External Affairs minister Pearson and were given public support by the Liberal party and its MPs.

The issue of nuclear warheads bedevilled Diefenbaker's six-year, three-term period as prime minister, culminated in a serious split within the government and resignations from three senior Cabinet ministers, and contributed to the return of the Liberals in 1963. In 1957 the Diefenbaker government had signed the NORAD agreement with the United States, binding the two countries to joint continental defence. Within two years the government decided to scrap the CF-105 Arrow, designed, engineered, and built in Canada, and to purchase the American Bomarc missile system, which required nuclear warheads to be effective. The Voodoo squadrons committed to Canada's NATO role also required nuclear-tipped missiles, as did the Honest John system employed by the Canadian army stationed in Europe. But the issue of Canada "going nuclear" had not been resolved.

In light of the defence White Paper presented to the House in the spring of 1959 and the heightened tensions of cold war politics, the concern for a foreign policy independent of the United States became the focus for extended and rather acrimonious Commons debates.[18] The issue was exacerbated by the Cuban missile crisis of October 1962, when it became apparent that Canada's unresolved nuclear policy prevented Canadian participation as an effective and credible NORAD partner. As Lester Pearson noted in his memoirs, "Canada's position [on nuclear warheads] was intolerable, or rather the fact that we had no position was intolerable."[19]

Although the June 1962 federal election—which kept the Conservatives in power, but as a minority—occurred in the shadow of the defence debate, the nuclear issue and Canada's role in NATO "did not, in fact, play a significant role in the campaign. . . ."[20] Yet within the year, these same issues brought an end to Diefenbaker's "years of achievement". The stridency of the Commons debates—pitting Diefenbaker, Howard

Green, and Douglas Harkness, among the more prominent government leaders, against Pearson, Paul Martin, and Paul Hellyer from the Liberal side—focused the nation's attention on a new role for Canada in NATO.

While none of the three major federal parties favoured nuclear weapons for Canada, the Liberal position argued for the need to address Canada's NATO and NORAD commitments to initial nuclearization and then to consider revision of these agreements. A U.S. State Department press release of 30 January 1963, setting forth the American perception of Canada's role, further complicated Diefenbaker's position since it brought into question, once again, the extent of Canada's latitude for independent policy formulation, as well as disclosed Diefenbaker's indecision. Throughout this period, both the NDP and the waning Social Credit Party opposed Pearson's position, yet neither party was approached by Diefenbaker during the critical period leading up to the last vote of confidence on 5 February 1963. The resignation of Harkness, Pierre Sévigny, and George Hees from the Conservative Cabinet brought to the fore the severe split within the Conservative caucus over Canada's fulfilment of its international commitments.

On 22 April 1963, the Liberal Party was back in power, under Lester Pearson. The importance of the defence policy debate in the overall political process should not be minimized, although, as one analyst has noted, "a survey of the [election] results suggests that the direct impact [of the nuclear warheads controversy] was probably not very great."[21] There is no evidence to suggest that Parliament or party politics changed the Diefenbaker government's foreign policy on this issue. Responsibility lay with Cabinet and so it remained. Rather, the profound disagreement in the House altered policy indirectly, through a dissolution of the government and a return to a better-informed electorate.

In the 1957, 1962, and 1963 electoral campaigns, foreign policy often made good platform issues, calling as it did upon longstanding concerns of sovereignty, independence, British or American sympathies, and visions of nuclear annihilation. But the absence of evidence linking such issues to the decisions of voters, combined with minimal disagreement on substance (though not on implementation or priorities) between the main parties, suggests that party influence on the determination of Canada's foreign policy was not distinct from the parliamentary debates. Although there was some dissension within the CCF/NDP on aspects of Canada's NATO commitment, and more serious disagreement within the Conservative Party on the relationship between NATO, NORAD, and nuclearization, none of the federal parties called for withdrawal from the Atlantic alliance or a change in commitment to the United Nations. As in the past, the question of Canadian–American relations loomed large, and the extent of anti-Americanism further divided the Conservatives. Until 1957, Canadian foreign policy was relatively unencumbered by partisan politics. The Diefenbaker period had changed that.

The Pearson Liberal minority governments of 1963 and 1965 were elected at a time of general disquiet both within Canada and in the international community. The defence debate had raised issues concerning Canada's external commitments, and had brought to the fore the continued tensions between East and West (exacerbated by the new French defence policy). The financial crisis during the Diefenbaker government placed immediate pressure on Pearson to address the question of domestic economic development and American financial penetration. At the same time, Quebec's Quiet Revolution was placing severe strain on the fabric of Confederation, as well as on the Liberal Party itself. By Pearson's second term as prime minister, Vietnam, the Middle East, and Canadian-American issues such as fisheries, automotive agreements, tariffs, and foreign investment were added to the agenda of foreign policy concerns.[22]

As in the past, while Parliament addressed many of these issues, especially those focusing on Canadian-American relations and economic development, it was the Cabinet that determined government policy. Parliamentary debate and committee hearings came after policy formulation and presentation to the House. In only one case—the withdrawal of the Gordon budget, which included specific directives on the control of foreign investment—was there any indication that Parliament directly affected foreign policy.

Prime Minister Pearson's "principal preoccupation in foreign affairs was with [Canada's] bilateral relations with the United States."[23] Because of the unique relationship between these two countries, bilateral issues almost inevitably fed into Canadian domestic politics and often onto the parliamentary agenda. The Columbia River Treaty is an example of a bilateral agreement that was completed through the process of parliamentary review, in meetings of the Standing Committee on External Affairs, and in spite of continued opposition from the NDP. Similarly, the defence agreements, including the clarification of the nuclear warheads issue, were presented to Parliament as policy when they were already signed and were not, in spite of Conservative demands, submitted for parliamentary ratification.

The issue of American economic penetration, however, is distinct from most other foreign policy issues because it so directly combines the sensitive concerns of diplomatic relations with the political symbolism of independence and the economic realities of Canada's sensitivity to the decisions of the American political and economic élite.[24] It was not a new issue in the Pearson years, having been addressed by politicians, academics, and the media at least since the 1920s. But after the Diefenbaker dollar devaluation, at a time of increasingly vocal antifederal activism in Quebec and a marked shift away from Canada's traditional Atlantic trade orientation, domestic politics became transfixed on the perceived threat of an expansionary United States, intent on continental control if not integration. Out of these concerns arose the Liberal caucus position, directed by Walter Gordon and supported by Pearson, of the necessity to assert Canadian control over Canada's economic development. Gordon's movement in and out of Cabinet reflected, after 1965, a growing division in the caucus on the extent of legislation needed to exert controls on foreign, primarily American, investment. However, with Mitchell Sharp in Finance, Gordon was brought back into Cabinet as president of the Privy Council to head, among other things, the Task Force on Foreign Ownership and the Structure of Canadian Industry, whose report was tabled in the House in February 1968.[25] This process, which so acutely reflected the linkage between domestic and foreign policy in Canada, was later to result in controversial legislation, again debated in the House but dictated by the Cabinet.

The 1968 election, which brought Pierre Trudeau to the forefront of Canadian federal politics, began an era of substantial increase in the activities of Parliament and political parties as contributors to Canadian foreign policy. It was Trudeau's foreign policy review that suggested Canada's activities abroad should be in pursuit of Canada's domestic national interests, and in implementing that goal, Parliament and the major political parties acted as conduits for constituency concerns as well as bodies of some expertise in their own right.

Partly because of the increased variety and quantity of international issues in the Trudeau years, but also because of the increased sophistication of elected officials, competing constituency interests, and the emerging prominence of House standing committees, most foreign policy pronouncements received careful public scrutiny, often including extensive debate and hearings before the Standing Committee on External Affairs and National Defence (SCEAND). For example, Parliament played "a highly significant role" in making the Canadian public intensely aware of the situation in Biafra in 1968; it encouraged citizens to urge the government to send aid to the civilians suffering as a consequence to the civil war.[26] The decision to send Canadian observers to Vietnam in 1973 was also closely examined by Parliament.

Members of Parliament and the parties and citizens they represented offered views on Canada's roles in NATO and NORAD and on accepting Indochinese refugees.[27] Special parliamentary task forces and subcommittees were established and reports issued on Canadian–American relations, North–South relations, and other issues.[28] In addition, the Parliamentary Centre for Foreign Affairs and Foreign Trade was established to provide research assistance to SCEAND, other committees and subcommittees, and individual House members.

Nevertheless, increased parliamentary involvement has not altered the fundamental fact that the Cabinet makes policy while others may advise, counsel, or otherwise try to influence decisions.[29]

Party differences on foreign policy shifted from questions of loyalty to Britain or the U.S. to more issue-specific concerns.[30] The NDP continued to be critical of Canada's NATO and NORAD commitments, of its close security ties with the U.S., of the government's hesitancy in supporting "liberation movements" in a number of LDCs, and of the lack of stronger action to curtail foreign ownership of major domestic industries. The Conservatives, generally more sympathetic to American concerns over global security and the Western alliance, were against proposed cutbacks on military spending, supportive of a greater Canadian presence in NATO, and critical of government policies that tended to discourage foreign direct investment in Canada. The plans of the Clark government to implement the Conservative Party platform included dismantling Petro-Canada, radically altering the mandate of FIRA, pushing forth on major equipment purchases and reconsidering the structure of the armed forces, and an overall foreign policy review.

But as the party in power for all but six and a half years since 1945, the Liberals have essentially made their platform the position of the government. The effect of the party structure, and especially the francophone caucus, can be seen in the significance placed on francophonie, especially its less developed countries, and in special measures to protect Quebec-based noncompetitive industries from the effects of the international marketplace. In general, however, the importance of their long reign is that the Liberals are dealing with standard operating procedures and consensus within the foreign policy community that they have established themselves.

In Canada's parliamentary system of government, the influence of elected officials and political parties on foreign policy is constrained by party discipline, Cabinet responsibility, and the government's ability to make policy without ratification by the House. Nevertheless, the House provides opportunity for debate and for the expression of constituents' views on current policy. The party structure, in turn, imposes some constraints and demands on Cabinet decisions. But except during minority governments, there is little evidence that either Parliament or the opposition parties influence foreign policy decision making enough to induce changes. The government caucus, on the other hand—especially with the overlapping regional, linguistic, religious, and economic divisions in the modern Liberal Party—has affected Canadian foreign policy in a direct and often significant way.

Associational Interest Groups and Labour

The right of individuals to organize into groups to represent their interests to the government is inherent in the participatory ethos of the

Canadian polity.[31] But because Parliament and the political parties have so little influence on policy, those who wish to affect Canada's external behaviour must address themselves to the key personnel and points of decision in the policy formulation process: the government caucus and the appropriate civil servants. Furthermore, since most policy is based on precedent, fundamental change is relatively rare and comes only as the result of long, persistent effort.

Interest groups are generally classified in terms of the permanence and professionalism of their organization, the extent of their economic interests, the scope of their concerns, and the specific sectors of society they represent.[32] Business, agricultural, labour, professional, and consumer associations nominally have economic self-interest as their dominant focus, while religious, ethnic, and general citizens' groups, as well as some functional groups, concentrate on noneconomic foreign policies. Some groups have sufficient expertise in their particular areas that they are asked by government to participate in the policy-making process, either with presentations or as advisory members of a task force or delegation. Most groups, however, must rely upon access to politicians and bureaucrats through meetings, position papers, and the electoral process or, more indirectly, through the media and constituent mobilization.

Access to one's government, it bears repeating, does not necessarily mean influence on government policy. Policy usually emerges as a consensus of opinion and analysis from diverse sources, and interest group intervention in the policy-making process is merely one of a number of stimuli. Even when a policy agrees with one group's position, moreover, it is rarely clear whether that group or some other factor—a political or economic consideration, for instance—made the difference in the government's decision.[33]

In the liberal-internationalist model, associational interest groups and labour are moderately significant, since they are balanced and mediated by equally significant governmental and external forces. These groups are minimally important in the peripheral-dependence model, where the external environment, especially a hegemonic power, severely constrains and effectively dictates the issues to pursue in foreign policy. They are centrally important in the complex neo-realist perspective, where key societal actors are seen to employ surplus capacity either directly, in the international marketplace, or in efforts to affect government policy in foreign affairs through domestic mobilization, coalition building, and élite influence within the parliamentary and governmental structures.

From the closing days of World War II to the Diefenbaker period, foreign policy stimulated little interest-group activity, except during the international security crises of Korea, Berlin, and Suez. These stimulated activity among specific groups such as the Zionist organizations, the

Eastern European communities, the outspoken anti-Communists, and those who questioned the efficacy of Canadian internationalism. The breakdown of bipartisanship over Diefenbaker's defence policies and Diefenbaker's cultivation of support among specific ethnic communities (especially the Ukrainians in western Canada, who had strong anti-Soviet feelings) started the practice of encouraging public participation in foreign policy. Foreign policy then received careful scrutiny by the few organized groups concerned with nuclear proliferation, Middle East politics, Soviet expansionism, American economic penetration, and the Vietnam war.

By the time Trudeau replaced Pearson, economic development arguments raised by Walter Gordon and his supporters had brought out articulate proponents of a combination of anti-Americanism and Canadian economic nationalism. Reinforced by the symbolism of the *Manhattan* Arctic expeditions in 1969 and 1971, the vision of an independent Canada with an independent foreign policy became the banner under which numerous interest groups and associations were formed. Furthermore, the heightened awareness within Canada, especially among church groups, of Third World activities pushed the Canadian government to the forefront in the early days of the North–South debate. "Anti-consensual" groups emerged to counter the conventional wisdom about Canada's role in the international community and its position on liberation movements, foreign aid, American definitions of global security, participation in military alliances, and so forth.[34]

Other coalitions of citizens were concerned with new nonmilitary, nonsecurity aspects of foreign policy, especially issues having to do with the environment. The *Manhattan* voyages and the American nuclear explosion at Amchitka in 1971 alerted many Canadians to issues of sovereignty and environmental degradation. Since then, concerns about nuclear radiation and wastes, oil spills and other marine pollution, acid rain, atmospheric pollutants, survival of seals and whales, flooding of lands for hydroelectric projects, preservation of spawning grounds, and disruption of Arctic communities by oil exploration and pipeline transport have been taken up by one or more societal interest groups. A sense of global community gave rise to support for the absorption of non-European refugees, resulting in a co-operative effort between interest groups and the federal government.

The relevance of many of these new issues to the Canadian public and to the foreign policy community is a striking feature of the Trudeau period. Nevertheless, traditional concerns of global security, nuclear proliferation, alliance cohesion, and United Nations performance still remained of central concern to many. Furthermore, in response to demographic factors, domestic legislation, and the changing economic realities in the OECD, this period also witnessed the rise of labour organizations addressing Canadian foreign policy on immigration, trade protection, interest rates, and other factors affecting conditions of economic expansion. Involved in nearly all these "new agenda" items have been academic and other professional and functional groups, reflecting the technical and complex nature of many of these issues but also the emerging competence of these groups, many of which have full-time professional staff.

Often a single issue is of concern to a number of disparate groups, resulting in coalition building. Evidence of the effectiveness of coalitions and pluralistic interest-group activity is found in the number and range of presentations made before SCEAND. On the whole, the number of associational interest groups recognized to have a legitimate, responsible, and active interest in participating in foreign policy making has grown dramatically.[35]

The lack of evidence for real influence of associational interest groups on foreign policy making suggests that the state apparatus of bureaucracy and Cabinet maintains its centralized control over this aspect of foreign policy. Where evidence does exist of the ability of associational interest groups to influence policy—as in issues concerning the Arab–Israeli conflict, refugee and immigration policies, trade barriers, fisheries and coastal boundaries, nuclear proliferation, human rights, and environmental protection—the apparent success is related to, among other things, significant sympathy within Cabinet and caucus, the absence of entrenched policy, the role of Quebec and Ontario MPs within the Liberal caucus, or public support with political value.[36]

Media

Broadcast and print media continue to be the main instruments that keep the citizens of mass societies informed. Three characteristics dominate any description of the Canadian media: ownership is concentrated; competition is minimal; and non-Canadian news comes predominantly from foreign news services.[37] The result is, among other things, that the Canadian media have relatively few experts in foreign affairs and that external events (except for periods of international crises) usually account for approximately 10 per cent of news content, about half as much as in major American networks and print media, and far less than in the media of Western Europe.

What significance do the Canadian media have in the Canadian foreign policy process?[38] Stairs argues that the press "has very little effect upon the substance of foreign policy *per se*, but . . . it exerts a very significant impact upon the day-to-day activities of the men who make it."[39] The impact is made up of coverage of external events themselves, reports of public debate on specific issues, and editorial positions.

Beginning with general (although not unanimous) press support for the establishment of the state of Israel, the key Canadian policies on

Berlin, Korea, NORAD, NATO, Suez, UN peacekeeping, nuclearization, refugees, and boundary disputes have all received substantial media coverage and editorial commentary. In these cases, the media disseminated information and provided opinion and sometimes prescription.[40] In issues such as the Nigerian civil war, refugees from Uganda, Chile, and Indochina, the UN conferences on crime (1975) and habitat (1976), and the Jerusalem embassy affair, the media also contributed directly to modification in Canada's policies.[41]

These examples suggest that even with the continued American dominance of foreign reporting, issues of specific and readily identifiable concern to the Canadian policy, calling for focused government policy, have been addressed by the print media from a Canadian perspective. Furthermore, in such cases as the offshore seal hunts, acid rain, the Indochinese refugees, the UN crime conference, and the Nigerian civil war, it is evident that both the actual reporting, in print and through broadcasting, and the ensuing editorials influenced Canadian policy.

Issues of the corporate structure of Canadian media and their degrees of foreign content have been addressed by the Davey and Kent commissions of the early 1970s and 1980s, in the tax decisions on *Reader's Digest, Time* magazine, and other foreign newsmagazines, and in various CRTC hearings. In the context of Canadian foreign policy, it is obvious that these issues have direct implications for the public at large and for the policy makers. Yet the actual independent influence of the media on Canada's foreign policy, outside of general political socialization and particular issues of importance, is impossible to ascertain. There is no doubt, however, that the instruments of mass information and opinion making are significant contributors to the participatory, pluralistic features of foreign policy articulation in the parliamentary system.

Business Community

Canada is a country intimately tied to the international marketplace, where economic development has been a foreign policy issue as much as one of domestic politics. Domestic market penetration, direct foreign investment, the need for external markets for Canadian goods and services, and currency and interest rates tied to the American economy have given the business community a longstanding concern with Canadian foreign policy. Long before the Gordon budget, the Watkins Report, and the Gray Report, Canadians recognized that Canada's economic development was not solely an internal affair. Whether the target was the British or, increasingly since the interwar years, the Americans, Canadian politicians and economic leaders have argued the pros and cons of the structure of the domestic economy and the availability of options. Interest in foreign economic policies has grown with the rapid expansion of the post–World War II economy, an expansion based on, among other things, massive developments in the resource industries, substantial population growth, rapidly expanding foreign markets, the entry of multinational subsidiaries and foreign capital, and the rapid adoption of new technologies.[42]

Individual firms and the associations that represent them have an interest in Canadian foreign policy because of the relatively extreme Canadian interdependence of the internal with the external economic environment. Domestic policies such as tax laws, wage and price controls, labour legislation, industrial incentives, interest rates, and currency supports, which are a primary political focus of most business communities, have an added importance to Canadian business because of the impact such policies have on the competitive viability of Canadian products and services, the ability of the internal market to absorb imports, and the country's balance of payments or international indebtedness. Decisions on tariff and nontariff barriers, subsidized export credits, preferential trade agreements, and so forth, which are clearly foreign economic policy matters, are affected directly by domestic economic policy and affect it in turn. Thus, in the business community, the perceived need to participate in and to influence foreign policy is an extrapolation of domestic affairs. It is in this area that Trudeau's dictum of foreign policy as an extension of national interest, with economic development being the pivotal concern, can be seen most clearly.

The economic community has always had a significant place in Canadian politics and foreign policy. From the days of early exploration and the opening up of the west and the north, both private and public capital and enterprise have directed the development and growth of Canadian society. Yet while in the early years of Confederation, the country's economic élites could deal individually with the government leaders, the rapid expansion of the Canadian economy has led to the emergence of associations to represent various interests within the business community. The close relationship among economic, political, and bureaucratic élites is no less close, but the connections are more numerous and complex, and the issues potentially conflictual. Furthermore, today there are counter-élites and counter-coalitions that compete for the allocation of a fundamentally scarce resource: a government policy decision favouring one party rather than others.[43]

The role of the business community in Canadian politics has provoked heated debate. In addition to the standard controversies about "who really governs" and the academic arguments about the applicability of Marxist, élite, and pluralist perspectives on state and society, these questions are of particular political relevance to the Canadian context because of substantial foreign direct investment and widespread foreign, primarily American, control.[44] The implication, of course, is that in a society whose economic infrastructure has substantial foreign involvement and whose economic leadership is part of the élite policy-making network, government decisions will further the interests of the *status quo,* implying continued foreign penetration. Hence foreign agents, insofar as they control economic factors, will influence government decisions. This argument assumes that such influence is at worst nefarious, certainly not in the interests of Canadian economic development, and at best a retardant to national independence.

Since the late 1960s, there have been consistent moves by the Canadian government to legislate constraints on further foreign penetration and to induce Canadianization of resource, manufacturing, and transportation industries.[45] These efforts have been paralleled by the growth of the government departments concerned with economic matters, both foreign and domestic, and the expansion of the number and variety of societal economic actors who wish to have their views considered as the government intervenes in shaping the Canadian economic structure.[46] In the realm of foreign policy, two types of business group actors stand out: those such as the Canadian Export Association that represent an aspect of the business community directly involved in and affected by international affairs in general, and organizations such as the Canada–Japan Trade Council that attempt to stimulate overall trade and investment between Canada and another particular country. In addition, many interest groups that represent sectors of the economy dominated by internal concerns will have occasion to participate in foreign policy debate, as will individual members of the Canadian corporate establishment.

It was not until after World War II—with the establishment and growth of the federal bureaucracy, a highly professional Department of External Affairs, and an independent and high-profile Canadian international involvement—that the business community at large found it useful to lobby the government on foreign policy matters. The first two major examples were the General Agreement on Tariffs and Trade (GATT) and the retention of the wartime Canadian Wheat Board.

The GATT talks, held in Geneva in 1947, established the trading regime of the OECD. It permitted a significant reduction in the costs of Canada's trade with its main partner, the United States; this was particularly important for the export of Canadian resources and agricultural products and the import of American manufactured goods. In his reflections on Canada's role in the establishment of the postwar international economic order, former Finance and External Affairs executive A.F.W. Plumptre noted:

> No country stood to gain more than Canada from the reduction of prewar and wartime trade barriers, from the establishment of codes of rules of international trade, payments and exchange rates, and from the introduction of more stable arrangements for international lending.[47]

In the negotiations, leading members of the business community—either directly or through sympathetic Cabinet members such as entrepreneur C.D. Howe and corporate lawyer Louis St. Laurent—advised the Canadian delegation and supported their efforts to move towards a multilateral, low-tariff trading regime. (The issue of protecting non-competitive Canadian industries primarily located in Ontario and Quebec would not become a major political problem until the following decade.)

The Canadian Federation of Agriculture, representing Canadian farmers, was especially concerned that the postwar economic restructuring would disrupt the buoyant wheat and produce market that had existed under the government's Canadian Wheat Board monopoly during the war years. Their concern, made more politically significant by the weakness of the Liberal Party in the west, contributed to the success of Minister of Agriculture James Gardiner's negotiations to continue the Wheat Board, ensuring market stability although at the cost of lower prices. At the same time, a long-term contract for export to Great Britain was extended.

Until the Diefenbaker years, the foreign policy agenda was dominated by East–West tensions, and Canadian policy retained its bipartisan quality because of the peace and security issues and the overwhelming Liberal majority under St. Laurent. Economic actors participated through the élite network that emerged from the wartime experiences. In contrast to later periods, a primary concern was the encouragement of foreign, especially American, investment in order to stimulate economic growth, employ new American technology, and guarantee access to the vast U.S. market. These were years of vigorous expansion.[48]

The Diefenbaker interlude brought new international economic realities as well as changes on the home front. The European Economic Community, created by the Treaty of Rome in 1957, established a new centre of economic influence; Japan was similarly on the rise. The old ties with Britain came under serious challenge as the relative importance of Canada–U.K. trade rapidly declined and Britain began to turn towards the EEC. And the United States government, facing the realization that its broadening overseas political, military, and foreign aid commitments were becoming permanent aspects of the international order, began to consider new methods to protect its domestic industries, especially since it needed to respond to its growing balance-of-payments deficit.

American attempts to curtail the external flow of its capital, beginning in 1963 as a response to this problem, necessarily concerned the Canadian government since they affected both access to American markets and the investment of American financial resources within Canada.[49] These policies, together with Walter Gordon's 1963 budget, exacerbated uncertainties over the Canadian economy and punctured the myth of central government planning, public service infallibility, and automatic economic growth under Liberal leadership, with American capital and technology.

The ensuing debate over American penetration rekindled the concern over nationalism and the Canadian identity. It also created a relatively new phenomenon in Canadian foreign policy: the emergence of a growing number of economic interest groups, intent on participating in the policy process and eroding the influence of the élite network, which had become less exclusive because of the expansion of the federal bureaucracy. Like other interest groups, business associations improved their competence by the use of professional staff and became a prominent new factor in the making and conduct of Canadian foreign policy.[50]

Since 1968, when economic issues began to be the central practical focus of much of the government's policy-making apparatus, economic interest groups have found a receptive ear in the halls of government. Indeed, new issues have even caused the government to request the establishment of interest groups for private-sector representation to tap their specialized knowledge, and to employ them for sounding out the acceptability of new positions.

Although little empirical research has been conducted on the growth and influence of the business community and economic interest groups on Canadian foreign policy, there is evidence to suggest that with expansion in variety and quantity has come an increase in importance.[51] Certainly, with the focus on economic development, all issues have been assessed in terms of both conventional foreign policy criteria and economic impact. Many new departments have been brought into the foreign policy process, each with a particular domestic constituency with both interests to service and expertise to employ. For example, the UN conferences on the law of the sea required participation from External Affairs, Energy, Mines, and Resources, Industry, Trade, and Commerce, Fisheries, and Environment, to name but the main departments. And their tasks were made more complex by the necessary consultations and presentations from associations representing major Canadian fishing, mining, and environmental groups, as well as individual economic actors such as Inco and Noranda.

More dramatic than the general inclusion of the business community in policy development has been the forceful intervention by representatives of business interests in particular policy issues with economic consequences. The Canadian Export Association and the Association of Consulting Engineers were vocal in the Jerusalem embassy affair and in the debate over possible federal legislation to combat Arab boycotts. The Mining Association of Canada has worked to encourage exports and to forward its position on the law of the sea. The Canadian Petroleum Association and the Independent Petroleum Association of Canada have also been involved with export policy and active in opposition to the National Energy Program.

As usual, there is little doubt about the increased participation and importance of these groups in the policy-making process, but there is only scant evidence by which to assess influence. For example, it is clear that in Prime Minister Clark's acceptance of the Stanfield Report, leading to the decision not to move the Canadian embassy in Israel from Tel Aviv to Jerusalem, the Canadian Export Association and the Association of Consulting Engineers, along with other corporate and financial actors, had substantial influence over the decision for the policy reversal. On the other hand, the protectionist, anti-GATT position of the Canadian Textiles Institute has been upheld, but this may be simply because potentially affected workers and their MPs are concentrated in Liberal centres in Quebec and Ontario. Similarly, in the policy reversals of 1981 and 1982 on leather and shoe imports, it is difficult to disentangle economic interest-group influence from the politics of the Liberal caucus.

Even with the lack of evidence on influence, other developments suggest the increased importance to the foreign policy process of the business community. Before the 1975 GATT meetings, the government initiated the establishment of a high-level consultative group representing the business community, the Canadian Business Group on Multilateral Trade Negotiations. And in 1977, again under the encouragement of the federal government, the Canadian Business and Industry International Advisory Committee (CBIIAC) was established as an umbrella organization for six major business and industry associations; its fundamental purpose is to co-ordinate the foreign policy interests of the economic community.[52] The importance of these groups lies in their institutional quality, their ongoing access to decision makers as a result of their professional expertise and the size of their constituencies, and the two-way flow of communications they maintain between government and their memberships, providing officials with a means to explore potential policy alternatives while the business sector is able to influence the parameters and potentially the choices of policy.[53]

Provincial Governments

The study of international relations has become complicated by the recognition that it is not always appropriate to assume that a state is a unified, rational actor where the central government expresses "the national interest" in its foreign policy. Our three perspectives on Canadian foreign policy clearly note the analytic importance of disaggregating the policy process into a number of components. For Canada, a federal system in which the sharing of powers continues to be the central political issue, policy making has become still more complex as the content of foreign policy has broadened to include functional interests of provincial governments.

Since Confederation, the provinces and the federal government have vacillated between co-operation, compromise, conciliation, confrontation, and conflict on matters of foreign policy. Among a long list of irritants, conscription, resource development and sales, foreign investment, import protection, export incentives, immigration, and representation at international meetings or on intergovernmental delegations have been prominent. These difficulties have been exacerbated by the coincidence of demographic and economic differences with provincial boundaries, so that arguments based on legal precedent have been confounded by a combination of tradition and changing socio-economic and political realities.[54]

The legacy of World War II included the perception, widely shared among the Liberal élite in Ottawa, that the provinces were not "rivals or antagonists, as they had been during the 1930s, but . . . irrelevancies to be stroked or prodded according to whether they had a Liberal government or not."[55] Except for the issue of a charter of human rights, raised during the United Nations founding conferences—which hinted at intervention in an area of provincial jurisdiction—and practical questions associated with the absorption of refugees from Europe, there were few federal-provincial foreign policy difficulties.[56] The government of Canada saw little need to include subordinate governments in foreign policy deliberations since the agenda was dominated by peace and security issues. To the extent that postwar economic recovery affected intergovernmental relations, foreign policy items such as trade, foreign investment, and market regulation remained under the control of Ottawa, and a strong central government with the confidence of the business community seemed necessary to prevent a postwar recession.

The Dominion-Provincial Conference on Reconstruction of 1945–1946 set the tone of federal-provincial relations for the next fifteen years. Unable to redesign the federal system, and with mounting and sundry prejudices emanating from the various regions, Ottawa and the provinces reverted to their prewar divisions of responsibility, although with a stronger, more interventionist central government that offered a wide range of social service packages, accepted or rejected at the discretion, and political cost, of each province. Foreign policy remained the responsibility of the central government and the élite Department of External Affairs.[57]

However, within a few years, the declining role of Great Britain and the overwhelming dominance of the United States in the economic fortunes of Canada became acutely clear through what was to become a central focus of foreign policy conflict between Ottawa and the provinces: discretionary management of natural resources. Two early examples were the development of the Columbia River in British

Columbia and the control of oil and natural gas, first discovered at Leduc in 1947. The presence of a third party, the United States, placed the issues not only in the context of federal–provincial relations but also in the equally contentious setting of North American continentalism. In these cases, the exploration, sale, taxation, and export of the resources and their products brought the provincial governments into direct conflict with officials in Ottawa. The resolutions also set uneasy precedents for the confrontations that were to occur over the next thirty years.[58] But these and most other foreign policy issues over the next decade or so remained secondary to the overwhelming preoccupation with security, defence, and the role of the United Nations in response to the perceived Soviet threat.

In the 1960s, federal–provincial tensions on issues relating to aspects of Canadian foreign policy escalated. Resources once again were of central concern. Control of offshore exploration and drilling rights was confounded by Canada's efforts to exercise sovereignty over Arctic waters and to extend its jurisdiction beyond the three-mile limit on fisheries and sea-bed mining. The Columbia River issue of earlier years remained unresolved, but pressure by the B.C. government relating to development plans for the Peace River and demands from Washington finally led to joint agreements between the three parties. The debate between Alberta and Ottawa over oil and natural gas became more vociferous and was joined by similar interests from B.C., Saskatchewan, the Maritimes, and the Yukon and Northwest Territories. Finally, and most significantly, the Quiet Revolution in Quebec began what was to become the most fundamental challenge to Canadian Confederation.

The defeat of the Union Nationale led by Maurice Duplessis in the Quebec elections of 1960 ended an era in Canadian politics. With the rise of Jean Lesage and the Quebec Liberals, a political and bureaucratic foundation was laid for the emergence of a distinct and articulate new Quebec presence. In the next two decades, the provincial governments of Lesage (Liberal), Daniel Johnson (Union Nationale), Robert Bourassa (Liberal), and René Lévesque (Parti Québécois) moved consistently towards challenging the very basis of Ottawa's legitimacy and power within the federal system. Foreign policy became increasingly important, at least symbolically, as Quebec attempted to gain international recognition, first of its special status within Confederation and then of its stature as an independent entity.

In October 1961, Quebec opened its *délégation générale* in Paris, beginning its increasingly aggressive overseas activity. Four years later, the special relationship between Quebec and France was furthered in the February 1965 signing of an educational *entente*, ratified by the exchange of diplomatic notes between Ottawa and Paris. That November, France and Canada signed an *accord cadre*, or umbrella agreement, which was meant to cover the interests of all provinces, but its purpose was soon undermined by another *entente* between France and Quebec, covering a broader set of understandings. This confirmed Pearson's worst fears; Quebec intended to bypass Ottawa in direct bilateral relations with France. Although Canadian displeasure was clearly manifest, President Charles de Gaulle and his representatives continued to acknowledge Quebec officials as if they were representatives of a sovereign state. In 1967, with Daniel Johnson's Union Nationale in power, de Gaulle made his famous visit to Montreal and, from a balcony at the Hôtel de Ville, concluded his speech to the crowds below: "Vive Montréal! Vive le Québec! Vive le Québec libre!"

Although Pearson had established the Royal Commission on Bilingualism and Biculturalism in 1963 as a sincere effort to respond to the emerging demands of the Canadian francophone community, numerous domestic problems seemed to undercut whatever credibility this effort had brought. Now, four years later, the Canadian government was faced with a nascent Quebec-based nationalist movement, with international diplomacy being employed as an instrument for its expression. In response, and in an effort to pre-empt Quebec, the Department of External Affairs that year established the Federal–Provincial Coordination Division. In the following months, Ottawa published two White Papers, *Federalism and International Relations* and *Federalism and International Conferences on Education.* These papers, while re-asserting federal primacy over Canada's external affairs, recognized the growing role of all the provinces in transboundary activities and hence the legitimate needs of provincial administrations to be informed, to be able to participate directly in areas of particular concern, to have a responsible voice in relevant negotiations, and to have access to appropriate personnel and organizational support in Ottawa. Within a short time, administrative structures were established in most provinces, usually located within departments of federal and intergovernmental affairs or of industry, trade, and economic development. Similarly, Ottawa appointed officials both at home and abroad (most importantly, in the United States and France) to assist the provinces and, of course, to provide the necessary linkage between provincial interests abroad and Ottawa's pre-eminent foreign affairs claims.[59]

In 1970, at the founding meeting in Niger of the Agency for Cultural and Technical Cooperation, Quebec unsuccessfully attempted to assert its right for independent status. Ottawa's ability to undercut this bid through the aid of the participating LDCs set a vital precedent for further federal–provincial understanding on representation at international conferences. By the 1972 meeting of the agency, Ottawa's policy of primacy in external affairs tempered by "pragmatic accommodation" allowed each province to assume the special status of a participating government within the unified Canadian delegation. Furthermore, where appropriate, such as in educational matters, heads of the

Canadian delegation could be provincial rather than federal officials. As one provincial government official noted, the 1970s were "the years of awakening" of the international involvement of the provinces.[60]

The first five years of the Trudeau administration witnessed the interaction of Ottawa's focus on economic development within the federal structure with the increasingly vocal demands of the provinces. Over the next few years, Quebec–Ottawa relations tended to dominate the debate, especially following the 1976 election of the Parti Québécois. The PQ victory caused concern not just in Ottawa but in the United States as well. Premier Lévesque travelled to New York and, in a speech to the Economic Club, tried to assure the American financial establishment of the reasonableness of his government and its policies. He claimed that sovereignty-association or Quebec independence from Canada would not undermine the credibility of its economic potential nor the stability of the long-term financial climate. Shortly thereafter, Prime Minister Trudeau addressed the United States Congress, attempting to reassert the pre-eminence of Ottawa and the cohesiveness and strength of Canadian federalism. The French government also became a central target of Quebec foreign policy, with reciprocal visits in 1977 between the French foreign minister and Lévesque; in an unprecedented event, the Quebec premier addressed the French National Assembly.

During this period the other provinces were neither acquiescent nor inactive in foreign policy. Official provincial missions abroad had grown from only six in 1960 to thirty-one in 1970 and thirty-nine by mid-1981; of these, seventeen were Quebec's (1980). Across the nation, provincial governments sponsored trade and cultural missions to a growing range of countries, received an equally broad representation of visiting foreign dignitaries, participated in important ongoing multilateral conferences, and ventured into new areas of interest, including joint federal–provincial foreign aid programs to Third World states.

The post-1973 focus on global scarcities of natural resources, especially fuels, contributed to an expansion of international activity in the western provinces. While Ontario continued to account for approximately 80 per cent of Canada's manufactured exports, the value of raw materials exports—including food, fuels, ores, and lumber—increased dramatically. The western provinces also became attractive centres for foreign investment in the resource extraction industries, in related capital-intensive high-technology processing facilities, and in land, service, and retail investment. One result was western disenchantment with Ottawa's constraints on foreign investment through the Foreign Investment Review Agency, its strict below-world-level pricing structure for oil and gas, its new taxation schemes on resource exports, and its legislation to Canadianize the energy industry, with disincentives for high-risk exploration.

The complexities in Canadian foreign policy became more evident over the 1970s. Provinces, individually or in coalition, often found their foreign policy interests to be at odds with Ottawa or with other provinces. For example, while Ontario and Quebec generally favoured protectionist measures to support their ailing manufacturing sectors, the western provinces, led by Alberta, condemned such anti-GATT policies, just as they argued against restrictions on foreign capital. Immigration policy became contentious as Quebec argued for a stance that would stimulate the growth of a francophone population. Provincial governments found it necessary to establish their own co-ordinative structures to deal both with federal–provincial transboundary issues and with foreign representatives. While disagreements occurred, the two levels of government more often than not found it mutually beneficial to co-operate, especially in the trade and investment areas, where a primary purpose of officials has been to facilitate economic expansion, often necessitating government support. In the expanding area of provincial relations with the LDCs, continuing government participation with the private-sector interests was often a prerequisite. This meant tangible contract support as well as symbolic ministerial visits with a joint private and public representation.[61]

The United States continued to be the dominant focus in long-term importance, because of standing agreements, such as the Auto Pact, and other fixed factors. Many of the more contentious Canadian–American disputes now involve areas of partial provincial jurisdiction, such as environmental pollutants, water resource management, and hydroelectric sales and transmission. The American market attracts more than half of Canadian direct investments abroad. The relative permanence of geographic contiguity and the resulting socio-economic interactions lead inevitably to day-to-day activities that require formal means of regulation—for example, transport taxes on transboundary commercial trucking and cable television regulation—as well as incentives, as in the tourist industries.[62]

Canadian foreign policy must increasingly take into account the interests of the provinces. Not only are legal requirements brought on by the expansion of international affairs into the realm of "low politics", but in a federal system, there are domestic political realities that must be considered—the most prominent one, but not the only important one, being Quebec. Most significant, however, are the linkages between Ottawa's focus on economic development, the expanding role of the provinces in this area, the relationship between domestic and external factors of production, and the socio-economic reality that neither Canada's economic wealth nor its means of productivity are equitably distributed across the country. These result in tensions between the provinces as well as with Ottawa on issues such as jurisdiction, trade, productivity, labour mobility, and boundary disputes, as well as on the broader concerns of multilateral agreements. Yet, while the provinces upgrade their administrative capacities to participate in the widening agenda of transboundary concerns, it is clear that the scope of most provincial activity and influence is constrained and directed by the interests of the federal government, usually complementary, and its far greater resources.

Conclusions

Over the past thirty-five years, societal factors have become increasingly salient in the making and conduct of Canadian foreign policy. Canada emerged from World War II as a major international actor concerned with the high politics of peace and security, with a foreign policy no longer linked directly to Westminster. Yet it remained supportive of British interests and sympathetic to its dilemma as a retiring power, while it focused on finding counterweights to a rising American hegemony. Canada thus pursued a foreign policy based on a reasonably clear definition of its role in the new world order and an understanding of its capacity to influence allies.

The wartime experience resulted in a massive mobilization of the country's productive capacity and the establishment of a sophisticated administrative apparatus to plan, co-ordinate, organize, and deliver the domestic output. Its legacy was a highly differentiated, increasingly specialized set of government and quasi-official institutions manned by an experienced, respected cadre of professionals; a Parliament and party structure with a reasonably clear perspective on the problems facing Canada and the world; and a Cabinet that intended to perpetuate Liberal domination. Under St. Laurent, it understood the intimate relationship between Canada's future prosperity and the fortunes of the international community.

Until the mid-1960s, American dominance of international politics provided moderate scope for the influence of societal actors on Canada's foreign policy. Except for Suez and the latter days of Vietnam, the American definition of world order and appropriate alliance behaviour complemented Canadian interests and reflected the sympathies of the electorate, thus giving Parliament and the political parties the central role of legitimating the policies of the government, with the support of the relevant associational interest groups. Where Canadian–American differences occurred, primarily on bilateral issues, these societal actors became crucial in the foreign policy process.

After 1965, with the gradual decline of American singular pre-eminence, the growing diffusion of the international system, and heightened concern over the strength of the federal structure, an articulated focus on Canadian economic development was formed. This focus, which judged foreign policy on criteria other than world order, global security, and ongoing multilateral commitments, also shifted the weight of societal influence away from traditional institutions to those that affected population mobilization and the factors of production directly—labour, economic interests—or indirectly—provinces, associational interest groups, and the media. In the categories provided by Stairs, this shift from pre-1965 activity was a movement from agenda setting, parameter setting, and limited policy setting to directly influencing policy and its implementation, or administration setting.

Although the evidence available makes it difficult to assess the extent of actual societal influence on Canadian foreign policy, it is clear that the degree of private-sector and provincial participation has shown a steady increase and that official Ottawa has been responsive to these interests. The general pattern of activity is indicative of a process of change from the behaviour predicted by the liberal-internationalist perspective to that inherent in the complex neo-realist perspective of Canadian foreign policy.

CHAPTER 6
THE GOVERNMENTAL PROCESS

The extensive changes in the external and domestic environments over the past three decades have posed a fundamental challenge to the traditional roles of responsible actors within the executive branch of the Canadian federal government. These actors have the tasks of calculating changing conditions at home and abroad, integrating the often conflicting requirements of the two spheres, and implementing the responses most appropriate to fulfilling domestic and international needs. In doing so, they may develop their own structures for perceiving outside events, determine their own framework of Canadian interests and values, and thus exercise considerable autonomy in defining the fundamental course of Canadian behaviour abroad.

The Three Theoretical Perspectives and the Governmental Process

In the liberal-internationalist perspective, these tasks of foreign policy are conducted with relative modesty and ease.[1] With clear imperatives in the external and domestic environments, and substantial compatibility between the two realms, actors in the state apparatus have an involvement that is more tactical than strategic. Attached to the pursuit of mediation, peacekeeping, and institution building, they focus on monitoring the international system, mobilizing their expertise in specialized, domestically related functional areas, and coping with the paradoxes inherent in securing incremental gains. Reinforced by a skepticism of formal planning and elaborate decision-making systems, state actors calculate the requirements of rational action individually within the broad yet powerful limits set by their internationalist vision of the world.

The liberal-internationalist perspective thus predicts a moderately salient, highly segmented, and broadly rational decision-making system within Ottawa. Because of the premium assigned to functional expertise and tactical flexibility, it suggests predominant influence for the Department of External Affairs career foreign service officers. It attributes a more routine involvement and less influence but a still substantial role to other foreign service and domestic departments whose functional resources are required, whose leaders are generally sympathetic, but whose expertise is not focused on the broad complexities of international politics themselves. This easy division of labour leaves the prime minister and his closest associates free to exercise a more passive oversight role, intervening to sustain the predominant internationalist predispositions of External Affairs only in those relatively rare instances when conflict arises.

More importantly, such co-ordination as is needed can be provided by the widespread consensus on the fundamental precepts of internationalism, the informal contact among senior officials in a small, intimate civil service, and their acquired skill in responding rapidly to crises. These factors in turn reduce interdepartmental conflicts and obviate the need for developed mechanisms for co-ordination or formal efforts to define the national interest.

From the perspective of peripheral dependence, the governmental process operates in a very different way. Indeed, proponents of this theory contend that the liberal-internationalist emphasis on an easy convergence of roles, pervasive interdepartmental harmony, and lack of strong central structures masks the existence of a weak and highly constrained state.[2] They see the internationalist consensus and procedural segmentation as permitting the state apparatus to function in the service of the dominant factions within society and their affiliates in dominant states abroad. The state itself has few resources and little expertise, no sophisticated capacity for research and planning, and an élite socialized into accepting the visions and legitimacy of its more powerful counterparts, first in the United Kingdom and later in the United States.

Such a state thus focuses on meeting the immediate needs of its powerful, if externally dependent, domestic "clients". Indeed, state actors accept the existing configuration of domestic interests, function in accordance with well-embedded standard operating procedures, pursue the goals of short-term efficiency, and largely neglect the broader structure of power through which their actions are constrained. As a result, the overall role of the executive branch in determining Canadian foreign policy is limited, passive, and unimaginative.

Within this framework, the perspective of peripheral dependence predicts that the primary influence resides in those organizations most directly dependent on dominant domestic constituencies. These are the former "foreign service" departments of Industry, Trade and Commerce (ITC) and Employment and Immigration (DEI), which focus on export promotion, industrial support, and labour supply. They also include the major domestically oriented departments—such as Agriculture, Fisheries, Transport, and to some extent National Defence—with specific societal interests to forward abroad. And they extend to Crown corporations serving as state traders, merchant bankers, and entrepreneurs (such as the Canadian Commercial Corporation, the Export Development Corporation, and Petro-Canada) and the regulatory agencies that rapidly develop supportive relationships with their domestic clients, such as the National Energy Board.

The support such bodies receive from interests within Canada and dominant powers abroad significantly reduces the ability of External Affairs to exert leadership or alter policy. Similarly, the prime minister and his associates are confined to passively arbitrating the frictions generated by the domestically oriented bureaucracy. Fundamental challenges come only from the occasional and largely unsuccessful efforts of isolated ministers, such as Walter Gordon, operating outside the prevailing policy framework. Most importantly, the operational orientation and dominance of the bureaucracy are sustained by the low levels of comprehensive co-ordination, resulting from an absence of research and planning capabilities and the *ad hoc* style of senior decision makers.

This portrait of a weak, dominated state is the antithesis of the government decision-making process predicted by a complex neo-realist perspective. This perspective points to a state apparatus with a highly salient impact on Canadian foreign policy, because of the intense debates conducted within it and the overall order imposed by strong central co-ordinative mechanisms.[3] It predicts a well-developed constellation of organizations pursuing their self-generated missions with considerable expansiveness, specificity, and skill. With no clear external imperatives, perceptual consensus, or domestic constituencies to define roles and engender harmony in the state apparatus, the intersection of these missions produces an intensely collective decision-making process, marked by competition and conflict. The need to control these cleavages and the vitality of the debate that produces them induce the government to act with autonomy to impose a transcending framework of values and priorities.

Domestically oriented organizations play a highly influential role. They develop a somewhat distinctive definition of their individual interests and the collective good, as well as an expertise in foreign affairs that enables them to forward these definitions in a wide range of policy spheres. A lesser influence is exercised by External Affairs, which, guided by its senior careerists, relies on diplomatic expertise to further its traditional mission of representation, reporting, and negotiation abroad. At the same time, less traditional components of External Affairs develop domestically linked missions and enter the interdepartmental debate. This induces the prime minister and his closest associates in central agencies, ministries of state, and major departments to develop an ongoing expertise and interest in foreign affairs and to regularly direct policy, rather than intermittently arbitrate it. Sustaining the centrality of this prime ministerial group is the powerful influence of formal, government-wide co-ordinative processes. Operating through the Cabinet and interdepartmental committee structure, comprehensive planning and budgeting exercises, and the ongoing leadership of central organizations, these processes permit not only a balancing of competing policy tendencies but also the autonomous creation and enforcement of an overriding national interest.[4]

During the past four decades, the Canadian government's foreign policy decision-making process has, in fact, conformed in some measure to the predictions of all three portraits. Yet it has experienced a steady shift away from the simple reflexive system predicted by peripheral dependence, through the dominant system of segmented harmony predicted by liberal internationalism, to the bureaucratic competition and overarching co-ordination predicted by complex neo-realism.

This progression has occurred during six distinct eras since 1948. The first era, covering the St. Laurent government from 1948 to 1957, was characterized by External Affairs leadership, segmented policy making, and informal co-ordination, as predicted by liberal internationalism. It also showed signs of the small, undifferentiated bureaucracy and perceptual constraints predicted by peripheral dependence, however. The second era, embracing the Diefenbaker regime of 1957 to 1963, saw a continuation of these patterns, supplemented by the emergence of major bureaucratic and ministerial cleavages over defence issues and the prominent, if unpredictable, involvement of a prime minister determined to impose new policy tendencies. In the third era, spanning the Pearson governments of 1963 to 1968, these cleavages were reinforced by the creation of new departments and broadened into ideologically based conflicts in the economic and politico-military spheres. These conflicts, in turn, spawned the first tentative efforts to impose overall order through prime ministerial advisers, a fixed Cabinet committee system, and a special foreign policy review.

It was during the Trudeau years that the most rapid shifts to a dominant complex neo-realist pattern occurred. In the fourth era, embracing the two Trudeau governments of 1968 to 1974, there was substantial expansion and institutionalization of these forces of competition and co-ordination, particularly before minority government in 1972. A proliferation of domestically oriented departments acquired expertise in international affairs. External Affairs came to embrace a broad range of domestic concerns. And the resulting interdepartmental conflict inspired and strengthened major attempts at overall co-ordination through a more structured Cabinet system, foreign policy planning exercises, more integrated foreign operations management and budgeting, and the exercise of greater leadership by External Affairs. The fifth period, covering the Trudeau and Clark governments of 1974 to 1980, strengthened this trend as External Affairs sought, with some success, to operate as a modern central policy agency on behalf of the prime minister. Finally, the sixth period, beginning with the return of Trudeau as prime minister in 1980, saw the clear dominance of a complex neo-realist approach. The major expansion and senior-level reinforcement of External Affairs in 1982 enabled it to act as a ministry of state for foreign affairs on behalf of the entire Cabinet, and to define and enforce the all-embracing conception of the Canadian national interest that this task demanded.

The Era of Harmonious Segmentation, 1948–1957

The foreign policy decision-making system that prevailed in Ottawa during the first postwar period was structured, in accordance with liberal-internationalist and some peripheral-dependence predictions, on three foundations.[5] These were routine executive-branch leadership, a comfortable segmentation of the major departments involved in foreign affairs, and highly informal co-ordination because of consensus among the actors most directly concerned. The result was a moderately salient role for the state apparatus, particularly when no international crises loomed.

During this era, the scars of the wartime conscription period and the imperatives of the cold war imposed deep constraints on the ability of the executive branch to manoeuvre at will in the foreign policy field. But the international power and commitment of the United States were now assured. Canada was tranquil and prosperous at home, and the Liberal government had both a secure electoral majority and a budgetary surplus. Thus, the state had considerable freedom to promote the internationalist orientation that Louis St. Laurent had proclaimed as orthodoxy in his 1947 Gray Lecture.

In this quest, the government functioned on the basis of an easy division of labour. External Affairs exercised unchallenged leadership over the "high" politics of peace and security. Other departments, notably ITC, Finance, and National Defence, assumed the predominant roles on internationally related matters within their functional spheres. The prime minister's role was secondary, as was demonstrated when a tightly knit group within DEA repudiated Mackenzie King's lingering isolationist instincts in 1947.

At the top of this edifice stood Prime Minister Louis St. Laurent. As secretary of state for external affairs from 1946 to 1948, St. Laurent had helped craft the early internationalist initiatives of the postwar era. This attachment to internationalism was first demonstrated in his successful threat of resignation to ensure Canada's fulfillment of its responsibilities on the United Nations Temporary Commission on Korea in 1947.[6] It continued in his Gray Lecture initiative, his enthusiasm for a nonmilitary North Atlantic Treaty, and his reservations over France's role in Indochina.

As the dominant francophone minister and a central participant in the 1944 conscription crisis, St. Laurent was much more reserved on issues that raised the spectre of large-scale commitments of Canadian ground forces to protracted conflict abroad, as in the Korean crisis in 1950. In most cases, however, his involvement was restrained by his preference for giving major ministers autonomy in their spheres and by his trust of professional civil servants. Moreover, as Mackenzie King's foreign minister, he had endured the discomforts of a relationship in which the prime minister left little room for independent manoeuvre. He had also developed, through daily contact with Undersecretary Lester Pearson and other senior officials in External, a considerable understanding of External's imperatives and confidence in its judgements.

St. Laurent's restraint gave Lester Pearson, now his own foreign minister, and his department undisputed leadership in the politico-military realm, as liberal internationalism predicts. External initiated the concept of the North Atlantic Pact, struggled to make NATO more than a mere military alliance, and devised and implemented the United Nations Emergency Force. Within this sphere, External tended to prevail against the conservatism of others in the occasional instances of interdepartmental conflict. Pearson successfully opposed older ministers and National Defence to secure Canadian participation in Korean peacekeeping and a Canadian supervisory presence in Vietnam in 1954. Indeed, Pearson's autonomy was limited only by the self-imposed restraints of maintaining his harmonious relationship with St. Laurent and keeping him fully informed in advance of major initiatives, as in the Suez crisis of 1956. The expanse of Pearson's influence was visible in his ability to moderate or even overturn St. Laurent's personal preference, notably over the Suez crisis and French role in Indochina.

In large measure, Lester Pearson's primacy was sustained by the experienced personnel, internal cohesion, and operational ethos of his department.[7] As the pre-eminent department in Ottawa, External had the most talented officials in the public service, with the possible exception of those at Finance. There were generalists like Norman Robertson, who had an intricate knowledge of trade and related economic affairs, and distinguished soldier-statesmen like Generals A.G.L. MacNaughton, Maurice Pope, E.L.M. Burns, and Victor Odlum to provide leadership in the military realm.

At senior levels of the department, creativity and cohesion were fostered by fluid supervisory arrangements. At lower levels, External, like its bureaucratic competitors, operated a highly cohesive organization in which matters were circulated rapidly and extensively among members and conflicts were quickly resolved. The department was relatively small and most of its officers came from similar social backgrounds, which reduced disparity of viewpoint and bureaucratic competition for involvement in priority issues. The harmony and overall consistency of Canadian policy was further enhanced by rapid rotation within the department and the encouragement of generalist career patterns. Although philosophic differences among conservative, liberal-moderate, and left-liberal tendencies existed within the department, the competition among them served to strengthen the intellectual sophistication and political appeal of departmental proposals.[8]

Of equal importance in inducing cohesion and defining organizational purpose was a common conception of External's proper policy concerns. It defined Canada as a middle power with sufficient capability to play a significant part in the international tasks of creating a new global order and defending Western values within it. With these priorities, the maintenance of international peace and multilateral institutions, through classic and coalition diplomacy, were the most important contributions a middle power could make. Operating as a mature foreign office focused on the challenges of global diplomacy, External thus played the major part in producing Canada's considerable successes in the multilateral security realm. As Ottawa's élite department, it exercised a dominant voice on the central issues that arose to disturb Canada's normal, more domestic relations with the United States, seldom consulting other departments beyond the core group of National Defence, Trade and Commerce, and Finance, and retaining the primary voice within this group. Interdepartmental consultation focused on the United Nations and defence-related subjects, and External used committees to mobilize the specialized advice of others and give them central policy direction.

A major beneficiary of this consultative process, and a general source of support for External's initiatives, was DEA's slightly junior ally, the Department of National Defence (DND). Brooke Claxton, the minister from 1948 to 1954, was a tacit political rival of Pearson who periodically contested the allocation of budgetary resources and the definition of priorities for Canadian overseas involvement. Yet his lack of interest in the External Affairs portfolio, his acquaintance with its work as acting minister in Pearson's absence, and his similar convictions about international affairs produced a close, friendly relationship between the two. Appointed by King to reduce military influence and budgets in the postwar era, and endowed with St. Laurent's complete confidence, the diligent Claxton did not hesitate to challenge his military advisers at the same time as he forwarded their requests for advanced weaponry and deferred to their expertise in military planning in the technological age.

Their recommendations to him were usually channelled via the Chiefs of Staff Committee, composed of officers and civilians from DND and representatives of the Privy Council Office, External Affairs, Defence Production, and Finance. The influential role of Air Force officers and scientists within this body and subordinate structures tended to generate military and ministerial perspectives that highlighted the North American region and the air defence task as the dominant elements of Canadian security, as the perspective of peripheral dependence suggests. Thus, whereas DND would reluctantly defer to External on low-cost involvements beyond Europe and jointly determine policy with it for the North Atlantic, it jealously guarded its primacy in matters within the continent and in Canada itself. DND prepared the 1950–1951 rearmament program, successfully warded off C. D. Howe's concerns about the CF-100, initiated and supported the expanding Avro Arrow project, refused External's 1955 request for a joint evaluation of North American security in the nuclear-missile age, and rejected DEA's proposal to improve NATO cohesion by inviting European forces to assume operational tasks in Canada's northern radar networks.[9]

Outside politico-military affairs, policy formulation was left largely to the other major departments, as External rapidly withdrew from its prewar participation in domestic policy. These trends were particularly pronounced in economic relations with the United States. Here, as liberal internationalism predicts, the bilateral interchange was seen as a separate and special sphere, linked to foreign policy for two purposes only: building continental resources for the large struggle with the Soviet Union, and creating a reservoir of goodwill for constraining the global assertiveness of the United States.

With External's interest intermittent and its involvement marginal, foreign economic policy was the preserve of the two major departments, Trade and Commerce and Finance. As minister of trade and commerce throughout the period and minister of defence production from April 1951 to June 1957, C.D. Howe had a legitimate interest in military-related areas, and he deferred automatically neither to DND requests nor to policy that lay in a colleague's realm.[10] However, Howe's reservations on such fundamental issues as the Arrow development and Korean peacekeeping were tentatively advanced and often circumscribed.

Much the same was true of Finance. In keeping with its statutory responsibilities for the tariff, its close relationship with the Bank of Canada, and the priorities of its Treasury Board Secretariat, it concentrated on multilateral trade issues, monetary affairs, and maintaining diplomatic, defence, and other expenditures within the overall fiscal framework. In the politico-military sphere, Douglas Abbott, minister from 1948 to 1954, and later Walter Harris functioned largely as domestic political ministers, remaining uninvolved in such diplomatic ventures as the quest for a North Atlantic Pact.

Sustaining the broad consensus among ministers and helping to solve their occasional differences with relative ease was a well-developed structure of consultation. This structure was grounded in a pattern of lead responsibilities within Cabinet, informal discussions on critical matters, and a network of interlocking committees and personal relationships at the Cabinet level and below. Crisis issues such as Canada's role in the United Nations Temporary Commission on Korea and in Korean and Suez peacekeeping were examined in informal, individual, advance discussions among the few ministers most directly concerned, with full Cabinet scrutiny given at regular intervals.

Less urgent matters were normally dealt with and developed through an extensive set of interdepartmental committees. In the politico-military sphere, the major body was the Cabinet Defence Committee, formed in August 1945. Some ongoing restraint on military perspectives was also imposed by the deputy ministerial-level Panel on Economic Aspects of Defence, a body that had become, by 1955, the primary interdepartmental forum for all defence questions. At more junior levels, the consultative mechanisms were increasingly informal, harmonious, and restricted to the DEA–DND core. These mechanisms included the Chiefs of Staff Committee and a well-developed network of informal personal and social contacts among DEA and DND professionals at all levels.[11]

Of much greater importance in ensuring effective, harmonious co-ordination and prescribing the framework within which consensus was to be achieved were the informal dynamics of a small, intensely interlocked bureaucracy. Effective power in Ottawa resided with a small group of individuals surrounding the half-dozen or so major Cabinet ministers; it was diffused through a "sub-Cabinet" of no more than three dozen members—senior officials in the Privy Council Office, External Affairs, National Defence, Finance, Trade and Commerce, the Bank of Canada, and Transport—to a bureaucratic élite of no more than two hundred people.[12] Their intuitive appreciation of one another's policy perspectives and of the limits on the collective good defined by their long-serving ministers fostered the degree of co-ordination that liberal internationalism predicts, but within some of the confines pointed to by peripheral dependence.

Beyond ongoing discussion in such interdepartmental forums and interpersonal relationships, the mechanisms to ensure co-ordination were virtually nonexistent. The framework set by St. Laurent's Gray Lecture and the antipathy towards formal policy review exercises obviated the need and the incentive to engage in any long-range, analytical foreign policy planning.[13] A steadily expanding foreign service and the principle of managerial autonomy in departments eliminated the need to chart broader directions and make costly interdepartmental trade-offs in allocating money and manpower for Canadian operations abroad.[14] And External's strong sense of confidence in its internationalist mission inhibited the tendency for major policy re-evaluations within departmental channels. As a result, the co-ordination of Canada's foreign policy was based on three quite fluid factors: the informal contacts within a small, permanent bureaucracy, the ability of its elected leaders to respond quickly to crises, and the belief of both groups in a traditional view of Canada's international behaviour. In short, while the relevance of various actors in the ongoing policy-making process conformed reasonably well to the predictions of liberal internationalism, the forms of overall co-ordination suggested some patterns of peripheral dependence.

The Era of Competitive Fragmentation, 1957–1963

During the six years of Progressive Conservative government under John Diefenbaker, the internal harmony and overall consistency that had prevailed in the St. Laurent era were severely eroded.[15] In considerable measure, this erosion could be attributed to a highly ambiguous external environment. Reductions in East–West tensions encouraged new executive branch initiatives in fields such as disarmament and decolonization, even as sudden eruptions of Soviet intrusiveness, as in Berlin in 1960 and Cuba in 1962, imposed the old constraints in more rigid form. Friction among departments and ministers increased, with primacy passing unevenly among the global disarmament initiatives favoured by External, the security and Europe-oriented concerns of Defence, and, at a lower level, the domestic imperatives advanced by the major economic departments.

Reinforcing this instability was a strong-minded prime minister. Before John Diefenbaker entered the office of prime minister, he had authored international proposals for United Nations peacekeeping forces, given strong support to the United Nations and NATO, and devoted himself to reinforcing Canada's ties with the United Kingdom and the Commonwealth, while reducing those with the United States. At the same time, his intensely political character and western Canadian power base, his government's minority status in 1957 and 1962–1963, and his personal responsibility for the massive majority in between, led him to calculate foreign policy for the prevailing domestic political effect. Moreover, his long years in opposition had bred in him a suspicion of civil servants, particularly in such presumed Liberal enclaves as External Affairs and Trade and Commerce.

As a result the prime minister's role in these years shifted towards the patterns predicted by both the complex neo-realist and the liberal-internationalist perspectives. At the outset of his government, John Diefenbaker took the leading role in the definition and announcement of major foreign policy initiatives. It was he who publicly reinterpreted Secretary of State for External Affairs Sidney Smith's statement of Conservative policy on Suez at Smith's first press conference in 1957. He defined and declared the government's intention to divert 15 per cent of Canadian trade from the United States to the United Kingdom; he announced himself the decision to retain Canadian forces in Europe. The acceptance of the Bomarc missile and the cancellation of the Arrow were decisions made and presented by Diefenbaker, albeit on the basis of considerable military advice. Yet he approved within an hour a proposal forwarded by Chief of Staff General Charles Foulkes through Defence

Minister George Pearkes to accept NORAD and, on the advice of others, rejected a tentative British proposal for a bilateral free trade arrangement with Canada.

The domestic political controversy aroused by the NORAD and Arrow decisions, combined with Diefenbaker's concern that he had been "stampeded" on the first and left uninformed of the political and economic dimensions of the second, reinforced his tendency to distrust his civil service advisers.[16] Therefore he took the initiative, with the support of Clerk of the Privy Council Robert Bryce, in opposing South Africa's continuing membership in the Commonwealth; he defined, despite the reluctance of External Affairs, Canada's opposition to British membership in the European Economic Community; he formulated Canada's firm response to Soviet moves on Berlin; and he engaged in a vigorous public condemnation of the Soviet Union on behalf of its persecuted minorities. Inspired by his deteriorating public relationship with U.S. President John Kennedy, and supported by the antinuclear sentiments held by the secretary and the undersecretary of external affairs, he showed Canada to be reluctant to support American behaviour in the Cuban missile crisis of 1962 and opposed the introduction of nuclear weapons into Canada until the fall of his government in February 1963.[17]

John Diefenbaker's personal convictions and political suspicions left little room for a distinctive, autonomous role for his foreign ministers or the department they headed. Diefenbaker chose to hold the External Affairs portfolio himself for two brief periods, and his first secretary of state for external affairs, Sidney Smith, lacked experience in government, Parliament, and international affairs. Undersecretary Norman Robertson, consumed with the task of educating his minister and under suspicion of harbouring Liberal sympathies, had no direct communication with the prime minister. He was forced to rely on the access and influence of his close contacts among senior officials in the Privy Council Office and elsewhere.[18]

The appointment to External Affairs in June 1959 of Howard Green—a parliamentary veteran, trustworthy friend of the prime minister, and equally devoted supporter of the British Commonwealth—combined with Diefenbaker's easing suspicions of Pearson's old department and Green's defence of his officials to restore External Affairs to some measure of its former influence. But its influence held mostly when its advice reflected and supported the predilections of Diefenbaker himself. Its major distinctive role, and one that converged nicely with Diefenbaker's electoral concerns, emanated from Green's passionate, if rather naive, commitment to disarmament.

Under Robertson's guidance, DEA succeeded in securing effective control of a new interdepartmental intelligence policy committee, in encouraging a reluctant Cabinet to authorize Canadian participation in the UN Congo peacekeeping force in 1960, and in drafting Diefenbaker's proposal for an international inspection force during the early stages of the Cuban missile crisis in 1962. Howard Green was also able to convince the prime minister that the acquisition of U.S.-built F-101 interceptors through a swap of Canadian CL-44s would create major political problems at home. With Robertson, he was able to hold up Cabinet approval of a DND draft agreement for Canadian acceptance of nuclear weapons, to counter pressure from DND and External's defence liaison divisions for interdepartmental agreement on the issue and for Cabinet consideration of it, and to sustain John Diefenbaker's reluctance to accept the weaponry until the end.

As the disarmament-oriented influence of External increased, the defence-oriented views of National Defence receded in persuasiveness and were expressed increasingly outside the overall policy framework. The department's first minister, Major-General George Pearkes, had been selected on the basis of his admirable military record, his support for Diefenbaker at the 1948 and 1956 leadership conventions, and his ability to control the military establishment. During Pearkes's leadership, Diefenbaker readily accepted DND proposals, including those that clearly reflected DND's pronuclear views. When Pearkes retired in 1960, the portfolio was given to Douglas Harkness, a competent administrator whose forthright style, Diefenbaker calculated, would be valuable in curtailing the enthusiasms of senior Defence officers. However, Harkness's readiness to accept the advice and adopt the views of his officers led him to become a strong advocate of the acquisition of nuclear weapons for the forces, to stretch the limits of authority by unilaterally allowing Canadian forces to go on alert in the Cuban missile crisis, and eventually, along with Associate Defence Minister Pierre Sévigny, to resign in February 1963 over Diefenbaker's refusal to accept nuclear weapons.

These tensions among ministers and departments over disarmament versus defence were compounded by the growing claims of domestic economic considerations and departments, both on defence resources and on the framework of foreign policy as a whole. The recession of the late 1950s and the austerity program of 1962 led members of the Cabinet to urge a quick decision on the Arrow and the acquisition of less expensive, nuclear-equipped, American replacements, which would free funds for civilian tasks at home. Throughout this period, Trade and Commerce—particularly after Deputy Minister Mitchell Sharp's resignation and George Hees's assumption of the portfolio—focused, with Diefenbaker's approval, on promoting Canadian trade with the United Kingdom, Latin America, and other overseas markets and on forging direct arrangements with counterparts in the U.S. on bilateral trade problems. Finance was largely left alone to impose constraints on Canadian representation and aid programs abroad, to deal with slow economic growth and government austerity, and to manage the exchange crisis with the United States in 1962.

In the Diefenbaker years, the decline of the traditional internationalist consensus, the tension between defence and disarmament, and the thrust away from a close relationship with the United States presented the Conservatives with a major problem: the need to actively promote government-wide foreign policy co-ordination. Given John Diefenbaker's distrust of officialdom and his penchant for personal, politically oriented decision making, this need was left to a Cabinet process and attendant interdepartmental network that operated with much less reliability than in the past. John Diefenbaker chose not to involve his Cabinet in such major decisions as NORAD and South Africa's withdrawal from the Commonwealth, rotated his major ministers far more frequently than in the past, and relied for policy advice within the Privy Council Office only on Robert Bryce and Basil Robinson. At senior levels of the civil service, the traditional undercabinet group became somewhat less cohesive. A 50 per cent growth in the civil service since the early 1950s, the creation of new institutions with specific interests, and a commensurate growth in stratification and intrabureaucratic conflicts severely strained the easy relationships of the earlier era. The task of forging a new consensus became dependent on the leadership of an increasingly isolated prime minister. In short, while the liberal-internationalist pattern of decision making established during the St. Laurent era continued to dominate, it was being challenged by two forces: an ongoing policy-making process more closely resembling the predictions of complex neo-realism, particularly in the new salience of the prime minister and the new conflict among ministers and departments below him, and a peripheral-dependence pattern of overall co-ordination, as prime ministerial co-ordination proved inadequate to overcoming DND's American-support demands in the nuclear weapons controversy of 1963.

The Era of Ideological Cleavage and Domestication, 1963–1968

The five years of Lester Pearson's Liberal regime witnessed an immediate attempt to impose coherence.[19] This partly successful attempt brought patterns of overall co-ordination—and hence the salience, scope, and sensitivity of the total government process—closer to the predictions of complex neo-realism, although a substantial gap remained. In large part, intensified trends towards the internal conflict but overall order predicted by complex neo-realism reflected the growing impatience at home and abroad with the Canadian role in the UN and NATO and the American government's behaviour in the world at large, especially in Vietnam.

These conditions enhanced the emergence of more deeply rooted ideological cleavages at the ministerial and senior official level over

Canada's international economic relationships and the country's traditional relationship with the United States in NORAD, NATO, and the conflict in Indochina. Although new co-ordinative processes began to arise at the Cabinet level, the prime minister's own frustrating preoccupations with the incessant Quebec dilemma made the adjustment to domestic concerns and the creation of a renewed foreign policy consensus an uneven, troubled, and uncompleted process. A rapidly growing bureaucracy, with a plethora of new domestically linked departments, made the task even more difficult.

Prime Minister Lester Pearson was propelled into a major role in foreign policy deliberations by the deference paid by his foreign counterparts and domestic colleagues to his expertise in international affairs, his 1963 electoral promises, and the need to provide allies with a reassurance of Canada's reliability after the Diefenbaker government's débâcle. However, the incessant demands of parliamentary management and electioneering, the increasingly strident challenges from Quebec City, the escalation of the Vietnam conflict, and his own experience in the St. Laurent government circumscribed Pearson's role at the same time. This was particularly true after the disappointing return of minority government in the 1965 election, which heightened Pearson's distaste for the burdens of office and his preoccupation with retirement.

In the politico-military sphere, Pearson tended to leave the initiation and determination of policy to his major ministers, confining his attention to the summit diplomacy, peacekeeping initiatives, and crisis mediation at which he excelled. He began his term by implementing his election pledge to acquire nuclear weapons and stabilizing the Canadian–American relationship through a visit with President Kennedy. With the aid of his policy adviser Tom Kent, he gave priority to peacekeeping and, among other things, resisted defence minister Paul Hellyer's demands for large increases in defence expenditure in formulating the defence White Paper of 1964.[20] After 1965, much of his time was spent mediating the growing disagreements among prospective claimants to his leadership within the Cabinet.

On the broader policy issues, Pearson's role was less pronounced.[21] Although he overrode foreign minister Paul Martin to call publicly for a pause in American bombing of North Vietnam in 1965, he issued only cautions against Martin's enthusiasm for mediatory efforts in Vietnam. Only late in the day did he rebuke Walter Gordon, in defence of the principle of Cabinet solidarity, after Gordon's public criticism of American involvement in 1967. Moreover, despite his private and public reservations about Canada's NATO involvement, he deferred to Paul Martin's opposition to his suggestions for a review of Canadian military participation in NATO and to Paul Hellyer's reluctance to delay implementation of the third stage of armed forces unification and renewal of the NORAD agreement. He commissioned the Robertson review of Canada's overall foreign policy, amid the hesitations of External Affairs, only in 1967.

Pearson's involvement in the determination of foreign economic policy was similarly circumscribed.[22] Although not personally committed to economic nationalist thinking, he reviewed Walter Gordon's 1963 budget containing such measures several times, sustained his finance minister against the objections of the governor of the Bank of Canada, Louis Rasminsky, and allowed Walter Gordon to continue in the portfolio despite the severe criticism the budget attracted. In the trade arena, he named a senior External Affairs official, Norman Robertson, as co-ordinator for the Kennedy Round of GATT negotiations, as a neutral between the opposing views of Finance and Industry, Trade and Commerce; Pearson kept a close watch on the bargaining as chairman of a special Cabinet committee and ultimately supported the position that his co-ordinator produced. Pearson's personal interest in the economic area was registered in his personal contacts with Lyndon Johnson to facilitate the conclusion of the Canada–U.S. automotive agreement, his authorization of an effort to secure an exemption for Canada from U.S. restrictions on capital outflows in 1963 and 1968, and his minor interest in the reform of the international monetary system in 1965.

Prime ministerial leadership was reserved pre-eminently, as complex neo-realism implies, for asserting Ottawa's control over foreign policy in the face of the growing relationship between Quebec and France.[23] Under Pearson's initiative, the new Liberal Cabinet decided that priority in Canada's external affairs must be given to strengthening the close ties that were developing with France. In fulfillment of this commitment, he and Martin visited de Gaulle in Paris in 1964, expanded Canadian activities with France, began to articulate Gaullist conceptions of NATO's structure, and directed Canadian aid towards the francophone world. By 1965 accumulating frictions propelled Pearson into a more intense, crisis-oriented involvement, as he produced a compromise policy on the sale of Canadian uranium to France, defined Canada's vigorous opposition to French withdrawal from the military component of NATO in 1966, and, with personal outrage, directed a Canadian protest against France's refusal to receive visits from Canadian representatives. His close involvement in defining the limits of Quebec's international presence and its flourishing relationship with France culminated in 1967. Pearson insisted upon a centennial year visit by de Gaulle to Ottawa as well as to Quebec City. He assumed personal responsibility through the Prime Minister's Office for the arrangements of the visit. And finally, over the objections of Paul Martin and Jules Léger, he produced the strong response to de Gaulle's declaration of support for a free Quebec.

In spite of his active involvement in these areas, Pearson left Secretary of State for External Affairs Paul Martin generally free to assert leadership in the politico-military sphere. Martin's widespread experience in several government departments, his personal concern for reconciling French and English communities within Canada, and the intensification of his quest for the party leadership in 1967 and 1968 led him during his five years in the portfolio to expand the boundaries of his mandate and policy interests to incorporate a broader range of the societal dimensions of Canadian policy.

The increased salience of societal considerations points to patterns of complex neo-realism, which became stronger because of developments within DEA. The appointment of Marcel Cadieux as undersecretary in 1964, as a francophone with a firm belief in strong federal government, and the formidable intellectual assistance of the similarly inclined director of the legal division, Allan Gotlieb, gave External a major domestically based role in countering Quebec's assertions of a separate presence abroad. Pearson's example and Martin's style, combined with senior-level appointments, tended to enshrine the pursuit of mediatory initiatives overseas as the department's dominant mission. Yet the addition of new divisions for cultural affairs, relations with francophone states, and federal–provincial co-ordination in 1966 and 1967, as well as the emphasis on recruiting francophone officers, began to broaden its concerns and re-orient its interests to the more specific challenges at home.[24]

With these assets, Paul Martin and his department started out by dominating daily policy making within the politico-military sphere, following the old liberal-internationalist trends. This was most notable on NATO-related questions and in peacekeeping involvements in Cyprus, Vietnam, and the Middle East. Martin overrode Pearson's doubts about mediation in Vietnam, his desire for an early NATO review, and his reluctance, shared by the clerk of the Privy Council, Gordon Robertson, to have Canada accept membership on the United Nations Security Council in 1966. Martin was equally successful in his relationship with DND, denying its requests for a significant reduction of peacekeeping forces in 1966. However, his propensity to urge accommodating responses to de Gaulle's slights led to a slow loss of control over policy in this most critical area, as registered in his failure to secure a mild statement from Pearson in response to de Gaulle's declaration on a free Quebec. And as the Pearson government progressed, External's policies in all spheres were increasingly subject to the criticisms of other ministers.

One vigorous claimant to involvement in policy formulation was defence minister Paul Hellyer. Believing that undue military influence had determined policy objectives in the past, Hellyer suspended all major purchases pending a DND review of defence policy when he entered office. After Cabinet's approval of the review's recommendations, he undertook an extensive reorganization of the armed forces, over the opposition of senior members of the defence staff and the growing reservations of Pearson himself. Within his department, where integration increased the influence of civilian officials, Hellyer was equally forceful, particularly in the 1965 purchase of the CF-5 ground support aircraft in place of a state-of-the-art interceptor.

A more far-reaching challenge came from Walter Gordon, minister of finance from April 1963 to December 1965 and leader of a left-wing coalition in Cabinet and caucus. Including Allan MacEachen, Edgar Benson, and, after 1965, Jean Marchand, Gérard Pelletier, and Pierre Trudeau, this coalition favoured redirecting Canadian defence away from its close association with the United States in NATO and NORAD and transferring defence resources to foster special welfare objectives at home.[25] Its major energies were devoted to arresting Quebec's movement towards an autonomous presence abroad and furthering Canadian economic independence from the United States. This last objective regularly pitted the leading advocate of economic nationalism against senior officials in the major economic departments. These conflicts arose with increasing regularity and sharpness over a number of issues, from the 1963 budget, multilateral trade policy, the tax status of *Time* and *Reader's Digest,* and the Mercantile Bank take-over attempt, to Canada's exemption from U.S. curtailments on the outflow of American capital in 1968, exchange rate policy, and the establishment of a broad policy on direct foreign investment in 1967.

The intensity of these cleavages was increased by the fact that there was little opportunity for conflicting perspectives to be properly reconciled and formed into unified policy during Cabinet discussions. Attempts were made by both prime minister and Cabinet. The major signs were the appointment of Tom Kent as a policy adviser to the prime minister, the work of Jean Beetz and Marc Lalonde on constitutional questions in the Prime Minister's Office, the formation in 1964 of nine Cabinet committees (including committees for external affairs and for defence), and the establishment of *ad hoc* committees. Yet the decline in Pearson's authority as leader after 1965 led to an increasing disorder in Cabinet business, a focus on reacting to crisis issues, and the absence of broad defence and foreign policy reviews, except on NORAD.

These trends were exacerbated by the tendency of Paul Martin to resolve all contentious issues in private discussion with the prime minister and only then bring them to Cabinet for ritual scrutiny and confirmation. Similarly, Paul Hellyer discussed defence issues with Pearson alone and negotiated an arrangement with Walter Gordon that minimized Treasury Board involvement in DND's budgetary affairs.[26] Thus the Cabinet Defence Committee focused only on major equipment purchases and administrative questions. In the government's latter years, the only major politico-military issue to be scrutinized in detail at the Cabinet level was the renewal of NORAD in 1967. A similar reliance on direct ministerial–prime ministerial contacts prevailed in the economic field, notwithstanding the tradition of consultation among Finance, Industry, Trade and Commerce, External Affairs, the Bank of Canada, and Agriculture.

Moreover, the stable consultative procedures at the official level, which liberal internationalism predicts, were significantly reduced by a rapidly growing bureaucracy and the creation of new departments with focused missions, precise demands, and domestic constituencies (notably Industry in 1963, Manpower and Immigration in 1966, and Energy, Mines and Resources in the same year). These developments eroded the coherence of Ottawa's tightly knit economic community and challenged major departments in the defence and diplomatic spheres. To be sure, the establishment of a Cabinet committee and task force on foreign investment and the initiation of the Robertson review towards the end of the Pearson government marked a move towards special policy planning exercises in particular areas.[27] Yet these initiatives were authorized with considerable reluctance, conducted in some secrecy, and developed and dealt with at one remove from the government's central decision-making process. In short, while both ongoing policy making and overall co-ordination moved closer to the predictions of complex neo-realism, in co-ordination especially the inherited liberal-internationalist patterns largely remained dominant.

The Era of Collective Policy Making and the National Interest, 1968–1974

The first fundamental effort to impose policy-making and co-ordinative patterns conforming to complex neo-realism came with the election of the Liberal government of Pierre Trudeau. Particularly during its first four years in office, the decline of the global pre-eminence of the U.S., its detachment from its newly assertive allies, and its cultivation of détente with the Communist world combined with Pierre Trudeau's dynamic leadership and secure parliamentary majority to provide an enhanced opportunity for the Canadian government to take a more salient and broader role.[28] It moved quickly to define new policy directions in considerable detail and to develop, as the mainspring of this effort, a precise, integrated conception of Canada's distinctive national interests. This process was sustained by the proliferation of new departments and bureaus with organized expertise in international affairs. It was also generated by the difficult reorientation of External Affairs from an exclusive pre-eminence in politico-military affairs to an expansive if variable involvement in the full range of domestically linked arenas. Although the convergence of interests of DEA and other departments created intense, persistent interdepartmental tensions, these did not, as in the Pearson years, overwhelm the coherence of overall government policy. Stimulating, structuring, and guiding these tensions was a new array of more powerful and precise co-ordinative mechanisms more typical of a principal power.

In their initial inspiration and application, these efforts towards redefinition and coherence were largely the work of a single individual. Although Pierre Trudeau entered office with little knowledge of international politics or interest in the field, he possessed a particular impatience with the concepts, priorities, and conduct of Canadian foreign policy in the past. His travels and his activity in Quebec intellectual circles had provided him with considerable sympathy for China's paramount place in the world community, an emphatic rapport with the developmental and social imperatives of leaders in small Third World states, and a publicly expressed antipathy towards defence and nuclear involvements. More importantly, his entry into politics, his work as Pearson's parliamentary secretary and minister of justice, and his quest for the Liberal leadership had been motivated by a deep-seated belief in the need for a strong federal government. Only under such a government, he felt, could the virulent and oppressive strains of narrow nationalism be contained, the virtues of ethnic pluralism registered, and the values of individual liberty and creativity expressed in full.

When applied to foreign affairs, this background translated into a repudiation of a systematically oriented concern with fostering global peace and security through mediatory initiatives and international institutional promotion. It inspired the creation of a policy in conformity with complex neo-realism, derived from Canada's domestically linked national interests and aimed at sustaining its existence as a strong federal state. Notwithstanding his attachment to classic concepts of liberalism and individual freedom, Trudeau viewed the political process as a forward-looking "radar of society" and a powerful instrument of innovation, capable of anticipating rather than merely reacting to environmental alterations and producing those new policies that would meet changing domestic needs.

From this foundation flowed Trudeau's commitment to a rational decision-making process in which the spheres and dimensions of foreign and domestic activity would be considered in a balanced fashion and integrated according to a defined policy framework in a way that ensured central political control. Reinforced by Trudeau's distaste for the disorder of the Pearson government, these predispositions dictated a continuous, wide-ranging, countervailing debate among a much broader group of officials, strong central agencies to ensure that competing bureaucratic proposals reached Cabinet, and a revised array of Cabinet committees and procedures in which political leaders could determine policy in an autonomous, co-ordinated, and creative fashion.[29]

This emphasis on creating counterweights, providing conceptual referents, and challenging prevailing orthodoxies was rapidly displayed in a series of far-reaching decisions initiated and determined by the prime minister himself. In this task he received support from a small group of sympathetic individuals, a strengthened Prime Minister's Office, and in particular from Ivan Head, who became a full-time special adviser on international relations after 1970. Shortly after entering office, Trudeau initiated a full-scale review of foreign policy that culminated in *Foreign Policy for Canadians.* Concepts developed in this statement were placed in a scale of priority by Cabinet. From this point, Trudeau's strong personal influence and decisiveness were brought to bear on individual issues throughout his term of office.

From the outset, Trudeau determined, on the basis of personal judgement, that Canada would seek to recognize the People's Republic of China and support its admission into the United Nations. Only then was the admittedly difficult task of implementation turned over to a sympathetic Department of External Affairs. Dissatisfied with the reports by civil service groups on Canadian participation in NATO, Trudeau asked Ivan Head for a highly confidential special study of Canadian defence policy. In accordance with its spirit, and in the face of substantial ministerial opposition, Trudeau decided on a reduction in the level of Canadian forces in Europe, a restructuring of Canadian defence priorities to emphasize the protection of sovereignty and the surveillance of Canada's territory and coast lines, and a three-year freeze on the defence budget and establishment. Trudeau and Head were also dominant in formulating Canada's claim to jurisdiction in the Arctic waters controversy of 1970 and in securing from a divided Cabinet an agreement to exclude Canada's application from the jurisdiction of the International Court of Justice. Perhaps the tightest prime ministerial control was exercised in all matters related to Quebec. Trudeau, his closest advisers, and his Quebec ministerial colleagues, notably Gérard Pelletier and Jean Marchand, defined in detail Canada's response to Quebec's interaction with France. In 1970 they suspended diplomatic relations with Gabon when that country threatened to give Quebec international recognition; in the fall, they contended with the international dimensions of the October Crisis.

Both the degree of prime ministerial pre-eminence and the direction in which Trudeau exercised it propelled the Department of External Affairs into a position of painful irrelevance at first, then revolutionary re-orientation in mission, *modus operandi,* and institutional structure, and, ultimately, renaissance as it attempted to regain its traditional centrality in a much broader policy sphere. Seeking to destroy the traditional primacy, exclusive processes, and narrow preoccupations of External Affairs, Trudeau gave the portfolio to Mitchell Sharp. Sharp's lengthy experience in senior government economic positions, decisive support for Trudeau at the 1968 Liberal leadership convention, and appointment as chairman of the new Cabinet Committee on External

Policy and Defence gave External new advantages in the economic sphere. Yet his relative lack of authority, compared with the charismatic prime minister, and his minimal knowledge of the dominant Quebec questions considerably reduced the department's previous stature. External's desire to retain Canadian forces in Europe at existing levels, its views on the Arctic waters issue, and its advice on Canada's response to Biafra's secession from Nigeria were effectively overturned or countered by recommendations from central agencies and Cabinet. The culmination of these assaults came on the budgetary front, when government austerity forced External Affairs to close missions and release personnel. And a new interdepartmental procedure for administering posts abroad seemed to prophesy a permanent reduction in the department's financial resources and administrative autonomy.

This swift, comprehensive attack on DEA's essential organizational mission devastated the morale of departmental officials raised under the traditional system, who viewed overseas "peace and security" diplomacy as their central mission and DEA's pre-eminence in these matters as a necessary right. However, after the initial shock, External responded with several initiatives designed to demonstrate the department's awareness of the new emphasis on close relationships between itself and other departments. The Policy Analysis Group was formed to answer the prime minister's criticism of the diplomat's function and to provide the overall foreign policy framework he desired. The department asserted its leadership over the new integrated procedures for managing operations abroad. And in 1971 it conducted a full-scale internal re-organization, designed to increase its control of overall policy, long-range planning, and key international and domestic issues as well as increase its links with organizations and individuals outside the bureaucracy. The culmination of this reform process came when the department was asked in 1972 to produce Canada's first comprehensive statement on its relations with the United States.

With the return of minority government from 1972 to 1974 and the largely successful registration of Trudeau's first wave of reforms, External's position was further enhanced. Although Mitchell Sharp had his own constituency and electoral preoccupations, the focus of the prime minister and his office on the intricacies of parliamentary management allowed External to regain some of its former leadership in the sphere of high politics.

However, despite their far-reaching character, these changes did not enable External Affairs to re-establish its traditional pre-eminence in a now vastly extended policy sphere. The major obstacle to External's re-emergence was the great expansion of the domestic departments of government in the resources and roles of their foreign affairs components. These departments were given direct authority over the international aspects of their activity and allowed to establish international units to act as focal points for foreign-related matters. The transfer of External Affairs officers to these new units provided the units with competitive diplomatic expertise as well as specialized functional skills. And a government doctrine defining foreign policy in complex neo-realist terms, as the extension abroad of domestic imperatives, legitimized the role of these units as the co-ordinative linchpins and advisory mainsprings of the Canadian foreign policy process.

The simultaneous expansion in the roles of DEA and the other departments soon replaced the many segmented processes of the past with an informal set of ten broadly based interdepartmental groups or systems. In the largest one, the economic system, the debates within the inner triad of Finance, Industry, Trade and Commerce, and External and the regular challenges from such members of the outer group as Agriculture, Manpower and Immigration, Consumer and Corporate Affairs, Labour, National Revenue, and Regional Economic Expansion reliably propelled issues upward. It gave the Cabinet Committee on Economic Policy and its supporting Privy Council Office secretariat a substantial voice in decisions and concentrated policy making within the central agencies and Cabinet itself.

In the new set of smaller systems, each based on a single domestically oriented department and a counterpart functional division in External Affairs, the pattern was more variable. Energy, scientific, and classic diplomatic matters tended to rise for Cabinet consideration and resolution. Environmental questions were handled in a close, co-operative, senior-level relationship between External and a domestic counterpart. Communications, transportation, and immigration issues were controlled by the leading domestic department. Only in the rather new and more amorphous field of public diplomacy was policy making centred in the Department of External Affairs alone.

This diversity in processes of ongoing policy making demonstrated high institutional differentiation and autonomy typical of a principal power. It also provided a major challenge to a prime minister who sought to have the full range of foreign policy activity surveyed and screened by a single centre, brought together into a general overview, common framework, and central plan, and endowed with operational force through selective control at the centre. The Trudeau government's search for a reliable method to achieve such co-ordination began, as complex neo-realism suggests, at the apex of government with the prime minister, his Cabinet, and their supporting central agencies. To meet its goal of exercising "a greater degree of planned, *collective,* political control over a large and complex government apparatus," the government separated the Privy Council Office from the Prime Minister's Office, doubled its size, and transformed it from a small group of individual troubleshooters into a formal organization with delineated functions and fixed procedures.[30] And the Treasury Board Secretariat was directed to focus on providing guidance throughout the year on the allocation of funds among programs and departments in the light of government-wide priorities.

A more important change came within Cabinet itself, where a new collegial system was introduced. To produce an orderly process of adversary policy making and central co-ordination, the number of ministers was increased, Cabinet committees were reduced in number and rationalized into five operating and four co-ordinating bodies, and meetings were scheduled at fixed times, with agendas, documents, and briefings given in advance.

The impact of the new system was soon registered throughout the politico-military arena, as exemplified by the six specific options, four separate policy reviews, and open disagreement among a large number of ministers over the NATO decision of 1969. Moreover, minority government added a further incentive to greater Cabinet control. This was reflected in Cabinet's introduction of a January 1973 House of Commons resolution publicly condemning renewed U.S. bombing of North Vietnam, and the long, concentrated, and agonizing debate in Cabinet that led to Canada's decision to participate in, and then withdraw from, a truce supervisory force in Vietnam.

Under the impact of minority government, the Cabinet system began to experience increasing difficulty in performing the integrative role its founders envisaged, particularly in many policy areas where bureaucratic dynamics did not naturally channel decisional activity towards the Cabinet structures. Rapidly rotating deputy ministers and senior officials among departments engendered not only countervailing debate, but also compromise in the higher reaches of the civil service. The central agencies, through active intervention in policy making below, assisted materially in having Cabinet presented with advice that did not distort the relevant facts or considerations, unduly foreclose the range of available alternatives, or, on the other hand, inspire such conflict that the evaluation and selection process became unmanageable. Yet they seldom created alternative policy advice themselves or produced the balancing, planning, and control efforts that the co-ordinative task demanded.

Within the Prime Minister's Office, only Ivan Head, as assistant principal secretary for international relations, had a continuous or major involvement in foreign affairs. He concentrated on overseas issues that aroused major domestic sensitivities or were of particular concern to the prime minister himself. The Privy Council Office, despite a more consistent and comprehensive role, rarely used its formidable powers of planning, assembling agendas, writing and interpreting Cabinet decisions, and briefing the prime minister, to provide advice that directly countered or replaced proposals from below. And the Treasury Board Secretariat focused primarily on screening foreign operations with particularly high expenditures. Within Cabinet itself, foreign impact was not routinely assessed. The overlapping membership of the committees and more informal devices produced no consistent integration. Moreover, neither the Priorities and Planning Committee nor the full Cabinet moved to fill this vacuum, despite their participation in the government's yearly priorities exercise and the policy planning reviews of 1970 and 1972.

These problems soon produced a shift in emphasis to the second co-ordinative mechanism of comprehensive policy planning. This took the form of a review of foreign policy as a whole, conducted from 1968 to 1970, and the 1972 paper "Canada–U.S. Relations: Options for the Future."[31] The review represented an unprecedented effort to prepare and publish papers aimed at producing a comprehensive, coherent statement of Canadian foreign policy objectives and a common framework to guide and integrate the diverse activities of otherwise separated officials. In practice, however, the perceptual process quickly became overwhelmed by organizational considerations, with both the content and the continuing relevance of the documents directly reflecting the interests and power of the actors that had sponsored them.

A similar process developed in the review of Canada–United States relations, the product of which was published during the election campaign in autumn 1972. External Affairs alone wrote the final document, consulting other departments only at a rather late stage and having the study published without the clear endorsement of Cabinet as a whole. As a result, the document's call for a comprehensive industrial strategy at home engendered no continuing commitment from the major economic departments in Ottawa, and its plea for an overseas diversification of Canada's relations remained dependent for its effectiveness on the intermittent willingness of the prime minister to invest his personal prestige and resources in the cause. Only in its call for arm's-length diplomacy towards the United States did it give its External sponsors a useful instrument with which to secure a more integrated management of the relationship as a whole.

The government's two exercises in comprehensive policy planning thus quickly shifted from co-operative interdepartmental efforts at policy co-ordination to means for asserting a leadership role for the Department of External Affairs. A similar result occurred in the government's program for enhancing co-ordination by integrating the administration of departmental operations abroad.[32] At the initiative of the central agencies, a carefully selected task force with a mandate to integrate was established in 1968. In 1969 it forwarded proposals for combining the separate foreign services of External Affairs, Industry, Trade and Commerce, Manpower and Immigration, and the Canadian International Development Agency into a "single comprehensive system of accountable management." The strong opposition of the various foreign service departments forced this integration program to be introduced without its central "superministry".

Lacking a strong organizational centre, and with little continuing attention from its Cabinet sponsors, integration was left to proceed on an incremental basis. This allowed External Affairs, as the most generally oriented foreign service department, to slowly acquire responsibility in country programming for devising overall Canadian foreign policy objectives, preparing specific country policy studies, and determining what requests to forward to the Treasury Board as part of the overall foreign affairs budget. This assertion led other departments, notably Industry, Trade and Commerce, to resist vigorously any extension of integrated procedures under the existing framework, which in turn prevented the integration program from developing into an effective means for planning or co-ordination.

As the results of these reform efforts unfolded, the government turned increasingly to External Affairs, as its foreign office, to serve as the primary centre for co-ordinating foreign-related activity throughout the bureaucracy.[33] However, the department's senior management, overwhelmed with crises at home and special negotiations abroad, was on the whole unable to produce broad plans or successfully support their subordinates against the experienced ex-DEA officers now situated in other departments. And while co-ordination was enhanced by several of the new features, proliferating numbers made direct middle-level consultation between functional and geographic officers an uncertain substitute for explicit direction from above.

Recognizing the unreliability of the department's normal working practices and accepting the need for greater integration advanced in the "Options" paper of 1972, the government moved to a much more ambitious program of co-ordinative reform, directed at the most difficult of relationships: that with the United States. Using External's U.S. division and its organizational allies as the leading instrument, it attempted the unprecedented task of addressing its extraordinarily broad and pervasive relationship with the United States on an ongoing basis, co-ordinating it to a greater degree than its other foreign relations, and creating a distinct executive procedure for this purpose. Thus in late 1974, External Affairs was given a clear mandate to manage the relationship with the United States as a whole, the power to see and clear all U.S.-related issues taken to Cabinet, and the responsibility to report periodically to Cabinet on the state of the relationship and the best way for Canada to approach it. The importance of this new regime was underscored at the bureaucratic level where DEA's United States division was staffed by forceful individuals, significantly expanded in size, and reorganized to emphasize the tasks of maintaining a continuous overview and central co-ordination of Canada–U.S. relations as a whole.

Beyond a reasonably comprehensive monitoring, however, integrative achievements were extremely rare. Forced to concentrate on such immediate questions as reducing the general level of friction in the relationship in the short term, External was unable to develop and apply reliable long-range strategies. This failure was due both to the unfamiliarity of many of External's foreign service officers with the co-ordinative task and to their traditional exclusion from many of the ongoing policy-making systems, where the real decisions were made. In short, the Trudeau government had done much to institutionalize a policy-making and co-ordinative process conforming to complex neo-realist predictions. Yet it had chosen as its major co-ordinative instrument an External Affairs organization unable to meet the need until it moved away from its traditional foreign office and foreign service role.

The Era of Central Agency Co-ordination, 1974–1980

External's move to a more central, co-ordinative role formed the overriding dynamic of the foreign policy decision-making process from 1974 to 1980.[34] The need for such a co-ordinative centre to direct Canada's external relations stemmed from several factors. The need for reduced government expenditure had led to heightened conflicts over allocating resources. The preoccupation of both Prime Ministers Trudeau and Clark with a limited set of priorities and a re-emphasis on the prerogative of individual ministers and deputy ministers reduced the prime minister's co-ordinating role. And outside Ottawa, the challenges of a separatist Quebec, resource-rich provinces, and a stagnant economy, together with the economic and security tensions bred by America's decline, demanded new foreign policy initiatives, even as the latter factor provided Canada with greater autonomy over a wider sphere.

With a secure parliamentary majority, the confidence of a renewed mandate, and six years of experience in operating a complex federal bureaucracy, Pierre Trudeau returned to office in July 1974. He entered with a considerably more sophisticated understanding of the type of decision-making system he desired and of the way in which it could be obtained. His revised conception began by stressing the need to conserve scarce ministerial time, to choose talented administrators as deputies, and to view government as a "confederacy of institutions".

The first element of this revised conception was soon registered at the Cabinet level, where senior ministers and committee chairmen were given greater responsibility. Greater use was made of special *ad hoc* committees for such complex, time-consuming questions as the Tokyo Round of GATT negotiations, the Canada–U.S. Alaska gas pipeline, and the east coast fisheries and maritime boundary dispute.[35] This shift was reinforced especially after November 1976 as the threat from the Parti Québécois government preoccupied the prime minister and his closest associates. It culminated in the summer of 1977 when the prime minister withdrew from actively guiding all policy spheres save those of national unity, economic recovery, and North–South international affairs. At the central agency level, a correspondingly greater reliance was placed on the transfer into influential positions of senior civil servants sympathetic to the prime minister's style of thinking and on procedural changes to enhance their influence.[36] Most importantly, three months after the 1974 election, Michael Pitfield replaced Gordon Robertson as secretary to the Cabinet, a move that placed in the most senior and sensitive post in the civil service an individual much closer to the prime minister in intellectual perspective, decision-making style, and personal rapport. At the deputy ministerial level, the new emphasis on deputies as specific administrators rather than general advisers led to a relaxation of the earlier rapid rotation of individuals among these positions and created a set of younger deputy ministers who had acquired central agency experience and would thus be responsive to prime ministerial direction.

This emphasis on individual ministers and deputies sensitive to the prime minister allowed Trudeau to focus his influence on his paramount concerns. He directed the federal response to Quebec's attempts to secure autonomous recognition abroad, conducted visits to the United States and France for this purpose, played an increasingly active role in the seven-power Western Economic Summits after 1976, and focused on resource transfer questions following Canadian co-chairmanship of the Conference on International Economic Co-operation in Paris in 1977.

While this enhanced role for the prime minister did not directly and dramatically compete with department prerogatives, it tended to confine the latter to a supporting role. Under Allan MacEachen, External Affairs gave complete support to the prime minister in furthering the quest for a North–South dialogue and a Canadian contractual link with Europe; in line with the latter objective, External supported the decision to buy the Leopard tank in advance of the final Cabinet decision. After Don Jamieson's appointment in September 1976, the minister's deep attachment to friendly relations with the United States and close personal relationship with U.S. Secretary of State Cyrus Vance led him to support DND on participation in a NATO Advance Warning and Control System. Despite DND reluctance, Jamieson also agreed to a Canadian contribution to UNIFIL, the United Nations force in Lebanon.

Prime ministerial prominence also had its impact on other major departments, particularly within the sensitive and costly sphere of defence. James Richardson, the first minister of national defence during this period, failed to secure an indefinite extension of NORAD and the closing of unneeded military bases, although he did obtain from Cabinet acceptance of the 1975 defence structure review and accompanying authorization of a major re-equipment program. Similarly, his successor, Barnett Danson, was overruled by the Cabinet when he opposed

Canadian participation in UNIFIL in 1978. However, he obtained an increase in force levels, military research and development, and advanced equipment procurement, even after a public prime ministerial commitment to limit annual growth in real defence expenditures to 3 per cent.[37]

Prime ministerial control, however, was exerted in ways considerably different from those heralded in 1968. From 1976 to 1980, and especially after the introduction of austerity measures in 1978, policy formulation and resource allocation were closely linked, and the prime minister's influence was exerted on the combined area through Cabinet and bodies set up to deal jointly with the two issues. One such body was the recently fused Priorities and Planning–Federal Provincial Committee, which alone controlled issues with a high conflicting impact on economic recovery, national unity, and North–South relations. The prime minister often intervened in this committee's areas, in unpredictable fashion, to forward his priorities and the government's re-election concerns. Overt control came from the increasing power and largely convergent views of Allan MacEachen, Jean Chrétien, and the functional committee chairmen, as well as from the transfer of activity to small, *ad hoc* groups of directly concerned or delegated ministers.

A far more direct and potent revision of the relationship between overall expenditures and foreign operations came in 1976 when Cabinet accepted a recommendation from the deputy ministerial-level Interdepartmental Committee on External Relations (ICER) that there be three years of no-growth in the foreign service abroad.[38] The resulting redeployment of officers to less expensive positions within Canada and the greater tension introduced into the resource allocation process induced External Affairs to take a much greater initiative in the 1977–1978 country programming process, by defining initial foreign policy objectives, engaging in greater interdepartmental consultation, and forwarding the combined requests for new resources to the Treasury Board. The prime minister speeded this trend towards integration by imposing government-wide austerity in the summer of 1978.

This increase in prime ministerial control was reinforced by changes in the bureaucratic-level planning process; senior officials at External were given high status, and the minister's primacy was reduced. After an interlude caused by the new Trudeau government's year-long ministerial effort to define overall government priorities and its subsequent preoccupation with the Quebec situation, the government returned to the foreign policy planning task in 1977, under the initiative of the new undersecretary for external affairs, Allan Gotlieb.[39]

The undersecretary's first step was to create the Committee of Deputy Ministers on Foreign Policy, a very restricted group of senior officials allowed to conduct a relatively free and informal exchange of views. The undersecretary next revived the External Affairs planning group, giving it the new name of the Policy Planning Secretariat (POL), and a mandate to review general foreign policy principles and practices and to stimulate options on current issues. It also had the opportunity to participate in all important deliberations before final departmental decisions were made. The undersecretary's third initiative, designed to create a new foreign policy framework similar in conceptual scope to *Foreign Policy for Canadians,* came in early 1978 when he asked POL to write a paper outlining the options of Canadian foreign policy for the 1980s, assigned it a general co-ordinative and central drafting responsibility, and asked for a review exercise in which specific individuals, largely in External Affairs, were to prepare eight papers in designated areas. But constrained by Jamieson's lack of interest, the Liberal government's public attachments to *Foreign Policy for Canadians,* and the uncertainties of an imminent federal election, the papers neared completion only by the time the Conservative government assumed office.

Although this initiative was slightly curtailed, External Affairs continued to provide policy planning and foreign service integration after 1977 as part of a broader concept of the leadership role that the department could exert on behalf of the prime minister in co-ordinating the foreign policy process.[40] To enable External to perform this role, Undersecretary Gotlieb moved on three interdependent fronts. Within the department, he created a new array of deputy undersecretaries with the status and full authority to deal with other deputy ministers in their spheres; he also gave lower-level units the responsibility and power to deal with emerging functional subjects. Within the interdepartmental community, he sought to serve as the senior foreign policy adviser to the government as a whole, giving advice to groups of ministers on a regular basis, contacting all ministers directly, clearing in practice all Cabinet memoranda with international implications, and encouraging his officers to become full, continuous participants in interdepartmental discussions related to their areas. And in regard to External's activities abroad, he sought to give practical force to External's formal right to conduct communications with foreign governments and international organizations, provide visible evidence of External's position as the key prime-ministerial adviser at summit conferences, be kept informed of direct head-of-government communications, and manage more actively Canada's operations and foreign service personnel abroad.

The new salience and scope of prime ministerial involvement established by Trudeau and Gotlieb largely continued during the nine-month minority government of Conservative Prime Minister Joe Clark. Prime Minister Clark entered office with little experience or interest in foreign affairs, beyond a strong overall attachment to a few general traditional Conservative beliefs, such as strong Canadian support for Israel, a close alliance with the United States, increased defence expenditure, sympathy for NATO, and a skeptical view of the UN. Procedurally, he was determined to shift the focus of Parliament from the PCO and the career bureaucracy to Cabinet, caucus, and Parliament. He also sought to control government expenditures, depressurize the central decision-making process, conduct comprehensive policy reviews in advance of individual decisions, and have individual ministers exercising control over their departments. As a result, he chose not to appoint a special adviser on foreign policy and called for the widest possible review of policy in the foreign affairs realm.

Yet Clark's desire to fulfill campaign promises and demonstrate control over the civil service led him, upon entering office, to announce his intention to move the Canadian embassy in Israel to Jerusalem, although he readily acceded to the advice of his foreign minister, Flora MacDonald, to appoint Robert Stanfield to study the issue and its ramifications; later he followed Stanfield's advice not to proceed with the move. Encouraged by electoral considerations and personal conviction, Clark emphasized Canada's friendly support for a militarily powerful NATO and the U.S. and sought to be helpful but not precipitous on the issue of possible Canadian involvement in a Rhodesian settlement. With the support of an otherwise unanimous inner Cabinet, he overrode Flora MacDonald to authorize Canada's attempt to sell a nuclear reactor to Argentina.

The integration of control over financial and policy planning that had developed in the latter days of the Trudeau government was also followed under the Clark regime. Indeed, it was strengthened by the creation of system management, which ensured that policy formulation and resource allocation were done together within financial "envelopes" fixed at Cabinet committee level; overall control was exerted by a new inner Cabinet over transfers across envelopes and disbursements from a central reserve.[41]

Spending constraints in defence operations also continued to be subject to prime ministerial control under Clark, although DND victories came somewhat more readily with Allan McKinnon as defence minister. Foreign service operations were subject to similar centrally controlled restraints. When Joe Clark entered office, he was immediately given a paper presenting the arguments for integration in foreign operations, suggesting alternative models, and arguing the need for immediate action. Motivated by his own strong and highly convergent views on government organization, Clark gave approval in principle of the earlier paper. Yet, aware of ITC's opposition, he created a carefully constructed task force to undertake further work.

However, with its attachment to ministerial control and public participation, the Clark government did not carry out the earlier Gotlieb approaches to foreign policy planning. In fact, the previous process and intellectual structure were replaced by a two-fold review of Canada's aid and foreign policy.[42] The general review, guided by a new paper on the external environment and what Canada faced in it, was steered towards the Cabinet committee and a subsequent parliamentary review. By the time of the government's fall, these papers and the Cabinet committee's deliberations had reached the stage where the review was about to be sent out for parliamentary scrutiny.

Although the recommendations for intellectual changes in foreign policy planning were not accepted by the Clark government, the role of the undersecretary as senior adviser to the prime minister was not substantially altered. However, his heightened position did not go unchallenged. By far the greatest challenge to the undersecretary's primacy was that posed by the secretary of state for external affairs, who had strong, discrepant views on policy and relied heavily on a strong team of personal advisers.

Flora MacDonald's claim to leadership stemmed from Prime Minister Clark's emphasis on individual ministerial responsibility, her experience at the National Defence College and the Committee for an Independent Canada, and her provision of crucial support of Clark at the Conservative leadership convention. In office, it was reinforced by her chairmanship in inner Cabinet and her strong attachment, somewhat compatible with the prime minister's, to Red Tory principles and such values as public participation in foreign policy. Although her deference to DND sensitivities produced a restrained involvement in policy and budgetary questions, she made largely individual decisions in many key issue areas. She skillfully secured an acceptable outcome to the prime minister's Jerusalem initiative and succeeded in formulating and securing the adoption of Canada's program to accept a large inflow of Indochinese refugees. She also helped define Canada's approach to the Tokyo Western Economic Summit, the Lusaka Commonwealth Prime Ministers' Conference, the Iranian revolution, and the Soviet invasion of Afghanistan.

MacDonald's independent approach was not compatible with the undersecretary's role as a prime ministerial adviser, a situation that produced considerable strains in her relationship with Allan Gotlieb. First apparent on procedural matters, they soon extended to major organizational issues, and in particular, the belief of the undersecretary and some of his closest associates that the role of External Affairs as a central agency required institutional expression through entities such as a strong centre of foreign operations management and a deputy ministerial "mirror committee" on foreign policy. However, believing from the start that Allan Gotlieb should perform only a classic deputy ministerial role, and interpreting such concepts as exercises in self-aggrandizement that foster interdepartmental conflict, Flora MacDonald repeatedly refused to accept them. Her refusal highlighted the limits to comprehensive co-ordination during this period. For while the undersecretary had done much to define the new role of External Affairs and introduce the patterns that complex neo-realism predicts in regard to overall co-ordination, his personal achievements remained largely devoid of permanent, institutional expression.

The Era of Continuous Central Management, 1980–

It was during the first two years of the new Trudeau government elected in the spring of 1980 that Gotlieb's achievements were embodied in institutional form. Combined with the ongoing policy-making process dominated by the prime minister, this development clearly indicated that complex neo-realist patterns of decision making had come to prevail.

Trudeau returned to office not only as an experienced prime minister with a secure majority but with several additional assets. The recent foreign policy performance of the Clark government, as seen by most Canadians, gave Trudeau an unusually large margin of manoeuvre. After twelve years in office, in what might be his last term as prime minister, he had an incentive to make fundamental and permanent innovations in the substance and processes of Canadian foreign policy. And his formidable international reputation as a statesman, combined with his unusually long experience in the Western Economic and Commonwealth summits, further suggested a leading role in areas of personal concern. A host of major events, notably the Ottawa Western Economic Summit of 1981 and the Cancùn meeting on the North–South dialogue, confirm that he played that role.

The centrality of the prime minister in ongoing policy making was sustained by his selection of Mark MacGuigan as secretary of state for external affairs. With no previous ministerial experience and a professorial, intellectual style, MacGuigan relied much more heavily than his immediate predecessor on the advice of his departmental officials and the directions that his prime minister set. With a general attachment to the principles of international law and organization, he was far less disposed than his Liberal predecessors to lead External into nontraditional fields such as energy policy. As a relatively strong anti-Communist, his instinctive approach to a host of East–West and North–South issues seemed a little discrepant with that of the prime minister himself. While these beliefs and longstanding interests led him to focus, with a moderate approach, on Canada–U.S. relations, there were limits to the degree of leadership in this sphere. The most formidable limit, seen when the National Energy Program was introduced and in the dispute over strengthening the Foreign Investment Review Agency, was the presence in other major economic portfolios of close Trudeau associates, notably Marc Lalonde in Energy, Mines and Resources and Allan MacEachen in Finance.

As a result, Canadian foreign policy generally and Canada–U.S. relations in particular were left to senior officials in External Affairs and the Privy Council Office who were sensitive to Pierre Trudeau's own approach. In the realm of formal foreign policy planning, it was Allan Gotlieb who again played the leading role. Even before the return of the Liberal government, the undersecretary had begun to prepare a philosophically oriented paper addressing such questions as what "foreign policy" meant, how appropriate policies were defined, and what themes could best guide Canadian foreign policy into the 1980s. The concept of bilateralism, developed as part of this paper, was subsequently selected as primary, partly on the grounds that it could be translated into specific policy and budgetary allocations. Following further development and ministerial approval, the paper was taken through the Cabinet process in the fall of 1980. Despite some reservations, the concept was given ministerial approval, and External was mandated to proceed towards the more detailed stage. Later a second theme contained in the undersecretary's concept paper, focusing on the management of Canada–U.S. relations, was developed by External's Policy Planning Secretariat and given public expression as well.

Within the government itself, these expressions of more comprehensive and detailed foreign policy co-ordination were given institutional force. The new Liberal government immediately authorized the creation of a mirror committee of deputy ministers on foreign and defence policy, with a secretariat located in External Affairs, to service the Cabinet committee in a way comparable to that of ministries of state in other policy spheres. The new government also moved almost at once to consolidate all the foreign service, except for ITC's Trade Commissioner Service, under the *de facto* leadership of External Affairs. As Canada–U.S. issues became more prominent, it gave the department more freedom to undertake comprehensive policy reviews in this realm.

The culmination of these developments occurred in January 1982 when the government conducted a major reorganization of External Affairs, centred on the absorption into the department of the trade and commerce components of the former Department of Industry, Trade and Commerce. This reorganization, devised for the prime minister by Secretary to the Cabinet Michael Pitfield, was prompted by several factors that converged to produce a change of unprecedented speed and scale. The most general was the need for the government to further its overall priority on economic development and concern with supporting the private sector by giving economic considerations a more central place in its foreign policy. More particularly, the need for economic development at a time of government expenditure restraint required a system that would allow ministers to define their priorities more sharply, eliminate recent cases of competitive spending between ITC and Regional Economic Expansion, and redirect trade policy from its industrial sector focus to the resource sectors—notably agriculture, fisheries, forestry, energy, and minerals—that promised to be the most vibrant sources of future growth.

Externally, the growing interaction of economic and political issues, their tighter relationship with domestic forces, and the government's policy of bilateralism suggested such an institutional amalgamation, particularly as an increase in global instability promised a more demanding environment abroad. In addition, the implementation of the incremental organizational reforms of the past few years—notably foreign service consolidation, the envelope system, and the proposals of the Royal Commission on Terms and Conditions of Foreign Service—suggested that further steps were necessary if their anticipated advantages were to be reaped. The leaders of both DEA and ITC, burdened with heavy line responsibilities and a large program load, had faced difficulties in developing the broad overarching policies on issues such as Canada–U.S. relations, Canadian sovereignty, and national unity that were needed in a large, complex government.

After careful consideration of several alternatives, the government decided to disband ITC, place its industry component along with Regional Economic Expansion into a new Department of Regional Industrial Expansion, and transfer its trade and commerce components to External Affairs. The resulting External Affairs federation was given three ministers: the secretary of state for external affairs, a minister for international trade, and a minister for external relations. This ministerial triumvirate was mirrored at the deputy ministerial level. The newly appointed undersecretary of state for external affairs, Gordon Osbaldeston, was charged not only with managing his department and advising his three ministers but with acting in an integrative central agency policy role across all areas of foreign policy, defence, aid, and trade. The new deputy minister for international trade was responsible for the department's trade and economic functions generally and was also named co-ordinator for international economic relations, with a mandate to blend economic and foreign policy, domestic and international considerations throughout the government's economic community as a whole. And the new deputy minister for foreign policy was assigned responsibility for the classic foreign office political functions as well as the task of serving as the prime minister's personal representative for the Western Economic Summit.

In addition to integrating economic and political considerations more closely within the new department, the re-organization of External had two crucially important effects. It endowed the department with the expertise and influence to interact and compete more effectively with the other departments of government, particularly the dozen or so departments in the economic sphere. Most significantly, by extending and institutionalizing External's central agency functions, it enabled the new departmental federation to perform *de facto* the role of a ministry of state for foreign affairs. At lower levels, this role was sustained by the absorption of the Trade Commissioner Service into a single, unified foreign service and by the creation of a central management core with functions broadly similar to those of the government's existing ministries of state. At the deputy ministerial level, the ministry of state role was strengthened by giving all three deputies co-ordinating and policy responsibilities on a government-wide basis. And at the top, it was furthered by having the ministerial triumvirate assume a dominant position in the Cabinet Committee on External Policy and Defence, with representation on all Cabinet committees in other policy spheres. Finally, by bringing all foreign operations within a single budgetary envelope and management regime and by giving External primacy on an annual foreign policy planning exercise linked directly with government-wide priority setting, the new structure gave External most of the essential powers of a government-wide ministry of state.

To be sure, the performance of the new system in its co-ordinating role depended critically on the creation of close working relationships between the trade and foreign policy wings, among the three deputy ministers, and among the three ministers at the top. To facilitate the first, the government gave central senior positions in the new department to individuals respected and trusted by trade officers and commissioners and by those in economic departments in the government at large. To ensure the second, it deliberately staffed the most senior positions with individuals who were the most talented in the entire government, broadly sympathetic to the new regime and known to be capable of working together. And to help alleviate initial problems in the third area, the government in September 1982 shuffled the relevant portfolios, naming Allan MacEachen secretary of state for external affairs, Gerald Regan minister of state for international trade, and Charles Lapointe minister of state for external relations. With a strong minister guiding an integrated departmental federation, Ottawa had achieved the institutionalized capacity for comprehensive co-ordination that the perspective of complex neo-realism predicts.

Conclusions

By 1982, the foreign policy decision-making process within Ottawa's executive branch had in large measure developed the autonomous force, internal pluralism, structural co-ordinative mechanisms, and defined conception of the national interest that the complex neo-realist perspective predicts.

The freedom of the state apparatus to formulate Canadian foreign policy, first evident in the thrust towards internationalism that emerged in 1947 and flourished thereafter, acquired increased force as the legacy of the conscription crisis and rigidities of the cold war diminished.

During the Diefenbaker era, the discernible if erratic decline in East–West tension and the use of electorally important domestic interest groups, largely at the prime minister's personal behest, enabled the government both to inject alternative policy tendencies (such as close relations with the United Kingdom, a new skepticism about the United States impact on Canada and global behaviour, and vigorous, publicly expressed anti-Communism) and to extend internationalist precepts to their experimental limits, responding, for example, to increasingly visible Third World concerns in the Commonwealth and United Nations and forwarding disarmament initiatives through to the nuclear weapons controversy of 1963. In the next decade, growing doubts about U.S. action in Indochina and NATO, domestic demands inspired by France's assault on American hegemony, Quebec's international assertiveness, and minority government led to a broader effort on the part of Prime Minister Pearson and a coalition of reformists to undertake basic policy redefinition.

By the late 1960s and early 1970s, the widespread international acceptance of détente and internal recognition of the legitimacy of societal priorities enabled a forceful and impatient prime minister, with a reoriented Cabinet and civil service, to undertake a conceptually integrated constellation of policy initiatives in major areas and a fundamental, comprehensive policy review. From 1974 onward, the end of America's global primacy and, to a lesser extent, the strength of separatism in Quebec permitted the prime minister and his closest associates in the civil service to adapt this vision of institutional permanence, operational force, and precision of implementation to internally engendered programs abroad, policy reviews, and structural reforms.

This cumulative transformation of the autonomy of the state apparatus was accompanied by increasing change in the relationship among the major foreign affairs actors within Ottawa and in the policy-making process they produced. The Department of External Affairs, as a standard foreign office, experienced a slow erosion from the primacy it enjoyed during the St. Laurent era, as other ministers and their departments acquired the resources, expertise, and assertiveness to challenge and surpass its leadership and as the prime minister himself acquired pre-eminence in the foreign policy sphere. Thus Sidney Smith, Howard Green, and their somewhat dispirited and divided officials met with the unyielding and eventually successful resistance of the Department of National Defence in the central peace and security arena; they exercised influence only by adapting to the variable preoccupations of a prime minister no longer content to allow his foreign minister a virtually free hand. Although in Paul Martin's tenure, an attempt was made to re-establish the traditional pattern, his leadership was continually constrained and periodically interrupted by the impatience of his colleagues and leader with the mediatory and federalist projections of internationalism and by ideologically based interministerial cleavages that extended from the politico-military sphere to the economic realm and the sphere of sovereignty.

The decisive transition came during Pierre Trudeau's first two governments, as a full-scale assault on External's traditional mission, prerogatives, and primacy, a proliferation of newly powerful and expert domestically oriented departments, and a prime ministerially guided process of policy redefinition and institutional reform yielded a collective, competitive policy-making process that generated interdepartmental conflict and propelled decision-making power to the top. These trends were extended during Pierre Trudeau's second two governments and Joe Clark's brief prime ministership. External Affairs, catalyzed by the interdepartmental conflict bred by resource scarcity and the ideas of Trudeau and his associates, withstood the efforts of the Clark government to impose more traditional patterns and transformed its role into that of a central government agency. During the subsequent Trudeau government, the central agency role was transformed into the structure of a ministry of state.

As the state's growing autonomy shifted the distribution of power in Ottawa towards domestically and prime ministerially oriented institutions, fostering intense internal debate, the government slowly developed mechanisms to impose overall co-ordination on a comprehensive and structural basis. As the informal consultations, crisis response processes, and perceptual consensus of the St. Laurent era were overwhelmed by the prime ministerial interventions and ideological cleavages of the Diefenbaker and Pearson governments, the executive moved to establish more formal Cabinet committees on major politico-military issues. During the first Trudeau governments these initiatives were intensified and broadened considerably. Cabinet's co-ordinative effectiveness was reinforced by a more differentiated structure and powerful central agencies. Full-scale review exercises generated new frameworks and processes to guide Canadian activities abroad and relationships with the United States and other countries. Integrated mechanisms of foreign operations planning and personnel management were added to ensure co-ordination abroad, interdepartmental procedures based in External Affairs were developed to engender and enforce coherence at home.

After 1974 these processes were endowed with bureaucratic permanence, integrated comprehensiveness, and managerial effectiveness, as Prime Minister Trudeau and his associates turned from unreliable Cabinet-level co-ordinative procedures to rely on a network of sensitive, senior-level officials and the far more coherent and effective foreign policy framework that its senior officials devised. External Affairs developed as a modern central policy agency managing foreign policy formulation and operations.

This development marked the culmination of a trend within Ottawa towards an overarching conception of the national interest, developed and applied in relatively autonomous fashion by the state apparatus itself. Although the internationalist vision articulated in St. Laurent's Gray Lecture had provided a set of principles and projections in major regions that faithfully reflected the foreign policy consensus and behaviour of the era, it lacked the conceptual precision, scale of priorities, and comprehensive applicability to survive the assaults of the Diefenbaker and Pearson periods. "Canada and the World," *Foreign Policy for Canadians,* "Canada–U.S. Relations: Options for the Future," and the personal elaborations of Prime Minister Trudeau slowly added these elements, but offered no calculus or interpretation to guide specific Canadian actions in all regions abroad, and no managerial centre to ensure faithful and consistent enforcement at home. Only with the definition within Ottawa of the concepts and applications of bilateralism and the emergence of External Affairs as a *de facto* ministry of state was the national interest endowed with autonomous, transcending, and enduring force.

PART II
CASE STUDIES

INTRODUCTION TO THE CASE STUDIES

Thus far our examination of Canada's international behaviour and the processes that generate it suggests that the perspective of complex neo-realism provides an increasingly accurate account of Canadian foreign policy in the Trudeau years. But do the general trends match the more detailed reality and changes below the surface? Political scientists have long been properly skeptical of relying exclusively on general patterns as the empirical basis for their conclusions. To provide a firmer foundation, they turn to the comparative case study approach. This method is especially useful in that it allows two critical theory-building tasks to be performed.

The first task is to ensure that a theoretical framework is sufficiently precise, sensitive, and interrelated to account for the complex dynamics of the real historical world. Specific case studies give an observer more detailed clues about the direction, pace, and causes of change. When explored through a particular framework—such as our seven basic questions and the answers given by our three perspectives—they show how a perspective can encompass fully the complex reality to which it applies.

The second task of case studies is to ensure that a theoretical framework is sufficiently strong to account for empirical evidence that would at first appear to challenge the theory. While cases that can be expected to conform to the perspective of complex neo-realism can usefully illustrate its features, other cases that appear to defy its predictions but conform to them upon closer examination demonstrate its theoretical value. Our case studies—in the areas of population, resources, technology, and Middle East policy—have been selected partly with this purpose in mind.

Although Canada is often regarded as a resource-rich society, its small population and weak technology seem to deny it the position of principal power that complex neo-realism ascribes. More importantly, Canadian foreign policy towards the Middle East, long regarded as the archetypical example of liberal internationalism or peripheral dependence, provides the strongest test of the complex neo-realist approach.

Traditionally, military and economic factors have been considered primary indicators of international political change and, as such, have dominated foreign policy case studies. Even a brief examination of the military and economic spheres of Canadian foreign policy provides substantial material to test the three theories presented in the preceding chapters.

In the investment field, the case of peripheral dependence is sustained by Canada's status at the OECD as the state with the largest relative share of direct foreign investment in its economy. Moreover, since at least 1948, U.S. firms have been by far the largest source of such investment, have acquired a dominant position in many basic manufacturing and resource sectors in Canada, and have thereby given the U.S. government a convenient vehicle for the extraterritorial application of U.S. law to Canada. Yet liberal-internationalist authors can point, since 1960, to Canada's ability to bargain informally and successfully with the United States on cases of extraterritoriality; also significant has been Canada's participation, in the OECD and United Nations, in erecting multilateral regimes to define rules of transborder investment flows acceptable to a broad range of home and host countries. And particularly in the 1970s, complex neo-realist theoreticians can point to Canada's ability to reserve vital economic sectors for Canadian control, to ensure "substantial Canadian benefit" through the broad screening mechanism of the Foreign Investment Review Agency, to serve as the base for a growing number of Canadian-owned multinational corporations, and even to become a net exporter of capital abroad.

In the area of the international balance of payments, a similar portrait emerges. Foreign exchange crises in 1947 and 1962, U.S.-induced balance-of-payments problems in 1963, 1965, and 1968, and Canada's reliance on U.S. funds or exemptions for a solution all lend credence to the case for peripheral dependence. But liberal internationalists counter that these cases are merely rare exceptions to the exchange-rate stability and increasing free convertibility provided by the International Monetary Fund—an institution that Canada, in a victory for functionalist principles, did much to create and manage. And complex neo-realists can point to Canada's stable position, enshrined in the fund, as one of the top seven or eight monetary powers in the globe since 1945, its continuous membership on the Board of Executive Directors, its representation of several other lesser powers in this capacity, and the ever-widening non-American or IMF sources of balance-of-payments support available to Canada as the 1970s progressed.

The case for complex neo-realism is somewhat more familiar in the area of trade. To be sure, peripheral dependence can claim as evidence aspects of Canada's move to sectoral trade liberalization in the 1960s with the U.S. alone, through the Defence Production Sharing Agreements and the Auto Pact; other evidence is its heavy concentration of trade on the U.S. as well as its limited influence in the Tokyo Round of the General Agreements on Tariffs and Trade. Yet the continuing use and success of the multilateral GATT process and Canada's central participation in it confirm the liberal-internationalist position. And since

1976, Canada's place as one of the seven states in the annual Western Economic Summit, and in related gatherings focused specifically on trade problems, confirms that Canada is acting as an equal principal power in new order-engendering concerts, as complex neo-realism predicts.

In contrast, the realm of politico-military or security affairs appears, at first glance, to provide little evidence of complex neo-realist patterns. For it seems difficult to argue that a country with no nuclear weapons, armed forces of well under 100 000, and a navy of only four modern destroyers can be a global principal power. Liberal internationalists argue that such capability is a sufficient contribution to make Canada's diplomatic voice effective in multilateral forums in the security sphere. But even they acknowledge departures from Canada's traditional enthusiasm for UN peacekeeping, from the NATO consensus, and from joint American defence since the late 1960s. The case for neo-realism is indeed more complex, as it emphasizes inherent, rather than in-place, military capability and the particular policy choices that Canadian governments have made, with increasing freedom, in the security realm. But the evidence is sufficient to demonstrate that complex neo-realism is capable of accounting for some, perhaps much, of Canada's foreign policy in the security sphere.

In the nuclear area, adherents of peripheral dependence point to Canada's lack of in-place, autonomous nuclear weaponry, its consequent dependence on the American nuclear umbrella, and its resulting exclusion from the great forums that negotiate the limitation or reduction of strategic arms. Liberal internationalists counter that it is the system of mutual deterrence, rather than a unilateral American guarantee, that protects Canada, and that Canada's functional assets—uranium, nuclear research, and seismography—have given it a leading place in UN arms control forums to this day. Complex neo-realist theorists begin by noting that there are now six nuclear-weapons states in the globe and that it is difficult to treat the sixth state, India, as a more advanced nuclear power than Canada, which had given India major nuclear assistance for two decades prior to 1974. They recall Canada's position as one of the three original participants in the development of nuclear weapons, its historical status as the fourth or fifth state in the globe capable of developing nuclear weapons, and its unique position as the only nonpermanent member of the Security Council to sit on the United Nations Atomic Energy Commission. And in the 1970s, they point to Canada's leading global rank in the scientific, industrial, and uranium resources from which nuclear weapons are forged, as evidenced by its seventh place in the global possession of peaceful nuclear reactors, its membership in the uranium cartel, and its leadership in devising a nuclear nonproliferation regime for the globe.

These brief sketches give some suggestion of the type of analysis that can be undertaken in relating theoretical precepts to economic and military facts. Similar trends away from peripheral dependence and liberal internationalism and towards complex neo-realism would be apparent in studies of other major sectors, such as foreign economic aid, peacekeeping and truce supervision, North Atlantic security (especially Canada's changing role in NATO), and the Canada–U.S. Aerospace Defence Command, which was considered in Chapter 2.

Although the understanding of economic and military activities is essential to foreign policy analysis, these two areas have not been chosen as the subjects of case studies here. These two traditional subjects of study provide the most sensitive and immediate gauges of power shifts, but they are not the primary generators of change. As we discussed in Chapter 4, international population distribution and changes in the technological and natural resources of individual countries have greater long-term effects on international power structures than economic or military activity. In fact, slower and less immediately obvious changes in population, resources, and technology lie behind any transformation in the distribution of military capability and economic growth. Therefore our case studies—with the exception of the final study, which tests the three theories in a domain of international behaviour traditionally thought to conform to liberal-internationalist precepts—treat each of the three master variables. It is to an examination of the postwar changes in these fundamental areas that we now turn.

CHAPTER 7

IMMIGRATION POLICY: THE CASE OF REFUGEES

Within the community of advanced industrial states, foreign policy rarely concerns the day-to-day lives of the citizenry. Other than during episodes of high international drama or of external events that have a special relevance to particular individuals or groups, foreign policy has far less salience to most people than, say, economic well-being or legal entanglements. Rarely does a country's external behaviour directly affect a citizen's support for the government or perception of the state's legitimacy. An issue area that clearly transcends the domestic/foreign policy dichotomy and impinges directly on the public is immigration.[1] The domestic economic and sociocultural implications of immigration make it a contentious, highly salient, political, and personal concern.

Immigration is an inextricable part of foreign policy since, by definition, it involves the transboundary movement of people, the purposeful governmental allocation of scarce resources to implement policy, and the establishment of criteria that define one state's position *vis-à-vis* the global community. As such, immigration policy can be viewed as a direct extension of a country's national interest, implicitly introducing domestic criteria to the formulation of a foreign policy. Since Canada, along with a number of other OECD states, determines annually the acceptable number of immigrants, immigration policy is always a potential political issue and may well be more sensitive than most government policies to the demands of domestic constituents and the exigencies of the day.

The case of refugees may be the most dramatic and controversial aspect of immigration policy because of its discreteness and humanitarian appeal and because of the political sensitivities that emerge when public attention becomes focused upon foreigners of varied racial or ethnic origin.[2] Immigration policy includes domestic economic and sociocultural factors in an effort to reflect the interests of the polity, but response to the plight of refugees may discount such factors in favour of other interests. In addition, the suddenness and immediacy of the problem introduces new demands to the standard operating procedures of the immigration process. Conventional criteria for admissibility may have to be waived; extra personnel and other governmental resources might be needed; new domestic constituencies may suddenly emerge and become politically active; new forms of co-ordination between levels of government may be deemed necessary; and new actors in the international arena could become centrally relevant to the implementation of policy.

Since the concluding days of World War II, the problem of displaced and persecuted people has been a constant feature of international politics. Canada's role since 1956 in responding to this ongoing human tragedy has been viewed as one of classic liberal internationalism, with an active and responsible participant offering aid and assistance under the aegis of the United Nations High Commissioner for Refugees (UNHCR). Before 1956 the Canadian position was far less flattering, with the government maintaining a very low profile of noncommitment, severe restraint, or outright refusal; the discriminatory nature of Canadian immigration policy reflected a fear of non-Anglo-Saxon infusion.[3] There is evidence to suggest that the more recent Canadian refugee policy formulation and implementation conforms more, though not entirely, to a complex neo-realist stance. This view highlights the ability of the government to commit scarce resources to respond unilaterally to a major international concern—the Indochinese "boat people"—while recognizing and co-ordinating the efforts of a large variety of societal interest groups.[4]

An Overview of Canadian Refugee Policy

Unlike the other cases examined in this volume, the issue of refugees focuses upon a series of discrete events that, while increasingly common in world politics, seem aberrant in comparison with the normal conduct of the immigration process. As seen in Figure 7.1, the general issue of immigration has always received a relatively substantial degree of official governmental attention. Since the 1950s, an increasing proportion of that attention can be accounted for by refugee concerns. (Were post-1978 data available at time of writing, this would probably be even more evident.) However, this reflects more the increase in refugee episodes and the politicization of the refugee issue than the institutionalization of the response, since during the nonrefugee years, such as 1964 through 1969, relative attention given to immigration increased. As shown in Table 7.1, the allocation of budgetary and personnel resources within the immigration sector grew in a steady and consistent manner, regardless of the number of new refugees. These data also reveal both the growing numbers of immigration offices and personnel abroad and the widening global coverage provided by the government, reflecting the expanding scope of overall involvement throughout the Canadian foreign policy sector.

Furthermore, as seen in Table 7.2, immigration activity after 1945 was subsumed under the standard operating procedures of the appropriate government departments and achieved a distinct role only in response to abnormal conditions such as the influx of displaced persons immediately after World War II. During such periods, the overriding self-perceived

FIGURE 7.1 Relative Attention to Refugee and Immigration Policy, 1944–1978

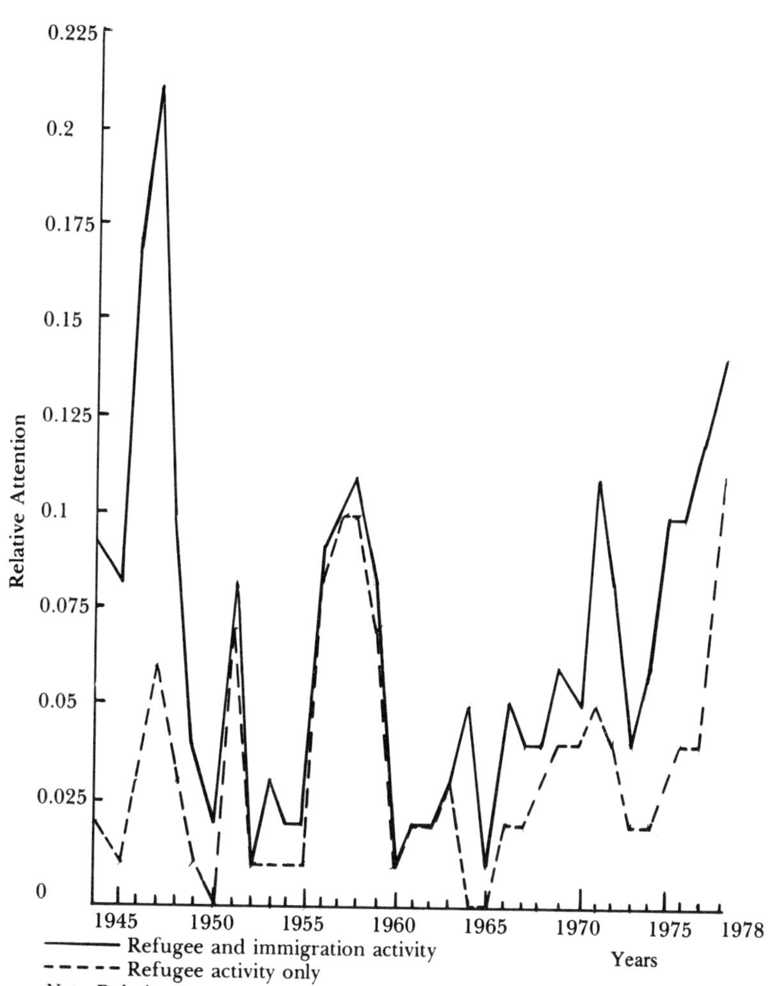

Note: Relative attention is measured by the number of paragraphs containing references to refugee and immigration policy, divided by the number of pages in each annual report.

SOURCE: Based on Department of External Affairs, *Annual Report*, 1944–1971; *Annual Review*, 1972–1978.

role, as expressed in official documents, was one of humanitarianism. Support for the multilateralization of the refugee phenomenon began in the mid-1960s, reflecting the exacerbation of the problem in the LDCs. A closer look at the 1970s, represented in Table 7.3, shows a movement away from this dominant liberal-internationalist ethos towards an overall complex neo-realist policy, reflecting Canadian domestic concerns for internal development, a review of immigration policy and practice, and

TABLE 7.1 Canadian Governmental Immigration Resources, 1948–1979

Year	Total Expenditures[1] ($ millions)	*Number of Immigration Offices Abroad* Europe	Western Hemisphere	Africa & Middle East	Asia & Pacific	Total
1948	2.7	5	—	—	—	5
1949	1.0	7	—	—	1	8
1950	5.0	11	—	—	1	12
1951	5.5	17	—	—	—	17
1952	8.2	17	—	—	1	18
1953	7.1	18	—	—	2	20
1954	7.3	18	—	—	2	20
1955	8.3	18	—	—	2	20
1956	8.0	18	—	1	2	21
1957	18.6	21	—	1	2	24
1958	22.0	23	2	1	2	28
1959	14.4	24	2	1	2	29
1960	11.7	24	4	1	2	31
1961	12.3	24	4	1	2	31
1962	12.0	24	4	1	2	31
1963	12.5	23	4	2	2	31
1964	13.2	25	4	2	2	33
1965	14.3	26	4	2	2	34
1966	14.3	27	4	2	4	37
1967	20.5	29	6	3	6	44
1968	21.6	26	7	3	6	42
1969	29.4	26	7	3	6	42
1970	24.0	26	5	3	6	40
1971	22.8	25	6	3	6	40
1972	22.7	25	6	3	6	40
1973	31.6	26	16	5	8	55
1974	34.2	26	18	5	8	57
1975	41.3	26	19	6	8	59
1976	51.5	26	19	6	8	59
1977	54.2	26	19	6	8	59
1978	62.0	23	19	5	8	55
1979	66.4	23	19	5	9	56

[1]For fiscal years ending March 31.

SOURCE: Based on annual reports of Department of Mines and Resources, Department of Citizenship and Immigration, Department of Manpower and Immigration, Department of Employment and Immigration, appropriate years. For 1966, 1978, and 1979, figures are taken from the Public Accounts Records. Figures on immigration offices by location from 1966 to 1974 are deduced from *Canadian Immigration and Population Study*, vol. 3; *Immigration and Population Statistics* (Ottawa: Department of Manpower and Immigration, 1974), Table 9.1.

TABLE 7.2 Canadian Roles in Immigration[1]/Refugee Activities, 1944–1978

In each pair, the first number represents immigration activities; the second represents refugee activities.

	'44	'45	'46	'47	'48	'49	'50	'51	'52	'53	'54	'55	'56	'57	'58	'59	'60	'61	'62	'63	'64	'65	'66	'67	'68	'69	'70	'71	'72	'73	'74	'75	'76	'77	'78
Role conception Not Apparent	6/2	7/0	10/3	15/5	7/2	3/1	2/0	1/5	0/1	2/0	1/1	1/1	1/4	0/9	1/10	0/5			0/1	0/2	4/0	1	2/0	2/1	1/2	2/2	1/3	6/3	4/0	2/1	4/1	5/3		5/3	2/6
Humanitarian	1/0	0/1	4/0	0/1	0/1			0/2					0/4	0/1		0/2	0/1	0/1	0/1		1/0		1/0				0/1	0/1	0/3					2/1	0/4
Promoter of Stability																		0/1																	
Supporter of Constructive Means to Solve World Problems																				0/1															
Supporter of/Contributor to Multilateral Assistance Schemes/U.N. Activities																							0/1	0/1	0/1	0/1		0/1	0/1	0/1	0/1	0/2			0/1
Developer																							0/1												
TOTAL ROLE REFERENCES	1		4	1	1			2					4	1		2	1	2	1	1	1		3	1	1	2	1	2	4	1	1	2	N/A[2]	1	5

[1]Immigration includes all relevant activity *except* for distinctly refugee issues.
[2]1976 data not available.

SOURCE: Department of External Affairs *Annual Reports/Reviews*, 1944-1978.

TABLE 7.3 Perceptions of Canadian Roles in Immigration/Refugee Activities, 1970–1978

In each pair, the first number represents immigration activities; the second represents refugee activities.

	1970	*1971*	*1972*	*1973*	*1974*	*1975*	*1976*	*1977*	*1978*
Humanitarian	0/1	1/0	0/11	1/6	0/8	4/5	0/4	1/9	0/13
Promoter of Internal Development	4/0	1/0	3/1	1/0	3/0	11/0	2/0	4/0	8/0
Protector of Quebec Interests–French Culture and Language	1/0								2/0
Tightening Policy on Immigration	3/0		6/0	2/0	3/0	5/0	12/0	4/2	2/0
Supporter of International Co-operation for Development	2/0								
Supporter of UN Activities							0/1		0/2
Mediator-Integrator/Supporter of International Understanding	0/1						1/0		
Anti-Communist								1/0	
Protector of Refugees									0/2
Role Conception Not Apparent	7/3	5/1	7/5	12/10	7/9	16/10	30/17	33/4	19/11
TOTAL ROLE REFERENCES	12	2	21	10	14	25	20	21	29

Note: Immigration includes all relevant activity *except* distinctly refugee issues.
SOURCE:: Based on Canadian Institute of International Affairs and Parliamentary Centre for Foreign Affairs and Foreign Trade, *International Canada,* 1970-1978.

the issue of Quebec culture and language in the context of federal policies. When refugee episodes occurred, the humanitarian position became dominant again. Towards the end of the 1970s, some evidence for a renewed Canadian concern with the role of multilateral and international factors was visible, undoubtedly reflecting the sudden dislocation of large numbers of Indochinese and African people as a result of local wars infused with East–West political, economic, and military proxies.[5]

The evolution of the Canadian position on refugees has been both dramatic and *ad hoc.* The Mackenzie King government initially approached the problem of displaced persons within the context of the traditional modes of immigration operation. However, while the Immigration Branch, housed at that time in the Department of Mines and Resources, pursued traditional policy, there began a broadly based movement within the Department of External Affairs, Parliament, and a number of societal groups to establish special criteria for displaced persons and refugees. These efforts culminated in a May 1947 statement by the prime minister, which "would prove to be the foundation upon which immigration policy rested [and] the umbrella under which hundreds of thousands of Europeans entered Canada during the next decade."[6] From then on, through the 1959–1960 efforts that began the liberalization of Canadian refugee policy, the government handled displaced persons and refugees solely under its regular immigration program.

The liberalization process continued through the 1966 White Paper on Canadian immigration policy and the 1974 Green Paper entitled *Canadian Immigration and Population Study*. By this time, Canadian policy had formally acceded to the guidelines of the UN Convention Relating to the Status of Refugees. To respond to major international crises, a "special movements" program was created in which normal immigration regulations and criteria for admissibility were relaxed and, in many circumstances, purposefully contravened in order to deal with particular humanitarian or hardship cases. These attempts at regularizing, rationalizing, and institutionalizing Canadian policy concerning refugees emerged in response to societal, governmental, and international demands in light of a series of tragic situations: postwar Europe, Hungary in 1956, Czechoslovakia in 1967, Uganda in 1972, Chile in 1973, and Indochina since the mid-1970s.[7] In this chapter, we examine the development and unfolding of Canadian refugee policy and performance during these six major refugee crises.

The Postwar European Refugees

In the immediate aftermath of World War II, the Atlantic community's efforts to restore some semblance of order, prosperity, and political freedom to war-torn Europe in the shadow of a perceived expansionist threat from Stalinist Russia included the enormous challenge of repatriating or resettling approximately 60 million displaced people. The United Nations Relief and Rehabilitation Administration (UNRRA) was successful in assisting almost all to return to their former homes, but about a million such persons remained in various locations throughout Europe.[8] This success of UNRRA, achieved in the four years following its founding in November 1943, was eventually undermined by the intrusion of East–West tensions into the United Nations and its specialized agencies. Acrimonious debate occurred over forced repatriation of East European and Soviet citizens, resulting in the abandonment of UNRRA and the July 1947 implementation of the International Refugee Organization (IRO), established under the Preparatory Commission the previous year.[9] While still under the auspices of the UN, the IRO was able to function without undue impediment since the Soviet Union and its Eastern-bloc satellites refused to sign the IRO constitution, leaving it essentially a Western-based organization. The IRO pursued its operations until March 1952, almost two years beyond the original mandate.[10]

Within Canada the Mackenzie King era was ending and a new Liberal government was established under Louis St. Laurent in November 1948. This government essentially continued the immigration policy articulated by King in his May 1947 address to Parliament. It focused on three fundamental factors: rate of population increase, absorptive capacity of the economy, and national and racial balance of the country. These elements, although flexibly interpreted by various orders-in-council over the years, remained the basis for policy until John Diefenbaker became prime minister in 1957.[11]

While Canada, a country of immigrants, had a history of being cautiously receptive to communities of refugees dating back to the United Empire Loyalists and including such groups as the Mennonites, Doukhobors, Hutterites, and Ukrainians, the fifteen years preceding King's 1947 declaration had been one of severe immigrant restriction for economic reasons and, more nefariously, preferential treatment for a few and exclusion for many because of racial, ethnic, and religious grounds.[12] The relaxation of these restrictions and Canada's acceptance of 165 697 displaced persons from Europe resulted partly from postwar domestic prosperity and escalating labour demand. The change in immigration patterns, particularly following King's retirement, also coincided with an emerging Canadian foreign policy committed to an active international presence and concerned with Canada's role in a newly defined global order and its ability to pursue national policies reflective of its new standing as a major postwar state.[13]

As a result, for the first time, immigration policy, tied as it was to issues of security and the rebuilding of Europe, became highly politicized within the governmental bureaucracy. Although it remained initially under the authority of J.A. Glen, minister of the Department of Mines and Resources, the Departments of External Affairs and Labour became directly involved in the question of the resettlement of displaced persons. This was indicative of the changing factors affecting immigration questions as well as of the evolving size, expertise, and importance of these two departments. The politicization of immigration policy also occurred in the House and Senate, as well as among large and diverse sectors of the Canadian public.[14] Nevertheless, the policy that gradually allowed the arrival of displaced persons remained rooted in the traditional criteria of economic absorptive capacity and concern over homogeneity of population characteristics.

External Affairs pushed for greater liberalization, conforming to its outspoken commitment—first under St. Laurent and then under Pearson—to internationalism, active participation, and responsible support for the UN and its special relief agencies and programs. In late 1945, the department established its own refugee committee, and the following year it convened an interdepartmental committee that included representatives from Labour, Health, and the Immigration

Branch of Mines and Resources. By May 1946, this committee sent a report to Cabinet containing short-term recommendations for immediate policy changes along with a request for a review of Canada's long-term population needs and the development of an immigration program reflecting the findings of the proposed study.

From this time forth, DEA officials began to express their increasing dissatisfaction with the performance of the Immigration Branch in the resettlement of European displaced persons.[15] External Affairs also differed with Labour on the number and type of immigrants required in the postwar Canadian economy. While Labour argued for the traditional policy of accepting unskilled and semi-skilled workers for labour-intensive employment, DEA argued for a resettlement policy based on a combination of humanitarian criteria and absorptive capacity, but with the latter category to include educated and professional persons as well as agricultural and industrial workers. Most serious of all were the conflicts between Immigration and Labour, based on perceptions by senior Immigration officials that the Department of Labour intended to intrude into jurisdictions held by the Immigration Branch.[16] Out of these bureaucratic positions, the interdepartmental committee drafted a policy statement that formed the basis for Prime Minister King's address to the House.

At this time, a wide-ranging public debate was occurring both within and outside Parliament. The Standing Committee on Immigration and Labour was reconstituted in April 1946, with its purpose, as expressed by Senator Arthur Roebuck, being "to discover whether Canada wanted, or needed, or could absorb, vast numbers of foreigners."[17] The committee hearings resulted in an official Senate report criticizing government policy and recommending a new immigration policy that would reflect the capacity of the Canadian nation to assist more effectively the international resettlement efforts, while also liberalizing the general criteria for immigrant admissibility. Within the House itself, opposition parties as well as government back-benchers criticized the government's lack of resolve and initiative in coming to the aid of the homeless in Europe.

The vigour and tenor of this public debate within Canada complemented the urgent requests coming to the IRO and the United Nations High Commissioner for Refugees, which began functioning in January 1951 as the successor organization to the IRO. The government of Canada responded to these expressions of concern and hope by relaxing a number of immigration criteria, by invoking special legislation through various orders-in-council, and finally, after the first seven years of the displaced persons program, by liberalizing the overall immigration policy so that, from 1952 on, "refugee arrivals from Europe were not singled out explicitly but formed part of the total [immigration] movement."[18] Although the Canadian response was considered generous and comparable to the positions adopted by the United States and Australia—taking into account Canada's active support for the IRO, the UNHCR, and the Intergovernmental Committee for European Migration (ICEM), founded in 1951—criticism was still forthcoming. Refugees continued to come under the general jurisdiction of standard immigration policy; therefore, immigration officers, encouraged by King's 1947 address, selected candidates on the basis of ease of resettlement and integration into Canadian society. This meant that Canada, along with other countries of resettlement, "bypassed thousands of European refugees due to their age, infirmities, and handicaps."[19] The IRO, the UNHCR, the ICEM, and DEA all argued unsuccessfully for further relaxation of requirements so that "hard-core" cases could be removed from countries of first asylum.[20] This restrictive position would remain the Canadian policy until the late 1950s.

The first Canadian experience after the war with displaced persons and refugees reveals a foreign policy highly conditioned by past prejudices and operational procedures. Canadian participation in international efforts to deal with Europeans fleeing from the conflict began with the infamous Evian Conference in July 1938. Until Mackenzie King's 1947 address, the Canadian position was one of ambivalence, noncommitment or open prejudice against non-Anglo-Saxons. Movement towards greater leniency, a broadening of the immigration program, and an overall liberalization of policy began shortly after the war's conclusion. The emergence of a new foreign policy on immigration evolved as a result of Canada's leading position in support of international organizations with which it was directly involved, especially the United Nations; the policy also grew out of its concern for the strengthening of the Atlantic community and the development of an increasingly strong and prestigious Department of External Affairs, embodying a commitment to active participation in shaping a new world order. But while these international factors provided the external context and the governmental capability, the parameters of opportunity and constraint clearly came from within Canada. The decisions and ensuing actions were rooted in the demands of politicians, parties, bureaucrats, and societal interest groups, as well as in the government's overall perception of the current state and future expectations of the Canadian economy.

Because of the special qualities of immigration policy, especially the implicit entwining of domestic and external politics in a country of immigrants, this aspect of Canadian foreign policy contains within it, almost by definition, factors of the complex neo-realist model. In particular, the domestic and governmental processes contribute significantly to any explanation. Nuances do exist, however, and these are what provide, along with the more dramatic changes, the test for the applicability of the three competing foreign policy perspectives.

It is evident that from the beginning of the process that led up to the May 1947 speech and beyond, Canadian refugee policy was part of the trend developing across the entire foreign policy spectrum: an increasingly active and responsible role, within a focus defined in consultation with Canada's allies, committed to joint action complementing the activities of others, and supportive of the multilateral institutional arrangements established to co-ordinate the general operation. However, in this special area of immigration/refugees, external factors, while having a prominent role, remained second to the overriding societal process as well as to governmental political and bureaucratic issues. This suggests that even at a time when a heightened internationalist ethos was pervading the Canadian foreign policy community, idealism was constrained by the pragmatism of domestic politics. Remnants of Canada's ties to an imperial power also continued to affect policy, especially in the definition of the United Kingdom as the "most preferred country" as a source of immigrants, a definition that helped close the doors to many non-Anglo-Saxon European refugees. But, in the final analysis, Canada did accept a large number of refugees from throughout Europe, continued to support international efforts for resettlement, and began the process of redefining both immigration policy and concomitant bureaucratic responsibility and division of labour in terms of Canada's new role in the changing global environment.

The Hungarian Refugees, 1956–1957

Although special migration arrangements for the refugees of World War II ended in 1953, Canada continued to admit such people under the Immigration Act of 1952, which codified and incorporated many of the measures that had been instituted through orders-in-council. In the fall of 1956, this procedure was severely tested as Canada, along with many other Western countries, began to respond to the crisis precipitated by the Hungarian uprising and the ensuing Soviet invasion. By the end of November, more than a hundred thousand people had fled Hungary, most seeking refuge in neighbouring Austria. In response to official Austrian requests, the UNHCR and the ICEM were asked to assist and co-ordinate the movement of Hungarian refugees to countries of second asylum and, where possible, to states that would provide permanent resettlement. "Of states accepting Hungarian refugees for permanent resettlement, none surpassed Canada."[21]

As part of its reorganization of the structure of government, the St. Laurent government had established the Department of Citizenship and Immigration (DCI) in 1950.[22] In 1954 Jack W. Pickersgill became the minister responsible for immigration, succeeding Walter Harris, the first minister of DCI. Both Harris and Pickersgill faced difficulties in formulating and implementing immigration policy, particularly because of the conflict over philosophy, approach, and shared jurisdiction between their own department and the Department of Labour. Labour was concerned that immigration policy should fluctuate in synchrony with the business cycle and unemployment statistics, while DCI believed in the long-term benefits to be derived from continuous efforts at expanding the immigrant population.[23] These issues spilled over into the Commons debates, providing easy targets and good press for the Conservative opposition at a time when the Liberal government was already facing an uncertain outcome in the approaching federal election, its position made even more difficult by the public debate over Canada's role in the Suez crisis of October 1956.[24]

The early official Canadian response to the events in Hungary came in the form of Pickergill's speech to the House of Commons on 26 November 1956; it was sympathetic, helpful, but cautious. Pickersgill indicated that the government had upgraded its Vienna office and provided assistance to those refugees willing to settle in Canada. While this was an improvement over earlier government positions, it remained far from sufficient for those parliamentarians, civil servants, citizen groups, and media personnel who were inclined to believe that Canada should and could do much more to alleviate the plight of the thousands of Hungarians scattered in refugee camps across Europe.[25] Furthermore, though Pickersgill had made Hungarian applicants the immigration priority, they were still required to conform to many of the standard criteria of admission.

In light of the changing circumstances, Pickersgill announced two days later that the government would provide free transportation, in place of an earlier loan scheme, and relax many of the bureaucratic, health, and economic criteria used for normal immigration processing. This announcement, which essentially committed the Canadian government to an active and large refugee admissions program, was greeted with much enthusiasm and support by those who had been lobbying the cabinet for a more humanitarian stance.[26] Nevertheless, within a few days of this speech and the minister's trip to Vienna to examine the situation personally, the St. Laurent government again came under severe criticism for what was perceived to be its somewhat cynical and opportunistic approach to refugee selection, an approach conditioned by concerns over resettlement costs and economic absorption as well as competition for the best candidates.[27] Yet policy was transformed to action, and by December 1958, 37 566 Hungarian refugees had arrived in Canada.

The Canadian response to the Hungarian refugees, after some initial hesitancy on the part of the Liberal government, was direct, forceful, and relatively well executed. The policy that permitted and facilitated the arrival of more than 37 000 refugees in less than ten months occurred as a direct result of the demands of large and vocal sectors of the Canadian public. The rapid evolution of the refugee program can be traced to specific instances of public comment and lobbying followed by commitment to assist in the absorption and settlement needs of the new immigrants.[28] Indeed, the government went so far as to host a number of receptions and mini-conferences with voluntary associations and provincial governments before Pickersgill's 28 November statement in order to ascertain how willing the public was to accept a large influx of Hungarians. Although longstanding differences in opinion and approach between DEA and DCI remained, these were effectively muted for much of this operation, at least partially because of the willingness of provinces and communities to share the work of successful resettlement.[29]

The activity that emerged, though affected by the responses of other Western countries, was foremost a domestic, interest-based policy, arranged bilaterally between the Canadian government and the Austrian officials working under the international co-ordination of the UNHCR, the Red Cross, and the ICEM. Even while relaxing Canadian immigration criteria, Pickersgill maintained that "the problem . . . that ought to worry every responsible member of the house [sic] and every Canadian . . . is what is going to happen to these people when they arrive."[30] Although this statement was open to criticism as giving priority to the skilled, tarnishing Canada's humanitarian ideals, it encouraged a multisector co-ordination to satisfy this governmental priority that did much to stimulate the success of the program.

The government's calculations, based upon a combination of its interests and capabilities, determined how many Hungarian refugees would be offered permanent asylum. The international context seemed to place Canada, along with its allies, in a position of responsibility to offer assistance to those who suffered at the hands of Communist repression. But, as the Conservative government demonstrated shortly after it came to power in 1957 and reduced the sponsored immigration program, the extent of Canada's open-door generosity was tempered by its own socio-economic and political climate. It may not be too harsh to suggest that had the domestic economic environment been different in 1954–1956, the Canadian response would have been far more cautious, hesitant, and restrictive, especially since the Liberal government was facing an uphill political struggle in the 1957 federal election. There is little evidence that significant international pressure existed to overcome major domestic reluctance, had any occurred. In this crisis, Canadian policy in both formulation and operation reflected a bifurcated perspective of liberal internationalism tempered by domestic socio-economic concerns.

The Czechoslovakian Refugees, 1968–1969

The defeat of the Diefenbaker Conservatives in the spring of 1963 signalled to many observers the resurrection of foreign policy as a priority in the affairs of government. Along with the revitalization of External Affairs, the Pearson Cabinet took on the task of examining a wide range of policy issues. Among them were the issues of immigration, minimized by Diefenbaker, and the relationship between population growth, domestic economic development, and external affairs.[31]

In 1966, after review by both Cabinet and the relevant civil servants—and in the spirit established by the Royal Commission on Government Organization (the Glassco Commission), the Senate Committee on Manpower and Employment, and the Economic Council of Canada—a new and powerful Department of Manpower and Immigration (DMI) was established, replacing Citizenship and Immigration and absorbing large areas of jurisdiction from the Department of Labour; citizenship returned to the Department of the Secretary of State. Following recommendations of a White Paper and the earlier Sedgwick Report, a special joint committee of the Senate and the House of Commons was appointed that resulted, albeit indirectly, in an internal departmental task force's proposal for a new set of immigration regulations. These regulations "established a point system for the selection of immigrants and three basic admission categories: independent applicants, sponsored dependents, and nominated relatives. . . ."[32] On 1 October 1967, these new regulations came into effect, ushering in, for the first time in Canadian history, an attempt to institutionalize objective criteria for an immigration program based on universality.

During the years between the end of the Hungarian crisis and the establishment of Manpower and Immigration, Canada continued to participate in refugee-related activities. The United Nations World Refugee Year, 1959–60, provided the impetus for the establishment of an ongoing private sponsorship program to aid European refugees. Canada continued to provide financial support for UNHCR and UNRWA at levels exceeded only by the United States for the former, and the U.S. and the United Kingdom for the latter. Although jurisdictional and budgetary problems existed between various federal government departments, between the federal, provincial, and municipal authorities, and between the public and private sectors concerning immigration policy, Canada continued to admit an average of two thousand refugees a year between 1959 and the mid-1960s.[33] These included not only Europeans but also, in 1962, a small number of Chinese refugees.[34] While refugees continued to be received and aided by the Canadian government, the White Paper on Canadian immigration policy "still did not contain specific provisions for accepting refugees."[35] Nor had Canada as yet acceded to the UN Convention and Protocol on Refugees.

One year after these new Canadian immigration regulations came into effect, a third Soviet-induced postwar European refugee crisis occurred. In August 1968, Warsaw Pact forces invaded Czechoslovakia and occupied the major cities; the Soviets subsequently removed the Dubcek government from office and imposed a new pro-Soviet hard-line regime in its place. Once again Austria, as well as other West European countries, became the place of first asylum for thousands of East European refugees, and once again, in response to requests from the UNHCR and the Austrian government and in consort with NATO allies, Canada embarked on a program of assistance and resettlement.

The Canadian response, similar to its response to the Hungarian situation of 1956, was to invoke a Cabinet-level directive to immigration officers in the field to relax the standard admissions procedures. After some initial hesitancy on the part of the government (which resulted in public condemnation), the final program opened the doors to approximately eleven thousand Czech and Slovak refugees.[36] On 3 September 1968, Secretary of State for External Affairs Mitchell Sharp announced that Canada would take all Czechoslovakian refugees who wished to come to Canada. Furthermore, recognizing the urgency of the situation and the fact that the majority of these people were technically skilled or professionals, and therefore desirable new Canadians under the conventional norms for immigration, the government committed additional personnel to Vienna and Belgrade to handle the growing number of visa enquiries. This special program continued until the middle of January 1969.[37]

The co-ordination of this five-month effort was handled by a special interdepartmental committee of representatives from Manpower and Immigration, External Affairs, National Health and Welfare, and the Solicitor General (RCMP).[38] Perhaps because NATO leaders abroad and Prime Minister Trudeau at home set the context of the problem within the East–West conflict, and perhaps because foreign minister Sharp was attempting to establish the primacy of DEA in foreign affairs and his own position within the newly elected Trudeau government, External Affairs took the lead in policy formulation. However, DMI, under its new minister Allan MacEachen, provided the operational co-ordination and expertise, including governmental support for resettlement upon arrival in Canada.[39] Except for the early caution in Trudeau's initial response, the Czechoslovakian refugee situation did not provoke much interest-group or private sector activity. Nor were parliamentarians or local politicians stimulated to offer the grandiloquent speeches so common in 1956. After condemnation of the Soviet action and support for the government's intention to aid refugees wishing to settle in

Canada, implementation of the program invoked little comment. Federal government machinery successfully co-ordinated the process of adjustment and absorption with local officials and representatives of the Canadian Czechoslovakian community.

The effectiveness of the government's response was based on five factors. First, the crisis evoked a sympathetic chord throughout Canada, a result of both the 1956 Hungarian episode and anti-Soviet feeling. Second, Trudeau's successful campaign to become leader of the Liberal Party and prime minister had created an air of excitement throughout much of Canada and belief in his leadership abilities. Third, during the preceding few years, the country had been involved in the debate over immigration policy and, in combination with the post-1963 expansionary policy, was receptive to a large influx of immigrants. Fourth, these refugees were perceived as being a homogeneous group of remarkably skilled Europeans, therefore easily assimilable and not a threat to the working person. Finally, a relatively large group of civil servants and voluntary personnel with experience and expertise gained through the two prior resettlement programs and the White Paper debate was in place. The efficiency of the Canadian response attested to this enhanced domestic capacity and the ability of the government to implement its foreign policy unilaterally.

The Ugandan Asian Refugees, 1972

Except for the admission of small numbers of Chinese refugees in 1962 and Tibetan refugees in 1970, Canadian efforts at assisting refugees since World War II had been limited to the three European movements. Peoples from Africa and Asia, while admitted under the standard immigration regulations—until the point system was introduced in 1967, openly prejudiced against non-Caucasians—had not been considered for refugee status or special movement programs. In 1972, the crisis provoked by Ugandan President Idi Amin's declaration on 4 August that all members of the Asian minority within his country who carried British passports would be expelled compelled Canadian authorities to consider, and ultimately to accept, the admittance of a large number of Ugandan Asian refugees. The urgency of the situation was compounded by two factors, the imposition of a ninety-day time limit on the expulsion order and the domestic difficulties the British would face if they were to accept the fifty thousand or more designated Ugandans within such a short period.[40]

Immigration minister Bryce Mackasey, in response to a British request for assistance, was authorized to admit Ugandan Asians as landed immigrants to Canada on an emergency basis. He announced that extra officials from DMI and National Health and Welfare, as well as a special medical unit, were being sent to Kampala to expedite immigration processing. While thousands of Ugandan Asians were being assisted by these extraordinary measures, they still were required "to pass the regulations of the Canadian Immigration Act before [being] approved for entry," although greater discretionary leniency was permitted, thereby reducing the restrictiveness of the point system.[41] Nevertheless, Canada was in the fortunate position, in the words of a member of the British high commission in Uganda, of "getting all the better-qualified ones" through careful selection.[42] By the end of this special movement, Canada had accepted more than seven thousand Ugandan Asians, more than all other countries combined apart from Great Britain.[43]

The entire process, taking less than six months, began with the direct initiative of the Prime Minister's Office. On 16 August the matter was brought before Cabinet, circumventing standard procedures of departmental and ministerial recommendation and setting the groundwork for the positive statement that emerged from Cabinet a week later. This was followed by the establishment of a special interdepartmental task force from DEA and DMI to oversee and co-ordinate the implementation of the government's policy on emergency admissions. While the government's stand won support from most sectors of society, some criticism was forthcoming from people in major urban centres, where concern was expressed over the increasing "ethnic presence" and fear of exacerbating the worsening unemployment situation was voiced. The government's policy was defended both in humanitarian terms and on the basis of the universal, nondiscriminatory nature of Canadian immigration policy.[44]

This refugee program, which could have been politically dangerous because of its non-European, non-Caucasian character and because it came at a time when the government was considering calling a federal election, received widespread support for a number of reasons. First, Prime Minister Trudeau and senior Cabinet ministers took a relatively quick and decisive stand on the issue, condemning Idi Amin for promulgating such a policy. Second, this was followed by a show of support for the British government in its dilemma of meshing legal responsibility and humanitarian obligation with domestic reality. Third, the Canadian government used anglophone sympathies and Commonwealth ties to provide support for an activist stand on aiding the British. Fourth, Canadians' exemplary behaviour in the Hungarian and Czechoslovakian crises provided a strong organizational network for motivating public support and assistance. In addition, it soon became evident that most of the Ugandan Asians would have qualified under standard immigration criteria anyway and that they were likely to be easily absorbed into Canadian society. Finally, because of the restrictions imposed by Amin's order, it was clear that the entire process would be relatively short-lived and therefore unlikely to impose a severe strain on the Canadian economy or the federal bureaucracy.

The Canadian performance was unique. Although Amin's decree was widely condemned and fifty foreign governments were approached by the British government to provide aid and to accept those faced with explusion, relatively few states, even leading members of the Commonwealth, offered anything other than transit facilities, limited financial assistance, or severely restricted admissions.[45] Nor did the UNHCR take as active a role as it had in previous crises, in co-ordinating refugee movements or mobilizing governmental response.

Except for the historical ties between Canada and Great Britain, which admittedly had much to do with the Canadian position, Canada's decision-making processes and its behaviour were indicative of an emerging complex neo-realist foreign policy perspective. Once initial policy calculations were made at the senior political levels, the governmental process reflected the highly specialized capabilities developed to deal with such exigencies. Within the society, specialized voluntary associations and committees took the leading role in assisting internal resettlement efforts, resulting in one of the lowest cost per capita admission programs initiated by the government.[46] The Canadian program was initiated, funded, and directed unilaterally, in consultation with the British but without any major intergovernmental or multilateral effort. Finally, the decision to admit one-seventh of all displaced Ugandan Asians was predicated on a combination of perceived responsibility to a main ally, a recognition of humanitarian ideals combined with special Canadian capabilities including absorptive capacity, and a pragmatic acknowledgement that the majority of the refugees could contribute to Canadian productivity.

The Chilean Refugees, 1973–1974

On 11 September 1973, the Chilean government of President Salvador Allende was overthrown by a military coup. Coups are domestic affairs of some frequency throughout much of Latin America, although uncommon in Chilean politics, but the fact that Allende's was the first democratically elected Marxist regime in the West attracted an unusual amount of international attention. His overthrow and assassination were followed by severe repressive measures against his supporters both in and out of government, many of whom were non-Chileans who had left other Latin American countries in order to participate in the Allende experiment of Marxist democracy in Chile. The military response three years after Allende's election was brutally effective, resulting in the imprisonment, torture, and death of many thousands. Many fled to neighbouring Latin American countries; others, following the diplomatic custom in Latin America, sought refuge in foreign embassies in Santiago. These efforts to seek first asylum based on fear of political persecution got officials from the UNHCR directly involved in providing resettlement assistance. Of greater difficulty were those Chilean citizens who were forcibly detained within their country since, by the United Nations Convention, they could not be considered refugees.

Canada's response to these events was unlike its participation in previous refugee crises. Government action came only after strenuous lobbying by a broad range of domestic interest groups, professional associations, and political organizations, beginning on 17 September when the Canadian Council of Churches presented a brief imploring the government to act "upon humanitarian and not political consideration."[47] Not until mid-October did the Canadian government announce its intention to send an interdepartmental team of officials to Chile for on-site inspection. By late November, the government had established DEA, DMI, health, and security personnel in Santiago for processing Chilean and non-Chilean refugees who wished to apply for admission to Canada. Furthermore, immigration minister Robert Andras announced that officials in Panama, Honduras, and Argentina had also been ordered to process such people "under the relaxed provisions of Canada's refugee program."[48] These actions, although indicating a commitment on behalf of the government to assist political refugees fearful of persecution, nevertheless received strong criticism from church, academic, and voluntary organizations, as well as from many members of Parliament. External affairs minister Mitchell Sharp, who had been the primary government spokesman on this issue, was accused of acting with undue restraint and establishing on-site security procedures that severely impeded processing, criticisms that had not been heard in the three previous refugee crises.[49] On the other hand, there were concerns in Parliament and among the public that such tight screening was necessary in order to prevent "criminals", "radicals", and "revolutionaries" from entering Canada.[50] By December 1973, of the approximately fourteen hundred visa applications received, only 184 had been granted.[51] But the Chilean authorities made it difficult for many who might have qualified for Canadian assistance to receive permission to leave the country, thereby distorting the numbers and characteristics of those who were actually allowed to apply for Canadian visas.

Throughout the following year, Chilean refugees continued to arrive in small numbers, assisted by Canadian government loans and free passage on chartered aircraft. By the fall of 1974, approximately twenty-nine hundred applications had been approved, and by the following February, 1188 refugees had arrived in Canada, although not all had received landed immigrant status.[52] The number of staff in the Santiago immigration office was gradually reduced, but over the next three years, Chileans, along with a number of other Latin American nationals, continued to request immigration into Canada. By 1978 almost six thousand had received Canadian visas, including many who had sought first asylum in other countries, particularly Argentina.[53]

This did not diminish the criticism levelled against the Canadian government for what was perceived to be an inhumane and complacent attitude in the face of mounting evidence of persecution and official UNHCR support for further assistance.[54]

Compared with earlier Canadian involvements with refugee resettlement, the Chilean case is perceived by many to be a blot on Canada's recent record as a humanitarian nation offering asylum to the persecuted. There is little doubt that Canadian behaviour differed markedly from the 1956, 1968, and 1972 episodes; almost as many Chileans as Ugandan Asians were admitted, however, although over a much longer time period. Nevertheless, the policy process conforms to the characteristics of the complex neo-realist perspective, more so than in any of the previous refugee cases. The Canadian government pursued a strictly interest-based policy, diverging significantly from its own previous behaviour and that of many West European states, most notably Sweden; it conformed more closely to security-related concerns of the Western hemisphere, which were traditionally fearful of any form of radical politics. The centrality of Cabinet and DEA in controlling the initial stages of the refugee situation reflected the unease many Western countries had felt in dealing with the Allende regime and further legitimating a Marxist presence in the hemisphere.

For Canada, the Chilean episode had additional significance in relation to the potential expansion of Canadian trade and investment in Latin America, a hoped-for result of Mitchell Sharp's recently articulated Third Option. Canada was reluctant to set a precedent by becoming directly involved in the domestic politics of another state, which might jeopardize future Canadian–Latin American relations. The forceful and articulate activities of societal groups and associations in Canada—especially the churches, which were part of an international network—did much to encourage the government to take a more active role. However, DMI officials in the field maintained a more rigorous position, following standard operating procedures with far less leniency than had been done with the Ugandans, Czechoslovakians, or Hungarians. And though criticized by some Canadians as well as by UN officials for this position, the government received widespread support from the Liberal, Progressive Conservative, and Social Credit/Créditiste parties both federally and provincially, as well as from many private citizens. As immigration minister Robert Andras noted, "Canadian politics are shifting to the right and . . . there will be 'hell to pay' over the Canadian decision to admit Chilean refugees."[55] These domestic factors were obviously important, considering the minority status of the 1973 Trudeau government, intent on calling a federal election to upgrade its position.

The Indochinese Refugees, 1975–1980

On 3 February 1975, the Green Paper on immigration policy was tabled in the House of Commons by Minister of Manpower and Immigration Robert Andras. The result of a two-year effort to provide the first comprehensive review of Canada's immigration policy, it led to Bill C-24, the new immigration act. The act came into effect on 10 April 1978, after being guided through review by Bud Cullen, who replaced Andras in DMI. During this same period, Bill C-27, the Employment and Immigration Reorganization Act of 1976 (promulgated on 14 August 1977), authorized the establishment of the new Canada Employment and Immigration Commission (CEIC) and the Department of Employment and Immigration (DEI) to replace the Unemployment Insurance Commission and DMI.[56]

These two acts were of direct significance to the Canadian involvement in the Indochinese refugee crisis following the April 1975 collapse of the South Vietnamese government. C-24 codified for the first time within domestic legislation Canada's international commitment to assist and protect refugees.[57] In addition, a structural reorganization combined with C-24 to allow for the institutionalization of long-term planning of Canada's immigration needs, with refugee admittance an integral part of this calculation.[58] Allan Gotlieb, who oversaw the drafting of the Green Paper and Bills C-24 and C-27 in his capacity as deputy minister of DMI, was transferred to DEA as its undersecretary. He was replaced in CEIC/DEI by his former colleague and senior assistant, J.L. Manion, thereby establishing an informal but crucial senior political and administrative link between these two foreign service departments.[59]

With the fall of Saigon, thousands of South Vietnamese tried to flee from the invading northern forces. The United States government offered asylum to many, and numerous others were received by Canada, Australia, and France as well as neighbouring Southeast Asian countries. From 1975 until the Hai Hong incident in 1978, most of the migration was overland movement between contiguous Asian countries, with relatively few "boat people" arriving in the Philippines, Singapore, Malaysia, Indonesia, Hong Kong, and even Japan and Australia.[60] Many of these people were not Vietnamese but refugees seeking asylum from the upheavals occurring in Laos and Cambodia (later Kampuchea), which were related to the Vietnam conflict and affected by the direct political and military involvement of the consolidated Vietnamese regime in their internal affairs.

The Vietnamese migration was relatively small until mid-1978, when the Vietnamese government's March declaration abolished "all trade and business operations of bourgeois tradesmen," effectively undercutting the livelihood of 80 per cent of the Hoa, the Chinese ethnics in Vietnam. This, combined with Hanoi's tilt away from China towards the Soviet Union and the later Chinese "punitive raid" into Vietnam, created a climate of fear and uncertainty within the Hoa communities. Between the fall of Saigon and the end of 1979, it was estimated, more than six hundred thousand people had fled Vietnam, 60 to 70 per cent Hoa. Most of these had used various forms of water transport (hence the "boat people" designation), ending up in refugee camps scattered across the Southeast Asian coastline, and as far adrift as Japan and Australia.

The Canadian action in the Indochinese refugee situation was one of incrementalism, responding to the changing international situation and Canadian public opinion over a five-year period.[61] Initially, the Canadian response to those claiming refugee status was reminiscent of the government's position regarding the Hungarian, Czechoslovakian, and Ugandan Asian crises. Admission was conducted by relaxing the point system, thereby restricting early applicants primarily to those Vietnamese and Cambodians with relatives already in Canada, followed one month later by an additional three thousand refugees already in countries of first asylum. Over the next year, in response to appeals from the UNHCR, Canada accepted 180 "small boat escapees" and 450 people from camps in Thailand.[62] In 1977 and 1978 the Cabinet, on advice from the DEI officials in the field and requests from the office of the UNHCR, instituted the Vietnamese Small Boat Escapee Program, which allocated additional immigration space to Indochinese refugees. Although neither procedures nor goals shifted significantly from the earlier program, this newly instituted program explicitly recognized that Indochinese refugees could no longer be considered a responsibility of the American government alone. By the end of 1978, under these two programs, Canada had admitted 9060 refugees, including those who had fled overland from Laos and Kampuchea into Thailand.[63]

The new immigration act that came into effect in April 1978 not only reaffirmed and codified Canada's postwar tradition of providing humanitarian assistance to the displaced and persecuted, but in addition introduced the policy of reserving a substantial portion of each year's immigration quota for refugees. The act also included "the innovative provision for private sponsorship of refugees and the designated class system whereby groups could be designated for admission on grounds similar to those applicable to the United Nations Convention on Refugees."[64] In December 1978, Cabinet designated the Indochinese refugees as such a class. Of the 10 000 spaces allocated for refugees in 1979, one-half were reserved for the Indochinese, with private group sponsorship to be in addition to this quota. Nevertheless, the Liberal government began to receive public criticism from leaders of church and other voluntary organizations, opposition MPs as well as some of its own back-benchers, and editorial writers.[65] Both Cullen and external affairs minister Don Jamieson were criticized and urged to extend Canadian financial aid and resettlement assistance still further, as evidence mounted that the numbers of refugees fleeing Vietnam were escalating from between ten and twenty thousand per month to more than fifty thousand per month. Nevertheless, throughout this time the government, while being criticized, still actively initiated, encouraged, and organized support from the public sector for increased refugee flows.[66]

The federal election campaign in the spring of 1979 dominated the news, and both on-site reporting and editorial commentary on the refugees ceased to receive significant attention in spite of the seriousness of the Indochinese situation.[67] However, within a month of the Liberal defeat, Prime Minister Joe Clark's new government faced constituency demands for a new Canadian initiative in response to the growing human tragedy.[68] On 22 June, foreign minister Flora MacDonald and Ron Atkey, minister of DEI, announced Cabinet approval for an upgrading of the Indochinese refugee quota from 5000 to 8000, with an additional 4000 to be admitted under a special private group sponsorship program. By the end of the month, officials from DEI were meeting with an increasing number of voluntary groups and organizations who wished to participate in this innovative sponsorship plan. The plan had received such tremendous public response that by early July, only two weeks after the Toronto-based Operation Lifeline had been launched, this voluntary group could count more than sixty affiliated groups within Ontario alone, with many more being formed from coast to coast.[69] In mid-July, MacDonald and Atkey issued a joint statement that further expanded and modified the original group sponsorship into a matching formula plan, with a 1980 target of 50 000 Indochinese refugees (the original 8000, and 21 000 privately sponsored, and 21 000 matched government-sponsored).[70] This announcement came as MacDonald was departing for a Geneva UN conference on the plight of the refugees and was clearly intended to establish a precedent to encourage other states to act in a like manner as well as to set the context for the strong condemnation of the Vietnam regime given by MacDonald at the Geneva meetings.[71]

The innovative program was the culmination of growing pressure within many sectors of Canadian society for a new and bold initiative to aid the Indochinese refugees. Internationally it not only established a precedent that showed Canada to be a responsible and leading Western ally, actively assisting those who suffered from Communist repression, but it also aided in restoring Canada's image in the wake of Prime Minister Clark's Jerusalem embassy proposal. Although criticism over the one-for-one policy ranged from a racially directed concern over admitting large numbers of ethnic Chinese, to the question of state versus private responsibility for sponsorship and settlement costs, to the issue of job security and employment, the feared backlash remained more an issue of media speculation and political anticipation than a widespread occurrence.[72] Clark, MacDonald, and Atkey actively defended the government's policy. Indeed, Ron Atkey voiced strong personal feelings concerning the humanitarian and ethical necessity of this generous policy, and the public record suggested initial widespread support for his stance.[73]

To the astonishment of many, private sector sponsorship achieved its goal of 21 000 in four rather than eighteen months. This was complicated by Flora MacDonald's public commitment, at a UN-sponsored fall meeting dealing with the plight of the Kampucheans, of $15 million of Canadian aid, $10 million beyond what she had been authorized to announce. The government was then faced with two questions. First, what should the policy be on the number of refugees admitted into Canada, in terms of both total numbers and the ratio of private to state sponsorship? Second, how was the government going to alleviate the $10-million shortfall? The government linked these two issues and the result was a decision on 5 December to cancel "future sponsorship of Indochinese refugees, leaving it to private sponsors to meet the bulk of the Ottawa target of 50 000."[74] This released substantial funds to aid in meeting the Kampuchean commitment while temporarily sidestepping the issue of limits.[75] Within a few weeks, however, MacDonald made it clear that the 50 000 commitment would not be altered, regardless of the oversubscription by the private sponsorship process. Atkey argued that this position was in line with prior policy as well as public opinion and the wishes of many provincial governments and not in response to a feared backlash.[76] Nevertheless, the pronouncement came at a critical time in the fortunes of the Conservative government, which was already facing serious problems with its budget statement of 11 December.[77] Any increase in refugee admissions would be seen as exacerbating economic fears and weakening still further the government's position.[78]

During the weeks leading up to this announcement, DEA and DEI civil servants had prepared various alternative policy recommendations to be presented to voluntary organizations, church leaders, and the two key ministers.[79] These were never presented for consideration nor were the groups consulted; instead, MacDonald informed all participants of the government's intentions. Although the personal conflict between MacDonald and her undersecretary, Allan Gotlieb, and the transfer of deputy minister Manion from DEI to Treasury contributed to the bureaucratic and interministerial conflicts over policy, the decision clearly came from Cabinet and reflected the political exigencies of an already troubled Conservative government concerned with preventing further erosion of public support.[80]

In the February 1980 federal elections, the Clark government was defeated after only 259 days in power. The returning Trudeau Liberals had considered reinstituting the matching formula program; however, before the decision could be made, the new minister of employment and immigration, Lloyd Axworthy, received a brief prepared by members of the private sponsoring organizations that proposed a new policy intent on continued refugee assistance while avoiding possible negative public reaction. No limit was placed on private placement, and the government sponsored an additional 10 000 refugees, with the understanding that any arrivals in excess of 3000 privately sponsored refugees would be carried over to the following year. By the end of 1980, almost sixty thousand Indochinese had arrived in Canada since the inauguration of the 1979 sponsorship plan, with an expected 1981 figure of 8000 government-sponsored and 5000 privately sponsored.[81] By mid-1981, while the influx of Indochinese refugees had subsided, the federal government increased its contribution to aid the resettlement of these new Canadians.[82]

The most significant aspect of the five-year "boat people" experience was the active role of the private sector in lobbying, supporting, and implementing a highly innovative, government-initiated refugee sponsorship program, culminating first in the Conservative government's one-to-one matching scheme and then in the Liberal government's continuation of a program without restrictions on total numbers of privately sponsored cases. The success of these programs, which spanned three governments, depended upon the receptivity of key senior ministers to these domestic voluntary efforts, the expertise and bureaucratic support for these initiatives from DEA and DEI officials, and the co-operation provided by the provincial governments—who would be most directly affected by refugee resettlement in the end. While the last two factors remained a positive constant throughout the period, the variability of the programs was a direct result of ministerial choice.

Although practical issues of logistics and cost were necessarily of concern, they were not a determining factor since expertise and resources were available and cost was simply a question of budgetary allocation.[83] Rather the progression from the early traditional but cautious response until early 1979 to the bold new July 1979 initiative must be seen in the context of the change of government as well as the increasing severity of the international situation. There is little doubt that the Clark Cabinet was genuinely moved by the tragedy occurring in Indochina. The early hesitation to act was due more to a combination of lack of experience in international affairs, mistrust of senior civil servants exacerbated by the Jerusalem embassy affair, and the suddenness of the new magnitude of the Hoa crisis than to any lack of humanitarian concern. The public encouragement of the churches, voluntary associations, and the media offered the government the motivation, popular support, and strength to take its unilateral initiative.

However, it must also be viewed in the context of the intraparty conflict between Prime Minister Clark, Flora MacDonald, and other key Conservatives. Many of them had been profoundly disturbed by Clark's handling of the Jerusalem embassy decision, which had also created great unrest within the civil service, especially at External Affairs. The refugee crisis provided a convenient albeit necessary opportunity for Clark to mend fences and recapture the image of Canada as an active yet responsible international actor, building upon a recognized area of Canadian expertise.

The Indochinese refugee policy was undermined by the ironic coincidence of its overwhelming success with a time of domestic uncertainty. The continuation of this policy was perceived as economically costly and politically unwise, in spite of continued active support from ever more private sector actors. The government's sudden retrenchment indicates its fear that the party would be vulnerable if it had to face a federal election.[84] The proven success of the refugee policy fell victim to the unproven and highly contentious politics of the budget.

Conclusions

Canadian refugee policy, although only recently codified within immigration law, has been an integral part of Canadian immigration since the eighteenth century. It has reflected many of the central tenets of immigration practice, especially economic, racial, and religious criteria and, more recently, political and ideological factors. There is little doubt that the crisis atmosphere surrounding the plight of refugees has influenced specific official decisions on priorities and admissions. Hand in hand with these decisions has developed a specialized capability within the federal government to mobilize and employ a wide range of public and private sector expertise to manage the complex logistics of external refugee assessment and delivery and, with the co-operation of provincial governments, internal resettlement.

Since the closing days of World War II, the spectre of the refugee has been a constant international political and economic presence. Canada's participation in assisting countries of first asylum or in providing permanent refuge has generally been perceived as second to none. In that light, humanitarianism looms large as a determining factor in Canada's refugee policy. But it is equally evident that standard economic, religious, racial, and ideological factors have dominated the context within which each decision was made. Furthermore, one must question the selectivity of many Western countries, including Canada, that have chosen to ignore the hundreds of thousands of refugees from more disadvantaged locales, such as those in the countries of the Horn of Africa, the highlands of South Asia, or certain parts of Central and South America.[85]

The Canadian record on refugees has been dominated by six factors.

First has been the emergence of specialized federal and provincial governmental capacity and expertise. Second, this expertise has become increasingly differentiated by department and level of government. Third, interdepartmental co-operation has become a standard operating procedure, codified into immigration law, so that jurisdictional disputes at the bureaucratic level are no longer a serious hindrance to performance. Fourth, because of the context of international crisis, senior Cabinet ministers, including the prime minister, have provided the policy direction, rather than civil servants as in the prewar years. Furthermore, while international agencies have offered co-ordinative structures, the nature of the problem has shifted the Canadian response from an IRO, ICEM, and UNHCR focus to direct bilateral arrangements between Canada and countries of first asylum. Finally, the roles of domestic voluntary agencies, the media, and Parliament have become more significant in stimulating concern and assuming responsibility for resettlement efforts.

This review of Canada's refugee experience conforms, over the years since World War II, to an emerging complex neo-realist perspective of Canadian foreign policy. The historical process and Canada's behaviour exhibit an ascending global involvement, through bilateral arrangements that often diverge from the behaviour of other OECD states, with an ever more diffuse set of actors and a decreasing reliance on international agencies and norms. The foreign policy is highly sensitive to the external process, even though the relevant actors do not include the United States and the United Kingdom except as indirect contributors, as in Uganda, Chile, and Vietnam. In no case did Canada respond to dictates from great-power states, and in every case the Canadian political and economic interests were an integral part of the decision-making calculus.

The societal process, with the increasingly significant role played by voluntary agencies, the media, and Parliament, was the determining constellation of factors that established the quality and quantity of the policy. Political calculations of the socio-economic and demographic impacts were paramount, and though nongovernmental actors became the stimulant for upgrading and expanding resettlement programs, governmental decision makers and operations experts provided the key policy decisions and necessary expertise for the evolving initiatives and policies. In the case of refugee policy, functional expertise—so central to Lester Pearson's vision of Canada operating in an order dominated by international multilateral institutions—is retained but employed in bilateral efforts defined by internal criteria and capabilities emerging from Ottawa's perception of the national interest.

CHAPTER 8

ENERGY POLICY: INTERNATIONAL OIL AND GAS EXCHANGES

In few sectors of Canadian foreign policy has the difference between the perspectives of liberal internationalism, peripheral dependence, and complex neo-realism been so acutely at the centre of scholarly and public debate as in the area of Canada's international oil and gas relations.[1] In large measure, this stems from the importance of resource relationships in reflecting and defining Canada's place in the North American region and the international economy.

Both the staple theory of economic growth, in which oil, gas, and minerals constitute the most recent element of a five-century trend, and the classic functional doctrine, in which uranium, agricultural, and other raw materials propel Canada's involvement in postwar international organizations, have highlighted the importance of resources in fuelling both domestic economic development and an active participation in multilateral economic management abroad.[2] The role of postwar energy and mineral resource development in stimulating vast inflows of primarily American direct foreign investment and new north–south trade patterns underscored the significance of resources as the leading sector in Canada's deepening dependence on the United States.[3] Most recently the vast quantities of Canadian energy supplies, in the context of apparently permanent American and global scarcity, have given Canada a new status as a "foremost nation" in international relations as a whole.[4]

In sheer quantitative terms, the dominant approach to the analysis of this area has flowed from the increasingly well developed concepts of peripheral dependence that were applied to Canada–U.S. energy and resource relations in the late 1960s and early 1970s.[5] Despite their disagreements, most of these authors begin with the portrait of a Canada whose energy policies have produced a pronounced, cumulative Canadian dependence on the United States and the global environment, punctuated only by reactive, short-lived attempts to create a national fuel market. In this vision, Canada's position is that of a highly fragmented country whose abundant overall supplies of energy are overwhelmed by geographic and economic realities that place domestic production and domestic markets far from each other but close to markets and suppliers abroad.

From this fragmentation flows an uncritical tendency to export large volumes to the United States alone and to create the integrated pipelines that render this dependence on a single market permanent, at the expense of fostering Canadian secondary manufacturing, further processing of resources, preserving low-cost energy supplies to meet future shortages, and keeping inflows of U.S. direct investment within manageable limits. In turn this exclusive continental concentration leads Canada to deal with the global energy situation through the mediating channels of the U.S. and its hemispheric partners such as Venezuela, to confine multilateral ventures to a passive role in the U.S.-dominated International Energy Agency, and to deal bilaterally only through specialized transgovernmental channels, with the aid of such acquiescent techniques as exemptionalism and quiet diplomacy. As a result, Canada has been portrayed as passively accepting an international energy order resting nominally on the precepts of free trade, investment, and prices, and in practice on the ability of U.S.-based multinational oil majors, aided by U.S. government incentives and statecraft, to manage the system to their benefit.

From this perspective, Canada's situation stems directly from a pervasive U.S. influence defined by U.S. oil import policies and the politics of the U.S. oil and gas industry that lies behind them. A strong contributing factor is a Canadian domestic process in which producing and consuming regions have markedly divergent interests, provinces act as free agents, and power normally resides with an Alberta government and a U.S.-controlled industry interested solely in short-term, regional economic development. Cementing this destructive marriage of foreign influence and internal fragmentation is a Canadian state reluctant to intervene to overcome geography, curtail foreign investment, or guide resource development. It is moreover a state that promotes a foreign-dominated sector with financial concessions, that is dominated by a National Energy Board dependent on data supplied by a U.S.-controlled industry, and that defers to the overarching principles of seeking continental economies of scale, exporting to foster internal exploration, maintaining an overall balance between exports and imports, and preserving "amity and comity" with the United States.

By the mid-1970s, this vision of Canada's energy dependence had been challenged by a series of writings emphasizing, from a liberal-internationalist perspective, the far more balanced interdependence of Canada's energy relationships with the outside world.[6] While noting ongoing cycles of concern about surplus and scarcity and phases of co-operation and conflict with the U.S., these writings emphasized Canada's continuing tendency to employ the economically necessary north–south energy exchanges as a means of financing internal exploration and east–west transportation systems. Portraying Canada as a resource-rich, industrialized country with persistent balance-of-payments problems, they further underscored the unique and vital mutual dependence of Canada and the U.S., both overall and in the energy field, with Canada providing large, proximate, relatively inexpensive, and secure supplies; the U.S. providing markets, financing, entrepreneurship, and skills; and both providing an economical, resilient, integrated network of pipelines.

As a result, Canadian activity in most continental and international forums was grounded firmly in a pluralistic web of transnational linkages and fundamentally common interests. Both Canada and the U.S. relied heavily, as charter members, on the multilateral frameworks of GATT, OECD, and IEA and undertook parallel responses to OPEC through the IEA. Through active roles in producer and consumer groupings, they rejected major alternative bilateral options; and with each other, they eschewed formal treaties and resource leverage in favour of factual understanding, advance consultation, and expanding potential supplies. Together with Canada's particular concern with further domestic processing of resources and its ambiguous international position between the North and the South, this strong co-operative structure led Canada to give global emphasis to reducing OPEC's share of world production, creating stability in international commodity markets, and engendering a consumer–producer dialogue in which both groups were fairly represented.

In explaining this characteristic Canadian orientation, liberal-internationalists assigned prominence to the reciprocal transnational and transgovernmental forces in the Canada–U.S. energy relationship. These forces transmit and help offset the effects of the important influences of the U.S. market, the U.S. government's policy and regulatory system, and the global energy situation. In the society they reinforce a pluralistic process in which concentrated influence and protracted conflict are substantially modified by the continuing tension between producing and consuming provinces, the mixed role of multinational corporations, the need for large industrial consortiums, the increasing role of more broadly focused interest groups, and the periodic great debates in parliamentary forums. Within the state apparatus, they induce a similar diffusion, reinforced by the normally reactive, noninterventionary stance of the federal government, the absence of a comprehensive natural resources policy, the involvement of several departments whose functional specialists dominate, and the departments' need for technical expertise, critical intelligence, and hence close linkages with counterparts at home and abroad.

Despite its attractiveness, this comfortable portrait has been subject, in the wake of the 1973 and 1979 global price and supply shocks, to a cascading series of revisions. Together these revisions have provided the foundation for a complex neo-realist perspective on Canada's international energy relationships.[7] Forwarded largely by governmental activists, this vision has pointed to Canada's steadily increasing prominence in a world situation marked by a secular shift to oil scarcity and the emergence of a neo-mercantilist order. This shift has made energy questions central to international politics and rendered Canada—with abundant new and old supplies, critical technology, and skilled manpower—one of the seven principal powers in the industrialized free world and a comparatively strong power in international relations as a whole.[8] Given the direct centrality of the energy challenge to a broad range of Canada's vital domestic and external objectives, Canada has risen to play a full, essential international role, on the basis of a long-term, global strategy that accords priority to satisfying Canadian needs first, then helping its allies and aiding the globe, particularly its less developed members, as a whole.

Such a strategy has required audacious efforts to ensure Canadian control over its energy industry and market, provide an example in conservation to other states, establish bilateral ties with OPEC members and other suppliers, deal with the U.S. confidently and realistically on a case-by-case basis, and employ energy for bargaining leverage in other issue areas. These efforts led Canada to be an active participant in a free-world concert centred in OECD, IEA, and, most importantly, the Western Economic Summit; a principal promoter of dialogue and technology transfers between the IEA and OPEC and between North and South generally; and an initiator in reducing systematic dependence by providing direct financial and technological assistance to the South.

Prompting these massive transformations were the profound external energy shocks of 1973 and 1979. These events produced a pervasive sense of global scarcity, insecurity, and instability leading to confrontation. They led to a loosening of the Western, Eastern, and Southern blocs; rendered far less relevant the old multilateral ties encased in the United Nations, International Monetary Fund, and network of multinational corporations; and spawned state-to-state bilateral relationships. Within Canada these developments diminished the centrality of foreign-controlled multinational corporations; increased the role of large Canadian-controlled corporations capable of mobilizing Canada's rich endowment of energy, technology, and manpower; and induced a bipartisan consensus on the goal of self-sufficiency and the need for a public sector corporation able to act internationally. Within the federal government, they created a powerful consensus about the need for concerted action and strong interventionary behaviour over the long term.

As in other areas of Canadian foreign policy, each of the perspectives of peripheral dependence, liberal internationalism, and complex neo-realism contributes to an explanation of Canada's international energy policy at certain historical periods and in certain component areas. Yet once again, general quantitative surveys and a detailed examination of individual periods strongly reveal a broad shift during the postwar era from patterns of peripheral dependence towards those of liberal internationalism and, more recently, of complex neo-realism. Thus the 1947–1956 period, characterized by the emergence of Canada's oil and gas exports to the U.S. and the creation of pipeline systems from Alberta to the U.S. and to central Canada, indicates a structure of peripheral dependence into which patterns of liberal internationalism were increasingly injected. The 1957–1963 period, marked by the establishment of the Royal Commission on Energy, the National Energy Board, and the National Oil Policy saw balanced decisions between the relatively equal alternatives of peripheral dependence and liberal internationalism, with the latter reinforced by the first major elements of complex neo-realism. The 1963–1968 period, defined by the strong promotion of exports to the United States, confirmed this pattern; the creation of the Department of Energy, Mines, and Resources and the 1965 Great Lakes pipeline debate demonstrated the growing force of complex neo-realism.

Subsequently, the pace of transition has quickened. The 1968–1973 period showed the growing strength of the complex neo-realist challenge, most notably in the denial of new natural gas export contracts to the U.S. in 1971, the flowering of EMR as a major policy-oriented department, and the first attempt at a comprehensive national energy policy in the spring of 1973. The 1973–1979 period, dominated by the price increase and supply curtailments of Canada's oil and gas exports to the United States and by the creation of Petro-Canada, witnessed the rise of complex neo-realism, even as the formation of the International Energy Agency and the Alaska Gas Pipeline project with the U.S. demonstrated the durability of a competing liberal-internationalist orientation. But Canada's response to the second OPEC shock, from 1979 onward, underscored the clear dominance of complex neo-realism. Most dramatically, the National Energy Program—with its threefold goal of energy independence, Canadianization of the industry, and stress on financial equity—affirmed Canada's autonomous global relevance, directly assaulted the major remaining element of peripheral dependence, and reinforced the power of the central state apparatus as a whole.

An Overview of Canadian Oil and Gas Policy

Historically, international oil and gas relationships have played a very minor and intermittent part in Canada's overall foreign policy concerns. As Figure 8.1 indicates, the federal government, through the Department of External Affairs, has usually devoted very little attention to these subjects, intervening only intermittently, as in 1961, 1966, and 1969, when major debates over pipelines or the general energy relationship with the United States erupted. Since 1970, however, there has been a massive and sustained increase in the prominence of this

FIGURE 8.1 Relative Attention to International Oil, Gas and Coal Relationships, 1960–1979

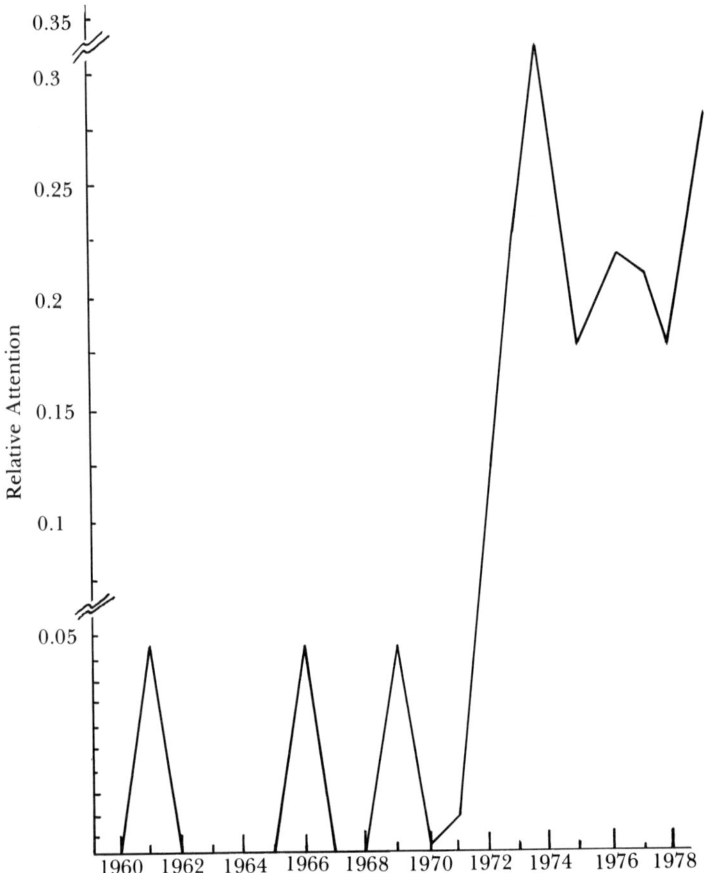

Note: Relative attention is measured by the number of paragraphs containing references to energy relationships, divided by the number of pages in each annual report.

SOURCE: Based on Department of External Affairs, *Annual Report*, 1960–1971; *Annual Review*, 1972–1979.

sector on the government's diplomatic agenda. Although largely fuelled by the two global price and supply crises of 1973 and 1979, this increase began a full two years before the Arab oil embargo of October 1973, as the government dealt with contentious national and continental energy issues. Moreover, as the high figure for the 1975–1978 period indicates, this relatively strong vigilance continued during the subsequent years of global calm and co-operative ventures with President Carter's administration in the U.S.

The tentative support for complex neo-realism provided by this significant and sustained increase in government attention in the 1970s

TABLE 8.1 Canadian Roles in International Oil, Gas, and Coal Policy, 1960–1979

	1960	*1961*	*1962*	*1963*	*1964*	*1965*	*1966*	*1967*	*1968*	*1969*	*1970*	*1971*	*1972*	*1973*	*1974*	*1975*	*1976*	*1977*	*1978*	*1979*
TOTAL NUMBER OF REFERENCES	1						4			3		1	6	11	16	11	20	18	18	20
NUMBER OF ROLE TYPES	1						3			1		1	3	4	5	5	5	5	5	4
INDIVIDUAL ROLES:																				
Organization Maintainer							2							4	5	2	5	2	4	7
Community Builder													1	2	2				2	
Community Builder/ Leader																		1	1	
Partner	1						1			3		1	4	4	3	2	6	8	5	6
Balancer							1						1	1	5	4	5	6	6	6
Community Builder/ Balancer																2	2	1		
Partner/Leader															1	1	2			1

SOURCE: Based on Department of External Affairs, *Annual Report*, 1960–1971; *Annual Review*, 1972–1979.

is strengthened to some extent by the shift in Canadian roles during the same period. As Table 8.1 reveals, before 1971 Canada's infrequent concern with international energy issues was expressed through the peripheral-dependent role of "organization maintainer" and the complex neo-realist roles of "partner" and "balancer". Since 1971 this duality has continued, with the new, liberal-internationalist roles of "community builder" and "community builder/leader" giving the patterns predicted by all three perspectives a substantial presence in the federal government's overall approach. Yet by far the most significant development has been the heightened prominence of a complex neo-realist orientation, as the roles of "partner" and "balancer" have intensified and those of "partner/leader" and "community builder/balancer" have been added.

A survey of Canada's policy process on international oil and gas matters, as presented in Tables 8.2 and 8.3, further reveals the recent emergence of a dominant complex neo-realist orientation. Taken together, these tables indicate that societal and governmental more than external actors had an increasing prominence from 1961 to 1969; by 1972 they had overtaken external actors as the most numerous factor noted. Apart from the crisis years of 1973–1974 and 1979, when external actors dramatically dominated government attention, internal actors maintained the new level they had acquired in 1972.

Far more convincing evidence for the emergence of complex neo-realist patterns comes from shifts in the composition of those external actors. As Table 8.2 shows, the scope of foreign actors relevant to Canada widened dramatically, from an average of five before 1973 to almost triple that figure in subsequent years. As peripheral dependence predicts, actors in states closely associated with the U.S. before 1972, such as Venezuela and the United Kingdom, dominated Canadian attention, with actors and organizations predicted by liberal internationalism—the United Nations and Canada–U.S. organizations—occupying a strong second place. These patterns continued through the period after 1972, with liberal internationalism driven to surpass peripheral dependence by the new emphasis given to the OECD, NATO, and the IEA.

Yet by far the most dramatic trend was the emergence of strong complex neo-realist patterns. Canadian attention spread around the globe, embracing individual states in Europe, the Middle East, Asia, and Latin America. Canada's associations through international organizations concentrated heavily on the more exclusive gatherings such as the Western Economic Summit, the Conference on International Economic Co-operation (CIEC), and bilateral organizations with states other than the United States.

A similar evolution occurs with respect to societal and governmental actors. As Table 8.3 demonstrates, even with rather fragmentary data,

TABLE 8.2 External Actors in Canadian Oil, Gas, and Coal Policy, 1961–1979

	1961	*1966*	*1969*	*1972*	*1973*	*1974*	*1975*	*1976*	*1977*	*1978*	*1979*
TOTAL NUMBER OF REFERENCES	6	6	4	7	25	34	25	33	22	37	39
NUMBER OF ACTORS NOTED	5	5	2	5	12	15	13	12	10	16	18
INDIVIDUAL ACTORS:											
U.S. in General				1	4	2	1	4	6	2	5
U.S. Executive Branch	2	1	2	3	4	1	4	4	2	5	1
U.S. Congress							1			1	
U.S. Private Sector								2			1
United Kingdom		1				1					
Europe, Industrialized Countries, the West					2	2	2	4			2
Denmark										1	1
Japan					2			1	4	2	1
Australia									1		
South Korea									1		
Rhodesia/South Africa	1	2									
OPEC and Oil Producers						3	1	2		2	
Egypt									1		
Palestinians						1					
Gulf States										5	1
Afghanistan											1
Iraq							1				1
Middle East, Arab States				1	2	5	2				1
Saudi Arabia				1						1	
Latin America					1	1	1	1			
Venezuela		1			2	1		4	1	1	2
Mexico										2	3
Asia	1										
China						2				1	
Canada–U.S. Joint Bodies, Channels, Projects	1		2		1	2				1	2
UN Political Bodies	1	1		1	2	4					
UN Functional Bodies					1	1	3		1	3	2
NATO, IEA, OECD					2	6	2	6	3	6	6
Western Economic Summit										2	3
Non-U.S. Bilateral Organizations							2	1		2	5
CIEC							3	3	2		
Third World					2	2	2	1			1

SOURCE: Based on Department of External Affairs, *Annual Report*, 1961–1971; *Annual Review*, 1972–1979.

the absence of relevant societal actors before 1971 has been replaced by a situation in which Parliament, then provincial governments, and finally Canadian business have become increasingly active. Within the government, occasional ministerial debate and the routine dominance of the

TABLE 8.3 Societal and Governmental Actors in Canadian Oil, Gas, and Coal Policy, 1961–1979

	1961	*1966*	*1969*	*1971*	*1972*	*1973*	*1974*	*1975*	*1976*	*1977*	*1978*	*1979*
TOTAL NUMBER OF REFERENCES	1	3	2	1	8	5	4	7	9	7	8	3
NUMBER OF ACTORS NOTED	1	3	2	1	4	4	3	4	6	5	4	3
SOCIETAL ACTORS:												
House of Commons					1							
Provinces							1					
Quebec								1				
British Columbia										1		
Alberta											1	
Dome Petroleum									1			
Business											2	1
Interest Groups												
GOVERNMENTAL ACTORS:												
Government, Prime Minister			1							1		
Cabinet	1					1			1			
Officials		1			2	1	2	3	4	2	4	
NEB		1						1	1			1
EMR		1				1				2	1	
DEA (including ambassadors)			1	1	4	2	1		1	1		1
MOE					1							
Finance								2				
Petro-Canada									1			

SOURCE: Based on Department of External Affairs, *Annual Report*, 1961–1971; *Annual Review*, 1972–1979.

functional specialists in the National Energy Board and Energy, Mines and Resources, as predicted by peripheral dependence and liberal internationalism respectively, have been replaced since 1971 by the involvement of a host of new departments and officials and the more vigorous participation of the central foreign policy managers in External Affairs, as complex neo-realism would suggest.

The Period of Diminishing Dependence, 1947–1957

During the first postwar decade, Canada's oil and gas policy was dominated by the federal government's efforts to develop its new-found oil and gas supplies in Alberta, to build the necessary pipeline systems, and to reduce the substantial dependence that had characterized Canada's international energy situation in the preceding twenty-five years. Throughout that time, Canada's own production had met only 2.5

per cent of domestic needs in 1920 and 15 per cent in 1940.[9] Moreover, its reliance on imports was heavily concentrated on the United States, which had become Canada's first supplier in the 1920s, and, to a lesser extent, on Colombia, Trinidad, and later Venezuela, which had begun to export in volume to Canada shortly before World War II and had quickly become the major source of crude for central and eastern Canada.

The demands and disruptions of World War II had prompted Canada to diversify its foreign sources, to harmonize energy relations with its continental ally, and to develop new production at home and exports abroad.[10] With wartime demand reducing access to U.S. exports, Canada had increased its imports from Venezuela. On the continent, it had authorized in 1941 a pipeline from Montreal to Portland, Maine, to transport these Venezuelan supplies; later Canada engaged in another joint project (CANOL) in the Canadian north and joined in a co-ordinated system of priorities.[11] And within Canada it had implemented stringent measures to encourage conservation and the development of alternative supplies. At the war's end many of these ventures came to an abrupt halt. But Canada was left with British Columbia and parts of southern Ontario dependent on American fields and a strong memory of supply insecurity, exacerbated by the growing need to import Middle East crude.

In 1947, three events sharpened the impact of this wartime legacy. An unusually cold winter in 1947 and America's new net importer status in the cold war era led the U.S. government to favour reduced exports, increased imports, and the development of indigenous new supplies from independent producers.[12] Secondly, the foreign exchange crisis of 1947–1948 prompted the Canadian government to search for alternatives to imported oil.[13] And most importantly, the discovery of large-scale Canadian oil supplies at Leduc, Alberta, provided an opportunity for Canada to meet both Canada's needs and those of the U.S. The Leduc discovery led to a Canadian policy regime in which an increasingly self-sufficient Canada emphasized promoting exports to U.S. markets, developing pipelines to carry supplies to the south and the east, and articulating, with growing ambitiousness, an overall policy of "Canada first".

As the magnitude of Alberta's reserves became known, Ottawa secured entry for Albertan supplies in both the Canadian and American markets. Beginning in 1951, the federal government granted export licences to Imperial Oil, Westcoast Transmission, and Transmountain Limited and urged an initially reluctant Alberta to declare a surplus of oil and gas available for export. Moreover, through personal contacts and joint Canada–U.S. organizations, the U.S. was pressed for greater market access, despite considerable opposition from American protectionist, high-cost oil producers.

The federal government's determination to seek large, assured export markets in the U.S. and in major Canadian population centres was evident in its formal authorization and informal promotion of four pipeline projects carrying Canadian oil and gas to the U.S. border.[14] The Interprovincial Pipeline Company, incorporated by the federal government in 1949, carried Alberta oil eastward, pushed the first quantities of Albertan oil into the U.S. at Minnesota and Wisconsin in 1951, and brought large volumes into Sarnia in 1954 through a U.S.-routed line. The small Canada–Montana line, built in 1951 at the request of U.S. defence authorities, was the first export-oriented natural gas project approved by the federal government. It was followed by the Transmountain Pipeline, incorporated in the spring of 1951, which transported Alberta oil into Vancouver by 1953, into Puget Sound by 1954, and into San Francisco by 1956. Finally, in 1952 the federal government granted Westcoast Transmission permission to export large quantities of gas to the U.S. and to build a pipeline from northern Alberta through Vancouver for this purpose.

By 1952 these four projects had given Canada a *de facto* policy aimed at securing both an east–west pipeline system to bring Albertan oil to Canadian markets and north–south systems to export rapidly expanding Albertan supplies to U.S. customers, thereby ensuring western Canadian economic development, the financial viability of the east–west lines, and the health of Canada's balance of payments. The effort to reconcile these potentially conflicting approaches formed the centrepiece of Canadian oil and gas policy over the next five years, as the government grappled with competing proposals to develop a new, large-scale natural gas pipeline from Alberta to the east.[15] Ottawa incorporated two major groups seeking to undertake the project: Western Pipelines, a Canadian-controlled consortium proposing a line to Winnipeg and then to the U.S. to finance further eastward extensions, and TransCanada PipeLines (TCPL), a U.S.-linked group offering a more expensive, all-Canadian line through northern Ontario to serve, exclusively and directly, the Ontario and Quebec market.

In October 1952, federal Minister of Trade and Commerce C.D. Howe decided that no Canadian gas exports to the U.S. midwest would be permitted until central and eastern Canadian needs were met first. And in March 1953, Howe declared a firm policy of constructing a single gas pipeline located entirely within Canada, offering government assistance, and threatening to withhold a construction licence until the rival groups could agree on a single plan.[16]

Policy was quickly backed by consistent action, in ever more interventionary and detailed forms. In 1953 and 1954, Howe used his power over exports and imports to sustain the viability of an all-Canadian line. In 1954 he induced the rival groups to merge into a single consortium and approved construction of the line through an all-Canadian northern route. Yet faced by mounting concerns over the project's financing and the need for rapid completion, he then allowed two U.S. companies with control over the necessary steel supplies — Tennessee Gas and Gulf Oil — a 50 per cent interest in the project. Driven by a desire to complete the all-Canadian line rapidly, the government also reluctantly agreed to construct, through a Crown corporation, the uneconomic northern Ontario section of the line and lease it to the consortium. And in June 1956, after a bitter parliamentary debate, the government provided a loan of $72 million to the sponsors to assist construction of the prairie section of the line.

These modifications and the basic decision on exports and pipeline construction were determined largely by the supply conditions, domestic oil and gas politics, and national security considerations within the United States. At the outset, the new U.S. deficit position, the cold war fear of raw material shortages, and the Korean war demand prompted the U.S. government to play a large part in defining its policy in accordance with national security objectives, and in ways largely compatible with Canada's export orientation. However, by the mid-1950s, security considerations had diminished to the point where Secretary of Defense Charles Wilson informed C.D. Howe that he could not get approval for imports from the Westcoast system on a national defence basis, nor could he produce a Canada–U.S. gas exchange plan that would help get Howe's TransCanada PipeLines financed. Indeed, security imperatives had become so marginal that the U.S. ambassador to the United Nations, Henry Cabot Lodge, could suggest that increased U.S. imports of Canadian oil would be allowed in return for Canadian diplomatic support for the U.S. position on admission of new members to the United Nations.[17]

As the importance of national security rationales diminished, control over U.S. oil and gas policy making returned to U.S. producers and their government's regulatory agency, the Federal Power Commission (FPC). Arguing that the U.S. market should be preserved for U.S. suppliers, especially at a time of American domestic oil and gas deficit, U.S. industry secured tariffs on imported oil; with reciprocal logic, the FPC was prepared to grant export licences, like the one that brought Texas gas to Windsor, with such stringent conditions of interruptibility and preferences for U.S. customers that only small supplies were sent.

While this had done much to convince Howe of the need for an all-Canadian gas pipeline, FPC actions and the internal dynamics of the U.S. industry continued to bedevil his effort to get the line built. Through licensing decisions, the FPC had given some life to the concept of an "invisible pipeline" of dual north–south exports that served largely as an alternative to Howe's all-Canadian east–west plan. By refusing to supply steel to a Canadian government-owned pipeline, Gulf Oil effectively eliminated Bank of Canada governor James Coyne's plan for a project with Canadian government equity participation. And because Tennessee Gas and Gulf Oil were the only companies willing and able to purchase the required amount of pipe at a time of U.S. steel shortages, but demanded 50 per cent of the project in return, they effectively turned Howe's all-Canadian pipeline, at least temporarily, into an American-controlled venture.

In addition to the powerful constraints imposed by American actors, Canadian government behaviour was also influenced by interests within Canada, and in particular by the divergent views of the major provincial governments. The government of Alberta owned most of the provincial oil and gas supplies, controlled their transportation within the province, and had the power to determine the amount, timing, and direction of gas exports beyond the province. Alberta's hope that its supplies would confer an advantage in consumer prices and industry location, the resistance of the Western Canadian Coal Operators Association and related railroads, and the advice of municipalities and a special provincial royal commission had made Alberta a very reluctant exporter at first. Although it provided, after some federal urging, the small volumes required for the Interprovincial, Transmountain, and Montana systems, only in 1952 did it accede to Howe's demands for a more general declaration of an exportable surplus.

On the major issue of the TransCanada gas pipeline, Alberta's recognition of a surplus, which was to assume major proportions by 1955, together with pressure from provincial producers and Prime Minister Louis St. Laurent led the province to permit the export of gas eastward and later to support a pipeline to Ontario, with Ottawa constructing the northern Ontario section. However Alberta really favoured a concept that would permit large, rapid exports to the U.S. by routing the TransCanada line south of the Great Lakes. It threatened to look for markets in the west, opposed an Ontario suggestion for a line built totally by government, supported a late proposal by an Alberta-based, Canadian-controlled group, and resisted Howe's proposal that Alberta purchase TransCanada PipeLine bonds. In contrast, Ontario, which had experienced U.S. supply interruptions during and after World War II and which, along with Quebec, faced acute fuel and power shortages, was an early advocate and consistent supporter of an all-Canadian route.

These differences over TCPL were even more pronounced, if less salient, within Parliament. The Progressive Conservatives, although divided into several factions, opposed a U.S.-located southern route and later criticized the heavy involvement of U.S. groups, the Liberals' opposition to government ownership, the inclusion of Gulf and Tennessee as temporary majority participants, and the government's provision of a loan to this group. The federal CCF, supported by the CCF government of Saskatchewan, was a more forceful exponent of

Canadian control and location, arguing for outright government ownership and operation of the line. Yet Conservative and CCF criticisms had little direct, immediate impact on the majority Liberal government's moves.

The Canadian corporate community and its interest-group allies also had internal divisions and a marginal impact. The issues of oil and gas exports through the early pipelines, the construction of an eastward gas line, and the ensuing financing problems had stimulated the involvement of competing consortiums, loosely structured on the dimension of Canadian-controlled groups opposing those with major American linkages and control. Yet the federal government was consistently able to control this competition. While the need for a U.S. import permit and U.S. steel exports led, respectively, to Westcoast's co-operation with its former American rival and the inclusion of U.S.-linked groups in TCPL, Canadians maintained control of Westcoast and by 1958 had secured over three-quarters of TCPL.

The ability of the federal government to override or modify the behaviour of private Canadian actors reflected not only the primacy of Ottawa in the oil and gas area but also the concentration of its internal decision-making process in the office of a single determined individual. For virtually this entire period, the minister of trade and commerce, C.D. Howe, served as the government's principal spokesman and negotiator on oil and gas questions, exercised oversight over the principal regulatory body, the Board of Transport Commissioners, headed the department with the ongoing policy-making responsibility, and assumed leadership in interministerial and Cabinet debate. Howe's initial approach was dominated by his belief in the need to develop the Canadian oil and gas industry as rapidly as possible, in accordance with the criteria of technical efficiency, the economics of the industry, and the continental supply–demand situation.[18]

With the lessening intensity of the Korean war and the growing strength of the Canadian oil and gas industry, Howe's approach broadened into a more comprehensive policy, containing wider referents and a more defined conception of the national interest as a whole. While his March 1953 speech left oil to the traditional criteria of economy and market development, it made gas exports and the east–west pipeline contingent on such factors as the future economic use of gas within Canada, the long-term economic viability of an all-Canadian line, and the historic unreliability of U.S. gas import policy. Moreover, he grounded his actions in a policy of "Canada always", dictated by the "long-range interest of the people of Canada" as a whole, yet mindful of Canada's association with the United Kingdom, the Commonwealth, and the United States.

While Howe continued to rely heavily on his departmental advisers in implementing this policy, the question of government financial guarantees for an east–west gas pipeline quickly catalyzed the participation of others and, on occasion, led to a rejection of Howe's advice. Howe's agreement with TCPL's initial request for a loan guarantee was opposed by younger members of the Cabinet, Finance, the Bank of Canada, and, ultimately, Prime Minister St. Laurent. In the spring of 1955, the Cabinet overruled Howe's proposal to allow imports from Tennessee Gas as a way of helping finance the east–west line. Yet Howe's deputy minister, Mitchell Sharp, subsequently produced a proposal, later approved by the prime minister, for government construction of the northern portion of the line. And Howe himself later secured Cabinet agreement for a government loan guarantee to a U.S.-controlled TCPL.

During the initial postwar decade, Canada's international oil and gas policy still displayed the substantial legacy of peripheral dependence from the prewar era, but with a steadily increasing emphasis on liberal-internationalist patterns and even tentative signs of complex neo-realist tendencies. This transition is first evident in Canada's dramatic shift from a concentrated dependence on U.S.-based supplies to diversified sources of imports. It was reinforced by Canada's ability, with the Leduc discoveries and Korean war climate, to balance its imports with exports to the United States and to construct the four pipeline systems that created not only the north–south export flows, but also the foundation of a national, east–west energy transportation system. It culminated in the TransCanada PipeLine project, which revealed Canada's structural dependence on U.S. entrepreneurship, investment, and materials, but also indicated Canada's increasing ability to bargain with U.S. actors and the primacy of an entirely national conception of Canada's energy transportation grid.

Liberal-internationalist patterns also appear in the process by which Canada's international energy policy was produced. While the behaviour of American government and private sector actors remained paramount as a determinant of Canadian action, the emergence of U.S. national security concerns gave Canada a useful point of access and enabled it to develop a domestic industry in which Canadian-owned as well as multinational firms had a place. Together with the growing debate between producing and consuming provinces, and among federal parties within Parliament, this diversity enabled the concept of an all-Canadian east–west supply system to compete equally with the earlier pattern, in which the north–south dimensions had been pronounced. The growing strength of the latter tendency was due not only, as liberal internationalism suggests, to C.D. Howe's skillful centrality as the relevant functional minister, but also, as complex neo-realism predicts, to his established conception of a "Canada first" policy and his dominance within the executive branch when the TransCanada PipeLine issue assumed overwhelming dimensions in the national political life.

The Period of National Compromise, 1957–1963

The principles of promoting exports, developing a north–south infrastructure, and creating an east–west supply system, forged during the 1947–1957 period, continued to provide the foundation for Canadian policy during the Diefenbaker years.[19] Yet the acrimony of the pipeline debate and the nationalist sentiment that led to the Conservative government's election prompted three major modifications of the earlier tenets. The first, reflected in the establishment of the Royal Commission on Energy in 1957 and the formation of the National Energy Board in 1959, was the emergence of a review and regulatory mechanism designed to relate specific projects throughout the energy area to a set of broad, specified principles of "national interest". The second, manifested particularly in the government's successful quest for an exemption for U.S. crude oil import quotas in 1959, was a drive to inject greater stability into the flow of oil and gas southward. And the third, seen in the debate preceding the adoption of the National Oil Policy in 1961, consisted of an effort to extend the "all-Canada" feeling of the gas pipeline debate to oil policy as well.

The government's move to formulate a more comprehensive and specific oil and gas policy began in 1957, when it established a royal commission on energy under the chairmanship of Henry Borden to review Canadian energy exports, pipeline operations, and the protection of Canadian requirements. With the wide discretion that these guidelines allowed, the commission focused on three major issues: the need for a new regulatory procedure; Canada's overall energy situation; and the desirability of serving the large Montreal market with Albertan rather than imported oil.

In its initial report, the commission resolved the first issue. Following the government's own predispositions, the commission recommended the establishment of a National Energy Board (NEB) with broad powers to advise the government on all matters regarding the development and use of energy resources and to regulate oil and gas production, distribution, and export, with a particular focus on the construction of new pipeline systems. In line with this recommendation, the government immediately legislated the NEB into existence and delegated to it the power to regulate Canada's interprovincial and international energy trade, subject to Cabinet approval, through the issuance of certificates for pipelines and licences for the export and import of oil and gas.

With the NEB in place, the government could resume the process of approving particular export and pipeline requests, which had been frozen pending the outcome of the commission's deliberations. The commission's review had foreseen a high domestic demand for gas and reaffirmed the need to serve first those parts of Canada within economic reach of the producers. Yet it argued that there would be an increasing surplus, which should be exported, partly to spur exploration in Canada and ensure the high level of reserves it had projected. The National Energy Board Act had accepted these principles, but defined the criteria for pricing gas exports as the price at which gas traded at the border, rather than the standards suggested by the commission, such as future price increases and the export prices for petroleum by-products. On this foundation, the NEB proceeded during the next decade to approve gas exports to the full amount of the estimated exportable surplus.[20]

Oil exports followed a similar pattern, although here the vagaries of U.S. energy politics made for an even more unstable course.[21] Canada's prompt increase in oil to the U.S. during the Suez crisis had helped it avoid serious quotas on its exports in the U.S. voluntary quota program of July 1957. When a more threatening extension of the program followed in December 1957, Canada responded by arguing in a protest note that its proximity to the U.S., the 1950 Canada–U.S. Principles of Economic Co-operation, the GATT agreement, and its NATO understandings rendered the reduction in Canada's voluntary quota unjustifiable. Canada then initiated informal discussions with the U.S. aimed at formulating a co-ordinated approach to oil in the light of free-world security.[22] These moves and the discussion in the Joint Committee on Trade and Economic Affairs had some impact. Six weeks after the United States had imposed a global mandatory system, Canada was able to secure, by presidential proclamation on 30 April 1959, an exemption on the grounds that its overland transportation route made its supplies as secure as U.S. domestic oil.

Seeing this exemption as the first step towards a highly desirable regime of free continental oil movement, the Borden commission urged Canadian producers to promote exports to the U.S., and the Canadian government began export negotiations.[23] Beginning in 1961, Canada, led by Minister of Trade and Commerce George Hees, pressed for increased exports. Canada resisted requests from the U.S. Department of the Interior for a fixed voluntary quota, arguing, among other things, that U.S. limitations would lead Canada to reduce its import of U.S.-owned Venezuelan oil and to supply Montreal with Albertan crude. The result was a regime in which the U.S. explicitly recognized the national security significance of Canadian supplies. Canada proceeded to permit new export pipelines, such as the Matador Line authorized in 1961, and promised to be reasonable in demanding a share of the U.S. market. The two sides also established co-operatively an informal understanding on Canadian export volumes on an annual basis.

As these bilateral discussions indicated, the third major issue of the Borden commission's deliberations—the Montreal market question—emerged into prominence during this period. As early as 1957, the final report of Walter Gordon's Royal Commission on Canada's Economic Prospects had recommended supplying Montreal with higher-priced Canadian crude if new U.S. markets were unavailable.[24] Somewhat similarly, the Borden commission's second report had argued against this on condition that the U.S. accept more partially Canadian-owned Albertan crude at the expense of more fully U.S.-owned and cheaper Venezuelan and Middle Eastern supplies. And as late as October 1960, the Canadian government, concerned that the domestic industry was operating at only 50 per cent capacity, declared that it was examining the economic feasibility of a line to Montreal.

Only when an expanding share of the U.S. market had been assured did the government formally set aside the "on-to-Montreal" alternative. Under the National Oil Policy announced by Hees on 1 February 1961, the government rejected a Montreal pipeline and created the "Ottawa Valley line", separating Alberta-supplied markets to the west from overseas-supplied markets to the east. Yet at the same time, it set forth steadily increasing production targets for Canadian industry, to be met by a growth in exports to the U.S., and noted the ability of the government to approve a Montreal pipeline in the future should these production targets not be met. By the fall of 1961, exports had in fact increased substantially, and by early 1962 they reached the targets established the previous year. The National Oil Policy thus led to a situation where, from 1961 through to the mid-1970s, Canada imported about half of its oil requirements, while its exports climbed from 21 per cent of net Canadian production in 1960 to a peak of 57 per cent in 1971.

During this period, Canadian policy continued to be heavily influenced by the United States. Yet increasing divisions within the United States, America's growing dependence on global supplies, and new Venezuelan assertiveness combined to give Canada significantly greater bargaining freedom.[25] Within the United States, a restrictionist coalition, led by independent oil producers, state governments, and line departments such as Interior, continued to argue that a healthy peacetime domestic U.S. oil industry was required to supply America and its Western European allies in times of crisis and war. Arrayed in consistent opposition were the major integrated oil companies with abundant low-cost reserves abroad, Pacific northwest and New England consumers served by relatively inexpensive Canadian supplies, and the president, the Departments of State, Defense, and Justice, the Council of Economic Advisers, and the Council on Foreign Economic Policy.

President Eisenhower had responded to increasing restrictionist pressure by appointing the Cabinet-level Special Committee to Investigate Crude Oil Imports; then, in July 1957, he imposed voluntary quotas on imports east of the Rockies under provisions that preserved Canadian markets in both the Pacific northwest and the midwestern states. As pressure increased, he exhibited considerable sympathy for a National Security Council recommendation that the U.S. "give preference, in any system of import restrictions, to imports of petroleum from Canada and other Western Hemisphere countries." He imposed the March 1959 mandatory quotas on Canada only because his advisers argued that an exemption for Canada alone would discriminate against Venezuela and violate GATT obligations.[26] Yet Eisenhower noted State's argument that the move constituted "an added inducement for the Canadians to build an uneconomic pipeline from their western oil field to the Montreal market," feared that such a move would produce Venezuelan protests to the U.S., and worried about the general state of Canada–U.S. relations and Pacific northwest reaction. Therefore, he quickly granted to Canada alone an exemption subject to "an understanding with Canada to the effect that, if imports should loom excessively large, or if the Venezuelans should be blocked from Montreal, this would be dealt with as a new situation."[27] (He was unable to secure such an exemption for Venezuela.)

The conditions of the exemption were soon implemented by the Department of the Interior, which pressed for voluntary limitations on rapidly increasing Canadian imports. That Canada was able to withstand such pressure was due to a shift of the new Kennedy administration's Office of Emergency Planning to the antirestrictionist coalition, the president's responsiveness to New England consumers and free trade values, his defence department's desire, heightened by the Cuban missile crisis, for freely available defence-related supplies, and the consistent antirestrictionism of State. As a result, the Kennedy administration recommended that the U.S. "discuss this problem with the Government of Canada with a view to obtaining co-ordination of U.S. and Canadian policies regarding North American petroleum security."[28] In the ensuing bargaining, leading to the creation of a co-ordinated system of informal allocation, Canada's position was heavily influenced by its insistence, exacerbated by the exchange crisis of that year, that the favourable U.S. balance of trade both overall and in the petroleum-related sector made any heavy U.S. constraints on Canadian crude exports unwarranted.

Canada's increased capacity for effective bargaining also reflected the growing salience of Canadian societal actors. To be sure, the decisions on major export projects after 1959, notably the Matador Pipeline, were made with no objections from Canadian provinces or companies, and throughout the period few aspects of Canadian oil and gas policy inspired widespread parliamentary debate. Yet the Borden commission, the National Energy Board, and the Montreal market question catalyzed the involvement of most directly involved provinces and companies, intensified the conflict between clear U.S.-linked and Canadian-based coalitions, and significantly strengthened the latter group.

The Borden commission's deliberation did see internationally related companies such as Shell and British-American Oil, the Canadian Petroleum Association, and Westcoast Transmission arguing against all others that vigorous exports would do the most to ensure domestic reserves. They and the provincial governments agreed, however, that gas exports should be allowed once Canadian requirements were met.

It was the Montreal oil market question that prompted the most intense debate. The Home Oil Company, a leading Canadian independent, proposed a guaranteed Edmonton–Montreal pipeline with support from other independents and the Alberta government. Imperial Oil, other foreign-controlled majors, and some Canadian independents argued that exports provided a better return to all producers and cheaper consumer prices in eastern markets. The Borden commission's acceptance of the export argument left the NEB free to devise and follow a standard formula for authorizing oil and gas exports for the next decade. While the producers, transmission companies, distributors, industrial consumers, and the Alberta and Ontario governments were regular participants in NEB hearings, important opposition to the dominant export orientation came only from the Ontario and Quebec governments, on behalf of their manufacturing, commercial, and thermal electric interests.

Within the executive branch, the routine dominance of Trade and Commerce under C.D. Howe in the earlier period was diffused to embrace the new National Energy Board and the Department of Finance.[29] The first challenge to Trade and Commerce's predominance came with the Borden commission. The very creation of the body, the appointment of a known Conservative nationalist as chairman, and the debate within it between advocates of the Montreal and export options demonstrated John Diefenbaker's suspicion of a Trade and Commerce–led bureaucracy and its export-oriented approach. This tension between east–west and north–south orientations arose once again, to even greater effect, within the interdepartmental committee considering the creation of the National Energy Board. Here the representatives of the Privy Council Office and the Department of Mines and Technical Surveys argued against those of Trade and Commerce that the latter's reflexive export orientation and internationally focused mission made it an unlikely organization to arbitrate such heavily domestically related matters as how to develop resources rapidly, what resources to develop, and how best to absorb provincial concerns.

In practice, however, the NEB soon came to behave in a similar fashion. Its first chairman, Ian MacKinnon, came to his new position from the Alberta Resources Conservation Board with a regional rather than national perspective and jealously preserved his prerogative of providing policy advice to the Cabinet in strict accordance with the NEB's technical calculations. Invariably this meant consistent recommendations for further exports as the NEB, after determining Canada's needs for the coming twenty-five years, emphasized the principles of economies of scale, resource and regional growth, current supply over future price, and amity and comity with the United States. Only in such rare, if significant, instances as the Montreal market question was policy dependent on the Cabinet's calculation of such broader political considerations as the need to support the balance of payments through exports and the need to develop the western industry in anticipation of the day when new markets in Canada could be economically supplied.

Taken together, the developments of 1957–1963 thus demonstrate the continuation of Canada's peripheral-dependence orientation, but also the emergence of a direct challenge from liberal-internationalist precepts and more substantial complex neo-realist tendencies. Although still focused on promoting exports to the American market alone, and hence dependent on the internal American debate between restrictionists and antirestrictionists, this posture was by no means reflexive or unchallenged. The creation of the Borden commission, its serious consideration of the Montreal market question, and the invocation of the National Oil Policy with its Ottawa Valley line broke the earlier stress on fostering exports on a north–south basis. In seeking access to the American market, Canada employed such liberal-internationalist devices as stressing Canadian–American commonality and the Venezuelan dimension to secure an exemption from mandatory oil import quotas, mobilizing existing joint organizations and summit contacts in the crusade, and developing an informal consultative process among functional counterparts to institutionalize the resulting special arrangement. Within Canada, the government began to legitimize neo-realist aspects of the decision-making process by giving serious consideration to Canadian independent producers' suggestions for a Montreal market extension and by creating the National Energy Board to define and protect Canadian interests on a comprehensive basis.

The Period of Growing Interdependence, 1963–1968

The increased capacity to bargain with the United States provided the central thrust of Canada's international oil and gas policy during the five years of Lester Pearson's Liberal governments.[30] Its primary manifestation was the success Canada enjoyed in engendering a stable regime with the U.S. within which Canada's traditional export orientation flourished. Equally important, this regime provided a framework within which Canada could keep alive its concern with constructing an east–west transportation system, secure a better bargain for its north–south transactions, and foster the internal institutional strength on which a more far-reaching national policy could be constructed.

Canada's enhanced bargaining power was most evident in the quest for expanded oil and gas exports to the United States. The new minister of trade and commerce, Mitchell Sharp, quickly announced that the National Oil Policy would not be altered in the near future and urged the industry to promote reasonable, nondisruptive exports to the United

States. By the end of 1964, Sharp's prediction of an increasing U.S. acceptance of Canadian crude was fulfilled when the flow southward exceeded even the levels tacitly agreed upon by Canada and the U.S. Department of the Interior.[31]

To some extent, this increase was due to the prime minister's service in the cause. Canadian oil exports were an agenda item at Pearson's May 1963 summit with President Kennedy. In January 1964, Pearson also pressed President Johnson for a greater inflow, countering Johnson's portrait of struggling independent Texas oil producers with a reminder of the damage to U.S.-owned Venezuelan oil should Canada, as a result of U.S. limitations, restrict imports into Montreal from that source.[32] This momentum was sustained when the April 1964 meeting of the Committee on Trade and Economic Affairs initiated studies by a joint working group on energy co-operation and when a later report by Livingston Merchant and A.D.P. Heeney identified energy as a fruitful area of continental collaboration.[33]

Yet by 1967 a familiar obstacle had arisen to impede Canadian access to U.S. oil markets and the comfortable procedure whereby Canada and the U.S. annually agreed on an import level. In May of that year, congressional pressure, reinforced by the attempted OPEC embargo during the June 1967 Middle East war, led the administration to include Canada in its overall quota system and to seek from Canada a commitment to voluntarily limit its producers' exports to U.S. regions east of the Rockies. In a secret, gentleman's "framework of agreement" in May 1968, Canada acceded to this request, but only after securing additional benefits from the U.S. In late 1967 and early 1968, Canada had secured the agreement of the administration and the Federal Power Commission to allow increased exports by looping Interprovincial's pipeline from Alberta and its extension directly into the Chicago area. And in February 1968, it induced the secretary of the interior to announce an increase in the target level of Canadian exports. Canada's acceptance of the gentleman's agreement was thus a response to a widely understood U.S. governmental linkage between authorizing the Chicago-destined projects in return for voluntary Canadian export restrictions. Yet growing U.S. demand and the absence of enforcement provisions in the understanding led to an increase in Canadian imports above the understood levels and American complaints as a result.[34]

In the field of natural gas, the legacy of the 1956 pipeline debate and the greater bargaining power resulting from America's shortages exercised a more powerful restraining effect on Canada's export push. These restraints were first evident in 1966, when TransCanada PipeLines proposed to meet a growing eastern Canadian demand by building a new gas pipeline south of the Great Lakes.[35] In this minor replay of the 1956 debate, the company's proposal for a U.S.-routed line, 50 per cent owned by U.S. companies, was first declared economical by the NEB but then rejected outright by the Liberal Cabinet. However, after an outburst of corporate and political criticism, Prime Minister Pearson announced Cabinet acceptance of a revised application. This application guaranteed the primacy of the existing northern line, its looping by 1970, and Canadian control of the southern project.

This growing Canadian resolve was also evident in the government's treatment of individual gas export applications.[36] While the NEB readily approved new applications, it demanded a higher price for gas volumes already contracted to the U.S. in dealing with Westcoast's request for additional exports in late 1967. U.S. refusal produced an escalating dispute. After Prime Minister Pearson briefly discussed the issue in Washington with Secretary of State Dean Rusk, the two regulatory agencies approved a revised application, which split the price difference.

Canada's stiffening stance in bilateral bargaining was accompanied by efforts to increase control over the oil and gas industry at home. In 1966 the government purchased a 45 per cent equity participation in Panarctic Oils of Calgary, to encourage Canadian-controlled exploration of its Arctic lands; and in 1967 it considered reducing the generous concessions given to the conventional and largely U.S.-controlled industry.[37] More importantly, in 1966, the government created the new Department of Energy, Mines and Resources (EMR), with authority over Canada's energy and water resources and a mandate to advise and co-ordinate policy on Canada's energy resources as a whole.[38] This replaced the technically oriented Department of Mines and Technical Surveys with a more broadly focused, policy-oriented body, while acknowledging the interests of such departments as Trade and Commerce, Finance, and External Affairs. The importance of this change was enhanced by Pearson's appointment, as EMR's first minister, of Jean-Luc Pepin, an MP with a broad economic understanding who rapidly developed a reputation as a good departmental leader.

To a considerable extent, this growth in Canadian initiatives, bargaining power, and national planning capacity was the result of a significant erosion in the previously powerful hold of the U.S.-defined international energy regime. As changing global conditions rendered the U.S. more responsive to events abroad and propelled it haltingly into greater government intervention, the ability of the administration to affect Canadian behaviour in a framework set by the American corporate community was correspondingly reduced. At the same time, these global alterations enabled Canada to respond directly to international fluctuations and allowed it to begin to deal directly, through both multilateral and bilateral channels, with other prospective partners overseas.

As American hegemony and multinational oil production in the Middle East combined to render uneconomic much of America's domestic oil and gas production, U.S. energy policy during the Johnson administration became dominated by three forces: the intensified complaints of U.S. oil producers over their diminishing market share; a steady decline in readily available U.S. oil and gas reserves; and, after the supply interruptions occasioned by the June 1967 war, the sudden need to find alternative secure sources to supply its domestic consumers, European and Japanese allies, and its forces in Vietnam.[39]

Within Washington, these preoccupations bred intensified involvement from the Department of the Interior (DOI) and the Federal Power Commission (FPC), the creation of new review bodies, and the growing participation of the Department of State. By late 1966, Interior had once again begun to press the restrictionist case, as Canadian exporters regularly surpassed their target levels of exports and as U.S. independents, through such bodies as the Independent Petroleum Association (IPA), demanded Canada's inclusion in the mandatory oil import program, the extension of the program to natural gas, and U.S. resistance to a new Canadian pipeline into Chicago. Reinforced by the Pearson government's handling of the Great Lakes affairs, Interior overcame State Department objections to strongly oppose the Chicago line in top-level exploratory discussion with Canada in May 1967 and to begin hearings on the oil import program.[40] However, the June war in the Mideast broke the impasse. Canada's demonstration of reliability, in a rapid increase in oil exports, and the Pentagon's search for alternative supplies for Europe and Vietnam led to renewed interest in Washington for the Chicago line and a sympathetic hearing for Pepin's forceful plea for increased access to U.S. oil markets.[41]

A similar transition took place with natural gas. The U.S. had been startled by the Pearson Cabinet's rejection, without advance warning, of the Great Lakes proposal and the accompanying rationale that Canada would not allow the supply of gas to its eastern consumers to be dependent, through the device of a U.S.-routed pipeline, on the legal authority of a foreign government. Canada's quick reversal of this decision compounded American doubts about Canadian reliability. As a result the FPC conducted extensive hearings on the Great Lakes application. Yet the shock of the Mideast war, together with American need for gas and other factors, soon led the FPC to grant and defend the application. Similarly, concern with security of supply and the shock of the 1967 war led the FPC to reject IPA demands to place gas under import controls and ultimately to accept the compromise proposal on the pricing of Westcoast's exports in 1968.

In other areas, the influence of U.S. behaviour was even more circumscribed. The U.S. government made no forceful response to the Canadian government's assumption of a 45 per cent equity participation in Panarctic, although it represented a potential challenge to American-based multinationals that had held many of the original exploration permits for the Arctic lands. Nor had it been concerned about the creation of EMR, a move partly occasioned by problems with the United States and concern over nationalist and continentalist paths in water resources. The diminishing salience of U.S. actions was most evident in Canada's reaction to the June war. The crisis led Canada to consider shipping Albertan oil eastward by rail, to take a renewed interest in the work of the OECD oil committee, and, with Albertan officials, to engage in contacts with Japanese and British government representatives about Canadian supplies to their countries and overseas participation in developing the Alberta oil sands.

The slowly diminishing salience and sensitivity of American forces was reflected in the increasing prominence of societal organizations as important participants in the debate. Parliament continued to exercise a vigilant oversight role on Interprovincial's application for the Chicago line, the Westcoast gas price dispute, and the creation of EMR. It also vociferously entered into the Great Lakes dispute of 1966. Here the desire of the minority Pearson government to appear decisive, as well as the growing nationalist thinking within parliamentary ranks, did much to prompt Cabinet's initial rejection of the Great Lakes application. Yet Parliament's influence on the substance of the subsequent compromise was reduced by severe intraparty divisions. Later most MPs agreed on the principle, expressed by Conservative Davie Fulton, that there be "progressive federal initiatives for action" that would give Canada control over its resources, ensure its future greatness, and prevent its slide down the continentalist slope.

A somewhat more influential vision was held by the corporate sector and its allies in the major provincial governments. Although small Alberta entrepreneurs had secured federal government participation in the Panarctic venture, virtually the entire industry remained united in its support of a southward export orientation. Alberta's independents, suffering through the supply glut of the mid-1960s, could argue through their 150-member Independent Petroleum Association of Canada that Alberta's prorationing scheme favoured the major multinationals and that Ottawa should preserve the on-to-Montreal option, should U.S. market restrictions not relax. Yet they readily joined Alberta and the major oil producers and gas companies to demand federal action to open U.S. markets. Moreover, in the Great Lakes controversy, this coalition attracted the support of Ontario, Quebec, and major Canadian industrialists in urging the Pearson cabinet to reconsider its initial rejection of a U.S. route. Yet the power of this coalition ultimately proved useful in sustaining the cause of a growing, if amorphous, Canadian nationalism, as it backed the NEB demand for higher prices in Westcoast's gas export application.[42]

It was within the federal government that the greatest moves towards challenging existing orientations occurred. Throughout the period, Walter Gordon waged a lonely crusade against the quest for exports led enthusiastically by EMR's Jean-Luc Pepin, the NEB, other economic ministers, and Prime Minister Pearson himself.[43] Yet slowly the weight of a competing logic began to be felt. In the Great Lakes affair, it was the fear of a new pipeline debate, the growing force of economic nationalism, fear of dependence on U.S. regulations, and the Cabinet's concern over its reputation for indecision that led it first to override the NEB and reject the U.S.-routed pipeline and subsequently to accept a revised proposal with firm conditions attached. In the creation of Panarctic, Minister of Indian and Northern Affairs Arthur Laing's fear of the nationalist critique, the attractiveness of a new area, and the knowledge that development would otherwise not be done led to Cabinet's acceptance of an equity position. By the time of the Westcoast price confrontation, the NEB, with Pearson's support, had added to its traditional principles the standard that the price of exported gas would be determined by the value of the commodity in the market served.

These changes were registered most decisively in the creation of EMR, an action that stemmed from Pearson's concerns that energy was becoming more important while difficulties with the U.S. were growing. It further derived from a feeling that policy could no longer be left to the quasi-judicial guidance of the NEB, especially in light of the body's continuing export orientation and links with Alberta, the broader political considerations surrounding the energy field, and the need to consider the country's total energy picture. Although the normal bureaucratic jealousies attended the birth of EMR, Pearson's conviction and the new perceptions meant that there was no active opposition from related departments.

Thus during the 1963–1968 period, the growing interdependence of the Canada–U.S. energy relationship reinforced the liberal-internationalist orientation of the previous period, while Canada's enhanced bargaining capacity and attainment of more balanced bargains demonstrated the increasing strength of complex neo-realism at a secondary level. The strength of liberal-internationalist patterns was reflected most clearly in the channels through which Prime Minister Pearson and his ministers successfully sought to keep American markets open to Canadian oil, the suggestions of the Merchant–Heeney report, the compromise decision in the Great Lakes affair, and the gentleman's agreement on oil exports. At the same time, complex neo-realist tendencies appeared consistently in the use of the Montreal market and Venezuelan interests as bargaining tools over oil exports, Canada's ability to increase the price of exported gas in the Westcoast case and secure entry into the Chicago market, its domestic intervention in its Panarctic participation, and the creation of Energy, Mines and Resources.

This two-tiered approach was further manifest in the process by which Canadian behaviour was determined. The emergence of a dominant liberal-internationalist process was evident in the continuing causal role of the United States and the influence of Parliament on the Great Lakes, Chicago, and Westcoast issues. Complex neo-realist dimensions were reflected in the growing sensitivity of the U.S. to global conditions, Canada's contacts with the British and the Japanese, and the continuing interest of the Canadian independents in the Montreal option. They were also seen in the influence of Walter Gordon and his nationalist Cabinet colleagues on the Great Lakes affair and later export questions, and Prime Minister Pearson's role in the creation of Energy, Mines and Resources.

The Period of Tentative Disassociation, 1968–1973

From 1968 to 1973, the growing unilateralism, bargaining strength, and national planning capacity of the Pearson years culminated in the first tentative moves to reduce the existing network of Canada–U.S. collaboration.[44] The leading sector in this transition was the area of oil exports to the United States.[45]

Following the 1967 gentleman's agreement, Canadian oil exports continued to rise above targeted levels, prompting a series of U.S. complaints and Canadian efforts to reduce producers' volumes. By 1969, President Nixon's appointment of a U.S. task force on oil imports stimulated stronger Canadian action. In March, Prime Minister Trudeau warned that U.S. restrictions could harm overall Canada–U.S. relations. In August, a Canadian note tacitly linked oil exports to gas exports by noting that Canadian producers required the former to finance exploration for the latter. And in December, a Canadian note to the U.S. Task Force underscored the interdependence of the two countries and their natural partnership in continental defence.

Such representations had little effect, for in March 1970, the U.S. imposed mandatory oil import quotas on Canadian crude and a severe reduction on the allowable level of imports from Canada. In response, Prime Minister Trudeau issued a strong protest and energy minister Joe Greene linked energy with Canada–U.S. defence and trade co-operation; in May, in a speech in Denver, Greene announced his conversion to a nationalist position. In November, a temporary accommodation was reached when the U.S., at the Joint Committee on Trade and Economic Affairs, agreed in principle to give Canadian oil "full and unimpeded access" to U.S. markets, established an immediate 20 per cent increase in Canadian export levels, and authorized discussions leading to a rapid agreement for security of supply, should flows from the Middle East be disrupted.[46]

These actions established a regime that lasted until the spring of 1972, when the first traces of an historic shift in Canadian policy appeared. In March, the NEB expressed concern over the decline in Canadian oil and gas reserves for the second consecutive year. In spring 1973, energy minister Donald Macdonald noted that Canada would curtail exports to the U.S. if Canadian production fell behind domestic needs. And in mid-June, temporary controls were placed on exports of gasoline and refined products. Later that month, EMR's policy paper, *An Energy Policy for Canada*, recommended a single price for oil in Canada, with importers of newly expensive eastern crude compensated by an export tax bringing U.S.-destined oil to world price levels.[47] And on 13 September, the government imposed an export tax of 40 cents per barrel on crude oil to insulate Canada from the rapidly rising U.S. and world price.

This reversal in Canadian policy was accompanied and aided by major disputes over two long-range integrative ventures: a U.S.-sponsored proposal for a *de facto* continental energy policy (CEP) and a Canadian proposal for a Mackenzie Valley Oil Pipeline as an alternative to the U.S. Trans Alaska Pipeline System (TAPS).

The CEP proposal for a more integrated and secure North American energy market constituted a far-reaching extension of the consultative pattern that had prevailed in the 1960s. This pattern had been reaffirmed by Prime Minister Trudeau and President Nixon at their March 1969 summit and reflected in the advance notice U.S. officials had provided of their intention to impose mandatory quotas in March 1970.[48] When it was first outlined by the U.S. in a December 1969 meeting, Greene had responded with great interest to a CEP, although by February 1970 both he and the secretary of state for external affairs were publicly favouring specific rather than comprehensive arrangements and denying any linkage between this issue and the oil import question. When American action in March contradicted this statement, Canada immediately suspended discussions on the CEP and publicly argued that comprehensive energy sharing would be an abnegation of sovereignty. When official-level discussions resumed in September, the Canadians firmly rejected the U.S. proposal. Following the U.S. trade surcharge of August 1971, Canada again suspended discussions to indicate its displeasure with the unilateral U.S. economic moves. While discussions resumed in November, Canada rendered its definitive negative judgement in January 1973.

TAPS evoked a much more ambivalent Canadian response. Here the government's concern over Canadian-controlled northern development conflicted with its desire to prevent the potential environmental danger to British Columbia coastlines posed by U.S. tankers carrying large quantities of newly discovered Alaskan oil from the pipeline's southern terminus at Valdez, Alaska, to refineries in the Pacific northwest.[49] In 1971, when it appeared the U.S. would proceed despite opposition from a consortium proposing an all-land route through Canada, Ottawa began to intervene. Prime Minister Trudeau, Joe Greene, and Mitchell Sharp all invited the U.S. to consider the alternative Mackenzie Valley route and asked for assurances about potential environmental damage, but they refrained from actively promoting the alternative route until Canada's northern development priorities had been established.

However, in late May 1972, Canada's stance changed significantly when Donald Macdonald met with U.S. Secretary of the Interior Rogers Morton to express Canadian opposition to tanker traffic along the British Columbia coast and to state Canada's readiness to consider investing in an oil and gas pipeline corridor from the Arctic to U.S. markets. Then the prime minister announced Canada's decision to construct an all-weather highway along the Mackenzie Valley, and Cabinet replaced its previous policy of passive promotion with active support for the Mackenzie Valley alternative. However, following Morton's May 1972 announcement that the U.S. had approved the construction of TAPS, Canada's focus shifted to limiting possible environmental damage. Canada's efforts to influence the internal U.S. debate on TAPS ended in July 1973, when a note sent to the U.S. embassy in Ottawa said, in a clarification of the Northern Pipeline Guidelines of 1970, that Canada would not require majority Canadian ownership of a Mackenzie Valley line.

These shifts in Canada's oil policy were mirrored in the area of natural gas. Although the government in the late 1960s began to insist on shorter-term gas contracts, it began the 1970s with its familiar policy, reaffirmed by Greene in April 1970, of exporting commodities that were surplus to Canadian needs.[50] Thus in February 1970, Cabinet approved a NEB decision, reached after two years of hearings, to approve four export applications totalling 6.3 trillion cubic feet (tcf), with terms of fifteen to twenty years, representing a 50 per cent increase over current levels. However, at the same time, the NEB rejected an export application for the first time and Greene warned that there would be no further exports unless Canada discovered more than the anticipated 3.5 tcf per year. More important, on 19 November 1971, the NEB announced its decision to deny all pending gas export applications, totalling 2.66 tcf, on the grounds that no surplus existed and demand in Canada was rising faster than reserves.

The increasing restrictiveness of Canadian energy policy was first evident on the domestic front in February 1970 when the minister of Indian and northern affairs, Jean Chrétien, announced that Ottawa was investing a further $13.5 million in Panarctic, in an effort to ensure that the government retained control of the corporation.[51] Two months later, in response to growing activity by U.S.-based Humble Oil in Canada's Arctic, the government unilaterally introduced antipollution regulations in the Arctic, asserted control over all shipping within 100 miles of Canadian lands, and declared that it would not abide by any judgement of the International Court of Justice on the international legality of these measures. In August, the government followed by promulgating a series of Northern Pipeline Guidelines declaring that only one gas pipeline and one oil pipeline would be constructed along the Mackenzie, seeking to maximize Canadian ownership and control of the lines, and favouring Canadian underwriters in the financing of the projects. The following year, the minister of EMR noted that any agreement on a Mackenzie Valley oil pipeline would require considerable Canadian content in the construction of the system. And in April 1971, the government demonstrated its commitment to this philosophy by intervening to secure a Canadian buyer for the Home Oil Company in the face of a proposed take-over by an American firm. The culmination of this trend came in EMR's June 1973 report, which argued that state participation in the oil and gas industry was important to secure adequate knowledge of the industry's operation in Canada and could exploit nonconventional sources while pursuing regional development and enhanced security of supply.

To a considerable extent, these steady moves towards national restriction stemmed from the government's development of a much more comprehensive and detailed policy for Canada's energy sector as a whole. Prompted by the American discoveries in Alaska, the government had established in 1968 the interdepartmental Task Force on Northern Oil Development, mandated to consider the implications of the discoveries for the National Oil Policy. Although the task force upheld the policy, a new philosophy soon emerged. Its impetus came from Prime Minister Trudeau's feeling, upon entering office, that there was a lack of knowledge within the government about Canada's actual energy supplies and about their relevance as instruments for actively furthering a broad range of national objectives. He thus directed EMR to initiate a comprehensive analysis of Canada's energy situation as a basis for producing a new energy policy. Begun in 1971, this analysis rapidly moved towards conclusions centred on the need for export restrictions. Foreshadowed in the NEB's February 1973 report, *Potential Limitations on Canadian Petroleum Supplies*, this view received its most ambitious expression in June 1973 when EMR's report *An Energy Policy for Canada* set forth the arguments for an export tax on Canadian oil, a single oil price within Canada, and state participation in the oil and gas industry.

The 1968–1973 period also saw the first major Canadian efforts to deal with energy questions beyond the western hemispheric context.[52] The initial move, taken in a North Atlantic multilateral forum, came in April 1973 when Donald Macdonald indicated that OECD members were negotiating an oil-sharing system to be instituted in the event of a curtailment of Middle Eastern supplies. Moreover in May, Canada established diplomatic relations with Saudi Arabia, and in June Macdonald announced that he would visit several major oil-producing states, notably Iran, Nigeria, and Venezuela, to discuss future oil supplies for Canada.

As these contacts in particular demonstrated, Canadian energy policy during the period became affected by an external environment that was considerably less U.S.-centred and rather less salient than the international constellation of previous years.[53] Within the United States, the declining ability of the government to meet its energy needs through a reliance on global open market regimes led to the development of comprehensive strategies in which foreign policy considerations and presidential and State Department actors were of greater concern. These trends were most apparent on the issues of oil imports and the CEP, where a presidentially appointed task force, under State Department guidance, sought to ensure that America's energy supplies would become less vulnerable to overseas price rises by developing with Canada an agreement for the assured free continental flow of oil and gas. More importantly, this coalition employed the device of drastically reducing Canada's oil import quota in March 1970 as a bargaining instrument to secure Canadian agreement to such a regime.

Canada responded to this linkage by maintaining its existing policy of refusing a comprehensive energy policy, by broadening the linkage through its refusal to discuss the concept before Washington's removal of import limitations and reconsideration of the August 1971 surcharge, and ultimately by shifting its own policy away from U.S. preferences, with the imposition of Canadian-based export restrictions. On the TAPS issue, the U.S. government's stress on an exclusively national transportation system was matched by a Canadian insistence on autonomously defining the direction and pace of its own northern development policy.

This increasing resistance to American stimuli was accompanied by the development of a direct concern with forces emanating from well beyond the American region. In rejecting a Montreal market extension in 1968, the government had noted the interests of Latin American and Middle Eastern producers in exporting to the region and the importance of such open markets to the process of Third World development. Subsequently, it had reacted to the Tehran agreement on increased Middle East prices by specifying their positive implications for energy and industrial investment in Canada. Both the NEB report of 1972 and the EMR report of 1973 had considered the possibility of supply interruptions from the Middle East; EMR had identified the consequent desirability of both a Montreal pipeline and direct state-to-state deals with overseas producers. Such deals gained considerable plausibility as Donald Macdonald visited major producing states, agreed that a direct deal with Venezuela was desirable, and noted the willingness of Canada's OECD partners to depart from their multilateral consensus in search of direct deals of their own.

This diffusion of external horizons was accompanied by an intensification of the domestic energy debate. Within Parliament, the New Democratic Party vigorously opposed the entire concept of a continental energy policy, and its views acquired considerable force after the 1972 election made its support critical to the survival of the minority Liberal government. Although the élite press, represented by the Toronto *Globe and Mail, Le Devoir*, and the *Financial Post*, continued to favour continental efficiency in energy development and sharing, the strong opposition of the Toronto *Star* and the Montreal *Star* to a CEP and growing public concern about American direct investment provided a persuasive counterbalance. Moreover, by 1971, the press and expert academics began to underscore Canada's declining reserves and high vulnerability to a disruption of Middle Eastern supplies.

The views of the business community, dominated by American-owned multinationals, also experienced a strong challenge. The 1970 NEB gas export hearings had marked the start of interventions by groups outside the oil and gas industry who were opposed to exports. By 1971, the Canadian Petroleum Association itself noted that Canada's reserves of conventional crude oil had fallen for the first time in two decades. Similarly, Alberta's strong export orientation attracted little support from other provinces. In 1969 the other provinces had objected to proposals to release reserved gas for export, and after 1971 the consuming provinces actively pressed for export restrictions and a low Canadian price for oil. The most dissatisfied consumer was the province of Quebec, which, dissatisfied with a federal policy that left it vulnerable, began in 1973 to explore with Saudi Arabia the prospects for a government-to-government deal.

Such conflicts helped enhance the power of an increasingly well organized federal government.[54] Under the impact of a determined prime minister, control over Canada's oil and gas policy passed decisively, after much interdepartmental consideration, conflict, and Cabinet attention, from an export-oriented NEB to a more comprehensively focused EMR. This transition began in full force in 1970, when Prime Minister Trudeau appointed Jack Austin deputy minister of EMR, with a mandate to assess Canada's inventory of energy, its dependence on international supplies, price relationships over the next three decades, and the impact of these factors on the development of the Canadian economy.

Austin's vigorous efforts to build EMR into a major policy department brought his organization into occasional conflict with Finance, the sole repository of economic expertise in the government; Industry, Trade and Commerce, the promoter of exports of all Canadian commodities; External Affairs, Canada's sole international negotiator and guardian of a stable relationship with the United States; and departments such as Indian Affairs and Northern Development, the proponent of rapid development of the Canadian north. More importantly, Austin propelled EMR into a major conflict with the NEB in the 1970–1971 debate over gas exports, when EMR, with prime ministerial support, succeeded in converting Cabinet, and ultimately the NEB itself, to a restrictive stance. Although Cabinet continued to devote considerable attention to such issues as TAPS, NEB recommendations and regulations, the 1973 EMR study, and overall Canada–U.S. relations, this victory left EMR with an unimpeded path to develop studies of Canadian oil and gas reserves, gas exports to the U.S., the world oil situation, and a national petroleum company. With these initiatives, the appointment of Donald Macdonald as minister, and the publication of *An Energy Policy for Canada*, Canada began to institute, several months before the oil embargo and price rise of October 1973, a more comprehensive policy regime based on a national price, transportation, and development system insulated from the vagaries of the world market.

The 1968–1973 period thus shows the growing force of the hitherto subordinate complex neo-realist elements, as Canada began to move towards bilateral detachment, national restriction, and global involvement. The limits of liberal internationalism in the Canada–U.S. relationship were clearly established when Canada rejected further integrative ventures such as a CEP, discouraged joint alternatives to TAPS, and began to reduce the existing trend of collaboration in the gas pricing decision of 1971 and the imposition of an oil export tax in September 1973. A complex neo-realist approach to activity and association generally began to emerge when Canada moved to strengthen its ties with Saudi Arabia, Mexico, and Venezuela, to counter expansion of the U.S. corporate presence in Canada on a case-by-case basis, and to produce a comprehensive policy emphasizing a unified Canadian pricing and transportation system distinct from the global environment. Perhaps the strongest evidence of this trend came in the policy-making proccss. Here Canada successfully withstood American pressure over oil exports on a CEP, absorbed the demands of oil-producing and Third World states in its external vision, responded to the preference of the New Democratic Party and the consuming provinces over oil and gas exports, and replaced the NEB with a well-staffed, policy-oriented Department of Energy, Mines, and Resources as the co-ordinating centre of the government's energy decision-making process.

The Period of Determined Detachment, 1973–1979

The philosophy established by *An Energy Policy for Canada* and the global oil shock of October 1973 provided a powerful foundation during the following six years for a determined, far-reaching Canadian effort to detach itself from the U.S.-defined energy system, to develop an oil and gas policy of fully global scope, and to create within Canada the intellectual and institutional structure for a more autonomous energy policy.[55]

The process of detachment was led by a series of sustained Canadian initiatives over the price and supply of oil and gas exports to the United States.[56] In order to insulate Canada from shortage-induced U.S. price rises in the wake of the Arab oil embargo, Canada rapidly raised its oil export tax from the 40 cents set in the autumn of 1973 to $1.90 in December, $4.00 in February 1974, and higher levels established by world market conditions thereafter. More importantly, it moved steadily to phase down the volume of crude oil actually exported, dropping the level from its peak of 1.2 million barrels a day (mbd) to 1.025 mbd in November 1973 and 305 000 barrels a day by January 1977. In similar fashion, it then moved to control the export price and level of natural gas, although in a substantially slower and more circumspect fashion. Prompted by British Columbia, the federal government announced in September 1974 an increase in the export price of gas to $1.00 per mcf effective January 1975; it later raised the price to $1.60 in May and $1.94 in January 1977. Movements towards supply reduction began with the October 1974 imposition of export control on propane and butane, continued with a January 1975 warning that a 20 per cent supply reduction would be necessary, and culminated in October 1975 when the NEB was granted the power, subject to government approval, to limit exports without conducting preliminary hearings.

By 1977, when the process of detachment was well established, a more co-operative emphasis began to prevail. During the preceding three years, Canada had based its price rises and supply controls on criteria such as national markets and security of supply, capturing the full value of exports according to the U.S. cost of substitution, providing advance warning and consultation where possible concerning new policies, to allow the U.S. time for adjustments, and giving special consideration to dependent refineries in the U.S. northern tier. Accordingly, it had kept oil exports above targeted levels in 1976, and it kept gas exports at existing levels in 1975 and 1976. In early 1977, it responded to U.S. pleas for emergency supplies during an unusually cold winter by providing additional quantities of gas and oil. In May 1977, it altered its policy to emphasize the continued export of heavy oil to the U.S. And in the next two years, responding both to new discoveries in West Pembina, Alberta, and to U.S. representations, it decided to continue light oil exports at stable levels for three years and increased the authorized levels of gas exports.

This stress on co-operation was reflected in attendant measures to define in greater detail the conditions of the bilateral energy exchange. A Joint Canada–U.S. Marine Contingency Plan, established through an official exchange of notes in June 1974, led to a voluntary tanker traffic separation plan in March 1975 and an agreement on tankers in the Strait of Juan de Fuca in December 1979. A joint working group created in June 1975 continued discussion over swapping western Canadian for eastern American oil and quickly produced an agreement. This was modified in December 1977 to exclude western crude destined for delivery to the Montreal market but to include "time" swaps for future considerations. Extensive diplomatic discussions produced a treaty guaranteeing the security of pipelines crossing each other's country. And throughout the period, three joint committees, established by Donald Macdonald and a U.S. presidential energy adviser in 1973, conducted information exchanges and identified areas of potential co-operation on specific projects.

The Mackenzie Valley gas project provided the clearest example of Canada's readiness to engage in new joint ventures after the detachment required to meet national needs had been secured.[57] Intense consideration of this project began in October 1974, after Canadian Arctic Gas Pipeline Limited and its American partner filed applications to construct a line to transport Canadian and American gas from Alaska and the Beaufort Sea through Canadian territory to American and Canadian markets in the south. Donald Macdonald, aware of a competing all-American proposal, offered assurances against unexpected provincial taxation, on proportional cost sharing, on supply apportionment in the event of disruption, and on guaranteed American flow-through in the event of additional Canadian discoveries. In January 1976, a draft agreement was initialled. In a February 1977 summit, President Carter and Prime Minister Trudeau agreed to harmonize the timing of their regulatory agencies' consideration of specific proposals. And in August, after a series of special inquiries, Canada authorized a proposal by a second group to build a line down a modified route. When final negotiations began on 17 August, Canada held forth the incentive of additional gas exports, and by September American agreement to a joint project had been secured. The following April, Canada moved to implement the agreement in a way consistent with national objectives by creating a Northern Pipeline Agency, headed by Mitchell Sharp, with a mandate to maximize benefits for Canadians.

Despite this intense concentration on bilateral matters, Canada was simultaneously engaged in developing direct dealings with participants in the global oil and gas market as a whole. Its initial thrust came through familiar multilateral channels.[58] Canada responded immediately to U.S. Secretary of State Henry Kissinger's December 1973 call for collaboration among the North Atlantic countries and Japan. In February 1974, led by the Department of External Affairs, Canada attended the Washington Energy Conference of thirteen consumer nations. While subscribing to the basic objectives of inhibiting direct bilateral consumer deals with producers, opposing Arab political interference in world trade, and enhancing the security of Western supply, Canada emphasized the need for consumer–producer dialogue rather than confrontation with OPEC, greater aid to non-oil-producing less developed countries, and a greater role for oil-producing states in multilateral organizations such as the World Bank and International Monetary Fund. Canada, as part of the seven-member Energy Co-ordinating Group, agreed to make oil available for an emergency pool, and in September joined the new eleven-member International Energy Agency, a body designed to formulate and manage an emergency oil-sharing plan among consumers, stimulate energy research, development, investment, and conservation, and promote co-operation with oil-producing nations.

Canada's emphasis on co-operation was reflected in Canadian initiatives in multilateral forums of a more global scope. Through Minister of Finance John Turner, it took a lead in prompting the International Monetary Fund to cope with the distribution among world capital markets of the large sums of surplus revenue accumulated by a few oil-producing states. More directly, it promoted the holding of a consumer–producer Conference on International Economic Co-operation (CIEC) in December 1975, accepted an appointment as co-chairman, with Venezuela, of the conference, and received seats on the commissions that the conference established on energy and development.[59]

Canada's prominence at CIEC was due in part to the strong bilateral relationships it had begun to forge with major oil-producing states, notably Venezuela and Saudi Arabia.[60] From 1973 through 1975, Prime Minister Trudeau and a steady stream of Cabinet ministers visited Venezuela, from whom Canada received 40 per cent of its oil imports, in quest of a long-term supply agreement covering Venezuelan exports and Canadian technology transfer and investment. In February 1976, a second visit by Prime Minister Trudeau furthered the process, through a suggestion that Petro-Canada play a greater role as a purchaser of oil imports. Beyond the hemisphere, action was equally intense. In December 1973, an embassy was opened in Saudi Arabia. The following year an embassy was opened in Iraq, relations were established with four Gulf states, Donald Macdonald was sent to Saudi Arabia and Iran, low-interest loans were extended to Mideast producers for the purchase of Canadian goods, and a joint committee was established with Iran. And in January 1976, Secretary of State for External Affairs Allan MacEachen visited Iraq, Egypt, Jordan, Israel, and Saudi Arabia and formed a joint committee for economic and technical co-operation with Saudi Arabia. Elsewhere, Canada attracted Japanese investment in the tar sands projects and forged closer ties through ministerial visits with Mexico.

The most significant Canadian initiatives during this period came on the domestic front. At the height of the oil embargo, the government authorized the Canadian Commercial Corporation to purchase any oil available on the tight international market and publicly criticized those multinational oil companies in Canada who were thought to be diverting Canadian-destined shipments to markets in the United States. The government committed itself to the Syncrude and Polar Gas projects, and on 30 July 1975, it created state-owned Petro-Canada, with an initial allocation of $1.5 billion and a mandate to increase domestic supply, help formulate Canadian energy policy, and increase the Canadian presence in the domestic oil and gas industry. Within its first year of operation, Petro-Canada had acquired U.S.-owned Atlantic Richfield of Canada, and in November 1978, with strong support from Prime Minister Trudeau and energy minister Alastair Gillespie, it purchased Pacific Petroleum from American interests.

Underlying these initiatives was the vision of Canada's energy future that the government had articulated with increasing vigour in policy papers and legislation from 1973 onward. The framework set forth in *An Energy Policy for Canada* was given legislative expression in the Energy Supplies Emergency Act of December 1973. This act officially stated the new policy goal of oil self-sufficiency by 1980 and security of supply in the interim period, created a national petroleum market by discarding the Ottawa Valley line, and advocated future price increases and the rapid construction of a Sarnia–Montreal pipeline. Following release of a NEB report on oil exports in 1974, the government instituted a new system of export controls to preserve supplies for the Montreal market and a more stringent formula for estimating exportable surplus. In 1976, the government unveiled *An Energy Strategy for Canada: Policies for Self Reliance*, which announced further movements to higher prices, an emphasis on frontier exploration, and increased Canadian participation in the oil and gas industry.[61] Subsequent legislation provided Petro-Canada with new optional working interests in renewal permits, provincial leases, and Crown land acquisitions, introduced new royalty schemes, and gave the minister of energy the power to require a 25 per cent minimum level of Canadian ownership in producible properties.

The emphasis on creating a made-in-Canada policy, insulated from the vagaries of American energy policy and the world petroleum market, reflected the diminishing potency of these factors in the determination of Canadian behaviour. The oil shock of 1973 did much to further Canada's previous determination to move towards self-reliance, and fluctuations in the world oil market continued to affect the pace and particular manifestation of this quest. Yet Canada's position as a net energy exporter and the support that higher world prices gave to vigorous domestic energy development provided a wide latitude for autonomous action. And the wide variety of external stimuli the government now received directly through its new network of multilateral and bilateral associations allowed far greater flexibility in preparing responses to events abroad.

Nowhere was this increased freedom of action more apparent than in

Canada's ability to engage in sustained unilateral action *vis-à-vis* the United States, withstand American criticisms, and alter the climate of the bilateral energy relationship in accordance with broader domestic needs. Although parts of the American executive and legislative branches had responded in strongly critical fashion to Canada's unilateral price rises and supply reductions, Donald Macdonald's representations to energy adviser William Simon, together with Henry Kissinger's geopolitical understanding of Canada's situation, did much to produce a grudging American acceptance of Canadian moves. After 1975, a period of relative price stability, Canada's co-operative emphasis, and the Carter administration's foreign policy vision reinforced American acquiescence in the new order. Thus President Carter made no effort to influence Canada's Mackenzie Valley pipeline route decision and promised his full support for the joint project. And Vice-President Walter Mondale emphasized the importance of close consultations, and urged that the U.S. follow Canada's lead in dealing with the global oil crisis.

Although the oil shock and the far-reaching changes in Canadian policy created a widespread politicization of oil and gas policy in Canada, that politicization did little to determine or change the course that the federal government had set. Parliamentary debate revealed a strong spirit of bipartisanship in the face of crisis, tempered by some ideological divisions over the degree of government intervention in the private sector. Similarly, public opinion consistently lent strong support to the government's initiatives.

The greatest conflict and changes came within the corporate sector, although here, too, the federal government was firmly and increasingly in control. The influence of U.S.-based multinational oil companies diminished considerably, as they responded poorly to Ottawa's efforts at ensuring rising export prices and secure import deliveries, fostering tar sands and frontier development, and increasing the Canadian presence in the oil and gas sector. In contrast, influence shifted to rapidly growing Canadian-controlled companies, whose success depended on government objectives.[62] The two major firms in this group, Alberta Gas Trunk Line and Dome Petroleum, succeeded in winning government approval for, respectively, the northern gas pipeline project and the continuation of drilling in the Beaufort Sea over U.S. government opposition.

Of considerably greater importance to federal calculations were the positions of the provincial governments. National unity considerations, thrust into prominence by the election of the separatist Parti Québécois government in the November 1976 provincial elections in Quebec, contributed at least indirectly to such decisions as developing a Canadian-supplied, price-subsidized Montreal market and co-operating with the United States on the northern gas pipeline venture. The crisis environment in the energy field prompted growing provincial unilateralism, with Quebec consulting Iran over a deep-water oil terminal on the St. Lawrence, the Atlantic premiers creating a joint working group on energy with the New England governors, New Brunswick assisting Maine with oil supplies, and British Columbia acting independently over west coast tanker traffic management, natural gas pricing, and oil swaps. By far the most influential and difficult province was Alberta, which opposed the initial oil export tax, demanded a greater share of the resulting revenues, and continually confronted the federal government over price setting, supply estimates, and oil and gas swaps.

Despite this determined provincial opposition, it was the intense debate within the federal executive branch that dominated the process by which Canada's energy policy was generated. Notwithstanding its early reflections and actions, the government had been surprised by the events of autumn 1973 and, viewing them in the image of the 1956 crisis, had responded in an *ad hoc* fashion. Yet that crisis inaugurated a period in which virtually all substantial decisions were propelled to Cabinet as the overall co-ordinator of policy, the integrator of political considerations, and the formulator of major actions. Cabinet regularly reviewed and often modified NEB recommendations on export pricing, supply, and swaps, and dealt with all price and overall policy decisions with provincial impact. Cabinet also co-ordinated the major decisions on the northern gas pipeline project—which occurred at the same time as the government's preoccupation with the national unity crisis—through a special Cabinet committee chaired by Allan MacEachen.

Within Cabinet, the prime minister assumed a more prominent role, taking personal charge of the response to the 1973 crisis, presenting the initial proposals to Parliament in December, and subsequently employing summit diplomacy to ensure a consultative energy regime with the United States, the northern gas pipeline agreement, and a bilateral energy relationship with Venezuela. Backed by growing expertise in the energy field and a 1974 Cabinet decision that assigned responsibility for the overall management of Canada–U.S. relations to the Department of External Affairs, DEA involvement generally grew, most notably in areas where its role as Canada's formal spokesman and negotiator was paramount, such as the International Energy Agency, CIEC, the Pipeline Transit Treaty, and the west coast tanker issue. However, its influence at its outer limits remained limited to advising on the political and international implications of others' proposals; these implications, insofar as they suggested accommodation in the interest of good relations with the United States, seldom carried determining weight.

A similarly expanded involvement but ultimately circumscribed influence was exercised by such other departments as Finance, which managed the petrodollar "recycling" process; ITC, which integrated energy with bilateral trade concerns; Environment, which was overruled by Cabinet on west and east coast tanker issues; and Indian and Northern Affairs and Transport, which contributed technical advice in their respective areas. As a result, policy and co-ordinative control became increasingly centred in EMR, which developed the overall policy strategies, recommended the major price and supply decisions, and forged its own relationships with counterparts in the United States.

The 1973–1979 period thus demonstrated the rise to predominance of complex neo-realist patterns in Canadian behaviour, and the continuation, within this new framework, of earlier liberal-internationalist tendencies. The strength of complex neo-realism was underscored initially by Canada's reasonably consistent and successful effort to raise the price and reduce the supply of its oil and gas exports to the United States, often through unilateral action and arm's-length bargaining. Furthermore, its new involvement in the IEA and other multilateral agencies and its successful pursuit of bilateral agreements in the Middle East and Latin America indicated the emergence of a fully global energy diplomacy, directed towards a genuine diversification of oil and gas relationships.

Within Canada, the creation of Petro-Canada, the Act of 1973, and the subsequent *Policies for Self Reliance* demonstrated a new stress on national interest as the basis for action, with internal modifications to enhance it. Only within this framework was freedom given to such liberal-internationalist activity as the emphasis on consultation with the U.S. after 1977, the joint northern gas pipeline project, Canada's role in the IEA, and its support within and outside this body for a co-operative world order in which the claims of the poor, energy-importing states would be accommodated.

Of equal importance was the emergence during this period of a process conforming strongly to complex neo-realist predictions. The reduced salience of the external environment was seen first in Canada's rejection of American complaints over price and supply issues, then more broadly in its freedom to set separate prices for energy commodities within Canada. Within a more potent domestic arena, the influence of producing provinces such as Alberta was felt less, while that of rapidly growing Canadian-owned firms increased. And within Ottawa itself, the involvement of a wide range of actors highlighted the co-ordinative centrality of EMR, the Cabinet, and the prime minister himself.

The Period of National Assertion, 1979–1981

The two-year period beginning in 1979 marked the culmination of the trend towards detachment begun during the 1970s.[63] After the second global oil shock in 1979, the Trudeau government, and to a lesser extent the short-lived Conservative minority government of Joe Clark, proceeded with greater vigour to alter price and supply relationships with the United States, limit collaboration to specific projects under well-defined rules, and develop alternative bilateral relationships overseas. More importantly it acted decisively to extend both the global reach and the national character of Canadian policy through its role in the energy deliberations of the Western Economic Summit and the moves towards independence, Canadianization, and equity heralded in the National Energy Program of 1980.

The initial steps in this process came in oil and gas trade with the United States. Through 1979 and 1980, Canada steadily raised the export price of oil by substantial amounts, with only the special case of heavy oils and a brief pause in July 1980 disturbing the trend. Oil exports in general and light oil exports in particular were subject to severe supply reductions; light oil exports were lowered significantly in September 1979 and virtually eliminated in December of that year. The price of exported gas also rose through 1979, and in January 1980 experienced a 30 per cent increase to a level of $4.47 per tcf. Afterwards U.S. complaints about insufficient advance warning and Canadian fears that lower-priced Mexican supplies might endanger completion of the northern gas pipeline led to a new consultative regime and a delay, until January 1981, in further price increases. Only in the area of exported gas volumes did Canada temper the trend towards detachment. Prompted by knowledge of increased Albertan reserves, fear of Mexican competition in the U.S. market, and above all a desire to facilitate financing of the northern gas pipeline, Canada began increasing its export volumes at the outset of 1979, provided greater flexibility in export licences in September 1980, and in the next three months authorized several additional applications.

In large measure, these increases were directly related to Canada's wish to secure prebuilding of the southern Canadian portions of the northern gas pipeline as a spur to the completion of the entire line.[64] Despite a series of general presidential assurances throughout 1979 and early 1980, Canada's doubts about the American government's commitment to proceed with its portion of the project were heightened by the American reluctance to allow Alaskan producers to join the pipeline consortium. The American government also refused to allow the sponsors to charge consumers higher prices in advance of the delivery of Alaskan supplies and gave no hint of whether government financial guarantees would be forthcoming if necessary. Canadian moves to modify the terms of the pipeline treaty and to issue public and private reminders of American obligations did little to speed progress on the American side. Thus, after obtaining a formal presidential commitment to the entire project, an assurance that the U.S. accepted Canada's right to set natural gas export prices, and a congressional resolution in support of the project, Canada on 17 July 1980 approved the prebuilding of the southern Canadian portion and the export of additional supporting quantities of conventional Canadian gas.

The exceptional nature of the prebuild venture was underscored by

Canada's cautious approach in related areas of bilateral exchange. While Canada consistently stated its preference for the environmentally preferable option—a joint overland pipeline to bring new supplies of needed Alaskan crude oil into the American midwest—it accepted with little protest the United States decision in favour of an all-American tanker and Northern Tier pipeline route. Similarly, Canada responded with increased oil swaps to new U.S. shortages induced by the revolution in Iran, but rejected exchanges in both oil and gas beginning in April 1979 because of perceived limitations of Albertan supply. It resumed shipments in the autumn only when the supply situation had eased. And throughout 1979 and 1980, Canada consistently rejected overtures by representatives of both the Republican and Democratic parties for a North American energy common market embracing Canada, the United States, and Mexico.

Consistent with Canada's caution towards continental collaboration was its expanded involvement in energy diplomacy overseas. At the IEA, Canada committed itself to a 5 per cent reduction in its oil imports and additional conservation measures in March 1979. At the OECD ministerial meeting in June 1979, Canada accepted the chairmanship of a working group on LDCs and renewable energy resources. And in May of that year, Canada acted as the Western spokesman on energy at the fifth United Nations Conference on Trade and Development (UNCTAD V).

Of greater importance was Canada's participation in the newly prominent energy agenda of the seven-member Western Economic Summit. At Tokyo in 1979, Prime Minister Clark successfully played a compromise role in a division over an appropriate energy plan for the seven industrialized powers, stated Canada's intention to achieve energy self-sufficiency by 1990, and acknowledged the need to adjust domestic oil prices upward towards world levels. And at Venice the following year, Prime Minister Trudeau helped achieve recognition of the need for a dialogue between producers and consumers and moderated a seven-power pledge requiring domestic prices to be based on world prices.[65]

The global scope of Canada's energy policy was reflected most fully in the intensified search for bilateral partnerships abroad. In the Middle East, oil shipments from Iraq were resumed following their suspension over the Jerusalem embassy affair, and in 1980, Canada received the Saudi Arabian energy minister in Ottawa and sent Prime Minister Trudeau to Riyadh in return. In a deliberate effort to reduce Canada's dependence on Middle Eastern crude, the government had Petro-Canada initiate talks with Venezuela and induced Gulf Canada to sign a contract directly with that state. In 1979, Canada began negotiations for a state-to-state oil deal with Venezuela; following the Liberals' return to office, the talks culminated in a March 1980 agreement for an initial Mexican shipment of 50 000 bpd to Canada.

Outside the major energy-producing regions, activity was similarly intense. Canada discussed energy supply arrangements with the European Community in December 1979, joined France in an exploration venture off the coast of China, and conducted energy talks with Germany and Italy. At the same time, it encouraged and initiated a broad series of ventures with Japan. Particularly through the Canadian International Development Agency, it inaugurated a large number of projects throughout the Pacific, Asia, and Africa.

By far the most ambitious action, however, came within Canada itself, where the goal of self-reliance was both reaffirmed and reinforced by substantive behaviour. Despite its dissatisfactions with Liberal energy policy and philosophy, the Clark government decided to retain Petro-Canada for state-to-state oil deals and participation in Panarctic Oils and the Polar Gas Project. It also moved decisively to raise domestic oil prices to world levels and employed the country's newly expanded gas reserves not only for exports to support the northern pipeline prebuild, but also to displace imported oil in Quebec and the Maritime provinces. Upon their return to office, the Liberals declared renewed determination to reduce Canada's dependence on imports and a desire to expand Canadian participation in the domestic oil and gas industry. On 29 October 1980, the government implemented its intention in a new National Energy Program (NEP).[66] In the most far-reaching and comprehensive set of actions taken to date, the government moved to ensure Canada's independence from the world energy market, to secure 50 per cent Canadian ownership of the petroleum industry by 1990, and to expand the government's proportion of that share.

The introduction of the National Energy Program highlights the low salience and diffuse scope of international factors in determining Canadian behaviour.[67] To be sure, the global oil shock of 1979 reinforced Canada's earlier determination to insulate itself from the global energy market and was fundamental to the generation of the NEP. Yet the NEP's stress on energy independence, the government's determination to keep domestic prices below world levels, and its actions at import reduction and extension of the national transportation system into Quebec and the Maritimes were aimed at insulating Canada from world disruptions and had some success. Within the multilateral forums of the IEA, the OECD, and the Western Economic Summit, Canada responded to the common interests of its industrialized and great-power allies, while helping define the consensus in its own interests and retaining its flexibility on the key issues of domestic pricing and the national treatment of foreign investment in the energy sector. Through bilateral discussions with industrialized states, bilateral agreements with energy producers, and development programs and multilateral diplomacy, Canada widened its energy horizons to global proportions and responded positively to the desires of energy producers and LDCs on such matters as state-to-state oil deals and co-operative, alternative energy development.

Within this global context, the significance of American behaviour diminished considerably. American pleas over Canadian actions on price and supply were generally to no avail, with the partial exception of the January 1980 gas price rise. Tentative American suggestions for a North American energy common market also met with an unaccommodating response. And while Canada remained vulnerable to American action in the case of the Northern Tier oil pipeline and the northern gas pipeline, it proceeded with the prebuild portion of the latter project only after receiving assurances of U.S. regulatory approval, of executive and congressional commitment to the entire project, and of Canada's right to set natural gas export prices.

This decline in American influence was matched by the emergence of an intense, sustained debate over international energy policy within Canada. The issues of domestic pricing, gas exports, and the prebuild gave rise to a structured cleavage among provincial governments, with Alberta, British Columbia, and other producing provinces influencing the Clark government's approach over the opposition of an Ontario government preoccupied with keeping plentiful supplies of inexpensive gas within Canada. At the same time, however, all provinces were united in the pursuit of direct relationships with major producing and consuming states abroad, a process led by Quebec's opening of an office in Venezuela and its efforts to secure a Quebec–Venezuela oil agreement.

Of greater importance were the divisions and shifting influence within the corporate community. The federal government's strong emphasis on expanding Petro-Canada's role was accompanied by direct and largely successful pressure on Canadian subsidiaries of multinational corporations to behave in accordance with national objectives. In contrast, the government did much to support the position of rapidly growing Canadian-owned firms, in part by acceding to their demands for new gas exports, thereby facilitating the prebuild project. This shift in influence resulted in the Canadianization provisions of the NEP, which significantly reduced the role of multinational corporations in favour of Canadian-owned and government-owned firms.

Within parliamentary channels, domestic pressures were equally intense but less influential. The NDP consistently opposed gas exports and the prebuild scheme. The Liberal opposition joined with it to confront the Clark government on these issues and to criticize the Conservative approach to the Northern Tier line. And in opposition, the Conservatives returned this criticism with complaints over the NEP. Only on the issue of higher domestic energy prices, where the Liberals joined with the NDP to defeat the Clark government, was the role of Parliament decisive.

These constraints on the influence of domestic actors stemmed partly from the emergence of a highly comprehensive and tightly co-ordinated process within the executive branch. The complexity of the northern gas pipeline issue spawned a distinctive decision-making process registered in the work of an *ad hoc* committee at the ministerial level and the appointment of Mitchell Sharp as federal pipeline commissioner. And the centrality of energy issues to the entire spectrum of national policy stimulated a more intense involvement on the part of numerous actors, from EMR, NEB, DEA, and ITC to Finance, Environment, Transport, Indian and Northern Affairs, and the Bank of Canada. Yet at the same time, it produced a strong incentive for high levels of overall co-ordination. This was reflected initially in the sustained involvement of the prime minister, within Ottawa, in visits to Saudi Arabia and Mexico, and in his active participation in the Western Economic Summits. It culminated in the National Energy Program, which was assembled by a small group of senior officials from EMR, Finance, and, at a lesser level, ITC.

The two years following the oil shock of 1979 marked the culmination of Canada's transition towards international oil and gas behaviour and processes conforming to complex neo-realist predictions. The Canadianization provisions of the National Energy Program represented a major assault on the one remaining area where peripheral-dependence patterns prevailed. Liberal-internationalist tendencies remained confined to Canada's authorization of the prebuild scheme and its supporting gas exports and to its involvement in the IEA and bodies such as UNCTAD.

Elsewhere, complex neo-realist patterns flourished. The reaffirmation of self-reliance as a pre-eminent policy and the development of new energy relationships with both the industrialized and the developing worlds pointed to a global pursuit of Canadian national interests. Unilateral initiatives on price and supply in North America, a domestic pricing policy at odds with that of Canada's IEA and Western Economic Summit partners, and the conclusion of state-to-state supply relationships with Mexico demonstrated a highly autonomous approach to the question of association. Canada's full role in the energy agenda of the seven-power economic summit, its focus on developing relationships with Japan and great powers on the European continent, and its formation through CIDA of direct energy programs in individual LDCs indicated a more exclusive approach to the definition of world order. Underlying these developments were those trends in the policy-making process that culminated in the National Energy Program, whose central objectives of independence, Canadianization, and financial equity highlighted, respectively, the low salience of external determinants, the new importance of autonomous domestic actors, and the overriding power of the central state apparatus.

CHAPTER 9

SPACE POLICY: INTERNATIONAL SPACE ACTIVITY

A critical test of the liberal-internationalist, peripheral-dependence, and complex neo-realist frameworks lies in those areas of Canada's international activity that require a great amount of advanced scientific and technological skills. The pursuit of such activities has long imposed a particularly stringent burden on the domestic political system, for they demand the societal resources, organizational skills, and political leadership to mobilize large amounts of disparate, costly, and scarce resources for highly specialized, risky missions over extended periods of time. In contemporary international politics, the successful performance of such tasks has been of central significance in furthering a broad range of external goals, from commercial prosperity and military security to national sovereignty itself. Throughout the history of the modern state system, the conduct of state-of-the-art science has done much to propel some states to a position of global hegemony while forcing others to serve as supplementary contributors to, or passive recipients of, the monopolistic resources that scientific innovation confers.[1]

In view of the centrality of scientific activity, it is hardly surprising that Canada's position in this area has been the subject of considerable internal debate. The dominant viewpoint, coinciding with a peripheral-dependence perspective, has highlighted Canada's profound weakness in advanced scientific capabilities, its resulting emphasis on rich endowments of raw materials as a source of international strength, and its deep dependence on the foreign technology, capital, and entrepreneurship required for discovery and exploitation of those materials.[2] A host of studies consistently confirm that Canada has ranked close to last among Western nations in exports in research-intensive groups and in its portion of GNP spent on research and development, production of significant innovations, patents abroad, and export performance in manufactured end products.[3] At the same time, other observers, operating in a liberal-internationalist or emerging complex neo-realist tradition, have offered a much more optimistic vision. They have noted Canada's position as sixth or seventh in the world in involvement in international scientific meetings, its high ranking in the number of publishing authors of scientific papers and the number of scientists and engineers per capita, the rapid increase since 1968 in the number of scientific attachés at its embassies abroad, in international science and technology agreements, and in the number of external partners with whom it deals.[4] These divergent perspectives have led to a vigorous discussion of appropriate strategies for Canada's future scientific development, with calls for a policy of "technological sovereignty" to overcome Canada's subordinate position, countered by a firm defence of an open, market-oriented regime.[5]

In an assessment of the merits of these competing perspectives, Canada's effort to develop and regulate outer space activities serves as a highly representative case of its broader involvement in the international scientific realm. Although not an area of massive investment or continuing controversy, space activity has been the subject of longstanding, regular state involvement and has commanded significant amounts of government attention, manpower, and money. As an integral component of the aerospace sector, it stands as a direct test of the dominant, peripheral-dependence portrait—symbolized by the cancellation of the Avro Arrow interceptor aircraft in 1959—of Canada's capacity, apparently irrevocably abandoned, to engage in the design, development, and production of internationally competitive, operational, integrated hardware systems.[6] As an activity initiated and guided by Canada's need for reliable information and communications in a vast airspace with particular atmospheric problems, it tests the ability of liberal-internationalist strategies to mobilize unique geographic advantages and needs for the conduct of specialized international ventures on a fully competitive and politically productive scale. As the subject of a sustained government commitment to the indigenous design and production of operational satellite systems, it tests the efficacy of complex neo-realist efforts to deploy state resources to secure fundamental national objectives in a highly exclusive sphere.

Throughout its postwar involvement in international space activity, Canada has in fact experienced the developments, pursued the approaches, and responded to the conditions highlighted by all three perspectives. During this time, the tendencies predicted by each perspective have co-existed in an uneasy constellation, each controlling Canadian behaviour in particular subfields and each striving to dominate the issue area as a whole. However, the peripheral-dependence pattern that strongly characterized Canada's initial involvement quickly receded before a strong liberal-internationalist orientation, which has more recently given way itself to a dominant complex neo-realist approach. Initially apparent in the general pattern of Canadian behaviour during the past two decades, this trend has been grounded in the particular policy innovations developed since 1945.

During the 1945–1956 period, Canada's intimate collaboration with the United States and the United Kingdom in defence-related research sustained the dominance of a peripheral-dependence orientation. From 1957 to 1967, however, Canada enthusiastically adopted the specialized national programs and roles in newly created multilateral organizations that stood at the heart of the liberal-internationalist tradition. Between 1968 and 1972, a sharp dispute over the domestic production of an operational communications satellite system promoted a direct challenge to internationalist premises from the tenets of complex neo-realism. And from 1973 to 1980, a sustained and successful effort to develop relations with the European Community and other overseas actors underscored the dominance of a complex neo-realist orientation in the international space sphere.

An Overview of Canadian Space Policy

The slow rise of complex neo-realism over its liberal-internationalist and peripheral-dependence competitors is first evident in the general trend of Canada's official diplomatic involvement in space issues during the past two decades.[7] As Figure 9.1 indicates, space subjects have occupied a steadily increasing place in the total framework of Canadian foreign policy, rising rapidly from obscurity before 1960 to a relatively high, stable, and slowly growing position from 1961 to 1973, and reaching an even higher if fluctuating pace from 1974 onward. Moreover, as Table 9.1 reveals, Canada has expanded, at a relatively steady rate, both its efforts to play a role and the number of roles it has sought to perform in this sphere. Such initiatory and innovative behaviour has been particularly pronounced in the 1967–1971 and 1973–1979 periods and of singular prominence in 1975 and 1976.

This greater activity and variety reflects in large measure Canada's shift towards roles that implement complex neo-realist tendencies. Although Canada's officially articulated roles reveal a strong attachment to a liberal-internationalist orientation, several trends are evident within this framework. The role closest to the passive approach of peripheral-dependence—that of "organization maintainer"—appeared during the mid-1960s and late 1970s, but was rarely dominant. The liberal-internationalist role of "community builder" has been consistently strong since 1960, but its more active "mediator" and "community builder/leader" affiliates ended in 1972. In contrast, since 1967 the more complex neo-realist roles of "community builder/balancer", "partner", "partner/leader", and "balancer" have steadily increased their position, with the most potent variant of "balancer" exercising clear predominance in 1975 and 1976.

This trend towards complex neo-realism is further apparent in the process by which Canadian behaviour is defined. As Table 9.2 indicates, the number of actors abroad that Canada has considered relevant to its international space behaviour has risen through several cycles to an ever-higher average level, suggesting a more sensitive appreciation of the external environment and its greater salience. Moreover, there has been a similar diffusion in the number of external actors that Canada

FIGURE 9.1 Relative Attention to International Space Activity, 1960–1979

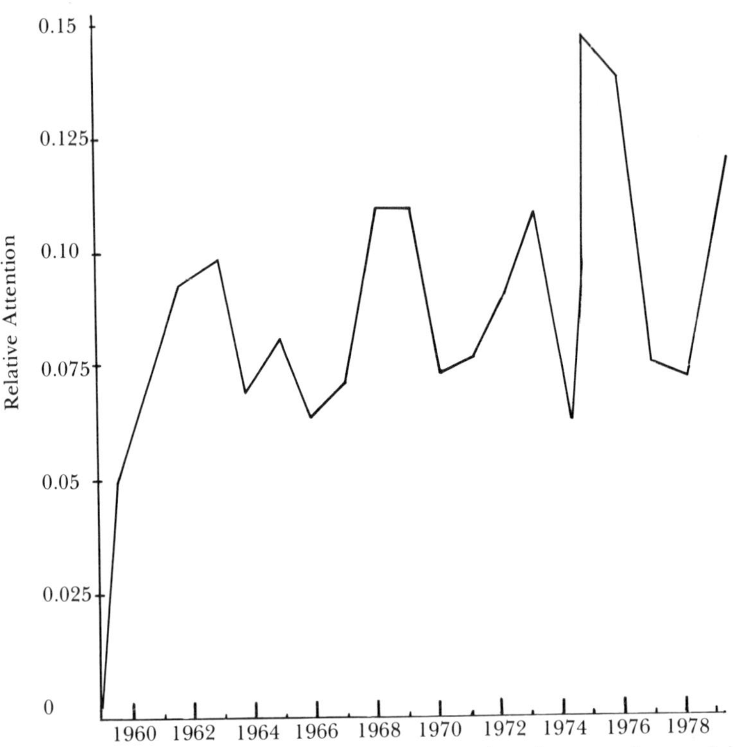

Note: Relative attention is measured by the number of paragraphs containing references to international space activity, divided by the number of pages in each annual report.

SOURCE: Based on Department of External Affairs, *Annual Report*, 1945-1971; *Annual Review*, 1972-1979.

has acknowledged as relevant, with a notably high dispersion in 1975 and 1976. Although Canada has remained interested in United States, United Nations, and interstate actors, the declining prominence of the United Kingdom, the Commonwealth, and the United Nations General Assembly since 1970 indicates some erosion of both dependent and internationalist processes. Despite the increasing attention devoted since 1968 to Canada's middle-power ally Sweden, the growing importance of France, Germany, Japan, and the European Space Agency suggests the emergence of a complex neo-realist orientation. As Table 9.3 indicates, this process has had a firm grounding within the state apparatus, as the specialized agencies of several domestic departments have become involved in the discussions that were previously the preserve of those in the prime ministerial group and the Department of External Affairs.[8]

TABLE 9.1 Canadian Roles in International Space Activity, 1960–1979

	1960	*1961*	*1962*	*1963*	*1964*	*1965*	*1966*	*1967*	*1968*	*1969*	*1970*	*1971*	*1972*	*1973*	*1974*	*1975*	*1976*	*1977*	*1978*	*1979*
TOTAL NUMBER OF REFERENCES	1	2	3	4	3	6	3	5	4	6	4	4	2	5	4	10	10	6	7	6
NUMBER OF ROLE TYPES	1	1	2	2	3	4	3	3	3	5	4	3	2	4	3	4	4	4	4	3
INDIVIDUAL ROLES:																				
Organization Maintainer					1	2	2	1	1	2				1	1		2	2	1	3
Community Builder		2	2	2	1		1	3	2	1		2	1	2	2	3	2	1	3	2
Mediator			1	2			1			1	1									
Community Builder/ Leader					1	1							1							
Community Builder/ Balancer	1									1	1	1		1	1	1		1		
Partner						2				1	1	1				2	1		1	1
Partner/Leader														1						
Balancer						1		1	1		1					4	5	2	2	

SOURCE: Based on Department of External Affairs, *Annual Report*, 1960–1971; *Annual Review*, 1972–1979.

TABLE 9.2 External Actors Involved in Canada's International Space Activity, 1960–1979

	1960	*1961*	*1962*	*1963*	*1964*	*1965*	*1966*	*1967*	*1968*	*1969*	*1970*	*1971*	*1972*	*1973*	*1974*	*1975*	*1976*	*1977*	*1978*	*1979*
TOTAL NUMBER OF REFERENCES	2	2	6	8	3	6	3	4	6	12	8	10	2	8	7	14	11	7	9	6
NUMBER OF ACTORS NOTED	2	2	5	5	3	6	3	4	5	7	7	10	2	6	6	10	10	6	8	6
INDIVIDUAL ACTORS:																				
Europe	1								1											
United Kingdom	1			1																
United States		1	1	2		1				2	2	1				1	1			
NASA, FAA, ISIS						1				1	1	1	1	2	1	2	1		1	1
United Nations General Assembly		1	2				1	1	1	2	1								1	1
United Nations Committees[1]			1	2	1	1	1	1	2	4	1	1		2	1	2	2	1	2	1
U.S.S.R.			1	2						1	1	1							1	1
Commonwealth			1		1	1							1							
INTELSAT					1	1	1	1	1	1	1	1					1	1	1	
France						1						1				2	1			
West Germany								1								1				
Sweden									1	1		1		1	1	1		2		
ESA (includes ESRO)											1	1		1	2	2	1		1	1
Japan												1				1	1			
IMCO, INMARSAT														1	1	1	1	1	1	1
AEROSAT												1		1	1	1		1		
Australia																	1			
China																	1		1	
Iceland																		1		

[1]Including UNCPUOS, its legal subcommittee, disarmament conferences, and ITU.

SOURCE: Based on Department of External Affairs, *Annual Report*, 1960–1971; *Annual Review*, 1972–1979.

TABLE 9.3 Governmental Actors Involved in Canada's International Space Activity, 1960–1979

	1960	*1961*	*1962*	*1963*	*1964*	*1965*	*1966*	*1967*	*1968*	*1969*	*1970*	*1971*	*1972*	*1973*	*1974*	*1975*	*1976*	*1977*	*1978*	*1979*
TOTAL NUMBER OF REFERENCES	1			1		2		1	1	1	1	1	1			2	2	1		
NUMBER OF ACTORS NOTED	1			1		2		1	1	1	1	1	1			2	1	1		
INDIVIDUAL ACTORS:																				
Cabinet Ministers	1																			
Prime Minister				1																
Department of External Affairs						1							1							
Defence Research Board						1		1			1									
Telesat Canada									1	1										
Canadian Overseas Telecommunications Corp.												1								
Canada Centre for Remote Sensing																1	2	1		
National Research Council																1				

SOURCE: Based on Department of External Affairs, *Annual Report*, 1960–1971; *Annual Review*, 1972–1979.

The Era of Imperial Collaboration, 1947–1956

Although this broad shift towards complex neo-realism is largely the product of the past two decades, its origins can be traced to Canada's involvement in international space in World War II. The wartime legacy, reinforced by the demands of the cold war, in large measure ensured that Canada's initial experience would be dominated by highly specialized research projects, directed at military imperatives, and conducted within the comfortable embrace of Anglo-American co-operation. At the same time, it spawned both the expertise in international scientific diplomacy and the capacity for indigenous scientific contributions that permitted a more prominent role in subsequent periods.

The character of Canada's international space activity during the first postwar decade was largely set by the wartime collaborative programs in electronics and ballistics.[9] Canada's National Research Council (NRC) had conducted experiments in upper atmospheric physics since the 1920s, and a radar research program and observation facilities for the Canadian armed forces had been in place since 1940, but it was a 1943 Anglo-American proposal for an ionospheric network throughout American and Commonwealth territory that prompted the NRC to join with the British Admiralty to construct a full set of observation stations across Canada. At the end of the war, this physical infrastructure and accumulated expertise induced the government to remain active in electronics and to transfer its scientists from naval headquarters to the new Defence Research Board (DRB) in 1947. Simultaneously, a joint Canada-U.S. technical conference requested by the U.S. State Department and a subsequent recommendation by the U.S. Bureau of Standards on behalf of the American armed forces prompted Canada to extend its facilities for ionospheric observation and to develop reliable systems for northern radio communication and navigation. By 1952, this program had expanded to include work on problems of communications equipment and long-term radar activity; by 1957, it had led to the construction of a radar laboratory at Prince Albert, Saskatchewan, for defence research and for tracking objects in space.

Within the field of ballistics, a similar process operated. Inspired by its wartime contribution and the usefulness of its large land mass for rocketry research, the Canadian government decided to continue its ballistics program on behalf of the alliance in the postwar period. It received a major assist in 1945 when the British, anxious to escape the confines of an obsolescent research plant, fostered the establishment of an advanced high-velocity projectile project at Valcartier that was used by the United States, as a substitute for a domestic facility, during the next ten years. In 1951, continental collaboration was furthered when a Canadian-initiated series of studies on re-entry physics led to a direct bilateral approach to the United States. And in 1956, the American presence was intensified with the construction of a rocket research range at Churchill, Manitoba, operated by the U.S. Army for Canadian and American scientists.[10]

This close collaboration with the United Kingdom and the United States also took place in ongoing research. The allocation of particular projects was normally made within a tripartite framework at annual meetings of the DRB and its British and American counterparts, according to which state could best perform the work. However, Canadian decisions were made only after further calculations, based on the information gathered at such meetings, as to what projects were of particular Canadian need, within Canadian capability, and unlikely to be overtaken by U.S. programs should the U.S. discover a pressing national need. Although the selection of projects that were not central to the United States produced some tendency for Canada to pursue less technologically advanced activity, it enabled Canada to pursue projects or paths to common objectives that represented innovative and internationally relevant research.

Underlying this collaboration was the broader system of tripartite information sharing and co-operation that infused the sphere of defence science as a whole. As early as 1940, the British had started to co-operate with Canada in military research on a fully integrated basis, and, through emigration, subsequently supplied Canada with a significant number of the scientists involved in postwar programs. Canada's first initiative had come in 1940 when the National Research Council established liaison offices in the United Kingdom and the United States. The DRB also created defence liaison offices in London and Washington in 1947 and in subsequent years it opened additional offices in the U.S. Outside the triangle, structured co-operation was conducted through the Commonwealth Advisory Committee on Defence Science, created in 1946, the Scientific Advisory Committee of the Western Union, established in 1947 with observers from the United States and Canada, and NATO, which, after its formation in 1949, acquired the Western Union's Subcommittee on Aeronautical Research.

This pattern of affiliation derived directly from an external environment in which the United States rapidly surpassed the United Kingdom as the globe's dominant scientific power. Although the United Kingdom had begun World War II with a significant lead in military electronics, the rapidity and openness of its war-induced transfer to the United States soon gave the U.S. superiority. By 1945 it had passed from direct applications of British inventions to U.S.-initiated work, with the aid of German scientists, in such new fields as missiles. Moreover, after 1947 the cold war, the Soviet atomic capability, the vulnerability of the United States to a Soviet attack over Canadian airspace, and Soviet advances in satellite technology produced an ever growing American technological lead and a direct stimulus to co-operative programs with Canada.

In contrast, the private sector space community within Canada was weak in influence and resources, fragmented in organization, and heavily dependent upon the state. The national scientific establishment had expanded tenfold from the start of the war, when its facilities had been placed at the disposal of the government, and hoped in 1945 to retain this capacity for civilian purposes, but Canadian industry remained directly reliant on governmental funding, facilities, and guidance. In keeping with its objective of making military research an organic part of Canada's industrial structure, the Defence Research Board included representatives of the University of Toronto, McGill, Laval, and Northern Electric, created an electronics advisory committee chaired by an official of Northern Electric, assisted the University of Toronto in opening an Institute of Aerophysics, and maintained liaison with the radio industry and the university community.

The DRB's leadership role, tight integration, and harmonious relationship with the private sector reflected its control over space activity with the government itself.[11] The board's centrality rested on its external reputation as an inventive, internationally respected scientific organization and on its position after 1948 as the exclusive conduit through which the United States placed contracts for research within Canada. It was reinforced by the stature and experience of its first chairman, O.M. Solandt, who served from 1947 to 1958, and by the chairman's position as a member, equal with the heads of the three military services, of the Chiefs of Staff Committee. Inside the government, consistent support from the outset came from the chief of the general staff, General Charles Foulkes. Within the armed forces, active opposition came only from the Royal Canadian Air Force, which, as the premier service, supported projects that were "all-Canadian" rather than collaborations with the Americans and the British. The RCAF feared that scarce funds might be diverted from its favoured project of developing an all-weather interceptor and argued that scientific research could best be conducted within the individual services.

Outside the military, the board's position was sustained by the close co-operation it developed with a major potential competitor, the NRC.[12] Despite the NRC's status as a co-ordinative centre for civilian space research, its president, C.J. Mackenzie, supported the board's creation and confined NRC's space-related activities to work in ionospheric physics. Similarly, the Dominion Observatories Branch of the Department of Mines and Technical Surveys limited its activity to meteorological research. In view of this self-imposed segmentation, the general sympathy of ministers of defence for defence science, and the secure channel the DRB had in reporting to ministers through the Cabinet Defence Committee, few space-related controversies emerged at the ministerial level.

The absence of high-level political conflict stemmed from the existence of a widespread and deeply rooted consensus about how Canadian defence science and its space-related component could best be conducted. The wartime experience had inspired a belief that Canada had passed from focusing on immediate operational problems, exporting talent, and importing results to initiating large-scale, decade-long projects, participating on an equal basis within the triangle, and making a proportionate contribution to the common scientific pool. But at the same time, it underscored the inevitability and desirability of close collaboration with the United Kingdom and the United States. Canadian leaders selected projects that not only facilitated a national industry based on unique climatic and geographic attributes and provided disproportionate benefits to Canada, but primarily served the interests of the alliance as a whole.[13] Within this context, they saw Canada following a middle path between British fundamental research and American applied activity. With the United States, they saw a special intimacy, based on the assumption that Canada's contribution and American generosity would produce both complete American openness and a tenfold return on all services performed on their behalf.

These beliefs and the behaviour they inspired produced a decade in which Canada's international space activity conformed essentially, although by no means exclusively, to the predictions of the peripheral-dependence perspective. Conducting a limited program focused on specialized research endeavours, dependent on access to the international scientific pool, and accepting the ongoing presence of American armed forces, Canada's position closely resembled that of a small and somewhat penetrated power. Confining its international activity largely to information flows and collaborative programs with the United States and the United Kingdom, readily accepting their proposals for joint activity, and concentrating on maintaining a flow of benefits from the United States, Canada operated within the limits and in response to the actions of its two imperial partners. By acknowledging American leadership in countering the threats of the cold war, centralizing its decision making within defence organizations, and facilitating domestic programs largely compatible with these purposes, it subordinated societal and state interests to the pressing demands of the external environment.

Within this framework, however, strong traces of competing tendencies, lodged particularly within the belief systems of responsible officials, were readily apparent. An emergent liberal internationalism was reflected in Canada's conduct of internationally competitive, specialized programs, selected on the basis of national advantage, the extension of its regular consultation with British and American counterparts into the Commonwealth and NATO spheres, and its conscious pursuit of a middle position and mediatory role. Finally, the seeds of a complex neo-realist orientation were contained in the emphasis placed on

Canada's distinctive geographic assets and problems, the enthusiasm of the Royal Canadian Air Force for a more complete national program of missile development, and the high degree of co-ordination, based on explicit rationales of national security, exercised within the state apparatus by the Defence Research Board.

The Era of Internationalist Co-operation, 1957–1967

These internal challenges to Canada's predominant dependent orientation formed the foundation for a major shift in Canadian policy from 1957 to 1967. Stimulated by the Soviet Union's launch of the first satellite, Sputnik, in October 1957, the resulting proliferation of American satellite programs, and the ensuing efforts at international regulation in the United Nations, this shift centred on a rapid and significant expansion in the technological sophistication, national control, and diplomatic arena of Canada's space activity. Its primary manifestation came in a national experimental satellite program that, with the launch of the Alouette in 1962, gave Canada the rank of the third space power in the globe. Its broader impact was felt in a steady reduction of the military orientation and United States presence in Canada's bilateral programs within North America. Its predominant expression was in the active role Canada assumed in furthering multilateral co-operation and mediating superpower differences in the new United Nations outer space committee.

The Canadian decision to design and construct an experimental satellite system stemmed from a convergence of internal advances in space technology with an external geopolitical rivalry that made Canada's contribution count. During the 1950s, Canadian research in electronics and ballistics had enabled DRB scientists to place compacted electronic components within a rocket projectile. At the same time, the momentum of the upper atmosphere physics program propelled them to employ this new capability in telemetry for ionospheric probes from space-based rather than ground-based sensors. Political support for moving to a satellite venture came quickly when, in response to the launch of Sputnik, Prime Minister Diefenbaker pledged that Canada would participate actively in space research for peaceful purposes to the extent that limited national resources allowed.[14]

A far more powerful stimulant was provided by a decision of the new National Aeronautics and Space Administration in the U.S. to secure a satellite for the specific task of ionospheric studies. By producing a rapid and technologically impressive response to this American decision, Canada secured a bilateral agreement in the spring of 1959 that enabled it to construct the original satellite, specify the experiments carried on it, and establish ground recording stations, in return for American financial support and the provision of launch services. Following the launch of the Alouette in 1962, the two countries signed a memorandum of understanding in which they agreed to construct, launch, and operate four further satellites—the ISIS series—under the management of a joint working group. Within Canada, the government deliberately used this program as a catalyst for the development of a domestic space industry, by funding the program through a special parliamentary vote, confining government involvement to the provision of management supervision, specifications, and specialized technical knowledge, and allowing much of the design and construction to be done by the major subcontractors, RCA Victor of Montreal and de Havilland Aircraft of Toronto.

This increase in Canada's technological competence and industrial capability was further reflected in Canada's broader programs of defence-related space science and observation.[15] John Diefenbaker had been an early proponent of a co-operative program with the United Kingdom, and had helped inspire a short-lived proposal for a joint satellite launching program valued at $125 million. Within North America, Canada acquired a much greater, civilian-based control over facilities within its borders and successfully employed its bilateral programs to secure a distinctive presence abroad.

Prompted by the needs and opportunities of the rapidly developing U.S. satellite program, the Canadian government employed the Prince Albert laboratory, until its closing in 1967, for tracking U.S. satellites, opened new tracking and ground communication facilities in Newfoundland and Nova Scotia under bilateral agreements, and contributed to experiments on U.S. satellites. In order to provide the Canadian armed forces with familiarity with the U.S. space effort, it concluded a technology exchange agreement with the United States in the early 1960s.[16] A high altitude research project, begun at McGill University in 1962 with funding from the United States Army Ballistics Research Laboratory, was expanded after the Canadian Department of Industry joined the program in 1964. Within the more traditional field of rocketry, the Churchill Rocket Range, managed after its reopening in 1962 by the United States Air Force Office of Aerospace Research, was transferred in 1965 to the NRC and opened to scientists from abroad doing directly relevant work. Previous research in re-entry physics, under DRB management and Department of Industry funding, culminated in the development of an operational Black Brant rocket, which was sold to the United States and Germany.

The tentative development of links with overseas partners received a far greater expression in Canada's first major moves in the multilateral realm. In part they consisted of a strengthening of previous pooling arrangements with Commonwealth countries and NRC membership in the nongovernmental committee on space research (COSPAR). Of much greater importance was Canada's leading role in the United Nations Committee on the Peaceful Uses of Outer Space (UNCPUOS).[17] In keeping with its consistent call for an active United Nations presence in space matters, Canada had assumed membership on a twenty-member *ad hoc* UN committee, formed in 1958, to develop a permanent structure in this field. Aware of Soviet objections to this body and seeking to involve all states most active in space research, Canada played an instrumental part in obtaining unanimous approval for the permanent, twenty-four-member UNCPUOS created in 1959, and Soviet participation in it.

Indicative of the Canadian approach to the work of the committee were Canada's 1961 initiatives to have the committee meet despite Soviet objections, to add four states from the developing world, to have the committee and the secretary-general maintain a registry of launches, and to have the specialized agencies involved. Canada also joined with the United States, Australia, and Italy to sponsor a resolution that recognized the United Nations as the focal point for global concern with the peaceful uses of outer space, affirmed the applicability of international law and the UN Charter to outer space, and declared space to be open for exploration and use by all. In subsequent years, Canada worked actively to secure a superpower consensus on principles governing the exploration and use of outer space. Except for a United States reservation restricting foreign states' access to national observation facilities, Canada secured this objective in 1967 when it signed the Treaty on the Peaceful Uses of Outer Space. Reflecting Canada's longstanding vision of an open, UN-based space regime, this treaty affirmed the principles of no national appropriation, freedom of scientific information, demilitarization, the extensions of international law and emergency collaboration, functional co-operation, and training programs for LDCs.

Canadian initiatives and success were somewhat less apparent in the commercially oriented International Satellite Organization (Intelsat).[18] Formed in 1964 at the initiative of the United States, Intelsat secured the participation of the United Kingdom and other European countries only after vigorous debates within these countries and consultations among them over the advisability of creating alternative satellite communications networks. Propelled by its proliferating growth in domestic telecommunications and by the limited capacity of its existing land-based circuits, Canada joined the twelve-member body at its inception, took a seat on the interim committee, and served as a reasonably influential member. However, it continued to share European reservations about the structure of an international organization in which the U.S. representative, COMSAT, also served as the manager of the operational multilateral system and remained subject to regulation by the U.S. Federal Communications Commission.

The new multilateral emphasis in Canada's space activity was due in large measure to a pronounced dispersion of power within the international space club. The United States maintained its previous dominance through a rapidly expanding program, and quickly assumed leadership in the most sophisticated field, that of manned orbit. But the emergence of a serious Soviet challenge produced an urgent and sustained need for mediatory activity at the United Nations and for an international space order based on a broader range of states. At the same time, United Nations involvement and the formation of Intelsat brought Canada into regular working contact with a host of great and middle powers and, after 1961, selected small states, with a shared interest in fostering multilateral regulation. These international organizations, particularly Intelsat, exposed Canada directly to the similar but more intense concerns of its French and British allies about an exclusive reliance on American leadership and control.[19]

The decreasing force and more diffuse impact of the external environment was reinforced within Canada by the development of a more organizationally diversified, technologically competent, and politically assertive domestic space community. Stimulated by the orbit of Sputnik, the government established in 1959 the Canadian Committee on Space Research, which integrated seven institutions under NRC leadership and furthered university research. In addition, responding to calls for increased activity channelled through the Canadian Aeronautics and Space Institute, the government facilitated the formation of special space research institutes at McGill and the University of Saskatchewan, funded McGill's development of a High Altitude Research Project (HARP), and concluded a continuing informal agreement between government and industry for the design and production of the ISIS-B satellite.

More importantly, the government deliberately sought to create a skilled, self-sustaining space industry in Canada. First manifest in the Black Brant rocket program, which Bristol-Aero Industries of Winnipeg had run with DRB assistance, this policy was underscored in 1963 by a special parliamentary vote to fund the ISIS program, a policy of involving Canadian industry as much as possible, and the award of the major subcontracts to Canadian firms. Indicative of the success of this policy were the performance from 1961 to 1967 of $29 million worth of space activity by RCA Victor, another $6 million worth of work for de Havilland, and the participation of eleven additional companies in domestic and export sales. Symbolizing the depth of the government's commitment to private sector development was the inclusion of one industry and two university representatives on a four-man task force, commissioned by the Privy Council Office in May 1966, to conduct the first comprehensive study of Canadian upper atmosphere and space programs.

The involvement of the Privy Council Office reflected the emergence within Ottawa of a significantly more diversified and senior-level decision-making process on space matters. During the late 1950s, the DRB and NRC had been joined as full members of the space community by the Department of External Affairs, as a consequence of its lead responsibility for United Nations matters, and by the Departments of Mines and Technical Surveys and Transport. In 1963, the new Department of Industry became involved as a result of its support for the experimental satellite and HARP programs. This expansion brought a steady civilianization of responsibility for the space program, hastened by the closing of spacecraft programs and facilities after 1962 and their transfer to civilian agencies and by the NRC's chairmanship of the Canadian Committee on Space Research.

The work of this committee and the rapidly expanding expenditures on space precluded intense interdepartmental conflict, but the sheer proliferation of activity and the new relevance of space to prime ministerial level objectives suggested the desirability of creating a central space agency. First raised by the 1963 Royal Commission on Government Organization, the establishment of such an agency received much greater prominence when it formed the central conclusion of the Privy Council Office's task force study, known as the Chapman report, issued in 1967.[20]

This call for a central agency stemmed from an acceptance throughout much of the government and relevant domestic community of a far more ambitious conception of Canada's international role in space. As expressed in the Chapman report, this conception began by juxtaposing Canada's relatively low level of space expenditures against its rapid progress through several scientific and industrial thresholds over the past decade and by pointing out the acute vulnerabilities and opportunities that this investment and external technological developments had bred. On this foundation, the report called for a 20 per cent annual increase in funding, domestic production of equipment to meet Canada's space needs, a national, commercially viable communications satellite system, leadership in resource-sensing technology, and, much less confidently, a domestic launch capability.

The importance of a nationally based program was underscored in a series of guidelines for Canada's international participation. The first was a belief that Canada's external involvements should use Canadian capacity, be directed towards specific national industrial, economic, and social advantages, and have a direct relationship to an indigenously developed, fully integrated, mission-oriented program. The second was an assumption that Canada could no longer afford to wait to purchase the results of programs in the United States, the United Kingdom, and France. The third, reflected in a call for development of major launch facilities on an international basis and an international agreement on the limited geosynchronous orbit, was a recognition that Canada's space program could not develop in partnership with only one nation. These views extended to a conception of a desirable global order in which Canada's traditional interest with maintaining the freest possible international exchange was joined by a new concern with rapidly developing international law, using national space facilities to aid less developed countries, limiting international law to areas where technology had rendered codifications feasible, and using Canada's knowledge and capacity to inhibit the evolution of regimes designed disproportionately for the benefit of the great powers.

Behind these precepts lay a perception of an external environment in which the Soviet Union and France served, along with the United States and the United Kingdom, as powers undertaking costly development activities, in which the United Nations reduced the danger of Canada being caught between American and Soviet rivalry, and in which France and, to a much lesser extent, Japan had emerged as referents for Canadian action. Moreover, in this context, the ability to develop and service domestic institutions became a far more central referent for Canadian behaviour. And a concern with a comprehensive, planned, integrated strategy grounded in a concept of the national interest underscored a vision of a governmental apparatus far more powerful, co-ordinated, and active than that which had so far emerged.

As a reliable, if ambitious, extrapolation of trends that had developed over the past decade, the Chapman report affirmed the declining relevance of peripheral dependence, the new dominance of liberal internationalism, and the emerging strength of complex neo-realism as a framework for Canadian behaviour. American fears generated by Sputnik had helped stimulate Canada's Alouette program and new bilateral ventures in space science, and American funding had largely sustained many Canadian activities such as HARP. But by 1964, these dependent patterns had been replaced by more multilateral concerns about the disproportionate influence of the U.S. in Intelsat and Canada's potential dependence, should it fail to keep pace with new satellite technologies.

Beginning in 1957, the dominance of a liberal-internationalist orientation was reflected in the wider affiliations Canada developed through membership in the multilateral forums of UNCPUOS and Intelsat, its mediatory role and pursuit of consensus within UNCPUOS, its emphasis on parity in continental relationships through the use of bilateral agreements, and its steady reduction of American-controlled facilities on Canadian soil. It was further apparent in Canada's effort to secure an international order based on the centrality of the United Nations, the strength of the secretary general, the active, supportive efforts of functional organizations, and the importance of a multilaterally defined international law based on a renunciation of national appropriation. And it was sustained by a new responsiveness to the views of the Soviet Union, France, and the middle powers in UNCPUOS and

Intelsat, by the emerging political salience of the domestic space community, and by the prominence within Ottawa of the Department of External Affairs, prime ministerial-level actors, and a wider range of domestic departments.

Of even greater visibility was the emergence during the decade of behavioural trends and beliefs that raised complex neo-realism to the position of a major, if not yet equal, competitor. The strengthening of these trends was most evident in the status Canada achieved with the Alouette program, which made it the third state to construct an orbiting satellite; in the development of a diversified, internationally competitive industry; and in the increasing concern, reaching the prime ministerial level, over the need for a central space agency to define, co-ordinate, and direct the national effort. Of even greater magnitude was the new philosophy, codified in the Chapman report, forwarding a very progressive view of Canada's space activity, calling for a program leading to Canadian primacy in selected areas through affiliations beyond the United States and guided by a process in which external stimuli would be subordinated to direct domestic forces and a central government strategy based on defined national interests.

The Era of National Assertion, 1968–1972

As heralded in the philosophy of the Chapman report, the dominance that liberal internationalism had achieved by 1967 was confronted by a major and sometimes highly politicized challenge during the first few years of the Trudeau government. First evident in Canada's bilateral space science co-operation with the United States, this challenge occurred most directly in the dispute over the decision to purchase Canada's first commercial communications satellite from American rather than Canadian firms. Although the immediate outcome of this dispute affirmed the legitimacy of liberal internationalism, the direct stimulus it provided for a subsequent domestic satellite program and for co-operation with European partners helped raise the competing precepts of complex neo-realism to an equal position.

The appeal of a complex neo-realist orientation was evident in Canada's bilateral co-operation with the United States.[21] Canada had responded to the January 1969 launch of the first satellite in their joint ionospheric research program (ISIS) by opening its data collection facilities to the global community and embarking on a successor satellite in partnership with the United States. It adopted a distinctly more cautious stance, however, to bilateral co-operation in the new field of earth resource sensing.

The possibility of Canadian–American collaboration here had been raised in informal discussions between the two countries in 1967 and became an imminent prospect following President Nixon's pledge at the United Nations in 1969 to allow international use of the United States

Earth Resources Technology Satellite (ERTS). Motivated partly by the calls of the Chapman report and the Science Council of Canada for an initiative in remote sensing, Canada responded favourably to the American proposal. However, it defined an arrangement in which its receipt of data from the American spacecraft would be matched by a Canadian contribution of equipment and a related research program. Constructed by Computing Devices of Canada and operated by the Departments of Communications and Energy, Mines and Resources, the equipment and accompanying program not only gave the United States a valuable ground site to aid in international data dissemination, but also enabled the Canadian government to provide a more rapid and widespread national distribution of data sensed over Canada. Canada raised its arrangement with the United States at the United Nations as an important example of international co-operation and argued for it as a way in which the new technology could benefit all nations.

By far the clearest evidence of the Chapman report's philosophy, however, came in the sharp controversy that emerged over the formation of a domestic, commercially oriented communications satellite system and over the choice of an American firm as the prime contractor for its first spacecraft.[22] The most authoritative call for such a system had come from a March 1968 White Paper, which had urged a Canadian initiative in this area as a means of ensuring technological progress, export sales, national identification, and the retention of skilled scientific manpower.[23] It had also specified the desirability of having control over the design and production of the satellites and Canadian-located earth stations and of having Canadian industry involved as much as possible. At the same time, it had affirmed the government's determination to operate the new system on a commercially profitable basis through a new corporation in which the government, major satellite users, and the public would participate.

The potentially conflicting goals of national control and commercial profitability were carried into the Telesat Canada Act after Minister of Communications Eric Kierans rejected proposals by the major commercial users for a system owned by private corporations. With the passage of the act in June 1969, Telesat Canada, created as a mixed government and private commercial corporation, moved to raise public capital in the specified amount amidst widely held expectations that the project would meet a broad range of national imperatives, from strengthening east–west communications, northern sovereignty, and French-language programming throughout Canada, to furthering national scientific and industrial capacity and export potential. These expectations were encouraged by a decision by Eric Kierans, his department, and Bell Canada to expand the system well beyond the six-channel facility the act envisaged; there were also public commitments by the ministers of communications and industry to employ a Canadian-designed and -built satellite. Moreover, they were given operational expression in the award to two Canadian-located companies, Northern Electric of Ottawa and RCA of Montreal, of preliminary contracts, a letter of intent in June 1969, and an accompanying promise that the companies would have a good chance to receive the prime contract for the satellites and ground stations themselves.

The first serious challenge to this expectation of a made-in-Canada project came in March 1970 when the two companies jointly submitted a bid for the system that was substantially above previous estimates, damaging Telesat's already deteriorating prospects of raising private capital for the venture. Compounding these problems were Telesat's doubts about RCA's technical ability to move from scientific to commercial satellites and about its chance of resolving patent disputes with its potential U.S. competitor, Hughes Aircraft, that could cause commercially damaging delays. By the summer of 1970, an external factor intervened. The death of French president Charles de Gaulle, the less conflictual style of his successor, and the severe difficulties encountered by the French satellite program reduced the Canadian government's fear that French and Quebec firms would beat them to French-language Canadian broadcasting and challenged its assumption that American technological supremacy could be threatened with relative ease.

The decisive change came in January 1970 when President Nixon, in a major policy reversal, declared a U.S. need for domestic communications satellites and the desirability of allowing anyone to buy, launch, and operate such systems within the United States. Hughes Aircraft and its U.S. competitors jumped into the task, eroding the earlier Canadian belief that the Americans would be forced for financial reasons to abandon some areas of space development and suggesting that a suitable, low-priced U.S. satellite could be available soon. This underscored the urgency of Canada's orbiting a satellite that could reap domestic and international sales before its American competitors and that could secure a position in the increasingly crowded geostationary orbit. By making available the large U.S. market, the American move also raised the possibility that RCA could construct a less expensive satellite itself in anticipation of a larger, U.S.-oriented production run.

The direct impact of the U.S. decision was felt in late April 1970, when RCA's proposal for a satellite was quickly countered by an unsolicited bid from Hughes Aircraft of California. After vigorous bidding, an RCA offer to construct a $42.8-million satellite, employing 55 per cent Canadian content, was juxtaposed against a Hughes proposal for a $30-million satellite, with 11.7 per cent Canadian content and an accompanying promise to allow Canadian firms to construct similar components on the next fifteen Hughes units.

The competition between RCA and Hughes and the surrounding

issues of economic nationalism and technological independence stimulated a widespread domestic political debate. The executives of affected Canadian electronics and aerospace firms made direct private representations to press their case, largely on behalf of RCA. The Electronics Industry Association of Canada argued for a national satellite program with maximum Canadian content, and the International Brotherhood of Electrical Workers demonstrated outside Parliament in support of RCA. In opposition, representatives of the Toronto-based financial community pointed to the need for the lowest-cost satellite if the public financing of Telesat Canada were to proceed without further delay.

Within the press, the Toronto *Star* and Toronto *Telegram*, noting RCA's American parentage, argued that only an experienced Hughes could build the system without delay. In contrast, *Le Devoir* and the Montreal *Star*, pointing to the space program's original Canadian objectives, the drift of economic activity to Toronto from Montreal, and Canada's increasing role as a satellite of the United States, pressed for an award to RCA in Montreal. In an effort at national synthesis, the *Globe and Mail* and the *Financial Times* suggested construction by a new Canadian industry–government coalition composed of RCA, Northern Electric, Spar Aerospace, and the Communications Research Centre of the Department of Communications. Within political channels, the debate was almost as intense, with the chairman of the Montreal Urban Community asking Prime Minister Trudeau for a Montreal location, the federal New Democratic Party offering consistent parliamentary criticism of Telesat Canada's corporate structure, and the Conservative Party demanding more information about the government's reversal on the issue of Canadian construction.

Within the executive branch, support for the RCA bid came from the Department of Communications Space Branch and Communications Research Centre, the Department of Industry, Trade and Commerce, and the Science Council of Canada, all of whom had a deep commitment to the development of an indigenous space industry. At the ministerial level, the RCA coalition was led strongly by Jean Marchand, who—as minister of regional economic expansion, head of the Quebec caucus, and one of Prime Minister Trudeau's closest confidants—was concerned about Toronto's ability to pull industries, particularly U.S. subsidiaries, away from Montreal. He received support in varying degrees from Minister of Industry, Trade and Commerce Jean-Luc Pepin, Minister of Labour Bryce Mackasey, Joe Greene, Herb Gray, and Bud Drury.

Arranged against this coalition was a bureaucratic-level group led by Telesat Canada. Skeptical of RCA's guarantees, anxious to raise private capital, and opposed to the cost-plus formula in a late RCA bid, Telesat Canada adamantly opposed the RCA bid, except in the unlikely event that the government provided an additional $20 million to meet the Canadian content requirements. The strength of this opposition was reflected in press reports that the selection of RCA would prompt several resignations from Telesat's board and in a visit by its president, David Golden, to Prime Minister Trudeau shortly before the final decision was taken. Ministerial support for Telesat's position came from Minister of Communications Eric Kierans, who declared his intention to resign if Cabinet accepted what he now considered an unrealistic RCA bid.

Throughout June and July, Cabinet debate produced continuing delays, deep divisions of opinion, reformulations of existing proposals, and intermittent bargaining with the companies. On 31 July 1970, the government announced the award of a contract to Hughes, on the condition that Spar Aerospace and Northern Electric be guaranteed work on subsystems of future domestic communications satellites constructed by Hughes. Hughes readily accepted this condition, and the subsequent decision of Canadian telecommunications companies and the CBC to participate in the system led quickly to the construction and launch of an operational satellite. The commercial success of the system enabled Telesat Canada, with parliamentary approval, to respond positively in 1973 to a request from U.S. companies to rent capacity on the Anik system; Telesat was able, too, to secure the resulting advantages in revenues, international credibility, and assured orbital positions.

A more significant consequence of the government's decision was its concomitant authorization of $12 million for an experimental Communications Technology Satellite (CTS) to be developed and constructed in Canada by the Communications Research Centre and RCA.[24] Conceived as the successor to Alouette and ISIS, and an experimental precursor to the next generation of Telesat Canada satellites, the CTS had been the subject of discussions between DOC and NASA for some time before the Anik controversy erupted. Its authorization, as a side payment to DOC and RCA, led rapidly to an April 1971 Canada–United States agreement under which Canada designed and constructed the $27-million spacecraft and the United States provided standard launch facilities and a critical electronic component.

Far more important, the CTS program prompted the European Space Research Organization (ESRO) to open negotiations in December 1971 for participation in the project, as a means of testing equipment for a telecommunications satellite system it was developing for Europe. Motivated by the opportunity of securing from the Europeans, at no cost, several advanced electronic parts that would otherwise have to be purchased in the United States and by the prospects of greater knowledge of their European counterparts, contracts for subsystems of European programs, an opening into the European Community's high technology industry, and ongoing participation in European space programs, Canada responded with enthusiasm. After NASA agreed to European participation and detailed negotiations with the Europeans in

February 1972, the Canadians concluded an agreement with ESRO in early May.

Canadian–European co-operation in the CTS program, reinforced by a simultaneous move towards joint participation by Canada, the U.S., and the ESRO in a North Atlantic aircraft navigation system, was a development of considerable significance.[25] Predating the announcement of Canada's Third Option policy by several months, it reflected the willingness of the Europeans to mount a challenge to American technological dominance in the space field, the emergence of a major Canadian space industry centred in Spar Aerospace and RCA, and the determination of a group of officials within the federal Department of Communications to develop a unique Canadian system that would maintain Canada's technological lead in a major area of domestic interest and secure export sales in such geographically similar middle powers as Australia, India, and Brazil. Equally important, it provided a solution to an internal challenge by the province of Quebec, with tacit support from France, to the federal government's international authority in the space area.

By registering the willingness of the Europeans generally, and the French government specifically, to deal with the federal government in a major program, the tripartite CTS agreement had provided a broader international legitimacy for Ottawa's denial of a Quebec government request to participate in an observer capacity in earlier CTS discussions with the United States. Quebec's demands for a direct international presence rested on the argument that provincial government responsibility for strengthening French language and culture enabled it to act internationally in the development of those satellite communications programs required for linguistic and cultural sustenance in the modern era. The federal government's first response to these claims, registered in an agreement with France on space matters during the Pearson government, had provided only a temporary resolution of the emerging dispute.[26] In late 1968, Quebec had countered by exchanging letters with France that enabled Quebec to participate in a French–German satellite program—the "Symphonie"—that would transmit cultural programs across the Atlantic. Although France had informed the Canadian government of its intention to sign this accord, it had neither responded to Ottawa's request to see and comment on a text in advance nor encouraged Quebec to engage in prior consultation with Ottawa. Ottawa countered by informing France, on a number of occasions, of federal constitutional prerogatives and demanding participation in the program.

Notwithstanding financial calculations that reduced Quebec's enthusiasm for participation and the start of federal–provincial consultations in late 1970, the dispute had expanded. France invited Quebec rather than Ottawa to join a related project in January 1971, and

Quebec's request to send an observer to Intelsat was met with a federal refusal. Moreover, the federal–provincial disagreement had quickly become fused with a broader France–United States dispute over France's plan to launch the Symphonie in an orbit capable of serving Europe, Africa, South America, and France. The plan was countered first by Intelsat's quiet insistence on its monopoly of commercial international communications satellites, supported by a tacit U.S. threat to refuse launching facilities for Symphonie, and secondly, by an autumn 1971 decision by Comsat to launch a satellite in the orbit that Symphonie would need to serve Quebec. Only in December 1971 was a compromise reached, in which Symphonie narrowly preserved an orbital position capable of servicing Quebec.

Although American predominance in Intelsat had been exercised in support of Ottawa's federalist objectives and Canada's individual functional needs, it had continued to be viewed by Canadian officials as inhibiting several states from becoming active members of the organization and encouraging a division of the world into two technically grounded, competitive cold war networks at the expense of a single global system.[27] During the 1970 negotiations to make Intelsat a permanent organization, Canada thus sought to make it genuinely international rather than American, by working for several objectives: a governing body in which voting power recognized a state's relative investment and use without allowing for control by a few members, a general body where all members would have equal representation, access by nonmembers to the organization's space segment, and the participation of a Soviet and East European bloc threatening to create a rival, technically incompatible system. These objectives, pursued by the deputy minister of communications and his delegation at conferences in Washington in 1970 and 1971, were partly achieved when Canada formally adhered to an August 1971 agreement specifying the replacement of Comsat by an international actor as technical manager of the system after an interim six-year period.

Canada's support for more equitable multilateral arrangements was also evident in its behaviour at the United Nations.[28] Here Canada saw the willingness of the United States and the Soviet Union to refrain from enshrining state practice in international law and the voluntary co-operation of the major space powers as only preliminary conditions for the international agreement that would enable most states to participate in the space field. It adopted the broader objectives of forwarding the principle of nonappropriation, rendering states' national, bilateral, and multilateral efforts complementary to the needs of the international community as a whole, and having the United Nations, through UNCPUOS and specialized agencies, play a central informational, analytical, and co-ordinating role.

Accordingly the Canadian delegation co-sponsored resolutions in the

1970 General Assembly calling for a convention regarding damage caused by objects launched into outer space, international co-operation on direct broadcast satellites, approval of the work of UNCPUOS on communications and earth resource satellites, and implementation of the World Weather Watch. Within UNCPUOS, it worked for a liability convention based partly on the domestic law of the victim and for voluntary adherence to a binding arbitration regime, as a precedent for developments in environmental and sea law. It promoted as a priority, in co-operation with France, a comprehensive, fully accessible system for the compulsory, prompt, and accurate registration with the secretary general of objects launched into outer space; it also sought through informal consultations to have the moon and other celestial bodies recognized as the common heritage of mankind and attempted to have the committee support the purposes of the emerging United Nations body on environmental protection. Canada worked with Sweden to establish a working group on direct broadcast satellites, beginning in 1968. Somewhat more cautiously, it participated actively in a working group on remote sensing to promote an incremental, pluralistic approach that included bilateral, limited multilateral, and ultimately international ventures.

Although there was a general continuity in Canada's United Nations behaviour, conflicts and changes in other areas reflected a major shift in power within the external environment, marked by France's assault on America's predominance in space within the Western world, the extension of this assault into a regional European effort, and the deliberate move of the United States to a broadly multilateral approach.

The French challenge, aimed at creating a European space capability independent of the United States and the Soviet Union, had begun in 1962 with the establishment of the Centre national d'études spatiales. In 1964, France had succeeded in forming the ten-member European Space Research Organization, to conduct research and development of experimental satellites for peaceful purposes, and the European Launch Development Organization, to construct a rocket capable of orbiting large satellites such as the Symphonie. In the next six years, individual members used these organizations to support domestic aerospace industries, the agencies suffered a series of expensive launch failures, and skepticism mounted about Europe's ability to develop a competitive space technology independently. However, prompted by the broader challenge of the new U.S. economic policy of August 1971, the major European nations agreed in December of that year to a much increased effort through ESRO in basic research, new operational space application programs, and independent launcher development.

At the same time, U.S. policy was moving away from the goal of maintaining global primacy in competition with the Soviet Union, particularly after the race to the moon was won by Apollo in July 1969.[29]

Motivated by the traditional American concern with rapid, depoliticized international dissemination of scientific information, and by the recognition that U.S. leadership could be sustained only with contributions from many other states, American policy acquired a strong emphasis on a greater co-operative sharing of the burdens and benefits of space exploration on a bilateral and multilateral basis. This emphasis was first registered in an American willingness to share space technology for developmental and political purposes in the Third World, reflected in the opening of the Earth Resources Technology Satellite to international use in 1969, training and experimental programs with Mexico, Brazil, and India, and the conclusion during the 1960s of bilateral science and technology agreements with ten foreign states. Of far greater importance was an American decision to seek co-operative opportunities on a much larger scale with its main allies. Beginning in 1969, this led to a strong effort to provide European states, Canada, Japan, and Australia with information about American plans for the post-Apollo period; these countries were asked to participate, using their own resources, in the U.S. program. By 1971 the U.S. moved to permit unclassified scientific exchanges with the People's Republic of China and negotiated co-operative agreements with the Soviet Union; this revealed its growing view of the global order as pentarchical, based upon the five powers of the U.S., the U.S.S.R., China, Western Europe, and Japan.

An equally powerful stimulus to the reorientation of Canadian behaviour came from the domestic environment. By 1972, the Canadian industry, centred in Northern Electric, Spar Aerospace, and foreign-controlled RCA, was capable of producing major space subsystems on an internationally competitive basis and could exercise sufficient autonomy to influence the government through private representations and through public action by the larger industry associations and labour unions. The intensity of this effort in the Anik controversy produced the first major debate over Canadian space policy in the press and led to a continuing parliamentary involvement, particularly over the creation of Telesat Canada and the Intelsat decisions. The provinces, too, had emerged as direct participants, at first through the tacit competition between Ontario and Quebec over the Anik decision, then through the assertion by both provinces of provincial rights *vis-à-vis* the federal government in the field of telecommunications, and ultimately in the direct challenge posed by Quebec to Ottawa's international authority in the Symphonie and Intelsat controversies.

Within Ottawa, a similar process of organizational proliferation and overt conflict emerged. The abolition of the previously central Defence Research Board at the outset of the 1968–1972 period had been followed by the creation of several new domestic departments and agencies with specialized space mandates. Led by a Department of Communications with strong ministerial leadership, an active Space

Branch, and a committed Communications Research Centre, these included Energy, Mines and Resources, Industry, Trade and Commerce, the Science Council of Canada, and Telesat Canada. Reinforced by the new relevance of space policy to those responsible for regional economic expansion, labour, direct foreign investment, and overall government policy, this specialization and expansion produced a major interministerial and bureaucratic conflict that took considerable political resources to resolve. The intensity of this conflict resulted in the involvement of actors at the prime ministerial level on an issue-specific basis, centrally directed efforts at the highest level to define overall policy, and an attempt to ensure middle-level co-ordination through the establishment in 1969 of an Interdepartmental Committee on Space.

The failure of this body to secure effective co-ordination and the major effort at overall policy direction pointed to the emergence of a set of perceptions in which a legitimate claim on Canadian space activity was held by a multitude of policy objectives, from east–west unity, northern sovereignty, bilingual programming, and national identification to the retention of skilled manpower, industrial and scientific progress, export promotion, and commercial profitability. More importantly, within this diversity there arose a tension between the aims of national development and commercial profitability as a framework for policy debate, with the interlinked imperatives of technological independence and national unity as overarching criteria.

The short period from 1968 to 1972 thus witnessed the decisive repudiation of the precepts and policy approaches of the peripheral-dependence framework, a rejection of liberal internationalism, and the emergence to an equal status of complex neo-realism. Traces of peripheral dependence did remain in the bilateral ionospheric research and earth resource sensing programs and in the reversion to a U.S.-produced domestic communications satellite backed by an organization with superior technological and financial resources, access to the U.S. market, and control of the requisite technology and patent rights. Moreover, a new form of peripheral dependence was seen in French penetration, through support for Quebec's claims in Symphonie, the CTS, and Intelsat, and in Ottawa's possible reliance on American dominance in Intelsat as a means of countering the France–Quebec link over Symphonie. However, the strength of liberal internationalism was demonstrated in all these cases by the opening of bilateral space science programs to international participation and discussion, the provision for specialized domestic participation and overseas sales in co-operation with American firms in the Anik contract, and Canada's consistent and somewhat successful pursuit of more broadly multilateral arrangements at Intelsat and the United Nations.

Of at least equal prominence, however, was the new strength of complex neo-realism in countering lingering peripheral-dependence patterns and in competing with liberal internationalism as a framework for new ventures. Canada's discretionary contribution of earth resource sensing facilities, its emphasis on indigenous technology, national unity, and international scientific assertiveness on the Anik and CTS programs, and its crisis-bred response to Quebec's challenge reflected the centrality of direct national interests as the foundation of Canadian behaviour and fostered involvements with European and other global actors outside the realm of traditional multilateral organizations. Notwithstanding its tripartite framework, the CTS program constituted a unilateral initiative that enabled Canada to diversify its international affiliations and sources of space technology from the United States to European partners. Despite the constraints of multilateral diplomacy, Canada's support for an international manager of the Intelsat system marked Canada's first major divergence from United States preferences and the successful pursuit, with European great-power allies, of an international order in which American predominance was no longer accepted.

Sustaining these complex neo-realist trends was a decline in the relevance of American behaviour and of the external environment in general. As the Anik and Symphonie controversies demonstrated, Canada remained dependent in specific instances on American domestic policy decisions and U.S. willingness to provide international support. Yet the American acceptance of a more multilateral framework, its pursuit of pentarchical arrangements, and the indirect effects of its August 1971 economic policy gave Canada the broader international affiliations and alternative great-power relationships that it used with effectiveness in the Intelsat and CTS cases. And the French challenge to American technological hegemony provided an external preoccupation that drew Canada's attention and later its co-operative international relationships beyond the American sphere.

Within Canada, the Quebec challenge provided the dominant focus, but the growth of a skilled domestic space industry enabled the federal government to mount an effective counter to Quebec's claims, forced it to respond to indigenous commercial as well as national unity objectives, and, in the case of Anik, enmeshed its initially preferred course of action in a full-scale political debate. Within the state apparatus, the involvement of new ministers and functional departments, the particular strength of the Department of Communications coalition, and the acceptance of a broader conception of the national interest provided a permanent foundation and expanding legitimacy for complex neo-realist initiatives.

The Era of Global Diversification, 1973–1980

During the remainder of the 1970s, complex neo-realism emerged to dominate Canada's approach to international space in virtually all its external relationships and in its policy as a whole.[30] Within North America, this trend was manifested in the achievement of a Canadian prime-contract capability for domestic communications satellites, a greater presence in bilateral programs, and an effort to embed Canada's relationship with the United States in a comprehensive formal agreement. Beyond the continent, it was reflected in a greater sympathy for the views of overseas great powers in North Atlantic organizations and at the United Nations, the establishment of a formal relationship with the new European Space Agency, and the quest for direct, co-operative bilateral relationships with space powers such as France and Japan. Its ultimate expression came in the development of an integrated, operationally effective Canadian space policy that confirmed in both its overall structure and its internal balance the paramount status of a complex neo-realist orientation.

The foundations for this complex neo-realist rise lay in the eventually successful moves towards a national capacity to design, develop, and construct operational communications satellites.[31] This process began in December 1975, when the Department of Communications Space Policy Branch persuaded Cabinet to fund a follow-on Anik satellite that went beyond the commercial needs of Telesat Canada to exploit the technological developments of the CTS program. It put Canada in the forefront of a new, higher radio-band communications technology and included significantly more Canadian content. These commitments were extended in April 1978 when the government, influenced in part by the Science Council's call for the prime contract to be awarded to a Canadian firm, acquired three further satellites for an Anik-C program. In response to the pattern of government support for space industries in other countries, the prospects of an expanding international business, the recommendations of an ITC-sponsored task force on electronics headed by the chairman of Spar Aerospace, and the urging of the Canadian press, the government later that year upgraded its satellite facilities to enable Spar Aerospace to assemble and test satellites in Canada rather than in the United States. And in May 1979, on the advice of MOSST, ITC, and DOC, but over the opposition of Finance and Treasury Board, it awarded Spar the prime contract for an Anik-D satellite and provided a direct subsidy to Telesat Canada to permit half of the work to be performed in Canada.

A less far-reaching but equally significant progression took place in bilateral programs with the United States. The first major issue was the degree and form of Canadian participation in the United States manned space shuttle program.[32] When the United States had first issued an informal invitation for participation, in early 1970, Canada had been far more reluctant than the European allies to offer a positive response, on the grounds that the program offered few direct benefits to Canada. However, President Nixon's authorization of the program in January

1972, as a stimulus to a depressed U.S. aerospace industry and an inexpensive alternative to distant manned flights, NASA's subsequent award to U.S. firms of feasibility studies on the shuttle's remote manipulator arm, and an accompanying emphasis on structuring the program to maximize U.S. domestic production prompted ITC to commission a feasibility study from Spar and an allied engineering firm. When the U.S. approached Canada for formal participation in the program, ITC and NRC argued that Canada must participate, because of its specialized expertise, to keep abreast of the new technology, and to ensure consideration of its bids for subcontracts and requests for space for experiments on the shuttle. In contrast, a coalition led by MOSST argued that scarce funds should be spent on defined Canadian objectives in communications technology and resources sensing. Still others argued that Canada lacked the resources to participate in any "big science" projects. This division made even minor Canadian involvement questionable for the moment.

In 1973, however, the NRC, which had been conducting informal shuttle-related studies with NASA, supported by ITC, which was interested in developing in international specialization, began talks with NASA about limited Canadian participation. Reinforced by industry demands and a growing feeling that nonparticipation would jeopardize Canada's continuing need for access to U.S. launch services, the government in the spring of 1974 decided to participate. Following a NASA–NRC agreement in 1975, the two governments formally agreed in June 1976 on a proposal similar to that signed between NASA and the European Space Agency. Under this agreement, Canada committed itself to design, develop, and construct the initial flight unit of the shuttle's remote manipulator system, in return for access to the shuttle for launches, service missions, and experiments, access to conventional launch systems in the interim, and entry into global markets for the RMS. Despite the subsequent cost overruns and delays in the shuttle program, the Canadian decision was proved correct when NASA awarded Canada and ESA a special rate for carrying experiments on the shuttle in August 1977. Furthermore, the program stimulated the domestic electronics industry and exports to West Germany, through the Canadian contractor Spar Aerospace; and NASA awarded Spar, in accordance with President Carter's space policy, a $63.6-million (U.S.) contract in April 1980 to construct three additional manipulator systems for further U.S. shuttles.

The initial hesitations and careful negotiations that characterized Canada's approach to the shuttle program were more pronounced in the case of the Earth Resources Technology Satellite (ERTS).[33] Canada's original 1971 agreement with the United States, signed when the relevant technology was at an experimental stage and international law quite underdeveloped, had contained only a minor Canadian reservation allowing for subsequent renegotiation of the document's dominant "free flow" regime. Canadian caution had since been reinforced by the spread of the technology into commercial applications, the success of a Canadian "quick look" facility at the Prince Albert ground station in generating information more rapidly than its U.S. rivals, resulting requests from U.S. firms to market Canadian-received data in the U.S., and a concern with making the bilateral arrangements consistent with rapidly evolving multilateral obligations at UNCPUOS.

By 1974, EMR's Canadian Centre for Remote Sensing, as the lead user agency, continued to favour the sale of data in accordance with the free information-sharing provisions of the agreement and reciprocal precedents whereby NASA supplied Canada with U.S.-sensed data about the Maritimes. However, within the government's Interdepartmental Committee on Space (ICS), the position of CRS was challenged by External Affairs, which was concerned about the implications for Canada's position at UNCPUOS. Such was the force of External's objections that Canada denied two requests from private U.S. companies for sales in 1974. Moreover, in the renewal of the overall ERTS agreement in May 1975, it inserted a significantly stronger reservation about its permanent acceptance of a free-flow regime.

This emphasis on the broader implications of bilateral co-operation was registered with equal force in a successful Canadian effort, extending from 1975 to 1980, to have the United States adopt a more co-ordinated, co-operative, multilateral approach to remote sensing with its allies. Canada's continuing representations to NASA on the virtues of multilateral co-operation stemmed from the belief of DOC's Space Policy Branch that effective Canadian participation in the first ERTS satellite, Landsat, had been precluded by insufficient prior notification of American plans. These representations received a major reinforcement in January 1979 when President Carter's space policy and a simultaneous reorganization of NASA indicated a rapid U.S. move to a commercially-oriented, user-pay ERTS system, operated by NASA and managed by a new committee on international co-operation similar to the Intelsat board.

This significant change in American policy led Canada to conduct a co-ordinated overview of its remote sensing activity in the context of overall Canada–U.S. space co-operation, its bilateral arrangements with ESA, Japan, and Australia, and its multilateral participation. On the basis of this review, Canada sought to reduce the oligopolistic features that an Intelsat-like system would entail by considering a substantial Canadian contribution to the new ERTS system. It further attempted to promote earlier Canadian access to information by pressing, with considerable success, for regular, high-level reviews of NASA's plans. Of greater significance was Canada's successful effort to encourage American moves towards internationalization. Canada's first initiative had come in the favourable response it had given to a request from ESA for a meeting of Canadian and ESA remote sensing experts. It thus readily accepted an American request for Canada to hold a multilateral meeting on remote sensing and, after some discussion about participants, hosted such a meeting in May 1980 among representatives of the United States, ESA, France, Japan, and India.

Accompanying this steady shift towards multilateralization was Canada's quest for a more formal framework agreement with the United States to structure its overall bilateral interchange. Initiated in January 1977, this effort was motivated by the general desire to accompany closer links with ESA with expanded bilateral ties with the U.S., by a direct interest in supplementing the network of informal ties by which Canada kept abreast of NASA plans, and by the specific concern with securing an equal opportunity to participate in American programs. It quickly resulted in a July 1977 bilateral space science review meeting, which ESA did not attend, although it had been invited. From this meeting flowed an April 1978 agreement to hold such discussions annually as well as a Canadian proposal, articulated by John Chapman before the U.S. House of Representatives, for an International Space Council, modelled after the NATO council, as a forum for such reviews. Throughout 1979, Canada continued to plan for a formal framework agreement with the United States, but it delayed intergovernmental negotiation pending the creation of an overall Canadian space policy.

These concerns on North American subjects had parallel expression in the North Atlantic realm. Here Canada's earlier concerns over Intelsat were reflected in a direct, balanced confrontation between the United States and Europe over the structure of new, operationally oriented international organizations and in significant Canadian shifts towards the European pole. These developments, which figured in the intergovernmental discussions over the establishment of an aeronautical navigation satellite system (Aerosat) and a search and rescue satellite system (Sarsat), became acute in negotiations over the formation of an International Maritime Satellite Organization (Inmarsat), a body of thirty-five seafaring countries created in 1979 to manage a satellite system together in aid of maritime navigation.[34]

From 1976 to 1979, Canada's position at Inmarsat had been the subject of internal debate. The Ministry of Transport and Teleglobe Canada favoured an inexpensive, U.S.-produced system, leased from Intelsat, to service the existing traffic. In contrast, the Department of Communications favoured an expansive system, provided equally by the United States and ESA, to develop the market and serve all Canadian territory. The Department of External Affairs balanced its recognition of the special Canada–U.S. space relationship by its acute awareness of Canada's pending application for membership in ESA, British and French complaints that Canada was adopting an excessively pro-U.S.

approach in Intelsat, and the European hope that the French Ariane rocket launcher would find an international market in Intelsat and elsewhere. In the end, the views of DOC and DEA were reflected in the Canadian position and in Inmarsat's adoption of a mixed U.S.–European system for its future requirements.

Similar shifts in Canada's orientation took place gradually at the United Nations.[35] On the issue of a legal regime governing the use of direct broadcast satellites, Canada adopted a position at variance with that of the Soviet Union, which insisted upon a rapidly established regime enshrining the prior consent of the receiving state. Nor did Canada fully subscribe to the position of the United States, which, supported by the United Kingdom, West Germany, Italy, Japan, and other Western countries, favoured the eventual establishment of a regime allowing for the free flow of information once the requisite technology had been developed. Rather, working with Sweden, France, and traditional middle powers, Canada sought an incrementally developed regime linked to the International Telecommunications Union, which all states could support, based on the maximum participation and co-operation of the targeted state. It further pressed for a full set of legal principles developed through working groups with a functionally limited membership. And it resisted occasional suggestions by the Americans and the British about the desirability of a co-ordinated Western position compatible with the allied emphasis on freedom of information at the Conference on Security and Co-operation in Europe.

Similarly, on the issue of remote sensing, Canada responded after 1973 to the hardening of positions between the "restrictionists", led by the Soviet Union, France, Mexico, and Latin American states, and the proponents of "open skies", led by the United States, by keeping the Canadian position open, presenting legal options for educational purposes, and working to secure intermediate agreements on specific issues. Guided by its belief in international co-operation, in the centrality of the United Nations and its outer space committee, in the widest use of the new technology, and in its relevance for environmental protection and development assistance, Canada offered balanced compromises that asserted the rights of sensed states to have access to data acquired over their territories and, after an appropriate delay, to have all data made available to the international community as a whole. Towards the later stages of the debate, Canada, resisting Department of National Defence suggestions that it support the views of its larger NATO allies and the U.S. Department of Defence, argued for co-operative projects and daily co-ordination among smaller groups of countries and the establishment of a panel of experts that, in the face of United States and Brazilian opposition, might be formed outside the United Nations.

A similar orientation was evident on other UNCPUOS issues. In the debate over the draft Convention on the Registration of Objects Launched into Outer Space, Canada forwarded a compromise satisfactory to the U.S. and France in 1974. In negotiations for a regulatory regime for activities on the moon, Canada, consistent with its earlier behaviour, decided in early 1980 to sign a draft treaty and ratify it after consultations with other Western countries, on the grounds that it affirmed the principle of the common heritage of mankind and anticipated rather than followed technological developments. In discussions of the use of nuclear power sources in outer space, Canada, supported by the United Kingdom, Italy, Japan, and a broad coalition of middle powers, worked for the creation of a working group to study the issue and a multilateral regime of strict, fully effective standards, safeguards, and restrictions paralleling the legal framework governing the use of nuclear materials on earth. On issues of paramount concern to the developing countries, Canada provided technical assistance while resisting requests for a major expansion of its program. Moreover, it supported a conference focused on the direct technical aspects of North–South outer space co-operation, rather than its broader economic and political issues; in a rough parallel with Brazil, Canada also supported limited planning, rather than the claims of equatorial states for national sovereignty over the use of the geostationary orbit.

The ability of Canada to enlist the support of France, the United Kingdom, and Italy in its middle-power-based coalitions at the United Nations reflected in part the growing compatibility between the Canadian and the European approaches to space activity as a whole. This compatibility was partly a consequence of a conscious, sustained Canadian effort to develop space affiliations with Europe, beyond the observer status in the European Space Conference that Canada had obtained in 1968. The quest for an enhanced link with Europe was proposed and consistently promoted by DOC, which, following on European participation in the CTS, saw the European states rather than the United States as the dynamic force in the future global development of communications satellite technology. It was strongly supported by MOSST, which favoured an expansion of Canadian industry through international sales. Moreover, the European link received significant support from DEA, which viewed it as a concrete way of expressing the Third Option policy, saw the potential role of the newly forming European Space Community in co-ordinating European views in UNCPUOS, and recalled the strong support the Europeans had given Canada in a dispute with the United States over the formation of Aerosat. DEA was satisfied, on the basis of information from NASA and the State Department, that the U.S. would not oppose such a link. The major opposition came from the NRC, which feared the diversion of scarce space science resources from productive programs with the United States, and from MOT, EMR, and the Department of Fisheries and Environment, which feared a disruption of their intimate bilateral co-operation with the United States.

Prompted by the knowledge that an integrated European Space Agency would be formed in April 1974, the DOC–MOSST coalition secured in March the approval of the Interdepartmental Committee on Space for a policy of strengthening Canadian space links with countries other than the United States and using the launching facilities of several countries rather than those of the U.S. alone. In January 1977, Cabinet gave formal approval, as part of a broad space policy review, for officials to begin exploratory discussions with ESA with a view to determining satisfactory terms for an upgraded Canadian membership. Following separate discussions with U.S. officials and ESA representatives, Canada decided on a somewhat limited associate membership that would allow for Canadian participation in all ESA planning committees and in its space science programs on an optional basis. After a delay occasioned by France's insistence on a reference to the use of ESA's launching facilities and by Canada's insistence on a full reciprocity of obligations despite the difference in capability between the two sides, an agreement incorporating both provisions was reached in 1978. The government's 1978 expenditure reduction program forced a temporary decline in Canada's participation in ESA programs, but it then moved rapidly to upgrade its representation to the agency, to begin negotiations for participation in ESA's remote sensing and large platform satellite programs, and, in January 1980, to provide the necessary funding for this involvement.

Canadian participation in ESA was but one component of a process that extended beyond association with overseas regional organizations to the creation of direct bilateral links with key great powers. This thrust towards bilateralism was first registered in the development of Canada's interaction with France into a regular, senior-level, co-operative relationship. The successful launch of the Symphonie and Canada's quest for a contractual link prompted a Canadian proposal for co-operation with France in science and technology generally and telecommunications specifically, issued by Prime Minister Trudeau during a visit to France in 1974, by Minister of Communications Gérard Pelletier during a visit to Paris later that year, and by Pelletier's successor, Jeanne Sauvé, during a visit to ESA headquarters and Paris in May 1976. As a result of these efforts, Canadian participation in the Quebec–France teleconferences employing the Symphonie was supplemented by a new 1976 agreement, between DEA and EMR on the one hand and the French Centre national d'études spatiales on the other, for co-operation in remote sensing. Reinforced by Canada's negotiation with France over Sarsat, this co-operation became regularized with the 1977 establishment of ongoing bilateral liaison arrangements and with the discussion of space co-operation during the 1978 session of the Canada–France Scientific Mixed Commission.

Bilateral liaison with West Germany, although less intense, proceeded in similar fashion.

Of greater potential significance was co-operation with Japan. Earlier ongoing discussions on space under the rubric of the Canada–Japan Technological Agreement were supplemented by exchanges of missions beginning in 1972, embassy contact commencing in 1973, Canada's dispatch of two space sector representatives to Japan, and the facilitation of business and governmental contacts in 1975. Following Prime Minister Trudeau's visit to Japan in 1976 and the conclusion of a framework agreement for economic co-operation, Canada began to assess Japanese interest in space co-operation with other countries and collaborative possibilities. Recognizing that Japan was on the verge of developing as an important member of the international space community, Canada established a liaison link and exchange of published information and sent senior officials to visit Japan. In return, Japan invited Canada to attend the next meeting of ongoing ESA–Japan space consultations, but it was forced to end this initiative by European objections and the cancellation of the meeting. By the end of 1978, the two countries had agreed to form a Canada–Japan panel on remote sensing from space, were consulting on possible Japanese involvement in Canadian operational systems, and were using one another's ground stations and rockets for experimental research.

At this time, Canada decided to examine co-operation with Japan in operational systems. This decision rested on Japan's policy of diversifying its space relations from the United States, the likelihood of Japan rapidly developing a full-scale program complete with an indigenous launch capability, its interest in Canadian participation in its commercial programs, and its particular interest in Canada's communication satellites. From Canada's perspective, it rested on an assessment that the Third Option policy and Cabinet's 1976 authorization for participation in ESA had legitimized by implication the development of links with Japan; the government also felt that ties with Japan were not competitive with those with ESA and that Canada's priority on space activity, the need to spread research and development costs, and the desirability of having alternative launch facilities available justified further collaboration. At the same time, however, an awareness of language barriers, superior Japanese internal organization, and the concern of the U.S. in imposing stringent conditions on technological transfers to Japan led Canadian officials to stress the need for care in transferring technology and securing balanced benefits and to rank collaboration with Japan after that with the U.S. and ESA.

The difficult questions of resource trade-offs and political balance that arose as a result of the proliferating diversity of Canada's international space activity culminated in a major move towards the construction of an overall space policy.[36] Despite earlier study documents and the 1968

White Paper, Canada's space program prior to 1974 had proceeded gradually, with the view that Canada was a rather small space power capable of performing little basic research. Informal practice mandated the maintenance of significant specialized expertise at the subsystem level in commercially relevant applications of particular interest to Canada, the transfer of technology and direct support from government to industry to promote an indigenous design and manufacturing capability in these areas, the purchase of full systems and launch facilities from the cheapest source abroad—in practice, the United States—and international co-operation with NASA, ESRO, and the United Nations.

Canada's first formal comprehensive space policy, announced by Minister of State for Science and Technology Jeanne Sauvé in July 1974, departed from this traditional approach by instituting a more clearly defined program, designed to contribute directly to Canadian economic and sovereignty goals. The policy called for a stronger Canadian role in basic space science, an indigenous capacity to design, develop, and construct operational systems in Canada, and a contracting and purchasing policy that would further promote Canadian industry. In international relations, the policy, while affirming Canada's continued reliance on foreign launch facilities and the utility of its longstanding relationship with NASA, noted the establishment of substantial launching facilities in other countries and Canada's willingness to consider involvement in these countries' space programs in order to ensure access to those facilities.

This emphasis on defining an overall program, developing national capability, and diversifying international relations was intensified in January 1980 when the minister of communications presented Cabinet with a five-year plan for space research and development. It committed the government to continuity in policy, stability in funding, and an increase in support for industry. On this basis, Cabinet authorized Canadian participation in a seven year co-operative space science program with NASA, the development with ESA of a large, multipurpose satellite, and the design with the Europeans of a new remote sensing system. This last initiative reflected a particular calculation that remote sensing was to replace communications as the dominant area of concern and that Canada should reduce its dependence on U.S. goodwill in this area by becoming an essential contributor to the European program.

The possible unreliability of American goodwill and the attendant need for co-operation with Europe was based most fundamentally on the emergence of a tripolar, competitive balance of space power in the Western world, in which the United States was being challenged as the leading non-Communist space power by Europe and Japan. This configuration stemmed from a gradual loss in American predominance in global space activities, manifested in the withdrawal of the United

States from such programs as domestic communications satellites in the early 1970s, and, after 1976, by a contraction in manned space exploration and a succession of real-dollar cuts in NASA's budget. Reinforced by a fear that the Soviet Union was securing disproportionate benefits from superpower détente and co-operation in space, these budget cuts led the United States to become more reluctant about transferring its best technology or complete information to allies. Compounding allied fears were the 1978 U.S. Space Policy Act, which declared retaining American technological leadership and creating technology for the benefit of mankind to be the dominant aims of American space policy, and the first unilateral cancellation of an international space project, designed to heighten fledgling NASA–ESA co-operation, by the U.S. Congress in May 1980.

The second element of an emerging tripolar structure was the success of the Europeans in becoming independent of the U.S. in space matters. By the end of 1972, the Europeans had secured the participation of their companies as suppliers for Intelsat and had decided to form an umbrella space organization, develop a new French satellite-launching rocket, and participate in the American post-Apollo space program. The implementation of these decisions was delayed for some time by divisions over launcher development and agency leadership among the French, the British, and the West Germans. However, following its establishment in May 1975, the new European Space Agency moved rapidly to develop a launch facility and a set of sophisticated programs. By 1980 these appeared to be competitive enough with American output to enable Canada to bargain with the United States over prices and access. Moreover, the tendency of France and West Germany to develop by themselves projects such as direct broadcast satellites and the resulting push of other ESA countries to proceed with programs such as a large-capacity satellite induced Canada to adopt a dual approach, in which direct bilateral ties with the two continental great powers supplemented those with the European community as a whole. Similarly, Japan's decision in the early 1970s to develop a full-scale space program to secure independence of the United States, its creation of a central space agency and launch capability, and its ability to progress to indigenous development of a state-of-the-art remote sensing system by 1986 provided a powerful pull on Canada's international activity.

The ability of Canada to respond effectively to these international alternatives was furthered by the emergence of a large, diverse, and expanding domestic space industry that was Canadian-controlled, internationally competitive at the major subsystem level, and sufficiently well organized to exert substantial influence on government policy. In the fifteen years prior to 1973, the Canadian space industry had grossed a total of $150 million in sales and maintained an average employment level of 700 persons. By 1980, the industry had reached an *annual* sales volume of $140 million and a direct employment level of 2240 workers. During this time, Canadian-controlled Spar Aerospace—formed initially from the Special Products and Applied Research Division of de Havilland and strengthened by the January 1977 acquisition of RCA Canada's space-oriented components—had grown to become the third-largest firm by sales in the Canadian aerospace industry. Moreover, with generous government support, it had acquired the capability to build full-scale space systems. By 1980, Spar had become the leading contributor to Canadian space industry exports of $56 million annually, had secured world leadership in its remote manipulator technology, and was considering bidding, in conjunction with U.S. companies, for major subsystems on NATO and Intelsat projects.

With this growing strength came political effectiveness. Industry demands were formulated and channelled to the government by the space subcommittee of the Air Industries Association of Canada. As expressed in August 1973, in a brief to the Interdepartmental Committee on Space, these demands centred on the need for much closer government–industry co-operation for export purposes and included requests for increased government-funded research and development, support for a Canadian prime contractor or consortium for operational space subsystems, a Crown or quasi-Crown corporation to help design and build such subsystems, procurement policies that increasingly favoured Canadians, bilateral trade agreements permitting the export of space products, a specific government agency to centralize and direct space activities, a mechanism for regular government–industry consultations, and a five-year government plan to provide stability for the industry. Reinforcing industry influence was the new involvement of a wide range of provincial governments and societal organizations in domestic applications of communications and remote sensing technology and the development of new projects, the importance of the space industry to the economies of six provinces, and the support of the national press for an active Canadian space program.

The apparent symmetry of industry demand and government response, however, was not due entirely to the influence of industry. Although it had gained financial strength, technical competence, general resilience, and the self-confidence with which to meet foreign competition, the domestic industry still needed a continuing policy commitment, ongoing direction, and direct support from the government. As in 1972, its success in securing such assistance stemmed partly from the effectiveness of such governmental supporters as ITC, DOC, and MOSST. Under their impact, the government's space budget tripled from just over $30 million in 1972/73 to $95.7 million (exclusive of Telesat expenditures) in 1978/79, and the number of government departments and agencies actively involved almost doubled, from six to eleven. Expansion bred a strengthening of the interdepartmental committee network and the revival of interest in a single space budget and agency. Despite numerous variations over specific issues, a fundamental cleavage emerged between the old operations and research-oriented bodies (NRC, DND, EMR, DFE, and Telesat Canada), which favoured special bilateral co-operation with the United States, and the new policy and co-ordination-oriented bodies (DOC, MOSST, the Science Council, DEA, and to a lesser extent, ITC), favouring expanded links with the Europeans and other overseas actors.

The need to integrate these conflicting tendencies resulted in a significant strengthening of the major co-ordinative body, the Interdepartmental Committee on Space. The ICS had been created in 1969 to review the space activities of federal departments and agencies, universities, and industries, to recommend the optimum use of resources and appropriate plans and proposals, to consider federal policy, and to disseminate information. During the next decade, it succeeded in changing its channel for reporting to ministers, from a Cabinet committee to the minister of state for science and technology, then to the more operationally committed and permanently concerned minister of communications. It acquired a permanent secretariat and the task of co-ordinating the government's spacecraft procurement in 1975, a Cabinet-mandated role of providing Treasury Board with an annual list of proposed space programs in order of priority in 1978, an ADM-level agreement not to put new space projects to Cabinet separately in October 1979, and the power to recommend co-operation in the space activities of foreign and international entities by 1980. In January of 1980, with the support of the four major program departments (DOC, NRC, EMR, and DFE) and all other members of the committee, it presented Cabinet with a five-year space plan and accompanying financial envelope and endorsed the concept of such a procedure for the future. Together these developments provided the ICS with the procedural power and philosophic vision to develop an overriding, integrated vision of Canada's national interest in the international space field.

Throughout the years from 1973 to 1980, Canada's international space policy thus shifted decisively towards a complex neo-realist orientation. Traces of peripheral-dependence patterns remained only in such limited areas as Canada's continuing need for access to U.S. launch facilities, information about U.S. plans, and special consideration in U.S. space programming as a motivation for its participation in the U.S. space shuttle and its quest for a bilateral space link. Within these areas, liberal-internationalist tendencies quickly developed an overriding force, as Canada secured international markets for its space shuttle subsystems, a competitive national capability, and stronger bilateral guarantees and multilateral participation in ERTS. Canada worked for formal consultative arrangements in this period under a multilateral structure in its overall relationship with the United States. Moreover, in overseas relations, liberal-internationalist tendencies continued to animate Canada's continued co-operation with Sweden on direct broadcast satellites, its effort to secure workable compromises on an international remote sensing regime, and its sensitivity to the concerns of leading Third World states on such North–South issues as the Space Conference and geostationary orbit.

Most striking, however, was Canada's new reliance on a complex neo-realist orientation in all spheres. Although it lacked a central space agency and indigenous launch capability, Canada entered the leading range of international space actors with its acquisition of an internationally competitive prime contract capability, albeit with the continuing participation of U.S. firms, for the construction of communications satellites. Global involvement with all powers active in international space was signalled by Canada's move beyond activity in the North American, North Atlantic, and United Nations realms to direct dealings with European states, Japan, and India; Canada also tried to sell Australia a Canadian domestic communications satellite system in 1980.

The centrality of a transcending conception of national interest was signified by the creation of comprehensive, detailed, and effective overall space policies in 1974 and 1980, the variability in Canada's interest in participating in the U.S. space shuttle as the trade-offs with ERTS and domestic communications satellites were assessed, and the delay in seeking a formal liaison link with the United States pending the definition of an overall Canadian space policy. Autonomous bilateral involvement was firmly evident in Canada's effort to penetrate the organizational consensus of ESA to develop direct, operationally relevant links with France and West Germany and in its establishment of ongoing co-operation with Japan.

The emergence of a defined, planned overall policy further led Canada towards unilateral approaches to ESA and Japan, in which consultation with the United States was confined to those diplomatic discussions required to gauge American reaction and ensure an effective implementation. It also bred clear divergence from American policy in numerous areas, as Canada supported a position closer to that of the Europeans in Inmarsat, aligned itself with France and Sweden on direct broadcast satellites and with a broader coalition of European great powers on nuclear-powered sources, and refused to adopt fully the "Western" position on DBS or the remote sensing regime. Moreover, it was underscored by a quest for diversification, as represented in Canada's 1974 policy of developing co-operation with countries other than the United States and securing access to their launch facilities, its attainment of associate membership in ESA, and its 1980 decision to participate in the European L-Sat and remote sensing programs.

Within the realm of international order, Canadian support for reduced institutionalization was evident in its consideration of taking discussions on remote sensing outside the United Nations. A move towards developing a great-power concert on the central issue of remote sensing was manifest in Canada's hosting of a meeting of the United States, the ESA, France, Japan, and India. And a shift towards modifying the structure of the international space order occurred in Canada's increasing reluctance to provide assistance through the United Nations and in its consideration of participation in the Japan–ESA consultations on space activity.

Changes in the Canadian foreign policy process further demonstrated the dominance of the complex neo-realist approach. External determinants became much less salient and considerably more diffuse, as Canada responded directly and equally not only to the actions of the United States and the United Nations, but also to those of Europe and Japan. Domestic determinants became increasingly influential as a large, Canadian-controlled, internationally competitive space industry developed the organized capacity and provincial and public support to secure major government funding for its programs. And the governmental process acquired a determining effect as a wide set of fully involved actors argued for their programs through a comprehensive co-ordinative structure that increasingly developed and imposed an overall concept of the long-range national interest, with attendant procedural and budgetary control.

CHAPTER 10

CANADIAN POLICY TOWARDS THE MIDDLE EAST

Within Canada's foreign policy agenda, few areas have so engrossed the Canadian government and people as events in the Middle East. Since the 1947 debates over the partition of Palestine, the ongoing Arab–Israeli conflict and recurrent crises in the broader region have been a continuing focus of Canadian concern. Moreover, in its skillful response to these dilemmas, Canadian policy towards the Middle East has provided most observers with an archetypical example of Canada's profound, enduring commitment to an enlightened, liberal-internationalist ethos.[1]

Portraying Canada as a stable middle power with no direct strategic and economic interests, historical commitments and animosities, or distinctive policy and instruments of influence, these observers have highlighted Canada's continued leadership and participation in peacekeeping, its even-handed mediatory role in search of peaceful settlement, and its generous contributions to promote functional accommodation, all through its favoured vehicle of the United Nations. In so doing, they have identified the wellsprings of Canadian behaviour as lying in a systemic concern with promoting global stability, United Nations legitimacy, and Western and Commonwealth solidarity and, equally, in the reinforcing internationalist commitment of the Canadian public and the policy community.[2]

Although official declarations and scholarly analyses have largely supported this portrait, they have also provided a basis for an assault upon the accuracy of this liberal-internationalist interpretation. This assault, which reflects the perspective of peripheral dependence, emphasizes the way in which Canada's reflexive neutrality, rendered precarious by its insensitivity to specific Arab perceptions and shifting coalitions in the world at large, has given it a steadily decreasing effectiveness and influence in the region. It points as a cause to the heavy constraints imposed by Canada's lack of knowledge and interest in the Middle East itself, its overriding preoccupation with maintaining harmony between the dominant United Kingdom and United States and retaining its own special relationship with both countries, and its resulting dependence on a specific historic interpretation of Judaism and Zionism, kept alive by the penetrative influence of a well-organized Jewish lobby within Canada.[3]

Despite the dominance of these two visions, considerable evidence suggests the need for a third perspective.[4] Beginning with the emphasis since 1973 on Canada's significant economic activities, reduced concern with the Arab–Israeli conflict, and expansion of bilateral relationships, this perspective highlights Canada's growing involvement and influence in Middle East affairs, the emergence of a defined policy grounded in the specific, wide-ranging interests of Canada and the Middle East states themselves, and the resulting tendency of Canada to undertake unilateral initiatives in pursuit of its particular objectives. While noting the recent attention Canada has given to a broader range of international actors involved in Middle East affairs, this perspective, which reflects complex neo-realist precepts, attributes a substantially greater weight to the vigorous debates within Canada's domestic community and, in particular, the concepts of overarching national interests developed by the Canadian government.

In order to assess the relative validity of the three competing perspectives, this chapter explores the evolution and determinants of Canadian behaviour towards the Middle East from the establishment of the state of Israel in 1947 through the controversy over the proposed move of the Canadian embassy in Israel to Jerusalem in 1979 and the immediate aftermath of that proposal.[5] This examination reveals that the patterns and processes of Canadian behaviour have undergone a significant evolution over the past three decades, through five distinct periods.

The first period, from 1947 to 1957, was characterized by diplomatic mediation, military peacekeeping, and intense concern over Anglo–American harmony, the NATO alliance, and the survival of the United Nations. It reveals aspects of both the dominant liberal-internationalist perspective and its peripheral-dependence competitor. The second period, covering the Diefenbaker governments of 1957 to 1963, was a time of reinforcing the internationalist role emanating from the Suez crisis and strengthening relations beyond the mediatory and peacekeeping framework. The third period, embracing Lester Pearson's tenure as prime minister from 1963 to 1968, witnessed first a reaffirmation, then a reconsideration of Canada's commitment to UN-sponsored peacekeeping operations, the extension of this role to Cyprus, and initiatives based on domestic Canadian imperatives in the new arena of North Africa.

The fourth period, spanning the first two Trudeau governments from 1968 to 1973, was dominated by the decreasing effectiveness of, and growing frustration with, UN mediatory and peacekeeping operations and by the formulation of a foreign policy framework centred on domestic economic interests as the foundation for subsequent initiatives. Finally, the fifth period, dealing with the Trudeau and Clark governments of 1974 to 1982, was highlighted by a proliferation of Canadian–Middle East relationships, a reduction in the centrality of the United Nations, the emergence of wide-ranging bilateral relations, and the primacy of domestic economic and political interests in Canadian policy formulation.

An Overview of Canadian Policy

A quantitative overview of Canadian involvement in the Middle East provides an initial opportunity to assess the validity of the three competing theoretical perspectives.[6] The emerging dominance of complex neo-realism is first suggested by the steadily increasing amount of attention the Canadian government has been devoting to Middle Eastern affairs in the context of its overall foreign policy concerns. As Figure 10.1 indicates, while intermittent crises have had their impact, the most striking trend is the steady increase in attention since 1969 to a historically high plateau. This portrait is sustained by the dramatic increase in the number of diplomatic representatives exchanged between Canada and Middle East states. Since 1948, Canada has almost doubled its representatives in the Middle East every decade, from a low of 11 in 1948 to a high of 89 in 1978, while Middle East countries have moved from a low of 14 representatives here in 1948 to a high of 121 in 1979.[7] These observations are reinforced by the substantial increase over the past decade in the number of Canada–Middle East bilateral summit meetings conducted between heads of government or at the senior Cabinet level.[8] Together these data suggest that, in conformity with the complex neo-realist perspective, the historical process of Canada–Middle East relations has grown in relative attention, in the concentration of diplomatic and governmental resources, and in interest and involvement at the highest level.

An examination of the context of Canadian involvement reinforces this appraisal. Table 10.1 indicates that while the United Nations has maintained its significance as a central focus for Canadian–Middle East concerns, since the late 1960s the Middle East itself has assumed a more broadly based relevance, tapping into the general foreign policy system and becoming linked to the more politically and economically sensitive areas of Europe and Africa. Of even greater importance is the sudden rise of the functional areas of security and economic affairs, indicating the more direct and intense connections that have grown between Canada and the Middle East.

Canada's roles and objectives with respect to the Middle East provide confirmation of this gradual shift in policy orientation. As Table 10.2 indicates, Canadian liberal-internationalist concern over regional conflict and its ensuing commitment to peacekeeping and other forms of conflict resolution remain constant. Yet Canada's preoccupation with a secure Atlantic community in the 1950s, characteristic of peripheral dependence, is replaced in the 1970s by Canada's complex neo-realist resolve to perform as an independent actor pursuing state interests and specific bilateral relations.[9]

TABLE 10.1 Context of Canada's Middle East Involvement, 1947–1978

	1947	1948	1949	1950	1951	1952	1953	1954	1955	1956	1957	1958	1959	1960	1961	1962	1963	1964	1965	1966	1967	1968	1969	1970	1971	1972	1973	1974	1975	1976	1977	1978
General	A				C	C	C	C	C									C	C	C	B	C				C	B	B	B	C	C	B
Geographic										B																						
Europe			A		A	B		A	A	B														C	A	A	A	B	B			B
NATO							A			B						A		B	B													
Commonwealth										B					C																	
United Nations		B			C	B	C	C	C	B	B	B	B	A	A	A	A	B	B	A	A	C	B	B	B	B	B	B	B	A	A	C
Middle East										B	B	B	B						B													
Africa																		B		B	B	A	B	B	B		B	B	B	B	B	B
Functional																																
Political		B																						C								
Security																											B	B	B			B
Economic																							C	B	B	B			C	B	C	C
Aid																		C					C									

A: Significant attention (more than one paragraph per page)
B: Substantial attention (one paragraph per page)
C: Minor attention (passing reference, less than one paragraph per page)

SOURCE: Based on Department of External Affairs, *Annual Review*; Canadian Institute of International Affairs and Parliamentary Centre for Foreign Affairs and Foreign Trade, *International Canada*, cross-referenced.

TABLE 10.2 Canadian Roles in the Middle East, 1947–1978

	1947	1948	1949	1950	1951	1952	1953	1954	1955	1956	1957	1958	1959	1960	1961	1962
Faithful Ally of United Kingdom					•					•						
Adjunct Regional Defender					•	•	•	•		•						
Defender of the Faith								•								
Mediator/ Integrator between:																
United Arab Republic/United Kingdom													•			
Commonwealth										•						
United Nations																
Jews or Israel/ Arabs	•	•			•		•	•	•	•	•	•	•	•	•	•
Inter-Arab																
Arab (Internal)											•					
Cyprus/Turkey/ Greece																
Consumer/Producer; North/South																
Liberator/ Supporter					•											
Developer																
Active/ Independent										•						

	1963	1964	1965	1966	1967	1968	1969	1970	1971	1972	1973	1974	1975	1976	1977	1978
Faithful Ally of United Kingdom																
Adjunct Regional Defender																
Defender of the Faith																
Mediator/ Integrator between:																
United Arab Republic/United Kingdom																
Commonwealth																
United Nations	•	•	•													
Jews or Israel/ Arabs	•	•	•	•	•	•	•	•	•	•	•	•	•	•	•	•
Inter-Arab	•	•														
Arab (Internal)														•		•
Cyprus/Turkey/ Greece		•	•	•	•				•		•	•	•		•	•
Consumer/Producer; North/South												•	•			
Liberator/ Supporter																
Developer		•									•					
Active/ Independent										•	•	•	•	•	•	

SOURCE: Based on Department of External Affairs, *Annual Report*, *Annual Review*, 1947/48 to 1978/79. Concept of state role categories derived from K.J. Holsti, "National Role Conceptions in the Study of Foreign Policy," *International Studies Quarterly* 14 (1970): 233–309.

FIGURE 10.1 Relative Attention to Middle East Affairs, 1948–1978

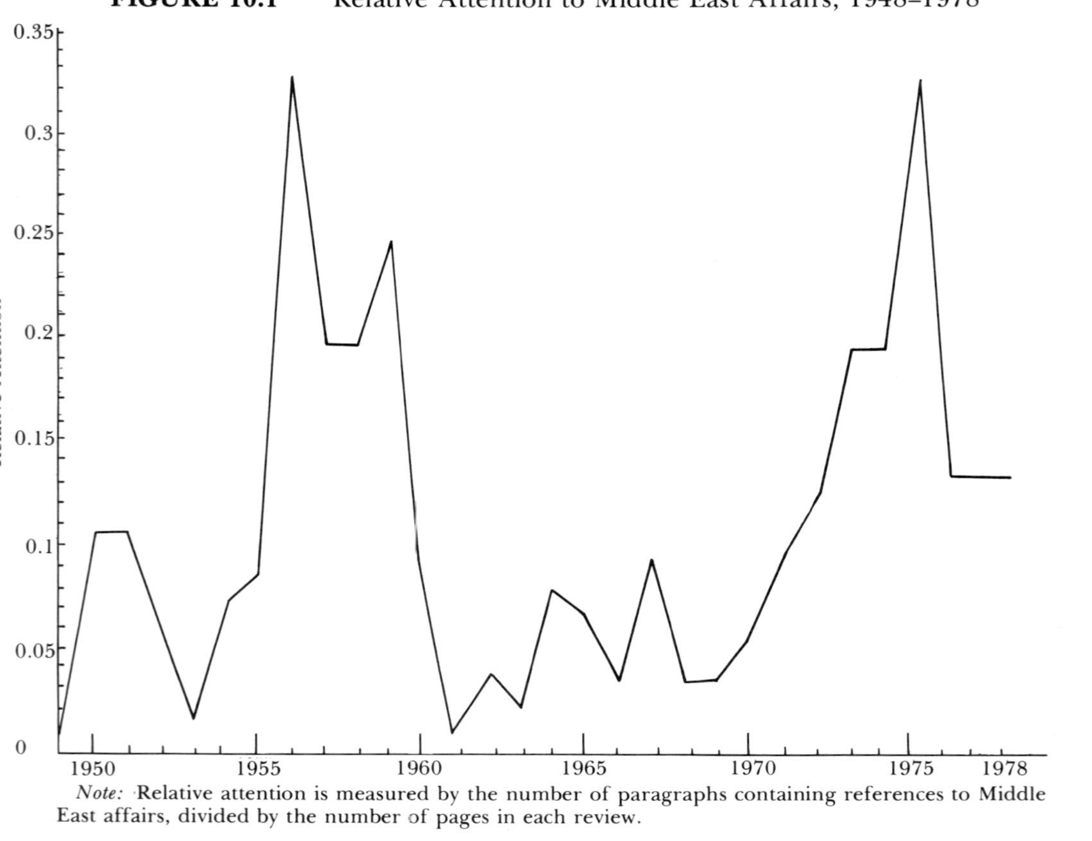

Note: Relative attention is measured by the number of paragraphs containing references to Middle East affairs, divided by the number of pages in each review.

SOURCE: Based on Department of External Affairs, *Annual Report*, 1948–1971; *Annual Review*, 1972–1978.

The specific ways in which Canadian foreign policy is implemented further substantiate the increasing applicability of the complex neo-

TABLE 10.3 Canada–Middle East Bilateral Activity, 1948–1978—Canada as Initiator

In each pair, the first number represents co-operative activities and the second represents activities of conflict.

	Israel	*Arab Confrontation States and PLO*	*Gulf States*	*Iran*	*North Africa*	*Turkey, Greece, Cyprus*	*TOTAL*
1948	4/0						4/0
1949							0/0
1950					1/0		1/0
1951		1/0				1/0	2/0
1952						1/0	1/0
1953							0/0
1954	1/0					1/0	2/0
1955		1/0					1/0
1956	4/2	3/1					7/3
1957	0/1	4/4			1/0	1/0	6/5
1958	1/0	2/0				1/0	4/0
1959		1/0					1/0
1960						2/0	2/0
1961	1/0	0/1				1/0	2/1
1962			1/0		1/1	1/0	3/1
1963	2/0						2/0
1964					2/0		2/0
1965		3/0					3/0
1966		2/0			3/0		5/0
1967	4/1	1/1			4/0	1/0	10/2
1968		1/0			7/0		8/0
1969		1/0			3/0	2/1	6/1
1970	1/0	1/0			3/0		5/0
1971					5/0		5/0
1972	2/0	0/1		1/0	1/0		4/1
1973			1/0	1/0		1/0	3/0
1974		4/1	1/0		2/0		7/0
1975			1/0			6/0	7/0
1976	2/0	6/1	2/0		3/0	1/0	14/1
1977	4/0	2/0		1/0	1/0	1/0	9/0
1978	1/0				1/0	8/0	10/0
TOTAL	27/4	33/10	6/0	3/0	38/1	29/1	

SOURCE: Conflict and Peace Data Bank project, University of North Carolina, Edward E. Azar, Chapel Hill, North Carolina, 1 January 1980.

realist perspective. As Tables 10.3 and 10.4 indicate, Canadian interaction with Middle Eastern countries focused throughout the 1950s upon the Arab–Israeli conflict. Except for the year following the Suez

TABLE 10.4 Canada–Middle East Bilateral Activity, 1948–1978—Canada as Target

In each pair, the first number represents co-operative activities and the second represents activities of conflict.

	Israel	*Arab Confrontation States and PLO*	*Gulf States*	*Iran*	*North Africa*	*Turkey, Greece, Cyprus*	*TOTAL*
1948							0/0
1949							0/0
1950							0/0
1951						1/0	1/0
1952						5/0	5/0
1953	2/0			0/1			2/1
1954	1/0						1/0
1955	1/0						1/0
1956	1/1	2/0					3/1
1957	1/1	1/1		0/1			2/3
1958				2/0			2/0
1959							0/0
1960		0/1				2/0	2/1
1961	1/0	2/0				2/0	5/0
1962	1/0				1/0	2/0	4/0
1963	1/0						1/0
1964					1/0		1/0
1965		3/0	1/0				4/0
1966		2/0			2/0		4/0
1967	2/1	1/1	0/1	1/0	4/0	2/1	10/4
1968		2/0			4/0		6/0
1969	1/0				2/0	1/0	4/0
1970	1/0				1/0	0/1	2/1
1971		0/1	1/0		4/0		5/1
1972	2/0	1/1		1/0		1/0	5/1
1973	0/1		1/0	1/0		1/0	3/1
1974		3/1	1/0	2/0	1/0		7/1
1975			1/0			5/0	6/0
1976		1/2	1/0		2/0	1/0	5/2
1977	1/0	1/0	1/0			1/0	4/0
1978	1/0					8/0	9/0
TOTAL	17/4	19/8	7/1	7/2	22/0	32/2	

SOURCE: Conflict and Peace Data Bank project, University of North Carolina; data supplied by principal investigator Edward E. Azar, Chapel Hill, North Carolina, 1 January 1980.

crisis, Canadian actions were advanced in a generally co-operative mode, reflecting the mediatory role designed by Pearson and supported by the Afro–Asian bloc. The other area of activity during this period was Turkey, indicating the importance of the debate within NATO over Turkey's role in the Western alliance and the question of vulnerability to Soviet expansion into the Mediterranean. These liberal-internationalist patterns were continued until the 1967 Six-Day War, with minor new activity occurring within the other areas of the region, especially North Africa.

The rise in activity with North Africa in the mid-1960s was the first indication of a changing Canadian profile, reinforced in 1971 and 1972 by the emergence of Iran and the Gulf states as areas for Canadian activity. From then on, Canada–Middle East behaviour became increasingly broad in scope, more co-operative and less conflictual in substance, although the Arab–Israeli issue remained evident. As early as 1964 but mostly in the 1970s, Canada can be seen as a more active initiator of relations, with a government policy more intent on the pursuit of self-defined interests.[10] Over half of all Canada–Middle East bilateral activities occurred in the most recent decade of the thirty-year period.

This acceleration in bilateral activity was reinforced by the willingness of governments to enter into formal agreements on political, economic, trade, technical, and cultural levels. Only since 1968 has the Canadian government entered into separate bilateral organizations with Tunisia (1968), Saudi Arabia (1978), Israel (1978), and Algeria (1979). In addition, there has been a substantial increase in summit visits, numerous trade delegations, and joint bodies for consultation on such matters as technology transfer and foreign aid programs.

The government's perception of the actors relevant to this bilateral behaviour casts further doubt on both the liberal-internationalist and peripheral-dependence theses. As Figure 10.2 indicates, external actors continue to dominate, but within this classification the UN and extraregional actors have decreased in importance while regional actors have become more prominent. In addition, societal and governmental actors have reached new levels of significance, excluding the four major Arab–Israeli wars and the Cyprus conflict. In the post-1970 period, extraregional concerns almost disappeared and domestic governmental and nongovernmental actors achieved approximate parity with regional actors.

The new salience of societal and governmental interests is confirmed by the pattern of expanding trade relations between Canada and the countries of the Middle East, as presented in Table 10.5. It is evident that trade, in both absolute and proportional terms, has witnessed a great increase since the early 1970s. To be sure, the countries of the Middle East account for less than 4 per cent of Canada's total global trade and, conversely, Middle East trade with Canada rarely exceeds 4

FIGURE 10.2 Canadian Perceptions of Relevant Actors in the Middle East, 1947–1979

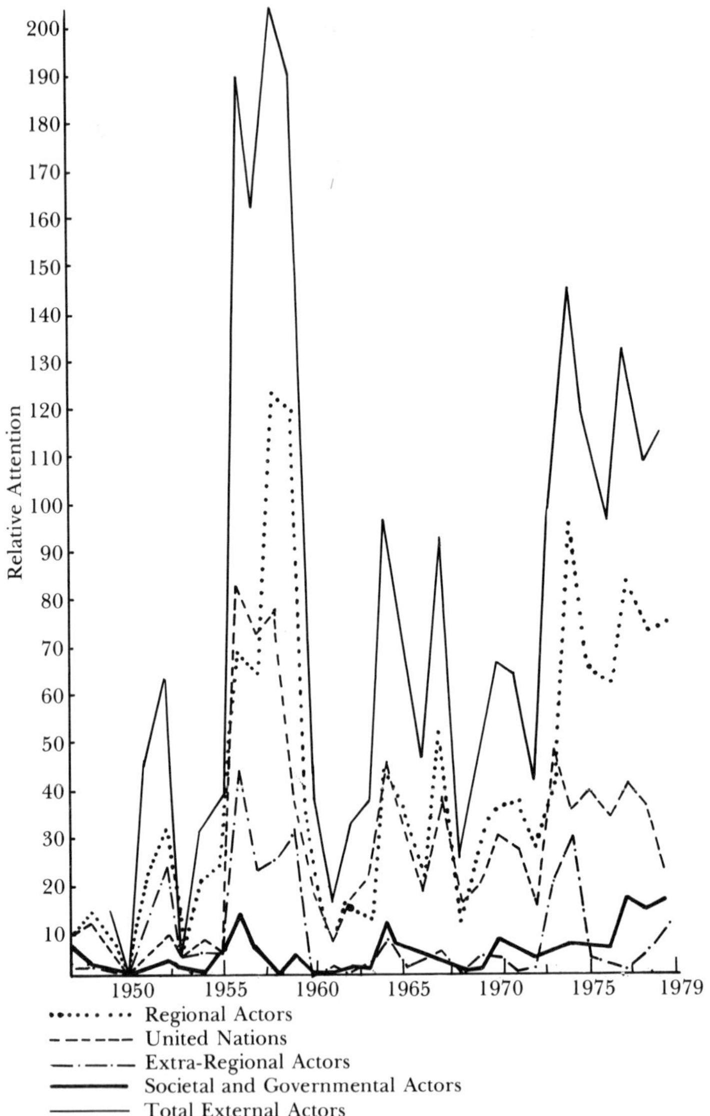

Note: Perceptions are measured as the number of references to relevant actors in the context of Canada-Middle East relations in each review.

SOURCE: Based on Department of External Affairs, *Annual Report*, 1947–1971; *Annual Review*, 1972–1979.

per cent of the total trade of those countries. Yet the resurgence of economic exchanges after 1973 is significant, going beyond dollar value to involve an expansion of political, commercial, and cultural ties.

TABLE 10.5 Canadian Trade with the Middle East, 1948–1981 (current C $millions)

	ISRAEL *Canadian*		*EGYPT* *Canadian*		*ARAB OPEC MEMBERS* *Canadian*		*IRAN* *Canadian*		*OTHER MIDDLE EAST* *Canadian*	
	Exports	*Imports*	*Exports*	*Imports*	*Exports*	*Imports*	*Exports*	*Imports*	*Exports*	*Imports*[1]
1948	5.0	0.0	10.2	1.5	0.8	0.8	0.7	1.0	10.5	5.8
1949	12.7	0.5	4.8	0.2	3.6	13.5	12.0	0.3	4.9	0.6
1950	12.1	0.5	3.7	0.7	1.3	29.3	1.0	0.2	3.2	0.8
1951	11.8	1.0	2.5	0.7	4.5	24.8	1.0	0.5	11.6	1.1
1952	11.9	1.2	19.4	0.5	3.2	8.6	0.6	1.2	14.6	16.4
1953	9.1	1.3	11.7	4.2	4.4	3.6	0.8	1.0	9.	20.2
1954	10.2	1.0	1.2	0.4	2.8	2.4	0.8	1.4	5.0	17.7
1955	4.6	1.2	1.3	0.3	2.5	8.3	0.6	2.1	4.1	19.7
1956	2.7	1.5	2.5	0.2	2.7	25.7	0.8	1.1	4.1	21.9
1957	5.0	1.6	1.2	0.3	2.9	34.7	1.7	0.5	2.7	0.5
1958	4.6	1.8	1.2	0.3	3.2	69.5	1.7	0.9	4.4	0.5
1959	4.6	2.3	1.6	0.2	7.6	71.8	2.2	11.9	4.7	0.4
1960	6.2	2.4	2.0	0.8	11.5	62.9	2.5	31.5	5.0	0.3
1961	8.7	3.1	3.0	0.5	11.5	71.3	4.5	21.6	4.3	0.5
1962	6.2	5.6	2.2	0.3	8.6	58.0	5.3	31.7	3.4	1.1
1963	8.2	6.0	2.5	0.2	12.7	66.0	3.6	42.8	6.3	1.0
1964	9.1	6.3	4.0	0.1	7.8	37.6	3.4	31.1	4.2	1.9
1965	6.3	6.7	4.8	0.2	11.2	63.4	3.3	31.7	4.1	1.3
1966	10.7	6.7	5.3	0.7	12.5	65.2	3.8	35.4	4.8	2.9
1967	6.6	9.2	1.0	0.3	11.4	54.2	3.1	33.7	7.6	3.1
1968	9.8	12.9	3.2	0.4	16.3	45.2	6.6	33.6	14.7	1.6
1969	17.7	15.1	3.0	1.1	19.1	65.3	5.5	30.2	9.6	1.7

TABLE 10.5 Canadian Trade with the Middle East, 1948–1981 (current C $millions)
(cont'd)

	ISRAEL Canadian		*EGYPT Canadian*		*ARAB OPEC MEMBERS Canadian*		*IRAN Canadian*		*OTHER MIDDLE EAST Canadian*	
	Exports	*Imports*	*Exports*	*Imports*	*Exports*	*Imports*	*Exports*	*Imports*	*Exports*	*Imports*[1]
1970	15.0	14.5	37.8	0.4	35.5	52.9	8.4	33.9	36.3	1.2
1971	20.7	15.4	10.2	0.3	73.3	56.3	17.8	66.6	36.2	3.2
1972	24.7	16.7	5.6	0.4	48.1	144.9	22.5	71.7	35.5	5.0
1973	35.8	22.5	3.1	0.5	59.4	178.6	53.7	131.7	41.5	27.6
1974	49.7	24.8	13.9	0.7	207.8	542.5	60.0	617.9	79.4	130.5
1975	63.1	28.2	6.6	0.3	254.6	1175.9	150.0	758.1	83.8	201.7
1976	57.1	38.4	35.2	10.3	304.2	872.3	144.2	695.4	46.3	205.0
1977	49.1	42.5	50.3	33.8	427.2	905.6	142.2	535.5	132.0	9.8
1978	77.8	44.8	56.9	81.9	511.6	939.4	155.6	593.7	135.0	3.2
1979	109.8	56.3	36.7	89.5	713.6	1511.2	22.4	335.1	183.5	8.0
1980	100.9	54.4	128.1	10.7	1060.2	2933.6	41.3	3.4	230.1	15.0
1981	124.4	51.3	126.0	6.6	1413.8	3075.8	21.9	2.7	254.2	17.2

[1]The increase in imports from 1974 to 1976 is the result of substantial crude petroleum imports from the People's Democratic Republic of Yemen.

Note: Canadian export figures do not include re-exports, only goods and services originating in Canada.

SOURCE: Based on Monthly bulletins from Dominion Bureau of Statistics and Statistics Canada: *Trade of Canada—Imports* (1948–1953); *Imports for Consumption* (1953–1962); *Summary of Imports* (1963–1974); *Exports* (1948–1952); *Domestic Exports* (1953–1958); *Summary of Exports* (1959–1974); *Imports by Commodities* (1975–1981); *Trade of Canada—Summary of External Trade* (1975–1981).

Although the rapid expansion of the oil-producing and exporting economies is the basis for much of the growth in activity, other states in the region are also involved. Furthermore, the fact that these increases occur not solely in dollar value but also in proportion of trade indicates that this growth is not merely a reflection of the rise in oil prices.

While a favourable balance of trade exists between Canada and the non-oil-exporting Middle East countries, this is overwhelmed by the asymmetry of Canada's economic exchanges with Arab oil-exporting states. However, this asymmetry is far less politically significant than the imbalances between these states and other OECD members. Not only are the proportions small relative to total Canadian trade, but the energy alternatives available to Canada markedly reduce whatever political vulnerability may seem to occur. Similarly, from the Middle East perspective, Canadian goods and services are neither so large, so strategically crucial in substance (as, for example, sophisticated integrated military systems), nor so irreplaceable as to create serious vulnerability. Hence, interests and foreign policy can be aggressively pursued throughout the Middle East in light of Canada's distinct domestic interests.

In summary, the pattern of Canadian behaviour towards the Middle East region and the relative importance of the various determinants of that behaviour have become more reflective of the predictions provided by the complex neo-realist perspective. We now turn to a detailed examination of the five major periods in Canada–Middle East relations.

The Emergence of Liberal Internationalism, 1947–1957

Canada's involvement in the Middle East, as elsewhere, grew out of the changing international structure emerging from World War II.[11] Before the war, Canada's quasi-isolationist instincts and the mandate system established under the auspices of the League of Nations following World War I left the Middle East area dominated by the residue of European neo-colonialism and great-power interests. However, after 1945, the establishment of the United Nations, the recognition of the need to pursue decolonization systematically, and the perception of an overwhelming Soviet threat to peace and world security provided stark background for the first real non-European test of the postwar international structure: the struggle over Palestine.

At the time, Canada was a founding member of the United Nations, the fourth-ranking country in the Western industrialized world at the close of global hostilities, a leader in the efforts to strengthen continental Europe against the ravages of economic collapse, political decay, and Soviet expansion, and the closest ally of both the United States and Great Britain. It was thus drawn into the question of the dissolution of the British mandate of Palestine and the establishment of replacement sovereign states.

In defining Canadian policy, both elected officials and civil servants of the Canadian government became subject to increasing pressure at home from articulate and well-organized Jewish and non-Jewish Zionist groups. Despite the Liberals' electoral dependence on Quebec, where anti-Semitism was exceptionally strong and pervasive, pro-Zionist sympathies in the Canadian public and media began to assume an expanding and legitimate presence. The Canadian Zionist Federation began to receive public support for its efforts from such organizations as the non-Jewish Canadian-Palestine Committee, established in 1944 and chaired by Sir Ellsworth Flavelle, and the CCF, whose leader in 1944, M.J. Coldwell, publicly endorsed the establishment of the state of Israel. However, not until Louis St. Laurent became secretary of state for external affairs in September 1946 and Lester B. Pearson became his undersecretary was there any indication that the government of Canada would move from Mackenzie King's entrenched policy of firm support for the British position in the Middle East.

Between 1946 and November 1948, when St. Laurent became prime minister and appointed Pearson to succeed him as foreign minister, Canada was drawn increasingly into the debate over the future of the Middle East. With Britain's April 1947 announcement that it would turn the Palestine Mandate over to the fledgling United Nations for resolution, the government of Canada took the first steps that would confirm, over the next decade, its role as an autonomous and responsible world actor apart from the United Kingdom and the United States. The establishment of the United Nations Special Committee on Palestine (UNSCOP) on 14 May 1947 and the leading role played by a Canadian jurist, Justice Ivan C. Rand, in drafting the majority report—which recommended partition of Palestine into Arab and Jewish entities within a single economic unit—was seen by some as indicating pro-Zionist leanings, since partition was unacceptable to the Arab bloc. Generally, however, the Canadian participants were viewed as objective and independent.

Pearson, as chairman of the First (Political) Committee, which sponsored UNSCOP, was unabashedly sympathetic to the plight of the survivors of the Nazi Holocaust and publicly expressed his emotional attachment to the Holy Land of his Sunday school days. But he was strident concerning the need to achieve a political solution fair to all and thereby avoid further escalation of violence and, perhaps more significantly, prevent a rift between the United Kingdom and the United States at a time when a solid Atlantic alliance was deemed essential for the survival of a non-Communist Europe. Furthermore, that the minority report of UNSCOP came from Iran, India, and Yugoslavia was one of a number of indicators that a successful UN-sponsored resolution was essential if the multilateral organization was to survive.

First within the General Assembly and then, from January 1948, on the Security Council, Pearson was crucial in the effort to resolve the dispute within the regional context of the Middle East; more significant still was his effort to prevent this issue from becoming the catalyst for a split between Britain and the U.S. or for a hardening of American–Soviet polarization. But the compromise he achieved on 10 November 1947 between the British, the Americans, and the Russians, concerning British withdrawal and the establishment of separate Jewish and Arab states, was undermined by the unanticipated early termination by Britain of its mandate powers and the Arab refusal to accept the United Nations partition plan. Thus in May 1948, Israel unilaterally declared its independence and the armies of five Arab countries crossed the borders of the new state.

Although the United States government gave *de facto* recognition to Israel on the day of its declared independence, the Mackenzie King government followed the position of the British delegation in withholding recognition. This disturbed many members of Parliament; in the course of Commons debates, they articulated a general predisposition of support and sympathy for the nascent Jewish state, a result of a combination of religious and emotional feelings towards the Holy Land, continued horror over the Nazi atrocities, recognition of the need for refugees to find security, and the lobbying efforts of the United Zionist Council of Canada. Nevertheless, Canadian efforts within the United Nations continued with General McNaughton, Canada's permanent representative, urging the conflicting parties on 14 November 1948 to accept an armistice and work towards a more permanent truce, which was adopted two days later.

Following the inauguration of the St. Laurent government, the Canadian position began to move more firmly towards the recognition that a quick end to hostilities required the expedient establishment of secure boundaries for all parties. When the Israelis applied for admission to the United Nations the following week, with the support of the United States and the U.S.S.R. but opposed by the British, Canada abstained on the vote and it then failed to pass. However, on 24 December, Canada did grant Israel *de facto* recognition. On 11 May 1949, Canada voted in support of the successful admission of Israel into the UN, thereby implying full recognition by the government of Canada of the new state.

While the debate over Canadian recognition flourished, the pro-Zionist organizations within Canada mounted a vigorous lobbying effort.[12] In the spring of 1948, the United Zionist Council of Canada (UZC) began to operate on a full-time basis in Ottawa, establishing much closer contacts than previously with ministers, politicians, government officials, and public relations persons in various centres across Canada. Despite charges from within the Zionist community that this approach was unduly elitist, *ad hoc,* defensive, and unsuccessful in fostering pro-Israel public opinion among the apathetic Canadian citizenry, it was reasonably effective in securing its major objectives, the most important being Canadian recognition of the state of Israel.

Calculating that "if Canada were to recognize Israel politically and economically, other middle powers would follow her lead since Canada is foremost among the middle powers," the UZC Public Relations Committee pursued several strategies. It sought further recognition by promoting trade, securing a Canadian loan for Israel, publicizing Israeli expenditures in Canada, arranging for the Israeli purchasing mission to contact government officials in August 1948, and lobbying directly for recognition with Deputy Minister of Finance Clifford Clark. As a result, the committee was able to report in September 1948 that Canadian recognition of Israel was inevitable and that a willingness to negotiate a trade agreement existed. Indeed, one well-placed observer could report that "certain departments were doing everything possible to compensate for the fact that political recognition of Israel had not yet been granted."[13]

During this same period, the Canadian Arab Friendship League (CAFL), established in 1944 under the direction of M.S. Massoud of Montreal, attempted to counter the increasingly active Zionist organizations. Through personal contacts and their publication, *The Canadian Arab,* the personnel of the CAFL pressed parliamentarians and DEA officials to reconsider the propriety of Canadian policies articulated by Pearson, Justice Ivan C. Rand, and others. Playing upon the Canadian affinity for the British position and reinforced by anti-Semitic feelings, especially in Quebec and within the Social Credit Party, the CAFL stridently condemned Canadian duplicity regarding the Arab position in Palestine. Nevertheless, this effort was not well received either within or outside Parliament.

Few other nongovernmental domestic organizations seem to have shown any consistent concern over the debate on recognition. Among these, the United Nations Association of Canada and the labour groups, particularly the Trades and Labour Congress of Canada (TLC) and the Canadian Congress of Labour (CCL), all demonstrated sympathy for a Jewish homeland, under the conditions of the mandate. Furthermore, they recommended full diplomatic and economic relations with Israel.

Yet despite these efforts and consideration of the Palestine issue by the Standing Committee on External Affairs, policy remained the domain of the prime minister and his Cabinet. Prime Minister King himself remained fearful of undue haste, of an escalation of Arab–Jewish violence, of a confrontation between British, American, and Soviet interests, of creating a rift in Anglo–American relations, and especially of committing Canadian resources to an area where Canada had no direct interests. Yet King did not preside over a Cabinet unhesitatingly committed to his position of inaction. For example, Cabinet ministers

J.L. Ilsley and St. Laurent were more inclined to uphold Pearson's initiatives at the UN, even to the point of implying support for an American initiative to assist in the implementation of the proposed partition plan, possibly requiring military resources. However, in the end, King's sympathies prevailed within Cabinet, although he became increasingly aware of the internal divisions. He noted that he "would like to have seen a direct opposition to supporting any idea of partition but felt it would be better to keep the Cabinet united and to fight that issue later if the course taken with the United Nations should render that necessary."[14]

The prime minister also faced some difficulty with his senior civil servants. While pleased with Pearson, he continually voiced his concern over his undersecretary's penchant for initiative and active diplomacy and DEA's recommended support for the American partition proposal. This concern reflected King's desire to go slowly and to retain his adamantly pro-British position on this issue, believing in British experience and longstanding interest in the region.

The Canadian policy became less close to that of the United Kingdom once Pearson assumed his place within St. Laurent's Cabinet. By this time, however, events in the Middle East had outpaced the machinations of UN diplomacy, so that Parliament, continually being briefed on the course of events by Pearson, became a forum for pronouncement and consensus with full agreement from most members and Cabinet. Close ties between the new secretary and his former colleagues in External Affairs, along with St. Laurent's open support, allowed policy to be directed and implemented with a unified voice. While the "crux of Canadian policy towards Palestine from the end of 1947 until King's retirement in November 1948 was . . . the relationship to Britain," the St. Laurent government pursued a stance less tied to a single foreign actor and more responsive to the evolving international context.[15] The tensions between the United States and the Soviet Union were the overriding concern, along with the need to solidify the Atlantic alliance quickly against the perceived expansionary interests of the Russians.

The years following the admission of Israel to the UN were occupied by the onset of the cold war and Canada's resulting concern for a strong NATO alliance. Decisions such as Canada's voting with France and Great Britain against immediate independence for Morocco and Tunisia were made on these new grounds. Nonetheless, UN-sponsored progress was made towards a stable pseudo-peace between the Middle East antagonists. In response to mounting instability in Egypt, Iran, Syria, and North Africa from 1950 to 1953, the United Nations in 1954 strengthened its Truce Supervision Organization (UNTSO). Canadian Major-General E.L.M. Burns was appointed chief of staff.

From the Canadian perspective, these years of global turmoil and unrest were tests both for the survival of the United Nations and for the resolve of the Western, non-Communist world. Canada's direct involvement in both arenas necessarily committed it to a gradual expansion of its ties with countries of the Middle East. Diplomatic exchanges and representation increased; Canadian loan guarantees were extended to Israel with encouragement for the development of economic exchanges; the region continued to receive official government attention; and trade with all Middle East countries, while less than 2 per cent of the Canadian total, began to show steady growth except when interrupted by the Iranian crisis.

Within Canada, the first three years following recognition of Israel in 1949 saw a decline in the active public relations program that the UZC had developed in the earlier period. But on the assumption that Canadian Zionists had a right to exert influence on behalf of Israel and could do so more positively than Israeli representatives in many instances, the UZC's Public Relations Committee revised its activities in 1952 under the impetus of three catalysts. The first was the continuing existence of the many economic and political threats to Israel. Secondly, in that year two Arab journalists stationed in Canada began publishing damaging items and were seen as intent on creating a network of friendly pro-Arab groups.[16] And thirdly, by 1952 there had been a marked drop in contributions to the United Israel Appeal and the United Jewish Appeal.

Under the influence of the committee's new chairman, Professor Maxwell Cohen of McGill University, the new leadership recognized the need to maintain a "rational balance" between the interests of Jews in Canada and in Israel, and included in its mandate the task of advising the Israelis of activities seen as damaging to the Zionist cause. However, explicit priority was given to "the continued creation of a climate of Canadian opinion, favourable to the existence and development of the State of Israel." This injunction translated into the fourfold aim of maintaining a "generally sympathetic" or "non-antipathetic atmosphere" among Canadians as a whole, a "positive favourable approach on the part of the Federal government," obtaining "specific Governmental or public support for very concrete projects," and maintaining among Jews, as a stimulus for continued financial support, "a healthy appreciation of the specific role that Israel is capable of playing in a resettlement of Jews and the recreation of a specific kind of Jewish life in the Near East." The tasks requiring immediate attention were to secure Canadian loans, grants, trade concessions, and so forth for Israel, to develop a sympathetic view of Israel's role as a Middle Eastern state, to co-ordinate a policy on Arab refugees and the question of the holy places, to address the particular role of French-Canadian Catholic opinion, and to provide the basis for a co-ordinated response to the emergence of North American interest in the Islamic world.

The revival of activity proceeded steadily under the direction of a newly organized national executive and with professional staff located in Montreal, Toronto, and Ottawa. The Canada–Israel Association had induced J.A. Bradette, chairman of the external affairs committee and the Liberal caucus, to deliver pro-Israeli speeches across the country and to arrange for a number of members of Parliament to visit Israel and give speeches throughout Canada upon their return. In addition, the association continued, under instructions from the PRC, to counter an increasing number of anti-Israeli speeches and press items across the country. More directly, a joint delegation from UZC and the Canadian Jewish Congress (CJC) met Pearson on 19 January 1953 to urge action against growing Soviet anti-Semitism and especially against the sale of heavy arms and jet planes to Egypt by the United Kingdom. The delegation reported that Pearson provided "a sympathetic and understanding reception, and promised to do what might be possible within the framework of existing Canadian policy."[17]

By early 1955, the revived PRC program had reached maturity and was functioning as a matter of routine. Its agenda had become centred on obtaining Canadian support for Israel abroad, in the UN, and in regard to the major powers, on developing effective co-operation between the Jewish community and official Israeli representatives, on explaining the significance of Israeli foreign policy *vis-à-vis* Canada, and finally on discussing the "two-way responsibility" between Jews in Canada and those in Israel.

This five-year period following the recognition of the state of Israel and the signing of armistice agreements between the antagonists can be seen as a period of regional consolidation of position and interests. Canadian policy during this time, therefore, was reflective of broader global issues. Canada's involvement was still one of indirectness, determined more by external factors than any single concern. The extent to which domestic considerations functioned in the conduct of foreign policy was limited to increasing the awareness of parliamentary, governmental, and lay leadership and, from the Zionist point of view, trying to ensure the sympathy of such people to Israel's plight. While pro-Arab sympathies existed and were developed along the lines of the earlier period, organized appeals and participation by relevant groups were minimal and remained essentially in the hands of M.S. Massoud and the CAFL, whose efforts were effectively countered by the Zionist and pro-Israel associations and supporters. The problem of Cyprus was dealt with primarily through the mediation efforts of Great Britain, while Iran was contained within the shadows of East–West antagonism. Both issues remained on the periphery of special Canadian foreign policy and evoked little domestic concern.

From late 1955 onward, the Arab–Israeli conflict intensified, culminating in the Suez crisis of October and November 1956.[18] Egyptian President Gamal Abdel Nasser's decision to seek military assistance from the Soviet Union led to America's refusal to finance the High Aswan dam, Nasser's nationalization of the Suez Canal, a failed effort at diplomatic settlement, and ultimately, a French, British, and Israeli invasion of the Canal Zone. During this time of international tension, Canada became directly involved, less as a faithful ally of Great Britain than as an initiator of compromise and conciliation through the United Nations.

The months prior to the Suez crisis had included a period of heated debate within the House of Commons over the sale of military equipment to Egypt and Israel.[19] In 1954 and 1955, total sales to Israel amounted to $2 067 685, primarily for munitions, spare tank parts, and anti-aircraft guns, all considered defensive equipment. At the same time, sales to Egypt totalled only $771 121, but the bulk of the transaction was fifteen Harvard training planes, considered by many both in and out of official circles to be offensive weapons, violating the Canadian government's position on neutrality in the area and arguably introducing a new element that could harm Israel's position, especially when Egypt was also then receiving arms through Czechoslovakia.[20]

Pearson's position, in response to strong questions and criticism from both the Progressive Conservatives and the CCF, indicated that Canada, though not directly involved, was willing to assist in the achievement of a peaceful settlement, and that so long as countries were considered friendly to Canada, arms transfers would not come under the stringent Sino–Soviet bloc arms embargo. The criticisms by the opposition parties within the Commons were soon toned down when it became apparent that their call for the House "to express its strong disapproval of the government's policy of authorizing the shipment of munitions of war to countries in that area not within the NATO alliance" jeopardized Israel's ability to receive Canadian materials so vital to its survival.[21] The debate then turned to the issue of supplying Israel with the F-86 Sabre jet fighters it had asked to buy. In July, Diefenbaker raised the issue of the F-86s out of concern for Israel's survival and in the light of Nasser's attitude. The government announced, on 26 September, its agreement to supply the jets; on 29 October, with the Israeli invasion of the Sinai, that order was suspended.

The Canadian reaction to the invasion and to the British–French ultimatum of the following day was uniquely intense, serious, and widespread. As James Eayrs observed, "Public criticism tended to decry Sir Anthony Eden's decision to intervene; official opinion seems to have been more distressed by the failure of his Government to let its allies and Commonwealth associates know in advance what it was up to."[22] Yet as the crisis continued, the Conservative and Social Credit parties voiced support for the invasion. In contrast, the government argued that the appropriate place and vehicle for resolution was the United Nations.[23] Nevertheless, the government was placed in the difficult position of being tainted as too supportive of the U.S. position. With the conclusion of the crisis, the massive extent of Soviet support to Egypt became evident and confirmed in the minds of many that the British–French moves had been warranted. In the June 1957 federal elections, the defeat of the St. Laurent government by Diefenbaker and the Conservatives was, according to some, at least partially attributable to the PCs' effective use of the Liberal betrayal of Mother England.

This period of escalating Mideast tensions in the context of cold war stridency, from 1954 to 1956, moved the Zionist and pro-Israeli organizations in Canada to focus on what they saw as a specific, harmful shift in Canadian policy after the announcement of the Soviet arms sales. In November 1955, a delegation met with St. Laurent and the acting external affairs minister. Although the reception was "consistently sympathetic and, in some instances very friendly," and there remained a "sense of moral responsibility on the part of all political leaders to Israel and her safety," on the arms sales issue the disagreement remained.[24]

The primary concern of the UZC Public Relations Committee during this time was the question of Israel's need for arms, in particular, the F-86 Sabre jet fighters requested but not yet decided upon.[25] The PRC combined its resources with those of the Canadian Jewish Congress in a concerted effort to enlist Canadian public opinion in convincing the Canadian government that a favourable decision was necessary in the interests of peace in the Middle East, to prevent an escalation of conflict by maintaining an arms balance sufficient to offer a credible deterrent, and in support of Canada's national interests.

Following the prime minister's return from the Commonwealth Conference in London, PRC information suggested that the government was leaning towards an unfavourable decision on the jets. This brought the PRC–CJC leadership into an intense consultative relationship with Israeli Ambassador Michael Comay. At the same time, however, the PRC advocated a posture of quiet diplomacy and self-restraint in order to avoid harming the sensitive intergovernmental negotiating process. A major breakthrough occurred with "the shift in the position of the two major opposition parties to support for the sale of the jets," partially an outcome of continuous and intimate contacts with high officials of the government and with leaders of all political parties. By early summer, "it became evident that a continuance of the restraints on public action would no longer serve."

Hence, on both the national and regional levels, the entire public relations system was mobilized "to acquaint public opinion with the dangers inherent in allowing Israel to suffer an arms imbalance against her." Parliamentarians and editors for the daily press were inundated by letters from across the country in an effort to make the government acutely aware of the "Jewish enmity" on this question. By early July, it became obvious that, together with events occurring internationally, the public relations program was contributing to a decisive shift in the government's position. "It was learned authoritatively (and indicated in press reports) that only certain 'formalities' regarding supporting actions by Washington and London remained to be completed, and the Government would announce its favourable decision on the jet request." However, the nationalization of the Suez Canal on 26 July restrained the timing of the decision, so that by September the official Canadian position was to announce a favourable decision on the jets as soon as the Suez situation was " 'clarified'." During this period of uncertainty, the PRC maintained close personal contact with government and opposition leadership in order to ensure a final positive outcome. But with the outbreak of war on 29 October, the sale became a nonissue as Canada suspended all military shipments to the combatants.

The events from 26 July to 4 November 1956, when the Canadian draft resolution in the United Nations General Assembly concerning a UN peacekeeping force was passed, indicated in the sharpest of terms the transition that Canada was facing. While it still acknowledged a special historical relationship with both the United Kingdom and, to a lesser extent, France, Canada's position in international affairs was not identical with either. At the same time, this movement towards distinctiveness could not be seen as merely one towards a new status of a dominant American linkage; rather it indicated a position of commitment to UN-based multilateral internationalism, recogition of a role unique to Canada, as well as responsible obligation and participation in Western security arrangements.

The path followed by the government during this period of intense international concern stimulated, within the Canadian polity, both support and serious opposition. Though Pearson was soon to receive the Nobel Peace Prize for his efforts in settling the crisis, at the time he and the government were the targets of severe criticism, reproached for betrayal of England and for playing into the hands of Soviet designs. From Pearson's perspective it had been these very reasons—the necessity to provide for Anglo-American reconciliation and thereby prevent further Soviet advancement—as well as the immediate concern for peace that prompted the active Canadian diplomacy under the umbrella of the United Nations charter. The international accolades that Pearson and the Canadian government received were not enough to see them through the 10 June 1957 general election, however, which brought John Diefenbaker's Progressive Conservatives to power. Indeed these very accolades, the new prime minister noted, were "an element in the Liberal Party's loss. . . ."[26]

The 1947–1957 period thus reveals a strong pattern of emergence from extreme sensitivity to British policy in the Mackenzie King era to an increasingly active, initiatory diplomacy in the context of the Western alliance and the United Nations. It was a period in which international facts dominated Canadian policy, when decision making centred on key Cabinet ministers, and when vital issues stirred domestic debate both inside and outside Parliament. The two issues that stand out as being directly affected by lobbying efforts, the 1948 *de facto* recognition and the 1956 F-86 sale, were policies made primarily in consultation with allies and in the context of international concerns.

While there is little doubt that the activities of special interest groups did play a role in shaping public and parliamentary sympathies, it is evident that the government's decisions were based on careful political and diplomatic calculation in the broadest sense. The government's activities within the UN focused on achieving consensus and introducing negotiated agreement with widespread support, while at the same time preserving the interests of the Western alliance. Although the interests of the United Kingdom and the United States were necessarily important aspects of the calculus of decision, British interests no longer overrode broader Canadian concerns, while U.S. concerns were important as part of the bulwark against Communism as well as being fundamental to any successful operation of the United Nations. With the increase in direct Canadian involvement in the Middle East through the expansion of diplomatic representation, coupled with the investment of Canadian diplomatic, military, and economic resources in that area under the auspices of the UN, Canadian foreign policy under Prime Minister St. Laurent and external affairs minister Pearson, emerged dramatically from the quasi-isolationist posture of the Mackenzie King era into an active, internationalist stance predicated on a particular vision of commitment and responsibility to a new postwar order. By 1956, the predictions of the liberal-internationalist perspective reigned supreme.

The Consolidation of Liberal Internationalism, 1957–1963

If the Suez issue provided the bench-mark of Pearsonian internationalism in the Middle East, it also revealed the rather different attitude held by the Diefenbaker Conservatives. From the early debate on the sale of jet fighters to Israel, it was evident that Diefenbaker's inclinations were markedly different from those of the former secretary of state for external affairs. In outlining the Conservative government's policy on Suez and the United Nations Emergency Force at his first meeting with the press, the newly appointed foreign minister, Sidney Smith, was suddenly interrupted by Prime Minister Diefenbaker, who proceeded to provide a much different and far less generous account.[27] The incident signalled both the prime minister's suspicions of Pearsonian internationalism and his intention to have the dominant voice within his government on international politico-military and diplomatic affairs.

The extent to which Canadian foreign policy during these years focused on the Middle East was more an outgrowth of the St. Laurent–Pearson legacy than of any major new initiatives. Five main issue areas concerned the Canadian government, two dealing with the UN, two with the expansion of bilateral relations, and one with regional stability and great-power intervention. Because of Diefenbaker's personal involvement in foreign policy, these issues were addressed under the fundamental guiding assumptions of vigilance against Communist penetration, support for Israel, particular sensitivity to the opinions expressed by specific Canadian ethnic groups, and concern for balancing, on the one hand, Canada's historic relationship to Great Britain and the role of the United States *vis-à-vis* Canada and in the containment of Communism with, on the other hand, the strong, moralistic commitments to both the Commonwealth and the United Nations.

In July 1958, when the United States landed two Marine battalions in Lebanon to quell a domestic civil war and counter an intervention by the United Arab Republic that appeared Soviet-inspired, Diefenbaker's government offered strong support for American actions, as it did for the landing two days later of British forces in Jordan. "Canadian policy became directed to getting the United Nations into the Middle East, and thus helping the two Western powers to leave."[28] This response was congruent with Canada's preference for conflict resolution through UN mediation and, if necessary, peacekeeping forces. It also allowed Canada to play a leading role, not only because of its special relationship with the British and Americans but also because UNEF (along the Sinai and Gaza borders between Egypt and Israel), UNTSO (along the Israeli–Syrian and Israeli–Jordanian borders), and UNOGIL (established in May 1958 along the Lebanese frontier) all had substantial Canadian contingents.[29]

Canadian involvement in these quasi-military UN operations, although somewhat less dramatic than the crisis-ridden days of Suez, highlighted both domestically and internationally Canada's continued commitment to this essential multilateral function. It also made it quite natural for the prime minister, on his 1958 world tour, to talk about arms exports to Israel with British Prime Minister Harold Macmillan, about the Algerian situation to French President Charles de Gaulle, and about the consequences for the Middle East of an India–Pakistan war to Pakistani President Ayub Khan and Prime Minister Pandit Nehru of India. The question of refugees was also of great importance to Diefenbaker, in the broad moral context of the suffering caused by natural or artificial disaster; but also, more specifically, Diefenbaker was concerned with the functioning of UNRWA in the settlement of the Palestinian refugees of the 1948 war. The unusually large Canadian contribution to these operations was causing the government to examine the cost-effectiveness and burden-sharing arrangement within the peacekeeping and refugee branches of the United Nations.

While Canada continued its responsible participation within the United Nations, the Conservative government began the process of strengthening bilateral relations with specific countries of the Middle East. It upgraded diplomatic missions in Egypt, Lebanon, and Israel and appointed Canada's first resident ambassador to Israel, providing some balance to the ambassador who had been resident in Cairo since before the Suez crisis. The prime minister also hosted an official five-day visit from Israeli Prime Minister David Ben-Gurion in May 1961, when the two leaders discussed the problems of the region, the Canadian and UN roles, the expansion of Canadian interest in the area, and the two countries' foreign aid programs.[30]

Efforts to strengthen Canada–Middle East economic relations were also of concern, particularly since Canada faced a regional trade deficit because of oil imports. In 1957, Israel appointed a trade commissioner to its Montreal consulate and upgraded its economic staff with the 1958 exchange of resident ambassadors. The following year, Israel participated in a number of Canada-wide trade fairs, and by the end of 1959, Canada–Israel trade, although relatively minor compared with the oil flows, began to show substantial improvement. Over the next three years, Canada–Israel trade and investment was aided by both governmental and private initiative, as missions were upgraded and expanded and various financing arrangements negotiated. Prime Minister Diefenbaker's special sense of affinity with Israel and sensitivity to the needs of the Jewish people encouraged these economic relations, and he often overrode objections from DEA and ITC officers. The Canadian Jewish community was also very active in this area, often providing the initiative or acting as a catalyst for official government action.

Despite his personal commitment, Diefenbaker's predisposition to employ the Commonwealth framework as a means for expanding Canadian ties with the newly emerging states meant that much of the operational resources and initiatives of the relevant government departments bypassed the Mideast region. Even within the UN context, it was displaced by Diefenbaker's concern for disarmament, in which Canada took a leading role under the guidance of external affairs minister Howard Green. It was left to domestic groups, especially the Canadian Jewish community along with other Israel supporters, to inform and stimulate official Canadian interest towards the Middle East in anything other than crisis management or peacekeeping.

As in the St. Laurent period, the Public Relations Committee of the Zionist Organization of Canada continued to co-ordinate the pro-Israeli activities of most Jewish and, indirectly, many non-Jewish organizations. They focused their efforts on parliamentarians and other community leaders, a result of the perceived need to address a number of chronic but potentially explosive issues, such as Israel's right to navigate through the Suez Canal, Canadian policy towards Arab refugees, and the UN-based attempt by the Arab League States to reactivate the Palestine Conciliation Commission. Attention was also given to responding to an increase in anti-Israeli as well as anti-Semitic articles in Canadian newspapers and mass-circulation magazines, to the spin-offs of the Eichmann episode and trial, and to the increased activity of the Arab Information Centre in Ottawa, funded out of New York.[31]

The leadership of the various Canadian Zionist organizations felt the need to maintain a high level of commitment to Israel within Canadian Jewish communities, an increasingly difficult task as Israel became more stable and secure within the international arena. To this end, programs for expanding direct economic ties with Israel were undertaken, an effort that, under the leadership of Samuel Bronfman, contributed to the establishment of the Canada–Israel Development Corporation in 1960 and the creation of the Canada–Israel Chamber of Commerce in 1961. This private sector interest and substantial monetary commitment, coupled with the prime minister's own predilections, had much to do with his decision, with the support of ITC's George Hees and against the advice of external affairs minister Green, to establish a Canadian trade mission in Israel, followed soon thereafter by the extension of Canadian export credits.

The relatively short Conservative interlude, although coming at a time of high international tension, did little to alter in any significant way Canadian foreign policy towards the Middle East. The prime minister's strong interest in specific issues of international concern, combined with his personal sympathies towards the state of Israel, introduced a Middle East policy that, although more staunchly supportive of Israel's needs, continued in the internationalist tradition he inherited from St. Laurent and Pearson, in spite of his distrust of some senior External Affairs personnel. Yet during this period the seeds for bilateral economic involvement and multilateral diplomatic participation clearly were planted.

Liberal Internationalism Challenged, 1963–1968

With the election of Prime Minister Pearson's Liberal government in 1963, the traditional internationalist orientation returned as the explicit foundation of Canadian policy. However, despite the success of an initial application of peacekeeping in the Cyprus dispute of 1964 and a reaffirmation of its priority in the defence White Paper of the same year, financing debates at the United Nations and the apparent ineffectiveness of Canadian diplomacy in the 1967 Arab–Israeli war produced widespread disenchantment. Perhaps more importantly, the challenge presented by Quebec's activities in francophone Africa to the authority of the federal government in international affairs created a direct national interest that propelled the government to develop relations with Arab states in North Africa.

The growing conflict between Greek and Turkish communities in Cyprus in early 1964, which threatened to erupt in full-scale violence and draw in other powers, prompted Secretary of State for External Affairs Paul Martin to take the initiative at the United Nations to secure the formation of a peacekeeping force (UNICYP) for the island.[32] Despite doubts about the organization, financing, and administration of the force, Canada readily agreed to contribute a battalion and worked to secure the participation of states other than the United Kingdom, in order to endow the operation with a genuine multilateral character. Moreover, both its duty to the UN and its estimation of the dangers of escalation led it to dispatch its troops to the region immediately after UN approval.

Canada's doubts about UNICYP's financial structure were intensified in the 1965 UN controversy over members' contributions to peacekeeping operations.[33] Faced with the refusal of several members, notably France and the Soviet Union, to support ongoing operations through compulsory assessment, Canada and the United States sought to promote a solution to the growing financial crisis by threatening to deprive those in arrears of their right to vote. Canada chaired and participated in special committees exploring the problem, worked for compromise with the nonaligned nations over British and American reservations, made a special contribution, along with the United Kingdom, Sweden, and Norway, to keep the existing operations in force, and took the initiative to get a General Assembly resolution of the general problem. Although Canada's objectives centred on reinforcing the secretary general's administrative control over operations and securing the widest possible contributions from members on a compulsory basis, it reluctantly acceded to the growing consensus that obligations could be met through voluntary contributions.

Difficulties with peacekeeping were registered most poignantly for Canada in the 1967 Middle East War.[34] Despite its growing disenchantment with its UNEF involvement, Canada's assumption that the force promoted stability within the region and its reluctant acceptance of membership in the Security Council in 1967 had reinforced the government's belief in the legitimacy and value of the peacekeeping enterprise and made it a public defender of UNEF. It thus came as a particular shock when, in May 1967, President Nasser requested the withdrawal of the UNEF forces interposed between Israel and the United Arab Republic.

Although its fellow UNEF contributors, India and Yugoslavia, complied, Canada responded with a warning to Egypt against hasty action. Canada joined in a British and American request for a Security

Council session, then asked for a meeting of the General Assembly to override Secretary General U Thant's desire to withdraw. In the face of continued Egyptian accusations of a neo-imperialist conspiracy led by the United States, the United Kingdom, and Canada, the Canadian government encouraged such proposals as a transfer of UNEF to Israel, strengthening of the UNTSO force, and an unsuccessful Security Council resolution calling for restraint from the warring parties. Yet when President Nasser, prompted by a declaration from Lester Pearson and President Lyndon Johnson, demanded that the Canadian contingent be the first to withdraw from UNEF and do so within forty-eight hours, Canada, faced with an erosion of Indian and nonaligned support, reluctantly complied. Only after the end of hostilities did Canadian diplomacy regain a broader measure of international responsiveness. Such traditional Canadian actions as accepting refugees, providing humanitarian assistance, and promoting a special UN mission were joined by a shift towards a "European" position in UN voting and Canadian support for a Pakistani resolution calling on Israel to rescind its annexation of Jerusalem.

Equally important, the Pearson years also witnessed the first major effort to develop more direct, ongoing relations with individual Arab nations in the North African region. Propelled by the Quebec government's greater international presence in the mid-1960s, Canada had determined that its development assistance programs should constitute "an outward-looking expression of the bilingual character of Canada" and "contribute to our sense of internal unity and purpose."[35] Within this framework, it began to develop significant bilateral relationships with Tunisia, Algeria, and Morocco, through embassies, economic missions, and aid. Although operated for the distinctive national purpose of countering Quebec's assertiveness, confined to functional channels, and impotent in contrast to the alignments formed by the Arab–Israeli conflict, these ventures provided the foundation for a gradual broadening and alteration of Canadian conceptions of the dynamics of the region and its interest therein.

The growing frustrations experienced by Canada in its classic internationalist approaches through the United Nations were due in part to the slowness with which it responded to shifting alignments within the international system. The traditionally strong emphasis Canada gave to the views of the United Nations collectively and to the secretary general in particular were well reflected at the outset of this period. The evidence includes Canada's prompt agreement to a UN request for a UNICYP contribution, its refusal of a U.S. presidential request to dispatch the force before UN authorization and multilateral participation were assured, and its quest, in accordance with International Court of Justice and General Assembly views, to devise a financing framework for peacekeeping operations that enshrined members' institutional obligations and the secretary general's autonomy. However, Canada's major conflict with Secretary General U Thant during the 1967 war ended the twenty-year special relationship between Canada and the UN as an entity apart from its individual members.

A similar decline occurred in Canada's ingrained sensitivity to fellow members of the middle-power coalition. To be sure, Canada readily joined with Britain, Italy, the Scandinavian countries, Ireland, Nigeria, and Latin American countries in seeking an end to the financing controversy; ultimately it supported a Pakistani resolution on Jerusalem in 1967. Yet it opposed Algeria and the nonaligned states on this issue, continued its peacekeeping involvement despite the prospect of Indian and Yugoslav withdrawal, and found itself in diplomatic conflict with these states, other nonaligned states, and the Arab world during the 1967 war. Its growing isolation was further highlighted by its differences with France on the financing issue, with Italy on Security Council membership, and even with the United States and Israel on the 1967 conflict. Only at the end of the period was this divergence stemmed by Canada's shift to a European stance over the diplomatic issues at the conclusion of the war.

In many ways, the difficulties experienced with external actors stemmed from the growing activity, salience, and divergent views of societal organizations. Although Parliament had not authorized Canadian participation in UNICYP before the troops were sent to the region, it provided a forum for the major opposition parties to criticize the United Nations, the government's management of the relevant issues, the external reception of Canada's peacekeeping role, and, somewhat paradoxically, the government's refusal to provide solid support for Israel's position. Complaints on this subject were found in the daily press, which was virtually unanimous in its pro-Israeli views on the war, and among the public, whose mail to the prime minister was overwhelmingly supportive of Israel.[36]

It also reflected, to a lesser degree, the work of major Jewish organizations within Canada. Led by the Joint Public Relations Committee and the Canada–Israel Association, the Jewish community had quickly forged links with Prime Minister Pearson and his ministers, continued their annual briefings and, partly on the basis of consultations with Israeli government representatives, made representations on specific issues. However, their effectiveness was increasingly circumscribed by internal divergences over tactics, by initiatives taken by DEA officials, and by the attitude of Pearson and Paul Martin, who were seen as taking "a much more reserved approach to Israel than Diefenbaker or Green ever did."[37]

A further constraint on Canadian behaviour, which did much to cause inflexibility in its diplomacy, was the divisions that emerged within the executive branch. Although Pearson tended to leave Middle East matters to Martin and the DEA professionals, Pearson's own stature as an international leader, growing doubts within Ottawa over the peacekeeping mission, and the divergent views between Pearson and Martin began to have an effect. Thus Martin was able to secure a reaffirmation of a full-scale UNEF contribution in 1966, Canadian membership on the Security Council in 1967, and a statement of Canada's continued acceptance of peacekeeping involvements following the 1967 war only over the opposition of the Department of National Defence, Secretary to the Cabinet Gordon Robertson, and Pearson himself. A more permanent cleavage also arose between Pearson and Martin, on the one hand, who as politicians in a minority government were more responsive to Jewish representations on behalf of Israel, and senior officials in External Affairs, on the other hand, who had wanted a strict neutrality between Arabs and Israelis before the 1967 conflict for fear that Nasser would demand the withdrawal of Canadian forces in UNEF.

By the end of Pearson's tenure as prime minister, the vigour of Canada's internationalist orientation had been undermined. At the UN, Canada suffered from frustrations over peacekeeping, the politicization of the specialized agencies, and the divergence of its traditional middle-power friends. At the same time, new forces within the Canadian government and society were beginning to challenge the conventional understanding of Canadian diplomacy, by expressing more direct interests in the broadening of relations with the Middle East region beyond the narrowly defined concerns of the Arab–Israeli conflict. Liberal internationalism was being confronted and challenged by the convergence of emerging societal and governmental interests and by a broader range of realities in the external environment.

The Decline of Liberal Internationalism, 1968–1973

The strains that had developed in Canadian policy towards the Middle East during the Pearson years reflected a much broader effort to redefine Canada's approach to international affairs in the globe as a whole. Middle Eastern issues themselves were neither a direct component of this quest for redefinition nor a particularly active aspect of Canadian foreign policy until the end of the 1968–1972 period. Yet the philosophy espoused by the newly elected prime minister, Pierre Trudeau, as codified in *Foreign Policy for Canadians,* had a clear impact on Canadian behaviour in the region.[38]

In particular, the stress on national interest, economic growth, and the need for counterweights was manifested in Canada's new reluctance to assume a prominent role in UN efforts to resolve the Arab–Israeli dispute, its efforts to develop economic ties with major states on the periphery of the region, and its restrained approach to the dilemmas created by the 1973 war and accompanying oil embargo. Its general orientation towards Middle East affairs was best summarized by

Secretary of State for External Affairs Mitchell Sharp, who noted that while Canada's Middle Eastern policy had "largely found expression through the United Nations," there were "great trading opportunities, particularly with Iran and Israel and . . . the United Arab Republic."[39]

At the United Nations, Canada continued to pursue a deliberate even-handed approach. Yet its reduced commitment to the traditional mediatory roles was seen in its emphasis on supporting the efforts of the big four to foster peace in the region, Sharp's disavowal of an "honest broker" role for Canada in his trip there, and the government's establishment of firm conditions for its future participation in peacekeeping operations. At the same time, the legacy of past orientations was evident in Canada's statements, as early as May 1973, that it would consider participating in a new truce supervisory force.

The more active pole of Canadian policy was the expansion of the bilateral economic co-operation that had begun in the previous period.[40] Co-operation with Israel remained largely ceremonial and functional in nature. Despite Sharp's visit to Iran and Egypt and a Canada–Iran agreement to facilitate joint ventures, Canada's priority partner in the Arab region remained Tunisia. Here a joint commission was established after a 1968 summit visit, and CIDA loans were granted to the country. And in Algeria, a Canadian embassy was opened in 1971, a long-term wheat agreement concluded, and CIDA aid disbursed.

These new relationships with Arab states had no major effect on Canadian behaviour during the 1973 Arab–Israeli war and oil embargo.[41] Guided largely by precepts of the past, Canada responded to the hostilities by requesting a cease-fire and the submission of the dispute to the UN. Later it stated its willingness to contribute to a peacekeeping force, sought to secure Canadian participation in any proposed operation, and agreed, when asked by the secretary general, to join for an initial six-month period under a fairly stringent set of conditions. Somewhat less successful was its effort to avoid the Arab oil embargo announced at the same time. Only with its subsequent opening of an embassy in Saudi Arabia did Canada begin to develop the contact required for a more fully sensitive appreciation of the Middle East.

The reduced vigour of Canadian activity at the United Nations and the somewhat functional nature of its bilateral involvements reflected the decreasing prominence of external factors in Canadian calculations. Although Canada continued to support the secretary general, it left the initiative more and more to the big four. While the visits of Israeli Prime Minister Golda Meir and Foreign Minister Abba Eban reflected the special importance Canada accorded to Israeli views, the pattern of Mitchell Sharp's meetings with Middle East leaders suggested the adoption of a broader and more balanced perspective. Moreover, Canada's concentration on fostering stable relations with Algeria and Tunisia, Mitchell Sharp's meetings with the respresentatives of Egypt,

Iran, Lebanon, Morocco, Algeria, and Tunisia during the 1973 war, and the subsequent expansion of representation in the Middle East indicated a slowly growing interest in Arab views.

The diminishing salience and broadening relevance of international factors allowed for a considerably greater role for domestic actions, especially from organized interest groups and the public. Within Parliament, the Conservatives and the NDP joined the government in affirming Israel's right to exist and in Canada's continued peacekeeping involvement. In an active debate over the 1973 war, they confined their criticisms of government actions to Canada's presumed deference to Egyptian demands for an inspection of the Canadian peacekeeping contribution and the government's apparent ignorance of the Arab oil embargo directed against it. Similarly, the press continued to voice strong pro-Israeli positions, although, led by the Toronto *Globe and Mail,* it raised several critical questions about Canada's peacekeeping involvement in 1973.[42]

It was among organized interest groups that a broader debate first began to appear. The Jewish community intensified its standard array of activities. Its views, however, received their first effective counter in an ultimately unsuccessful effort by the editor of the United Church *Observer,* the Reverend A.C. Forrest, to highlight the alleged pro-Zionist bias of the Canadian press through the pages of his publication and in his testimony before the Senate Special Committee on Mass Media. More importantly, the Arab community in Canada developed a much greater level of organization, activity, and effectiveness with other groups. Through such major vehicles as the Canadian Arab Federation and the Federation of Arab Societies in Canada, it urged Mitchell Sharp to include the Middle East in Canada's foreign policy review and called for greater restrictions on the Jewish community's financial support of Israel. More importantly, it attracted more sympathetic support from Parti Québécois leader René Lévesque and leaders of the Confederation of National Trade Unions in Quebec. Indeed it joined with the CNTU to meet Palestinian leaders in a tour of the Middle East.

In contrast to this societal diversity, the government's executive branch approached Middle East issues with a new coherence, grounded in an altered conception of its central foreign policy interests. Although the government's foreign policy review contained no separate treatment of Canadian relations with the region, its de-emphasis of Canada's role as a "helpful fixer" and the priority it assigned to economic growth provided clear referents for all ministers and officials to follow. Furthermore, while foreign minister Mitchell Sharp continued to offer leadership on all diplomatic and UN-related questions, the review's stress on the many themes affecting policy outcomes, and the collegial style of decision making favoured by Prime Minister Trudeau, increasingly legitimized the involvement in Middle East affairs of other ministers, notably those from Industry, Trade and Commerce and Manpower and Immigration. These formative years of the Trudeau era established the foundations upon which Canada began a concerted move towards expanding direct interests, involvements, and bilateral relations with Middle East countries beyond the context of the Arab–Israeli conflict.

The Emergence of Complex Neo-Realism, 1974–1982

Following the shocks of 1973–1974, Canada's policy underwent several major shifts. In the sphere of global peace and security, Canada moved slowly away from the pursuit of compromise, stability, and institutional development that had long characterized its behaviour in the United Nations. Closer to home, the government proved capable of withstanding the pressure presented directly by domestic Jewish groups and indirectly by American example; it also defined its position on hosting UN conferences and on the Arab boycott of Israel on the basis of broader national interests.

The strongest expression of the new approach came in the government's creation of an overall policy of strengthening relations with all states in the Middle East region, development of new bilateral relationships promoting Canadian economic interests, and modification of Canada's traditional arms export policy in accordance with these objectives. The depth and durability of these trends were reflected in the 1979 controversy over moving the Canadian embassy in Israel to Jerusalem, where the government initiated a unilateral action designed partly to fulfill widely shared systemic interests and ultimately deferred to its direct national interests at home and within the region itself.

Canada's reconsideration of its behaviour at the UN began with the classic expression of internationalism: peacekeeping.[43] Although Canada accepted the revised arrangements for financing peacekeeping forces and extended its participation in UNEF and the UN Disengagement Observer Force (UNDOF), it gave growing emphasis to its views that peacekeeping merely preserved an uneasy *status quo* in the absence of negotiations among the parties directly concerned. It further stressed its demand that the conflicting parties work towards a comprehensive settlement, its condition that Canadian participation required the consent of all parties, and its emerging justification of the value of peacekeeping in facilitating the creation of co-operative bilateral relationships in the economic sphere. This growing skepticism culminated in 1978 when, to the surprise of its major allies, Canada hesitated before joining the United Nations Force in Lebanon (UNIFIL) and withdrew its forces after a short term of only six months.

A somewhat more complex evolution occurred in Canada's diplomatic activity at the UN and, in particular, in its votes on the crucial question of Palestinian rights and representation. In a Cabinet document, the government declared its intention of pursuing a policy of objectivity and balance in its comments and actions regarding this issue.[44] In practice, this meant that Canada, like numerous other international actors, moved slowly towards a greater recognition of the collective rights of the Palestinians and of the role of the PLO as their legitimate representative, outside the rigidly balanced framework of obligations in Resolution 242 and the approval of all parties to the conflict.[45]

Canada began the period by requesting the postponement of the 1975 UN Crime Congress with PLO representation, which it was to host in Toronto, and by abstaining on or opposing UN resolutions that affirmed the rights of the Palestinian people to independence and sovereignty, granted the PLO permanent observer status, and linked racism with Zionism. However, in 1976, it hosted Habitat, a UN conference on human settlements, with PLO representation. In 1974, it began to approve or abstain on measures favouring PLO participation in UN bodies not exclusively intergovernmental in character; on other crucial votes, it abstained or shifted its voting alignment away from Israel and the United States and towards Europe.[46] And despite Canada's appearances in the late 1970s in coalitions with Israel containing as few as four members, by 1980 its position was sufficiently flexible to cause anxiety and action on the part of Jewish organizations within Canada.

Of greater importance than Canada's revised multilateralism was the development of its first comprehensive policy towards the Middle East as a distinct region. A Cabinet decision developed in the autumn of 1975 and approved by full Cabinet in February 1976 stated Canada's desire to engage in trade and economic co-operation with all states in the region.[47] In keeping with this emphasis, Secretary of State for External Affairs Allan MacEachen toured the Middle East in January 1976. Building upon the strengthening of Canada's diplomatic relations with Saudi Arabia, Iraq, Jordan, Bahrain, Qatar, and the Emirates during the preceding two years and upon the work of a Canada–Iran joint commission established by his colleague in ITC during an April 1974 visit, MacEachen stressed the importance of moving beyond the Arab "forest" to deal with the individual state "trees". He also provided aid to Egypt and established a Canada–Saudi Arabia Joint Commission.[48] Under the impact of these initiatives and SSEA Don Jamieson's visit to the Middle East in October 1977, Canadian trade with the region rapidly expanded and increased.

The significance of these initiatives was highlighted by the government's willingness to adjust its traditional multilateral approach to economic exchange in a way that sustained these flows. In 1978, it conducted a review of its policy on the export of military-related equipment. While reaffirming a restrictive approach, this review placed additional demands on those opposing such sales and led to a more accommodating response to those with prospective contracts in specific cases. More significantly, the government repeatedly resisted demands for legislation to counter the Arab boycott of Israel. However, under the considerable pressure of prior Ontario and U.S. legislative actions as well as the impending federal election, the federal government did introduce reporting requirements. And it partially yielded to domestic demands with a promise to introduce antiboycott legislation.[49]

In many ways, Canada's shifting multilateralism, growing unilateral initiatives, and developing bilateral economic relations were seen most clearly in the Clark government's actions over the issue of moving the Canadian embassy in Israel from Tel Aviv to Jerusalem.[50] Canada's interest in a comprehensive peace settlement in the Middle East, combined with expanding relationships with Arab states, led Prime Minister Trudeau to refuse Israeli Prime Minister Menachem Begin's request for Canada to move its embassy during Begin's visit to Canada in November 1978. However, a major shift in Canadian policy towards Israeli positions and a response to domestic pressures were reflected in Prime Minister Joe Clark's promise in June 1979 to undertake such a move. This decision also represented a new willingness to engage in unilateral action to further both the peace process itself and Canada's relationships in the region. Clark's subsequent decision against a move of the embassy underscored this attitude.

The initial determinants of these substantial shifts in Canadian policy came from the broader range of states acquiring relevance to Canada, the shift in government attention from the United States and Israel to major European powers and specific Arab states in the region, and the freedom that this altered vision allowed. Within the United Nations, it was the growing strength and legitimacy of Arab and Third World state views, rather than those of Canada's traditional allies or of the secretariat and the organization itself, that defined the consensus to which Canada increasingly, if slowly, responded. The diminishing impact of the United States, both directly and indirectly, was seen in the failure of its antiboycott legislation to inspire similar Canadian action, American surprise at Canada's reluctance to accept ongoing UNIFIL obligations, and Canada's UN voting record. It was further evident in the restrained reaction of the United States to Prime Minister Clark's announcement of the Jerusalem embassy move. Indeed U.S. leaders deliberately confined their response to a conversation between Secretary of State Cyrus Vance and External Affairs Minister Flora MacDonald at the United Nations, designed to provide information on American concerns about the implications and hence to strengthen MacDonald's position in the internal Canadian government debate.[51]

Helping to moderate American influence was the increasing importance Canada attached to major European states. Their positions were considered and their views canvassed on the Arab boycott and Jerusalem embassy questions. Their votes at the United Nations showed a position that Canada found more compatible with its own. Of greatest importance, however, was the more sensitive understanding Canada developed of the views of individual Arab states, through its expanding network of bilateral ties. The representations that Arab states made on the antiboycott issue through the Arab League Information Office in Ottawa were insufficiently focused and too early to affect Canadian actions. Yet the vigorous, widespread criticism by Arab states on the proposed transfer of the embassy to Jerusalem helped secure a rapid shift in the government's policy.

To an increasing degree after 1973, Middle East questions also became the subject of a well-developed, ongoing, and more balanced debate among a broad range of organizations within Canada. These developments were first evident in the activities of Parliament and the federal parties. As reflected in ongoing debates, question period, comments in committee, and Parliament's unanimous approval of a 1975 resolution introduced by John Diefenbaker condemning the United Nations linkage of racism and Zionism, all major parties were consistently more supportive of Israel than the government itself. The NDP tended to be the most firm and vocal, followed by the Progressive Conservatives. Together with Herb Gray of the Liberal Party, the spokespersons of these parties pressed to refuse entry to PLO representatives for the 1975 crime congress, praised the decision to postpone Canada's hosting of the congress, and sought the rapid introduction of strong legislation, similar to that in the U.S., prohibiting compliance with the Arab boycott. The more moderate position of the Liberal Party as a whole was accounted for in large measure by the split within their parliamentary caucus between anglophone members, who were inclined to be supportive of Israel, and francophone representatives, who had greater and more active sympathy for the Palestinian position. Partly because of these variations, the general parliamentary consensus limited but did not determine the direction of government policy. The exceptions were those instances, such as the 1978 introduction of a strong antiboycott policy, where the imminence of a close election allowed the parties, as transmitters of other interests, a more salient if brief influence on Cabinet calculations.

Although the press and the public also continued to demonstrate a sympathetic understanding of the Israeli government's position during this period, its views were by no means stable nor sufficiently unanimous to reliably affect Canadian policy. The government's postponement of the crime congress received the strong disapproval of Canada's largest daily, the Toronto *Star*. Even the linkage of Zionism with racism produced a fairly even division of opinion among respondents to a poll by the Canadian Institute of Public Opinion, and a large segment who professed no knowledge of the issue.[52] The virtually unanimous support of the Canadian press for strong federal antiboycott measures and the prominence the daily press gave to news items on the issue were factors in Cabinet deliberations on the subject. However, on the Jerusalem embassy issue, the press, with the exception of a somewhat more cautious Montreal *Star* and Montreal *Gazette*, strongly opposed a move of the embassy and gave full attention to the criticism of this action voiced by governments abroad.

As press views became more complex, the Canadian Jewish community, led by the Canada-Israel Committee (CIC) and its sponsoring organizations—the Canadian Zionist Federation, the Canadian Jewish Congress, and the B'nai Brith—found its freedom of action somewhat more circumscribed. The CIC had the advantage of a growing and skilled professional staff and close contacts and information exchanges with such bodies as the Canada-Middle East Trade Council, corresponding organizations in the U.S., the Israeli government, and the Israeli embassy in Ottawa. Its primary resource, however, was the immediate access it had to MPs, media, and influential citizens across Canada through its own committee structure, the eighteen organizations in the CZF and other sponsors, and Jewish citizens throughout Canada, especially the ten thousand members of Canadian Zionist organizations and the hundred and fifty thousand Jewish citizens in the province of Ontario.[53] And within Ottawa, CIC professionals, with systematic expert information, a reputation for reasonableness, and a sophisticated knowledge of Ottawa's decision-making process, were able to maintain ongoing communication with responsible officials in DEA.

The greatest success of the Jewish community came over the 1975 UN crime congress issue. A meeting of representatives of Jewish organizations with the secretary of state for external affairs the day before a crucial Cabinet meeting, the careful consideration given by MacEachen to the views expressed in a letter from the CIC's national director, the fear of massive demonstrations and legal action by Jewish organizations, and the electoral sensitivities and official position of the Ontario government helped lead to a postponement of the congress in Toronto, contrary to the recommendation from External Affairs. However, despite the widespread distaste for a UN resolution linking racism with Zionism, the forceful views expressed at an emergency National Jewish Leadership Conference in Ottawa, and the supportive actions of the Vancouver City Council, the government proceeded to host the UN Conference on Human Settlements the following year.

Elsewhere, the Canadian Jewish community succeeded in raising and keeping the issue of antiboycott action in the press and in Parliament, slowly moving the government towards a more restrictive stance. With the examples of American and Ontario legislation, the imminence of a close federal election, letter-writing campaigns and petitions in Montreal and Toronto, and close contacts with sympathetic Cabinet ministers, the CIC was able to produce a promise of antiboycott legislation from John

Roberts and Barney Danson and to start lengthy discussion with ITC officials over the contents of the proposed bill.

Similarly, the expectation that the federal election would be decided in Ontario enabled the CIC to create an atmosphere in which Joe Clark, prompted by prominent individual Jewish citizens, declared his support for an embassy move during the campaign and affirmed the policy as prime minister. However, in the face of the resulting domestic and international criticism, the CIC proved unable, and indeed unwilling, to prevent the appointment of the Stanfield mission and the acceptance of his report.

In some measure, the limited success of the Jewish community was due to the emergence within Canada of Arab organizations somewhat more effective than in previous periods. The Canadian Arab community operated through organizations perceived to be much less effective than their Jewish counterparts, and it was beset by internal divisions, such as those caused by Lebanese Maronites and various Islamic sects. Its primary constituency was only about nineteen thousand Arabs, backed by a hundred thousand Canadian Muslims, of whom sixty thousand resided in Ontario.[54] Its primary organization, the Canadian Arab Federation, warning of its ability to disrupt Canadian-Arab business and, supported by the Quebec-Palestine Association, succeeded in securing a meeting with Allan MacEachen during the crime congress controversy and sent numerous letters and telegrams on the Jerusalem embassy question. With organizations such as the Canadian-Palestine Committee, the Arab-Canada Chamber of Commerce, and the Council of Muslim Communities of Canada, it was also active on the boycott issue. However, only on such relatively nonpolitical issues as the admission into Canada of Lebanese nationals at the time of the 1975-1976 civil war in Lebanon did the Arab community have a discernible direct impact on Canadian action.

A somewhat greater constraint on both Jewish community influence and Canadian government action came from the growing involvement of provincial governments. The Ontario government's initiative and participation in the aborted arrangements to host the crime congress and its unanimous resolution condemning the UN linkage of racism and Zionism helped sustain federal government predispositions. Moreover, the Ontario government's firm antiboycott policy and its subsequent enactment of legislation were substantial determinants of proposed federal government action on the boycott issue. However, the growing interest of the other provinces—the three western provinces and Quebec, in particular—in trade and financial relationships with the Middle East and the representations made by the Quebec government on behalf of its business community active in the Middle East had an important offsetting effect on the Arab boycott and Jerusalem embassy issues respectively.[55]

Perhaps the most potent societal influence as the period progressed came from a relatively new source: the Canadian business community. The focused quest of Canada's service industries and high technology manufacturers for exports, together with macroeconomic and regional development considerations, prompted the government to adopt a less restrictive approach to military-related exports in 1978. In contrast, given the internal divisions and the preference for discretion and moderation of the business community, the Canadian Manufacturers Association's opposition to antiboycott legislation had no major effect on the Ontario government's decision to proceed along these lines. However, the government's concern with the possibility of a concerted public media campaign, mounted by the business community and focused on the principle of government interference in the private sector, was an important factor in the federal government's reluctance to proceed with similar legislation.[56] Public criticism and numerous private communications to DEA and ITC over the Jerusalem embassy move from Canadian exporters, banks, and other commercial interests also helped prompt the government to appoint the Stanfield mission and accept its conclusions.

A similar trend towards wide-ranging involvement, balanced debates, shifting priorities, and greater influence took place within the executive branch. These trends were first visible on issues within the traditional UN framework of Canadian diplomacy. Cabinet had routinely approved at an early stage Canada's hosting of the crime congress and had established within the Ministry of the Solicitor General (MSG) a normal secretariat to deal with implementation. But Cabinet's involvement increased rapidly as the questions of attendance by PLO observers prompted conflicting advice and intense debate among officials from MSG, the RCMP, Justice, and particularly Manpower and Immigration, as well as among the UN, legal, and consular divisions of DEA and very senior government officials. The conflict among these officials and their failure, under DEA's guidance, to produce recommendations acceptable to Cabinet led to a highly unstructured, Cabinet-dominated process. Officials produced more than a dozen draft memoranda and Cabinet itself debated the issue on six occasions, finally producing a decision that did not coincide with the recommendations forwarded by officials through DEA.

Somewhat similarly, the issue of PLO attendance at the Habitat conference also reached the Cabinet or the prime minister through External Affairs on at least four occasions. Significantly, however, it led the prime minister, determined to prevent a repetition of the unstructured process on the crime congress issue, to intervene personally, ordering a fusion of the two responsible co-ordinative centres in DEA and the Ministry of State for Urban Affairs. By putting representatives of the two bodies on an equal footing, clarifying reporting relationships to Cabinet, and fostering the orderly presentation of a firm, functionally grounded recommendation to Cabinet, this move reduced the scope for some ministers' domestic political considerations to influence unpredictably the Cabinet's final decision.

Issues of high politics at the UN also attracted the regular involvement of the prime minister and Cabinet ministers, but with a stronger reliance on the advice and official-level co-ordinative centrality of External Affairs. Through External Affairs, Canada strongly supported the initiative of Egyptian President Anwar Sadat that culminated in the Camp David accords, by having Trudeau and Jamieson send a letter to Begin and Sadat, by pointing out to Israel and Egypt areas, such as the West Bank settlements, where their actions were unhelpful, and by maintaining an open and active dialogue with American officials and states in the region. More generally, the need for careful handling and consideration of significant nuances led the external affairs minister to instruct Canada's UN delegation personally on all Middle East issues.

On peacekeeping issues, the professional calculations of the minister of national defence and the general orientation of the prime minister were the decisive influences. Partly in response to the growing disagreements between an increasingly reluctant DND and a still-committed DEA, recommendations suggesting renewal of Canada's participation in UNEF and UNICYP were regularly sent to Cabinet from 1974 to 1977. However, an intensification of these departmental disagreements over the question of a contribution to UNIFIL propelled the issue further upward. It received the close personal attention of the prime minister and occasioned a meeting among Prime Minister Trudeau, Secretary of State for External Affairs Jamieson, Minister of National Defence Danson, and the vice-chief of the defence staff, unusual because military personnel are not normally involved in such events.

Although the defence minister, as a political leader from Canada's Jewish community, was concerned about the domestic dimension, his position was guided by the unanimous advice of his officials and everyone's serious reservations about the force's conception, terms of reference, command structure, prospects for success, and particular demands on Canada's military establishment. He thus successfully insisted, against a somewhat hesitant prime minister and external affairs minister, that the British and Australians assume the commitment, that Canada enter for only six months, and that other demands on DND be set aside for this period. Only the prime minister's intervention, after a phone call from UN secretary general Kurt Waldheim, ensured that Canada joined the force at all.

The increased influence of other departments, External's new orientation, and the shifting Cabinet and prime ministerial consensus were even more pronounced on economic matters. This began in the autumn of 1975, when a memorandum proposing strengthened bilateral relations with *all* states in the Middle East was prepared with heavy contributions from the economic ministers and DEA's economic divisions and considered in Cabinet committee. It was Secretary of State for External Affairs MacEachen who, after ministerial consultation, decided in 1976 to establish a joint committee with Israel as a symbolic gesture. But his department supported ITC's quest to secure a "fair share" of the new Arab oil dollar markets through participation in trade fairs and acceded to ITC's demand that the trade commissioner resources withdrawn from South Africa be used to open a trade post in Kuwait.

A similar transition took place over the more difficult question of arms exports. Here DEA had traditionally taken the lead in defining overall policy, joined with DND to control the advice to Cabinet on specific cases, and generally sustained a restrictive policy over the competing and more complex claims of ITC, Supply and Services, and the Export Development Corporation. In the spring of 1978, however, a government review of arms export policy added the minister of ITC to the group that had to be consulted before a decision was made. The impact of this altered procedure was registered in several cases, notably one dealt with in full Cabinet in which the minister of ITC, supported by the minister of DND, overcame Don Jamieson's initial reluctance to authorize a sale in the event of a successful Canadian bid.

The tensions produced by the new configuration of influence were registered most directly in the debate over measures to counter the Arab boycott in 1978. Before 1978, the management of this issue had been confined to officials and ministers in ITC, DEA, Finance, and EDC, who had easily reconciled their objectives of securing maximum Canadian exports without accepting the extraterritorial application of foreign laws or provoking a domestic political debate. In 1978, however, the issue became the subject of interdepartmental political co-ordination and Privy Council Office (PCO) involvement, the most active item in the Cabinet Committee on External Policy and Defence, and, ultimately, the subject of intense discussion in full Cabinet. At the Cabinet level, advocacy for a strong antiboycott policy came from John Roberts, Barney Danson, and ministers from constituencies with large Jewish populations in Toronto, Vancouver, and Montreal. The opposition was led by Allan MacEachen and Don Jamieson, and included Jean Chrétien, other economic ministers, and those Quebec ministers aware that most of the Middle East export business from their province went to the Arab world. Although the prime minister, in keeping with his general approach in Cabinet, attempted to remain neutral, his resentment at being pressured by the Jewish community—a resentment reinforced by the substantive arguments advanced by DEA—led him to express opposition to strong antiboycott measures and force the formulation of a compromise policy.

The strength of new departmental priorities, the professional judgements of External Affairs, and the prime minister's broader conceptions were tested most severely, and ultimately sustained most convincingly, in the government's debate over the movement of the Canadian embassy in Israel from Tel Aviv to Jerusalem. Trudeau refused to respond to the urgings of Israeli Prime Minister Menachem Begin on his state visit to Canada in November 1978 and to the similar urgings of close associates, who were sensitive to Trudeau's worsening domestic political situation and anxious to reward an Israeli prime minister who had come so far in furthering the peace process. Similarly, opposition leader Joe Clark, on his tour of Israel in January 1979, had abided by the advice of U.S. officials, DEA, and the Canadian ambassador to Israel, rather than that of the personal advisers and the candidates who accompanied him, in rejecting Prime Minister Begin's request for a move.

Joe Clark's promise to move the embassy, issued immediately before his meeting with the Canada-Israel Committee during the 1979 campaign, was made personally and individually. It was made partly on the basis of Clark's calculations of Conservative electoral fortunes in southern Ontario and in those Toronto ridings with large Jewish populations, following the favourable views of his closest political advisers, and despite the opposition of other Conservative strategists and candidates. His decision to implement this promise immediately upon assuming office as prime minister was also made personally, over the objections expressed in a DEA-PCO briefing paper and by his external affairs minister, Flora MacDonald. However, the decision itself, the supporting advice given immediately prior to its announcement in a note from Clark's personal adviser Lowell Murray, and the context of its announcement were grounded in the more general procedural issues. These included firm prime ministerial control over the civil service and the need to implement electoral promises, to demonstrate determined leadership to the party and public, and to follow a presumed electoral mandate to undertake fundamental change. Moreover, the policy itself stemmed partly from a personal belief on the part of the prime minister that such an initiative would help remove the paralysis in Middle East negotiations, further the Camp David peace process, and permit Canada to take some further balancing moves in favour of the Palestinian cause.[57]

However, Clark soon became convinced of the need to alter the firm promise he had made. This shift was aided by the assessments he had received from the PCO, by Flora MacDonald's conviction that some change was required to reduce the disruption to her department, and by the virtually unanimous views of officials in DEA and elsewhere in the government. After consideration at senior levels of DEA, MacDonald and her closest associates, together with the responsible experts in her department, developed the idea of appointing a mission to secure a report. The prime minister accepted the idea and her subsequent suggestion that Robert Stanfield be named to head the mission. Moreover, on the advice of her closest associates and departmental experts, she also intervened to secure the prime minister's agreement to an important and not unanimously supported change in the Stanfield mission's terms of reference. When Robert Stanfield wrote his October letter suggesting the embassy not be moved, it was the prime minister who, after consulting with his political staff, decided to accept this recommendation and publicly announced his decision in Parliament.

On 18 February 1980, the Conservative government of Prime Minister Clark was defeated in the federal election called over its proposed budget. The return of the Trudeau Liberals brought back a prime minister intent on constitutional reform and economic recovery.[58]

To support the priority of economic recovery, the Trudeau government pursued an active agenda of high-level visits to the Gulf states, Egypt, and Iraq, as well as Israel. Trade missions from provincial governments, especially Alberta, Ontario, and Quebec, including senior representatives from the business community, toured much of the Middle East. Major contracts were signed, often with the assistance of ITC, CIDA, and EDC. Formal meetings of joint bilateral organizations were held with the Israelis, the Tunisians, and the Saudis. Aid programs with Tunisia and Egypt were either renewed or enhanced, and new initiatives were sought. A new resident embassy in Jordan enhanced still further Canada's expanding interests in the area.

These economic initiatives received support from the top. Senior Cabinet officials travelled widely throughout the Middle East and other LDCs, and Prime Minister Trudeau visited a number of countries himself, including Saudi Arabia. Canada also successfully negotiated increased Saudi participation within the International Monetary Fund, and secured a $300-million, 5-year loan to aid the Canadian balance of payments. At the same time, Canada balanced these initiatives towards the Arab world with continuous support for the Camp David peace process, with the furthering of economic ties with Israel through visits by federal and provincial ministers (including delegations from Alberta and Quebec), by negotiations over aid programs with Egypt, and with an innovative trilateral aid scheme with Canadian money, through CIDA, and Israeli technology joining together in co-operative ventures with Third World countries.

The active pursuit of autonomous bilateralism was advanced still further by the Canadian decision to decline an American invitation to participate in the U.S.-sponsored Sinai force. Although the force was part of the Camp David accords, which Canada supported, the Canadian position reflected a concern over non-UN sponsorship, a recognition that an American-directed initiative could create political difficulties in other Canadian external ventures, a belief that it would rekindle the Arab perception of a pro-Israeli bias, jeopardizing economic gains, and a recognition that Canadian participation was unnecessary given the extent of confirmed West European involvement.

The priority given to the expansion of bilateral economic arrangements received further confirmation after the return of the Liberal government; antiboycott legislation was avoided, no compliance data were tabled, and official high-level Canadian visits were all led by senior economic ministers, including ITC minister Ed Lumley and EMR minister Marc Lalonde. In addition, when Trudeau visited Saudi Arabia prior to the Cancùn conference, he was pointedly informed by his hosts that discussions would focus not on the politics of North–South relations but on trade, commerce, and investment. While the peace process and a stable international order remained Canadian concerns, Canada–Middle East relations in the first two years of the 1980s were led by an economic imperative emerging from the dynamics of domestic economic development.

Conclusions

Whether from circumstance or design, the development of an autonomous Canadian foreign policy has been very closely entwined with the forces of nationalism and statehood in the Middle East. From the closing days of World War II, Canada emerged as a major international actor concerned with global peace, Western cohesion, a stable and orderly process of decolonization, and commitment to a functioning United Nations as the central instrument for conflict resolution. When applied to the maelstrom of Middle East–United Nations politics, these concerns brought a Canadian profile of internationalism, articulately engineered by its principal architect, Lester B. Pearson.

The quantitative overview of Canadian behaviour towards the Middle East provides strong evidence of a steady movement from Pearsonian liberal internationalism towards the behavioural patterns predicted by complex neo-realism. Official government attention to and involvement in the Middle East has shown a consistent increase, matched by a similar growth in reciprocal activity towards Canada. Multilateral forums no longer constitute the principal mode of operation, as formal meetings between leaders of government, new bilateral agreements and bodies, and an increasingly diversified trading pattern have begun to overshadow such traditional concerns as peacekeeping and UN-based mediation.

The relevance of international factors has also shown a marked shift since the Mackenzie King era. King's overriding foreign policy concerns were support for British interests, fear of Communism, and a reluctance to get entangled in external issues that did not bear directly upon Canadian interests. His appointment of St. Laurent as secretary of state for external affairs, with Pearson as undersecretary, began the shift away from a policy that perceived Canadian foreign policy as conceptually focused on and responsive to the United Kingdom, towards the Pearsonian ideal of Canada as a middle power tied to the network of Western alliance interests and committed to the UN and the Commonwealth. The seven-year St. Laurent–Pearson partnership revealed a lessening of great-power dominance over Canadian behaviour towards the Middle East and a concern with conflict mediation, NATO consolidation, and UN legitimacy. Nevertheless, as peripheral dependence suggests, the Canadian positions on recognition of Israel and on arms sales to Israel were directly influenced by the wishes of Great Britain and the United States, although this took the form of consultation between allies more than direct compliance to external demands.

The Suez crisis confirmed Canada's ability to pursue the fine line between alliance commitment and an autonomous foreign policy stance. The Diefenbaker interlude continued in this tradition of balancing alliance concerns, including the UN and the Commonwealth, with an aggressive attempt to stake out a position independent of the United States and reflective of specific internal Canadian values. The Pearson period of 1963 to 1967, while a time of vibrant internationalist activity, reflected growing frustration with the functioning of the United Nations. The Canadian government became less tied to the traditional middle-power coalition, initiating bilateral arrangements in pursuit of its growing interests in the region.

The first Trudeau governments of 1968 to 1973 brought these concerns to a climax. There was an explicit and growing tendency towards establishing relationships outside the UN context and giving greater weight to internal demands and interests. Canada's willingness to pursue its traditional UN mediatory role was less automatic, Canada was less inclined to follow the increasingly divergent paths of states within the Western alliance, and it showed more interest in enhancing chosen bilateral relationships. Since 1973, there has been still further decline in the direct relevance of international actors. Canada has not converged in any consistent manner—except on the question of Israel's existence—with its traditional coalition partners or leaders. It did not follow the American antiboycott legislation; it did not support the European Venice Declaration on the status of the PLO; and it took its Jerusalem embassy initiative outside the UN and Camp David context. Furthermore, Canada has not maintained its automatic positive response towards peacekeeping, nor has it consistently voted in the UN in accordance with the United States.

A contrasting pattern has emerged with respect to societal determinants of Canadian foreign policy towards the Middle East. Jewish and non-Jewish organizations had been active and articulate since before World War II. In the first postwar decade, their influence was felt on the issues of recognition of Israel, arms sales, support for Israeli security, Canadian performance at the UN, and the extension and strengthening of diplomatic and economic ties with Israel; later the Zionism-as-racism issue played an important role in Canadian decision making. Yet it would be an overstatement to say that their influence has been either the sole determining factor or a distortion of the dominant Canadian perception of the day. Rather, they have been working within a democratic political system that is largely sympathetic to their interests, supportive of their rights as citizens to pursue those interests within the boundaries of that system, and responsive to their efforts.

The UN Crime Congress, PLO recognition, and the initial Jerusalem embassy decisions were clear examples of the direct success of Zionist efforts, while Habitat, antiboycott legislation, and the embassy reversal balanced the pattern. The boycott and embassy incidents further indicate the increased concern of the business community over Canadian policy towards the Middle East. Over the entire postwar period, political parties and parliamentarians alike have moved from a minor involvement in foreign policy during the King era through a moderate participation under St. Laurent, Diefenbaker, and Pearson to an increasingly active involvement in debate and attempts at influence.

The third set of foreign policy determinants, the governmental decision-making process, offers further evidence of Canada's thrust beyond liberal internationalism. With each successive government, Canadian–Middle East policy has become increasingly politicized, with the prime minister and senior Cabinet colleagues involved in policy decisions. While the Department of External Affairs remains a central actor, other departments have found themselves drawn into the arena as the country broadens its interests and upgrades its commitment of government and private sector resources. DEA, in its role as a standard foreign office, has thereby become less dominant relative to other agencies, forced increasingly to compete to register its departmental priorities, and therefore more insistent in its pursuit of a co-ordinative role in support of overarching national interests.

Until the Trudeau era, the UN focus of Canadian policy underscored the primacy of DEA, National Defence to a lesser extent, and a sympathetic prime minister when external crises demanded. The expansion of bilateral relations and the post-1973 politics of oil, with all its attendant socio-economic, diplomatic, and political consequences, significantly altered that situation. Once domestic interests expanded and drew into the policy-making process a wider range of concerned citizens and their elected representatives, the central structures of government and key personnel, especially Cabinet, necessarily became more directly involved.

In short, the last decade has seen the demise of the Pearsonian legacy of a liberal-internationalist, middle-power Canadian foreign policy. In its place has arisen a complex neo-realist pattern to dominate the one policy area where Canada's internationalist tradition was born and long reigned supreme.

CONCLUSION

Foreign Policy for Canadians established two central precepts: that "there is no natural, immutable or permanent role for Canada in today's world" and that foreign policy and external behaviour "should be directly related to national policies pursued within Canada, and serve the same objectives."[1]

The statement brought Canada into the Trudeau era with a sharp break from the past. No longer were Canada's external activities to be defined by the middle-power, helpful-fixer role; no longer would foreign policy decision making be isolated from the central concerns of the Canadian state and society. Although the mere assertion of the new policy did not automatically ensure its full implementation, the symbolism of making a formal pronouncement did more than merely dissociate this government from the policies of its predecessors. Prime Minister Trudeau effectively altered the expectations of the foreign policy community, and placed on notice all those who had assumed the continuation of the *status quo*. The policy review set in motion a process, still continuing more than a decade later, in which emphasis was placed "on policies, domestic and external, that promote economic growth, social justice and an enhanced quality of life for all Canadians."[2]

This sharply different emphasis in foreign policy direction was due, in the minds of most Canadians, to the impact of a determined new prime minister and his government, and to the enhanced strength and self-confidence of the society that they governed. Yet in many ways, it was a more dimly perceived yet profound transformation in the external environment that was the central engine of this change.

During the first postwar decade and a half, Canada's foreign policy had been largely defined by the skilled, diplomatic professionals in the Department of External Affairs, backed by the resources of a country that had emerged unscathed and strengthened by the war. To be sure, the United States' effective postwar global monopoly of many critical capabilities produced some tendencies towards peripheral dependence on the part of a country less than one-tenth America's size. Yet the new rise of the U.S. towards an internationalist foreign policy, and its need for allies in its newly acquired international tasks, enabled Canada to perform with distinction its dominant liberal-internationalist role.

By 1960, however, a changing global environment had begun to impose severe strains on this role. On the one hand, the emergence of the U.S. as a global imperial power—a vision proclaimed in President John Kennedy's inaugural address and pursued in Vietnam—rendered less relevant Canada's stress on combination, consensus, and constraint, and threatened to push it into a more peripheral and dependent position. Yet at the same time, the share of global capability held by the U.S. began to diminish, propelled primarily by the revival of Europe and by the assertions of Japan. This enabled a more autonomous and domestically based Canadian foreign policy to emerge.

During the first five years of Pierre Trudeau's government, the prospects for such a foreign policy were undeniable, as the 1968 Tet offensive in Vietnam, the 1971 surcharge crisis, and the 1973 oil shock gave the United States a rapidly diminished presence in the globe. Within Canada, a more vibrant and vocal society, led by Quebec, made demands for change. And in Ottawa, a strong, self-confident, and sophisticated government responded by instituting the process of foreign policy change.

During its first five years in office, the Trudeau government firmly established the foundations of its new, complex neo-realist approach. Its expanding aid programs, directed largely at the francophone world, thrust it into global involvement. The philosophy summarized in *Foreign Policy for Canadians* underscored the legitimacy of interest-based involvement. And its initiatives towards China, NATO, and the Arctic set in motion a broader shift towards unilateral behaviour, divergence from U.S. policy, and a revision of those multilateral institutions whose interests Canada had long accepted as its own.

Yet the true extent of the Trudeau revolution became apparent, even to its practitioners, only in the years since 1974. For as the United States retreated rapidly towards a modest position and isolationist stance, Canada was able to complete its transition to a complex neo-realist approach. The policy of bilateralism, practised during the 1970s and proclaimed as general doctrine in 1981, underscored the pre-eminence of autonomous bilateral involvement in Canada's activity abroad. Canada's successful quests for contractual links with Europe and Japan demonstrated its ability to secure diversification from the United States. And its pursuit of renewed and revised global order—in the West, in the North–South dialogue, and in distant regional theatres—confirmed its place within new concert structures as one of the principal powers of the globe.

As far-reaching as these changes have been, however, one critical task remains. It concerns the character of the modified world order that Canada, as one of the globe's principal powers, is seeking to promote. The attainment of diversified bilateral partnerships throughout the world does not, in itself, define a preferred concept of international order on a regional or global scale. And the influence of concert memberships can, in the absence of such definitions, be used all too easily to preserve and enhance the privileges of those already in the top tier of the global hierarchy and of those now moving into it.

To be sure, the Trudeau government's central involvement in the East-West debate over the distribution of security and in the North-South dialogue over the security of distribution suggest that these dilemmas are being faced. And Canada's entrenchment in a full global range of bilateral relationships provides some guarantee that specific self-interested voices closer to home will not be the dominant influences on Canada's behaviour abroad. Yet it remains the task of a strong state apparatus to define how, in accordance with Canada's national interests and values, the global order is to be transformed.

OPENING PAGE QUOTATION

The opening page quotation is from a speech given at The Christian A. Herter Lecture Series, The Johns Hopkins School of Advanced International Studies, by Allan Gotlieb, Canadian Ambassador to the United States and formerly Undersecretary of State of External Affairs. The speech was subsequently printed in the *SAIS Review* 17 (summer 1982): 177, 178–180.

FOOTNOTES

INTRODUCTION

1. This great debate was inaugurated in the modern era with James Minifie's very popular work, *Peacemaker or Powder-Monkey: Canada's Role in a Revolutionary World* (Toronto: McClelland and Stewart, 1960). It has been reflected in a plethora of subsequent works, notably J. L. Granatstein, ed., *Canadian Foreign Policy Since 1945: Middle Power or Satellite* (Toronto: Copp Clark, 1970); and, most recently, Peyton V. Lyon and Brian W. Tomlin, *Canada as an International Actor* (Toronto: Macmillan, 1979).

2. More precisely, what is new is not the perspective of complex neo-realism but its comprehensive specification and application to Canada's experience. Within the scholarly community on Canadian foreign policy, we gratefully acknowledge the contribution of the writings of James Eayrs, especially his seminal article "Defining a New Place for Canada in the Hierarchy of World Powers," *International Perspectives* (May/June 1975): 15-24; the introductory theme in Norman Hillmer and Garth Stevenson, eds., *Foremost Nation: Canadian Foreign Policy and a Changing World* (Toronto: McClelland and Stewart, 1977); the concluding suggestions in Stephen Clarkson, ed., *An Independent Foreign Policy for Canada?* (Toronto: McClelland and Stewart, 1968); some of the themes in John W. Holmes, *Canada: A Middle-Aged Power* (Toronto: McClelland and Stewart, 1976); and much of the evidence in Lyon and Tomlin, *Canada as an International Actor*, and John W. Holmes, *The Shaping of Peace: Canada and the Search for World Order, 1943-1957*, 2 vols. (Toronto: University of Toronto Press, 1979, 1982). However, in many ways our deepest intellectual debt is to the later scholarly writings of Allan Gotlieb, notably (with Charles Dalfen), "National Jurisdiction and International Responsibility: New Canadian Approaches to International Law," *American Journal of International Law* 67 (April 1973): 229-58; "Canadian Diplomatic Initiatives: The Law of the Sea," pp. 136-51, in Michael Fry, ed., *Freedom and Change: Essays in Honour of Lester B. Pearson* (Toronto: McClelland and Stewart, 1975); *Canadian Diplomacy in the 1980's: Leadership and Service* (Toronto: Centre for International Studies, University of Toronto, 1979); (with Jeremy Kinsman) "Reviving the Third Option," *International Perspectives* (January/February 1981): 2-5; and "Canada/U.S. Relations: The Rules of the Game," Christian A. Herter Lecture Series, The Johns Hopkins School of Advanced International Studies, 1 April 1982, Washington.

3. The growth of the field is evident in the number and focus of the works compiled in successive editions of the basic bibliographies in the field: Don Page, ed., *A Bibliography of Works on Canadian Foreign Relations, 1945-1970* (Toronto: Canadian Institute of International Affairs, 1973); Page, ed., *A Bibliography of Works on Canadian Foreign Relations, 1971-1975* (Toronto: Canadian Institute of International Affairs, 1977); and Jane Barret and Jane Beaumont, eds., *A Bibliography of Works on Canadian Foreign Relations, 1976-1980* (Toronto: Canadian Institute of International Affairs, 1982).

4. See Ian Lumsden, ed., *Close the 49th Parallel Etc.: The Americanization of Canada* (Toronto: University of Toronto Press, 1970); and Michael Tucker, *Canadian Foreign Policy: Contemporary Issues and Themes* (Toronto: McGraw-Hill Ryerson, 1980).

5. Each perspective or set of conceptions is a theory in the sense that it offers an explicit framework of analysis whose concepts embrace the full range of major questions, are fully consistent and partially interrelated with one another, and are sufficiently distinctive and precise to be assessed against the available evidence. At this stage they do not meet the more ambitious goals of providing an axiomatic structure yielding deductive propositions falsifiable by the strict canons of positivist, scientific logic. When we use such terms as "liberal-internationalist behaviour", for terminological convenience, we mean merely empirical patterns conforming to the predictions of a particular perspective, liberal internationalism in this case.

6. For assessments of the theoretical quality of the field of Canadian foreign policy, see Roger Frank Swanson, "Systematic Analysis in the Study of U.S.-Canadian Relations," *SAIS Review* 14 (winter 1970): 1-4; Stephen Clarkson, "Lament for a Non-Subject: Reflections on Teaching Canadian-American Relations," *International Journal* 27 (spring 1972): 265-75; and Arpad Abonyi, Ivan Sylvain, and Brian Tomlin, "L'état des études internationales au Canada: Un survol de la recherche scientifique," *Etudes Internationales* 9 (septembre 1978): 337-60.

7. In particular, we are indebted to the theoretical traditions reflected in George Liska, *Imperial America: The International Politics of Primacy* (Baltimore: Johns Hopkins University Press, 1967); and Robert C. North and Nazli Choucri, *Nations in Conflict: National Growth and International Violence* (San Francisco: W.H. Freeman, 1975).

CHAPTER 1

THREE THEORETICAL PERSPECTIVES

1. R.A. MacKay and E.B. Rogers, *Canada Looks Abroad* (Toronto: Oxford University Press, 1938). See also Robert Bothwell and Norman Hillmer, eds., *The In-Between Time: Canadian External Policy in the 1930's* (Toronto: Copp Clark, 1975). The most authoritative history of this period is contained in C.P. Stacey, *Canada and the Age of Conflict*, vol. 1, *1867–1921* (Toronto: Macmillan, 1977), and vol. 2 *1921–1948* (Toronto: University of Toronto Press, 1981).

2. John W. Holmes, *The Shaping of Peace: Canada and the Search for World Order, 1943–1957*, 2 vols. (Toronto: University of Toronto Press, 1979, 1982). On the move towards the war and its legacy, see James Eayrs, *In Defence of Canada*, 4 vols. (Toronto: University of Toronto Press, 1964, 1965, 1972, 1980).

3. See Dale Thomson and Roger Swanson, *Canadian Foreign Policy: Options and Perspectives* (Toronto: McGraw-Hill Ryerson, 1971); Peter Dobell, *Canada's Search For New Roles: Foreign Policy in the Trudeau Era* (Toronto: Oxford University Press, 1972); Peyton V. Lyon, "A Review of the Review," *Journal of Canadian Studies* 5 (May 1970): 34-47; Lyon, "The Trudeau Doctrine," *International Journal* 26 (winter 1970/71): 19-43; James Hyndman, "National Interest and the New Look," *International Journal* 26 (winter 1970/71): 5-18; and Kal Holsti, *Proceedings* of the Standing Committee on External Affairs and National Defence, Statement no. 7, 19 July 1971.

4. The most influential framework provided by students of general foreign policy analysis is presented in James N. Rosenau, "Pre-theories and Theories of Foreign Policy," in R.B. Farrell, ed., *Approaches to Comparative and International Politics* (Evanston, Ill.: Northwestern Universtiy Press, 1966), pp. 27-92. For a view of the development and application of this framework, see Patrick McGowan and Howard Shapiro, *The Comparative Study of Foreign Policy: A Survey of Scientific Findings* (Beverly Hills, Calif.: Sage Publications, 1973); and James N. Rosenau, ed., *Comparing Foreign Policies: Theories, Findings and Methods* (Toronto: John Wiley & Sons, 1974).

5. The prevalence of such myths and models in the social sciences is noted, by specific example, in Larry Ward et al., "World Modelling: Some Critical Foundations," *Behavioral Sciences* 23 (May 1978): 135-47. The major traditions in Canadian historical writing are discussed in Carl [illegible]er, ed., *Approaches to Canadian History* (Toronto: University of Toronto [illegible], 1967); and Berger, *The Writing of Canadian History: Aspects of English-Canadian Historical Writing: 1900 to 1970* (Toronto: Oxford University Press, 1976). A brief portrait of the implicit models on the writing on Canadian foreign policy is offered in John W. Holmes, "After 25 Years," *International Journal* 26 (winter 1970/71): 1-4.

6. Kal Holsti, *International Politics: A Framework for Analysis*, 3d ed. (Englewood Cliffs, N.J.: Prentice-Hall, 1977), p. 390; Maurice East and Charles Hermann, "Do Nation-Types Account for Foreign Policy Behaviour?" in Rosenau, ed., *Comparing Foreign Policies*, pp. 269-303.

7. The best treatment of the classic formulations of relative capability, position,

and status is provided in Martin Wight, *Power Politics* (Harmondsworth, England: Penguin, 1979). For modern extensions and applications, see Klaus Knorr, "Notes on the Analysis of National Capabilities," in James N. Rosenau et al., eds., *The Analysis of International Relations* (New York: Free Press, 1972); Knorr, *The Power of Nations: The Political Economy of International Relations* (New York: Basic Books, 1975); and Ray Cline, *World Power Trends and U.S. Foreign Policy for the 1980's* (Boulder, Col.: Westview Press, 1980). Recent applications to individual states include Ezra Vogel, *Japan as Number One: Lessons for America* (Cambridge, Mass.: Harvard University Press, 1979); and Wolfram Hanrieder, "Germany as Number Two? The Foreign and Economic Policy of the Federal Republic," *International Studies Quarterly* 26 (March 1982): 57-86. Yet to appear is a piece in this tradition arguing the case for "Canada as Number Seven."

8. See K.N. Waltz, *Theory of International Politics* (Reading, Mass.: Addison-Wesley, 1979); Charles Pentland, "The Regionalization of World Politics: Concepts and Evidence," *International Journal* 30 (autumn 1975): 599-630; William Zimmerman, "Issue Area and Foreign Policy Process: A Research Note in Search of a General Theory," *American Political Science Review* 67 (December 1973): 1204-12; William C. Porter, "Issue Area and Foreign Policy Analysis," *International Organization* 34 (summer 1980): 405-28; A.F.K. Organski, *World Politics*, 2d ed. (New York: Knopf, 1968); and W.W. Rostow, *The World Economy* (Austin: Univeristy of Texas Press, 1978).

9. Following the treatment in Joseph Frankel, *International Relations in a Changing World* (Toronto: Oxford University Press, 1979), pp. 8-27, security is defined as the possession of defined, externally recognized boundaries unlikely to be changed in the short term by outside force. Sovereignty is defined as the capacity of the central government to enforce its jurisdiction and preserve the identity of its major societal institutions, and legitimacy as its ability to attract regularly high degrees of voluntary compliance from its citizenry.

10. The three basic categories of externally oriented behaviour are formed by viewing state behaviour at progressively higher levels of analysis: activity (acting state), association (state in interaction with other states), and order (system of interacting states). Each of these categories is divided in turn by the three stages of behaviour offered in events data analysis: emission, transmission, and reception or impact. See J. David Singer, "The Level of Analysis Problem in International Relations," in Klaus Knorr and Sidney Verba, eds., *The International System: Theoretical Essays* (Princeton, N.J.: Princeton University Press, 1961), pp. 77-92; and Charles Hermann, "What is a Foreign Policy Event?" in Wolfram Hanrieder, ed., *Comparative Foreign Policy: Theoretical Essays* (New York: David McKay, 1971), pp. 295-321.

11. Diffusion is defined more specifically as the number of, balance among, and intensity of relations with the targets of Canadian action abroad. Analytically, the impact of Canadian behaviour on a target transforms Canadian "activity" into "relations". It thus leads to the next level of analysis—association—in which attention is directed at the internal character of a pattern of relations (or a "relationship").

12. Analytically, because the overall focus of Canadian behaviour is directed at the distribution of power in the international system and can affect that distribution, it gives rise to the subsequent concern with order, or the structure of the international system that a given distribution of power yields.

13. The basic concept of world order is discussed in Hedley Bull, *The Anarchical Society: A Study of Order in World Politics* (New York: Columbia University Press, 1979). See also Robert Tucker, *The Inequality of Nations* (New

York: Basic Books, 1977). For a current debate on regimes, see *International Organization* 36 (spring 1982), entire issue.

14. The importance of systemic attributes, such as the actions of individual states on a state's international activity, is argued in James Harf et al., "Systemic and External Attributes in Foreign Policy Analysis," in Rosenau, ed., *Comparing Foreign Policies*, pp. 235-50. Evidence that the relative status and salience of external actors has a particular impact on Canadian foreign policy behaviour is contained in Don Munton, "Lesser Powers and the Influence of Relational Attributes: The Case of Canadian Foreign Policy Behaviour," *Etudes Internationales* 10 (septembre 1979): 471-502. Salience includes the concept of vulnerability, which refers to "the relative availability and costliness of the alternatives that the actors face." It is defined as "an actor's liability to suffer costs imposed by external events even after policies have been altered" and is measured by "the costliness of making effective adjustments to a changed environment over a period of time." Rober O. Keohane and Joseph S. Nye, Jr., *Power and Interdependence: World Politics in Transition* (Boston: Little, Brown, 1977), p. 13.

15. Compare the concept of sensitivity as degree and speed of costly impacts from, and responsiveness to, outside events, including social, political, and economic contagion effects, "before policies are altered to try to change the situation." Keohane and Nye, *Power and Interdependence*, pp. 12-13.

16. For an introduction to the literature on domestic sources of foreign policy, see Henry Kissinger, "Domestic Structure and Foreign Policy," *Daedalus* 95 (spring 1966): 503-29; James N. Rosenau, ed., *Domestic Sources of Foreign Policy* (New York: The Free Press, 1967); McGowan and Shapiro, *Comparative Study*, pp. 107-32; and Peter J. Katzenstein, ed., "Between Power and Plenty: Foreign Economic Policies of Advanced Industrialized States," *International Organization* 31 (autumn 1977).

17. For societal determinants, a further breakdown of scope includes the concepts of institutional differentiation and autonomy derived from Samuel Huntington, *Political Order in Changing Societies* (New Haven: Yale University Press, 1968), and the discussion of penetrated political societies in Rosenau, "Pre-theories and Theories." On the dual nature of the influence relationship between domestic and governmental actors in the Canadian case, see Denis Stairs, "Publics and Policy Makers: The Domestic Environment of the Foreign Policy Community," *International Journal* 26 (winter 1970/71): 221-48; and Stairs, "Public Opinion and External Affairs: Reflections on the Domestication of Canadian Foreign Policy," *International Journal* 33 (winter 1977/78): 128-49.

18. See Richard Snyder, H.W. Bruck, and B.M. Sapin, eds., *Foreign Policy Decision Making* (New York: Free Press, 1962); Graham Allison, *Essence of Decision: Explaining the Cuban Missile Crisis* (Boston: Little, Brown, 1971); McGowan and Shapiro, *Comparative Study*, 65-106; and, most usefully, Stephen D. Krasner, *Defending the National Interest: Raw Material Investments and U.S. Foreign Policy* (Princeton, N.J.: Princeton University Press, 1978); Alfred Stepan, *The State and Society: Peru in Comparative Perspective* (Princeton, N.J.: Princeton University Press, 1978); and Eric A. Nordlinger, *On the Autonomy of the Democratic State* (Cambridge, Mass.: Harvard University Press, 1981).

19. "A principal task of research is to determine the extent to which any particular state (a) is procedurally neutral and allows an autonomous and competitive process of interest aggregation to present binding demands on the state, (b) is a class instrument in which the full range of its coercive, administrative and legal powers is used to dominate some class fractions and

protect others, or (c) achieves some degree of autonomy from civil society and thus contributes its own weight to civil society." Stepan, *State and Society*, pp. xii-xiii.

20. These three groups emerge from most empirical analyses of a state's foreign policy apparatus; for example, I.M. Destler, *President, Bureaucrats and Foreign Policy: The Policy of Organizational Reform* (Princeton, N.J.: Princeton University Press, 1972).

21. These co-ordinative structures and processes are staffed by what Stepan terms the "strategic elite" and depend for their efficacy on the "ideological and organizational unity of that elite." Stepan, *State and Society*, p. xiii.

22. Although there have been a wealth of liberal-internationalist contributions to the literature on Canadian foreign policy, the presentation here of its underlying structure and mainstream tenets have been derived from the published work of John W. Holmes, the senior practitioner with the longest record of publication relevant to scholars in the field of Canadian foreign policy. See, in particular, *The Better Part of Valour: Essays on Canadian Diplomacy* (Toronto: McClelland and Stewart, 1970); *Canada: A Middle-Aged Power* (Toronto: McClelland and Stewart, 1976); and *Shaping of Peace*.

23. The first major direct critique and defence of the core liberal-internationalist concept—the middle-power tradition—came only with J. King Gordon, ed., *Canada's Role as a Middle Power* (Toronto: Canadian Institute of International Affairs, 1966).

24. House of Commons, *Debates*, 9 July 1943, p. 4558.

25. See A.J. Miller, "The Functional Principle in Canada's External Relations," *International Journal* 35 (spring 1980): 309-28; Douglas Anglin, "Canadian Policy Towards International Institutions, 1930-1950" (Ph.D. dissertation, Oxford University, 1956), and David Mitrany, *A Working Peace System: An Argument for the Functional Development of International Organization* (London and New York: Royal Institute of International Affairs, 1946).

26. On the transfer of the Pearsonian style and the peacekeeping imperative into a general ethos in the Department of External Affairs, see A.E. Gotlieb, "Canadian Diplomatic Initiatives: The Law of the Sea," in Michael G. Fry, ed., *Freedom and Change: Essays in Honour of Lester B. Pearson* (Toronto: McClelland and Stewart, 1975), pp. 136-51.

27. This theme was first given major emphasis by Escott Reid, who long served as the intellectual leading indicator of new forms of liberal internationalism, in "Canadian Foreign Policy, 1967-1977: A Second Golden Decade?" *International Journal* 22 (spring 1967): 171-81.

28. This stress on continuity appears in most of the mainstream liberal histories of Canada.

29. The classic concept of a middle power is discussed in Wight, *Power Politics*, pp. 61-67. More relevant to this study is the modern formulation, presented in Carsten Holbraad, "The Role of Middle Powers," *Co-operation and Conflict* 7:2 (1971): 77-90. For an application of the concept to the Canadian case, see Brooke Claxton, "The Place of Canada in Postwar Organization," *Canadian Journal of Economics and Political Science* 10 (1944): 409-21; Lionel Gelber, "A Greater Canada Among the Nations," *Behind the Headlines* 4:2 (Toronto: Canadian Institute of International Affairs, 1944); Gelber, "Canada at San Francisco," *The Round Table* 138 (March 1945): 382-65; Gelber, "Canada's New Stature," *Foreign Affairs* 24 (October 1945–July 1946): 277-89, George Glazebrook, "The Middle Powers in the United Nations System," *International*

Organization 1 (June 1947): 307-15; R.C. Riddell, "The Role of the Middle Powers in the United Nations," *Statements and Speeches* 48:40 (Ottawa: Department of External Affairs, 1948); Edgar McInnis, "A Middlepower in the Cold War," in Hugh Keenleyside et al., *The Growth of Canadian Policies in External Affairs* (Durham, N.C.: Duke University Press, 1960); pp. 149-63; James Eayrs, *Northern Approaches* (Toronto: Macmillan, 1961); John W. Holmes, "Canada and the U.S. in World Politics," *Foreign Affairs* 40 (1961): 105-17; Theodore Ropp, "Politics, Strategy and the Commitment of a Middlepower," in David Deener, ed., *Canada–U.S. Treaty Relations* (Durham, N.C.: Duke University Press, 1963), pp. 81-101; F.H. Soward, "On Becoming and Being a Middle Power: The Canadian Experience," *Pacific Historical Review* (1963): 111-36; Holmes, "Canada in Search of its Role," *Foreign Affairs* 41 (July 1963): 659-72; Holmes, "The Diplomacy of a Middle Power," *Atlantic Monthly* (November 1963): 106-12; R.A. MacKay, "The Canadian Doctrine of the Middle Powers," in H.L. Kych and H.P. Krosby, eds., *Empire and Nations* (Toronto: University of Toronto Press, 1969), pp. 133-43; Mitchell Sharp, "A Middle Power in a Changing World," *Statements and Speeches* 69: 16 (Ottawa: Department of External Affairs, 1969); Sharp, "The Role of Middle Powers in a Changing World," *Statements and Speeches* 69:3 (Ottawa: Department of External Affairs, 1969); Arthur Andrew, *Defence by Other Means: Diplomacy for the Underdog* (Toronto: Canadian Institute of International Affairs, 1970); and Annette Baker Fox, *The Politics of Attraction: Four Middle Powers and the United States* (New York: Columbia University Press, 1977).

30. See Holmes, *Shaping of Peace*, vol. 1, pp. 105-36, especially p. 255.

31. Illustrations of the direct relevance of Canada's basic infrastructure and specialized skills in ensuring this rapid transferability of resources include Canada's ability to mobilize diplomatic and military personnel for truce supervision in the distant and largely unknown Indochina region in 1954, the ability to open new posts in the Middle East at the time of the Arab oil embargo of 1973, the use of longstanding Canadian expertise in seismology and geologic survey in initiatives in disarmament discussions, and the importance of an Arctic ice-breaking capability in ensuring the protection of Canadian sovereignty at the time of the *Manhattan*'s voyage in 1969.

32. An example of penetration above this threshold is the direct, ongoing presence of large numbers of United States troops operating in the Canadian north with minimal Canadian supervision during World War II. Examples below it include Canadian fear at the 1944 Chicago conference on civil aviation that an open, largely unregulated Canadian Arctic would be potentially available for regular, unchallenged use by foreign aircraft, and the concern during the 1970s that existing Canadian capacity would not be fully able to prevent illegal operations within Canada's maritime boundaries.

33. On peacekeeping, see Alastair Taylor, David Cox, and J.L. Granatstein, *Peacekeeping: International Challenge and Canadian Response* (Toronto: Canadian Institute of International Affairs, 1968). Examples of mediatory extensions include Lester Pearson's 1955 visit to the Soviet Union and Canada's role at the 1960, 1966, and 1971 Commonwealth prime ministers' conferences.

34. The classic statement is Denis Stairs, *The Diplomacy of Constraint: Canada, the Korean War, and the United States* (Toronto: University of Toronto Press, 1974).

35. The classic formulations are presented in Livingston Merchant and A.D.P. Heeney, "Canada and the United States—Principles for Partnership," *Atlantic Community Quarterly* 3 (fall 1965): 373-91; and Kal Holsti, "Canada and the United States," in K.N. Waltz and S.L. Spiegel, eds., *Conflict in World Politics*

(Cambridge, Mass.: Winthrop, 1971), pp. 375-96.

36. However, on the importance of the distinction between promotion and protection in the eyes of U.S. officials, see Roger Frank Swanson, "Canadian Cultural Nationalism and the U.S. Public Interest," in Janice Murray, ed., *Canadian Cultural Nationalism* (New York: New York University Press, 1977).

37. Examples of these components of multilateralization are, respectively: Canada's instincts to place the bilateral North American Air Defence Command within the multilateral framework of NATO in 1957; Canada's quest for the admission of sixteen new members to the United Nations in 1955 and its support for the membership of the People's Republic of China in 1969; and its initial ambivalence about the membership in NATO of such dubiously democratic North Atlantic states as Italy and Portugal and the extension of NATO's security guarantee to Algeria, Greece, and Turkey.

38. See Ronald St. John Macdonald, Gerald Morris, and Douglas Johnston, eds., *Canadian Perspectives on International Law and Organization* (Toronto: University of Toronto Press, 1974).

39. Keohane and Nye, *Power and Interdependence*.

40. Thus liberal-internationalists assign a moderate salience to each of the external, domestic, and state processes. The precise boundaries of "moderate", and hence those of "low" and "high", cannot be specified on a theoretical basis but must be derived from the empirical pattern. This latter task is guided by the emphasis placed by liberal-internationalists on "the recognition of complexity and acceptance of paradox." In practice, this maxim produces the referent by which moderate influence can be seen—an equal emphasis, in considering the factors from a single environment relevant to a specific decision, on those suggesting further or greater behaviour and those suggesting less.

41. Emphasis is given to two components of the United Nations system—the General Assembly, as the preferred forum for middle-power mediation, and the first generation of specialized agencies (in particular those not dominated on a functional basis by the United States)—as the appropriate framework for functionalism.

42. On the relevance of moral considerations, see John W. Holmes, "Morality, Realism and Foreign Affairs," *International Perspectives* (September/October 1977): 20-24.

43. The foundation for this synthesis of the peripheral-dependence perspective is the work of those who highlight the most prevalent assumptions and positions and who relate their analysis explicitly and centrally to Canadian foreign policy. The most useful works are Stephen Clarkson, *An Independent Foreign Policy for Canada?* (Toronto: McClelland and Stewart, 1968); Kari Levitt, *Silent Surrender: the Multinational Corporation in Canada* (Toronto: Macmillan of Canada, 1970); Garth Stevenson, "Continental Integration and Canadian Unity," in Andrew Axline et al., eds., *Continental Community?: Independence and Integration in North America* (Toronto: McClelland and Stewart, 1974) pp. 194-217; Wallace Clement, *Continental Corporate Power: Economic Linkages Between Canada and the United States* (Toronto: McClelland and Stewart, 1977); Jeanne Kirk Laux, "Global Interdependence and State Intervention," in Brian Tomlin, ed., *Canada's Foreign Policy: Analysis and Trends* (Toronto: Methuen, 1978), pp. 110-35; Clarkson, "Anti-Nationalism in Canada: The Ideology of Mainstream Economics," *Canadian Review of Studies in Nationalism* 5 (spring 1978): 45-65; and Clement, "Continental Political Economy: An Assessment of Relations between Canada and the United States," *Canadian Review of American Studies* 10 (spring

1979): 77-88. Of the vast literature in this tradition, see also Ian Lumsden, ed., *Close the 49th Parallel Etc.: The Americanization of Canada* (Toronto: University of Toronto Press, 1970); John Warnock, *Partner to Behemoth: The Military Policy of a Satellite Canada* (Toronto: New Press, 1970); Phillip Resnick, *The Land of Cain: Class and Nationalism in English Canada, 1945-1975* (Vancouver: New Star Books, 1977); and John Hutcheson, *Dominance and Dependency: Liberalism and National Policies in the North Atlantic Triangle* (Toronto: McClelland and Stewart, 1978).

44. An important distinction between instrumental and structural Marxism is outlined in Krasner, *Defending the National Interest*, pp. 20-26.

45. See, for example, Archibald MacMechan, "Canada as a Vassal State," *Canadian Historical Review* 1 (December 1920): 347-53; Hugh Keenleyside, "The American Economic Penetration of Canada," *Canadian Historical Review* 8 (March 1927): 31-40; and League for Social Reconstruction, *Social Planning for Canada* (Toronto: Nelson, 1935).

46. The general literature is well codified in James Caporaso, ed., "Dependence and Dependency in the Global System," *International Organization* 32 (winter 1978). Modern Canadian political economy is represented by Leo Panitch, ed., *The Canadian State: Political Economy and Political Power* (Toronto: University of Toronto Press, 1977).

47. For the initial analysis, see Royal Commission on Canada's Economic Prospects, *Final Report* (Ottawa: Queen's Printer, 1957). A description of the underlying political tension is contained in Irving Brecher, "Canada-U.S. Economic Relations," *International Perspectives* (November/December 1975): 29-37. See also Walter Gordon, *Troubled Canada: The Need for New Domestic Policies* (Toronto: McClelland and Stewart, 1961); Gordon, *A Choice for Canada: Independence or Colonial Status* (Toronto: McClelland and Stewart, 1966); and Gordon, *A Political Memoir* (Toronto: McClelland and Stewart, 1977).

48. James M. Minifie, *Peacemaker or Powder-monkey: Canada's Role in a Revolutionary World* (Toronto: McClelland and Stewart, 1960); and Clarkson, ed., *Independent Foreign Policy.*

49. George Grant, *Lament for a Nation: the Defeat of Canadian Nationalism* (Toronto: McClelland and Stewart, 1965); and Grant, *Technology and Empire: Perspectives on North America* (Toronto: House of Anansi, 1969).

50. The drift-into-dependence or transfer-of-dependence theme is embraced by writings as diverse as Roger Frank Swanson, "The United States as a National Security Threat," *Behind the Headlines* 26:6 (Toronto: Canadian Institute of International Affairs, 1970); and Standing Committee on External Affairs and National Defence, *Eleventh Report to the House*, no. 33, 27 July 1970. For a history of Canada based on this theme, see Donald Creighton, *Canada's First Century, 1867-1967* (Toronto: Macmillan, 1970).

51. Examples include, respectively, Canada's hesitation in opening new missions in the late 1950s, its deliberations over participation in truce supervision in Indochina in 1954, and its reluctance to become involved in the issue of Biafra's secession from Nigeria in 1968.

52. On the "excessive" preoccupation of Canada with the United States, a favourite theme of liberal-internationalists, see Peyton V. Lyon, "Second Thoughts on the Second Option," *International Journal* 30 (autumn 1975): 646-71; and, in a prescriptive sense, Peter Dobell, *Canada's Search.*

53. More specifically, private organizations include the Canadian-American Committee and International Chamber of Commerce, international organizations include the United Nations during the 1950s and NORAD since its

inception in 1958, and regions include Central and Latin America and Europe before 1965.

54. Specific examples of factors inducing imperial concentration are Canada's 1959 exemption from U.S. oil import quotas, the U.S. Trading with the Enemy Act, the exchange reserves agreement of the mid-1960s obliging Canada to hold official reserves in non-negotiable U.S. government securities, and special bilateral regimes for trade in agricultural machinery, defence products, and automobiles.

55. Vietnam serves as the archetypical example. See Kenneth NcNaught, "From Colony to Satellite," in Clarkson, ed., *Independent Foreign Policy*, pp. 173-286.

56. On the concept of "exemptionalism", see R.D. Cuff and J.L. Granatstein, "The Perils of Exemptionalism," in their *Canadian-American Relations in Wartime* (Toronto: Hakkert, 1975), pp. 156-63.

57. Levitt, *Silent Surrender*, p. 52.

58. The absence of intermediate groups is discussed in Franklyn Griffiths, "Opening up the Policy Process," in Clarkson, ed., *Independent Foreign Policy*, pp. 110-18. The theme of "closed-circuit decision-making" is highlighted in this article; the prevalence of brokerage parties is discussed in Clarkson, "Anti-nationalism"; financial contributions from U.S.-controlled resource corporations to provincial political parties are highlighted in K.Z. Paltiel, *Political Party Financing in Canada* (Toronto: McGraw-Hill, 1970), pp. 5-6. The weakness of an autonomous public opinion is discussed in Abraham Rotstein et al., "Retaliation the Price of Independence," in Clarkson, *Independent Foreign Policy*, pp. 43-56; and Clement, "Continental Political Economy."

59. Stevenson, "Continental Integration," pp. 194-217.

60. Rotstein et al., "Retaliation." This portrait of the federal government as an active facilitator of American domination is presented in Clement, *Continental Corporate Power*. See also Laux, "Global Interdependence"; and Charles Hanly, "The Ethics of Independence," in Clarkson, *Independent Foreign Policy*, pp. 17-28. The prevalence of *ad hoc* decision-making procedures is noted in Stevenson, "Continental Integration."

61. Hans Morgenthau's classic work is *Politics Among Nations: The Struggle for Power and Peace* (New York: Knopf, 1948). Other classic works in the realist tradition, broadly conceived, are E.H. Carr, *The Twenty Years' Crisis, 1919–1939: An Introduction to the Study of International Relations* (New York: St. Martin's Press, 1939); Raymond Aron, *Peace and War: A Theory of International Relations*, (New York: Praeger, 1967); and Bull, *Anarchical Society*.

62. Carl Berger, *The Sense of Power: Studies in the Idea of Canadian Imperialism, 1867-1914* (Toronto: University of Toronto Press, 1970).

63. Don Page, "Canada as the Exponent of North American Idealism," *The American Review of Canadian Studies* 3 (autumn 1973): 30-46.

64. John H. Herz, "Rise and Demise of the Territorial State," *World Politics* 9 (July 1957): 473 ff; and Herz, *International Politics in the Atomic Age* (New York: Columbia University Press, 1959). See also the criticisms summarized in Stanley Hoffman, *The State of War: Essays on the Theory and Practice of International Relations* (New York: Praeger, 1965).

65. This broadening of the concepts of security and national interest and the introduction of a more prominent role for values and moral considerations were

led by Arnold Wolfers, *Discord and Collaboration* (Baltimore: Johns Hopkins University Press, 1962).

66. For example, R.J. Sutherland, "Canada's Long-Term Strategic Situation," *International Journal* 17 (summer 1962): 199-233; James Eayrs, "Sharing a Continent: the Hard Issues," in J.S. Dickey,. ed., *The United States and Canada* (Englewood Cliffs: Prentice-Hall, 1967), pp. 55-94; Klaus Knorr, "Canada and Western Defence," *International Journal* 18 (winter 1962/63): 1-16; and Melvin Conant, *The Long Polar Watch: Canada and the Defence of North America* (New York: Harper and Row, 1962). From an earlier period, see the great classics, J.B. Brebner, *North Atlantic Triangle: The Interplay of Canada, the United States and Great Britain* (Toronto: Ryerson, 1945); "A Changing North Atlantic Triangle," *International Journal* 3 (autumn 1948): 309-19; and Harold Innis, *Great Britain, the United Nations and Canada* (Nottingham, England: University of Nottingham Press, 1948).

67. For the best summaries, see Keohane and Nye, *Power and Interdependenc*; and Stanley Hoffman, *Primacy or World Order: American Foreign Policy Since the Cold War* (New York: McGraw-Hill, 1978).

68. Wight, *Power Politics*, pp. 30-40; and Jeffrey Hart, "Dominance in International Politics," *International Organization* 30 (spring 1976).

69. Hans Morgenthau, *The Purpose of American Politics* (New York: Knopf, 1960); Arnold Wolfers, "Statesmanship and Moral Choice," *World Politics* 1 (January 1949): 175-95; and Wolfers, *Discord and Collaboration*. While this broader conception of interests and values follows many of the recent extensions of realist thinking, it does *not* embrace the globally derived, universally common or inherent "cosmopolitan values", argued in John H. Herz, "Political Realism Revisited," *International Studies Quarterly* 25 (June 1981): 182-97, and suggested in Stanley Hoffman, *Duties Beyond Borders: On the Limits and Possibilities of Ethical International Politics* (Syracuse, N.Y.: Syracuse University Press, 1981). Essentially, our argument asserts that balance-of-power dynamics do not usually prevent a state from acquiring a position of hegemony, that such states have "milieu" goals, and that such goals are partially determined by a historically engendered conception of national values.

70. The major works that provide the basis in the general literature for our complex neo-realist model are George Liska, *Imperial America: The International Politics of Primacy* (Baltimore: Johns Hopkins University Press, 1967); Raymond Aron, *The Imperial Republic* (Englewood Cliffs, N.J.: Prentice Hall, 1974); and David Calleo, *The Imperious Economy* (Cambridge, Mass.: Harvard University Press, 1982). Equally important is a stream of literature focusing on the dynamics within and between states, which give rise to processes of hegemony. See, in particular, Nazli Choucri and Robert C. North, *Nations in Conflict: National Growth and International Violence* (San Francisco: W.H. Freeman, 1975).

71. See A.F.K. Organski, *World Politics*, pp. 364-67; and Wight, *Power Politics*, pp. 30-40.

72. On great powers, see Wight, *Power Politics*, pp. 41-53.

73. The concept of surplus capability is drawn from Charles Kindleberger, "Dominance and Leadership in the International Economy," *International Studies Quarterly* 25 (June 1981): 245. In our formulation, it is not only an absolute criterion based on internal capability but also a criterion relative to domestic demands, external security threats, and ultimately the demands for creating international order that different external distributions of power breed.

74. Collectively, a particular configuration of interests and values is termed

"the national interest". The traditional, security-focused concept of national interest has met with considerable skepticism from scholars of international politics, for reasons well summarized in James N. Rosenau, "National Interest," in David L. Sills, ed., *International Encyclopedia of the Social Sciences*, vol. 11 (New York: Crowell, Collier and Macmillan, 1968), pp. 34-40. Our concept derives from subsequent efforts to defend and refine the concept, such as Joseph Frankel, "National Interest: A Vindication," *International Journal* 24 (autumn 1969): 717-25; Donald Neuchterlein, *National Interests and Presidential Leadership: The Setting of Priorities* (Boulder, Col.: Westview Press, 1978); and, especially, Krasner, *Defending the National Interest*. In our conception, the national interest is a set of premises, perceptions, and policy-relevant priorities that is durable (extending for a minimun of, say, five years), comprehensive (in embracing interests from several issue areas or sectors of society), interrelated (in specifying the relationships among interests), internally prioritized (in providing a particular scale of order or weighting to components), and general (in relating directly overarching values that structure the scale of priorities). In process terms, "the national interest" is seen in broad foreign policy declarations, doctrines, or the calculus underlying seminal decisions when these endure beyond the electoral cycle, actively involve a number and range of government departments, require extensive interdepartmental interaction, engender interdepartmental conflict or major efforts at harmonization, and stimulate more than formal authorization, monitoring, or servicing activities from the chief executive group or central co-ordinative structures. Thus "the national interest" embraces both "interests", which are specific to societal sectors and government departments and affected by decision in a direct and immediate way, and "values", which are general to society and the state and produced by the chief executive group and central co-ordinative structures. Because society lacks unified control and central co-ordinative structures, interests are primarily the preserve of society, while values reside primarily in the state.

75. The concept of specialized capabilities is drawn from Choucri and North, *Nations in Conflict*, pp. 14-43.

76. In short, they present the possibility of leadership, as conceived in Kindleberger, "Dominance and Leadership."

77. In addition to the works cited in the Introduction, our presentation of complex neo-realism draws on the following literature in the Canadian foreign policy field: Hyndman, "National Interest and the New Look"; Ivan Head, "The Foreign Policy of the New Canada," *Foreign Affairs* 50 (January 1972): 237-52; "Dossier Canada," *Politique Internationale* 12 (summer 1981): 181-302; A.E. Gotlieb, "The Western Economic Summits," Notes for remarks to the Canadian Institute for International Affairs, 9 April 1981, Winnipeg; and Charles Doran, "Politics of Dependency Reversal: Canada," Paper prepared for the International Studies Association Annual Meeting, 21–24 March 1979, Toronto.

78. Note the co-existence of the two themes in the prescriptions of Reid in "Canadian Foreign Policy, 1967-1977." Distinctive cultural groups included, most notably, the francophone countries and the People's Republic of China.

79. See Clarkson, ed., *Independent Foreign Policy*, pp. 253-69; and Hyndman, "National Interest and the New Look."

80. See Head, "Foreign Policy of the New Canada"; and James Eayrs, "Defining a New Place for Canada in the Hierarchy of World Powers," *International Perspectives* (May/June 1975): 15-24.

81. More particularly, we see the United States acquiring hegemony from

1945 to 1960 and exercising stable, virtually unchallenged "high" hegemony from about 1960 through 1967.

82. Robert Bothwell, Ian Drummond, and John English, *Canada Since 1945: Power, Politics and Provincialism* (Toronto: University of Toronto Press, 1981).

83. "Canada is a large power; to call us a 'middle power' is inaccurate. . . .As an immigrant country, with a barely developed national resource base to our economy, and a rapidly adapting capability in technology and processing, we are to some extent only now beginning to reach our true potential." A.E. Gotlieb, "Canada/U.S. Relations: The Rules of the Game," Christian A. Herter Lecture Series, The Johns Hopkins School of Advanced International Studies, 1 April 1982, Washington D.C., pp. 4, 10. The term "principal power" is used by Marc Lalonde, "Le Canada et l'indépendance energetique du monde libre," *Politique Internationale* 12 (summer 1981): 206.

84. A.F.K. Organski and Jacek Kugler, *The War Ledger* (Chicago: University of Chicago Press, 1980), p. 43.

85. For an illustration of this calculation, see Gotlieb, "Western Economic Summits."

86. For an example of a national capabilities presentation, see Peyton V. Lyon and Brian W. Tomlin, *Canada as an International Actor* (Toronto: Macmillan, 1979), pp. 56-76.

87. Such groupings include the Western Economic Summit, the Namibia Contact Group, and, less clearly, the four-power Caribbean Consultative Group, the 1970 uranium cartel group, the initial London Suppliers Group on nuclear materials, the executive directors of the International Monetary Fund, and historically, the United Nations Atomic Energy Commission.

88. These groupings include states in the Commonwealth and francophonie, particularly those from the Caribbean and Africa and, less clearly, small and middle powers from the North Atlantic region. One very stringent measure of such states are those that Canada has represented at one time as an executive director on the International Monetary Fund: Norway, Iceland, Ireland, Jamaica, Guyana, Barbados, and the Bahamas. From this perspective, the standard observation of Canada—as a "regional power without a region" because of the dominating presence of the United States—overlooks the three major poles of Canada's regional sphere: as a transcontinental and trans-Atlantic power, beginning with Confederation in 1867 and culminating in the admission of Newfoundland into the Dominion in 1949; as a northern power, symbolized by the Arctic Waters Pollution Prevention Act of 1970 and conceptualized in Franklyn Griffiths, *A Northern Foreign Policy* (Toronto: Canadian Institute of International Affairs, 1979); and as a Caribbean power, based on this historic Canada-West Indies trade and currently registered in Canada's leading role in development assistance in the region.

89. More precisely, within the United Nations, greater emphasis is given to the Security Council and to the new generation of organizations and special conference groupings created in the 1970s to deal with new "global" issues.

CHAPTER 2
MAJOR DOCTRINES AND DECISIONS

1. On the concept of doctrines, see William Overholt and Marylin Chou, "Foreign Policy Doctrines," in Richard Merritt, ed., *Foreign Policy Analysis* (Lexington, Mass.: D.C. Heath, 1975), pp. 149-53. It should be noted that Canadian doctrines have tended to lack the firmness and precision of their American equivalents, such as the Monroe, Truman, and Nixon doctrines, perhaps primarily because doctrines of this sort tend to emanate from large, particularly hegemonic powers in the international system.

2. For a discussion of Conservative foreign policy before 1945, see Donald Story, "The Foreign Policy of the Government of R.B. Bennett: Canada and the League of Nations, 1930-35" (Ph.D. thesis, University of Toronto, 1976). The initial efforts within Ottawa to define Canada's role in the postwar order are explored in Don Page and Don Munton, "Planning in the East Block: the Post-Hostilities Problems Committees in Canada, 1943-5," *International Journal* 32 (autumn 1977): 687-726; and John W. Holmes, *The Shaping of Peace: Canada and the Search for World Order, 1943-1957*, vol. 1 (Toronto: University of Toronto Press, 1979).

3. It was this set of reservations that sustained James N. Rosenau's classic critique of the concept of national interest in "National Interest," in David L. Sills, ed., *International Encyclopedia of the Social Sciences*, vol. 11 (New York: Crowell, Collier and Macmillan, 1968), pp. 34-39. Similar concerns in the case of Canadian foreign policy, stimulated primarily by the Trudeau government's 1970 foreign policy review, are presented in Denis Stairs, "Dreary Product of Consensus Decision-Making," *Behind the Headlines* 29 (August 1970): 21-23; Robin Ranger, "New Myths for Old Realities: The British and Canadian Foreign Policy Reviews Reviewed," *Queen's Quarterly* 77 (summer 1970): 274-78; Peyton V. Lyon, "The Trudeau Doctrine," *International Journal* 26 (winter 1970/71): 19-43; Harald von Riekhoff, "The Recent Evolution of Canadian Foreign Policy: Adopt, Adapt, and Improve," *The Round Table* 62 (January 1972): 63-76; and Denis Stairs, "Pierre Trudeau and the Politics of the Canadian Foreign Policy Review," *The Australian Outlook* 26 (December 1972): 274-90.

4. The survival of "national interest" as a central concept in foreign policy analysis and the conceptual elaboration required to endow it with operational utility are reflected in Stephen Krasner, *Defending the National Interest: Raw Materials Investments and U.S. Foreign Policy* (Princeton, N.J.: Princeton University Press, 1978); Donald Neuchterlein, *National Interests and Presidential Leadership: The Setting of Priorities* (Boulder, Col.: Westview Press, 1978). The utility of articulated government statements as a meaningful basis for political analysis is argued and demonstrated in Kal Holsti, "National Role Conceptions in the Study of Foreign Policy," *International Studies Quarterly* 14 (September 1970): 233-309. For the application of the role concept and its more precise variant of objectives in the analysis of Canadian foreign policy, see Don Munton, "Much Ado About the Dependent Variable: Goals, Roles, and Actions as Foreign Policy," Paper presented to the Workshop on Approaches to the Study of Canadian Foreign

Policy, Centre for Foreign Policy Studies, Dalhousie University, May 30–June 1, 1974; Peyton V. Lyon and David Leyton-Brown, "Image and Policy Preference: Canadian Elite Views on Relations with the United States," *International Journal* 32 (summer 1977): 640-71; and Peyton V. Lyon and Brian W. Tomlin, *Canada as an International Actor* (Toronto: Macmillan of Canada, 1979), pp. 9-55.

5. Charles Hermann, "International Crisis as a Situational Variable," in James N. Rosenau, ed., *International Politics and Foreign Policy*, 2d ed. (New York: The Free Press, 1969), pp. 409-21.

6. For evidence in the Canadian case, see A.E. Gotlieb, "Canadian Diplomatic Initiatives: The Law of the Sea," in Michael G. Fry, ed., *Freedom and Change: Essays in Honour of Lester B. Pearson* (Toronto: McClelland and Stewart, 1975), pp. 136-51.

7. Louis St. Laurent, Secretary of State for External Affairs, "The Foundations of Canadian Policy on World Affairs," *Statements and Speeches* 47/12. For analysis from the period, see W.L. Morton, "Canada and Foreign Affairs," *Canadian Historical Review* 18 (June 1947): 183-93; William Wade, "Canada's New Role in World Affairs," *Foreign Policy Reports*, 15 July 1951; and R.A. Spencer, *Canada in World Affairs: From UN to NATO, 1946–1949* (Toronto: Oxford University Press, 1959). The major historical sources on the period are Holmes, *Shaping of Peace*, vol. 1, and the *Canada in World Affairs* series. The most useful are Spencer, *1946—1949*, and James Eayrs, *October 1955 to June 1957* (Toronto: Oxford University Press, 1959). Of the major personal accounts, see in particular Lester B. Pearson, *Mike: The Memoirs of the Right Honourable Lester B. Pearson*, vol. 2, 1948–1957, ed. John A. Munro and Alex I. Inglis (Toronto: University of Toronto Press, 1973); Dale C. Thomson, *Louis St. Laurent: Canadian* (Toronto: Macmillan, 1967); J.W. Pickersgill, *My Years with Louis St. Laurent: A Political Memoir* (Toronto: University of Toronto Press, 1975); and J.L. Granatstein, *A Man of Influence: Norman A. Robertson and Canadian Statecraft, 1929-68* (Ottawa: Deneau, 1981).

8. This aspect is emphasized retrospectively, as a deficiency, in Pearson, *Mike*, vol. 2, pp. 25-28.

9. As cited in Holmes, *Shaping of Peace*, vol. 1, p. 62; emphasis added. Canada's experience in the creation of the United Nations system is drawn primarily from this source and James Eayrs, *In Defence of Canada*, vol. 3 (Toronto: University of Toronto Press, 1972), pp. 137-67, 258-318; and A.F.W. Plumptre, *Three Decades of Decision: Canada and the World Monetary System, 1944–75* (Toronto: McClelland and Stewart, 1977).

10. See Holmes, *Shaping of Peace*, vol. 2, pp. 3-75, 123-42; and Don Page and Don Munton, "Canadian Images of the Cold War, 1946-7," *International Journal* 32 (summer 1977): 577-604. See also James Eayrs, *In Defence of Canada*, vol. 4, *Growing Up Allied* (Toronto: University of Toronto Press, 1980); Escott Reid, *Time of Fear and Hope: The Making of the North Atlantic Treaty, 1947–1949* (Toronto: McClelland and Stewart, 1977); Holmes, *Shaping of Peace*, vol. 2, pp. 98-122, 221-250; and Pearson, *Mike*, vol. 2, pp. 38-106.

11. Holmes, *Shaping of Peace*, vol. 1, pp. 141-58, vol. 2, pp. 165-87; James Eayrs, *In Defence of Canada*, vol. 3, *Peacemaking and Deterrence* (Toronto: University of Toronto Press, 1972), pp. 201-57; Pearson, *Mike*, vol. 2, pp. 107-33; and Escott Reid, *Envoy to Nehru* (Toronto: Oxford University Press, 1981).

12. Denis Stairs, *The Diplomacy of Constraint: Canada, the Korean War, and the United States* (Toronto: University of Toronto Press, 1974); Holmes, *Shaping of*

Peace, vol. 2, pp. 143-64; and Pearson, *Mike*, vol. 2, pp. 150-214.

13. John W. Holmes, "Geneva: 1954," *International Journal* 22 (summer 1967): 457-83; Holmes, *Shaping of Peace*, vol. 2, pp. 200-20; James Eayrs, *In Defence of Canada*, vol. 4; Douglas Ross, "In the Interests of Peace: Perception and Response in the History of Canadian Foreign Policy Decision-Making Concerning the International Commission for Supervision and Control for Vietnam, 1954–1965" (Ph.D. thesis, University of Toronto, 1979); and Ross, "The Dynamics of Indochina Diplomacy: Pearson, Holmes and the Struggle with the Bureaucratic Right, 1955," in Kim Nossal, ed., *An Acceptance of Paradox: Essays on Canadian Diplomacy in Honour of John W. Holmes* (Toronto: Canadian Institute of International Affairs, forthcoming), pp. 56-85.

14. William Willoughby, *The St. Lawrence Seaway: A Study in Politics and Diplomacy* (Madison, Wisc.: University of Wisconsin Press, 1961); Lionel Chevrier, *The St. Lawrence Seaway* (Toronto: Macmillan, 1959) and Holmes, *Shaping of Peace*, vol. 2. pp. 259-63.

15. Holmes, *Shaping of Peace*, vol. 2, pp. 348-70; Pearson, *Mike*, vol. 2, pp. 239-316; Terence Robertson, *Crisis: The Inside Story of the Suez Conspiracy* (Toronto: McClelland and Stewart, 1964); Robert Reford, *Canada and Three Crises* (Toronto: Canadian Institute of International Affairs, 1968); and David Cox et al., *Peacekeeping: International Challenge and Canadian Response*, (Toronto: Canadian Institute for International Affairs, 1968), pp. 115-42.

16. The centrality of foreign policy to John Diefenbaker and his desire to create a distinctive Conservative approach are apparent in two sources that must otherwise be treated with caution: John G. Diefenbaker, *One Canada* vol. 2, *The Years of Achievement: 1957–1962* (Toronto: Macmillan, 1976), and vol. 3, *The Tumultuous Years, 1962–1967* (Toronto: Macmillan, 1977). The basic historical source for this period is John McLin, *Canada's Changing Defense Policy, 1957–1963: The Problems of a Middle Power in Alliance* (Toronto: Copp Clark, 1967). Of the relevant *Canada in World Affairs* series, see in particular Peyton V. Lyon, *1961–1963* (Toronto: Oxford University Press, 1968). Useful personal accounts, in addition to John Diefenbaker's own memoirs, are Patrick Nicholson, *Vision and Indecision: Diefenbaker and Pearson* (Toronto: Longmans, 1968); Peter Stursberg, *Diefenbaker: Leadership Gained, 1956–62* (Toronto: University of Toronto Press, 1975); Stursberg, *Diefenbaker: Leadership Lost 1962–67* (Toronto: University of Toronto Press, 1976).

17. The Diefenbaker government's statements on foreign policy, on which this analysis is based, are: "Great Issues in the Anglo-Canadian-American Community, Statement by Prime Minister John G. Diefenbaker, at Dartmouth College, Hanover, New Hampshire, September 7, 1957"; "Canada and the United Nations: Statement by Prime Minister John G. Diefenbaker in the General Assembly of the United Nations, September 23, 1957"; "Commonwealth Trade and Economic Conference, 1958: Statement made at the Commonwealth Trade Conference, Montreal, September 18, 1958, by Prime Minister John Diefenbaker"; and "A Canadian View of NATO: Statement by the Secretary of State for External Affairs, Mr. Howard Green, to the NATO Council, October 28, 1959." All are reprinted in Arthur Blanchette, ed., *Canadian Foreign Policy, 1955–1965: Selected Speeches and Documents* (Toronto: McClelland and Stewart, 1977). For a discussion of the Diefenbaker government's early objectives, see Trevor Lloyd, *Canada in World Affairs, 1957–1959* (Toronto: Oxford University Press, 1968).

18. Robert Bothwell, Ian Drummond, and John English, *Canada Since 1945:*

Power, Politics, and Provincialism (Toronto: University of Toronto Press, 1981), pp. 203-207.

19. See McLin, *Canada's Changing Defense Policy*, pp. 3-105; William Willoughby, *The Joint Organizations of Canada and the United States* (Toronto: University of Toronto Press, 1979); and Neil Swainson, *Conflict over the Columbia: The Canadian Background to an Historic Treaty* (Montreal: McGill-Queen's University Press, 1979).

20. Bothwell, Drummond, and English, *Canada Since 1945*, pp. 210-12.

21. James Dow, *The Arrow* (Toronto: Lorimer, 1979). On defence production sharing arrangements, see John J. Kirton, "The Consequences of Integration: The Case of the Defence Production Sharing Arrangements," in Andrew Axline et al., eds., *Continental Community? Independence and Integration in North America* (Toronto: McClelland and Stewart, 1974), pp. 116-36; Danford Middlemas, "Economic Defence Co-operation with the United States, 1940–63," in Nossal, ed., *Acceptance of Paradox*, pp. 86-114; and Middlemas, "A Pattern of Co-operation: the Case of the Canadian-American Defence Production and Development Sharing Arrangements, 1958–1963" (Ph.D. thesis, University of Toronto, 1976).

22. Peter Harnetty, "Canada, South Africa and the Commonwealth, 1960–61," in *Journal of Commonwealth Political Studies* 2 (November 1963): 33-43; Clarence Redekop, "Canada and Southern Africa, 1946–1975: The Political Economy of Foreign Policy" (Ph.D. thesis, University of Toronto, 1977); and Frank Hayes, "South Africa's Departure from the Commonwealth, 1960–61," *International History Review* 2 (July 1980): 453-84.

23. Reford, *Canada and Three Crises*, pp. 147 ff; Lyon, *Canada in World Affairs*, pp. 27-64; and Jocelyn Ghent, "Canada, the United States, and the Cuban Missile Crisis," *Pacific Historical Review* 48 (May 1979): 159-84.

24. House of Commons, *Debates*, 22 October 1962, pp. 805-806.

25. Lyon, *Canada in World Affairs*, pp. 76-222; and Jocelyn Ghent, "Canadian-American Relations and the Nuclear Weapons Controversy, 1958–1963" (Ph.D. thesis, University of Illinois, 1976).

26. "Defence Policy and Foreign Policy: Statement by Mr. Paul Martin, Secretary of State for External Affairs, to the Special Committee on Defence of the House of Commons, July 25, 1963," in Blanchette, *Canadian Foreign Policy, 1955–1965*, pp. 179-92. For background on this period, see Charlotte Gerard, *Canada in World Affairs, 1963–1965* (Toronto: Canadian Institute of International Affairs, 1980); and especially John English, *Canada in World Affairs, 1965–1967* (Toronto: Canadian Institute of International Affairs, forthcoming). Personal accounts include Lester B. Pearson, *Mike: The Memoirs of the Right Honourable Lester B. Pearson*, vol. 3, 1957–1968, ed. John A. Munro and Alex I. Inglis (Toronto: University of Toronto Press, 1975), Peter Stursberg, *Lester Pearson and the Dream of Unity* (Toronto: Doubleday, 1978); Stursberg, *Lester Pearson and the American Dilemma* (Toronto: Doubleday, 1980); Walter Gordon, *A Political Memoir* (Toronto: McClelland and Stewart, 1977); and Denis Smith, *Gentle Patriot: A Political Biography of Walter Gordon* (Edmonton: Hurtig, 1973).

27. Gordon, *Political Memoir* (Toronto: McClelland and Stewart, 1977); Smith, *Gentle Patriot*; Gerald Wright, "Persuasive Influence: The Case of the Interest Equalization Tax," in Axline et al., ed., *Continental Community?*, pp. 137-63; Maureen Molot, "The Role of Institutions in Canada-United States Relations: The Case of North American Financial Ties," in Axline et al., eds., *Continental*

Community? pp. 164-93; and James Keeley, "Constraints on Canadian International Economic Policy" (Ph.D. thesis, Stanford University, 1980). See also John J. Kirton, "The Politics of Bilateral Management: The Case of the Automotive Trade," *International Journal* 36 (winter 1980/81): 36-69; and A.E. Safarian, "The Task Force Report on Foreign Ownership," *Journal of Canadian Studies* 3 (August 1968): 50-56.

28. Pearson, *Mike*, vol. 3, pp. 147-88; and English, *Canada in World Affairs.*

29. Gordon, *Political Memoir*, pp. 277-88; Granatstein, *Man of Influence*, pp. 364-81; and Bruce Thordarson, *Trudeau and Foreign Policy: A Study in Decision-Making* (Toronto: Oxford University Press, 1972), pp. 22-27.

30. English, *Canada in World Affairs*, E.L.M. Burns, "The Withdrawal of UNEF and the Future of Peacekeeping," *International Journal* 23 (winter 1967/68): 1-17; and Henry Wiseman, "Peacekeeping: Début or Dénouement," *Behind the Headlines* 31 (February 1972).

31. Pearson, *Mike*, vol. 3, pp. 278-90; and John Schlegel, *The Deceptive Ash: Bilingualism and Canadian Foreign Policy in Africa, 1957-1971* (Washington: University Press of America, 1978).

32. See Department of External Affairs, *Foreign Policy for Canadians* (Ottawa: Queen's Printer, 1970); and Mitchell Sharp, "Canada-U.S. Relations: Options for the Future," *International Perspectives* (autumn 1972).

33. *Foreign Policy for Canadians*, p. 9. Discussions of the document, in addition to those listed in note 3 above, include Thordarson, *Trudeau and Foreign Policy*; Thordarson, "Trudeau and Foreign Policy," *International Journal* 33 (spring 1978); the seventeen authors' symposium in "Foreign Policy for Canada: Comments on the White Paper," *Behind the Headlines* 29 (August 1970); Standing Committee on External Affairs and National Defence, *Fourth Report*, no. 31, 23 June 1971; Peyton V. Lyon, "A Review of the Review," *Journal of Canadian Studies* 5 (May 1970): 34-47; Robin Ranger, "Canadian Foreign Policy in an Era of Superpower Detente," *The World Today* (December 1972): 546-54; Garth Stevenson, "For a Real Review," *Current Comment* 2 Occasional paper, Carleton University School of International Affairs, n.d.; Gilles Lalande, "En guise d'introduction, réévaluation ou rationalisation," *Etudes Internationales* 1 (juin 1970): 2-5; Louis Sabourin, "L'influence des facteurs internes sur la politique étrangère canadienne," *Etudes Internationales* 1 (juin 1970): 41-64; John W. Holmes, "After 25 Years," *International Journal* 26 (winter 1970/71): 1-4; James Hyndman, "National Interest and the New Look," *International Journal* 26 (winter 1970/71): 5-12; A.F.W. Plumptre, "Canada and the International Monetary Fund," *International Journal* 26 (winter 1970/71): 109-12; James Eayrs, "A Foreign Policy for Beavers," in *Diplomacy and Its Discontents* (Toronto: University of Toronto Press, 1971), pp. 45-48; Bruce Thordarson, "Post Pearsonian Directions," *The Lakehead University Review* 6 (fall/winter 1973): 172-81; Ivan Head, "The Foreign Policy of the New Canada," *Foreign Affairs* 50 (spring 1972): 237-52; T.A. Keenleyside, "Canada and the Pacific: Perils of a Policy Paper," *Journal of Canadian Studies* 8 (May 1973): 31-49.

34. Sharp, "Canada-U.S. Relations," p. 1. Discussions of this options paper are contained in Dale C. Thomson et al., "Symposium on Canadian-U.S. Relations," *International Perspectives* (January/February 1973): 3-13; William Diebold, Jr., et al., "Canada-U.S. Relations: Options for the Future: 1. American Reaction," *Behind the Headlines* 32 (February 1973); Solange Chaput-Roland et al., "Canada-U.S. Relations: Options for the Future: 2. Canadian Reaction," *Behind the Headlines* 32 (April 1973); R.M. Fowler, "Canadian-American Relations," *International Perspectives* (May/June 1973): 35-39; and Maxwell Cohen, "Canada

and the United States—Possibilities for the Future," *Columbia Journal of Transnational Law* 12 (1973): 197-292. Commentary from the "second wave," which focuses on the question of a "special" relationship between Canada and the U.S., includes Denis Smith, "Choosing the Third Option," *Journal of Canadian Studies* 10 (February 1975): 1-2, 63-64; Alex I. Inglis, "Recent Statements on the Relationship," *International Perspectives* (March/April 1975): 3-11; Christopher Young, "Special Relations Won't Go Away," *International Perspectives* (March/April 1975): 12-15; Irving Brecher, "The Myth and the Reality of Canada-U.S. Relations," *International Perspectives* (November/December 1975): 29-37; Peyton V. Lyon, "Second Thoughts on the Second Option," *International Journal* 30 (Autumn 1975): 646-70; Lyon, "The United States: Good Friend and Benevolent Neighbour," *International Perspectives* (Special Issue 1976): 14-25; and Harald von Riekhoff, "The Third Option in Canadian Foreign Policy," in Brian W. Tomlin, ed., *Canada's Foreign Policy: Analysis and Trends* (Toronto: Methuen, 1978).

35. Department of External Affairs, "Canada and the World," Policy statement by Prime Minister Pierre Elliot Trudeau, 29 May 1968, *Statements and Speeches* 68:17.

36. Ibid, p.3.

37. John Harbron, "Canada Recognizes China: the Trudeau Round, 1968–1973," *Behind the Headlines* 33 (October 1974). For the historical background, see Kim Nossal, "Business as Usual: Relations with China in the 1940's," in Nossal, ed., *Acceptance of Paradox*, pp. 39-55.

38. Thordarson, *Trudeau and Foreign Policy*, pp. 121-66.

39. A.E. Gotlieb and C. Dalfen, "National Jurisdiction and International Responsibility: New Canadian Approaches to International Law," *American Journal of International Law* 67 (April 1973): 229; and Maxwell Cohen, "The Arctic and the National Interest," *International Journal* 26 (winter 1970/71): 52-81.

40. G.L. Reuber, "Canadian Independence in an Asymmetrical World Community: A National Riddle," *International Journal* 29 (autumn 1974): 535-56; Ian Drummond, "The Implications of American Economic Nationalism," in Norman Hillmer and Garth Stevenson, eds., *Foremost Nation* (Toronto: McClelland and Stewart, 1977); and R.M. Dunn, "Canada and its Economic Discontents," *Foreign Affairs* 52 (October 1973): 119-40.

41. Charles Pentland, "Linkage Politics: Canada's Contract and the Development of the European Community's External Relations," *International Journal* 32 (spring 1977): 207-31; E.E. Mahant, "Canada and the European Community: The New Policy," *International Affairs* 52 (October 1976): 551-64; Robert Bothwell, "The Canadian Connection: Canada and Europe," in Hillmer and Stevenson, eds., *Foremost Nation*, pp. 24-36; and Michael Donnelly, "Growing Disharmony in Canadian-Japanese Trade," *International Journal* 36 (autumn 1981): 879-97.

42. Ashok Kapur, "India and the Bomb," *Bulletin of the Atomic Scientists* 30 (September 1974): 27-30; Michael Tucker, *Canadian Foreign Policy* (Toronto: McGraw-Hill Ryerson, 1980), pp. 203-8; and Barrie Morrison and Don Page, "India's Option: the Nuclear Route to Achieve Goal as a World Power," *International Perspectives* (July/August 1974): 23-28.

43. John J. Kirton, "Canada and the United States: A More Distant Relationship," *Current History* 79 (November 1980): 117-20, 146-49; Harald von Riekhoff et al., *Canadian-U.S. Relations: Policy Environments, Issues and Prospects*

(Montreal: C.D. Howe Research Institute, 1979); Canadian-American Committee, *A Time of Difficult Transitions: Canada-U.S. Relations in 1976* (Montreal: C.D. Howe Research Institute, 1976); and Canadian-American Committee, *Bilateral Relations in an Uncertain World Context: Canada-U.S. Relations in 1978* (Montreal: C.D. Howe Research Institute, 1978).

44. R.B. Byers and David Leyton-Brown, "The Strategic and Economic Implications for the United States of a Sovereign Quebec," *Canadian Public Policy* 6 (April 1980): 325-41.

45. R.B. Byers, "Defence and Foreign Policy in the 1970's: The Demise of the Trudeau doctrine," *International Journal* 33 (spring 1978): 312-38.

46. Linda Freeman, "Canada and Africa in the 1970's," *International Journal* 35 (autumn 1980): 794-820. Clarence Redekop, "The Limits of Diplomacy: The Case of Namibia," *International Journal* 35 (winter 1979/80): 70-90.

47. For an early assessment of the Clark government's approach to foreign policy, see Peyton V. Lyon, "New Directions in Canada's Foreign Policy," *The Round Table* 277 (January 1980): 28-32. The Conservative government's major policy statements came in "Canada in a Changing World: Part 1," Discussion paper, 30 November 1979. See also Jeffrey Simpson, *The Discipline of Power: The Conservative Interlude and the Liberal Restoration* (Toronto: Personal Library, 1980).

48. "Text as Delivered of an Address by the Secretary of State for External Affairs, Dr. Mark MacGuigan, to the Empire Club of Canada, Toronto, Ontario, January 22, 1981." Elements of the new policy were stated publicly on earlier occasions by MacGuigan in "Canada and Latin America—Past, Present and Future," (Windsor, Ontario, 29 March 1980), *Statements and Speeches* 80:4, "Current Issues in Canadian Foreign Policy," (Ottawa, 10 June 1980), *Statements and Speeches* 80:11; "Canada Looks West—Increasing Links Across the Pacific," (Hong Kong, 2 July 1980), *Statements and Speeches* 80:4; and "Notes for a Speech by the Secretary of State for External Affairs, Dr. Mark MacGuigan, at the Pacific Rim Opportunities Conference, Vancouver, November 19, 1980," *Statements and Speeches* 80:32.

49. A.E. Gotlieb and Jeremy Kinsman, "Reviving the Third Option," *International Perspectives* (January/February 1981): 2-5.

50. A.E. Gotlieb, "The Western Economic Summits," Notes for remarks to the Canadian Institute of International Affairs, 9 April 1981, Winnipeg.

51. David Wright, "Lessons of CIEC," *International Perspectives* (November/December 1977): 7-12.

CHAPTER 3

ACTIVITY, ASSOCIATION, AND APPROACHES TO WORLD ORDER

1. The research program on international conflict under the direction of Robert C. North, begun at Stanford University in the late 1950s, provides a cumulative record of the importance of this distinction between professed and operational policy. See, for example, Nazli Choucri and Robert C. North, *Nations in Conflict: National Growth and International Violence* (San Francisco: W.H. Freeman, 1975), Introduction and Part I. For an additional approach to this problem area, see Alexander L. George, "The Operational Code: A Neglected Approach to the Study of Political Decision-Making," *International Studies Quarterly* 13 (June 1969): 190-222. In addition, see an article by Naomi Bailin Wish that examines the relationship between role conceptions of national leaders and political behaviour: "Foreign Policy Makers and Their National Role Conceptions," *International Studies Quarterly* 24 (December 1980): 532-44.

2. The data on which this paragraph is based came from *Yearbook of International Organizations*, 19th ed. (Brussels: Union of International Associations and International Chamber of Commerce, October 1981).

3. See Steven J. Brams, "The Structure of Influence Relationships in the International System," in James N. Rosenau, ed., *International Politics and Foreign Policy* (New York: The Free Press, 1969), pp. 583-99. The formulation adopted in the present analysis derives from its focus on Canada's tendency to break with past patterns in the conduct of new initiatives or the search for new associations.

4. Our observations concerning foreign policy initiative are supported, with regard to Canadian-American relations, in a recent study by Michael B. Dolan, Brian W. Tomlin, and Harald von Riekhoff, "Uneasy Interdependence: Integration and Fragmentation in Canada-U.S. Relations," Paper prepared for the International Studies Association Annual Meeting, 18-21 March 1981, Philadelphia.

5. This stress on the willingness to take the initiative in conflictual as compared to co-operative behaviour derives from Canada's tendency to forward unilaterally incompatible objectives, with commensurate friction, rather than adhere in co-operative fashion to existing associations. For further evidence on Canadian-American conflict, see Dolan, Tomlin, and von Riekhoff "Uneasy Interdependence," pp. 20-21, and their discussion of discordance.

6. Joseph S. Nye, Jr., "Transnational Relations and Interstate Conflict: An Empirical Analysis," *International Organization* 28 (autumn 1974): 961-96.

7. Nye, Jr., "Transnational Relations." For further evidence, see Dolan, Tomlin, and von Riekhoff, "Uneasy Interdependence," p. 22.

8. Thomas Keating and T.A. Keenleyside, "Voting Patterns as a Measure of Foreign Policy Independence," *International Perspectives* (May/June 1980): 21-26. For a contrasting analysis, based on voting during the 1957/58 General Assembly and strongly suggesting that Canada behaved as a loyal Western ally and developed state rather than as a mediator, see Don Munton, "Myths of Middle Power Mediation: Canada in the General Assembly," Paper presented to the

Canadian Political Science Association Annual Meeting, June 1980, Montreal.

9. P. Terrence Hopman and Barry Hughes, "The Use of Events Data for the Measurement of Cohesion in International Political Coalitions: A Validity Study," in Edward Azar et al., *Theory and Practice of Events Research: Studies in Inter-Nation Actions and Interactions* (New York: Gordon and Breach, 1975), pp. 81-94.

10. Despite Canada's persistent opposition to U.S. conceptions of strong allied support within NATO, constraints on Canadian behaviour are imposed by NATO membership. These are documented in Robert Matthews, "Canada and Anglophone Africa," in Peyton V. Lyon and Tareq Ismael, eds., *Canada and the Third World* (Toronto: Macmillan, 1976), p. 113; and Robert Matthews and Cranford Pratt, "Canadian Policy Toward Southern Africa," in Douglas Anglin et al., *Canada, Scandinavia and Southern Africa* (Uppsala: Scandinavian Institute of African Affairs, 1978), p. 165. It should be added that the decreased level of U.S. predominance in pan-American bodies after 1968 makes Canada's increased involvement after this time at least partially an element of diversification..

11. This overall shift is calculated from yearly changes in the ratio of multilateral to bilateral affiliations, as aggregated from the figures under the "multilateral" and "bilateral" headings in Table 3.7. The figures under "other"—which include all additional memberships, predominantly those of minor character—do not significantly disturb this trend.

12. David Leyton-Brown, "The Multinational Enterprise and Conflict in Canadian-American Relations," *International Organization* 28 (autumn 1974): 733-54. On the dimensions of policy co-ordination, distribution of benefits, and affect (friendship or hostility), Dolan, Tomlin, and von Riekhoff confirm our own findings with regard to Canadian-American relations. See their "Uneasy Interdependence," pp. 21-24.

13. Robert Angell, "National Support for World Order—A Research Report," *Journal of Conflict Resolution* 17 (September 1973): 429-54.

14. Brian W. Tomlin, "Polarization and Alignment in the General Assembly: The Effects of World Cleavages on Canadian Foreign Policy Behaviour," in Brian W. Tomlin, ed., *Canada's Foreign Policy: Analysis and Trends* (Toronto: Methuen, 1978), pp. 51-68.

15. Chadwick Alger, "Interaction and Negotiation in a Committee of the United Nations General Assembly," *Papers of the Peace Research Society (International)* 5 (1966): 141-59; "Interaction in a Committee of the United Nations General Assembly," in J. David Singer, ed., *Quantitative International Politics* (New York: Free Press, 1968), pp. 141-59; and "Negotiation, Regional Groups, Interaction, and Public Debate in the Development of Consensus in the United Nations General Assembly," in James N. Rosenau et al., eds., *The Analysis of International Politics* (New York: Free Press, 1972).

16. Thomas Volgy and Jon Quistgaard, "Correlates of Organizational Rewards in the United Nations: An Analysis of Environmental and Legislative Variables," *International Organization* 28 (spring 1974): 179:205.

17. Peyton V. Lyon and Brian W. Tomlin, *Canada as an International Actor* (Toronto: Macmillan, 1979), ch. 9, especially Figures 9.2 to 9.4.

18. The initial increase is detailed in Economic Council of Canada, *For a Common Future: A Study of Canada's Relations with the Developing Countries* (Ottawa: Supply and Services Canada, 1978), ch. 5, p. 91.

19. Ibid.

20. The World Bank, *World Development Report, 1980* (Washington: The World Bank, 1980), pp. 140-41, Table 16.

21. Ibid., and the North–South Institute, *In the Canadian Interest? Third World Development in the 1980s* (Ottawa: North–South Institute, 1980).

CHAPTER 4

POPULATION, ENERGY, AND TRADE

1. See, for example, "Trudeau and Foreign Policy," *International Journal* 33 (spring 1978), particularly the lead article by Harald von Riekhoff, "The Impact of Prime Minister Trudeau on Foreign Policy," pp. 267-86; Bruce Thordarson, *Trudeau and Foreign Policy* (Toronto: Oxford University Press, 1972); and Ivan Head, "The Foreign Policy of the 'New' Canada," *Foreign Affairs* 50 (January 1972): 237-52. The few examples of an alternative perspective include Denis Stairs, "Pierre Trudeau and the Politics of the Canadian Foreign Policy Review," *Australian Outlook* 26 (December 1972): 274 90; and Peter Dobell, *Canada's Search for New Roles* (Toronto: Oxford University Press, 1972), pp. 23-37.

2. This point and that of the primacy of the external environment are basic to standard realism as outlined, for example, in Hans Morgenthau, *Politics Among Nations*, 4th ed. (New York: Knopf, 1967). For leading examples of applied work in relative capability analysis, including Canada's place in the global scale, see Ray Cline, *World Power Assessment, 1977* (Boulder, Col.: Westview Press, 1977); Peyton V. Lyon and Brian W. Tomlin, *Canada as an International Actor* (Toronto: Macmillan, 1979), pp. 56-76; and, in the field of natural resources, Harald von Riekhoff, "The Natural Resource Element in Global Power Relationships," *International Perspectives* (September/October 1974): 63-76.

3. For the classic discussions of possible structures of the international system, see Morton Kaplan, *System and Process in International Politics* (New York: Wiley, 1974); Richard Rosecrance, *Action and Reaction in World Politics: International Systems in Perspective* (Boston: Little, Brown, 1963); and K.N. Waltz, *Theory of International Politics* (Menlo Park, Calif.: Addison-Wesley, 1979). See also the classic debate on the implications of alternative configurations, set forth in Karl Deutsch and J. David Singer, "Multipolar Power Systems and International Stability," *World Politics* 16 (April 1964): 390-406; and K.N. Waltz, "The Stability of a Bipolar World," *Daedalus* 19 (summer 1964): 892-907.

4. Robert Gilpin, *War and Change in World Politics* (Cambridge, England: Cambridge University Press, 1981), especially pp. 29, 110-11, 116, 144-45, and 156; and George Modelski, "The Long Cycle of Global Politics and the Nation State," *Comparative Studies in Society and History* 20 (1978): 214-35.

5. Gilpin, *War and Change*, pp. 197-209, 232-44.

6. This paragraph is based on Tony Smith, *The Pattern of Imperialism: The United States, Great Britain and the Late Industrializing World Since 1815* (Cambridge, England: Cambridge University Press, 1981.

7. The two major positions in the new "great debate" can be seen in Stanley Hoffman, "Notes on the Elusiveness of Modern Power," *International Journal* 30 (spring 1975): 183-206; Hoffman, *Primacy or World Order: American Foreign Policy Since the Cold War* (New York: McGraw-Hill, 1978), especially pp. 105-34; Klaus Knorr, "Is International Coercion Waning or Rising?" *International Security* (spring 1977): 92-110; and Knorr, "On the International Uses of Military Force in the Contemporary World," *Orbis* (spring 1977): 5-27.

8. See, for example, A.F.K. Organski and Jacek Kugler, *The War Ledger* (Chicago: University of Chicago Press, 1980); and Klaus Knorr, *The Power of Nations: The Political Economy of International Relations* (New York: Basic Books, 1975).

9. For the pre-eminent statement, see Nazli Choucri and Robert North, *Nations in Conflict: National Growth and International Violence* (San Francisco: W.H. Freeman, 1975).

10. This discussion is based on: Katherine Organski and A.F.K. Organski, *Population and World Power* (New York: Knopf, 1961), p. 4; A.F.K. Organski, Bruce Bueno de Mesquita, and Alan Lamborn, "The Effective Population in International Politics," in Richard L. Clinton, William S. Flash, and R. Kenneth Godwin, eds., *Political Science in Population Studies* (Lexington, Mass.: D.C. Heath, 1972), pp. 80-81; John Barratt and Michael Louw, eds., *International Aspects of Overpopulation* (London: Macmillan, 1972); Richard Clinton, *Population and Politics* (Lexington, Mass.: D.C. Heath, 1973); Quincy Wright, *A Study of War* (Chicago: University of Chicago Press, 1965); Marcel Leroy, *Population and World Politics* (Leiden, The Netherlands: Martinus Nijhoff, 1978); Leon F. Bouvier, with Henry S. Shryock and Harry W. Henderson, "International Migration: Yesterday, Today, and Tomorrow," *Population Bulletin* 32 (September 1977): 3; Julian L. Simon, *The Economics of Population Growth* (Princeton: Princeton University Press, 1977), p. 4; and Leroy, "Population and International Relations: A Framework for the Future," Paper presented to the Canadian Population Society Annual Meeting, 1-2 June 1979, Saskatoon, pp. 4-5; Kinsley Davis, "The Migrations of Human Populations," *Scientific American* 231 (September 1974).

11. W.W. Rostow, *The World Economy* (Austin: University of Texas Press, 1978), pp. 3-6. See also John D. Durand, "The Modern Expansion of World Population," *Proceedings of the American Philosophical Society* 3 (June 1967); *World Development Report* (Washington: The World Bank, August 1979 and August 1980); U.S. Council on Environmental Quality and the Department of State, *The Global 2000 Report to the President: Entering the Twenty-First Century*, 3 vols. (Washington: U.S. Government Printing Office, 1980). Also relevant is the work of the Club of Rome, notably D.H. Meadows et al., *The Limits to Growth* (Washington: Potomac Associates, 1972); M. Mesarovic and E. Pestel, *Mankind at the Turning Point* (New York: E.P. Dutton, 1974); A.O. Herrera et al., *Catastrophe or New Society? A Latin American World Model* (Ottawa: International Development Research Centre, 1976). Most recently, see Willy Brandt, *North-South: A Programme for Survival* (London: Pan Books, 1980).

12. This discussion of the dependency ratio is based on the guidance offered in Leroy, *Population and World Politics*, ch. 2, while effective population is based on Organski, Bueno de Mesquita, and Lamborn, "Effective Population." For a discussion relevant to Canada, see Science Council of Canada, *Population, Technology and Resources*, Report no. 25 (Ottawa: Minister of Supply and Services, 1976). For a comparison between dependency ratios and the concept of effective population and their significance for international affairs, see Leroy, *Population and World Politics*, pp. 48-52.

13. Leroy, *Population and World Politics*, p. 27. In its original formulation, demographers defined the active age group as from 20 to 64 years old. Leroy, however, argues that a demarcation of 15 to 64 is more representative of the employment and productive sectors of the vast majority of the world's population. For various uses of the dependency ratio as well as assessments of its reliability and validity, see *Population and World Politics*, p. 36; David R.

Kamerschen, "The Total Dependency Ratio Approach to 'Overpopulation': A Statistical Critique," *Social and Economic Studies* 13 (December 1964): 488-501; E. Kleiman, "A Standardized Dependency Ratio," *Demography* 4 (1967): 876-93; Ralph Thomlinson, *Population Dynamics: Causes and Consequences of World Demographic Change* (New York: Random House, 1965).

14. Organski, Bueno de Mesquita, and Lamborn, "Effective Population," pp. 80-81. Our definition, which is based on the number of nonagricultural workers in the labour force, differs slightly from Organski, who uses the number of employed nonagricultural workers.

15. *Global 2000 Report*, vol. 2, pp. 29-38. See also Bouvier, "International Migration," p. 4; Kinsley Davis, "The Migrations of Human Populations," *Scientific American* 231 (September 1974): 101; and Donald T. Bogue, *Principles of Demography* (New York: John Wiley & Sons, 1969), p. 801. It is interesting to note that most global models do not include migration as part of the population component.

16. John A. Jackson, ed., *Migration* (London: Cambridge University Press, 1969), p. 19.

17. Davis, "Migrations of Human Populations," pp. 100-103. For a discussion on competing theories, the difficulties in interpreting demographic data, and relating empirical findings, see, among others noted above, Simon, *Economics of Population Growth*, especially chs. 1–2, 7–8, 12–14, 23–24, and Appendix.

18. Reinhard Lohrmann, "European Migration: Recent Developments and Future Prospects," *International Migration* 14, no. 3 (1976): 229-38.

19. *Canada Year Book 1976-77, Special Edition* (Ottawa: Minister of Supply and Services, 1977), Table 4.2, p. 185.

20. Ibid. For details of Canadian trends and policy, including internal migration, see ibid., Table 4.21, p. 193, and Table 4.57, pp. 212-13; For LDC figures, see Economic Council of Canada, *For a Common Future* (Ottawa: Minister of Supply and Services, 1978), pp. 115-16; and C. Michael Lampier, "A Study of Third World Immigrants," study prepared for the Economic Council of Canada, 1978. For the importance of immigrant labour as a main ingredient in postwar European economic growth, a probable argument for Canada as well, see Charles P. Kindleberger, *European Post-War Growth: The Role of Labour Supply* (Cambridge, Mass.: Harvard University Press, 1967). In addition, see Science Council of Canada, *Population, Technology and Resources*; Freda Hawkins, *Canada and Immigration: Public Policy and Public Concern* (Montreal: McGill-Queen's University Press, 1972); C.D. Howe Research Institute, *Policy Review and Outlook, 1979: Anticipating the Unexpected* (Montreal: C.D. Howe Research Institute, 1979); L.O. Stone and Claude Marceau, *Canadian Population Trends and Public Policy Through the 1980's* (Montreal: McGill-Queen's University Press, 1977); Department of Manpower and Immigration, *Internal Migration and Immigration Setttlement* (Ottawa: Ministry of Supply and Services, 1977), p. 5.

21. V. Kerry Smith and John V. Krutilla, "The Economics of Natural Resource Scarcity: An Interpretative Introduction," in V. Kerry Smith, ed., *Scarcity and Growth Reconsidered* (Baltimore: Johns Hopkins University Press and Resources for the Future, 1979), pp. 4-5. For the original work upon which this volume is focused, see Harold J. Barnett and Chandler Morse, *Scarcity and Growth* (Baltimore: John Hopkins University Press and Resources for the Future, 1963).

22. Nicholas Georgescu-Roegen has written two provocative books on this and related issues. See his *Energy and Economic Myths* (New York: Pergamon, 1976)

and *The Entropy Law and the Economic Process* (Cambridge, Mass.: Harvard University Press, 1971).

23. Howard T. Odum, *Environment, Power, and Society* (New York: Wiley-Interscience, 1970), p. 26.

24. Charles F. Park, Jr., *Earthbound: Minerals, Energy, and Man's Future* (San Francisco: Freeman, Cooper, 1975), p. 20.

25. Ibid., chs. 1, 8–10. See also, among others, Jeremy Rifkin, *Entropy: A New World View* (New York: Viking, 1980); Robert C. North, *The World That Could Be* (New York: W.W. Norton, 1977); Smith, ed., *Scarcity and Growth Reconsidered*; and John W. Bennett, *The Ecological Transition* (New York: Pergamon Press, 1976).

26. Park, *Earthbound*, p. 214. For an interesting discussion, see Jeffrey Hart, "Three Approaches to the Measurement of Power in International Relations," *International Organization* 30 (spring 1976): 289-305. See also North, *The World That Could Be*; Robert C. North, "Toward a Framework for the Analysis of Scarcity and Conflict," *International Studies Quarterly* 21 (December 1977): 569-91; Oystein Noreng, *Oil Politics in the 1980s* (New York: McGraw-Hill and Council on Foreign Relations, 1978), p. 2.

27. James Eayrs, "Defining a New Place for Canada in the Hierarchy of World Power," *International Perspectives* (May/June 1975): 15-24; and von Riekhoff, "Natural Resource Element."

28. In addition to the works of Georgescu-Roegen cited above, see Amory B. Lovins, *Soft Energy Paths: Toward a Durable Peace* (Cambridge, Mass.: Ballinger, 1977), and his well-known essay, "Energy Strategy: The Road Not Taken?" *Foreign Affairs* 55 (October 1976): 65-96; William W. Hogan, "Energy and Economic Growth," in John Sawhill, ed., *Energy Conservation and Public Policy* (Englewood Cliffs, N.J.: Prentice-Hall, 1979), pp. 9-21. For competing and often directly conflicting views on this issue, see the discussion in Smith, *Scarcity and Growth Reconsidered*. The problem of uncertainty is definitive and manifest in efforts at prediction, and creates very significant difficulties when attempting to link forecasts to policy. See, for example, *Global 2000 Report*, parts II and III; and U.S. Central Intelligence Agency, Office of Economic Research, "The World Oil Market in the Years Ahead," Research paper (Washington: August 1979), Appendices. See also B.A. Rahmer, "World Energy: Long-Term Outlook Hopeful," *Petroleum Economist* 46 (March 1979): 92.

29. Rifkin, *Entropy*.

30. International Bank for Reconstruction and Development, *World Economic and Social Indicators* (Washington: World Bank, 1980), p. 12.

31. See Noreng, *Oil Politics in the 1980s*, ch. 2; Peter R. Odell, *Oil and World Power*, 5th ed. (Harmondsworth, England: Penguin Books, 1979); and John M. Blair, *The Control of Oil* (New York: Pantheon Books, 1976).

32. On the energy strengths of OECD countries, see Carroll L. Wilson, *Energy: Global Prospects 1985–2000* (New York: McGraw-Hill, 1977), pt. I; International Energy Agency, *Energy Balances of the OECD Countries 1974/1978* (Paris: Organization for Economic Co-operation and Development, 1980), p. 155, as well as specific country tables.

33. On the Soviet situation and its possible implications for expansionism, see Odell, *Oil and World Power*, especially chs. 2, 3, and 9. An example of the range of implications drawn from these analyses can be found by comparing the previously cited works of Odell and Noreng with Bridget Gail, "The World Oil

Crisis and U.S. Power Projection Policy: The Threat Become a Grim Reality," *Armed Forces Journal International* (January 1980): 25-30.

34. "The LDCs' Big New Role in the Dollar's Future," *Business Week* (5 May 1980): 119-22.

35. *World Energy Outlook: A Reassessment of Long-Term Energy Developments and Related Policies* (Paris: Organization for Economic Co-operation and Development, 1977), p. 34.

36. For a recent statement, see Walter J. Levy, "Oil and the Decline of the West," *Foreign Affairs* 58 (summer 1980): 999-1015.

37. For a discussion of the IEA and the Western Economic Summit, see International Energy Agency, *Long-Term Co-operation Program* (Paris: Organization of Economic Co-operation and Development, n.d.), pp. 1-28.

38. Department of Energy, Mines and Resources, *The National Energy Program 1980* (Ottawa: Supply and Services Canada, 1980); and Daryll G. Waddingham, *The Canadian Balance of Payments to the Year 2000* (Global Energy and Minerals Group, Royal Bank of Canada, n.d.), pp. 23-24. The following discussion draws upon Waddingham's compilation of statistics and partially upon his analysis.

39. Waddingham, *Balance of Payments* pp. 27-28. See also R.F. Key and D.W. Fischer, "Assessing the Development Decision-Making Process: A Case Study of Canadian Frontier Petroleum Development," *American Journal of Economics and Sociology* 36 (April 1977): 147-48.

40. The following figures are drawn from *National Energy Program* and Department of Energy Mines and Resources, *The National Energy Program: Update 1982* (Canada: Minister of Supply and Services, 1982).

41. See, for example, Albert O. Hirschman, *National Power and the Structure of Foreign Trade* (Berkeley: University of California Press, 1945). A more recent statement in the context of the debate over the new international economic order is Brandt, *North–South*; see also Roger D. Hansen, *Beyond the North–South Stalemate* (New York: McGraw-Hill and Council on Foreign Relations, 1979).

42. Joan Edelman Spero, *The Politics of International Economic Relations* (New York: St. Martin's Press, 1977), pp. 5, 11; George Modelski, ed., *Transnational Corporations and World Order* (San Francisco: W.H. Freeman, 1979); Raymond Vernon, *Sovereignty at Bay: The Multinational Spread of U.S. Enterprises* (New York: Basic Books, 1971); Charles P. Kindleberger, ed., *The International Corporation* (Cambridge, Mass.: M.I.T. Press, 1970); Jack N. Behrman, *National Interests and the Multinational Enterprise: Tensions Among the North Atlantic Countries* (Englewood Cliffs, N.J.: Prentice-Hall, 1970); C. Fred Bergsten and Lawrence B. Krause, eds., *World Politics and International Economics* (Washington: Brookings Institution, 1975).

43. Rostow, *World Economy*, p. 247.

44. For an interesting political examination of postwar economic recovery, see Organski and Kugler, *The War Ledger*.

45. Michael Hudson, *Global Fracture: The New International Economic Order* (New York: Harper & Row, 1977), pp. 186-87.

46. Spero, *International Economic Relations*, pp. 12-17; see also David H. Blake and Robert S. Walters, *The Politics of Global Economic Relations* (Englewood Cliffs, N.J.: Prentice-Hall, 1976).

47. This discussion of East–West trade is based, among others, on Thomas A. Wolf, "East-West Trade Credit Policy: A Comparative Analysis," in Paul Marer, ed., *U.S. Financing of East-West Trade: The Political Economy of Government Credits*

and the National Interest (Bloomington, Ind.: International Development Research Centre, 1975); John Pinder, "How Active Will the Community Be in East–West Economic Relations?" in Leuan John, ed., *EEC Policy Towards Eastern Europe* (Westmead, England: Saxon House, 1975), pp. 71-92; and R.S. Mathieson, *Japan's Role in Soviet Economic Growth: Transfer of Technology since 1965* (New York: Praeger, 1979).

48. Edwin R. Carlisle, "New Trends in World Exports," *The World Today* 32 (November 1976): 428-33; and Spero, *International Economic Relations*, ch. 10.

49. This discussion of North–South relations is based on International Monetary Fund, *Direction of Trade Statistics, Yearbook 1982* (Washington: International Monetary Fund, 1981); United Nations Conference on Trade and Development, *Handbook of International Trade and Development Statistics* (New York: United Nations, 1979); United Nations, *World Economic Survey, 1981–1982* (New York: United Nations, 1981); International Bank for Reconstruction and Development, *World Tables*, 2d ed. (Baltimore: Johns Hopkins University Press, 1980). See also Edwin M. Martin, *The United States and the Developing Countries*, Atlantic Council Policy Series (Boulder, Col.: Westview Press, 1977); and Carol Cosgrove Twitchett, *Europe and Africa: from Association to Partnership* (Westmead, England: Saxon House, 1978), pp. 148-49.

50. Spero, *International Economic Relations*, pp. 12-13.

51. Arthur Lewis, *The Evolution of the International Economic Order* (Princeton, N.J.: Princeton University Press, 1978), ch. 6.

52. Stephen D. Cohen, *The Making of U.S. International Economic Policy: Principles, Problems, and Proposals for Reform* (New York: Praeger, 1977); Charles W. Kegley, Jr., and Eugene R. Wittkopf, *American Foreign Policy: Pattern and Process* (New York: St. Martin's Press, 1979); and R.T. Green and J.M. Lutz, *The United States and World Trade: Changing Patterns and Dimensions* (New York: Praeger, 1978).

53. Henry Kissinger, *Years of Upheaval* (Boston: Little, Brown, 1982), p. 238.

54. For a brief introduction to trade from the perspective of the United States government, see John C. Kimball, ed., *The Trade Debate*, Publication no. 8942 (Washington: Department of State, 1978).

55. This paragraph is based on David Calleo, *The Imperious Economy* (Cambridge, Mass.: Harvard University Press, 1982).

56. For a discussion of Japan's situation, see Kiyoshi Kojima, *Japan and the New World Economic Order* (Tokyo: Charles E. Tuttle, 1977); Terutomo Ozawa, *Multinationalism, Japanese Style: The Political Economy of Outward Dependence* (Princeton, N.J.: Princeton University Press, 1979); and Saburo Okita, *Japan in the World Economy* (Tokyo: The Japan Foundation, 1975). For an interesting study on the spread of Japanese interests to middle-income emerging states and the OECD, see Zavis Zeman, *Men With the Yen* (Montreal: Institute for Research on Public Policy, 1980). For a focus on Canada, see, in addition to Zeman, Keith A.J. Hay and S.R. Hill, *Canada–Japan Trade and Investment* (Ottawa: Economic International, December 1978) for the Canada–Japan Trade Council.

57. This discussion of Europe's situation is drawn from Richard Bailey, *The European Community in the World* (London: Hutchinson, 1973); and Werner J. Feld, *The European Community in World Affairs: Economic Power and Political Influence* (New York: Alfred, 1976), pp. 105-106.

58. The basic sources for Canada include Robert Bothwell, Ian Drummond, and John English, *Canada Since 1945: Power, Politics, and Provincialism* (Toronto: University of Toronto Press, 1981), ch. 5. This discussion of Canadian trade

relies heavily upon the data and text provided by the Department of Industry, Trade and Commerce, Economic Intelligence Unit, Policy Analysis Branch, in *Canada's Trade Performance, 1960–1977*, vol. 1, *General Developments* (Ottawa: Minister of Supply and Services, 1978), as well as on Waddingham, *Balance of Payments*.

59. On the Third Option, see Mitchell Sharp, "Canada–U.S. Relations: Options for the Future," *International Perspectives* (autumn 1972). See also Peyton V. Lyon and Brian W. Tomlin, *Canada as an International Actor* (Toronto: Macmillan, 1979); "Trudeau and Foreign Policy," *International Journal* 33 (spring 1978); Department of External Affairs, Policy Planning Secretariat, *Canada's Bilateral Relations: Some Key Statistics* (December 1980), Tables 9 and 13. A.E. Gotlieb and Jeremy Kinsman, "Reviving the Third Option," *International Perspectives* (January/February 1981), which appeared after this text was written, tends to support our analysis.

60. *Canada's Trade Performance*, vol. 1, p. 87. Note that this has remained the case; for example, with the 1982 negotiations concerning production-sharing arrangements as part of a contract for new fighter aircraft.

61. See Waddingham, *Balance of Payments; Canada's Trade Performance;* Economic Council of Canada, *Looking Outward: A New Trade Strategy for Canada* (Ottawa: Minister of Supply and Services, 1976); Peyton V. Lyon, *Canada–U.S. Free Trade and Canadian Independence* (Ottawa: Economic Council of Canada, 1975); and Richard H. Leach, "Canada and the United States: A Special Relationship," *Current History* 2 (April 1977); 145-149, 180.

62. On direct foreign investment, see *Foreign Direct Investment in Canada* (Ottawa: Information Canada, 1972), (known as the "Gray Report"). See also C.D. Howe Research Institute, *Investing in our Own Future: A Staff Report* (Montreal: C.D. Howe Research Institute, 1980); Kari Levitt, *Silent Surrender: The Multinational Corporation in Canada* (Toronto: Macmillan, 1970); A.L. Calvet and M.A. Crener, "Foreign Business Control: The Canadian Experience, 1973–1977," *Canadian Public Administration* 22 (fall 1979): 417-19; Allan Tupper, "The State in Business," *Canadian Public Administration* 22 (spring 1979); David Perry, "Uncrowned Institutions," *The Financial Post 500*, 14 June 1980, pp. 51-54; and *Report of the Royal Commission on Corporate Concentration* (March 1978), p. 182.

63. The following discussion of the crucial services account relies heavily on Waddingham, *Balance of Payments*, pt. 1.

64. On the structural problems of the Canadian economy, see *Canada*, OECD Economic Surveys (Paris: Organization for Economic Co-operation and Development, 1979); and G.K. Helleiner and Douglas Welwood, "Raw Materials Processing in Developing Countries and Reductions in the Canadian Tariff," Discussion paper no. 11 (Ottawa: Economic Council of Canada, 1978), pp. 9-10.

CHAPTER 5

THE SOCIETAL PROCESS

1. See *International Organization* 31 (autumn 1977), special issue edited by Peter J. Katzenstein, entitled *Between Power and Plenty: Foreign Economic Policies of Advanced Industrial States*; Robert O. Keohane and Joseph S. Nye, Jr., *Power and Interdependence: World Politics in Transition* (Boston: Little, Brown, 1977); Peter Gourevitch, "The Second Image Reversed: International Sources of Domestic Politics," *International Organization* 32 (autumn 1978): 881-911.

2. See, for example, *International Studies Quarterly* 25 (March 1981), special issue edited by W. Ladd Hollist and James N. Rosenau, entitled "World System Debates."

3. See, for example Stephen D. Krasner, *Defending the National Interest: Raw Materials Investment and U.S. Foreign Policy* (Princeton, N.J.: Princeton University Press, 1978); Eric A. Nordlinger, *On the Autonomy of the Democratic State* (Cambridge, Mass.: Harvard University Press, 1981); Gourevitch, "Second Image Reversed"; Patrick J. McGowan and Howard B. Shapiro, *The Comparative Study of Foreign Policy: A Survey of Scientific Findings* (Beverly Hills, Calif.: Sage, 1973); Maurice A. East, Stephen A. Salmore, and Charles F. Hermann, eds., *Why Nations Act: Theoretical Perspectives on Comparative Foreign Policy Studies* (Beverly Hills, Calif.: Sage, 1978); and Nazli Choucri and Robert C. North, *Nations in Conflict: National Growth and International Violence* (San Francisco: W.H. Freeman, 1975).

4. Garth Stevenson provides a brief but very illuminating overview in "The Determinants of Canadian Foreign Policy," a chapter in a forthcoming volume edited by Paul Painchaud. For domestic capability and foreign policy, see our Chapter 4.

5. Franklyn Griffiths, "Opening up the Policy Process," in Stephen Clarkson, ed., *An Independent Foreign Policy for Canada?* (Toronto: McClelland and Stewart, 1968), p. 111.

6. Denis Stairs, "Public and Policy-Makers: The Domestic Environment of Canada's Foreign Policy Community," *International Journal* 26 (winter 1970/71): 246-47.

7. "Policy Statement by the Prime Minister," 29 May 1968, as cited in James E. Hyndman, "National Interest and the New Look," *International Journal* 26 (winter 1970/71): 5.

8. See Paul Martin, *Federalism and International Relations* (Ottawa: Department of External Affairs, 1968); and Mitchell Sharp, *Federalism and International Conferences on Education* (Ottawa: Department of External Affairs, 1968).

9. See Denis Stairs, "Public Opinion and External Affairs: Reflections on the Domestication of Canadian Foreign Policy," *International Journal* 33 (winter 1977/78): 128-49. Also see his chapter "The Foreign Policy of Canada," in James N. Rosenau, Kenneth W. Thompson, and Gavin Boyd, eds., *World Politics: An Introduction* (New York: The Free Press, 1976), pp. 178-98.

10. Alan C. Cairns, "The Governments and Societies of Canadian Federalism,"

Canadian Journal of Political Science 10 (December 1977): 695-725.

11. Robert A. Spencer, *Canada in World Affairs: From UN to NATO, 1946–1949* (Toronto: Oxford University Press, 1959), pp. 403-4.

12. James Eayrs, *Canada in World Affairs, October 1955 to June 1957* (Toronto: Oxford University Press, 1959), p. 10.

13. John W. Holmes, *The Better Part of Valour: Essays on Canadian Diplomacy* (Toronto: McClelland and Stewart, 1970), pt. I, ch. 5.

14. See Spencer's comment to this effect in *Canada in World Affairs*, ch. 9; also, by implication, the discussions provided in Michael Tucker, *Canadian Foreign Policy: Contemporary Issues and Themes* (Toronto: McGraw-Hill Ryerson, 1980), ch. 1; and Dale C. Thomson and Roger Frank Swanson, *Canadian Foreign Policy: Options and Perspectives* (Toronto: McGraw-Hill Ryerson, 1971), chs. 2 and 3.

15. For the reader interested in specific examples and the historical context within which such issues arose, the best place to begin is the series *Canada in World Affairs*, sponsored by the Canadian Institute of International Affairs; there are, to date, thirteen published volumes, the latest covering the 1963–1965 period.

16. For an introduction to the events surrounding the Canadian government's positions on Suez, see our Chapter 10. The appropriate volumes in the *Canada in World Affairs* series provide background on the Suez and nuclear warheads issues. For Lester Pearson's own recollections and his surprise in facing such strong opposition from Howard Green and John Diefenbaker, see Lester B. Pearson, *Mike: The Memoirs of the Right Honourable Lester B. Pearson*, vol. 2, 1948–1957, ed. John A. Munro and Alex I. Inglis (Toronto: University of Toronto Press, 1973), pp. 273-78. A third example of considerable importance is the pipeline debate; see our Chapter 8.

17. For a view of this crisis as the beginning of a shift in the Conservative Party from its traditional pro-British, anti-American posture to a pro-American position, see Garth Stevenson, "Foreign Policy," in Conrad Winn and John McMenemy, eds., *Political Parties in Canada* (Toronto: McGraw-Hill Ryerson, 1976), ch. 14.

18. For overviews, see Trevor Lloyd, *Canada in World Affairs, 1957–1959* (Toronto: Oxford University Press, 1968), ch. 2; Richard A. Preston, *Canada in World Affairs, 1959–1961* (Toronto: Oxford University Press, 1965), ch. 3; Peyton V. Lyon, *Canada in World Affairs, 1961–1963* (Toronto: Oxford University Press, 1968), ch. 3.

19. Pearson, *Mike*, vol. 2, p. 69.

20. Lyon, *Canada in World Affairs*, p. 111.

21. Ibid., p. 211.

22. Lester B. Pearson, *Mike: The Memoirs of the Right Honourable Lester B. Pearson*, vol. 3, 1957–1968, ed. John A. Munro and Alex I. Inglis (Toronto: University of Toronto Press, 1975).

23. Ibid., p. 117.

24. Ibid., ch. 5; see also Keohane and Nye, *Power and Interdependence*.

25. Pearson, *Mike*, vol. 3, pp. 226-35.

26. See Donald Barry, "Interest Groups and the Foreign Policy Process: The Case of Biafra," in A. Paul Pross, ed., *Pressure Group Behaviour in Canadian Politics* (Toronto: McGraw-Hill Ryerson, 1975), pp. 117-47.

27. On the NATO debate, see Bruce Thordarson, *Trudeau and Foreign Policy: A*

Study in Decision-Making (Toronto: Oxford University Press, 1972), ch. 5. On refugees, see our Chapter 7.

28. For example, Parliamentary Task Force on North-South Relations, *Report to the House of Commons on the Relations Between Developed Countries and Developing Countries* (Ottawa: Supply and Services, 1980).

29. Tucker, *Canadian Foreign Policy*, pp. 39-52, makes the same point.

30. Stevenson, "Foreign Policy"; and Stevenson, "Determinants of Canadian Foreign Policy."

31. At the same time, it is important to recognize the impact of the structures of government on the political functioning of societal actors. See Cairns, "Governments and Societies"; and Nordlinger, *Autonomy of the Democratic State*.

32. There is, as yet, relatively little published research on interest groups in Canadian foreign policy. Among research currently under way, the following unpublished manuscripts have been most helpful. See W. Blair Dimock, "The Involvement and Influence of Domestic Interest Groups in Canadian Foreign Policy Making" (M.A. thesis, Carleton University, 1980); Elizabeth M. Dixon, "The Domestic Mosaic: Domestic Groups and Canadian Foreign Policy," Paper presented to the CIIA Conference on Domestic Groups and Foreign Policy, June 1982, Carleton University. An important collection of papers is the volume edited by A. Paul Pross, *Pressure Group Behaviour in Canadian Politics*.

33. See Dixon, "Domestic Mosaic," for a comprehensive list of foreign policy interest groups in Canada and for a statement addressing the methodological problems associated with this research. See Dimock, "Involvement and Influence," chs. 3 and 4, for a discussion on involvement and influence.

34. This observation and term was pointed out to us by Professor Cranford Pratt.

35. One rough assessment of the growth of foreign policy-related interest groups can be made by comparing the number of groups presenting briefs to SCEAND during the foreign policy review in 1971—77—and the number provided by Dixon, "Domestic Mosaic," in her thorough review of such activity—196. The expanding variety of foreign policy concerns and the perceived need to spend more time on these issues can be observed by an examination of the SCEAND hearings, where topics and witnesses are noted. For example, even including the anomaly of the Columbia River hearings in 1964 (thirty-nine days), the years 1950 to 1967 averaged fourteen days of committee or subcommittee sittings, while from 1968 to mid-1982 the yearly average was twenty-six.

36. Neither the secondary literature nor the ongoing research of which the authors are aware provides a reliable empirical basis upon which to draw anything other than speculation and hypotheses for further research. This may mean not simply that it is an untapped area for study, but that it has been, to date, a "null cell"; much of the common understanding suggests that associational interest groups, with some notable exceptions (for example, in the Arab-Israeli conflict or in fisheries), do not play a major role in Canadian foreign policy. For an example of how domestic political factors affected fisheries policy, see Stephen Greene and Thomas Keating, "Domestic Factors and Canada-United States Fisheries Relations," *Canadian Journal of Political Science* 13 (December 1980): 731-50. For the role of labour, see John Clark, "Canadian Labour Congress as an International Actor," *International Perspectives* (September/October 1980): 9-12. For the impact of domestic sectors on Canada's policies on the law of the sea, see Barbara Johnson and Mark W. Zacher, eds.,

Canadian Foreign Policy and the Law of the Sea (Vancouver: University of British Columbia Press, 1977).

37. See, for example, John W. Warnock, "All the News it Pays to Print," and Frank Peers, "Oh Say, Can You See?," both in Ian Lumsden, ed., *Close the 49th Parallel Etc: The Americanization of Canada* (Toronto: University of Toronto Press, 1970), pp. 117-56.

38. There are now no published systematic studies of the relationship between the Canadian media and Canadian foreign policy. For an initial consideration, however, see the appropriate essays in *International Journal* 33 (spring 1976), a volume devoted to "news and nations". In particular, see the article by Denis Stairs, "The Press and Foreign Policy in Canada," pp. 223-43. Broadcast media are not examined in this volume.

39. Stairs, ibid., 238.

40. Stairs offers three analytic categories for the functioning of the press: bearer of intelligence, source of prescription, and policy maker's instrument for manipulating the political environment both at home and abroad; ibid., p. 224.

41. On the Nigerian civil war, see Barry, "Interest Groups." On refugees and the Middle East, see our chapters 7 and 10, respectively.

42. For a very readable and informative overview of the postwar development of the Canadian economy, and a postive view about the impact of foreign investment on Canadian development, see Robert Bothwell, Ian Drummond, and John English, *Canada Since 1945: Power, Politics, and Provincialism* (Toronto: University of Toronto Press, 1981), especially chs. 2–5, but also chs. 9, 19, 23, 27, 30, and 33.

43. For background on Canadian élites, see Dennis Olsen, *The State Elite* (Toronto: McClelland and Stewart, 1980).

44. A very interesting discussion of these and related issues can be found in Cranford Pratt, "Corporate Bias, the National Interest or Pluralist Reconciliation in Canadian Foreign Policy Towards the Third World," Draft paper prepared for the Conference on Domestic Groups and Foreign Policy, Ottawa, 9-11 June 1982. Standard Canadian sources are noted in our discussion of the peripheral-dependence perspective in Chapter 1. In addition, for specific data on foreign ownership, see A.E. Safarian, *Foreign Ownership of Canadian Industry* (Toronto: McGraw-Hill, 1966).

45. See our chapters 1, 4, 8, and 9.

46. For example, see Peter Aucoin, "Pressure Groups and Recent Changes in the Policy-Making Process," in Pross, ed. *Pressure Group Behaviour*, pp. 174-92.

47. A.F.W. Plumptre, *Three Decades of Decision: Canada and the World Monetary System, 1944-75* (Toronto: McClelland and Stewart, 1977), p. 30.

48. This was especially true for the development of the Canadian petroleum and natural gas industries; see our Chapter 8. For the 1950–1956 period and the crucial importance of the "Clark boys" in the Department of Finance, see Plumptre, *Three Decades*, ch. 6.

49. This material can be found most easily in ibid., chs. 7–9.

50. For the importance of institutional association as opposed to issue-specific ones, see Pross, ed. *Pressure Group Behaviour*.

51. For a list of such groups and their Canadian headquarters, see Dixon, "Domestic Mosaic," Appendix B. A number of the following observations also have been made by Pratt in his paper, "Corporate Bias," especially pp. 13-16.

52. CBIIAC was an outgrowth of the Canadian Business and Industry Advisory Committee, created in the early 1960s with Thomas Bata as its first president. As it grew, it focused more on the relationship between domestic economic growth and the international community. Its new mandate as CBIIAC focuses explicitly on ensuring that the government is made aware of business viewpoints, that appropriate international bodies are aware of the concerns of the Canadian business community, and that economic leaders are aware of their government's activities.

53. Although it is difficult to ascertain, it is likely that the Canadian corporate sector is exerting more rather than less influence today. A comparison over the years detailing Canadian ownership among the largest Canadian-based corporations shows a dramatic rise in corporations having more than 50 per cent ownership in Canadian hands. In the latest compilation, reported in the June 1982 issue of the *Financial Post 500*, 55 per cent reported primarily Canadian ownership. If this trend towards Canadian ownership of the domestic corporate sector continues, it seems not unreasonable to argue the likely increase in their participation and influence in policy making.

54. A central issue in the study of Canadian political behaviour revolves around how one divides the Canadian polity—for example, into provinces and territories or into five regions—and whether it makes a difference, and if so, what kind, in political analysis. See, for instance, David Elkins and Richard Simeon, *Small Worlds: Provinces and Parties in Canadian Political Life* (Toronto: Methuen, 1980); Donald E. Blake, "The Measurement of Regionalism in Canadian Voting Patterns," *Canadian Journal of Political Science* 5 (March 1972): 55-81.

55. Bothwell, Drummond, and English, *Canada Since 1945*, p. 74.

56. See John W. Holmes, *The Shaping of Peace: Canada and the Search for World Order, 1943-1957*, vol. 1 (Toronto: University of Toronto Press, 1979), pp. 290-95.

57. See Bothwell, Drummond, and English, *Canada Since 1945*, chs. 8-10, 14.

58. On the oil and natural gas sector, see our chapter 8; on the Columbia River project, see Neil Swainson, *Conflict over the Columbia: The Canadian Background to an Historical Treaty* (Montreal: McGill-Queen's University Press, 1979).

59. For discussions of federal-provincial relations on foreign policy matters, see the following, which have served as the secondary source materials for much of this section: Ronald G. Atkey, "The Role of the Provinces in International Affairs," *International Journal* 26 (winter 1970/71): 249-73; P.R. (Roff) Johannson, "Provincial International Activities," *International Journal* 33 (spring 1978): 357-78; Richard Simeon, *Federal-Provincial Diplomacy: The Making of Recent Policy in Canada* (Toronto: Holt, Rinehart and Winston, 1973); Tucker, *Canadian Foreign Policy*, pp. 52-60; Thomas Hockin, "Federalist Style in International Politics," in Clarkson, ed., *Independent Foreign Policy*, pp. 119-30; Louis Sabourin, "Special International Status for Quebec?" in ibid., pp. 97-109; Howard Leeson and Wilfried Vanderelst, *External Affairs and Canadian Federalism: The History of a Dilemma* (Toronto: Holt, Rinehart and Winston, 1973); Luigi Di Marzo, "Legal Issues Connected with the Agreements Canadian Provinces Conclude with Foreign Entities," Paper prepared for the Conference on the Provinces and International Relations, Carleton University, November 1975; Wayne Clifford, "The Western Provinces of Canada: The Importance and Orientation of their International Relations," Paper prepared for the government of Alberta, October 1981.

60. Clifford, "Western Provinces."

61. The importance of provincial authorities as links between foreign actors and the provincial private sector is crucial and is recognized as such by both provincial administrations and Ottawa bureaucrats. From confidential interviews with senior provincial and federal trade officials, winter 1981/82. Although accurate data are difficult to gather, there is substantial impressionistic evidence that the last decade has witnessed a dramatic rise in official visits given and received by provinces. Additional circumstantial evidence is the substantial increase in the number of consulates-general, consulates, vice-consulates, and information offices established in Canadian cities (outside of Ottawa) since the early 1970s. Perhaps most striking is the upgrading of the western provinces, especially Alberta, which in 1975 had only two consulates-general but has since received upgraded representation from France, Germany, and the United Kingdom, the latter establishing a trade commission office in Calgary and consulate-general in Edmonton.

62. For a discussion on Canadian direct investment abroad, see I.A. Litvak and C.J. Maule, *The Canadian Multinationals* (Toronto: Butterworth, 1981).

CHAPTER 6

THE GOVERNMENTAL PROCESS

1. See Graham Allison, *Essence of Decision: Explaining the Cuban Missile Crisis* (Boston: Little, Brown, 1971), pp. 10-39; and John Steinbruner, *The Cybernetic Theory of Decision: New Dimensions of Political Analysis* (Princeton, N.J.: Princeton University Press, 1974), pp. 25-46.

2. The decision-making process portrayed by peripheral dependence thus largely coincides with the predictions of the organizational process model on cybernetic and cognitive paradigm outlined in Allison, *Essence of Decision*, pp. 67-101, and Steinbruner, *Cybernetic Theory*, pp. 47-87. It adds, however, the requirement that the dominant organizational structures are established by the processes emanating from external imperial actors and their penetrative agents within Canada, and from the constrained, deeply embedded, previously foreclosed thought processes that they breed according to the cognitive paradigm.

3. The complex neo-realist conception of the decision-making process thus begins with the governmental politics model presented in Allison, *Essence of Decision*, pp. 114-84, but attributes actors a considerable capacity for creative and collective learning. More importantly, it emphasizes the existence of value integration and autonomously engendered coherence through strong control by the chief executive and structured co-ordinative mechanisms that render him effective. In this latter requirement, it follows the models of strong presidential leadership outlined in Stephen Krasner, "Are Bureaucracies Important? (Or Allison Wonderland)" *Foreign Policy* 7 (summer 1972): 159-72; Alexander George, "The Case for Multiple Advocacy in Making Foreign Policy," *American Political Science Review* 66 (September 1972): 751-86; Robert Art, "Bureaucratic Politics and American Foreign Policy: A Critique," *Policy Sciences* 4 (December 1973): 467-90; Amos Perlmutter, "The Presidential Power Center and Foreign Policy: A Critique of the Revisionist and Bureaucratic Political Orientations," *World Politics* 27 (October 1974): 87-106; I.M. Destler, *Presidents, Bureaucrats and Foreign Policy: The Politics* (Princeton, N.J.: Princeton University Press, 1974); and I.M. Destler, "National Security Advice to U.S. Presidents: Some Lessons from Thirty Years," *World Politics* 29 (January 1977): 143-76. The link of internal state behaviour to environmental forces follows the relationships outlined in Peter Cowhey and David Laitin, "Bearing the Burden: A Model of Presidential Responsibility in Foreign Policy," *International Studies Quarterly* 22 (June 1978): 237-66.

4. The conventional objections to the concept of the national interest as an analytical tool are well summarized in James N. Rosenau, "National Interest," in David L. Sills, ed., *International Encyclopedia of the Social Sciences*, vol. 11 (New York: Crowell, Collier and Macmillan, 1968), pp. 34-40. In contrast, this chapter follows the logic of the statist tradition and in particular Stephen D. Krasner's *Defending the National Interest: Raw Material Investments and U.S. Foreign Policy* (Princeton, N.J.: Princeton University Press, 1978).

5. The most detailed summary account of this period is provided by James

Eayrs, *The Art of the Possible: Government and Foreign Policy in Canada* (Toronto: University of Toronto Press, 1961). See also James Eayrs, *In Defence of Canada*, vol. 3, *Peacemaking and Deterrence* (Toronto: University of Toronto Press, 1972) and vol. 4, *Growing Up Allied* (Toronto: University of Toronto Press, 1980). The numerous revealing accounts by and about those involved include Dale C. Thomson, *Louis St. Laurent: Canadian* Toronto: Macmillan, 1967); Lester B. Pearson, *Mike: The Memoirs of the Right Honourable Lester B. Pearson*, vol. 2, *1948–1957*, ed. John A. Munro and Alex I. Inglis (Toronto: University of Toronto Press, 1973); J.W. Pickersgill, *My Years with Louis St. Laurent: A Political Memoir* (Toronto: University of Toronto Press, 1975); Robert Bothwell and William Kilbourn, *C.D. Howe: A Biography* (Toronto: McClelland and Stewart, 1979); A.D.P. Heeney, *The Things That Are Caesar's: Memoirs of a Canadian Public Servant* (Toronto: University of Toronto Press, 1972); J.L. Granatstein, *A Man of Influence: Norman A. Robertson and Canadian Statecraft, 1929–68* (Ottawa: Deneau Publishers, 1981); John W. Holmes, *The Shaping of Peace: Canada and the Search for World Order, 1943–1957*, vol. 1, (Toronto: University of Toronto Press, 1979); Escott Reid, *Time of Fear and Hope: The Making of the North Atlantic Treaty, 1947–1949* (Toronto: McClelland and Stewart, 1977); John Swettenham, *McNaughton*, vol. 3 *1944–1966* (Toronto: Ryerson, 1969); George Ignatieff, "General A.G.L. McNaughton: A Soldier in Diplomacy," *International Journal* 22 (summer 1967): 402-415; Maurice Pope, *Soldiers and Politicians: The Memoirs of Lt.-Gov. Maurice A. Pope* (Toronto: University of Toronto Press, 1962); E.L.M. Burns, *Between Arab and Israeli* (Toronto: Clarke, Irwin, 1962); and A.F.W. Plumptre, *Three Decades of Decision: Canada and the World Monetary System, 1944–75* (Toronto: McClelland and Stewart, 1977).

6. Bruce Thordarson, "Posture and Policy: Leadership in Canada's External Affairs," *International Journal* 31 (autumn 1976): 666-91. On Canadian participation in the Korean conflict, see Denis Stairs, *The Diplomacy of Constraint: Canada, the Korean War and the United States* (Toronto: University of Toronto Press, 1974). The Indochina transshipment issue is described in James Eayrs, "A Blind Eye: The Canadian Position in Indochina," Toronto *Star*, 20 January 1975.

7. On the Department of External Affairs during this period, see John J. Kirton, "The Conduct and Co-ordination of Canadian Government Decision-making Towards the United States" (Ph.D. dissertation, Johns Hopkins University, 1977), pp. 16-29; and Eayrs, *Art of the Possible*.

8. The existence of these competing tendencies within External Affairs is explored in Douglas Ross, "In the Interests of Peace: Canadian Foreign Policy and the Vietnam Truce Supervisory Commission" (Ph.D. dissertation, University of Toronto, 1979). See also Don Page and Don Munton, "Canadian Images of the Cold War, 1946–7," *International Journal* 32 (summer 1977): 577-604.

9. The Avro Arrow case is outlined in James Dow, *The Arrow* (Toronto: James Lorimer, 1979); on the joint evaluation incident, see George Ignatieff, "NATO, Nuclears and Canada's Interests," *International Perspectives* (November/December 1978): 3-9.

10. The first assessment is C.D. Howe's; see House of Common, *Debates*, 2 March 1951, 836-39; the second is that of James Eayrs in *Peacemaking and Deterrence*, p. 10. Some indication of Howe's assertiveness can be seen, however, in the debate over whether responsibility for Canada's foreign aid program should rest with External Affairs or Trade and Commerce, as sketched in Eayrs, *Art of the Possible*, pp. 58-59.

11. For the network of fixed interministerial committees and clearance

procedures, see Eayrs, *Art of the Possible*, pp. 17-19.

12. Ibid.

13. Ibid., pp. 150-59. See also Page and Munton, "Canadian Images."

14. For the existing tensions, see Eayrs, *Art of the Possible*, p. 58.

15. The major sources for this period are: Eayrs, *Art of the Possible;* Thordarson, "Posture and Policy"; John McLin, *Canada's Changing Defence Policy, 1957-1963: The Problem of a Middlepower in Alliance*, (Baltimore: Johns Hopkins University Press, 1957); Peyton V. Lyon, *Canada in World Affairs*, vol. 12, *1961-1963* (Toronto: Oxford University Press, 1968); Trevor Lloyd, *Canada in World Affairs* vol. 10, *1957-1959*, (Toronto: Oxford University Press, 1968). See also Jocelyn Ghent, "Canadian-American Relations and the Nuclear Weapons Controversy, 1958-1963" (Ph.D. dissertation, University of Illinois, 1976); and Howard Lentner, "Foreign Policy Decisionmaking: The Case of Canada and Nuclear Weapons," *World Politics* 29 (October 1976): 29-66. Memoir material, while less useful than that from the earlier period, includes John Diefenbaker, *One Canada*, vol. 2, *The Years of Achievement: 1957-1962* and vol. 3, *The Tumultuous Years: 1962-1967* (Toronto: University of Toronto Press, 1976); R.H. Roy, *For Most Conspicuous Bravery, A Biography of Major-General George R. Pearkes, V.C., Through Two World Wars* (Vancouver: University of British Columbia Press, 1977); E.L.M. Burns, *A Seat at the Table: The Struggle for Disarmament* (Toronto: Clarke, Irwin, 1972); and Granatstein, *Man of Influence*.

16. The characterization of the government being "stampeded" by the military is that of General Charles Foulkes, as cited in McLin, *Canada's Changing Defence Policy*, pp. 45-46. Diefenbaker's much later account is provided in *One Canada*.

17. Granatstein, *Man of Influence*, pp. 322-56.

18. For an account of External Affairs during this period, see ibid., especially pp. 324-26.

19. The basic literature for this period consists of Robert Bothwell, Ian Drummond, and John English, *Canada Since 1945: Power, Politics, and Provincialism* (Toronto: University of Toronto Press, 1981); and Peter Dobell, *Canada's Search for New Roles: Foreign Policy in the Trudeau Era* (Toronto: Oxford University Press, 1972): 10-12. See also McLin, *Canada's Changing Defence Policy*, pp. 193-220; R.B. Byers, "Executive Leadership and Influence: Parliamentary Perceptions of Canadian Defence Policy," in Thomas A. Hockin, ed., *Apex of Power: The Prime Minister and Political Leadership in Canada* (Toronto: Prentice-Hall, 1971), pp. 163-82; Byers, "Canadian Civil-Military Relations and Reorganization of the Armed Forces: Whither Civilian Control?" in Hector Massey, ed., *The Canadian Military: A Profile* (Toronto: Copp Clark, 1972): 197-229; Vernon Kronenberg, *All Together Now: The Organization of the Department of National Defence in Canada, 1964-1972* (Toronto: Canadian Institute of International Affairs, 1973); and Thordarson, "Posture and Policy." Material on individuals, in addition to that previously cited, includes Lester B. Pearson, *Mike: The Memoirs of the Right Honourable Lester B. Pearson*, vol. 3:, 1957-1968, ed. John A. Munro and Alex I. Inglis (Toronto: University of Toronto Press, 1975); Walter Gordon, *A Political Memoir* (Toronto: McClelland and Stewart, 1977); and Judy LaMarsh, *Memoirs of a Bird in a Gilded Cage* (Toronto: McClelland and Stewart, 1969).

20. Bothwell, Drummond, and English, *Canada Since 1945*; and John English, *Canada in World Affairs, 1965-1967* (Toronto: Canadian Institute of International Affairs, forthcoming).

21. This papagraph is based largely on Bothwell, Drummond, and English, *Canada Since 1945*.

22. This paragraph is based on Gordon, *Political Memoir*, and Granatstein, *Man of Influence*.

23. English, *Canada in World Affairs*.

24. A.E. Gotlieb, "Canadian Diplomatic Initiatives: The Law of the Sea," in Michael G. Fry, ed., *Freedom and Change: Essays in Honour of Lester B. Pearson* (Toronto: McClelland and Stewart, 1975); and Kirton, "Conduct and Co-ordination," p. 30.

25. Gordon, *Political Memoir*, pp. 262-63.

26. Ibid., p. 279. Hellyer also maintained a direct relationship with Paul Martin, who had suggested, when the Cabinet was formed, that divisive defence issues be reconciled in advance private discussion between the two, as a means of avoiding the defence minister–foreign minister conflict that had led to the fall of the Diefenbaker government.

27. On the Robertson review, see Granatstein, *Man of Influence*, pp. 374-79.

28. Within the voluminous literature on this period, the best summary accounts are provided in Peter Dobell, *Canada's Search for New Roles: Foreign Policy in the Trudeau Era* (Toronto: Oxford University Press, 1972), especially pp. 10-22; Harald von Riekhoff, "The Impact of Prime Minister Trudeau on Foreign Policy," *International Journal* 33 (spring 1978): 267-86; John Kirton, "Foreign Policy Decisionmaking in the Trudeau Government: Promise and Performance," *International Journal* 33 (spring 1978): 287-311; and Thordarson, "Posture and Policy," pp. 681-91. More detailed empirical information is contained in Bruce Thordarson, *Trudeau and Foreign Policy: A Study in Decisionmaking* (Toronto: Oxford University Press, 1972); Garth Stevenson, "L'élaboration de la politique etrangère canadienne," in Paul Painchaud, ed., *Le Canada et le Québec sur la scène internationale* (Montreal: Les Presses de l'Université du Québec, 1977), pp. 51-79; and Michael Henderson, "La gestion des politiques internationales du gouvernement fédéral," in ibid., pp. 81-107. See also Rod Byers, "Defence and Foreign Policy in the 1970's: the Demise of the Trudeau Doctrine," *International Journal* 33 (spring 1978): 312-38; George Radwanski, *Trudeau* (Toronto: Macmillan, 1978); Michael Tucker, *Canadian Foreign Policy: Contemporary Issues and Themes* (Toronto: McGraw-Hill Ryerson, 1980); Kirton, "Conduct and Co-ordination"; and Peter Dobell, *Canada in World Affairs, 1971–1973*, (Toronto: Canadian Institute of International Affairs, forthcoming). For initial interpretation of the Trudeau government initiatives, see Peyton V. Lyon, "The Trudeau Doctrine," *International Journal* 36 (winter 1970/71): 19-43; James Hyndman, "National Interest and the New Look," *International Journal* 26 (winter 1970/71): 5-18; and Peter Dobell, "The Management of a Foreign Policy for Canadians," *International Journal* 26 (winter 1970/71): 202-20.

29. These general objectives and the corresponding innovations are outlined in G. Bruce Doern, "Recent Changes in the Philosophy of Policy-making in Canada," *Canadian Journal of Political Science* 4 (June 1971): 243-64; G. Bruce Doern, "The Development of Policy Organization in the Executive Arena," in G. Bruce Doern and Peter Aucoin, eds., *The Structures of Policy-Making in Canada* (Toronto: Macmillan, 1971), pp. 39-78; and Michael Pitfield, "Instruments for Policy Formulation at the Federal Level," *Canadian Public Administration* 19 (spring 1976): 8-20.

30. Marc Lalonde, "The Changing Role of the Prime Minister's Office," *Canadian Public Administration* 14 (winter 1971): 521; Gordon Robertson, "The

Changing Role of the Privy Council Office," *Canadian Public Administration* 14 (winter 1971): 504-6; and A.W. Johnson, "The Treasury Board of Canada and the Machinery of Government in the 1970's," *Canadian Journal of Political Science* 4 (September 1971): 346-9. Also relevant are Thomas D'Aquino, "The Prime Minister's Office: Catalyst or Cabal? Aspects of the Development of the Office in Canada and Some Thoughts about Its Future," *Canadian Public Administration* 17 (spring 1974): 55-79; and Michael Hicks, "The Treasury Board of Canada and Its Clients: Five Years of Change and Administrative Reform 1966–71," *Canadian Public Administration* 16 (summer 1973): 182, 205.

31. The exercises and their impact are discussed in Thordarson, *Trudeau and Foreign Policy*; André P. Donneur, "Politique et technique: le rôle du groupe d'analyse politique du ministère canadien des affaires exterieures," *Res Publica* 16 (1974): 209-20; Daniel Madar and Denis Stairs, "Alone on Killers' Row: The Policy Analysis Group and the Department of External Affairs," *International Journal* 32 (autumn 1977): 727-55; G.A.H. Pearson, "Order Out of Chaos? Some Reflections on Foreign-Policy Planning in Canada," *International Journal* 32 (autumn 1977): 756-68; Harald von Riekhoff, "The Third Option in Canadian Foreign Policy," in Brian W. Tomlin, ed., *Canada's Foreign Policy: Analysis and Trends* (Toronto: Methuen, 1978), pp. 87-109.

32. The introduction and results of the program are examined in J.R. Maybee, "ICER and its Two-Year Search for an Approach to Integration," *International Perspectives* (September/October 1972): 40-3; Michael Henderson, "Planning in Canadian External Affairs," Paper prepared for the Canadian Political Science Association, June 1974, Toronto; and Arthur Andrew, "The Diplomat and the Manager," *International Journal* 30 (winter 1974/75): 45-56.

33. For a public statement of some of the logic behind this thrust, see Standing Senate Committee on Foreign Affairs, *Canada–United States Relations*, vol. 1, *The Institutional Framework for the Relationship* (Ottawa, 1975).

34. The basic literature on this period consists of John Kirton, "Les contraintes du milieu et la gestion de la politique étrangère canadienne de 1976 à 1978," *Etudes Internationales* 10 (juin 1979): 321-49; W.M. Dobell, "Interdepartmental Management in External Affairs," *Canadian Public Administration* 221 (spring 1978): 83-102; Denis Stairs, "Responsible Government and Foreign Policy," *International Perspectives* (May/June 1978): 26-30; and George Radwanski, *Trudeau* (Toronto: Macmillan, 1978) for the Trudeau government; for the Clark government, see Flora MacDonald, "Notes for Remarks," Address to the annual meeting of the Canadian Political Science Association, 3 June 1980, Montreal; Jeffrey Simpson, *Discipline of Power: The Conservative Interlude and the Liberal Restoration* (Toronto: Personal Library, 1980); and David Humphreys, *Joe Clark: A Portrait* (Ottawa: Deneau and Greenberg, 1978). See also Michael Pitfield, "The Shape of Government in the 1980's: Techniques and Instruments for Policy Formulation at the Federal Level," *Canadian Public Administration* 19 (spring 1976): 8-20; M.J.L. Kirby and H.V. Kroeker, "Policy-Making Structures and Processes in Canada," *Canadian Public Administration* 21 (autumn 1978): 407-17; and A.W. Johnson, "Public Policy: Creativity and Bureaucracy," *Canadian Public Administration* 21 (spring 1978): 1-15.

35. On the use of special negotiators and co-ordinators, see Gilbert Winham, "Bureaucratic Politics and Canadian Trade Negotiation," *International Journal* 34 (winter 1978/79): 80.

36. On the operation and structure of central agents during this period, see Colin Campbell and George Szablowski, *The Superbureaucrats: Structure and Behaviour in Central Agencies* (Toronto: Macmillan, 1979).

37. See. C.J. Marshall, "Canada's Defence Structure Review," *International Perspectives* (January/February 1976): 26-29; Hugh MacDonald, "Canada, NATO and the Neutron Bomb," *International Perspectives* (March/April 1979): 9-11; Albert Legault, "Disappointment and Satisfactions," *International Perspectives* (September/October 1978): 9; G.T. Skinner, "Canada's Approach to Disarmament Session," *International Perspectives* (May/June 1978): 30-5; William Epstein, "Canada's Disarmament Initiatives," *International Perspectives* (March/April 1979): 3-8).

38. Prime Minister's Office, Press release, 21 March 1980, and "Background Paper on Foreign Service Consolidation," 12 March 1980.

39. For evidence of the enduring impact of the preceding foreign policy reviews, see R.B. Byers, David Leyton-Brown, and Peyton V. Lyon, "Canadian Elite Images of the International System," *International Journal* 32 (summer 1977): 608-39; and Peyton V. Lyon and David Leyton-Brown, "Image and Policy Preference: Canadian Elite Views on Relations with the United States," *International Journal* 32 (summer 1977): 640-71.

40. A.E. Gotlieb, *Canadian Diplomacy in the 1980's: Leadership and Service* (Toronto: Centre for International Studies, University of Toronto, 1979); Kirton, "Conduct and Co-ordination"; William Dobell, "Is External Affairs a Central Agency? A Question of Leadership Controls" *International Perspectives* (May/June, July/August 1979); and Klaus Goldschlag, "The Notion of Sovereignty, in an Evolving World System," address to the Canadian Institute of International Affairs, 29 January 1978, Toronto.

41. Details of the Cabinet committee and envelope systems are presented in, respectively, Privy Council Office, "Cabinet Committee Membership," 31 July 1979; and Treasury Board, *Guide to the Policy and Expenditure Management System* (Ottawa: Supply and Services Canada, 1980).

42. Secretary of State for External Affairs, Discussion paper, 30 November 1979, Part I, "Canada in a Changing World," and Part II, "Canadian Aid Policy."

CHAPTER 7

IMMIGRATION POLICY: THE CASE OF REFUGEES

1. This chapter is not intended as an in-depth definitive study of Canadian refugee policy, but rather as an overview of a series of cases that elucidate the emergence of Canadian foreign policy perspectives, with regard to one neglected area of foreign policy activity. For an excellent presentation of the evolution of Canadian refugee policy, see Gerald E. Dirks, *Canada's Refugee Policy: Indifference or Opportunism?* (Montreal: McGill-Queen's University Press, 1977).

2. The definition of refugees as a distinct migrant category has roots in both humanitarian and legal concerns. The displacement of large numbers of people as a result of World War I prompted efforts to codify the status of such persons. The realization that the evolving conflict-prone state system was exacerbating this problem and making it a chronic phenomenon rather than an acute but transitory one has resulted in a series of proposed legal definitions, the single most important one coming out of the 1951 UN Convention Relating to the Status of Refugees, partially amended by the Organization of African Unity in 1969. The central theme in the basic 1951 definition is the phrase "a well founded fear of being persecuted." For a clear discussion on this issue, see Dirks, *Canada's Refugee Policy*, ch. 1; *Canadian Immigration and Population Study*, 4 vols. (Ottawa: Department of Manpower and Immigration, 1974), vol. 2, *The Immigration Program*, ch. 4. Hereafter cited as *CIPS* 2. The 1951 Convention defines a refugee as "any person who, owing to well-founded fear of being persecuted for reasons of race, religion, nationality, membership of a particular social group or political opinion, is outside the country of his nationality and is unable or, owing to such fear, is unwilling to avail himself of the protection of that country; or who, not having a nationality and being outside the country of his former habitual residence is unable or, owing to such fear, is unwilling to return to it."

3. See John W. Holmes, *The Shaping of Peace: Canada and the Search for World Order, 1943-1957*, vol. I (Toronto: University of Toronto Press, 1979), pp. 96-104; Dirks, *Canada's Refugee Policy*, chs. 3-6; Irving Abella and Harold Troper, "The Line Must Be Drawn Somewhere: Canada and Jewish Refugees 1933-9," *Canadian Historical Review* 60 (June 1979): 178-209; and Constantine Passaris, "Canada's Record in Assisting Refugee Movements," *International Perspectives* (September/October 1981): 6-9.

4. Howard Adelman, "Canada and the Boat People," unpublished manuscript. See also Edmund Gress, "Canada Leads World as Refugee Haven," Chicago *Sun-Times*, as reported in Edmonton *Journal*, 10 August 1981.

5. When data become available for the post-1978 period, they will probably show these patterns to an even greater degree as a result of "boat people", Kampuchea, the worsening situation of the refugees in Somalia, and the heightened profile of the Palestinians as a result of the deteriorating situation in Lebanon. This is borne out by a cursory examination of House of Commons debates concerning immigration and refugees.

6. Dirks, *Canada's Refugee Policy*, p. 147 and p. 150; see chs. 5–7 for a review of this period.

7. In other refugee crises of the period, the Lebanese civil war, flaring up intermittently since the late 1960s, resulted in a large number of Lebanese being displaced. In 1976 the government of Canada provided special dispensation to Lebanese visitors to Canada and Lebanese relatives of Canadian citizens or landed immigrants, creating a situation somewhat different from the six cases examined in this chapter. Nevertheless, Canada has accepted more than ten thousand Lebanese since 1976 as a special movement, for humanitarian reasons. See Rhoda Howard, "Contemporary Canadian Refugee Policy: A Critical Assessment," *Canadian Public Policy* 6 (spring 1980): 361-73. The Tibetan refugee issue of 1970–1971, while of interest, cannot be considered a major crisis.

8. These figures are cited in *CIPS* 2, p. 100. Dirks uses 30 million, citing J. Vernant, *The Refugee and the Postwar World* (New Haven: Yale University Press, 1953), p. 30, although Dirks agrees with the figure of 1 million.

9. For a competent and detailed assessment on this period, see Dirks, *Canada's Refugee Policy*, ch. 5, on which our summary is based.

10. L.W. Holborn, *The I.R.O., A Specialized Agency of the United Nations* (New York: Oxford University Press, 1956).

11. Alan G. Green, *Immigration and the Postwar Canadian Economy* (Toronto: Macmillan, 1976), pp. 16-33.

12. Dirks, *Canada's Refugee Policy*, chs. 2–3; Freda Hawkins, *Canada and Immigration: Public Policy and Public Concern* (Montreal: McGill-Queen's University Press, 1972), chs. 1–4.

13. See our Chapter 2.

14. See, for example, *Proceedings of the Senate Committee on Immigration and Labour*, 1946; and Dirks, *Canada's Refugee Policy*, ch. 6.

15. Ibid., pp. 138-50; see, for instance, the quotation cited on p. 144.

16. Ibid., pp. 168-71.

17. As paraphrased in ibid., p. 131.

18. Green, *Immigration and the Postwar Canadian Economy*, p. 28.

19. Dirks, *Canada's Refugee Policy*, p. 172.

20. Ibid., pp. 173-75.

21. Ibid., p. 192.

22. See Hawkins, *Canada and Immigration*, ch. 4.

23. For example, see "Men (and Women) Wanted," Toronto *Globe and Mail*, 15 April 1955; and Hawkins, *Canada and Immigration*, pp. 98-114.

24. See our Chapter 10.

25. See Dirks, *Canada's Refugee Policy*, pp. 193-99.

26. Ibid.

27. See, for example, "Stamp of Approval," Toronto *Globe and Mail*, 5 December 1956; "Only Money," *Globe and Mail*, 11 December 1956; "Hungarian Refugees Immigration Dream, Pickersgill Reports," *Globe and Mail*, 24 December 1956; "Immigration Versus Inflation," Winnipeg *Free Press*, 28 December 1956.

28. It is difficult to ascertain the cause-and-effect relationship, but it is clear that the public's activities in support of policy changes did at least provide a positive stimulus to government action.

29. Hawkins, *Canada and Immigration*, pp. 114-18.

30. J.W. Pickersgill, Statement to the House of Commons, 28 November 1956 *Statements and Speeches* 56:37.

31. For a review of immigration policy in these two periods, see Hawkins, *Canada and Immigration*, chs. 5 and 6.

32. Ibid., p. 162. Much of this discussion is based on Hawkins, whose work focuses on a critical in-depth analysis of Canadian immigration policy.

33. *CIPS* 2, p. 107; "Our Aid-Refugee Drive Bogged Down in Hassle," *Financial Post*, 20 February 1960; "Canada to Admit More TB Families," Toronto *Globe and Mail*, 3 March 1960; Department of External Affairs, "World Refugee Year—the Government Programme," *Statements and Speeches* 60:28; United Nations, Office of Public Information, "New Group of Tuberculous Refugees to Go to Canada," Press release, 19 July 1960.

34. "Canada to Take Chinese," Montreal *Daily Star*, 23 May 1962; "Canada and Chinese Refugees," Toronto *Globe and Mail*, 14 May 1962; "Outstretched Hands," Winnipeg *Free Press*, 18 May 1962.

35. *CIPS* 2, p. 106.

36. "A Certain Urgency, Please," Toronto *Globe and Mail*, 31 August 1968.

37. "Canadians to Meet Refugees in Vienna," Toronto *Globe and Mail*, 4 September 1968; "Rush of Czech Refugees Handled in Crash Program," *Globe and Mail*, 16 September 1968; "Canada Harvests Big Crop of Skilled Czech Refugees," *Christian Science Monitor*, 1 November 1968; "Haven Granted to 10,000; Czech Program to End," *Globe and Mail*, 4 January 1969.

38. *CIPS* 2, pp. 108-109.

39. Ibid.; Dirks, *Canada's Refugee Policy*, pp. 233-35.

40. Dirks, *Canada's Refugee Policy*, pp. 238-44; "For Once, Let Canada Be First: Help Uganda's Asians Now," Toronto *Star*, 11 August 1972.

41. "Ugandan Asians in Thousands Seek Canada Entry," Toronto *Star*, 7 September 1972.

42. "11,000 Seek Canada Entry," Montreal *Star*, 8 September 1972.

43. *CIPS* 2, p. 111.

44. "Trudeau Right on Ugandans," Montreal *Star*, 22 September 1972; Dirks, *Canada's Refugee Policy*, p. 243; "How Canada Moved Fast," Toronto *Star*, 14 September 1972.

45. "UK Asks 50 Countries to Help in Settling the Expelled Asians," London *Times*, 5 September 1972.

46. Dirks, *Canada's Refugee Policy*, p. 244; Freda Hawkins, "Ugandan Asians in Canada," *New Community* 2 (summer 1973): 268-76.

47. Canadian Council of Churches, Press Release, 17 September 1973, as cited in Dirks, *Canada's Refugee Policy*, p. 246. For an overview of the Canadian policy and behaviour, see ibid., pp. 244-50; and Gerald E. Dirks, "The Plight of the Homeless: The Refugee Phenomenon," *Behind the Headlines* 38 (1980): 17-19.

48. "Ottawa to Help Chile Refugees in Move North," Toronto *Globe and Mail*, 1 December 1973.

49. "Parliament: Excerpts from Yesterday's House of Commons Proceedings," Toronto *Globe and Mail*, 17 November 1973; "Ottawa Investigators Advise Helping Out," *Globe and Mail*, 28 November 1973; Dirks, *Canada's Refugee Policy*, pp. 247-48; also Howard, "Contemporary Canadian Refugee Policy."

50. Ibid., "Ottawa to Help Chile Refugees in Move North," Toronto *Globe and Mail*, 1 December 1973; "Andras Says Ottawa Will Give $650 Loans to Chilean Refugees," Toronto *Star*, 1 December 1973; "Liberal Urges Screen on 'Radicals' from Chile," Toronto *Star*, 31 December 1973.

51. "1,400 Chilean Immigration Queries Received But Many Specify Spring Move, Andras Says," Toronto *Globe and Mail*, 22 December 1973.

52. Dirks, *Canada's Refugee Policy*, p. 250; "Chilean Refugees 'in Limbo' Waiting for Landed Status," Toronto *Star*, 27 July 1974.

53. Dirks, "Plight of the Homeless," p. 19; "Three MPs Report Argentina Refugees Need Speedy Entry," Toronto *Globe and Mail*, 12 October 1976; "Stranded Chileans Find Canada Slow to Help," *Globe and Mail*, 21 December 1976; "MPs Challenge Cullen Statements on Movement of Chilean Refugees," *Globe and Mail*, 21 December 1976.

54. Dirks, "Plight of the Homeless"; "Ottawa Charged with Complacency Toward Chilean Refugee Plight," Toronto *Globe and Mail*, 5 March 1974; "Would-be Chile Immigrants Face Grilling on Politics," Calgary *Herald*, 10 April 1974; "Chilean Exodus Slowly Subsides," *Globe and Mail*, 2 April 1974; "Andras Studies Demand to Allow 10,000 Chileans into Canada," Ottawa *Citizen*, 10 October 1974; "Canada Rejects Many Chileans," Montreal *Star*, 22 December 1976; "Chilean Refugees Are Being Red-taped," Toronto *Star*, 27 December 1976; "Canada Hit over Delay on Chile Immigrants," Montreal *Star*, 26 January 1977.

55. "Andras Says There Will Be Hell to Pay over Decision to Admit Chile Refugees," Toronto *Star*, 21 January 1974.

56. See Department of Manpower and Immigration, *Annual Reports*, 1974/75, 1975/76, 1976/77 (Ottawa: Minister of Supply and Services); and Department of Employment and Immigration, *Annual Reports*, 1977/78, 1978/79, 1979/80 (Ottawa: Minister of Supply and Services).

57. DEI *Annual Report*, 1978/79, p. 20.

58. DEI *Annual Report*, 1979/1980, pp. 20-21.

59. The importance of this relationship was stressed in a number of confidential interviews with senior officials in both departments; Ottawa, August 1978 and 1979.

60. See Barry Wain, "The Indochina Refugee Crisis," *Foreign Affairs* 58 (fall 1979): 160-80, upon which much of this paragraph is based.

61. Much of this section is based on information and analysis contained in Adelman, "Canada and the Boat People." Professor Adelman, founding member and first director of Operation Lifeline, kindly made his manuscript available to us, providing a collection of data and insight enriching our own analysis. For his view on Canadian decision making, see in particular his Chapter 4.

62. Canada Employment and Immigration Commission, "Vietnamese/Cambodian Special Programme," Memorandum, 28 February 1978; cited in Adelman, "Canada and the Boat People," ch. 4, n. 1.

63. Canada Employment and Immigration Commission, "Vietnamese Small Boat Programme," Memorandum, 28 February 1978; cited in Adelman, "Canada and the Boat People," ch. 4, n. 1. In this memorandum, the federal government received from Quebec an offer to settle 30 per cent of all Indochinese refugees, subject to review by appropriate Quebec personnel. "Ottawa Opens Door to 'Boat People'," Montreal *Star*, 27 January 1978; "Canada

Joining Move to Resettle the Boat People," Toronto *Globe and Mail*, 18 November 1978; "At Our Own Door," *Globe and Mail*, 6 December 1978.

64. Adelman, "Canada and the Boat People," ch. 4, p. 7; "Refugee Priority under Study," Vancouver *Sun*, 20 March 1975; "Priority for Refugees Studied for New Immigration Policy," Vancouver *Sun*, 25 March 1975; "Canada Ready to Open Doors to Refugees," Toronto *Star*, 3 April 1975; "Canada Trying to Arrange Immigration Plan for Viets," Toronto *Star*, 23 November 1976; "New Law will Create Quotas for Immigration to be Decided in Consultation with Provinces," Toronto *Globe and Mail*, 25 November 1976.

65. "Canada's Vietnamese: Waiting for Ships That May Never Come In," Toronto *Globe and Mail*, 9 December 1978; "Canadians Demanded Boat People be Helped," Toronto *Star*, 15 January 1979; "Canada's Refugee Efforts Hindered," *Globe and Mail*, 15 February 1979; "Immigration Official Is 'Not Proud' of Charging Vietnamese for Fares," *Globe and Mail*, 29 January 1979; "The Montreal–Vietnam Connection," *Globe and Mail*, 20 February 1979; "An Integrated Policy is Needed for Refugees and Immigrants," Toronto *Star*, 25 February 1979; "Refugee Policy 'Unacceptable'," Montreal *Star*, 4 March 1979.

66. Adelman, personal communication; Adelman, "Canada and the Boat People," ch. 4, p. 8.

67. Laura Heller, *Newspaper Scan of the Southeast Asian Refugees in Canada*, (Toronto: Greater Toronto Southeast Asian Task Force, April 1980).

68. "We Have to Help the Helpless," Toronto *Star*, 14 June 1979; "Canada to Take More Refugees," Toronto *Globe and Mail*, 20 June 1979; "Admit 30,000 Vietnamese a Year, Canadian MDs Urge Government," *Globe and Mail*, 21 June 1979; "Idealism and Realism," Calgary *Herald*, 25 June 1979; "The Refugee Crisis," *Globe and Mail*, 27 June 1979; "It's Up to Us," *Globe and Mail*, 28 June 1979; "Canada Willing to Take More Refugees," *Globe and Mail*, 29 June 1979; "We Can All Help the Refugees," Toronto *Star*, 30 June 1979.

69. Adelman, "Canada and the Boat People," contains an in-depth analysis of voluntary groups and nongovernmental organizations.

70. Ibid., ch. 4, p. 11 and n. 15.

71. "Ottawa's Challenge: Triple Flow of Refugees to 50,000," Toronto *Globe and Mail*, 19 July 1979; "Refugee Plan Makes Atkey 'Proud to be a Canadian,'" Toronto *Star*, 19 July 1979; "Response to Crisis," Montreal *Star*, 19 July 1979; "Rescuing Boat People," Ottawa *Citizen*, 19 July 1979; "MacDonald Assails Vietnam for Outrageous Rights Violations," *Globe and Mail*, 21 July 1979; "Keep Heat on Viets, MacDonald Urges," Toronto *Star*, 22 July 1979; "Critical Murmurs Follow Canadian Generosity," Montreal *Star*, 27 July 1979.

72. "You'll Determine Refugee Entry," Toronto *Star*, 19 July 1979; "Critical Murmurs Follow Canadian Generosity," Montreal *Star*, 27 July 1979; "Refugees Are Canada's Gain," Toronto *Star*, 29 July 1979; "Ad on Asian Refugee Policy Racist, Atkey Says," *Globe and Mail*, 24 August 1979; "Coalition Charges about Refugees Draw Sharp Protest," *Globe and Mail*, 28 August 1979; "Let's Not Turn Our Backs," Toronto *Star*, 26 August 1979; "Refugees and Citizens," *Globe and Mail*, 29 August 1979; "Boat People: a Policy for Canadians," Winnipeg *Free Press*, 3 October 1979.

73. Adelman notes that Atkey "wanted to make sure he did not go down in history in the same way Canadian ministers have been recorded in history with respect to their treatment of the Jews in the 1930s." Atkey's officials were required to read Abella and Troper, "The Line Must Be Drawn Somewhere," which documented the anti-Semitism of Director of Immigration F.C. Blair,

anti-Semitism that had prime ministerial and ministerial backing. Adelman, "Canada and the Boat People," ch. 4, pp. 13-14.

74. "Ottawa Won't Sponsor More Refugees," Toronto *Globe and Mail*, 6 December 1979.

75. Although Flora MacDonald denied this linkage, earlier statements from Ron Atkey's office plus Adelman's research provide substantial support for this hypothesis. In addition to Adelman, "Canada and the Boat People," see "PCs Accused of Bowing to Backlash by Dropping Refugee Sponsorship," Toronto *Globe and Mail*, 7 December 1970; "Flora Denies Aid Based on Sponsorship Savings," Winnipeg *Free Press*, 8 December 1979; "National Refugee Policy is Urgently Required," *Globe and Mail*, 8 December 1979.

76. See Adelman, "Canada and the Boat People," chs. 1 and 4–6, especially concerning the inconsistencies of Atkey's statements.

77. Jeffrey Simpson, *Discipline of Power: The Conservative Interlude and the Liberal Restoration* (Toronto: Personal Library, 1980), ch. 1.

78. "Boat People will Create Jobs for Canadians," Toronto *Globe and Mail*, 28 December 1979.

79. This is reported in Adelman, "Canada and the Boat People," ch. 4, pp. 17-18.

80. See Simpson, *Discipline of Power*, chs. 1 and 5.

81. Adelman, "Canada and the Boat People," ch. 4, pp. 19-21. "Canada Plans Fuss over 'Last' Refugees," Winnipeg *Free Press*, 3 December 1980; "Canada Cuts Refugee Total for Next Year," Toronto *Globe and Mail*, 1 November 1980; "Refugee Flood," Calgary *Herald*, 24 May 1980.

82. "Ottawa Increases Funds for Refugees," Winnipeg *Free Press*, 16 June 1981.

83. See Adelman, "Canada and the Boat People"; also, Department of Employment and Immigration, *Annual Reports* 1976 through to 1980.

84. Simpson, *Discipline of Power*.

85. Although in some of these situations, such as the crisis in the Horn of Africa, international or local decisions have been made not to resettle refugees, it is unclear whether such decisions have been based on simple practicality or on the belief that these peoples would be "unsuitable" for resettlement in more prosperous parts of the world. The underlying rationale and criteria employed in such decisions are worthy of investigation.

CHAPTER 8

ENERGY POLICY: INTERNATIONAL OIL AND GAS EXCHANGES

1. The issue area of Canada's international oil and gas relations is defined to include Canadian federal government actions dealing directly with the exchange between Canada and the outside world of oil, natural gas, and associated products in essentially unprocessed form. In all cases, greater weight is given to those activities, such as natural gas and pipeline projects, that involve large volumes, diverse forms of investment, high risk, and long-term commitments.

2. The staple thesis, invented by W.A. Mackintosh and developed by Harold Innis, is codified by Mel Watkins in "A Staple Theory of Economic Growth," *Canadian Journal of Economics and Political Science* 29 (May 1963): 141-58. It is given a partial application to Canada's international energy relationships in W.T. Easterbrook and Hugh Aitken, *Canadian Economic History* (Toronto: Macmillan, 1956) and Hugh Aitken et al., *The American Economic Impact on Canada* (Durham, N.C.: Duke University Press, 1959). For a detailed exploration of the application of the functional doctrine, see John W. Holmes, *The Shaping of Peace: Canada and the Search for World Order, 1943–1957*, vol. 1 (Toronto: University of Toronto Press, 1979).

3. See, for example, Abraham Rotstein and Gary Lax, eds., *Independence: The Canadian Challenge* (Toronto: Committee for an Independent Canada, 1972); Abraham Rotstein and Gary Lax, eds., *Getting It Back: A Programme for Canadian Independence* (Toronto: Committee for an Independent Canada, 1974); and Kari Levitt, *Silent Surrender: The Multinational Corporation in Canada* (Toronto: Macmillan, 1970).

4. Notably James Eayrs, "From Middle to Foremost Power: Defining a New Place for Canada in the Hierarchy of World Power," *International Perspectives* (May/June 1975): 15-21.

5. See James Laxer, *The Energy Poker Game: The Politics of the Continental Resources Deal* (Toronto: New Press, 1970); Philip Sykes, *Sellout: The Giveaway of Canada's Energy Resources* (Edmonton: Hurtig, 1973); "Energy Sell-Out: A Counter-Report," *The Canadian Forum* 53 (June/July 1973); Eric Kierans, "Utilizing Canadian Natural Resources," *American Review of Canadian Studies* 3 (spring 1973): 96-100; Mel Watkins, "Resources and Underdevelopment," in R.M. Laxer, ed., *Canada Ltd.* (Toronto: McClelland and Stewart, 1973), pp. 107-26; James Laxer, *Canada's Energy Crisis* (Toronto: James, Lewis and Samuel, 1974); Edgar Dosman, *The National Interest: The Politics of Northern Development, 1968–75* (Toronto: McClelland and Stewart, 1975); Abraham Rotstein, "Canada: The New Nationalism," *Foreign Affairs* 55 (October 1976): 97-118; Larry Pratt, *The Tar Sands: Syncrude and the Politics of Oil* (Edmonton: Hurtig, 1976); François Bregha, *Bob Blair's Pipeline: The Business and Politics of Northern Energy Development Projects* (Toronto: James Lorimer, 1979); Ian McDougall, "Energy and the Future of Federalism: National Harmony or Continental Hegemony?" in R.B. Byers and Robert Reford, eds., *Canada Challenged: The Viability of Confederation* (Toronto: Canadian Institute of International Affairs, 1979); and Ian McDougall, "Energy, Natural Resources and the Economics of Federalism:

National Harmony or Continental Hegemony?" in Elliot Feldman and Neil Nevitte, eds., *The Future of North America: Canada, the United States and Quebec Nationalism* (Ottawa: Institute for Research on Public Policy, 1979). See in particular these works by John McDougall: "The National Energy Board and Multinational Corporations" (Ph.D. dissertation, University of Alberta, 1975); "Regulation Versus Politics: The National Energy Board and the Mackenzie Valley Pipe Line," in Andrew Axline et al., eds., *Continental Community? Independence and Integration in North America* (Toronto: McClelland and Stewart, 1974), pp. 250-73; "Canada and the World Petroleum Market," in Norman Hillmer and Garth Stevenson, eds., *Foremost Nation* (Toronto: McClelland and Stewart, 1977), pp. 85-125; "North American Interdependence and Canadian Fuel Policies," in Brian Tomlin, ed., *Canada's Foreign Policy: Analysis and Trends* (Toronto: Methuen, 1978), pp. 70-86; and "Prebuild Phase or Latest Phase? The United States Fuel Market and Canadian Energy Policy," *International Journal* 36 (winter 1980/81): 117-38.

6. Leonard Waverman, "The Reluctant Bride: Canadian and American Energy Relations," in Edward Erickson and Leonard Waverman, eds., *The Energy Question: An International Failure of Policy*, vol. 2, *North America* (Toronto: University of Toronto Press, 1974), pp. 217-38; Ted Greenwood, "Canadian-American Trade in Energy Resources," in Annette Baker Fox et al., eds., *Canada and the United States: Transnational and Transgovernmental Relations* (New York: Columbia University Press, 1976), pp. 97-118; Philip Trezise, "The Energy Challenge," in H. Edward English, ed., *Canada–United States Relations* (New York: Academy of Political Science, 1976), pp. 113-23; Carl Beigie, "The Optimum Use of Canadian Resources," in ibid., pp. 164-76; Carl Beigie, "An Introductory Overview," in Carl Beigie and Alfred Hero, Jr., eds., *Natural Resources in U.S.–Canadian Relations*, vol. 1, *The Evolution of Policies and Issues* (Boulder Col.: Westview Press, 1980), pp. 1-11; Paul Daniel and Richard Shaffner, "Lessons from Bilateral Trade in Energy Resources," in ibid., pp. 305-35; and William Diebold, Jr., "What Are the Issues?" in ibid., pp. 337-62.

7. The central, seminal exposition is provided in Eayrs, "From Middle to Foremost Power." See also Hillmer and Stevenson, *Foremost Nation*; Harald von Riekhoff, "The Natural Resource Element in Global Power Relationships," *International Perspectives* (September/October 1974): 18-22; A.E. Gotlieb, "Energy and International Relations," *Statements and Speeches* 79:23 (November 1979); and Marc Lalonde, "Le Canada et l'indépendance energétique du monde libre," *Politique Internationale* 12 (summer 1981): 201-10.

8. The phrase "principal power" is employed by Lalonde, "Le Canada et l'indépendance," p. 206.

9. John Davis, *Canadian Energy Prospects: Study Prepared for the Royal Commission on Canada's Economic Prospects* (Ottawa: Queen's Printer, 1957), p. 130; and, more generally, Edward Shaffer, *The Oil Import Program of the United States* (New York: Praeger, 1968).

10. Royal Commission on Energy, *Second Report* (Ottawa: Queen's Printer, 1959).

11. See J. Copeland, "Portland-Montreal Pipeline," February 1949, Imperial Oil Library, Toronto; Copeland, "Portland/Montreal Pipe Line System," Public Affairs Department, Imperial Oil Limited, 1978; and Copeland, "Portland-Montreal Pipeline: New 236-Mile Pipeline Will Release Tankships for Britain," *Imperial Oil Review* 25 (summer 1941): 2-3. Also see C. Cecil Lingard and Reginald C. Trotter, *Canada in World Affairs, September 1941–May 1944* (Toronto: Oxford University Press, 1950) pp. 69-71; and R. Warren James, *Wartime*

Economic Co-operation: A Study of Relations Between Canada and the United States (Toronto: Ryerson, 1949), pp. 46-49.

12. The U.S. experience during this period is described in Crawford Goodwin, ed., *Energy Policy in Perspective: Today's Problems, Yesterday's Solutions* (Washington: Brookings Institution, 1981), pp. 1-204.

13. The exchange crisis did prompt a suggestion that Canada, for exchange reasons, import from British-owned wells or use sterling to pay for its imports from Venezuela, then valued at $26.7 million (U.S.) annually.

14. The development of these four lines is described in John McDougall, "The National Energy Board."

15. See in particular William Kilbourn, *Pipeline: TransCanada and the Great Debate—a History of Business and Politics* (Toronto: Clarke, Irwin, 1970), which provides the basic account of the entire TransCanada PipeLine issue.

16. House of Commons, *Debates*, 13 March 1953, 2927-31.

17. Donald C. Masters, *Canada in World Affairs, 1953-1955* (Toronto: Oxford University Press, 1959).

18. Howe's beliefs and role are well described in Robert Bothwell and William Kilbourn, *C.D. Howe: A Biography* (Toronto: McClelland and Stewart, 1979).

19. The basic sources for this period consist of John McDougall, "The National Energy Board"; Royal Commission on Energy, *First Report* (Ottawa: Queen's Printer, 1958); Royal Commission on Energy, *Second Report* (Ottawa: Queen's Printer, July 1959); and confidential interviews with federal officials in 1979 and 1980.

20. The NEB and the Cabinet approved a TransCanada PipeLines application for the export of gas at Emerson, Manitoba, in April 1960; granted a second export application by the Canada-Montana line in June 1960; authorized an export application representing over 30 per cent of Canadian gas exports by the newly formed Alberta and Southern system; and opened Canada's Arctic Islands to oil and gas exploration in 1961. The Borden commission had recommended that TransCanada's application be withdrawn pending the completion of NEB hearings. Kilbourn, *Pipeline*, p. 170.

21. This section relies heavily on William Barber, "The Eisenhower Energy Policy: Reluctant Intervention"; Barber, "Studied Inaction in the Kennedy Years," in Goodwin, ed., *Energy Policy in Perspective*, pp. 205-236; and Alan Plotnick, *Petroleum: Canadian Markets and U.S. Foreign Trade Policy* (Seattle: Washington University Press, 1964).

22. Plotnick, *Petroleum*, p. 115.

23. Trevor Lloyd, *Canada in World Affairs, 1957-1959*, (Toronto: Oxford University Press, 1968), p. 86.

24. Royal Commission on Canada's Economic Prospects, *Final Report* (Ottawa: Queen's Printer, November 1957), pp. 123-48.

25. This section relies heavily on Barber, "Eisenhower Energy Policy."

26. United States, National Security Council, "Certain Aspects of U.S. Relations with Canada," NSC 5822/1, 30 December 1958, p. 7.

27. Barber, "Eisenhower Energy Policy."

28. Ibid., p. 307.

29. This section is based primarily on 1979-1980 confidential interviews with federal officials.

30. The basic source for the 1963–1968 period is John McDougall, "The National Energy Board."

31. John Garbron, "Business and Industry," in John Saywell, ed., *Canadian Annual Review* for 1963 (Toronto: University of Toronto Press, 1964), p. 246; and Plotnick, *Petroleum*, p. 127.

32. Roger Frank Swanson, *Canadian-American Summit Diplomacy, 1923–1973: Selected Speeches and Documents* (Toronto: McClelland and Stewart, 1975), pp. 217-66; and Lester B. Pearson, *Mike: The Memoirs of the Right Honourable Lester B. Pearson*, vol. 3, 1957–1968, ed. John A. Munro and Alex I. Inglis (Toronto: University of Toronto Press, 1975), p. 131.

33. Department of External Affairs, *Canada and the United States: Principles for Partnership* (Ottawa: Queen's Printer, 1965).

34. Bruce MacDonald, "Pepin Hopeful About U.S. Oil Line," Toronto *Globe and Mail*, 30 May 1967; and these articles by W.L. Dack: "Alta.-Chicago Crude Oil Line?" *Financial Post*, 5 November 1966, p. 1; "Oil's 'On-to-Chicago' Plan May Be Shelved," *Financial Post*, 13 May 1967, p. 1; "We Could Weather Oil Pinch," *Financial Post*, 10 June 1967, pp. 1-2; "Gulf Coast and Canadian Crude Could Clash for Chicago Market," *Oilweek* 17 (6 June 1966): 10-12.

35. Kilbourn, *Pipeline*, pp. 167-86. "Washington's Balk Hurts TransCanada," *Financial Post*, 13 August 1966, p. 1; W.L. Dack, "We Face Gas Shortage, May Import From U.S.," *Financial Post*, 3 September 1966, p. 1; Knowlton Nash, "All-Canadian Pipeline Rule May Hit Energy Sharing," *Financial Post*, 3 September 1966, p. 3; Nash, "Prospects Darken for TransCanada Pipeline," *Financial Post*, 22 October 1966, p. 56; Nash, "More Details Wanted on Gas Pipeline Through U.S.," *Financial Post*, 5 November, 1966, p. 35; W.L. Dack, "Here's Why the U.S. Gave Green Light to TransCanada," *Financial Post*, 29 June 1967, p. 5; and House of Commons, *Debates*, 28 October 1966, 9223-32 and 31 October 1966, 9314-29.

36. John McDougall, "The National Energy Board," pp. 110-32; "Last Obstacle Gone," Winnipeg *Free Press*, 22 June 1967; "Time to Stand Firm," *Financial Times*, 30 August 1967.

37. Dosman, *National Interest*, p. 44; Patrick Deutscher, "Panarctic Oils Ltd: The Government and the Energy Business," *Canadian Forum* 53 (June/July 1973): 32-34; Deutscher, "Backers of Arctic Oil Hunt Get Two Financing Choices," *Financial Post*, 20 May 1967, p. 30; and Clive Baxter, "Mine, Oil Men Soon to Lose Tax Jitters," *Financial Post*, 13 May 1967, p. 3.

38. Clive Baxter, "Plenty of Power in These Four Top Jobs," *Financial Post*, 22 October 1966, p. 8; House of Commons, *Debates*, 3 March 1966, 2107-15; and 1979-80 confidential interviews with federal officials.

39. James Cochrane, "Energy Policy in the Johnson Administration: Logical Order Versus Economic Pluralism," in Goodwin, *Energy Policy in Perspective*, pp. 337-94; and Shaffer, *Oil Import Program*.

40. Material derived from 1979–1980 confidential interviews with federal officials.

41. National Energy Board, *Annual Report* (Ottawa: Queen's Printer, 1966, 1967).

42. The financial press, not surprisingly, reliably supported industry positions, with the Toronto *Daily Star* serving as the most faithful exponent of the nationalist cause.

43. Pepin's arguments for exports, shown most clearly in the Chicago pipeline

case, included the logic of markets and geography, mutual benefits of continental security, the effect on Canada's balance-of-payments deficit with the U.S., Middle East disruptions, Canada's stable political system, and the closeness of the Canada–U.S. defence alliance.

44. The basic literature for the 1968–1973 period consists of Laxer, *Energy Poker Game*; Sykes, *Sellout*; J.J. Greene, "Canadian Resources: To Share or Exploit?" *SAIS Review* 14 (summer 1970): 32-36; David Crane, "The Pressing Need for Canada to Define Its Energy Policies," *International Perspectives* (July/August 1973): 32-37; D.A. Seastone, "The Potential Impact of Canada on North American Energy Supplies," *American Review of Canadian Studies* (spring 1973): 135-45; Dosman, *National Interest*; James Keeley, "Constraints on Canadian International Economic Policy," (Ph.D. dissertation, Stanford University, February 1980). pp. 328-505; and 1979–1980 confidential interviews with federal officials.

45. David Crane, "NEB Plans Action to Keep Oil Exports Inside Quota," Toronto *Globe and Mail*, 30 April 1969.

46. Joint Canada–United States Committee on Trade and Economic Affairs, Communiqué, November, 1970.

47. Department of Energy, Mines and Resources, *An Energy Policy for Canada, Phase I*, 2 vols. (Ottawa: Information Canada, 1973).

48. This account of the continental energy policy proposal is based on William Calkins, "Towards a Continental Energy Plan? A Vital Issue in Canadian-United States Relations," *ACSUS Newsletter* 1 (autumn 1971): 17-35; and confidential interviews with federal officials in 1981.

49. Dosman, *National Interest*.

50. Eric Kierans, "The Day the Cabinet Was Misled," *The Canadian Forum* (March 1974): 4-8; National Energy Board, *Energy Supply and Demand in Canada and Export Demand for Canadian Energy, 1966 to 1990* (Ottawa: Information Canada, 1971); John MacDougall, "The National Energy Board."

51. Dosman, *National Interest*.

52. *International Canada* and confidential 1979–1980 interviews with federal officials.

53. Neil de Marchi, "Energy Policy under Nixon: Mainly Putting Out Fires," in Goodwin, ed., *Energy Policy in Perspective*, pp. 395-474; and confidential 1981 interviews with federal officials.

54. Dosman, *National Interest*; Jack Austin, "An Overview of Canadian Energy Policy in the '70's and the Role of Petro Canada," Address to "Options 80," Halifax, 5 November 1979; and confidential interviews with federal officials in 1975–1976, 1978, and 1979–1980.

55. The basic literature for the 1973–1979 period consists of Ronald Ritchie, "Assessing the Energy Issues from a Canadian Perspective," *International Perspectives* (March/April 1974): 13-18; Greenwood, "Canadian–American Trade"; Waverman, "The Reluctant Bride"; John McDougall, "Canada and the World Petroleum Market"; John McDougall, "North American Interdependence"; Trezise, "The Energy Challenge"; Pratt, *The Tar Sands*; Ian McDougall, "Energy, Natural Resources and the Economics of Federalism"; Helmut Frank and John Schanz, *U.S.–Canadian Energy Trade: A Study of Changing Relationships* (Boulder, Col.: Westview Press, 1978); and Larry Pratt, "Petro-Canada," in Allan Tupper and Bruce Doern, eds., *Public Corporations and Public Policy in Canada* (Ottawa: Institute for Research on Public Policy, 1981), pp. 95-148.

56. The record of Canadian action on the price and supply of oil and gas is contained in *International Canada*. See also National Energy Board, *Canadian Natural Gas Supply and Requirements* (Ottawa: Information Canada, 1975).

57. On the northern gas pipeline, see Don Peacock, "Negotiating the Pipeline," *International Perspectives* (January/February 1978): 12-16; Bregha, *Bob Blair's Pipeline*; Peter Pearse, ed., *The Mackenzie Pipeline: Arctic Gas and Canadian Energy Policy* (Toronto: McClelland and Stewart, 1974); National Energy Board, *Reasons for Decision: Northern Pipelines*, 3 vols., (Ottawa: Supply and Services Canada, June 1977); Christina Newman, "The Long Ordeal of William Wilder," *Saturday Night* 92 (July/August 1977): 16-20; Joel Sokolsky, "The Canada–U.S. Alaska Highway Pipeline: A Study in Environmental Decisionmaking," *The American Review of Canadian Studies* 9 (autumn 1979): 84-112.

58. John McDougall, "Canada and the World Petroleum Market," pp. 94-99.

59. David Wright, "Lessons of CIEC," *International Perspectives* (November/December 1977): 7-12.

60. *International Canada*; and Stephen Scott, "MacEachen Finds His Policy Acceptable in Middle East," *International Perspectives* (May/June 1976): 3-6.

61. Department of Energy, Mines and Resources, *An Energy Strategy for Canada: Policies for Self Reliance* (Ottawa: Supply and Services Canada, 1976).

62. G.R. Berry, "The Oil Lobby and the Energy Crisis," *Canadian Public Administration* 17 (1974): 600-35. For a journalistic account, see Peter Foster, *The Blue-Eyed Sheiks: The Canadian Oil Establishment* (Toronto: Collins, 1979).

63. This account of the 1979–1981 period is based heavily on Diebold, "What Are the Issues?"; Daniel and Shaffner, "Lessons from Bilateral Trade"; Lalonde, "Le Canada et l'indépendance"; Gotlieb, "Energy and International Relations"; and confidential 1979–1980 and 1981 interviews with federal officials.

64. John McDougall, "Prebuild Phase or Latest Phase?" See also National Energy Board, *Canadian Natural Gas Supply and Requirements* (Ottawa: Supply and Services, 1979).

65. Michel Vastel, "Report on Venice Summit," *International Perspectives* (July/August 1980): 3-6; and A.E. Gotlieb, "The Western Economic Summits," Notes for remarks to the CIIA, 9 April 1981, Winnipeg.

66. Department of Energy, Mines and Resources, *The National Energy Program: 1980* (Ottawa: Supply and Services Canada, 1980), and subsequent "Update" (1982). See also Larry Pratt, "Energy: The Roots of National Policy," *Studies in Political Economy* 7 (winter 1982): 27-59.

67. This account of the policy-making process is based heavily on confidential 1981 interviews with federal officials.

CHAPTER 9

SPACE POLICY: INTERNATIONAL SPACE ACTIVITY

1. Robert Gilpin, *France in the Age of the Scientific State* (Princeton, N.J.: Princeton University Press, 1968); Eugene Skolnikoff, *International Imperatives of Technology*, Technological Development and the International Political System Research Series, no. 16 (Berkeley, Calif.: Institute of International Studies,

University of California, 1971); and Geoffrey Barraclough, *An Introduction to Contemporary History* (Harmondsworth, England: Penguin Books, 1967), especially ch. 2.

2. James Caporaso, ed., "Dependence and dependency in the global system," *International Organization* 32 (winter 1978).

3. Organization for Economic Co-operation and Development, *Review of National Science Policy: Canada* (Paris: Organization for Economic Co-operation and Development, 1969); and Canada, Senate, *A Science Policy for Canada: Report of the Senate Special Committee on Science Policy*, 2 vols. (Ottawa: Queen's Printer, 1971, 1972).

4. Science Council of Canada, *Canada, Science and International Affairs*, Report no. 20 (Ottawa: Information Canada, 1973); and Jocelyn Ghent, "Science, Technology and Trudeau's Foreign Policy," *Behind the Headlines* 36 (1978).

5. See John Bretton and James Gilmour, *The Weakest Link: A Technological Perspective on Canadian Industrial Underdevelopment* (Ottawa: Science Council of Canada, 1978); Steven Globerman, "Canadian Science Policy and Technological Sovereignty," *Canadian Public Policy* 4 (winter 1978): 34-35; and Kristean Palda, *The Science Council's Weakest Link* (Vancouver: Fraser Institute, 1979). It should be noted that proponents of technological sovereignty base their arguments on precepts grounded in complex neo-realism as well as in the peripheral-dependence approach.

6. For a discussion of the Arrow case, see John McLin, *Canada's Changing Defense Policy 1957–1963: The Problems of a Middle Power in Alliance* (Baltimore: Johns Hopkins University Press, 1967); and James Dow, *The Arrow* (Toronto: James Lorimer, 1979).

7. The sources for this trend, the *Annual Reports* and *Annual Reviews* of the Department of External Affairs, record the official view of an actor seldom centrally involved in the full internal debate. But they offer a standard base from which to draw reliable comparisons over time and across issue areas, provided by an actor charged with a general responsibility for managing all Canadian behaviour in the international realm.

8. The relative absence of references to actors within Canada, evident in Table 9.3, is even more pronounced in the case of domestic organizations, where only three references occurred throughout the entire period.

9. This section is based primarily on D.J. Goodspeed, *A History of the Defence Research Board of Canada* (Ottawa: Queen's Printer, 1958); Lt.-Col. T.A. Spruston, "Science and Politics: The Evolution of Canadian Space Policy," (M.A. thesis, Royal Military College, 1976); and confidential interviews with federal officials from 1979 to 1981.

10. Science Council of Canada, *A Space Program for Canada*, report no. 1, (Ottawa: Queen's Printer, 1967).

11. The Board's formation, operation, and organizational relationships are discussed in Goodspeed, *Defence Research Board*; O.M. Solandt, "The Defence Research Board's Untimely End: What It Means for Military Science," *Science Forum* 8 (October 1975): 19-21; and A.M. Fordyce, "How It All Started: The Goforth Paper," *Canadian Defence Quarterly* 1 (spring 1972): 15-16.

12. On the NRC, see Wilfred Eggleston, *National Research in Canada: The NRC, 1916–1966* (Toronto: Clarke, Irwin, 1978).

13. These unique problems began with the need for reliable radio service in the north, the communications problem and scientific puzzles generated by the

aurora borealis, and the general need for communication over large, sparsely populated areas. The cold war and the Soviet Union's acquisition of deliverable atomic weapons added communications needs stemming from the increased dispersion of land and sea forces, preparation for air interception far from Canadian population centres, the advent of electronically guided missiles, service demands for improved electronic countermeasures, and the recognition that Canada had an empty land mass sufficiently large for missile research.

14. Ministry of State for Science and Technology, *Canada in Space* (Ottawa: Supply and Services Canada, 1982).

15. The basic information for this section is provided in the *Canadian Annual Review* from 1960 to 1970; Science Council of Canada, *Space Program*; and Ministry of State for Science and Technology, "Inventory of Canada-United States Agreements in Science and Technology," mimeographed, circa 1975.

16. Spruston, "Science and Politics," p. 62.

17. Department of External Affairs, *Canada and the United Nations* (Ottawa: Queen's Printer, 1959–1966 annually).

18. Department of Communications, *The Role of Canada in Intelsat and Other Relevant International Organizations*, Telecommission Study (3) a, International Implications of Telecommunications (Ottawa: Information Canada, 1971).

19. In February 1961, before the American launch of Telstar, a group of British companies formed the British Space Development Company, which developed plans for an operational Commonwealth communications satellite system, apparently secured promises of financial support from the British banking community, but failed to secure government approval. Although in March 1963, the British government declared its intention to move away from buying time on a foreign satellite and to involve British industry in the highest level of space technology, no effective action was taken before Britain joined Intelsat. Raymond Palmer, "Why Britain Never Got into Orbit," *Business Observer*, 2 July 1972.

20. Royal Commission on Government Organization, *Report*, vol. 4 (Ottawa: Queen's Printer, 1963), p. 274.

21. This section is based on Science Council of Canada, *Space Program*; Science Council of Canada, *Second Annual Report*, June 1968; Canada, Department of Communications, *Annual Review*, 1970; William Rogers, "U.S. Foreign Policy in a Technological Age," Text of an address to the twelfth meeting of the Panel on Science and Technology of the House Committee on Science and Astronautics (United States Information Service, 29 January 1971); Jeff Carruthers, "Canada to 'Plug in' to U.S. 'Eye in the Sky' Program," Ottawa *Journal*, 18 February 1971; and *International Canada* (October 1972), p. 174.

22. This discussion of the Telesat-Anik debate is based primarily on interviews; Prime Minister's Office, Press Release of 14 July 1967; House of Commons debates; and press reports, notably "Anik: Too Many Questions," Toronto *Globe and Mail*, 8 November 1972; Ian Rodger, "Ottawa Seeks Political Way to Accept Highest Bid on Telesat," *Financial Post*, 25 July 1970; "Our Satellite First of a Global Series," *Financial Post*, 6 May 1971; and John Rolfe, "Telesat Contract Loss May Cost Canada $100 Million in Exports," *Globe and Mail*, 9 October 1970. On the corporation itself, see Bruce Doern and James Brothers, "Telesat Canada," in Allan Tupper and Bruce Doern, *Public Corporations and Public Policy in Canada* (Ottawa: The Institute for Research on Public Policy, 1981), pp. 221-50.

23. C.M. Drury, *A Domestic Communications Satellite System for Canada* (Ottawa: Queen's Printer, 1968).

24. On the CTS, see Jeff Carruthers, "Europe Eyes Canadian Satellite," Ottawa *Journal*, 16 February 1972; Jeff Carruthers, "Canada, Europe Join Space Efforts," Ottawa *Journal*, 12 May 1972; and "Reserve Rights on Satellites, L'Allier Says," Toronto *Globe and Mail*, 21 April 1971.

25. The North Atlantic Aircraft navigation satellite system (Aerosat) had been formed at an August 1971 meeting between the U.S. Federal Aviation Administration and ESRO. Although Canada had been asked to attend this meeting, it joined in December 1971. Through MOT, it provided $10.5 million for the first phase of a five-year, $200-million experimental system beginning in 1974 that would require, among other things, several geostationary satellites, a ground station in eastern Canada, and airborne testing by CP Air and Air Canada.

26. *International Canada* (January/February 1969 and December 1970); and "Rocky Road to Space Independence," *Financial Post*, 6 May 1972.

27. On Intelsat, see Department of External Affairs, "Canada Signs the New Intelsat Agreements," Communiqué, 20 August 1971; "Notes for a statement by A.E. Gotlieb, Deputy Minister of Communications for January 29, 1970 meeting of the Canadian Institute of International Affairs (New York Branch) on some current satellite questions"; and Lester B. Pearson, "The Political Implications of Satellite Communication," Address to the Century Association, New York, 19 October 1971.

28. *International Canada* (December 1973).

29. William Rogers, "U.S. Foreign Policy," p. 6; and George Low, "International Aspects of Air Space Program," Remarks at the National Space Club luncheon (United States Information Service, 26 January 1971), p. 2.

30. Much of the material for this period is based on twenty confidential interviews from 1974 to 1980 with Canadian government officials involved in space activity, and documents made available by the Department of External Affairs.

31. Gordon Hutcheson, "New Radio Frequency to be Tried with Fourth Telesat Satellite," *Financial Post*, 17 January 1976; Robertson Cochrane, "Ottawa Opts Out, Gives U.S. $67 Million Contract," Toronto *Star*, 29 April 1978.

32. This account of Canada's involvement in the space shuttle program is based on "Nixon Approves 6-year, $5.5-billion Program to Develop Craft for Routine Space Shuttle," Toronto *Globe and Mail*, 6 January 1972; Jeff Carruthers, "Canada Unlikely to Join U.S. Space Shuttle Program," Ottawa *Journal*, 11 January 1972; Jeff Carruthers, "Canadians Hope for Robots in Space," Ottawa *Journal*, 24 June 1972; Jeff Carruthers, "Did Canada Miss the Boat on Space Shuttle Project?" Ottawa *Journal*, 11 August 1972; Lydia Dotto, "Canada May Shun Major Role in U.S. Space Shuttle Program Because of High Costs and Few Benefits," *Globe and Mail*, 22 August 1972; Department of External Affairs, "The National Research Council of Canada Joins with the National Aeronautics and Space Administration in the Development of the Space Shuttle System," Communiqué, 23 June 1976; Bruce Levett, "Canada forgoes spaceship deal," Ottawa *Citizen*, 24 June 1976; Lydia Dotto, "Tale of Woe for NASA's Space Shuttle," *Globe and Mail*, 29 August 1979; and "Spar to Get $63.6 Million for Providing Cranes under Pact with NASA," *Globe and Mail*, 15 April 1980.

33. Robert Steklasa, "The Satellite Revolution," *Financial Post*, 15 September 1979; and David Salisbury, "New Space Satellite to Peer Down on World's Oceans," *Christian Science Monitor*, 20 June 1978.

34. In the case of Sarsat, a Canada–U.S.–France project to establish a search and rescue satellite system, Canada opposed a provision proposed by NASA for a free flow of information, with a specific exemption for commercial purposes, and sought to ensure the mutual operability of the system with a Soviet equivalent.

35. "Notes for a Statement by the Canadian Representative, Mr. E.B. Wang," U.N. Committee on the Peaceful Uses of Outer Space, Legal Sub-Committee, 11 May 1976; "Statement on Remote Sensing by the Canadian Representative, Mr. E.B. Wang," UNCPUOS Legal Sub-Committee, 18 May 1976, Geneva; "Remarks by Mr. Erik Wang," Symposium on Legal Implications of Remote Sensing from Outer Space, McGill University, 17 October 1975; Jeanne Sauvé, "Relationship of Space to the Environment," Symposium on the Legal Implications of Remote Sensing, McGill University, 16 Ocober 1975; and "Statement by His Excellency R. Harry Jay," UNCPUOS Legal Sub-Committee, 14 March 1978, Geneva.

36. See Jeff Carruthers, "Space Policy under Study: Canada May Get Its Own NASA," Ottawa *Journal*, 23 June 1972; "Statement by the Honourable Jeanne Sauvé," News Release (Office of the Minister of State for Science and Technology, 16 July 1974; "New Directions for Space Policy," News Release Ministry of State for Science and Technology, 16 July 1974; and Department of Communications, *The Canadian Space Program: Five-Year Plan (80/81–84/85)*, Discussion paper DOC-6-79DP, January 1980.

CHAPTER 10

CANADIAN POLICY TOWARDS THE MIDDLE EAST

1. See, for example, Peter Dobell, *Canada's Search for New Roles* (Toronto: Oxford University Press, 1972); Peyton V. Lyon and Brian W. Tomlin, *Canada as an International Actor* (Toronto: Macmillan, 1979); and Michael Tucker, *Canadian Foreign Policy* (Toronto: McGraw-Hill Ryerson, 1980).

2. Tareq Ismael, "Canada and the Middle East," in Peyton V. Lyon and Tareq Ismael, eds., *Canada and the Third World* (Toronto: Macmillan, 1976), especially pp. 240-41; and Janice Stein, "La politique étrangère du Canada au Moyen-Orient: Stimulus et réponse," in Paul Painchaud, ed., *Le Canada et le Québec sur la scène internationale* (Montreal: Les Presses de l'Université du Québec, 1977), especially pp. 379-81.

3. Ismael, "Canada and the Middle East," pp. 250, 258, 264-68; and Dobell, *Canada's Search* p. 17. See also Peyton V. Lyon, "Canada's Middle East Tilt," *International Perspectives* (September/October 1982): 3-5.

4. Janice Stein, "Canadian Foreign Policy in the Middle East After the October War," in *Social Praxis* 4, nos. 3-4 (1976/1977): 271-97; L.A. Delvoie, "Growth in Economic Relations of Canada and the Arab World," *International Perspectives* (November/December 1976): 29-33; and Laurence Grossman, "The Shifting Canadian Vote on Mideast Questions at UN," *International Perspectives* (May/June 1978): 9-13.

5. In addition to the standard array of secondary and primary sources, this analysis draws upon material contained in four confidential interview programs on Canadian foreign policy decision making conducted by the authors in 1975–1976, 1978, 1979–1980, and 1981–1982 with foreign policy officials in the Canadian federal government. The authors also conducted a selective review of the files of major Canadian Jewish organizations in 1980 and 1981. We gratefully extend our appreciation to those who spoke with us and made material available to us, especially Professor Maxwell Cohen, who provided free access to his personal papers in the Public Archives of Canada; John English, for his permission to cite his forthcoming volume in the *Canada in World Affairs* series; and the professional staff of the Canada–Israel Committee for permission to examine and use their files.

6. The selection and use of quantitative data follow the prevailing focus and standards in the literature, as expressed for example in Robert O. Keohane and Joseph S. Nye, Jr., *Power and Interdependence* (Boston: Little, Brown, 1977); and E. Azar and T. Sloan, *Dimensions of Interaction* (Pittsburgh: International Studies Association, 1975). Despite the use of single sources for some variables, and the relatively low degree of variation in material drawn from general data banks, the use of occasional validity checks and the overall consistency of the results across variables strongly suggest that the data are sufficiently reliable for the purposes for which they are employed in this chapter.

7. These figures have been compiled from annual editions of two Department of External Affairs publications, *Canadian Representatives Abroad* and *Diplomatic Representation in Canada*.

8. As recorded in *International Canada* (Toronto: Canadian Institute of International Affairs and Ottawa: Parliamentary Centre for Foreign Affairs and Foreign Trade, monthly) and the *Annual Report*s and *Annual Review*s of the Department of External Affairs.

9. These conclusions are sustained by a separate analysis, from the DEA *Annual Report* and *Review*, of Canada's "objectives" towards the region.

10. This trend towards increased Canadian initiation and unilateral action is further suggested by the ratio of Canadian action received on the measures of diplomatic representation, summit visits, and event interaction. We are grateful to Edward Azar for providing event-interaction data from the Conflict and Peace Data Bank (COPDAB) for the period beyond 1975, as well as for his earlier data set.

11. The analysis in this period is based primarily on Zachariah Kay, *Canada and Palestine: The Politics of Non-commitment* (Jerusalem: Israel Universities Press, 1978); published accounts of leading Canadian participants; the relevant volumes in *Canada and World Affairs* (Canadian Institute of International Affairs); and selected materials from the files of major Jewish organizations. See also Anne Hillmer, "Canadian Policy on the Partition of Palestine, 1947," (M.A. thesis, Carleton University, 1981).

12. These paragraphs and quotations, unless otherwise noted, are based on material from the Cohen Papers, in particular, "Report on Public Relations, submitted by M.A. Appel to the United Zionist Council of Canada," 1952; "Memorandum on Zionist Public Relations," 1948; and "Minutes of the National Public Relations Committee of the United Zionist Council of Canada," 11 September 1948.

13. David Croll, "Memorandum to the PRC," September 1948, Cohen Papers.

14. J.W. Pickersgill, *The Mackenzie King Record*, vol. 4 (Toronto: University of Toronto Press, 1970), p. 164.

15. Kay, *Canada and Palestine*, p. 149.

16. The following two paragraphs are based on Maxwell Cohen, "Public Relations Problems and Methods," November 1952, Cohen Papers.

17. "Report of the Public Relations Committee to the National Executive," 23 January 1953, Cohen Papers.

18. A few of the more useful general works on Suez are: Chester L. Cooper, *The Lion's Last Roar: Suez 1956* (New York: Harper & Row, 1978); Daniel Hofstadter, ed., *Egypt and Nasser,* vol. 1, *1952–1956* (New York: Facts on File, 1973); Walter Z. Laqueur, *The Middle East in Transition* (New York: Praeger, 1958); Kenneth Love, *Suez: The Twice Fought War* (New York: McGraw-Hill, 1969); John Norton Moore, ed., *The Arab–Israeli Conflict* (Princeton, N.J.: Princeton University Press, 1977); Terence Robertson, *Crisis: The Inside Story of the Suez Conspiracy* (Toronto: McClelland & Stewart, 1964); Hugh Thomas, *The Suez Affair* (London: Weidenfeld & Nicholson, 1967).

19. Donald C. Master, *Canada in World Affairs, 1953–1955* (Toronto: Oxford University Press, 1959), chap. 6.

20. The following materials were taken from James Eayrs, *Canada in World Affairs, October 1955 to June 1957* (Toronto: Oxford University Press, 1959), chap. 6; and Eayrs, "Canadian Policy and Opinion during the Suez Crisis," *International Journal* 12 (spring 1957): 97-108.

21. As cited in Eayrs, *Canada in World Affairs*, p. 256.

22. Ibid., p. 183.

23. See J.W. Pickersgill, *My Years with Louis St. Laurent* (Toronto: University of Toronto Press, 1975), pp. 313-17.

24. "Report of the Public Relations Committee to the 33rd Convention of the Zionist Organization of Canada," March 1956, Cohen Papers.

25. The following information comes primarily from "Report on Public Relations Program and Activities, March–September, 1956," September 1956, Cohen Papers.

26. John G. Diefenbaker, *One Canada* vol 1, *The Crusading Years, 1895–1956* (Toronto: Macmillan of Canada, 1975), p. 281; Lester B. Pearson, *Mike: The Memoirs of the Right Honourable Lester B. Pearson*, vol. 2, 1948–1957, ed. John A. Munro and Alex I. Inglis (Toronto: University of Toronto Press, 1973), pp. 244-78.

27. Trevor Lloyd, *Canada in World Affairs, 1957–1959* (Toronto: Oxford University Press, 1968), pp. 18-19. The major sources for this period are James Eayrs, *The Art of the Possible: Government and Foreign Policy in Canada* (Toronto: Univeristy of Toronto Press, 1961); John McLin, *Canada's Changing Defence Policy, 1957–1963: The Problems of a Middlepower Alliance* (Baltimore: Johns Hopkins University Press, 1967); Peyton V. Lyon, *Canada in World Affairs, 1961–1963* (Toronto: Oxford University Press, 1968).

28. Lloyd, *Canada in World Affairs*, p. 141.

29. In his memoirs, Diefenbaker observed that his strong support for American intervention came after he had been consulted by President Eisenhower, one day before the landing. Eisenhower indicated that the action was being taken in direct response to an urgent appeal from Lebanese President Chamoun, who feared a Communist-directed uprising that he could not control alone. This confirmed in Diefenbaker's mind the necessity for immediate action, especially since the Soviets would block any such move within the United Nations forum. See Diefenbaker, *One Canada*, vol. 1, p. 74.

30. A useful monograph on Canada-Israel relations from a particularly positive viewpoint is Shira Herzog Bessin and David Kaufman, eds., *Canada-Israel Friendship* (Toronto: Canada-Israel Committee, 1979), pp. 11-78.

31. "Report of the Public Relations Committee to the 34th Convention of the Zionist Organization of Canada," 1 June 1958; "Report of the Public Relations Committee to the 35th Convention of the Zionist Organization of Canada," n.d.; "Memorandum to Inner PR Committee from Maxwell Cohen (jointly signed by Saul Hayes)," 8 June 1959; Cohen Papers.

32. This account of the Cyprus issues is based on Lester B. Pearson, *Mike: the Memoirs of the Right Honourable Lester B. Pearson*, vol. 3, *1957-1968*, ed. John A. Munro and Alex I. Inglis (Toronto: University of Toronto Press, 1975), pp. 134-35.

33. This account of the financing dispute is drawn from John English, *Canada in World Affairs, 1965-1967* (Toronto: Canadian Institute of International Affairs, forthcoming); and Peter Bishop, "Canada's Policy on Financing of U.N. Peace-Keeping Operations," *International Journal* 20 (autumn 1967): 463-83.

34. This account of the 1967 war is based largely on English, *Canada in World Affairs*; and Andrew Boyd, *Fifteen Men on a Powder Keg: A History of the U.N. Security Council* (London: Methuen, 1971).

35. As cited in Delvoie, "Growth in Economic Relations," p. 29.

36. English, *Canada in World Affairs.*

37. "Draft Notes on the Public Relations Workshop Conference of April 19, 1964," Cohen Papers.

38. Department of External Affairs, *Foreign Policy for Canadians* (Ottawa: Queen's Printer, 1970).

39. Department of External Affairs, "Visit to the Middle East," Press release, 19 November 1969.

40. Delvoie, "Growth in Economic Relations"; and Antoine Ayoub, "How Should Canada Approach the Many Faces of the Magnet?" *International Perspectives* (May/June 1972): 36-40.

41. Ismael, "Canada and the Middle East."

42. Press views were, however, not sufficiently unanimous to prevent complaints by Jewish leaders about the anti-Israeli bias of several publications, notably the Montreal *Gazette*, Vancouver *Sun*, Edmonton *Journal*, Ottawa *Citizen*, *La Presse*, and *Le Devoir*.

43. This account of peacekeeping is based on Stein, "Canadian Foreign Policy in the Middle East," and Henry Wiseman, "Lebanon: The Latest Example of UN Peacekeeping Action," *International Perspectives* (January/February 1979): 3-7.

44. Confidential interview with federal officials, May 1981.

45. Stein, "Canadian Foreign Policy in the Middle East," pp. 286-93.

46. Grossman, "The Shifting Canadian Vote."

47. Confidential interview with federal officials, May 1981. See also Stephen Scott, "MacEachen Finds His Policy Acceptable in Middle East," *International Perspectives* (May/June 1976): 3-6.

48. Scott, "MacEachen."

49. This account of the boycott issue is based largely on materials in files of the Canada-Israel Committee, supplemented by confidential interviews with federal officials.

50. This account of the Jerusalem issue is based substantially on George Takach, "Clark and the Jerusalem Embassy Affair: Initiative and Constraint in Canadian Foreign Policy," (M.A. thesis, School of International Affairs, Carleton University, 1980); Howard Adelman, "Clark and the Canadian Embassy in Israel," *Middle East Focus* 2 (March 1980): 6-18; Jeffrey Simpson, *Discipline of Power: the Conservative Interlude and the Liberal Restoration* (Toronto: Personal Library, 1980), pp. 145-59; Yaacov Glickman, "Political Socialization and the Social Protest of Canadian Jewry: Some Historical and Contemporary Perspectives," in Jorgen Dahlie and Lissa Fernando, eds., *Ethnicity, Power, and Politics in Canada* (Toronto: Methuen, 1980), pp. 123-50; and Harold M. Waller, "The Political Process in Canadian Jewish Community Organizations," *Viewpoints* 2 (fall 1980): 10-19.

51. Information about the involvement of the U.S. government is based largely on interviews about the American foreign policy process towards Canada, conducted with middle and senior-level U.S. government officials in the spring of 1981.

52. John Benesh, "Canadian Images of the Middle East: Conflict and Implications for Canada's Middle East Foreign Policy to 1977," (research essay, School of International Affairs, Carleton University, 1979).

53. Canadian Jewish Congress, "Brief to the Standing Committee on Justice, Legislature of Ontario," 18 September 1978; and "Brief Submitted by the Canadian Zionist Federation, Central Region, to the Standing Administration of Justice Committee in support of Bill 112, 'An Act to Prohibit Discrimination in Business Relationships'", Canada-Israel Committee files, n.d.

54. Although public estimates of the number of Arabs in Canada vary, these numbers on Canada's Islamic population are contained in Council of Muslim Communities of Canada, "Brief Submitted to Justice Committee on Bill 112," 6 September 1978, Canada-Israel Committee files.

55. Confidential interview with federal officials, May 1981.

56. Confidential interview with federal officials, May 1981.

57. Confidential interviews with Canadian government officials, 1979-1981. See also Takach, "Clark and the Jerusalem Embassy Affair," p. 39.

58. These paragraphs are based on confidential interviews with federal officials in the winter of 1981/82 and supplemented by reports in the Toronto *Globe and Mail* and *Financial Post* spanning 1981 and the first six months of 1982.

CONCLUSION

1. Department of External Affairs, *Foreign Policy for Canadians* (Ottawa: Queen's Printer, 1970), p. 8.

2. Ibid., p. 32.

INDEX